The Po

The American Revolution

IN CONGRESS, JULY 4, 1776.

The unanimous Declaration of the thirteen united States of America.

The Political Economy Of the American Revolution

Nancy Spannaus and
Christopher White

EDITORS

Executive Intelligence Review

Washington, D.C.

1st edition: 1977
2nd edition: 1996

Please direct all inquiries to the publisher:

Executive Intelligence Review
P.O. Box 17390
Washington, D.C. 20041-0390

ISBN 0-943235-14-6

Library of Congress: 95-83922

Printed in the United States of America

EIB 95-001

Contents

Part II
The Founding Fathers

Why We Must Reprint The PEAR Book Today

It would be a only a small exaggeration to say that the American population has undergone a lobotomy relative to its real history. Americans in general have absolutely no knowledge of the distinct and positive qualities of the Declaration of Independence, the U.S. Constitution, and the American System of Economics, and where they come from. Many have actually bought the line that British free-trade lackeys like Adam Smith and John Locke, were part of the positive heritage of this country. Such ignorance has created a very dangerous weakness that anti-American zealots parading as patriots—such as Rep. Newt Gingrich and Sen. Phil Gramm—are currently able to exploit.

The actual lineage of the American System is the concept of the commonwealth, an idea which emerged with force out of the period of the Italian Golden Renaissance, which was itself based on the Platonic republican tradition from the Greek Classical period, as well as Christianity. The concept of the commonwealth was built on the idea that a sovereign nation-state must be dedicated to the education and improvement of its population through scientific and technological progress. It was an idea that defined a positive role for the state, in its fostering of conditions that would benefit the individual, and which understood the individual for the first time in history, as being made in the image of God the Creator, and thereby worthy of being treated as such in social and economic policy.

If you understand the principle of the commonwealth, you then understand the coherence of the Declaration of Independence and the U.S. Constitution, and the undeniable fact that the fledgling

American republic was a rejection of John Locke and British free-trade policies, and an embrace of republican values. If you know the real history of the commonwealth tradition, you then understand where the concept of "general welfare" in the U.S. Constitution comes from, and how it commits the United States to rejecting the Confederate Constitution and its modern-day imitators. You are able to resolve the allegedly irreconcilable conflict between the interest and freedom of the individual and of states, through the concept of a republican nation-state based on God's natural law.

Historian Christopher White and I first sought to document this assertion when we published the first edition of this book in 1977. We decided to present primarily selections of original sources on economy, many of which were unavailable elsewhere. We found that there were very few who had read Alexander Hamilton's original economic writings, not to mention that of his predecessors.

The first edition has long been out of print, and in many respects the misunderstanding of American history and economics is much worse today. The U.S. population has been virtually brainwashed into believing that "free trade" is an American tradition. History is barely taught any more. And this author has been told that the original economic papers of Hamilton, including the Report on the Subject of Manufactures, which we reproduce in large part in this book, are almost unavailable in local libraries around the country, and non-scholarly, including paperback editions, of the Hamilton reports, which used to be available, are no longer in print.

Since 1977, with the aid of economist-philosopher Lyndon La-Rouche and many of his and our associates, the picture of the roots of the American System has been filled out considerably.[1] The fundamental breakthrough was made in the period of the 1439 Council of Florence, which saw an explosion of creativity not only in the arts and sciences, but also in the understanding of statecraft. A school of thinkers developed who called themselves cameralists, since they

---

1. Two full-length books and innumerable magazine articles have been produced from the voluminous researches of members of the International Caucus of Labor Committees, the philosophical association based on LaRouche's ideas. The books are: W. Allen Salisbury, *The Civil War and the American System, America's Battle with Britain, 1860–1876* (Washington, D.C.: Executive Intelligence Review, 1992); and H. Graham Lowry, *How the Nation Was Won, America's Untold Story 1630–1754, Vol. 1* (Washington, D.C.: Executive Intelligence Review, 1988).

formed chambers of advisers to local rulers. The task of the cameralists was to devise the policies which would guide the ruler in economic policies in particular.

Their thinking spread from Italy into France (Louis XI to Jean Bodin to Jean-Baptiste Colbert) and Germany-Austria (Melchior von Osse to Veit Ludwig Seckendorff to Gottfried Leibniz to Johann Heinrich Gottlob von Justi and Joseph Sonnenfels). These thinkers, as well as commonwealth adherents in England, played a direct role in transmitting the idea to the American colonies where, with the benefit of immense distance from the European oligarchy, a distillation of their republican ideas was put into practice. It was a great, though by no means perfect, step toward the realization of the ideas of the Renaissance.

At the present time, the American population—degraded in its self-conception as well as its culture and living standards—is in great danger of betraying its heritage. The opponents of the American Revolution knew that, if they destroyed the *ideas*, they could destroy the reality. In this brief introduction are traced the leading intellectual forebears of the American republic and its system of economics and statecraft. In most cases, it is very difficult to find mention made of them, much less their writings, in any history or economics book, and even in libraries. Yet, an understanding of the thinking of these men is absolutely integral to understanding what the United States of America represented in its founding, and what it must again represent today.

Then, we urge you to read the original essays and documents, which follow. While, having learned a good deal in the meantime, we might write them somewhat differently today, we have maintained the original text, with minor additions and subtractions. We have added the Declaration of Independence, Franklin's writing on wages, and the two Leibniz essays.

The Cameralists in Italy

It is likely that the republican notions of statecraft that arose in the Golden Renaissance derive from the wide-ranging work of that era's most seminal figure, Cardinal Nicolaus of Cusa.[2] The cardinal's

2. William F. Wertz, Jr., "Man Measures His Intellect Through the Power of His Works," *Fidelio*, Winter 1994. How Nicolaus of Cusa's revolution in the Platonic

groundbreaking work in science was supplemented by writings on statecraft, and the museum dedicated to his life in Bernkastel Kues, Germany, contains a display on his pioneering ideas of representative government. In the same period, a Platonist of Greek nationality, George Gemisthos Plethon, was active in Florence, and discussed the principles by which a proper government must deal with different sections of society—those engaged in agriculture, manufacturing, and trade—in order to provide for the general welfare.

The core concept behind cameralist statecraft was that the prosperity of a state depended upon the adoption of policies which fostered the improvement, materially and spiritually, of the citizenry. This was a revolutionary idea at the time—and remains so in many parts of the world today. It meant that a ruler had to devise a means of increasing wealth by making the citizenry more productive, but not by looting them. It meant changing from a situation where the vast majority of the population were slaves, or virtual slaving beasts, to one in which people were assumed to be educable and improvable—and therefore to a state policy which sought to implement such a policy.

Thus, as opposed to a situation of virtual war between rulers and their subjects, there was conceived to be a scientifically knowable common interest between them. The first purpose of the ruler was to provide for the prosperity of his subjects.

At the highest level, with the cameralists there came into being a school of statecraft and economics based upon the idea that man's nature was *imago viva Dei,* in the living image of God. Man's innate dignity and his creative capabilities were not simply to be recognized in church, but were to be understood as the foundation for sound economic and social policies.

The cameralists are sometimes known as the school of statecraft or economics which based itself on expanding population. This was directly related to their view that each individual was a net producer, rather than a drain on society, and that the source of wealth in society is not raw materials or land, but the productive powers of labor of individuals. It was a short step from there to the requirement to

Christian concept of natural law laid the basis for the Renaissance invention of the modern nation-state.

improve that productive power, through education and infrastructure and technological advance.

The eighteenth-century cameralist Antonio Genovesi put it this way: "The first aim of Political Economy is the increase in population. The most important part of Political Economy is to discover through what means one can increase the population. The ways to increase the population are manufacture and the improvement of agriculture through the teaching and application of agricultural mechanics."[3]

The most prominent Italian cameralist was Antonio Serra, who wrote his Treatise of the Sources of Wealth of State without Gold or Silver Mines in 1613. Serra's work was known to the German Hamiltonian Friedrich List (nineteenth century), but undoubtedly his work around Naples also spread to France, Germany, and Italy much earlier. Serra distinguished two kinds of wealth: *accidenti propri* and *accidenti communi*. *Accidenti propri* he categorizes as follows: 1) wealth from bullion coming from gold and silver mines; 2) wealth resulting from an extraordinary geographical endowment, such as fertile agricultural land; and 3) wealth from extraordinarily strategic location for trade, as in the case of Venice. But clearly none of these sources of wealth can provide a general concept of how to create wealth, Serra argued, since only a few states are endowed with these special characteristics.

Then Serra discusses *accidenti communi*, which he describes as follows: 1) crafts and manufactures; 2) the quality of the population; and 3) the character of the policy of the state. These are elements of policy which any state can develop properly, regardless of geographical, climatological, or related conditions. Serra defines crafts and manufactures as the most important element for creating wealth, *above agriculture*. He argues that this is true because they guarantee a surplus, unlike agriculture, since they depend upon human work alone, not upon nature; because they can be expanded almost without limit; and because they can be transported over long distances.

Improving the quality of the population is the second policy Serra discusses. This means that the state has an interest in improving and educating people, and giving them the capability to learn and

3. The quotes from Genovesi and other cameralists (not including Leibniz) come from an unpublished speech given in the early 1980s by Michael Liebig of *EIR*'s German affiliate.

advance. His associate Tommasso Campanella[4] expressed the concept
this way:

"God's will is that science is taught not only to noble men but
to all people. . . . Doesn't that painter paint better who knows mathematics and other sciences, compared to the one knowing only the
craft of painting? In the same way, the wise man cultivates the land
more profitably than the ignorant peasant, who knows nothing about
the peculiarities of soil, water, and air, or the different seeds, plants,
grasses, etc. . . . If bricklayers, shoemakers, and other craftsmen
would know about scientific ideas on the subject and proceedings of
their work, and therefore rely not only on tradition, we would have
better workers and a happier life."

The third determinant of the state's prosperity is whether the
government, or ruler, followed such policies.

What we see in Serra, overall, is an anti-oligarchical policy—
one that demands constant progress for the population as a whole,
and an active effort by the state to create conditions permitting that
progress.

The French Cameralist School

While there were many Italian Renaissance influences into France,
including through the Brothers of the Common Life and other institutions and individuals who influenced the great Louis XI,[5] one of
the major theorists of the school of national economy (or national
economic development) which came out of this, was Jean Bodin
(1539–96). Bodin's work and that of his better-known successor,
Louis XIV's General Controller of Finances Jean-Baptiste Colbert,
are extensively reviewed by Christopher White in his essay, which
introduces Part I.

---

4. Tommasso Campanella was born in southern Italy in 1568, and died in 1626. He
   was an extremely controversial figure, who served as a monk, was condemned by
   the Inquisition and Spanish monarchy, spent many years in prison, and wrote
   voluminously on subjects of religion and statecraft.
5. King Louis XI (reigned 1463–83) created the world's first modern nation-state in
   France. His national projects included the first postal system, the first national
   military not based on the private armies of the feudal nobilities, and a project for
   a national bank (unfortunately never realized). Under his 20-year reign, in a country
   otherwise devastated by the Hundred Years' War and Black Plague, the national
   income was doubled. Louis XI was closely allied with both the Renaissance forces
   in Italy and with the Brothers of the Common Life in the Low Countries.

Bodin begins from the concept that an expanding and improved population is the principal basis for wealth, and then asserts that the growth of wealth depends upon increasing the amount of work done on nature (e.g., crafts and manufactures). Both of these ideas led him to reject the leading practice of the day—looting bullion to increase wealth. Instead he had to insist upon the state taking actions to promote an increase in knowledge on the part of the population, and an increase in the means by which the population could produce wealth, through tax policy, education, subsidies, and so forth.

These policies were continued by Colbert in particular, who used his period of political power to unify the French nation with infrastructure, to promote self-sufficiency in necessities such as food and clothing, and to foster technological advance through academies, fairs, and so forth.

Colbert was a direct influence on Alexander Hamilton, America's first secretary of the treasury and the acknowledged founder of the American System of Economics. Colbert's policies are generally considered the prototype of mercantilism, meaning state protection of industries against the free trade, or trade war, and the control of terms of trade. What is usually ignored, however, is that the Colbertian—and American—view of mercantilism was not undertaken in pursuit of buying cheap and selling dear (effectively, theft), but for building up the productive power of the nation.

The German Cameralist School

German cameralist writings have been traced to the period as early as 1555, when Melchior von Osse, a court judge in Leipzig, wrote his "Testament."[6] Von Osse outlined the obligations for a ruler who wished to run a prosperous, successful state. Here is a sample of his thought:

"A lord and ruler is in three respects under obligations to the people divinely intrusted to him, namely, that he should maintain the same in good prosperous circumstances, which occurs when

---

6. The following history of cameralist writers, with the exception of the material on Leibniz, comes from Albion W. Small, *The Cameralists, The Pioneers* (Chicago: University of Chicago Press, 1909). While Small maintains the inaccurate view that cameralism was merely a pragmatic, rather autocratic reaction to the situation in the German feudalities, he is one of the few English-language writers on this subject, and includes invaluable quotations from original sources.

the people live virtuously, and some among them are promoted to learning, and to good arts, and many wise and learned people are in their numbers, from whom the rest may receive good instruction, and they are not left to wander in the darkness of ignorance, and everything through which such promotion of things useful to the community is hindered is either prevented or averted by the ruler."

Von Osse's ideas should not be thought of as abstract. He was fighting specifically for policies of caring for widows and orphans, of controlling prices for necessities, and of curing abuses in prisons and courts—all policies which could teach Gingrich a few things today. His successors, like Veit Ludwig von Seckendorff (1626–92), were even more explicit—demanding government provisions for doctors, clean water, sewage treatment, a good education, the abolition of usury, suppressing parasites (such as gamblers), and providing the means by which everyone could make a decent living. Von Seckendorff wrote two major books on cameralist theory and policy, *The German Prince's State* and *The Christian State*.

The concept of "general welfare" as the touchstone of public policy for the cameralists is so clear, that even those who deny the universal nature of this school of statecraft, like author Albion W. Small, feel forced to deal with it.[7]

Another leading cameralist in the seventeenth century was Johann Joachim Becher (1635–82), a doctor who traveled throughout Europe, and collaborated with many leading scientific intellects, including Christiaan Huygens and that towering genius Gottfried Wilhelm Leibniz, who worked at the same Mainz court at which Becher resided in the 1660s and 1670s.

Becher wrote a *Political Discourse—On the actual reasons determining the growth and decline of cities, states, and republics. How to make a state populous and productive and to make it into a real Societam Civil.* The piece is remarkable in its explicit advocacy of the Christian principle underlying a successful state, which today is only advocated by LaRouche in his *The Science of Christian Economy.*[8] The preamble cites Genesis 1:28, with its injunction to "Be fruitful and multiply. . . ." And in describing the role of

7. *Ibid.*, p. 86.
8. Lyndon H. LaRouche, Jr., *The Science of Christian Economy* (Washington, D.C.: Schiller Institute, 1991).

government, he says, "Government is said to be the means by which man is enabled to live according to his nature, which is created in the divine image."

Becher conceives of society as being divided into three parts: its soul, its mind, and its body. The soul is comprised of the government and the church; the mind, of the scientists and teachers; and the body, of the peasants, craftsmen, and merchants. The health of the soul and the mind are absolutely dependent, Becher insists, on the health of the three productive classes, the peasants, craftsmen, and merchants. To define the right proportions, Becher uses the following beautiful image:

"Just as when one is to play on a violin, one must first examine and tune each string, so when its sustenance is to be assured to a community, attention must be paid to every sort of human being that there is, and nothing appears to be more remarkable than that in many places no thought whatever is given to these most difficult points."

Becher promotes a policy of expanding population, nourished by an increased living standard. He targets three systematic enemies of this objective—monopoly, polypoly, and propoly. Monopoly, he notes, checks population and is therefore evil. Polypoly, which means the unrestricted competition for scarce resources (including jobs), reduces living standards too much. And propoly, which means a society in which individuals amass huge quantities of goods for speculation, divides the community.

What a difference from today's free marketeers, or from the oligarchs of the time, who wanted to see wages driven down to the lowest possible level, and let the economy be dominated by the speculators or monopolists!

Nor was Becher, a doctor, limited to mere administrative or political affairs. The concluding chapters of his *Discourse* survey 14 major areas of physical economy which must be attended to, and he also wrote several books on mining, chemistry, and mechanics.

Becher's father-in-law, Philip Wilhelm von Hornick, was also a leading German (in this case Austrian) cameralist. Differentiating between private and public economy, von Hornick developed nine rules of public economy, most of which involve ensuring maximum production of national necessities at home, minimum dependence on foreign nations, and full exploitation of domestic natural resources.

The Genius of Gottfried Wilhelm Leibniz

Working closely with Becher and von Hornick was Gottfried Wilhelm Leibniz. Leibniz is primarily known as a philosopher and scientist, but his role as a genius in statecraft cannot be overlooked. Leibniz, like Benjamin Franklin after him, was at the center of massive international political networks which intervened on behalf of the republican idea of statecraft. Because of his work in physics and technology, as well as philosophy and science, LaRouche describes him as the founder of modern economic science.

Leibniz wrote two seminal documents on economic policy. The first was composed in 1671, while he resided at the court of Count Johann Philipp von Schoenborn in Mainz. It is called "Society and Economy,"[9] and in it can be found the very antithesis of the free-market economics which runs rampant today. The second is a proposal for founding an academy for the promotion of arts and sciences, in which Leibniz's ideas of how a society should progress are outlined at some length. (We have added both in this second edition.)

"After all, is not the entire purpose of Society to release the artisan from his misery?" Leibniz asks in his short, incomplete, essay on "Society and Economy." He then outlines the principles by which this aim can be accomplished, which include ensuring that the farmer gets a fair price for his produce, and that there is no shortage of food. He also argues that individuals be provided with sufficient resources to care for their families.

With the proper measures, Leibniz says, "we eliminate a deep-seated drawback within many republics, which consists in allowing each and all to sustain themselves as they please, allowing one individual to become rich at the expense of a hundred others, or allowing him to collapse, dragging down with him the hundreds who have put themselves under his care."

What is striking about Leibniz's view in this small sketch is its total opposition to the views of British economy which argue that only need, misery, or punishment will force a person to work hard. Leibniz argues as follows:

"One might object that artisans today work out of necessity; if all their needs were satisfied, then they would do no work at all. I,

9. Published in *Fidelio*, Fall 1992, p. 54.

however, maintain the contrary, that they would be glad to do more than they now do out of necessity. For, first of all, if a man is unsure of his sustenance, he has neither the heart nor the spirit for anything; will only produce as much as he expects to sell (which is not very much given his few customers); concerns himself with trivialities; and does not have the heart to undertake anything new and important. He thus earns little, must often drink to excess merely in order to dull his own sense of desperation and drown his sorrows, and is tormented by the malice of his journeymen."

A good description of industrial England, or even the poor in American cities today? To prevent such problems, Leibniz promotes a policy of full employment, adequate wages, continual conferences of scholars, universal education, and the promotion of morality in all locations.

Leibniz's longer discussion of principles of economy comes within his 1671 paper "On the Establishment of a Society in Germany for the Promotion of the Arts and Sciences."[10] The extensive introduction to a listing of specific measures in this paper makes explicit the philosophy underlying his economic measures: the fact that man is created in the image of God. We quote briefly:

"For God creates rational creatures for no other reason but that they should serve as a mirror, in which His infinite harmony would be infinitely multiplied in some respects. . . . Now reason and power can be used for the glory of God principally in three sorts of ways, exactly as I can meet a man in three sorts of ways; that is, with good words, good thoughts, and good works. . . ."

Leibniz explores all three ways of serving God, first as orators and priests, second as natural philosophers (or scientists), and third as moralists and politicians. The highest value he puts on the third, because the moralists and politicians establish the framework of society which facilitates the other two kinds of professions. For example, he notes, "evil institutions, carelessnesses, and distractions" are permitted to make useful discoveries useless to people, if the moralists and politicians don't do their work. His inspired description of the worthy task of statecraft goes as follows:

". . . The third way to seek the glory of God, namely those who

---

10. Published in *Fidelio*, Spring 1992, p. 63.

serve Him as moralists, as politicians, as those who guide public affairs, is the most perfect, since those not only endeavor to find the radiance of God's glory in nature, but also seek to emulate Him through imitation; and thus seek to honor Him not only through praise and devotion, or with words and thoughts, but also with good works, not only to consider the good He has done, but to sacrifice themselves to Him and offer themselves as an instrument and through that to do more good for society and in particular for the human race, as the best of all visible creatures, in those things which we have the power to effect, and for which we are ordered and created.

"These are the ones who apply the discovered wonders of nature and art to medicine, to mechanics, to the comfort of life, to materials for work and sustenance of the poor, to keeping people from idleness and vice, to the operations of justice, and to reward and punishment, to preservation of the common peace, to the increase and welfare of the fatherland, to the elimination of times of shortage, disease, and war (insofar as it is in our power and is our responsibility), to the propagation of true religion and fear of God, indeed, to the happiness of the human race; and who endeavor to imitate in their domain what God has done in the world."

After this motivation, Leibniz details his ideas on how manufactures, commerce, and the arts and sciences should be promoted and improved. Under the first, he includes his crucial concept of "continuous cheap fire and motion as the basis of all mechanical effects," as well as a listing of the various divisions of manufacturing which he describes as "all those inventions which help the working people doing manual labor."[11]

Under the section on commerce, Leibniz deals with the mercantilist principles against free trade, including the need for food reserves, for immigration, for a bank, and government measures to promote innovation in manufacture.

Under the "promotion and improvement of arts and sciences," Leibniz insists upon the collection and publication of ideas and experiments, an education system available to the poor and orphans as well as to others, and the improvement of medical sciences.

Clearly, what Leibniz is talking about in this paper is the germ

---

11. This section of the Society paper is not included in the *Fidelio* selection, but comes from the unpublished speech of Liebig, *op. cit.*

form of a society or a national economy based on scientific and technological progress. It is composed from the standpoint of the responsibility of political leaders, or government, to provide the basis for every citizen to contribute to society, and be cared for by society. From this plan comes the idea of the "general welfare" of society, as opposed to a Hobbesian universe of each citizen against the other, or a government limited to minimal interference in each person's affairs. There is a higher purpose to society, and the economic system must serve it.

From Leibniz to America

The influence of Leibniz's ideas went far beyond Germany. He had correspondents in the American colonies, in England, in Russia, and many other places. And although the British and other oligarchical forces did their best to wipe out his name and ideas, they did not succeed.

The standard line of incompetence these days, of course, is that the American economic system and revolution were the spawn of the English moral philosophers John Locke and Adam Smith. Yet, even a short glimpse at the ideas of these two characters, in relation to the founding institutions and acts of the fledgling republic, should disprove this notion.

John Locke was not unknown in America. As a member of the Board of Trade appointed by King William of Orange, he had advocated revoking the charters of all the American colonies, a royal dictatorship over their economic activity, and a ban on the manufacture of any finished goods.[12] He had also at one time drafted a constitution for the colony of South Carolina, which declared the purpose of the government to be the defense of "life, liberty, and property." Part of that "property," of course, was the population of slaves, as Locke did not find that institution at all incompatible with his idea of the liberties of Englishmen. Locke's constitution established a hereditary nobility (outlawed by the U.S. Constitution, you'll recall!). After about 18 years, Locke's constitution was abandoned.[13]

12. Lowry, *op. cit.*, p. 75.
13. John Marshall, *The Life of George Washington, Vol. 1* (Fredericksburg, Virginia: The Citizens' Guild of Washington's Boyhood Home, 1926), pp. 154–159.

But the U.S. Declaration of Independence and Constitution did not follow Locke's lead in either respect. Not only did the Declaration anticipate the development of an industrial nation, but the inalienable rights which it asserted were the Leibnizian "right to life, liberty, and the pursuit of happiness."

Leibniz, himself a lawyer among other vocations, considered happiness as the "end" of society, and to be the object of the highest form of law. "The most perfect society is that whose purpose is the general and supreme happiness," he wrote in a piece on natural law.[14] In a longer piece on "Meditation on the Common Concept of Justice," written in 1702–03, Leibniz distinguishes three levels of law: the *ius strictum*, equity, and piety.[15] The crafting of the U.S. Constitution, especially the statement of purpose in the Preamble, reflects a higher concept of law than mere contracts or equity, and thus stands in the Leibnizian, not Lockean, tradition.

Of course, one can find innumerable American revolutionaries, as well as Tories, who quoted Locke and his ostensibly anti-absolutist views during the period of the Revolution and the formation of the Constitution. But that does not relieve you of the obligation to look at the content of the ideas. There may be many "patriots" today who adhere to the slogan "Life, Liberty, and Property," but the patriots of the American Revolution were about a higher moral purpose.

Even more outrageous is the argument that the economic system of the most advanced colonies, and the early republic, followed the ideas of Adam Smith and English liberals. Smith's *The Wealth of Nations* was published in 1776, and was a polemic *against* everything the American colonists were fighting for—the right to manufacture and achieve economic development, most prominently. While Smith permitted the central government to play a role in defense, his explicit argument on the economy was to keep the government out, and let the private entrepreneurs (might we say privateers?) do what they would without interference. Although such a free-trade outlook was not at all England's imperial practice, Smith was writing for the

---

14. Gottfried Wilhelm Leibniz, "On Natural Law," in *Leibniz, Political Writings*, translated and edited by Patrick Riley (Cambridge: Cambridge University Press, 1972, 1988), p. 77.
15. Leibniz, "Meditation on the Common Concept of Justice," in *Leibniz, Political Writings, op. cit.*, pp. 45–64.

mickeys, such as us Americans. We were supposed to buy it, and
continue to let England dominate world finances and trade.

But the American System of Economics, which Benjamin Franklin represented before the founding of the Constitution, and Alexander Hamilton represented afterwards, was at direct loggerheads with
Smith's propaganda. Nothing demonstrates this more sharply than
the Preamble to the U.S. Constitution, with its commitment to "form
a more perfect Union, establish Justice, insure domestic Tranquility,
provide for the common defence, promote the general Welfare, and
secure the Blessings of Liberty to ourselves and our Posterity." Under
Smith's philosophy, we had no right to talk about the "general welfare" as an aim of government policy, much less put the federal
government in charge of promoting it.

To the contrary, the ideas of the government's role in promoting
the general welfare of the citizenry had to come from another tradition—the tradition of Leibniz, Colbert, and their English co-
thinkers.

The Cameralist School Continues

While the United States of America is the only republic to have been
founded in the spirit of the cameralist tradition, the tradition survived
in Europe, primarily in Germany and Austria.

In 1727, the first Professorship of Cameralism was established
at Frankfurt an der Oder. The first individual to hold that position
was Justus Christoph Dithmar, who began as a professor of history.
With the appointment came the idea that there was a cameral science,
dealing specifically with how to raise and improve the income of the
principality, and apply it for the maintenance of the community.

One of Dithmar's successors, George Heinrich Zincke, described
the "new" science as follows:

"Cameral science is a learned and practical science, first, of
inventing, improving, and introducing all sorts of good police [sic]
laws and institutions drawn from the nature and condition of the
means of livelihood of a land; second, a science partly resting upon
die Öconomie (economics), partly upon special rules and maxims
which set forth the rights and duties of a ruler, of wisely, prudently,
rightly, and skillfully founding, maintaining, increasing, and administering the necessity, comfort, and riches of a land, and at the same

time and thereby the ready means needed by the ruler for the good of the state and its ruler."[16]

The most famous of the official cameralists, however, was Johann Heinrich Gottlob von Justi, who had a widely variegated career, from the Austrian Court of Maria Theresa to Göttingen, Denmark, and Berlin. Justi, who wrote the book *Staatswirtschaft* (*State Economy*) in 1758, conceived of himself as a "universal cameralist." The first principle of his profession he described as follows: "Hence follows the first and universal principle, namely all the governmental activities of a state must be so ordered that by means of them happiness of the state must be promoted."[17] He argued that "subjects do not exist for the sake of the ruler," and the ultimate aim of the republic has to be the common happiness of the population.

The state's happiness depends upon providing conditions of freedom, assured property, and flourishing industry to the population, Justi said. That means that the state has to have enough wealth to make such a provision. He proceeds to outline various ways to increase the wealth of the state—all of which could usefully be studied by the decorticated professionals called "economists" today.

The first way is to increase population. Justi says, "The larger the number of people living in the country, therefore, the greater will be the means and power of the republic. Hence the duty of the ruler to promote an increase of population."

The second way is to provide for flourishing commerce, manufacturing, and trade. Justi was clearly thinking of dirigist measures here, as he writes, "A wise ruler will not leave the food supply and employment of subjects to take care of themselves, but will see that they are systematically made abundant." He also argues that regulations governing medicine, municipal sanitation, and food hygiene be enforced. He also discusses the need to regulate trade, and the need for good infrastructure, like harbors, roads, navigable rivers, canals, and a postal system. He insists upon the promotion of domestic production.

Justi is fully confident that an emphasis on such objectives will increase necessary state revenues. As he puts it, the "best and surest

16. Small, *op. cit.*, p. 254.
17. *Ibid.*, p. 310. Other quotations from von Justi are from the same source.

means to increase revenues comes from encouraging the laboring class."

The last prominent self-professed cameralist was Joseph von Sonnenfels, an Austrian who lived between 1733 and 1817. Sonnenfels was a great promoter of industry from the theoretical standpoint that the development of manufacturing was a boon to increasing population, and to increasing the component of "artificial labor," i.e., technology, in society. Sonnenfels, unlike many other cameralists, is cited in economics textbooks. What we know today as the Vienna School of economics—a slew of British liberal monetarists—has done its best to bury or subvert practically every tenet of Sonnenfels's thinking.

The American System of Economics Today

It is not necessary for American or other national political leaders today to rush into the local library, dust off their German and Italian, and read the writings of the cameralist school of economics. Fortunately, they can turn to the much more elaborated and advanced work of the modern physical economist in the cameralist tradition, Lyndon H. LaRouche, Jr.

But it is critical, in this time of extraordinary failure of economics to serve and improve the human condition, to know that there is a tried and tested tradition of moral economics, Christian economics—a tradition which found its expression in the first hundred years of the America republic, and can therefore be revived today.

—*Nancy B. Spannaus*
April 18, 1995

Uncovering
the Treason School
of American History

by Nancy B. Spannaus

> To *cherish and stimulate the activity of the human mind, by multiplying the objects of enterprise*, is not among the *least considerable* of the *expedients*, by which the *wealth* of a nation may be promoted. — comes from Pericles 5th c. B.C.
>
> "towards things that will bring about Everlasting fame" - Pericles
>
> Alexander Hamilton, *Report on the Subject of Manufactures*, 1791.

Throughout the twentieth century a succession of pathological liars have "revised" American history down to a point where the founding ideas of the American republic have been nearly buried with its Founding Fathers. Substituting reliance on Lockean empiricists for continuity with the English Renaissance, disguising the pursuit of scientific progress as "pragmatism," and upbraiding the republican form of government for its deviations from pure democracy, the Beards, Arnolds, Williamses and countless others have attempted to undermine the very heritage that can preserve a society based on technological advance.[1] It is high time that the treason school of history be exposed for precisely what it is.

1. Beard, Charles A., *The Economic Interpretation of the Constitution*, The Free Press, New York, 1941. Arnold, Thurman W., *The Folklore of Capitalism*, Yale University Press, London, 1937. Williams, William A., *Contours of American History*, The World Publishing Co., New York and Cleveland, 1961.

1

Above all, what our American revisionist historians have told us is that there were no *universal values* represented by the American revolutionaries who established the U.S. Constitution, that every occurrence can be either explained or principle discarded, as being motivated by narrow group or individual self-interest. It is fortunate for both them and the entire world that they are totally wrong. Without the break from governments dedicated to the looting rather than the production of wealth, the break represented by the revolution resulting in the United States of America, the world's future under the East India Company and French monarchy was headed straight for a worldwide recurrence of the Black Death, and worse.

The American Revolution was successful because its leaders pursued the *science* of political economy and government. The evolution undergone by America's greatest genius, Benjamin Franklin, best illustrates this process. From his own understanding of both the delights and necessity of man's mastery over nature, Franklin determined to devote his early career to establishing the social institutions such as hospitals and libraries which would extend that mastery. Simultaneously, he was constantly studying nature itself in hopes of discovering its laws and putting them to the use of society, and disseminating his knowledge through newspapers and pamphlets.

Up until the period of the Seven Years War between Britain and France, Franklin's strategic view of capitalist progress was that the American colonies—as an *extension* of the British nation—would serve as the rapidly expanding and modernizing agricultural base to fully industrialize the more developed *island* portion of the nation. This would then accelerate the export of technological and industrial development to the American continent, all guided by a policy of increasing the production and productive reinvestment of surplus wealth for the English-American nation. With his entirely correct perception that by 1763 the British were committed to the imperialist looting of America instead of its development, Franklin turned strategically to France. He continued to organize weakening pro-development layers in the British Parliament, at the very least to buy time— time to implement a war-winning strategy for American independence. The French Physiocrats, with an agrarian notion of absolute (social) profit though not of industrial progress, became the lawful political-intellectual circle for Franklin's organizing in France, especially since only a combination of French military support and rapid

American agricultural development would make independence from Britain possible.

While Franklin's successors had neither his scientific nor political depth, they followed him in their determination to mold a society based on intellectual and technological progress. Alexander Hamilton, slandered at the time and today as a monocrat and servant of "moneyed interests," went the farthest in conceptualizing and implementing the political and economic institutions necessary for an advancing society. Without Hamilton, there is no doubt that neither the Constitution nor a rudimentary, competent credit system would have been implemented, and the English financiers who were destroying human civilization in India would have had a free hand in America. Hamilton's archrival, Thomas Jefferson, made his indispensable contribution because he refused to apply the standards of vulgar democracy that tainted his 1790s behavior to his conduct of the presidency, and to science and education. If the Founding Fathers had not fought to educate the American population to what their self-interest was, British manipulation of the "popular will" would have ensured that the republic did not survive.

Thus, when Charles Beard in *The Economic Interpretation of the Constitution* denounces the framers of the U.S. Constitution for lining their own pockets, we must ask why he opposes the establishment of a credit-worthy central government which has the means to counter economic, political and military subversion of the young country. Is it because he really doesn't understand the benefit to the country as a whole of entrepreneurs building canals and roads, or investing in a national bank which will support those projects, the government, and industry? Does he really not understand that human progress depends on an absolute increase in wealth, not a redistribution and dissipation of the same? One suspects that his intimated preference for a government less concerned with property, coincides with his desire to have some other power determine how that property will be disposed of.

More openly treasonous was famous revisionist and Assistant Attorney General Thurman Arnold, who wrote *The Folklore of Capitalism* in order to justify Franklin Roosevelt's 1937 plan to pack the Supreme Court. The Founding Fathers set up a government replete with checks and balances that would leave the least opportunity for action by passion, rather than by the considered judgment for the good of the nation. Arnold demands attention to the cries for food and shelter from the population instead of "a search for universal truth." "The old creed of democracy as our fathers knew it was a *useful slogan* to bind together those who rose to fill the gap left by an incompetent aristocracy,"[2] writes Arnold in his demagogic attempt to win support for dismantling the Constitution. Arnold's traitorous threat survives him in the Institute for Policy Studies which he co-founded, and which pursues its aim of dismantling "capitalist industry" through appeals to Hitler's "Volksgemeinschaft" and terrorist bombings.

Those Tories who operated as a fifth column within the United States found it generally convenient to take the part of "anti-capitalists" in their appeal for popular support. The relevant alternative which they sought to impose up through their defeat in the Civil War was mercantilism, the system by which America's economy would depend on the provision of raw materials to Europe, and be free of "oppressive" technology and industry while running progressively into greater and greater debt. The alternative that Thurman Arnold and his allies were trying to impose was and is fascism, the regimentation and gutting of *industrial* capitalism by financiers interested only in protecting their property titles by their collection of debt. Fascism has always been anti-capitalist—as even a cursory study of Germany or Italy in the 1930s shows.

But the Grand Prize for Historical Psychopathy must go to William Appleman Williams. When describing the consolidation of a national government in the United States whose uniqueness lay precisely in its opposition to mercantilist looting as a form of social reproduction, Williams writes the following:

> Not only may the concept *feudal* be used, it provides the most accurate insight into the true nature of the Constitution. It is a document based on feudal principles. Just as in the feudal age, the individual citizen was beholden to, but was also the responsibility of, the highest lord (or the national government). He had the same relationship with his state government (a lower lord), which in turn had (as a vassal

2. Arnold, Thurman W., *The Folklore of Capitalism*, Yale University Press, London 1937, p. 42 (emphasis added).

to the top lord) reciprocal ties with the national government. As long as the citizen participated directly and actively at both levels, and as long as the states remained significant elements in the political economy of the system, the individual was protected and at the same time able to play a meaningful role in government himself.[3]

The fact that James Madison, co-author of the *Federalist Papers* with Alexander Hamilton, can be cited as speaking of "the (Constitution's—N.B.S.) aspect rather of a feudal system of republics" provides no excuse for Williams' lunacies. Like the founder of his line of thought, John Locke, Williams cannot conceive of any individual, not to mention societal, relationships that are not based on feudal-style contracts. His paranoid perception of existence through propitiatory relationships has a certain correspondence with the mental workings of the local citizen confronting his state and national governments, but it sheds no light on the actual social and material basis for the existence and continuation of American society under the Constitution. And even so, the vast majority of the American population supported the Constitution because they understood that a national government with an income and a uniform commercial policy would provide the best basis for the country's prosperity—not, like some 1960s suburbanite, because they were looking for "meaningful" roles to play.

From its beginnings, America has been the concrete realization of the humanist conception of progress—a political system wedded to technological advance, and to the republican form of government on which its assimilation depends. Its shortcomings have resulted from the necessity of industrial capitalism to wage a battle for its survival again and again—the deliberate stultification of the rate of material and cultural growth by infestations of mercantilists, slave-traders, financiers and Naderites demanding their democratic rights to sabotage. The revival of the concepts behind the American Revolution is the first step toward a capitalist renaissance that will once again put science at the center of politics, and pave the way for the elimination of capitalism's anarchic features in due time.

3. Williams, William A., *Contours of American History*, The World Publishing Co., New York and Cleveland, 1961, p. 160 (emphasis in original).

An Education for Independence

The lengths to which illiterate or lying historians will go to deny the power of ideas in shaping events is truly astounding. Hence, according to the school of thought that attributes the once-glorious British Empire to the fact that Britain is an island, America rose to greatness because it was a big continent! The revisionists' variant on this theory is that it was the physical challenge of the vast frontier of the colonies that led to America's emergence as a wealthy republic.

Frederick J. Turner's acclaim as author of this theory has been fed by positive connotations of the frontier concept that unfortunately were totally unintended by Turner. To the mentally alive individual the existence of a frontier is a challenge, be it physical or in a domain of knowledge. He responds then to the frontier by searching for the new concepts through which it can be brought under his control, or developed. Hence, exploration at the frontiers of knowledge holds the promise of resituating everything which is already known, as one searches to determine the coherent lawfulness of the entire universe. It is the mental quality one brings to the frontier that determines its yield.

To Turner, on the other hand, the frontier was the "every man for himself" environment which spawned an Andrew Jackson—that uncouth murderer who marched, stinking buckskins and all, into the White House to dismantle the only financial establishment available for developing the frontier *out of* homestead poverty into a network of cities and towns.[4] It is largely to Turner that we owe the adulation of the "individualist" American who serves as a law unto himself, bites his opponent's ear off in a brawl, disdains "booklarnin," and shoots the stranger who sets one foot on his land. *American history is a battle against this rural bestiality*. The backwoodsmen participated in the building of this nation under the leadership of Americans wielding the very highest culture that Europe had to offer.

Much of the early American population was created out of waves of extraordinarily thoughtful and heavily urbanized European immigrants. In New England and the Middle colonies, they were descendants of Protestants who had risked their very lives in order to possess

---

4. Turner, Frederick Jackson, *The Frontier in American History*, Henry Holt and Co., 1920 and 1947 *passim*.

and read an English Bible; many others were close relatives of the Cromwellian army which for a brief moment established a republic in seventeenth-century England. Beyond the Bible, their literary fare included heavy doses from Shakespeare, Milton, John Bunyan and their Whig heirs in the eighteenth century. Their rate of literacy is estimated by all to have been extraordinarily high even by general standards today: nine out of ten adults could read in New England; three out of four in the much less developed area, Virginia.

The population as a whole, then, had a deep respect for education, what Hamilton calls a "genius for mechanics" and a religious sense of purpose about their lives. Relatively free of royal attention during Britain's wars with the Dutch and the French and Indian wars, the colonists approximated the republican traditions of the Cromwellian interlude under more prosperous material conditions. Science and education were high public priorities, as shown by local ordinances requiring schooling for boys and girls, and public funding of such activities as the study of eclipses. No wonder that they spawned a generation of intellectual and political giants—the men who took on the organizing of a new republic.

I number among those giants John Adams, Sam Adams, Benjamin Franklin, Thomas Jefferson, Alexander Hamilton, Thomas Paine and George Washington. Without any one of these men, America would not have won her freedom and established a stable form of republican government. Of these only four were educated through the nation's universities, but the drive of each to acquire the very most knowledge he could about the universe, and apply that knowledge to the benefit of mankind, qualifies each as an intellectual. With the exception of Jefferson's 1790s retreat, each was characterized by that hubris which scorns so-called public opinion, and concentrates instead on educating that opinion to the necessary course for the public good. They were not democrats, but republicans.

And educate they did. Beginning in the 1720s, Franklin, who left a Boston family of Puritans and craftsmen to become a Philadelphia printer, began to establish a chain of newspapers, in which the public could find the latest controversy in astronomy, the deliberations being taken in their local legislature, and a sprinkling of aphorisms and jokes—often enough culled from the literary genius of François Rabelais or Erasmus. At the same time, he pulled together a small group called the "Junto" which met every week to discuss their

political and intellectual undertakings of the previous week, and
how their accomplishments could be disseminated more generally.
Simultaneously, Franklin himself, self-educated by this time in both
the English classics and five other languages, was establishing close
contact with certain members of the generally stagnant Royal Society
of London around questions of electricity, metabolism and the like.
Contrary to general custom (scientists' huffy possessiveness about
"*their* discoveries" was already a time-honored tradition), Franklin's
correspondence was composed primarily of hypotheses and suggested
experiments which he encouraged those with more time and equipment to take advantage of and try out.

By the 1740s, Franklin had shifted his primary attention to the
stimulation and upgrading of cultural and scientific improvements
in America. His *Proposal for Promoting Useful Knowledge Among the
British Plantations in America* helped organize what was previously
only an informal network of scientists and physicians into an increasingly political grouping, a network which as the American Philosophical Society, came to include Jefferson, Hamilton and many other
revolutionary leaders. Franklin now began publishing and organizing
for certain immediate improvements in Philadelphia. These included
Pennsylvania's first militia, organized on the Cromwellian model;
the first sanitation department in America; a hospital; a public library;
and the Academy that later became the University of Pennsylvania—
all realizations of his goal to maximize the "power of man over
nature."

Franklin—by 1750 recognized as a successful businessman, a
leading American intellectual, experimental scientist, and accomplished inventor—is already the epitome of the American spirit, a
man whose creativity is constantly being exercised and directed toward elaborating the knowledge and the institutions required for
human progress. Would you have guessed it from the tales of the
old miser moralizer and womanizer you read about in the common
American history text?

In 1750, the British clamped down a new barrier to America's
development, issuing regulations strictly prohibiting the production
of finished iron products in America. The presses of both Franklin
and Sam Adams in Boston quickly tore into this issue, as they had
on the British prohibition of colonial currencies the decade before,
from the standpoint of its crimp on the productive powers of the

entire empire. Franklin's winning of the job of Deputy Postmaster General for the colonies in 1753 vastly aided his ability to organize and educate opposition. Under his administration, mail service was extended to Quebec and time of delivery was reduced by 75 per cent—an achievement as critical as his insistence on freedom of the mails in light of the intense period of coordinated continental political action ahead.

It was in direct response to Britain's slap at colonial progress that Franklin planted the first concrete proposal for continental union during this period. The plan was clearly conceived as a way of creating colonial unity against Britain's policy of enforced backwardness as well as in immediate response to the danger of Indian wars. The Albany Conference of 1754 reviewed the Franklin-authored plan to be united under one governor, elect one grand council and tax itself through a liquor tax. Long after both the Parliament and the local assemblies had vetoed the plan, Franklin's cartoon and slogan "Join or Die" was used to underline the need for colonial solidarity against British depredations.

By 1763, the Iron Act had proven to be only the beginning of a *total military, political and economic assault* on the colonies' development. By the end of that year—supposedly the close of British military operations on the American continent as a result of the conclusion of the French and Indian War—the Parliament had imposed new taxes on the valuable molasses trade, had closed off the frontier to colonial expansion, had authorized Church of England missionary activities in "wildernesses" such as the city of New York, and had left a substantial complement of His Majesty's troops who, along with Crown-appointed officials, were trampling right and left on colonial legal safeguards. The Americans could again justly complain that the British—who preferred to loot furs and other natural resources from the Indians rather than develop the capacity in America for social reproduction at higher levels—were treating the Indians better than loyal British subjects. The same issue had touched off the famous and quickly crushed Bacon Rebellion in Virginia in 1676![5]

This time, the center of resistance to these policies was Boston,

5. Bacon, Nathaniel, *Declaration in the Name of the People*, in Ver Steeg, Clarence L. and Hofstadter, Richard, eds., *Great Issues in American History, From Settlement to Revolution 1584–1776*. Vintage Books, New York, 1969, pp. 104–107.

where Sam Adams and James Otis originally took the lead, well supported by the Virginians and other urban centers. It was in the cities where the troops were quartered, and the taxes had the most immediate impact on survival. It was also in the cities that the nuclei of political intellectuals had arisen.

The propaganda war began in earnest in 1763. The first task of the American leaders was to educate the population that the attacks on Boston and the other coastal cities were only the first step in British subjugation of the entire population of the colonies. The merchant class itself paid for much of this propaganda and a great deal of the "mass action" which came later on in the fight, as the revisionists gleefully point out. The treason school of history merely ignores the fact that the propaganda was nevertheless correct: it *was* upon the prosperity of the merchants that expanded employment, improved technologies and the upgrading of living standards depended. The town artisans and laborers were readily organized to oppose the British measures. The farmers were convinced more slowly, and some, especially tenant farmers, not at all, for two reasons: 1. their lower cultural level made them "naturally" hostile to any "outsiders"; and 2. they were often affected by the fact that their "immediate" self-interest pitted them against their patriotic landlords, and by British incitement and promises of rewards. Much of the frontier area was actually contested or neutral throughout the war, due to the threat of British-inspired Indian raids and preoccupation with their own local affairs.

Overall, however, the education campaign was successful. Franklin, while remaining adamantly critical of frontier behavior, like the brutal raids against peaceful Indians carried out by the most backward Scotch-Irish frontiersmen, succeeded in overcoming a great deal of the nascent town-vs-country split in Pennsylvania by elaborating the mutual benefits of expanded markets and trade. Sam Adams concentrated more on the political commonality of interest against increased repression. The Virginia planters were more than anxious to end their total dependency for cash and goods on British companies, a plight strikingly similar to that of raw materials-rich, industry-poor Third World countries today.

No one is more underestimated as a political leader from the beginning to the end of the American Revolution than George Washington. One cannot help but judge that it is indeed an intense hatred of greatness that leads the revisionists to revile Washington as a bumbling general, a selfish land speculator, and then the mouthpiece for everything which Alexander Hamilton put in his ear.

Washington, in his youth a surveyor and colonel in the Virginia militia, had groomed himself to be a statesman from adolescence. Having been given only one year of formal schooling, he delved on his own into his favorite subject of mathematics, as well as the political and philosophical classics. Washington's central self-conception was that of a nation-builder, and by 1758 had gotten himself elected to the Virginia House of Burgesses to pursue that undertaking.

From his position as a legislator, an exporter and a landowner, he felt keenly the effects of Britain's renewed vigor in looting the colonies by more taxes, frontier expropriations, etc. By 1769 he had begun to diversify into manufactures and to propose the building of the Potomac canal for commercial use. Nor were these measures conceived by him as merely personal expedients. He wrote the following to James Warren around 1774:

> Let vigorous measures be adopted to punish speculators, forestallers and extortioners, to promote public and private economy and to encourage manufactories, measures of this sort, gone heartily into by the several states, would strike at once at the root of all our evils.[6]

Washington's deserved selection as the new nation's commander-in-chief becomes more understandable also if one realizes that he co-authored the Fairfax Resolves in response to Britain's imposition of the Coercive Acts against Boston in 1774. The Fairfax Resolves called for the establishment of a Continental Association; the non-importation of goods from Britain and committees to enforce this measure; a ban on slave importation; and an embargo against Britain if the above measures were not effective within one year in stopping Parliament's repressive actions. Washington not only shepherded these through the Virginia Assembly, but they were passed by the First Continental Congress. As commander-in-chief, he was recognized to be the nation's only executive in far more than narrow

6. Ritter, Halsted L., *Washington as a Business Man*, Sears Publishing, 1931.

military affairs, but also in decisions concerning foreign affairs, navigation and highways, commerce, and manufacturing.

Hamilton's position as chief aide was obviously significant in aiding Washington to conduct a brilliant *political* fight and in holding an unpaid, underfed and underclothed rotating army together, but no one yet dares suggest that he ran the army through the "puppet" George Washington. Moreover, in the face of open and covert Tory sabotage and disruption, Washington organized his forces from a *political* war-winning standpoint, angrily refusing an "offer" from Congress of dictatorial powers to dragoon men and supplies (making the American forces "indistinguishable from the king's," as Washington retorted).

Following the war, Washington again turned to the task of economic development. A trip to the west in 1784 resulted in a report on what routes could best be developed for stimulating internal commerce, and on the desirability of Detroit as a future center for commerce and trade. Before his attempt to get interstate collaboration on his Potomac venture in 1786, he corresponded and consulted on canal building as far away as New York State.

Washington combined, in diluted form, the strengths of both Hamilton and Jefferson, using his executive authority to foster the unity and advancement of the U.S. through proposals for manufacturing and for a national university; and unlike his colleagues, he almost never allowed his judgment to be overruled by his emotions. When the new nation's survival depended on economic development and avoidance of war, Washington overrode factional clamorings and maneuvers by both Britain and France to pit the United States against one or the other, notably in the destabilizing furor over Jay's Treaty. The ex-general set up the Alexandria Academy in 1785, and later donated money to build a national university on the site chosen for the new capital. To Lafayette in 1788, he expressed his desire "to indulge the contemplation of human nature in a progressive state of improvement and melioration." After doing his best to create that progressive state, he concluded his presidency with a farewell address that demanded unity around the nation's highest goals, including scientific education:

> promote then as an object of primary importance, institu-
> tions for the general diffusion of knowledge. In proportion

as the structure of a government gives forces to public opinion, it is essential that public opinion should be enlightened.[7]

As compared with the revisionists' portrait of Washington, the Weems' cherry tree story and so forth look positively plausible.

There were two other sides to the political education process which America's revolutionary leaders were conducting: organization, and the activities of the British themselves. The first continent-wide meeting since the Albany Conference was the Stamp Act Congress of 1765, of which the Adams cousins and Patrick Henry of Virginia were prime organizers. As conservative as it was—the Congress defeated resolutions by Virginia to affirm the colonial assemblies' total sovereignty and to declare supporters of the Stamp Act traitors to America—the Congress provided an effective lesson in favor of *national* organization. Between the national refusal to use the stamps, the boycott of British goods and Franklin's spokesmanship in London, the Stamp Act was overturned in a matter of one year. From 1765 to 1774, however, most of the organization was local, consisting of small networks of Sons of Liberty and Committees of Correspondence, who did little traveling and much writing. Organizing for explicit solidarity between the colonies was primarily focused on getting colonial assemblies to pass Circular Letters or resolutions that would be sent both to Parliament and also to other colonial legislatures. Washington and Jefferson joined the Adamses in playing key roles in this organizing.

Just as significant in creating a proto-national unity among the Americans was the British intransigence. No sooner had the Parliament backed down on the Stamp Act than it passed the Declaratory Acts, whose purpose was solely to assert parliamentary authority over the colonies in every matter whatsoever. It then proceeded not only to widely increase the range of taxes, but also to make governors financially independent of the legislatures, and increase the military presence, especially in the Boston area. Who could still argue that this was merely a question of a little increase in taxes? In fact, in light of the scope of the conspiracy, the patriots believed that the smaller any particular tax, the more insidious it was.[8]

---

7. Washington, George, *Farewell Address, 1796.* See any version of collected works.
8. Dickinson, John, early colonial pamphleteer cited in Bailyn, Bernard, ed., *Pamphlets of the American Revolution, 1750–1776*, The Belknap Press of Harvard University Press, Cambridge, Mass., 1965.

Equally powerful were the reports of the actual parliamentary attitude being sent over by Franklin, now formally representing Massachusetts as well as several other colonies. The most explosive was the Hutchinson letter, a clever tactic for which Franklin and Sam Adams are generally underestimated; Franklin's transmittal of the Massachusetts governor's statement that "There must be an abridgement of what are called English Liberties" had to have been intended by Franklin to reach every colonial newspaper—just as Sam Adams insured that it did.

What kept the consolidation of national sentiment from moving even faster than it did was the lack, in the minds of the leaders of the continental movement, of a practicable alternative to membership in the British Empire. Franklin and Jefferson held out the longest, in hopes that sufficient pressure and persuasion could be applied to Britain to have to realize that *her own* self-interest called for allowing America to develop her wealth, instead of having it siphoned off to pay the British debt. America's revolutionary leaders disappoint our revisionists because they are responsible intellectuals, not Yippee protestors.

But even Franklin's piercing wit failed to arouse the intelligence of the parliamentarians to the fact they were systematically dismantling their own empire. So necessity demanded a scheme of colonial development which would work against British opposition. Both Sam Adams and George Washington had conceptualized the necessity for the colonies to develop an independent manufacturing capability as early as 1768, but the political instrument for even considering this course was lacking. In fact, it took the acceleration of the Boston struggle to a point of military occupation to dramatize the necessity for a semipermanent national coordinating body. At that point, the question before Congress was more pointed than development as such—how to mobilize everything necessary to win a war.

The final step in the education of the population is widely attributed, and correctly so, to Tom Paine's pamphlet *Common Sense*. But was Tom Paine a lowly tradesman who caused a radical break in the process of the American Revolution because he dared to, for the first time in the propaganda war, center his fire on the king? No. *Federalist* Tom Paine's circle in Philadelphia was Franklin's circle, frequented as well by Drs. Rittenhouse, Rush and Thomas Jefferson; his manuscript was not only checked over by these supposed "compromisers," but was also by all evidence most likely commissioned by them! The publication of *Common Sense* was a *strategic* decision taken by representatives of the very grouping who had begun as much as 20 years before to prepare the American colonists to decide whether or not America's progress was compatible with her allegiance to the king.

What the revisionists variously obscure or abstract into mere logic is the development of advanced principles of government to serve the goal of progress. The colonialists' reaction to British measures after 1763 was not simply to the amount of taxation, but was focused with intensity on British assertion of a *policy of looting*. Colonial propaganda and legalistic remonstrances on this point theoretically and tactically concentrate on defining the powers of Parliament, and appropriately insist that those powers are *void* when they serve to "enslave" or "subjugate" the American population by abrogating its *right to development*.

During the first phase of this process, until approximately 1771–72, the emerging Revolutionary leadership pours forth pamphlets and treatises on the "English Constitution," demanding that Parliament adhere to notions of liberty and *standards of policy-making* defined by a humanist commitment to progress. (The revisionists frequently treat all of this as evidence that the American colonists were merely inheritors of an already prescribed English Constitution, and thus deny the uniquely advanced ideas that *made* the Revolution.)

During the second phase (roughly through 1774), with British depradations now occurring with military enforcement as well, American propaganda points directly at a *conspiracy* against English liberties, and against the institution of Parliament itself. This accusation, oft cited by revisionists to fuel the slander that the Revolution was a paranoid, irrational episode, was entirely correct respecting the subversion and suppression of pro-development factions *in England* and Parliament's prominent role in carrying out the looting policies. Politically, the American propaganda assault also defined the commitment to fight for constitutional government, *independently creating one if necessary*.

From 1774 onwards, Americans properly regarded Britain strictly as an imperialist *monarchy*, stripped of all vestiges of constitutional government and of all prospects of freedom for development. It is then that polemics against the king are launched broadside, frequently portraying him physically *devouring* the peoples of the Empire and comparing America's fate to India! That fate, and for the world worse, was assured if the American Revolution, the one successful capitalist revolution, had not secured freedom for a nation to accomplish scientific progress and industrial development.

This then is how a revolution—"this radical change in principles, opinions, sentiments and affections of the people" relative to English rule—occurred before even a single shot was fired, as John Adams pointed out on reflection in 1818. Its leaders were scientific inventors—Paine, Franklin, Jefferson; lawyers steeped in the republican experiments of Rome, Florence and Cromwellian England—Jefferson, the Adamses, Hamilton; businessmen and tradesmen—Washington, Franklin, Sam Adams. Above all they were intellectuals who understood that material progress and human freedom were of one and the same piece, intellectuals who would not rest until they found a strategy for winning the world's frontier for human progress.

The Battle for the Constitution

Despite the fact that a good two-thirds of the representation at the Constitutional Convention was the same as that which adopted the Declaration of Independence—a fact that would seem unequivocal enough to capture empiricist Charles Beard's attention—the revisionists and their Institute for Policy Studies offspring do not blush to lie that the Constitution of the United States is a document of counterrevolution because it supports the rights of property. It is profitable to look back at who was mouthing this line at the time when the Constitution was being debated—they were none other than the Tory traitors!

Having failed to split the merchants from the farmers and one group of merchants from the others, the British strategists of the Revolutionary War determined that their main fallback position would be to protect states' rights! The strategy was not dissimilar to the one which they had tried and had failed—that of pitting the farmers against the cities—during the period leading up to the Declaration of Independence. Now, however, under conditions of all-out warfare, they had high hopes that they would be able to sabotage the functioning of a wartime command center, without which no army could fight effectively. So, throughout the Revolutionary War the loudest cries against "tyranny" and the taxes demanded by the Continental Congress in order to prosecute the war came from enclaves of British sympathizers who were too frightened to come out openly and fight with the Redcoats, but were anxious to do their part to restore monarchical rule.

This fifth column action came dangerously close to succeeding, especially in the years after the war was technically over. But for the prescience and determination of George Washington, Alexander Hamilton and Tom Paine, in particular, in producing the propaganda and organizing the meetings that led to the Constitutional Convention, the coordinated economic pressure being applied both from Britain herself and the traitors within the young nation might have resulted in an actual counter-revolution in the name of economic salvation.

Despite the overwhelming popular support for the Declaration of Independence, it was clear to Congress at the very beginning that the difficulties in mobilizing sufficient men, materiél, and sustenance would be immense, if not insurmountable. America had been totally dependent on Great Britain for textiles, gunpowder, muskets, finished iron products such as cannon, and innumerable other small, but crucial supplies for a war economy. Now Britain would not only not supply those goods, but was patrolling the east coast line in hopes of preventing goods from other countries from making it into port. This meant that there was little choice but to do two things: mobilize the country to produce for the needs of the army as much as possible—including the establishment of new industries; and two, achieve foreign loans of materiél and supplies that could be privateered by skilled American seaman past the British blockade. Accordingly, the first task of the committee set up by the Continental Congress to procure supplies for the army was to send Benjamin Franklin to France, and the second was to go about exploring new ways of manufacturing gunpowder.

The lack of national economic and political integration, however, meant that not even those supplies which could be met easily by the American population were easy to get to the right place at the right time. Requisitions from Congress could be sabotaged 1. by the colonial legislature; 2. by Tories with access to or control over supplies and their means of transportation; and 3. by political scandals manufactured so as to destroy public confidence in the war's management both by Congress and the commander-in-chief. The Tories went for all three. Legislatures quibbled over the equity of the congressional requisitions. Rotten flour was delivered to the army while edible meat and warm blankets would be held back due to "lack of wagons" to transport them. The Conway Cabal tried to wrest control of the Continental Army from Washington in order to put it in the traitorous hands of General Charles Lee.

One of the most devastating blows was the pseudo-left mobilization of the population against the very merchant "profiteers" who were responsible for buying and delivering crucial supplies from France and other countries. The cause célèbre was the case of Silas Deane, the man who handled the business end of Franklin's diplomatic mission for the first two years of the war. The fact that Deane profited by his business of supplying the American Army—while other Americans swallowed the illusion that French aid ought to, and was, being given free—was made into a serious Congressional inquiry. One of the main suckers in what smells like a sophisticated disruption by British agents, aided by ingenuous Americans, was Tom Paine himself, then employed as foreign secretary of the Congress. The clamor and abuse ultimately did drive Deane into the arms of the British, despite no evidence of any traitorous sympathies previously. But the upshot was not only considerable embarrassment and jeopardy for Franklin's Paris operation, but also a concomitant wave of riots against high prices in the colonies—riots which just happen to have targeted Robert Morris of Philadelphia and other major suppliers of the American war effort. When real profiteering was going on, Washington and Hamilton were among the first to lead the political attack.

In the face of such operations, Washington had little choice but to give major attention to the propaganda front, since he was supplied to advance on few others. The main weapon in his arsenal was the pen of Federalist Paine, who travelled with the Revolutionary Army for a while, and produced 13 *Crisis Papers* between 1776 and 1783, which ripped apart the British propaganda and mobilized the superhuman effort needed to get through "the times that try men's souls." Paine touched on every issue, including that of the demands Congress was making on the states to fulfill their requisitions for funds.

Paine's words on this subject, written in May of 1780 when noncompliance by the states had brought the nation to a point of extraordinary crisis, ruthlessly expose his nominal admirers, who seem unable to tell the difference between taxation by Britain and taxation by the Congress:

> So extensively right was the ground on which America proceeded, that it not only took in every just and liberal sentiment which could impress the heart, but made it the direct interest of every class and order of men to defend the country. The war, on the part of Britain, was originally a war of covetousness. The sordid and not the splendid passions gave it being. The fertile fields and prosperous infancy of America appeared to her as mines for tributary wealth. She viewed the hive, and disregarding the industry that had enriched it, thirsted for the honey. . . .
>
> Britain did not go to war with America for the sake of dominion, because she was then in possession; neither was it for the extension of trade and commerce, because she had monopolized the whole, and the country had yielded to it; neither was it to extinguish what she might call rebellion, because before she began no resistance existed. It could then be from no other motive than avarice, or a design of establishing, in the first instance, the same taxes in America as are paid in England (which, as I shall presently show, are above eleven times heavier than the taxes we now pay for the present year, 1780) or, in the second instance, to confiscate the whole property of America, in case of resistance and conquest of the latter, of which she had then no doubt. . . . It is not so much my intention, by this publication, to propose particular plans for raising money, as it is to show the necessity and the advantages to be derived from it. My principal design is to form the disposition of the people to the measure which I am fully persuaded it is in their interest and duty to adopt, and which need no other force to accomplish them than the force of being felt.[9]

By and large, the Washington strategy was effective, given the aid of extraordinarily well-built fortifications which Franklin's engineer

---

9. Paine, Thomas. "The Crisis Extraordinary," in Foner, Philip S., *The Life and Major Writings of Thomas Paine*, Vol. I, The Citadel Press, Secaucus, N.J., 1948, pp. 172 and 182.

recruits and American skilled workmen put together, and the support given by the population. When France entered the war, and it became clear that the British would not be able to rally any significant portion of the population to join their military forces, the succession of stodgy, indecisive British generals could not hope to win the war, no matter how many individual battles they might leave in triumph.

The next question was whether the Americans could survive the peace. Documents from behind-the-scenes negotiations that were going on in Europe between 1781 and 1783 prove beyond all doubt that significant sections of both the French and English governments were agreed to 1. deprive America of lucrative fishing rights off Newfoundland; 2. prevent the extension of her boundaries to include Canada, the West Indies, Florida or other strategic launching points for future harassment of the new country; and 3. if possible, to divide the country up into New England versus the rest of the country.[10] Through playing Britain and France off against one another, Franklin, Jay and Adams succeeded in negotiating territorial integrity, recognition of independence, and the fishing rights. Britain immediately retaliated with full-scale trade warfare. They dumped cheap goods, put prohibitive restrictions on American imports into Britain, looted America of hard cash, and waited for the resultant social unrest to force America's leaders to cry "uncle!"

A central government with significant control over national economic and political policy had the same military-strategic significance which it had during open hostilities, but it was even harder now to mobilize common action in the absence of a flesh-and-blood enemy army. The Confederation had just gone into effect in 1781, thanks to Paine's and others' mobilization to get Virginia to cede her claim to all land west of the Alleghenys to the national domain. A battle had begun simultaneously to increase the central government's powers beyond those which had been proposed in the original Confederation proposal of 1776. Hamilton wrote a series called the *Continentalist*, demonstrating the necessity for uniform commercial regulations and federal taxes for the survival of America. Congress battled valiantly within itself to adopt measures that would give them enough revenue to pay the army, and the debt, only to find their proposals ship-

10. Morris, Richard B., *The American Revolution Reconsidered*, Harper and Row, New York, Evanston and London, 1967, section on diplomacy.

wrecked by one or two states who put their own short-term prosperity above that of the nation which had kept them free to enjoy it.

In the overall depression caused less by any decline in American productivity, than by the economic warfare being carried out by Britain, British agents found fertile field for their dirty work. Impoverished farmers without markets for their produce were encouraged to revolt against equally insolvent legislatures. Military takeover plots were barely avoided. Each legislature bid to carry out policies that would give it an advantage in foreign trade, enacted laws that prevented free transport of goods across state lines, and put innumerable roadblocks up against proposed internal improvements in those few cases where there was sufficient capital accumulated to undertake them. By 1785, the situation had degenerated to its lowest point. Continental Congress-backed legal tender was so worthless that barter deals predominated. The three banks that had been established— two in Philadelphia and one in New York—were objects of populist agitation. The charter on the Bank of North America was successfully revoked by reactionary, and undoubtedly British-influenced forces in Pennsylvania, and pro-development legislators were not able to revoke the repeal for two years.

The end result of tolerating this deteriorating situation was no mystery to the perspicacious. As Hamilton laid out in the *Federalist Papers* after the Constitution had been adopted, such internecine competition would inevitably lead to manipulation by foreign powers and reconquest.

It was to deal with this real threat that Hamilton, Morris, Madison and others developed the economic and political conceptions that led to the U.S. Constitution. But before getting to the genesis and content of the Federalist program, let's eliminate one oft-cited "proof" of Hamilton's restorationist program—his defense of Tory property-owners from an official witchhunt in New York after the war. The only coherent explanation for this braving of public scorn to defend those people whom he had just been fighting in the trenches of Yorktown is, amazingly enough, just what Hamilton himself puts forward. In the face of what were, in everyone's estimation, the most anarchist populists in the country, he was determined to end what could turn into an endless battle for existing property in order to put people back to work in the kind of environment where they could create new wealth. The other principle involved had more lasting value as it was decided in the groundbreaking *Wadsworth* v. *Rutgers* case: Hamilton established the precedence of the *national* treaty just concluded by the Congress over the local laws, where they might conflict. Is it believable that a secret Tory would argue a case on the basis of the absolute authority of the government he was devoted to wiping from the face of the earth?

What lay on the agenda in the 1780s was the *completion* of the revolution against aristocracy and its right to subordinate the prosperity of its subjects that had been declared with the 1776 Declaration of Independence. What had swept the country throughout the war had been a mood of dismantlement—dismantling of the feudal vestiges of quitrents and property entails, progressive banning of the slave trade, a dropping of the debts owed to British creditors and expropriation of many a Tory estate abandoned by its fearful owner. New constitutions had also been adopted in many of the colonies with fewer restrictions on suffrage, but local measures to generate the necessary *credit* for economic expansion or even taxes fell flat on their face. What remained to be discovered was that the economic welfare of the country, like its physical security, depended upon the development of a national political center with a national economic policy.

The policy which Hamilton, et al. devised was the government's defense of private capital in return for the mobilization of private capital to back the government economically and politically. Wealthy merchants and landowners had the desire to invest in the development of agriculture, manufacturing and infrastructure. The government needed this investment in order to secure the prosperity and growth of its population. The government, then, in Hamilton's view had to provide the conditions in which this investment could take place; at the same time, it would lay out the guidelines and general goals that would discipline the naturally heteronomic functioning of the capitalists. In reality, the Constitution was a statement of political agreement among those capitalists and the intellectuals of the society to discipline themselves within the bounds of the national interest.

Without the juridical forms imposed by a federal system of government, the nascent capitalism of America had already had a universalizing effect on the country's economy. Technological advances made *for profit* in one part of the country affected the general rate of profit available in the country, and tended to spread the innovations, raising the standard of living despite Britain's deliberate embargo on both machine blueprints and skilled artisans. Benjamin Franklin, for example, had devoted considerable expenditure to improving agricultural methods through rotation of crops—an innovation that was being taken up *for profit*. But the pursuit of more absolute surplus for the society as a whole through investment in more technological advances in agriculture and industry was constantly threatened by mercantilist and slave-owning interests, who could offer what appeared to be more spectacular profits through looting land and labor. The advantages of the former could only be explained by a scientific view: profit by looting meant that the society would very rapidly run out of the human and physical means to reproduce itself.

Thus, as capitalists, Hamilton, Washington and the other fathers of the nation judged the effects of their economic and political measures by what kind of *future* they would produce. They could see that the prevention of an accumulation of wealth would stymie the development of new technologies and higher material and cultural levels. They knew that the government had to have the ability not only to collect taxes, but to attract and create credit for building infrastructure that would aid commerce and future self-defense. Surplus beyond the immediate needs of the population had to be generated through investment, and then reinvested in the areas that would again yield to an expanded rate of surplus production. The problem lay in controlling the heteronomic individual capitalists according to national necessity; this meant control through a coherent, strong national government, the object which British and other anticapitalists put under most vicious attack.

The relative strength of a capitalist outlook is reflected in the differences among the participants at the Constitutional Convention on the question of debt. The southerners in general could see it as nothing but a lodestone around their neck, in line with their experience with the British. They demanded utter cancellation. Hamilton, on the other hand, acted both to reduce the debt and to harness it for generating future credit, hence maintaining a political tie between America's creditors and her government based on a common interest in America's prosperity. Hamilton's view of the subject is most clearly delineated in his *Report on Public Credit* to Congress in 1790; government funding of the debt through the issuance of bills based on that debt and the placing of official authority behind their repayment will not only raise the value of government stock, and hence lower the interest that the people must pay, Hamilton argued. It will also allow us to use the money of our foreign or domestic creditors in carrying out agriculture, commerce and manufacturing that *will produce more value for us than the income which the creditors will receive.* Hamilton was fond of pointing out how well his scheme worked. Interest rates went down to six per cent, and loans that would previously have had to be paid back completely could now be carried along for such small interest payments.

Despite its apparent contradiction with the debt moratorium program of the LaRouche movement today, Hamilton's program must be endorsed as coherent with the main justification for today's demand—the elimination of barriers to expanded investment in socially useful production. Over half the new nation's debt was to internal creditors; bankrupting them would only cut the nation's throat. As for Britain, Holland and France, the nation's other main creditors, Hamilton was confident that they could be induced to provide credit for America's expansion if approached with a political harness, rather than a political stick. In fact, if debt is maintained on the books with payment merely of the interest, that debt does function as a credit. It is precisely this transformation which Hamilton's Bank of the United States made and that the world needs through the establishment of an International Development Bank today.

It was Jefferson who suffered from a pay-back-the-past concept of debts. He had fantasies about wiping the books clean every 25 years, so as no obligation from the past would taint the future. This idea was so silly that he too was forced to abandon it after a few years in the White House. The maintaining of the debt, managed through the establishment of the national Bank of the United States, in fact vindicated Hamilton's point of view. It was invested so productively in the U.S. economy that the nation was able to retire it substantially within the projected 20 years, despite the reduction of taxes overall and a moderate level of internal improvements.

It was with the needs of a growing economy in mind that Hamilton, Washington and the others devised the shape of the new government. While several significant battles took place within the chosen framework, there was little disagreement on the choice of republican-

ism, above either monarchy or democracy. The following quote from
Tom Paine's *Rights of Man* cogently expresses the reason why:

> . . . the question naturally presents itself, *What is the best
> form of government for conducting the RESPUBLICA, or the
> PUBLIC BUSINESS of a nation, after it becomes too extensive
> and populous for the simple democratical form?*
>
> It cannot be monarchy, because monarchy is subject
> to an objection of the same amount to which the simple
> democratical form was subject.
>
> It is possible that an individual may lay down a system
> of principles, on which government shall be constitutionally
> established to any extent of territory. This is no more than
> an operation of the mind, acting by its own powers. But the
> practise upon those principles, as applying to the various
> and numerous circumstances of a nation, its agriculture,
> manufacture, trade, commerce, etc., requires a knowledge
> of a different kind, and which can be had only from the
> various parts of society.
>
> It is an assemblage of practical knowledge, which no
> one individual can possess; and therefore the monarchical
> form is as much limited, in useful practise, from the incom-
> petency of knowledge, as was the democratical form, from
> the multiplying of population. The one degenerates, by ex-
> tension, into confusion; the other, into ignorance and inca-
> pacity, of which all the great monarchies are an evidence.
> The monarchical form, therefore, could not be a substitute
> for the democratical, because it has equal inconveniences.[11]

No one doubted, either, that the most intelligent men of the nation,
not the most common, should represent the public good in the nation's Congress. The issue of representation is not replication of every
spontaneous inspiration that might strike the country's fancy, but
the putting forward of the most *competent* ideas for furthering the
nation's welfare as a whole. Hamilton and Jefferson would find ludi-
crous Jimmy Carter's inaugural plea to the population that "Your

11. Paine, Thomas, *Rights of Man*, Part I, in Foner, Philip S., *op. cit.*, p. 371 (emphasis
   in original).

strengths can compensate for my weakness and your wisdom can help to minimize my mistakes."

With the nation in danger of a total collapse of agriculture, trade and credit in the mid-1780s, Washington, Hamilton and Madison had to create a new institution which could begin to address the public welfare competently. Congress itself had been virtually abandoned by anyone who wanted to accomplish anything. The state legislatures also were more often roadblocks than helps. In 1786, for example, George Washington addressed the assemblies of both Virginia and Maryland to get authorization of his privately financed venture to widen the Potomac River into a waterway navigable for cargo boats. Unable to resolve the problem, he called a conference at his home to discuss means of creating a political climate or structure compatible with projects such as his. If the conference had come off, it would most likely have been the scene for the first call for a Constitutional Convention.

Instead, James Madison took up the idea and called a meeting of businessmen for Annapolis, Maryland for later in the year. Although only five states attended, Hamilton seized the occasion to promulgate a call for a convention of all the states to be held as soon as possible. The declaration from the meetings, written by Hamilton, motivated the convention by citing the general need to "consider how far a uniform system in their commercial relations and other important matters might be necessary to the common interest and permanent harmony of the several states."

The convention itself was the scene of compromises with the industrial capitalist outlook represented most cogently by Hamilton and strongly supported by Franklin and Washington. The Federalists were too practical to let the whole union go down the drain because they refused to compromise. So the economic questions were left for the first session of Congress, while they were approached tangentially through the battles over state vs. individual representation, and the mode and regularity of elections.

But, say the revisionists, if this was no reactionary convention, why was slavery still suffered in the Constitution? In reality opposition to slavery was far more advanced by the time of the Constitutional Convention than it was in 1776, when the assembled delegates eliminated mention of it altogether. Several states had abolished it, and Hamilton and several other prominent New York citizens had petitioned the New York State legislature to eliminate the slave trade in 1786—a move "populist" Governor Clinton aided in blocking. It is a baldfaced lie that the hard-nosed capitalist Federalists were soft on slavery. Discounting a faction of throwbacks to English mercantilism who had captured a certain section of Massachusetts, the Federalists hated slavery as a degradation of labor power, and hence an intolerable impediment to industrial and agricultural advancement. Hamilton himself had advocated giving slaves their freedom for fighting with the Continental Army as early as 1779!

Yet, the Federalists decided to compromise, creating a structure of a union with the details of its commitment to capitalist progress still to be filled in. The commitment to promoting science and inventions was stated clearly under the responsibilities of Congress. The commitment to a national defense and a national commercial policy was there. The right to tax was there. With these minimal requirements they were fairly certain they could win the support of the nation. Their plan to save the nation from anarchy won more than that—it sent the advocates of zero-growth and mercantilism into an evil tantrum from which they have not yet recovered.

Behind the Hamilton-Jefferson Fight

The political battles that rent the United States during its first decade under the Constitution can only be understood in the context of the international strategic situation which the young nation faced. To pose the struggle between the Federalists and the Republicans as the eternal fight between the principles of autocracy and democracy is to perpetuate a pathological lie. On the contrary the Hamilton-Jefferson fight emerged because the American state faced some uncomfortable choices about how to survive under a virtual state of siege.

America was surrounded by hostile armies—British forts to the west and north, Spanish to the south, French to the west. American vessels, regardless of their captains' beliefs in free trade, were considered fair game by both British and French warships, especially after the French initiated new international hostilities in 1793. Within the country itself the state of industry and agriculture, while promising, was totally insufficient to provide an adequate defense for commerce or territory, and to compensate for the scarcity of hard currencies which also complicated international purchases. As the later plans for military adventures against America by both the Spanish and Napoleon show, it was not paranoia on Hamilton's and Washington's part to insist upon the development of a strong navy and a well-trained national army along with the roads, canals and industries which could serve both war and peace.

The exigencies of the situation demanded that the U.S. conduct its foreign policy in an exceedingly hard-nosed fashion, putting primary emphasis on rapid internal development that would free it from dangerous dependencies and build up its capability for self-defense. Congress, in fact, motivated its request for Hamilton to prepare the *Report on Manufactures* by alluding to the necessity for the nation to provide an independent means for its defense. Unfortunately an unhealthy combine of New England mercantilism and southern slave owners succeeded in rejecting the recommendations of that report, sparking instead a hysterical contest between "Jacobins" and "Monarchists" that left serious discussion of the necessary economic program totally out of the picture.

Hamilton and Jefferson never considered resolving their dispute by dismantling the Union—the necessity for preserving the nation was the bedrock of both their programs. In his virtuous self-righteous complaints against the Hamilton-Washington regime, however, Jefferson never succeeded in putting forward a viable economic program and several times let himself be "captured" by totally indefensible popular assaults on the constitutional government. While from the vantage point of the presidency, Jefferson matured to the point of actually extending Hamilton's economic development program, his weaknesses have been apotheosized into the hallmark of the Democratic Party. For these vulgar democrats demanding independence from the central government, President Jefferson would have the same charge he pressed against Aaron Burr in 1808—*treason!*

The personality struggle that has been the object of disgusting chit-chat and analysis by so-called historians rather had its roots in the discrepancy between Hamilton's and Jefferson's understanding of political economy. Hamilton's elaborated understanding of how industrial capitalism would benefit the welfare of the nation as a whole informed all of his proposals to stabilize public credit (of which the National Bank was part two) and to stimulate manufacturing. He had determined that a wedding of the "moneyed interests" to the state was essential for the society's progress. The following ex-

cerpts from his private correspondence demonstrate that Hamilton
was not looking at his proposals as short-term inducements or rip-
offs, but as a scientifically determinable necessity for a developing
nation.

> The tendency of a national bank is to increase public and
> private credit. The former gives power to the state for the
> protection of commerce among individuals. Industry is in-
> creased, commodities are multiplied, agriculture and manu-
> factures flourish, and herein consist the true wealth and
> prosperity of a state.[12]
>   Whenever, indeed, a right of property is infringed for
> the general good, if the nature of the case admits of compen-
> sation, it ought to be made, but if compensation be impracti-
> cable, ought not to be an obstacle to a clearly essential
> reform.[13]

What most disturbs the revisionists about Hamilton's economics
is that he asserts them as the realization of precisely those universal
values which the revisionists insist do not exist! The cynicism that
drips from Thurman Arnold's pen when he refers to those who seek
a standard beyond their immediate gratification is reserved especially
for the term "universal truth." Williams cannot conceive of an economic system that advances and yet aspires to improve the general
welfare—hence industrial capitalism as put forward by the Founding
Fathers is interpreted by him as the corporate state, or feudalistic.
One suspects that even the caveman had a higher morality or sense
of society than these champions of fascism's "little man."

By contrast with Hamilton, Jefferson's understanding of economics was an incoherent mishmash of mercantilist saws, adulation
of agricultural life and a dedication to the advancement of the means
of production and existence through fostering science and inventions.
So while he insisted that the quickest way to increasing national
wealth was to stick to the exchange of American raw materials for
European manufactured goods, he fought for the increase in skill

12. Lodge, Henry Cabot, ed., *Collected Works of Alexander Hamilton,* letter to Morris,
    1781.
13. Cooke, Jacob E., ed., *Alexander Hamilton, A Profile,* Hill and Wang, New York,
    1967, p. 157.

level and education for the population that was compatible with
advancing both agricultural and industrial technologies. Jefferson's
advance beyond Physiocratism—his knowledge of and belief in the
development of the human mind—was what impelled him not to
dismantle Hamilton's National Bank and program of internal improvements, after years of tooth-and-nail battle against them.

The lack of a developed economic perspective left Jefferson with
an inadequate basis on which to judge both domestic and foreign
policy decisions. He had no strong overall perspective on which to
motivate a whiskey excise tax, or a treaty preference for England or
France. Under these circumstances he yielded, as President Washington suggested in his *Farewell Address*, to a pro-France foreign policy
based on "womanish affections." His utter frustration with economic
policy is best seen in his total commercial embargo of 1808, which
was like saying to the world that "the game's not going my way, so
I quit." As to domestic policy, his lack of vision left him vulnerable
to constituency pressures of the most heteronomic sort—up until,
and no farther than, the point at which they openly threatened the
union.

Despite Jefferson's agrarian proclivities, Hamilton initially
thought that at least through the mediation of Washington, he could
work with the secretary of state. After all, the central ambition of
both was to guide the United States to wealth and greatness as
measured not by military superiority, but by the qualitative and
quantitative improvement of the nation's productive powers. Their
economic policy even found a common ground around the conception
laid out by Benjamin Franklin in his Pennsylvania Society for Manufacturing and the Useful Arts, and the American Philosophical Society. But while Hamilton arrogantly—and correctly—pressed forward
the necessity for the government to take an active, directive role in
achieving these worthy ends, Jefferson and Madison immediately
began to drag their feet—unwilling to take on the strong political
opposition within their own state and unaware of the strategic consequences of leaving the nation without a strong economic center. And
heavy strategic consequences there were. Jefferson's championship,
however passive, of rebellion against Hamilton's economic development program had its directly traceable effect in the miserable state
of the navy and other military necessities—setting the United States
up for not only a continuous beating by the British and others on

the seas, but also the hideous destruction of the War of 1812. Even more significantly, it postponed the defeat of the mercantilists— giving them the opportunity to challenge the supremacy of industrial capitalist advancement, and hence leaving the institutions intact that would cause the nation's economic policy to be fought out in the Civil War.

Economic Policy. The most serious mistakes made by Jeffersonians were in the realm of economic policy. While they made a deal to allow Hamilton's first *Report on Public Credit* to be approved, this did not occur until considerable hoopla had been raised throughout the country about the "conspiracy of the rich" against poor Revolutionary War veterans. In reality, the point was moot. Veterans who had sold their bonds could not be assured repayment, and in fact, the consolidation and payment of the debt to the current holders would provide the maximum opportunity for a solvent government and growing economy—the best aids for the veterans.

Although Jefferson cooled Madison's oppositionist ardor on the public credit report, he committed himself to preventing the institution of the national bank. Unable to stop the measure in the Congress, he instead made a fuss within the cabinet which resulted in Washington's requesting statements on the constitutionality of the bank by Chief Justice Randolph, Secretary of the Treasury Hamilton, and Secretary of State Jefferson. Jefferson's argument was directly counter to his own personal philosophy of human progress; he argued that as long as it was possible to accomplish an end (such as collecting taxes) through inefficient, unsynchronized, and generally backward state banking institutions, the federal government could not establish a corporation that would carry out the same aim more effectively and provide additional benefits to the general welfare of the nation. The argument had about as much validity as the stand that the federal government had no right to muster a navy or an army until the enemy had already attacked, an argument Hamilton and Madison had already given short shrift to in the *Federalist Papers* three years previous. Jefferson's *Opinion on the Bank* was the first influential airing of the talmudic, constructionist view of the U.S. Constitution, that ignores the intent of its guidelines for promoting the general welfare, in favor of minute examination of its commas, semi-colons and colons. He had many occasions himself to be glad that Washington ignored his views and agreed with Hamilton that the bank was not only useful in carrying out the enumerated powers of the federal government, but that the exercise of such sovereign authority as to establish an institution was not explicitly prohibited by the Constitution. With Washington's refusal to veto, the Bank of the United States was established by law.

Hamilton's elaboration of the economic measures to build a strong nation did not end there. Proposals to establish a mint, begin construction of a navy, collect an excise tax on whiskey, and promote manufactures by a combination of bounties and moderate tariffs followed in rapid succession. Hamilton put his most intense effort into the *Report on Manufactures*, a brilliant theoretical, comprehensive, and practical discussion of how the fostering of manufactures would contribute to the wealth, culture and defense of the nation. It was the *Report on Manufactures* that the Jeffersonians, with the aid of a faction of New England merchants, moved to block.

Jefferson had no rational explanation for blocking the policy. He had no alternative internal development policy to offer. By this time—the end of 1791—he rather begins to ride on the crest of an unprincipled opposition that was united only by its resistance to what temporary inconveniences Hamilton's program for development would mean for them. This opposition reached its peak in 1794–1796, with the fomenting of open rebellion against federal authority on the question of excise taxes. The test legal case chosen by the southern plantation owners who correctly saw the taxes as discriminatory against the slave economy, was the carriage tax, a case Hamilton had the pleasure of winning before the Supreme Court in 1796. The political test case was the Whiskey Rebellion of 1794.

The scene of the Whiskey Rebellion was western Pennsylvania, where whiskey distilled from the local grain crop was the primary cash crop, and often the medium of exchange. It would be mistaken, however, to view the incident as an outpouring of spontaneous local resentment. The defying of federal authority to collect the taxes was organized by Democratic-Republican Clubs which at this time had been engaged in a demagogic campaign against "monarchists" Washington and Hamilton for at least two years. And after the local residents had used armed force against the federal excise officers, the Republican governor of the state refused to do anything to restore respect for federal authority!

Since Congress was out of session, Hamilton and Washington determined to seek extraordinary authority from the Supreme Court to requisition militia forces to intimidate the rebels into their rightful respect for federal law. Hamilton's argument—both in court and before the public in the national press—won general public support. The Republicans were forced to disassociate themselves from the rebellion, and their ranks provided much of the overflow of volunteers who flocked to join the disciplinary force, led by Hamilton himself.

Although not itself an immediate danger to the federal government's integrity, the Whiskey Rebellion would have established an extremely dangerous precedent had it not been suppressed. As it was, Jefferson allowed his Republican Party to circulate the charges that Hamilton had fomented the rebellion himself in order to increase the authority and taxing power of the federal government! Even after President Washington's forthright attack on such irresponsible activity by the Democratic societies, Jefferson spread the following filth:

> . . . And with respect to the transactions against the excise law, it appears to me that you are all swept away in the torrent of governmental opinion, or that we do not know what these transactions have been. We know of none which, according to the definitions of the law, have been anything more than *riotous*. There was indeed a meeting to consult about a separation. But to consult on a question does not amount to a determination of that question in the affirmative, still less to the acting on such a determination; but we shall see, I suppose, what the court lawyers, and courtly judges, and would-be ambassadors will make of it. The excise law is an infernal one. The first error was to admit it by the Constitution; the second, to act on that admission; the third and last will be, to make it the instrument of dismembering the Union, and setting us all afloat to chuse (sic) which part of it we will adhere to . . . I expected to have seen some *justification* of arming one part of the society against another; of declaring a civil war the moment before the meeting of that body which has the sole right of declaring war; of being so patient of the kicks and scoffs of our enemies, and rising

at a feather against our friends; of adding a million to the
public debt and deriding us with recommendations to pay
it if we can, etc . . . etc.[14]

Keep in mind that Jefferson had left the Washington cabinet rather
than fight for his views in 1793. From the standpoint of a "pure"
outsider, he was acting both stupidly and very dangerously.

Although Jefferson used the economic issue in a demagogic way
throughout the rest of the decade, he never lent his support again
to a *practical* assault against Hamilton's economic infrastructure.
Indeed, his return to high office, this time the vice-presidency, in
1796 seems to have been the beginning of a slow reconciliation to
the necessity of those measures. While he eliminated the liquor excise
tax upon being elected President, he already had a more mature view
of the necessity for federal intervention into the national economy—
centered on the goals of education, infrastructure, and science.

Foreign Policy. As the new government's secretary of state, Jefferson's proper sphere of influence was foreign policy. But here his
"womanish affections" left him incapable of formulating a sound
perspective for avoiding both war and anarchy. The only sound
policy was to avoid entanglements in European wars, while acting
quickly to create the conditions for an American victory against the
looting wars which would inevitably be waged against the U.S. by
Britain or France. For a secretary of state who "hated" England and
"loved" France, this path to national security was impossible to
traverse.

Ironically, it was the French Revolution that most complicated
the formulation of a consensus on foreign policy in the United States.
While the French Revolution's highest accomplishments were directly inspired by the American Revolution and its spokesmen Tom
Paine and Ben Franklin, its fracturing into a British-controlled
"right" and "left" made it a mortal danger to the American Revolution
by no later than 1793. Jefferson could not have been aware of this
when in 1791 he received a copy of Paine's *Rights of Man* (Part I)
with its dedication to George Washington, and proceeded to have it
printed for wide circulation all over America. The contents of Paine's

14. Jefferson, Thomas, letters in *The Portable Thomas Jefferson*, edited by Merrill D.
    Peterson, The Viking Press, New York, 1975, pp. 468–469 (emphasis added).

pamphlet only underlined Jefferson's own judgment that the French scuttling of the unchecked monarchy would win unqualified support in all arenas of American life:

> If government be what Mr. Burke describes it, 'a contrivance of human wisdom,' I might ask him if wisdom was at such a low ebb in England, that it has become necessary to import it from Holland and from Hanover? But I will do the country the justice to say, that was not the case; and even if it was, it mistook the cargo.[15]

> The Revolution in France is attended with many novel circumstances, not only in the political sphere, but in the circle of money transaction. Among others, it shows that a government may be in a state of insolvency, and a nation rich. So far as the fact is confined to the late Government of France, it was insolvent; because the nation would no longer support its extravagance, and therefore it could no longer support itself; but with respect to the nations, all the means existed. (The difference between France and England is) . . . The people of France refused their aid to the old Government; and the people of England submit to taxation without inquiry.[16]

> Public measures appeal of themselves to the understanding of the nation, and, resting on their own merits, disown any flattering application to vanity. *The continual whine of lamenting the burden of taxes, however successfully it may be practised in mixed governments, is inconsistent with the sense and spirit of a republic.* If taxes are necessary, they are of course advantageous; but if they require an apology, the apology itself implies an impeachment. Why then is man thus imposed upon, or why does he impose upon himself?[17]

> Whether the forms and maxims of governments which are still in practise, were adopted to the condition of the world at the period they were established, is not in this case

15. Paine, Thomas, *Rights of Man*, in Foner, *op. cit.*, p. 326.
16. *Ibid.*, p. 336.
17. *Ibid.*, p. 340 (emphasis added).

the question. The older they are, the less correspondence
can they have with the present state of things. Time, and
change of circumstances and opinions, have the same progressive effect in rendering modes of government obsolete,
as they have upon customs and manners. Agriculture, commerce, manufactures, and the tranquil arts, by which the
prosperity of nations is best promoted, require a different
system of government, and a different species of knowledge
to direct its operations, than what might have been required
in the former condition of the world.

   . . . it would be an act of wisdom to anticipate their
(revolutions') approach, and produce revolutions by reason
and accommodation, rather than commit them to the issue
of convulsions.[18]

But France did not follow the constitutional model which Federalist Paine proposed, and in fact the beheading of the king was the
signal for unleashing a bevy of British-controlled ultra-lefts who
tried to exterminate the entire circle of Franklin's followers (e.g.,
Lavoisier) and Paine's co-thinkers, and nearly got Paine himself.
British agents such as Marat and Danton carried out an orgy of
blood and hysteria that ran circles around even the Revolution's most
human representative, Maximilien Robespierre. The chaos, self-initi-
ated war with Britain, and emasculation of republican institutions
are the tragic vision, *writ large*, of what could have happened to the
United States if qualified economic thinkers like Hamilton and
George Washington had not overruled the likes of Thomas Jefferson.
   Jefferson's view of the French Revolution always maintained a
romantic veil that prevented him from productively evaluating that
revolution for the working people who supported it. Hamilton knew
what it lacked—an economic program that would both develop and
unify the country. But his fury at the blanket calls for revolution
being issued by the French government and the mindless anarchy
of successive governments received no sympathy from Jefferson.
Instead Jefferson continued in the irresponsible vein which he had
begun in 1787:

18. *Ibid.*, p. 344.

I own that I am not a friend to a very energetic government. It is always oppressive. The late rebellion in Massachusetts has given more alarm than I think it should have done. Calculate that one rebellion in 13 states in the course of 11 years, is but one for each state in a century and a half. *No country should be so long without one.*"[19]

Not until 1800, when Napoleon practically had his ships loaded with men to secure French control of the Mississippi and Louisiana, did Jefferson perceive the reality that post-1793 France was no more bound by feelings of loyalty to the U.S. than the U.S. was to Britain.

The greatest danger in Jefferson's softness for the French government was that it would have inevitably led to a premature war with Great Britain. Edmond Genet's provocative activities as French ambassador to the U.S. during 1793 followed precisely the lines he would have had to take to provoke war between the U.S. and Britain. On top of Britain's continual interference with American commerce with France, the complaints by the British about Genet's harboring privateers in American ports escalated American hostility to its overbearing ex-rule to the boiling point.

War with Britain was what Hamilton and Washington knew had to be avoided. It was a war that would deal America, still surrounded by British-manned forts not only in Canada but also on the western frontiers, and totally outclassed at sea, a crushing blow. Hence, Hamilton and Washington determined that they would send John Jay to England to make a pact with the devil. While they did not foresee that the British would force such an unpalatable settlement down their throats, they knew there was little choice but to accept it as a way to *buy time*. With the Jeffersonians screaming "sellout to the monarchists" all around the country, they stuck firm. The gains obtained by the Jay Treaty were seemingly insignificant—primarily the guarantee of some safe trading with both Britain and France. But it was by virtue of the Jay Treaty, as well as Napoleon's military genius, that the next hostilities in the ongoing war between the British imperialists and American capitalists were delayed until 1812.

War with France was still a possibility on the agenda, however.

19. Jefferson, Thomas, *Letters*, in Peterson, *op. cit.*, letter to Madison, Dec. 20, 1787, written from Paris, pp. 431–432 (emphasis added).

In 1795, French government representative Adet campaigned for Jefferson on a platform that demanded a new revolution in the U.S.! Diplomatic relations were considerably strained because America had consented by treaty—the Jay Treaty—to British seizure of contraband goods headed for France. Talleyrand's XYZ Affair brought the two nations very close to the outbreak of war. In this case, it was Hamilton's turn to be ruled by affections.

Leaving the federal government with Washington in 1796, Hamilton continued to head the Federalist party while practicing law in New York. But he became increasingly embittered against both the Jeffersonians and the increasingly hegemonic New England mercantilist tendency in his own party. By 1795, he had had to abandon his attempt to build a prosperous industrial complex in New Jersey. In 1797, the despicable John Beckley of the Jeffersonian party paid a whorish journalist to expose Hamilton's extramarital affair with Maria Reynolds, itself a setup by her conniving shyster of a husband. Hamilton responded with dignity but he was sorely wounded. Within Hamilton the rage seethed and boiled—only waiting for the opportunity to be unleashed. Daily the press would lambast him as a "monarchist"; few came to his defense.

Under these pressures Hamilton made the foolish and dangerous resolution to himself that he would seek an opportunity to lead an army into battle again—either against France herself or against French and Spanish colonies in the Americas, or even against the recalcitrant anti-Federalists in Virginia. His chances of realizing his ambitions were considerable, as he managed to get himself appointed second-in-command in the armed forces, again Washington's first subordinate, in 1798. Fortunately, Washington never turned over the reins to Hamilton, who, despite his resolve not to be the obvious aggressor in a war with France, was chafing to throw his newly organized and efficient army into battle. President Adams' continuous efforts for peace gave France a chance to back down, and eliminated one military adventure. General Washington himself nixed Hamilton's proposal to "liberate" certain French and Spanish colonies with an armed band of men. The third opportunity disappeared when Jefferson prevented Virginia from using her militia to resist the Alien and Sedition Acts in 1799—an act of sedition that Hamilton was only too eager to put down.

The disbanding of the army by Washington upon the reaching

of a peace agreement with France ended the nation's war mobilization—not to be revived until the War of 1812. When Jefferson took up the reins as President, he rededicated himself to Washington's policy of neutrality. His only failure on that front was that he did not prepare to win the next war as well.

Democracy vs. Republicanism. When opposition to the Federalist policies first began to take shape in 1791-2, the new party gave itself the name the Democratic-Republican Party. It is not surprising that whereas Jefferson's grouping shortened this name to "Republican," the Jacksonians and Rooseveltians who claim lineage from Jefferson identified themselves as "Democrats." Those who cannot understand the difference cannot fathom the actual content of the fight between Hamilton and Jefferson on the question of political organization.

In a strict sense, Hamilton and Jefferson were both republicans. Knowing intimately, if not sufficiently, the qualities of intellect, experience and judgment that were necessary to govern, and knowing them gravely lacking in most of the population, they favored a government by the best qualified representatives of the people. They agreed—as Hamilton had laid out plainly in the *Federalist Papers*—that the population must chose its most qualified men, especially intellectuals, to run their government. Too much direct dependence on the masses would lead to government instability, as everyone knew who knew their history—mobs could be bought and controlled by men of evil design. A democracy would suffer the same fate as that of ancient Athens, Rome and Florence—takeover by a tyrant and elimination of all participation and virtue in public affairs.

But how does one ensure that the population in a representative republic chooses the leaders who will implement good policies? Through what process can the idea of good government be realized in social institutions? It was the answering of these questions which brought Hamilton and Jefferson into opposition with each other on the issue of political rights.

Hamilton expressed in his notorious and only substantial speech at the Constitutional Convention his conviction that good legislators should rule for life—both in the Senate and in the presidency, although not in the Assembly. It is ridiculous to think that Hamilton expected his plan to be adopted, especially since the only plan on the floor of the convention when he introduced his was the Virginia plan for popular and frequent election of the Senate, the House and the President. It does reflect the problem he had in comprehending the *process* of developing good leaders. Hamilton had no certainty or self-conscious program of mass *quality* education as a means of narrowing the gap between the men of excellence who should be chosen to lead the country, and the lesser educated majority of the population. Although he could see empirically that the implementation of the ideas he knew were right—like the *Report on Manufactures*—depended upon their assimilation and support by the general population, he grew impatient at the population's current backwardness. There was a bit of Bonapartism in him. His impatience made him open to suggestions that the sources of dangerous and false ideas simply be repressed, a "solution" which simultaneously undermined the moral authority of the government.

Jefferson, on the other hand, held as the highest value the propagation of education and ideas. Jefferson was responsible for the setting aside of space for schools in the Northwest Territories. During his term as governor of Virginia, he tried to implement a state-wide education plan that would guarantee every child a primary school education, and erect a system of secondary schools and universities on top of that. Although his idea was rejected then and at least twice afterwards, Jefferson maintained his perspective of *creating* an intelligent electorate, as his turning of government surplus over to education during his presidency indicates. What Jefferson understood was the cardinal principle of why benevolent dictatorships seldom work for very long: no glorious plan will succeed without the assimilation of the ruler's advanced ideas, or at least the *process of assimilation* going on among the population which must carry them out.

Jefferson's failures come precisely where he yields to vulgar democracy, embodied in British agent Aaron Burr's buy-an-immigrant's-vote societies in New York. That kind of constituency was manipulable and dangerous to the national interest if led by the wrong men. The fact that Aaron Burr could turn that constituency over lock, stock and barrel into the ranks of August Belmont's Democratic Party of Slavery and Treason provides sufficient proof of that.

The issue of furthering the ideals of republicanism was first raised between Hamilton and Jefferson in the former's *Report on Manufactures*. Jefferson did not recognize it, but Hamilton's report explicitly aimed to raise the quality of intelligence within the American population through the mechanization of agriculture and industry, and the diversification of industries and employment. An opportunity for creating optimal social conditions for national mass education was lost with the report's defeat.

The next time was the Whiskey Rebellion—in which Jefferson shamefully capitulated to heteronomic reaction among the uneducated population.

The most mature battle came over the Alien and Sedition Acts, passed in 1798 by a Congress that was convinced that the raging hostilities going on between Britain and France were about to spill over and involve the United States. Hamilton supported the Alien and Sedition Acts in hopes of ridding the country of undesirable foreigners and newspaper editors, but *he did not initiate the Sedition Act*. To the contrary, when Hamilton first heard that such an act had been proposed, he urged that it be dropped because such repression would only strengthen the Jeffersonian opposition. Failing to get it dropped, Hamilton went to Philadelphia,[20] and soon afterwards, a congressman who was known to be very close to him politically introduced the following stipulations to the bill:

1. No punishment could be inflicted until a jury had been satisfied that the publication was false; and
2. that the accused, knowing it to be false, had published it with an evil purpose.

With the passage of these stipulations in the law, America's seditious libel law became the first in the world to allow truth to be a defense. The same rights were not recognized in England until 1843, and they are still not in effect in Germany today! In 1798 in America, however, the Republicans often did not have the social forces to back up the law, and prevent even their truthful publishers from going to jail.

Hamilton's more wholehearted support of the Alien Act, which allowed the President to have someone deported without any proof of overt acts against the government being required, came from his central concern not with stopping internal dissension per se, but with establishing national security against foreign meddlers.

20. Miller, John C., *Alexander Hamilton and the Growth of the Nation*, Harper Torchbooks, 1959, p. 484.

Jefferson's understandable alarm at the passage and practice of these acts led him to organize conventions in Kentucky and Virginia which asserted the states' democratic right to "nullify" federal laws—in particular the Alien and Sedition laws. In doing so, he too was deserting the republican principles that built the nation in what appeared to him to be a dire emergency. Jefferson stopped short of backing any secessionist moves, however, just as Hamilton was to do six years later in response to a Federalist secession plot.

The Hamilton and Jefferson tradition that we inherit today is that of republicanism. Jefferson was no mindless democrat; that was left for Andrew Jackson and his traitorous heirs today.

In 1801, after succeeding in stopping both John Adams and Aaron Burr from acceding to the presidency, Hamilton drops from prominence in national politics—more remembered for his negative reactions than for his only partially fulfilled positive plans for national development. Ironically, his genius lives on not through any successors in the Federalist Party, many of whom have now abandoned the dreams of industrial capital for the cash returns available for serving Britain's carrying trade, but through his arch-enemies Thomas Jefferson and Albert Gallatin. Unlike that pseudo-"Jeffersonian" Andrew Jackson, Jefferson and Gallatin refused to yield to populist and British-inspired pressures to dismantle the national bank and halt internal improvements and "big spending." Jefferson spent more than the Federalists ever did when he bought Louisiana in 1803—an acquisition which Hamilton had rather aspired to take by force some five years previously.

Despite the dilution of the national banking system character of the Bank of the United States by the proliferation of private banking for "mechanics and agriculture," Hamilton's dream of using foreign investors' money to produce a wealthy America began to come true. Even as the British Barings Company acquired two-thirds of the stock of the Bank of the United States, its control was severely limited by the fact that *foreign stockholders had been given no vote!* The greatest discontinuity between the reign of the Federalists was not in the realm of commerce or even political freedom (the Sedition Act continued to be prosecuted against Federalists on the state, rather than the federal level), but in the lack of investment in supplying the armed forces. Jefferson followed up Hamilton's idea to establish a military-engineering academy, and received the congressional backing which

Hamilton was denied. Simultaneously, he allowed the navy especially to go to pot, and refused to eliminate many of the vulnerabilities that let the British nearly devastate the U.S. in the War of 1812.

Above all, Jefferson's assumption of the responsibility of the presidency was decisive in allowing his qualities as an inventor and believer in science and progress to win out over what Washington had identified as his "womanish affections." There had never been any reason to doubt Jefferson had those qualities; he had devoted his career to the fight for mass education, to abolishing feudal restrictions on land and religion, to patronizing inventors like Tom Paine, to improving agricultural techniques and architecture, and to providing solutions on problems of money and land that would obviate internecine quarrels between the states. But he had simultaneously indulged himself in self-destruction from the harsh realities involved in formulating correct and practical economic programs for the country as a whole, and in winning their acceptance; time and time again he would retreat to his home to study his plants and buildings, and nurse his grief about his wife's early death. Like a man who shields his eyes so as not to see what his boat might hit in the stormy seas ahead, he did not confront reality effectively until he was forced to take the helm himself.

Jefferson wants no lying praise from those who attack his "aristocratic" mind and fawn over his championship of the "little man" against the federal government. Let the Treason School of History come out openly in praise of its fascist heroes. They have nothing to do with the elitist intellectuals Thomas Jefferson and Alexander Hamilton, whose goal was to build a nation that would progress in excellence.

The Issue of Freedom

The enemies of the American Revolution have never changed their line that the problem with the federal government of the U.S. was that it did not give sufficient "freedom" to "the people." In the 1780s, their issue was "freedom from taxation and government"; during the next four decades, it was "freedom from national banks and autocrats"; in the 1820s and 1830s it was "free trade"; from 1840 through to their defeat in the Civil War, it was "freedom for slave-holders!"

One can imagine the revisionists chortling secretly with delight over the fact that their "histories" have convinced both "right" and "left" of the un-Americanness of "big government." What hypocritical, sneaking liars! Government intervention for national industrial growth is the Washington-Hamilton-Jefferson tradition of progress and has nothing to do with Franklin D. Roosevelt's zero-growth corporatism. Until Roosevelt's accession to the presidency, in fact, the proponents of an active government role in the economy were consistently the strongest *opponents* of the looting school of political economy.

Before the emergence of Abraham Lincoln himself into politics, there were two major warriors in favor of this tradition, both of whom have been not-so-strangely downplayed and maligned by most American histories. They were John Quincy Adams—the direct intellectual heir of Benjamin Franklin, who undertook his European education—and Henry Clay, a most diligent student of Jefferson and J.Q. Adams. Top on their agendas for this country were education, science and industrialization of the United States. From this standpoint, they pressed for national sponsorship of public improvements, the preservation of the national bank, and government sponsorship of science and education through its military academy and its expenditure of profits from western land sales on mass education. These men stood out above their parties, which were fraught with inconsistent policies and easy victims of the British counterinsurgents' policy to destroy all national parties. In fact, the clearing away of the party structure allowed for the creation of a new national party based on the consistent and inspiring principles of development that Adams and Clay had stood for. They are the intellectual ancestors of the Republican Party as it was founded in 1856.

Henry Clay cut his teeth in Congress by fighting for the re-establishment of a national bank after the debacle of the War of 1812. He opposed the military adventures which the British were using to draw America into the Monroe Doctrine, a doctrine that provided protection for *British* looting in Latin America. He demanded the protection of American manufacturing through the establishment of reasonable tariffs at a time when British interests, working through August Belmont and the Democratic Party, were hellbent on keeping the United States as a natural resources exporter, like all the rest of its colonies. Clay's vision of the United States included vast criss-crosses of roads and canals to facilitate trade and travel—

and led him into occasional opposition with his own Kentucky constituency to impose the eminent domain of the federal government.
His stumbling block was the issue of slavery itself; there, partly
because of his constituency pressures and partly because of his own
personal inadequacies, he refused to draw the consequences and
imperatives from the secessionists' assault.

Those who opposed slavery fell into two categories—the abolitionists and pro-industrial moderates. The fact that the abolitionists
were essentially ruled by their affections, like Jefferson himself in
foreign policy, made their groupings exceptionally vulnerable to pen-
etration by agents and agents-provocateurs. Yet many were honest
people who suffered hideously because they insisted on calling for an
immediate end to slavery. The pro-industrial moderates concentrated
first on preventing the spread of slavery, and then on looking for an
economic program which would allow this blight to be eliminated
once and for all.

What lay behind the moderates' stance was that there was no
way in which "freedom for slavery" could be compatible with the
development of an industrial society based on free labor. The degradation of labor power—the quality of labor's ability to reproduce
itself—in the slave economy would necessarily debase the value of
all labor. As economist Henry Carey points out in the 1840s, an
advancing society must invest much more in its labor than a slavoc-
racy in order to achieve greater productivity. We must eliminate
"cheap labor," Carey demands. He is right, even though he fails to
point out that the greater investment in labor and technology will
ultimately cheapen the cost of production relative to the total product
obtained. One is reminded appropriately of Gresham's law that the
very existence of cheap currency (labor) threatens to drive the more
valuable specie out of circulation.

From a competent economic standpoint—yes, from a competent
human standpoint—the concept of freedom for slavery absolutely
contradicts the *necessary* laws of human development. No one who
has contributed to the line of humanist thought in political economy
has ever dallied long in the realm of freedom in such a heteronomic
sense. Freedom lies in man's ability, and necessity, to come up with
creative solutions to the problems of man's own continued existence
that arise within each mode of social reproduction. "Solutions" which
move toward the reduction of the human race's capacity to reproduce

itself in future generations may be "unique," but they are not creative, or human. If the human race had ever accepted man as he was—either the caveman or the slave-holder or the slave—it would not have existed to listen to the obscenities of the revisionists today. No one has the right to demand the freedom to live like an animal, or maintain a system which requires treating whole sections of the human race like dumb, happy beasts of burden. Yet William A. Williams in his latest book has the gall to criticize Abraham Lincoln for "oppressing" the South into giving up slavery and becoming part of a U.S. industrial economy.[21] One can barely control one's stomach.

There are, of course, those fakers who criticize Abraham Lincoln from the other side of the fence. They castigate him for acting insincerely, for waiting so long to free the slaves that his actual Emancipation Proclamation becomes a mere "political tactic" without conviction. They are incompetent.

Lincoln was committed from his earliest days in politics to the concept of free labor, constitutional government, and progress, taking much of his inspiration from Henry Clay. He hated the side of the frontier which meant slavery to the land and to alcohol. He detested the anarchy on the part of the abolitionists and the anti-abolitionists alike—basing himself firmly on the intent of the Constitution that slavery was not to be extended out of the South, and would probably die out there as well. He believed that individual labor was the road to individual and social progress, a view which put him in the camp of those who despised slavery and encouraged public improvements, not in the "let's-eliminate-public-services-and-welfare-cheats" den. He waited perhaps too long before issuing the Emancipation Proclamation, but he waited until he was sure that it would accomplish the ends of northern industrial victory, not merely self-righteous justification for the slavery-hater.

The North's victory in the Civil War established the hegemony of a government committed to industrial capitalism in the United States, but the monetarists—both Britain's Rothschilds and their new branch offices in the United States, including the Rockefellers—did not give up. In the hopes of getting Britain to intervene on their side, they had not hesitated to provoke the Civil War. Now they

21. Williams, William A., *America Confronts A Revolutionary World*, William Morrow, New York, 1976.

carried out every trick in their counterinsurgency manuals to prevent a political alignment in the U.S. corresponding to the central line of conflict between the forces of progress and those of retrogression. We have seen the muckrakers, the Know-Nothings, the Progressive Movement, the New Dealers, the New Leftists—every one an insidious diversion away from the issue of industrial progress and the necessity for political alliances involving all classes precisely on that basis. Their latest attempt is epitomized by the spectacle of James Schlesinger, Nelson Rockefeller, Marcus Raskin, and Ralph Nader coming together in support of Carter's demands to dismantle America's constitutional commitment to industrial growth by shutting off energy to every factory, home and school!

We can no more afford to give the revisionist historians the freedom to continue their lies than we can let the Rockefeller crew save their empire through the ravages of slave-labor or war. It is the kind of lies that they spread that have allowed the gutting of the American labor force and industry for the last 20 years, that have allowed the American population to be pitted against the rest of the world that wants nothing more or less than what the early Americans did—industrial progress. Now is the time to put both revisionists and their masters on trial for their crimes of high treason.

We presume they won't object to the inclusion on the jury of Mr. Hamilton and Mr. Franklin. It would be only just.

Bibliography

Adams, John Quincy. *The Selected Writings of John and John Quincy Adams*, edited with an introduction by Adrienne Koch and William Peden, New York, Alfred A. Knopf, 1946.

Carey, Henry. *The Slave Trade, Domestic and Foreign; Why It Exists and How It May Be Extinguised*, Philadelphia, A. Hart, Carey and Hart, 1853; and *The Harmony of Interests: Agricultural Manufactures and Commercial*, Philadelphia, J.S. Skinner, 1851.

Clay, Henry. *The Papers of Henry Clay*, edited by James F. Hopkins and Mary W.M. Hargreaves, The University Press of Kentucky, 1973.

Franklin, Benjamin. *Collected Works*. (The Jared Sparks edition, in particular.)

Hamilton, Alexander. *Collected Works*, edited by Henry Cabot Lodge; and *The Papers of Alexander Hamilton*, edited by Harold C. Syrett and Jacob E. Cooke, New York, Columbia University Press, 1962.

Jefferson, Thomas. *The Portable Thomas Jefferson*, edited by Merrill D. Peterson, New York, The Viking Press, 1975; and *Crusade Against Ignorance, Thomas Jefferson on Education*, edited by Gordon C. Lee, New York, Teachers College Press, Columbia University, 1961.

Lincoln, Abraham. *The Life and Writings of Abraham Lincoln,* edited by Philip van Doren Stern, New York, The Modern Library, 1940.
Paine, Thomas. *The Life and Major Writings of Thomas Paine,* collected, edited and annotated by Philip S. Foner, Secaucus, N.J., The Citadel Press, 1948.

Secondary Sources

Bailyn, Bernard, editor. *Pamphlets of the American Revolution, 1750–1776,* Cambridge, Mass., The Belknap Press of Harvard University Press, 1965. This work is primarily of value because of the reprints of sermons and pamphlets therein. The introduction by Bailyn is useful in providing leads, but mixes apples and oranges when trying to identify the philosophical sources of the American Revolution, e.g. Milton and Locke. The keystone to Bailyn's confusion is the fact that the Glorious Revolution of 1688, which was in fact an occupation of England by the monetarist Dutch, is treated as a progressive step toward the American revolution instead of the retrogression it was.

Bowers, Claude G. *Jefferson and Hamilton, The Struggle for Democracy in America,* Boston, Houghton, Mifflin, 1953. A hideous, and unfortunately very popular account of the 1790s, which so romanticizes the two heroes that any resemblance with the actual events is purely coincidental.

Edwards, Newton and Richey, Herman G. *The School in the American Social Order, The Dynamics of American Education,* Boston, Houghton Mifflin Co., 1947. An informative review of the development of education from the Puritan period forward, with concentration on the legal provisions and institutional forms of education.

Hawke, David. *Paine,* New York, Harper and Row, 1974. A relatively complete and accurate biography, although it approaches Paine from the standpoint of having to defend him from charges of being a drunken atheist. Clear on his Federalist and scientific contributions, as well as his role in producing effective war propaganda.

Hendrickson, Robert. *Alexander Hamilton,* Vol. I, New York, Mason Charter, 1976. Proceeding from the standpoint that Hamilton did more than any other Founding Father to shape the accomplishments of the American Revolution, Hendrickson does an exhaustive job, with much documentation, in delineating Hamilton's military, programmatic and economic contributions up to 1789. After that period Hendrickson claims that Hamilton goes somewhat haywire, but the second volume of this work which deals with that period has not yet been published.

Hindle, Brooks. *Science in Revolutionary America,* New York, W.W. Norton and Co., by arrangement with University of North Carolina Press, 1974. Exhaustive, but useful review of who's who in science circles in the mid-eighteenth century.

Miller, John C. *Sam Adams, Pioneer in Propaganda,* California, Stanford University Press, 1936; *Origins of the American Revolution,* Boston, Little, Brown and Co., 1943; and *Alexander Hamilton and the Growth of the Nation,* New York, Harper Torchbooks, 1959. Miller is an uneven, but valuable resource, his books improving vastly in quality over the years. While Miller's work on Adams is laced with paranoia about how Adams was virtually a one-man conspiracy to cause the revolution, his latest work on Hamilton is a full well-researched account of the entire post-1776 period. Despite the lack of full appreciation of Hamilton's contributions, he correctly locates the Colbert link and avoids the usual personal, "anti-capitalist" slander. The *Origins* is unexceptional, to be read only for an overview on how the break with Britain developed, giving no conceptual insight into the dynamics behind the break.

Ritter, Halsted L. *Washington as a Business Man,* Sears Publishing, 1931. A very positive discussion, including some documentation, of Washington as an industrial capitalist and statesman.

Morris, Richard B. *The American Revolution Reconsidered*, New York, Evanston, and London, Harper and Row, 1967. Morris's book is an invaluable attack against revisionist history, asserting clearly, if somewhat timorously, the progressive capitalist nature of the revolution and its leaders. One of a kind.

Schlesinger, Arthur M. *Birth of a Nation, A Portrait of the American People on the Eve of Independence*, and *Prelude to Independence, the Newspaper War on Britain, 1764–1776*, Knopf, 1958. As a Fabian, Schlesinger understands the political importance of ideas, the literacy rate and tradition of the American population, etc., and therefore is useful reading. The thesis for which he marshals these facts is that the revolution was not a revolution, but a war of independence—totally wrong, and therefore to be ignored.

Sosin, Jack M. *The Revolutionary Frontier, 1776–1783*, Holt, Reinhart and Winston, 1967. Sosin's thesis is that the frontier produced "no new systems of government, religion or agriculture," and that its significance was determined in different areas of the country and overall by the culture of those who colonized it. This is an effective, if somewhat boring, explicit antidote to Turner's frontier thesis, and invaluable as such.

Sumner, William Graham. *The Financier and Finances of the American Revolution*, Vol. I, New York, Burt Franklin, 1891. Unfortunately, this is one of the very few extant biographies of Robert Morris, the Philadelphia banker who was the first national treasurer of America and a close collaborator of Ben Franklin, Hamilton and others. Any facts learned are purely accidental. Sumner, one of the popularizers of Social Darwinism in America, was totally insane, arguing that the revolution was on such an unsound financial basis that he couldn't understand how leading Americans committed themselves to it. He never understood as much as the leading merchants of the day—that prosperity is a question of the investment in future production, not current in-pocket wealth.

PART I

The European Roots of the American Revolution

Jean-Baptiste Colbert and the Origins of Industrial Capitalism

by Christopher White

The rehabilitation of the reputation of Louis XIV's Contrôleur-Général des Finances Jean-Baptiste Colbert (1619–1683) is an urgent, and, important task. Colbert, his ideas and influence are of seminal importance in the development of the outlooks associated with and corresponding to industrial capitalism in its origins and subsequent development. As such he is, ironically, an important contributor to the evolution of the current from which republican democracy emerged.

Colbert's innovative interrelated conceptions of political economy and sovereignty, are the mediation of earlier such efforts by the currents associated with the Frenchman Jean Bodin (1530–1596) and the Englishman Thomas Gresham (1519–1579). His efforts contribute in part to the line of development which is later brought to fruition in the struggles of Alexander Hamilton and the Federalists to draft the U.S. Constitution and frame a practical policy for the scientific and industrial progress of the newly born United States and its peoples. Colbert's creative contributions, and the humanist tradition they embody provide a recurrent leitmotif in more contemporary European, especially French political outlooks as identified by that tendency of republicanism and Gaullism which embraces such figures as Gabriel Hanotaux and General DeGaulle himself.

It is by celebrating, through reasserting the contributions of gifted statesmen such as Jean-Baptiste Colbert, his predecessors and his successors, that we can know both the qualities of intellect and will which have made human progress out of feudalism's bestiality possible, and know the content of the life and death political struggle out of which such relatively gigantic but fundamentally human figures shaped themselves and their decisive contributions.

Colbert, in that light represents the last in a line of European political and intellectual figures whose identities had been shaped in a struggle, which lasted nearly 150 years, to free that continent from the stranglehold of the genocidal policies of the Imperial House of Hapsburg and its rapacious banker allies, the Fuggers, Welsers, Hochstetters, and their seventeenth century Dutch and English successors. It is out of that struggle that the outlooks and instrumentalities which we now associate with the current "industrial capitalism" are formed.

The political tendency which informed and shaped such struggles, in the fight to free Europe from the Hapsburg boot, is the humanist current which defined its own origins in the Florentine and Paduan Renaissances of the fifteenth and early sixteenth centuries. That is the tendency which creates the notions of political economy and sovereignty as the effective weapons with which to root out the Hapsburg-Fugger threat to human survival itself, while posing in the form of an apparent paradox the problem which is resolved under the government of a capitalist political democracy.

As the last representative, in a sense of certain aspects of that struggle, Colbert's example points relentlessly forward to the achievements of Alexander Hamilton and the Federalist current of the American Revolution. Such a view might seem peculiar to those afflicted with the myth that the American Revolution was rooted in the French Enlightenment political struggle against what is known as absolutism.

In a fundamental sense, Hamilton's enemies were also the enemies of Colbert. Colbert's political-economic outlook was premised on the necessity to free France from the grips of Dutch financial and commercial control. Essential aspects of Hamilton's struggle to free the United States of America from English monetarism were equally so founded. It is not accidental that Adam Smith, whose *The Wealth of Nations* canonized the tenet that the U.S. was properly to be kept in agricultural backwardness, should have been the epitome of everything Hamilton hated and despised, just as Smith's text is, in part, a monetarist's factional polemic against the surviving influence of *Colbertisme*.

Actually, such similarities in outlook are more direct than the reflections of shared concerns would indicate. Hamilton turned directly to the traditions of *Colbertisme* in order to inform his struggle against the monetarism represented, on the one hand, by Adam Smith and, on the other hand, by the relative bestiality of Smith's allies from the ranks of the Physiocrats.

The irony in Hamilton's factional use of the Colbert tradition should be immediately apparent to anyone who studies the divergent courses of the respective French and American revolutions in the nineteenth century. Where the French nation ended up rooted in small-scale industry and small-scale agriculture, condemned by the policies of English-based monetarists, such as the Rothschilds, to technological backwardness, the American, by dint of a century of struggle and effort, built up a scientific, technological and agricultural capability that was literally the envy of the world.

It is not necessary to review here in detail the evolution of each respective revolution. The point is simple, but more fundamental. The differences in outlook we have adduced between humanist and monetarist currents are not mere matters for informed opinion or taste, they are real. Equally the different consequences of such outlooks are real. The Federalists' achievement in fostering the outlooks among the American population in favor of scientific, technological and industrial progress made such progress possible, and demonstrates that Jefferson's "sturdy yeomen," his French Physiocratic allies and Adam Smith were absolutely wrong.

Those two fundamentally irreconcilable outlooks are predicated on fundamentally irreconcilable notions of society's wealth.

For the Hapsburgs, for the Fuggers, for Adam Smith, for certain of the Physiocrats, wealth is fixed and finite, represented in the nominal claim on society's output of useful goods and services of paper monetary instruments. Theirs is essentially the outlook expressed in the shopkeeper's well-known refrain, "buy cheap and sell dear." Under such a view, the maintenance of the money-income derived from such paper titles to wealth takes precedence over all else, including the output of such goods and services which ultimately underwrite the integrity of the paper instruments themselves. Such outlooks treat wealth as mere loot to be scooped from the blood and bones of the peoples so subject.

The humanist outlook we have identified resists the ravages of such a bestial view. In its evolution, humanism defines wealth as a necessary, predicated aspect of the perfection of the human species as a whole. The humanist orients himself not to the relatively finite agglomerations of the output of fixed technology, but, instead, to those fundamental areas on the frontiers of existing science and technology which pose the problems whose material solution, as assimilated for practice by broader layers of the population, will contribute to the progress and perfection of the species as a whole. Success in those terms can be represented crudely as that process by which population growth is fostered and material conditions of life improved.

It is from that standpoint that we examine the contribution of M. Jean-Baptiste Colbert, not as a representative of perfected humanity (that, of course, would be a horrendous travesty). Colbert provides a convenient locus for an investigation of the evolution of that humanist current, and its specific refraction in the political development of industrial capitalist outlooks.

But, first, we must restore his reputation to its rightful standing.

The Achievements of Colbert

Colbert's lasting achievement, and the subject of his lasting importance for posterity, is the development and application, to the extent that he was able, of a competent notion of society's wealth. To the extent that he successfully implemented and realized the policies which flowed from such a notion, he must be considered among the founders of political economy. To the extent that his policies were sabotaged and relegated into secondary or tertiary positions of importance by the imbecility of Louis XIV and the bellicose impulsions of his Ministers of War Le Tellier and then Louvois, with their unemployed idle aristocratic backers, then Colbert, of course, can be numbered among accountants' causes of the French Revolution. That other contribution, is however, distinctly secondary to our concerns.

The policies which we will address were elaborated in a series of administrative memoranda, letters, decrees and drafts of decrees in the period encompassed by the dates 1663–1680.

Most often, unfortunately, he is remembered and quoted for his memorandum on the kingdom's finances, which was written in 1670. This is the memorandum which includes the famous phrase, "Commerce is the source of public finance, and public finance is the vital nerve of war." That phrase is most often ripped out of its context in both the evolution of Colbert's policies and the actual development of real historical processes, to become by fallacy of composition the slogan chosen to characterize Colbert's policies as a whole. There is scarcely a general survey text of that period in European history, or even a relatively specialist work, which does not make use of that phrase in the fashion indicated. As if history could be written in the manner soap-powders are sold.

Yet, the absurdity of such a fallacy of composition, which is evident from a superficial comparison of the cited text with others, whether from earlier or later phases of his career, goes much deeper than that mere dishonesty would suggest. In the traditional view of the matter, the seventeenth century is the period in which a triumphant capitalism, previously shackled in the fetters of feudal outlooks and institutions, breaks free of its chains and establishes the domination of a hybrid-form known as mercantilism. That variant, in turn, is defined as the basis for the evolution of the modern state, in both its English revolutionary and French absolutist forms, and as such provides the jumping-off point for real capitalist development in the eighteenth century.

In that light, Colbert, who has been maligned, since the days and writing of Adam Smith, as the principal proponent of the reactionary mercantilism relative to the subsequently "progressive" nature of capitalism, is understood to characterize a principal feature of the period as a whole, with the quotation we have cited defined in its turn as the principal battle slogan of the contending forces. As usual, there is in that, as in all such vapid commonplaces, a certain amount of truth, though not enough to qualify the term paper of the student of such generalities for a pass-mark.

Colbert's cited statement is in fact a factional document. It does not characterize the thrust of his policies as a whole, not in the sense attributed by the authors of general survey textbooks and other such writings. Already, by 1670, when the document was authored, it had become apparent, after one war with the English, and on the eve of another with the Dutch, that the financial resources of Louis XIV's monarchy could not sustain both Colbert's economic-policy efforts and an aggressive foreign policy. The memorandum most often quoted to define Colbert's policy as a whole, is in fact designed to protect the means for the implementation of his policy from the growing depredations of the Ministry of War.

As that fact would suggest, Colbert was not the architect or principal exponent of any so-called mercantile system. His policies as such were not mercantilist in any respect. Nor can such notions illuminate any historically identifiable process of the period under consideration.

Responsibility for the indicated sorry state of scholarly affairs must be traced back to Adam Smith, the sly author of *The Wealth of Nations*, and to those political scientists, economists and historians who persist in viewing his work as some kind of objective statement of economic theory. Smith's text is itself a political factional document. Economically and historically it is a fraud. In that document, Smith attacks the then-dominant English and Dutch monetarist currents, labeling that tendency "mercantile or commercial," using Colbert to underscore his factional points, the better to make his case for the destruction of France as England's principal global competitor.

To the extent that subsequent generations were duped by Smith into seeing Colbert and *Colbertisme* as the reality of the English-Dutch brand of monetarism that was hegemonic (after the Dutch coup d'etat and counter-revolution in England in 1688 which brought William of Orange to the throne of England), and more or less absolute (after the same interests won exclusive right for their East India Company to ship slaves into Spanish possessions after the wars against France which ended in 1715), then Colbert and *Colbertisme* is a variant of monetarism in the form of mercantilism. But only in that case; otherwise such views represent the associative methods of schizophrenia.

Smith's own definition of mercantilism establishes that doctrine as a subsumed aspect of the development of monetarism. Mercantilists, for Smith, know only wealth derived from the proceeds of trading. Real wealth is identified as the result of buying cheap and selling dear. The measure of such wealth is the amount of bullion, whether gold or silver to hand, when the transaction is completed. If there is a surplus, the trader is wealthier. If there is a deficit, the trader's wealth has been diminished to the advantage of the competitor who has gained his bullion.

These shopkeeper-like superstitions are then extended by Smith to subsume the inter-relationships of various national economies. In that view, for Smith's mercantilist the wealth of a country is a determined expression of the balance of trade measured in bullion. The country that exports more than it imports, and has a surplus of bullion to hand as accounts are settled is wealthier than the country which imports more than it exports and is graced with a relative drop in its bullion holdings when accounts are settled.

Smith was not actually so naive as that view might otherwise represent. His concern was to demonstrate that wealth lay not in such simple notions of profit, but in the ability to reinvest the expanded mass of bullion at a further profit—primarily through wrecking the French by dumping cheap English manufactures on them, but more importantly, in the long-term, through the loot extracted from colonial populations, through the extension of interest-bearing loans to finance imports of manufactured goods and raw materials extraction.

With those concerns in mind, Smith then identified in an aspect of Colbert's policies "mercantilist barriers" which would have to be overcome if his own policy was to be implemented successfully. Such was the jungle of legislative measures, excise taxes, prohibitions of certain kinds of foreign imports, and so forth, which by the time of Smith's writing effectively protected the French economy from itself. This then became, and has remained for scholars the legacy of Colbert and *Colbertisme,* summed up in the word "protectionism."

The view we have just identified, is as uninformed about the workings of actual economies as it is about anything else. This we shall demonstrate from the writings of Colbert himself. For Colbert, like Smith, was concerned above all else with breaking the stranglehold of especially Dutch, but also emergent English financial and commercial interests over the French economy. Unlike Smith, he approached the problem from a political and economic standpoint which was conceptually way beyond anything Smith, the English customs official in Scotland and Professor of Moral Philosophy in the University of Glasgow, could have dreamt of.

Where Adam Smith's policies define a bridge between the modern monetarist advocates of zero-growth economies, and their forefathers, the sixteenth-century Augsburg banking family of Fugger, in that the practical consequences of all three such outlooks will tend to converge more or less rapidly on large-scale genocide of human populations (through the rapacious destruction of sources of raw materials, farming and manufacturing capabilities in favor of augmenting the nominal wealth represented by paper property titles and money-lucre), Colbert reasserted the notion that wealth is an expression of political determination to reinvest in new sources of raw materials and manufacturers, to expand the goods and services available to society as a whole.

To implement his policies, Colbert zeroed in on the point of fraud which should have discredited Smith's approach even before *The Wealth of Nations* was published, an approach which Smith himself no doubt knew to be fraudulent. The point was that even during the middle of the seventeenth century, trade and finance were not under the control of an agglomeration of various national, or what could for the sake of argument be called national-interest groupings. International trade and financial resources were predominantly concentrated in the Dutch Republic of the Netherlands, as indeed they had been since the Hapsburg Emperor Charles V developed the port city of Antwerp as the entrepôt for European trade and finance in the second quarter of the sixteenth century.

A French merchant with goods to sell did not therefore go directly to an English buyer to, for example, negotiate a price, and exchange his product for gold. That French merchant instructed his agent *in Holland* to obtain a bill of exchange, drawn most often on the Bank of Amsterdam, and concurrently undertook to supply the money equivalent of the bill of exchange in goods to the issuer of the note within a certain time period. The issuer of the bill would then use the promised appearance of the goods to generate further such credit issuances in the form of bills of exchange. The merchant's agent would either use the bill of exchange to purchase produce to import to France, or would use it as a speculative instrument, to be discounted and rediscounted among the Amsterdam commercial and financial houses in efforts to increase his nominal profit from the original sale of goods.

The terms of trade, and even the ability to trade, were defined through that process in Amsterdam. Anyone, who is in the least informed, will recognize that such a process is in all essential respects similar to what prevails in, for example, Lower Manhattan or the

City of London to this day. Furthermore, they will be no doubt delighted to know, that process in the same form had existed, whether in Antwerp or in Amsterdam, for the entire preceding period of nearly 150 years before Colbert even took office in 1663.

The financial and commercial role and power of those two cities was borne of the union in and preceding 1525 of the feudal power of the Spanish monarchy and Austrian Hapsburgs with the moneyed lucre-wealth of the Fugger banking house and its allies and rivals, the Welsers and Hochstetters. That combination defines the essence and origins of monetarism. That alliance, in one way or other, was hegemonic in Europe down to 1659, when Colbert's predecessor Cardinal Mazarin finally separated the Austrian and Spanish feudalist branches of the combination in the Treaty of the Pyrenees. At that point, Dutch financial and commercial interests, with their foreign allies and debtors, succeeded in their own right to the mantle that had otherwise been wrested from the Hapsburgs. If that was mercantilism, then mercantilism is subsumed properly under the development of monetarists' outlooks and institutions.

As Smith's use of Colbertian protectionist measures would suggest, the intent and effect of Colbert's policies was to break France free from the clutches of the financial and commercial interests in Amsterdam. His systematic efforts were directed towards providing France with independent sources of raw materials, commercial shipping and manufacture, built on the kind of domestic economic infrastructure which could support such efforts. To achieve that end, he returned to the economic policies and strategies which had been elaborated in the sixteenth century, in the collaboration between the French faction known as the *politiques* represented by Jean Bodin and the English faction epitomized by Thomas Gresham. Their concern, like his, had been how to free their respective nations and economies from the ravages of an earlier phase of such financial and commercial hegemony as represented by the Hapsburgs' Fuggery.

If that process, in turn, is supposed to represent a so-called mercantile, or commercial school, then mercantilism as a phenomenon is a subsumed aspect of the development of European humanism. In either case, the notion of "mercantilism," which has thus far been the characteristic feature in the analysis of especially European seventeenth-century history, bridging the transition from feudalism

to capitalism, itself has no independent existence separate from either
of the principal currents we have identified. As such it does not
explain anything of primary importance, whether it be about Colbert,
the origins of the modern state, or the transition from feudalism to
capitalism. Rather it is the political and military fight between the
associated representatives of the two tendencies we have identified,
which defines the outcome of that process.

Colbert's fight against Dutch financial and commercial power,
locates him squarely in the current of European humanism, not
simply because he challenged that power, but because in doing so
he made use of the weaponry developed by the humanist-industrialist
current, and therefore reasserted that current itself. As such, an
examination of his policies will help us to examine the evolution of
the current as a whole, and enable us to evaluate its relative strengths
and weaknesses.

It is from that standpoint that we can turn to Colbert's policies
as he himself elaborated those policies. There are three documents
available in the Municipal Archives of the town of Nantes in Brittany
which are relevant to that effect, and worth reproducing more or
less fully.

The first is a letter received by the Chamber of Commerce at
Nantes and dated September 29, 1665. It reads in part,

I have spoken to M. Colbert about the memorandum you
sent me in which you requested that foreign merchants be
prevented from marketing products other than those which
are worked up from the raw materials of their own countries.
He indicated that he would be favorably inclined on condition that you were to give assurances that you could implement what you advocate. It is therefore relevant that you
duly apply yourselves in assembly to a careful examination
of all factors, and therein determine the number of vessels
you can put to sea to undertake the business of the said
foreigners, and contribute by this means to the failure of
the Dutch, for they are accustomed to transport in their
vessels all the materials which are necessary to us. We are
both going to make a tour of the coast and should finish at
Nantes where we will contribute what is necessary from our
side to make the project a success. Meanwhile you should

make everything ready for examination by us when we arrive.[1]

The second document is in the form of an *arrêt*, an order from the king's council having the effect of law, dated December 5, 1664 and "given in favor of all those merchants or others who will hereafter, build ships or do business by sea." By this order a business council is established out of the ranks of provincial businessmen and merchants to coordinate the development and implementation of policy from Paris. The purpose of the council is defined as being the examination of the causes for the diminution or destruction of commerce and manufacture and the adoption of efficient means for their re-establishment. Beyond that, the king encourages nobles to take part in commerce and manufacture, and undertakes to subsidize the development of a shipbuilding industry, to subsidize the purchase of ships abroad, and to subsidize trade in the raw materials that make such ship-building feasible, provided such materials are shipped directly into French ports from their ports of origin in Scandinavia and the Baltic. (This order, incidentally also set subsidies for successful settlement in North America at the rate of 100 sols for a male and 3 livres for a woman.)[2]

The third document is a royal declaration dated August 26, 1664, which reads in part,

> . . . having considered how much it would be useful for this kingdom to re-establish commerce both within and beyond the borders of the same, and that beyond our support and protection nothing could contribute better to the success of such a good plan, we have resolved to that end to have held and give over in its entirety every two weeks a special commercial council in which the interests of businessmen and merchants in making such a re-establishment succeed will be examined and resolved, as also everything which concerns the manufacturing industry . . . We also inform you that we have allocated from the expense of our State one million livres annually for the re-establishment of manufactures and for the increase of shipping capacity without

1. Archives Départmentales de la Loire-Atlantique, Côte C610.
2. Archives Départmentales de la Loire-Atlantique, Côte C663.

including in this allocation more considerable sums which we will make available to establish companies for the East and West Indies; we will also work tirelessly to abolish all tolls levied on navigable water-ways.

The declaration then outlines already allocated funding for repairing and improving internal road and river communications, offers royal financial backing to all those seeking to establish or create forms of manufacture, and undertakes to protect the freedom of trade.[3]

The overall design which these documents intimate is that of the unifier and builder, not that of feudal incompetent or nincompoop. Starting with internal road and river communications a unified infrastructure was to be built up, encompassing the expansion or creation of port facilities, a commercial fleet was to be designed from scratch, for both fishing and trade with a navy built to protect it. A supporting infrastructure in the manufacturing industries was to be developed, requiring the establishment of iron and steel processing capabilities, the encouragement of sail and rope manufactures, even the development of new kinds of heavy fishing net for catching flounder and plaice. Such measures were complemented in the sphere of agriculture by specialist measures designed to increase and improve bloodstock in both horses and cattle, and facilitate the manufacture of woolens.

A parallel drive was launched to standardize procedures in the stupendously entangled French fiscal, judicial and legal administrations. Colbert's fiscal reforms, the last such overhaul to be seriously attempted before the final years of the *Ancien Régime,* resulted in the concentration of what are still referred to politely as tax collecting procedures within the amalgam known as the *Cinq Grosses Fermes,* the independent collection agencies which extended credit to the crown, and like his concomitant attacks on legal and judicial institutions, were principally designed and shaped as efforts to assert royal authority to the detriment of local aristocratic and other interest groups by dismantling the privileges which gave such groups effective veto rights over the implementation of royal policy.

Beyond this, overseas trading companies were established to secure sources of raw materials independently of Dutch and English

3. Archives Départmentales de la Loire-Atlantique, Côte C694.

financial and maritime power. Such were the East and West Indies Companies founded by royal decree in the mid-1660s. These companies were financially underwritten by royal grants, and forced, if nonetheless interest-bearing, levies from the members of the court aristocracy and its associates. Special ports were established and equipped for them in Brittany, at Port-Louis and L'Orient. They were not sustained, however, because financial guarantees could not be continually levied from the nobility without some tangible, monetary return.

Education and training programs were adopted to raise the skill levels of the work force which was recruited into the implementation of that grandly conceptualized outline. In Brittany, for example, English and Dutch sailors and shipwrights were imported to train the native population in navigation and ship construction. In Paris and major provincial urban centers, Chambers of Arts and Crafts were established to educate workers in the skills necessary for the manufacturing industry. The Chamber in Paris still stands as a testament to that policy.

Even contemporary tourists to Brittany can see certain of the results of the process set in motion by such policies. The drydock in the naval arsenal at Brest, which was built in the 1660s and was in its time the largest in Europe, is available for inspection, even if foreigners can do no more than look from a distance. The elegant little fortress designed by Vauban, the great military architect, still stands guard over the fishing village of Camaret across the sound from Brest, even if it is now overshadowed by the wreckage of Rommel's bunkers from World War II. That notwithstanding, the salt pans of Croisic and Guérrande, from which salt was extracted by evaporation for the gabelle, still silently testify as to the political constraints on the implementation of such policies.

More important, however, is the very outline of the policy which Colbert conceived. This is not the work of a mind whose productions are inspired by the ethics of the mentality "buy cheap and sell dear." Neither is it the work of a mind whose conception of national wealth, or indeed wealth, is located in the filthy piles of bullion which balance international trade.

Here, in outline, produced under the conditions of a seventeenth-century monarchy, is a policy which embodies in fundamental features modern political economy. For Colbert, as opposed to his later

Physiocratic detractors, wealth was not fixed, nor was it limited to the produce of certain branches, as was argued in the case of agriculture by the Physiocrats themselves. It is on that basis that Colbert can be defined as a humanist relative to the more backward, in fact bestial tendencies that were represented in the dominant currents of the eighteenth-century Physiocrats.

Those Physiocrats' notion of wealth, as defined by the relatively fixed produce of agriculture, is in fact as feudal in outlook as William the Conqueror's *Domesday Book*, since it merely includes the efforts of human labor as an additive to the productive activities of nature and rural animal life itself. Such views were in fact more backward than the notion of "net profit" developed by the Commissioners who prepared the valuation of England's Church lands when Henry VIII ordered their confiscation in 1534. As the document in which that latter undertaking was recorded, the *Valor Ecclesiaticus* shows Henry's commissioners' net profit in terms of the income and expenses needed to keep such concerns operating profitably and usefully. In turn, it was that feudal outlook of the Physiocrats which defined their susceptibility as both the allies and victims of the policies elaborated by Adam Smith.

Colbert, in distinction from the grandfathers of the propagators of such views, rejected the notion that wealth was represented by the fixed array of agglomerations of objects available for use and disposal: he asserted that the ends of policy should be defined by the need to create new useful sources of such wealth, while expanding what is available from existent sources of production of useful goods and services. Wealth for him, both in conception and in his efforts to implement that conception, was based on the potentiality accorded by existing circumstances and resources to innovate and therefore expand and change such resources and materials as were otherwise defined as the fixed products of finite notions of wealth.

Colbert's policy intentions, as we have deduced those intentions from amid the available abundance of archive and related material, demonstrate without the shadow of a doubt the existence of a body of human knowledge concerning the proper area delineated by the field of political economy and associated social policy which is superior to anything concocted by the followers of Adam Smith from among the ranks of the monetarists since the late eighteenth century. Any responsible citizen of the twentieth century should shudder at the irony that the policies which informed even the government of a seventeenth-century monarchy were by and large conceptually superior, in design if not implementation, to those policies and the so-called body of knowledge which have regulated even republics in the course of the twentieth century. That irony reflects the actual legacy of Colbert.

As one might be expected to infer, such a body of knowledge does not lie around the nearest royal court waiting for passing powdered courtiers to avail themselves. The body of ideas from which Colbert informed himself was the result of a brutal and often bloody struggle to develop for practice the kind of intellectual weapons necessary to free Europe from the oppressive yoke of the Hapsburg dynasty and its banker allies. It was that process of human struggle which shaped the industrial-capitalist nationalist outlook of Colbert, from its roots in the humanism of fifteenth-century Florence and Padua and the early sixteenth-century England of Henry VII and Henry VIII.

The Anti-Hapsburg Front

It is now fairly widely conceded, even by historians who do not have a glimmer of insight into the context of what they assert (like M. Roland Mousnier of the Sorbonne, or M. Emmanuel LeRoy Ladurie of *Le Nouvel Observateur*), that the seventeenth century was a century of profound crisis. The usual process by which such a conclusion is adduced is more or less as useful as the normal process by which the relative balance of strategic forces between the Soviet Union and the United States is calculated. The enumeration of separate categories of the kind of evidence that might suggest one thing or another is not in itself particularly useful. Like present U.S. strategic thinkers, historians who embark on that process need a concept of the overall process of development before they can begin to weigh the various categories of evidence they might find near at hand.

The little paperback volume, *Crisis in Europe,* edited by Trevor Aston[4] is such a work. In essay after essay, the evidence for and against the title is enumerated and arrayed. That period is defined as a water-shed between feudalism and capitalism, clearing the way for the industrial revolution in England and the Revolution in France.

4. Trevor Aston, ed., *Crisis in Europe, 1560–1660*, Anchor Books, 1967.

A crisis between state and society is discerned out of which the modern state is born. The role of religion is noted. But other than the specious reasoning of *post hoc, ergo propter hoc*, not one of the contributors of the volume hazarded his reputation in an effort to discern a principle for the development of what was really going on.

The key to making good, where such contributors renege, is provided by their own emphasis on war. With the exception of three years the entirety of the seventeenth century, that means the other 97 years, were given over to warfare. That does not mean that war itself is the determinant of historical development. Warfare's most constant contributions are typified by the famines, plagues and wholesale destruction which swept Europe as a whole in the seventeenth century. The Thirty Years War, which raged backwards and forwards across central and northern Europe between the years 1618 and 1648, is most obviously cited in that regard, and it is from that standpoint that the question of religion is most often broached. The Thirty Years War was nominally fought out between contending Catholic and Protestant forces.

In reality, the Treaty of Westphalia, which is supposed to have ended that war in 1648, did not, much to the discomfiture of those who like to label the Thirty Years War a religious war. That treaty ended the hostilities between Holland and Spain, which had been more or less a chronic feature of European life since 1555. The actual character of the previous decades of constant warfare is revealed by the fighting between French and Spanish monarchies down to 1659. The Treaty of the Pyrenees signed with much pomp and majesty by the royal houses of both kingdoms in that year, on the Island of Pheasants in the river which divides Spain from France, with the Spanish king in his territory, the French king in his, and the border running directly through the center of the table on which the peace document was signed, illustrates what the war was all about.

Under the terms of that treaty, the hereditary possessions of the Hapsburgs, in central Europe and its Spanish holdings, were forever split apart into separate entities. Beyond that was inscribed the provision that the heir of Louis XIV have first claim in marriage to the appropriate female offspring of the Spanish crown, and that Spanish dominions revert not through the usual channel of the male line but through the female. Louis XIV's son was thereby supposed to become not only king of France, but king of Spain and its dominions. The treaty broke up the Hapsburg power base, and laid a future claim for the abrogation of the base by the French.

It is also that last ten years of warfare which blows the lid off the cover-story that these were religious. The Spanish Catholic crown at that point financed French Huguenot upsurges against the Mazarin administration of Louis XIV's minority. Such most unCatholic activities of succouring the heretics were not an aberration borne out of Spanish necessity in the last years of warfare. Before the Treaty of Westphalia, for example, the Calvinist Protestant Dutch had sent their navy to repress Spanish-financed French Huguenots who had again been induced to revolt against Mazarin's rule.

The wars, however, can be subsumed under a common process, and that process is definitively not characterizable as "Wars of Religion." From approximately the year 1527, when the Emperor Charles V marched into Rome and laid the eternal city to waste in an orgy of pillage and plunder, Europe had fought to free itself from the ravages of Hapsburg rule. It is the effort to put together a coalition of interests capable of achieving that end and remaining independent of Hapsburg rule, at the point that whichever particular war is formally considered to be over, which provides the essential common thread. It is that process which shapes the beginnings of the industrial capitalist outlook, and defines the problems solved in the notion of political democracy established by the American Revolution.

The hideous effects of such a line of development can even now only be contemplated with horror. Consider only those regions of Germany which include northern Bavaria, the mining regions of the Harz mountains, the cities of Nuremburg and Augsburg—the Fuggers' home base. Between 1450 and 1520, innovative craftsmen from that area, such as Gutenberg, invented the printing press, refined metalworking techniques to the effect that reliable and functional firearms and clocks could be almost mass-produced, improved the instrumentation available to experimenters in the natural sciences, and produced the breakthroughs in metallurgy and mining techniques which forced Henry VIII and Elizabeth to call for German experts when they established mining and metallurgy sectors in England.

Those areas were utterly destroyed from the German Peasants' Wars of the early 1520s onwards. There are many statistics available to document that process. We will simply take those available in

Carl J. Friedrich's *The Age of the Baroque*.[5] Between the years 1623 to 1652, the numbers of males capable of bearing arms in Wurtemburg was reduced from 65,000 to 14,800. In areas of Thuringia, half the population was destroyed. In Wurtemburg again, half the buildings were destroyed, 36,100 houses in what would politely be called cities, and 318 castles. In Munich, the number of clothiers fell to one third of the levels prevalent at the beginning of the period, the number of weavers dropped by 50 per cent.

The figures themselves cry out with the anguish of the population thus afflicted. But then consider the armies of the period, as for example that monstrosity fielded by Wallenstein to fight on behalf of the Hapsburgs. The troops of such armies were mercenaries paid out of the loot they themselves could plunder in primarily the periods between set-piece battles. They were provisioned from the produce of the countryside they were billeted in, or marching through. No community of peasants, or small town would fight such an army. They would either flee, and returning face their ravaged fields, butchered and stolen livestock, plundered supplies of feed and seed grains, etc, and look death in the face for the next year. Or they would join such an army, to buy time as it were, until either battle would put them out of their misery or they could desert.

In either case, the long-term effects of their choice would contribute to the aggravation of the dislocation of rural and urban life. Pestilence and famine stalked along the trail of such armies. Then apply, for pedagogy's sake, the German figures to the other regions in which that war was fought out, Lithuania, Latvia, Poland, Bohemia, Austria, Northern Italy, Switzerland, France and Spain itself, the Netherlands. There is a crude but nonetheless approximate costing to the human race of the effort to expunge the Hapsburgs.

The title of nominal victors in that horrendous process of bloodletting and destruction must be awarded to the Dutch, and more particularly to the House of Orange and its constant rivals in the financial and commercial oligarchy which ruled over Amsterdam. The burghers of the city of Amsterdam emerged from that series of wars holding in their own hands what they had previously mediated on behalf of the Hapsburgs and the Fuggers, namely the strings of European finance and commerce.

5. Carl J. Friedrich, *The Age of the Baroque, 1610–1660*, Harper Torchbooks, 1962.

The Bank of Amsterdam, whose deposit system was considered by Adam Smith in 1776 to be fool- and run-proof under most conditions, was founded in 1609 and rapidly became Europe's premier source of loan funds. It was the center of a web of discount and rediscount operations in bills of exchange and other letters of credit which underwrote a far-flung network of trading operations, from Japan, through southeast Asia to India and Africa, through Latin America to the North American cod fisheries and embraced the British Isles, the Scandinavian countries, the Baltic littoral and what was known then as Muscovy.

The bulk of the world's trade in basic raw materials such as bullion, grains, spices, woods pitch, and salted or pickled fish, and certain manufactured weapons such as cast iron weapons, agricultural implements and clothes passed through that port, whether directly, as merchandise, or indirectly as a bill of exchange or letter of credit. When, in 1639, Dutch Admiral Tromp wiped out the Spanish navy, destroying nearly 70 ships and a 20,000 man invasion force bound for his homeland, in the battle known as the "Scandal of the Downs" (he pursued the stormstruck Spanish fleet into English territorial waters to exterminate them), Dutch financial and maritime hegemony was complete.

Ironically, it was through the process by which the Dutch achieved the financial and commercial hegemony they wrested from the Hapsburgs that the body of knowledge from which Colbert derived his anti-Dutch political economic policy was formed and shaped. The Dutch themselves were the principal catalyst and mediation of the development of that body of knowledge itself.

Ordinarily that process is referred to as "The Revolt of the Netherlands."[6] For a period of nearly 100 years, from 1555 to 1648, the predominantly Protestant Dutch were locked in the bloody grip of what is always described as a struggle for their national liberation from the brutal military occupation policies of the Catholic Spanish monarchy and the Hapsburgs. In a restricted sense that view is correct. But the restrictions are such that the commonplace view is not helpful at all.

At the point in 1519 when the Hapsburg Charles V united his dynastic holdings in central Europe, which included what are now

6. Peter Geyl, *The Revolt in the Netherlands.*

Belgium and Holland, with the kingdom and territories built up by the wicked Ferdinand of Castile, he made the Netherlands into the political cockpit for Europe as a whole. The issues fought out in that little corner of the continent reclaimed at such cost from the seas, which straddles the vital north-south shipping routes and is divided by the major Rhine, Scheldt and Meuse rivers, the life lines into central Europe, were never purely local or national. It is literally the case that from 1525 until 1648, and even thereafter, the Netherlands were the center of gravity of European politics as a whole.

Charles V and the Fuggers built up the port city of Antwerp as the entrepôt for Europe's credit finance and commerce, as a lever for political control of the continent as a whole. They matched inflowing bullion from Latin America in that city, with the grains of central Europe, the wools and cloth of England, the wood and iron of Scandinavia. The malevolent Fuggers, who controlled the spigots of finance and credit from their home base in Augsburg, were the actual masterminds of the whole show. As their own records show, the annual profit they extracted from their credit and finance operations, which were extended to more customers than just Charles V, was in the order of 53 per cent.

It was their rapacious appetite for lucre, as mediated by the political-economic insanity of Charles V and his successor Philip II, and expressed in that annual figure of 53 per cent, which defined the life or death issues for Europe, as well as for the native populations of Peru, Guyana, Venezuela, Colombia, Mexico and parts of Africa and Asia. The fight around those issues was concentrated in the Low Countries, until the Hapsburgs' Empire was broken up in 1658, when the question was posed differently.

Hapsburg policies for Europe, as defined by that rapacious figure of 53 per cent demanded by the Fuggers, were not a bit different than those applied in Mexico and Peru under Cortes and Pizarro, both in conquering those countries and in the genocidal regime under which bullion was extracted from the fabled mines. The horrifying repression of the German peasants in the early 1520s, when more than 100,000 were reported to have been directly put to the sword, stands as a vivid testimony to that fact, as do the similar measures applied in Spain, the destruction and pillage of Charles' march on Rome, the grisly activities of the Hapsburg-allied, Fugger-financed Catholic Guise faction in the French so-called Wars of Religion, the bloody-handed suppression of successive revolts in the Low Countries themselves as epitomized by the Council of Blood used by Alba and Requesens to root out and burn opponents of Hapsburg rule, and, of course the Thirty Years War itself.

The political issue that was fought out in and around the Netherlands, beginning in 1525, but more especially from 1555 in the conjuncture of the first Netherlands Revolt and the first Great Spanish Bankruptcy of the same year, was the question of whether Europe as a whole would be ground down under the Hapsburgs' bloody boot, and if not, what were the terms and policies under which the Hapsburgs could be defeated.

At the end of that process it is the French monarchy which for a brief period emerges as progressive, relative to the new version of the Fuggers' rapacious political outlook concocted by the alliance of English and Dutch trading interests through the period of the 1660s and 1670s. Where the Dutch and the English assumed the full legacy of those who had been their persecutors over that entire period, the French under Colbert attempted to make use of the weaponry which had been forged in the struggle against the Hapsburgs and Fuggery to prevent the emergence of such an alliance.

Some, among whom would be included many so-called professional historians, would no doubt protest vigorously against such a sweeping characterization. Let them. The evidence does not fit any other analysis.

It is the case that violent pulsations of the struggle in the Netherlands, which form an otherwise mostly subterranean current in the history of that people, as exemplified by the political careers of William "the Silent" of Nassau, John Oldenbarnevelde and William's son Maurice of Nassau, not only produce expanding ripple effects measured more and more in direct support from other anti-Hapsburg European factions, but also coincide with the periodic bankruptcies of the House of Hapsburg itself.

It is also the case that each such bankruptcy of the House of Hapsburg, beginning, but excepting for the moment, 1557, that is to 1575, 1593, 1609–1610 and then more or less regularly every ten years down to 1648 and the Treaty of Westphalia, at which point Spain, France and the English were all plunged into bankruptcy, coincides with a more or less conscious effort on the part of the forces opposed to the Hapsburgs and Fuggery to pull together an armed coalition to be fielded in the Low Countries themselves.

Thus, in the early 1570s negotiations were underway for such a joint venture between William the Silent, with Walsingham and Walter Ralegh representing the English and the Duc de Coligny a pro-Dutch, anti-Hapsburg French faction. Similarly, in the 1580s and 1590s, the years of William's marriage alliance with the French Anjou family, the years of the defeat of the Spanish Armada and of Walter Ralegh and Cecil's lightning strike against a Spanish naval build-up in the harbor of Cadiz, Spanish capability to resupply troops by sea as opposed to the far longer overland route was destroyed. Again, in 1609–1610, Oldenbarnevelde for the Dutch, Henry IV and Sully for the French, and certain selected German Protestants attempted to mount the same effort. Finally, it is the shaping of such anti-Hapsburg alliances which characterizes the process of the Thirty Years War itself, when Dutch financial support for the French under Richelieu was parlayed into French subsidies for the European armies of Gustavus Adolphus of Sweden and George of Saxony's Protestant League.

Hapsburg counter-measures merely emphasize the point. The most infamous such example is, of course, the St. Bartholomew's Day massacre in France in 1572. That foul pogrom was not simply a matter between the Catholic Guise family and Coligny's Huguenots. Guise was subsidized by the Hapsburgs. The Spanish ambassador coordinated the atrocities in Paris. The purpose of the bloodletting was to prevent Coligny leading the army he had promised against the Hapsburgs' exposed southern flank in what is now Belgium. The dagger of the assassin Ravaillac ended Henry IV's plans to march to the assistance of Oldenbarnevelde in 1610. The ritual beheading of Walter Ralegh was the result of the same influences. James I could only buy peace with the Hapsburgs by eliminating the political faction which stood for their destruction. Ralegh was therefore outmaneuvered and incarcerated on charges of being a Spanish agent in 1603, the very year the idiot James acceded to Elizabeth's throne. He was kept on suffrance as a bargaining chip, and disposed of in the manner of the times.

The year 1555 is the exception to this process, which in fact proves the case beyond the shadow of a doubt. It is true that no one directly intervened to support the Dutch in the years of their first revolt. But it is the case nonetheless that the armamentarium of policy, which was subsequently brought to bear internationally against the Hapsburgs, was forged in that period. It is the policies elaborated by respective factions beginning in about 1555 and running through 1575 which surface more or less forcefully in subsequent years whenever the rapaciousness of the Hapsburgs transformed political pressure into bloody shove.

Religion and the Origins Of the "Industrial" Outlook

It is in the years prior to and between the first and second Dutch Revolts that the essential aspects of the policies of such heroic figures as Thomas Gresham and Jean Bodin were formulated. The two were mutual correspondents, and therefore knew of each other's work, whether or not they actually met. Such shared knowledge is directly reflected in Bodin's writings themselves and in the thinking and writing of the Gresham faction in England, including such figures as William Cecil, Humphrey Gilbert and Thomas Smith.

The political-economic efforts of the two were based on a return to common shared roots, in particular to the utopian program formulated between 1511 and 1516 in the collaboration between Thomas More and his Chelsea study group and the Dutchman Erasmus. Those two endeavored to draw up a practical program to realize in this world the scientific advances of the Italian humanists Marsilio Ficino and Pico della Mirandola. As the title of Thomas More's best known work, *Utopia*, implies, and indeed reveals, they did not succeed.

It is instructive in that light to read Thomas More's *Utopia*. One cannot but be struck by the prescience with which he, through the mouth of the character "Raphael" foresees the future course of events in sixteenth-century Europe, and analyzes the policies available to the contending forces he thus defines. Equally it is instructive to see why More and his collaborators could not succeed. For More, as with Erasmus, who located his life's work in the effort to realize the notion of "perfection" developed by Ficino and Pico, could only, in effect, offer his personal example in efforts to achieve that end.

For More, as for Ficino before him, the quality of "perfection" which fundamentally distinguished the human soul from the lower beasts is known only as a fixed state of rest. That being the case, how does one proceed from the evident imperfections and rampant heteronomy which characterize the present to a future perfected state of rest? That problem confronted More as a fundamental paradox leering at his every effort. It is the effort to resolve that paradox which is the intellectual mainspring of sixteenth-century humanist efforts to secularize the conception of perfection for this world rather than for the next. And it is in that struggle that the beginnings of the modern republican political, as with modern economic outlooks are formed.

That is the struggle which defines the ensuing process as fundamentally religious.

For no one would qualify either of the contending secular institutions which were accorded the name church, whether Protestant or Catholic, with the title "religious." By the sixteenth century, the papacy had reached depths lower than imaginable for such an institution, as more than simply the practices of Borgias reveal. The papacy was in fact a pawn in the game of European politics as a whole, to be seized and deployed by whoever was strong enough to take it at the time, and thereby avail themselves of both its financial resources, and the effects of its reputation in terrifying the credulous. It is not accidental in that regard that the French and the Spanish dynasts had their own, independently controlled Inquisitions—the Capuchins and the Jesuits, whose criteria for orthodoxy were strictly secular, no matter what ritual verbiage they employed.

Similarly with the Protestants, whether Calvinists or Lutherans; both excised what was fundamental to the humanist current, namely the notion of "free will," without which man can be no more than an animal in this world. The Calvinists became the principal purveyors of human flesh across the face of Europe, in the supply of mercenaries made available on cash payment, from the depths of Switzerland and southern Germany. The Lutheran faction in Germany, betrayed by their pastor in the Peasants Wars, in which he had urged revenging aristocrats to kill and kill again, suffered as the passive victims of a political process which played itself out over their heads.

The humanist current is the only one concerned with the fundamental questions of religion during this period. The others are simply more or less effective rationalizations for more or less temporary political arrangements.

Bodin is unabashed about his intellectual origins as his constant references to the works of Thomas More, in preference to other contemporary authors, reveal. As for Thomas Gresham, his father John was an intimate of Thomas More's intellectual circle up to the time that More's execution broke up the circle—but, as Henry VIII's subsequent policies show, with the consequences of strengthening the ideas. Gresham's father, an associate of Thomas Cromwell, was a pioneer and principal beneficiary of Henry VIII's confiscation and sale of church lands in England. As a member of the London Mercers' Company, he was an early advocate of expanded cloth production in England, and subsidized the translation of the Bible into English by William Tyndale and Miles Coverdale from Erasmus' prepared version of the Greek texts of the New Testament.

Comparison of the works of Bodin and the Gresham circle shows how much such concerns had developed by the 1560s and 1570s. Bodin's *Résponse aux Paradoxes de M. de Malestroict* established for the first time a correlation between the inflow to Europe of the gold bullion from Latin America, and the inflationary explosion that was then ravaging Europe. The famous *Memorandum on the Exchange* produced by the Gresham circle in England demonstrates how backward the kind of thinking represented in Philips Curve-style economic nostrums is in regard to the finest levels of Elizabethan England. The shared concern motivating both efforts is the need to find an effective policy to defeat the Hapsburgs and the Fuggers at the source of their power. Equally, the answers developed by both individuals provide a shared competent notion of the political measures necessary to ensure a functioning national economy.

Both had seen previous attempts fail. Gresham knew that the confiscation, and cloth production policies of his father and Thomas Cromwell, had dissolved into a pile of debt owed to the Fugger in Antwerp. This was exacerbated by Fugger control of the exchange to the point that English internal credit was wrecked in the Great Debasement of the years 1545–1555, when the English coinage was stripped of its bullion content in order to free such bullion for debt payment in Antwerp. The result was to accelerate the collapse of the pound sterling on the Fugger-controlled exchanges, thereby repeating in more aggravated fashion the cycle of destruction of internal credit and liquid means of payment.

Bodin likewise knew of the absurd efforts of the pathetic House of Valois to defeat the Hapsburgs at their own game, by embarking on an ambitious policy of military conquest aimed at keeping Spanish and Central European possessions separate by forcefully appropriating chunks of Italy—as epitomized by the alliance in the 1520s of Francis I, the papacy and the Turks. Through that and similar forms of insanity, what was to become France was reduced to bankruptcy and civil war among gangs of aristocrats and paid thugs: the one side financially and politically backed by the Hapsburgs and known to posterity as "the Catholics," their opposition, the Huguenots.

Gresham and his faction gave priority to taking control of English manufacture and trade from the Fuggers. They engineered the great Reform of the Coinage in 1560, by which the nominal value of the country's debased silver coinage was reduced by decree to levels at which it would be practicable to remint a standardized currency. At the same time, the country's chronic problem of indebtedness was tackled on the basis of the eminently sound principle that the country's annual debt service could no longer exceed income from current production of real tangible wealth in the form of the output of agriculture and manufacturing industries. The implementation of that policy gave Elizabeth's government the margin of increased maneuver which freed it from abject servitude to the powers of Fuggery who controlled the Antwerp exchanges, and created the basis for undoing the ravages of the same forces which had so ruinously depleted the country's economic base.

In so doing, the Gresham circle established the modern science of political economy. They refused to bow down before externally imposed objective conditions and definitions of wealth as represented by the Fugger's purse. They triumphantly asserted that key parameters which determine a country's credit, and its investment policy, are subjective and therefore susceptible of deliberate change by the intervention of the human decision-making process and its instrumentalities.

This was the foundation on which was built a period of sustained development in science and technology, itself the outcome of such legislative documents as William Cecil's *Industrial Program* and *The Statute of Artificers*. Such development was fueled by the scientific concerns of Humphrey Gilbert and Walter Ralegh, who pulled together a team of scientists and engineers to build the navy they designed, equip it with the necessary levels of technology to outgun and outsail the Spanish fleet, and train the crews. Under the auspices of these two, the *common AB's of the Elizabethan navy were educated with courses in astronomy, navigation and mathematics.*

That effort was the front end, as it were, of the broader programmatic concerns of the Cecil-Gilbert grouping, who deployed themselves to their utmost to develop contemporary technologies in mining and metallurgy and other manufacturing processes, such as glass manufacture. The corporation known as the "Mines Royal," under the terms of whose charter all ores and minerals found anywhere on English soil were the property of the crown, to be developed as per royal government instruction, was established for that purpose, and German specialists in extraction and metal-working processes imported to make the effort succeed.

Consistent attention was focused on the problem of switching from the use of wood in the fueling of manufacturing processes to coal. This policy was designed to conserve trees—for ship-building and to gain tree independence from the sources of Hapsburg-controlled raw materials for the armaments industry in northern Europe. As a by-product of that concern, coal-fired glass and iron-smelting processes were developed.

Coal consumption under Elizabeth was higher than at any time subsequently down to the so-called "industrial revolution." At the end of Elizabeth's reign, experimental work towards the development of a steam engine was begun. (See Appendix.)

The results of Bodin's work do not show up so immediately or so dramatically as the inspiring advances of the Tudors. Nevertheless that should not detract from his importance. The hideous effects of the St. Batholomew's Day Massacre cannot be neglected in that regard. The intellectual and political cream of sixteenth-century France was drowned in blood. Yet, the very fact that such an event could occur at all is itself suggestive of the fact that, though the problems he considered were similar to those which faced the Gresham circle in England, the solutions to those problems were prioritized very differently. Where Henry VII and Henry VIII in England eliminated the foci of aristocratic discontent towards effective policies of central government by confiscating estates and disbanding private aristocratic armies, and thereby eliminated successfully some of the internal sickness of venality and cupidity which could have been useful to Hapsburg and Fugger alike, the idiot House of Valois was concerned with an altogether different notion of grandeur. Their wars of conquest merely aggravated the chronic tendency of aristocrats to buck authority and revolt.

Bodin was motivated above all by the need to settle the semipermanent chronic state of civil war between competing aristocratic factions in a way which would permit some kind of civilized life to subsist. His *Six Books of the Commonwealth* were written as a contribution to that end. In his judgment, an end would have to be put to the senseless blood-letting of aristocratic factions each competing for supreme power.

He, therefore, distinguished conceptually in his writings between the interests of the state, or commonwealth (in the Latin usage of Thomas More and Erasmus, et al., his use of the word "Res Publica" is actually better rendered by the English commonwealth or republic than state), and the interests of whatever monarch happened to be on the throne at a given time. In consequence, he was able to derive permanent interests for the subsistence of the commonwealth, which could then be effectively juxtaposed to the notion that the exercise of power was no more than a short-term rip-off which was violently propagated in practice by both the aristocratic groups which headed up the opposing factions in the civil war. Like the Gresham circle in England, Bodin therefore asserted that the political arrangements under which men's affairs are regulated are neither God-given, nor immovable, but themselves subject to wilful change, and themselves the instrumentality through which such humanly initiated change is to be implemented.

With that accomplished, Bodin and the other members of his faction, who were known and styled themselves as the *politiques*, to distinguish themselves from the advocates of internecine strife, fought for a policy which would beef up central authority by taxing the hell out of the aristocracy in order to make fissiparous factions impossible. They simultaneously advocated Gresham-style measures to encourage the development of a manufacturing and commercial basis that would be independent of the Hapsburgs.

Bodin did not live to see his work or policies implemented successfully. Nonetheless his labors, as complemented by his successors Laffemas and Montchrétien, are the authority to which successive French regimes turned as they were forced into war for their own survival by the insane Hapsburgs. Henry IV and Sully, before Ravaillac's dagger put an end to such potentials, based their conceptions and outlook on the work of Bodin and his allies in the ranks of the *politiques*. Cardinal Richelieu adopted the principles of that same faction when he threw down the glove and challenged the Hapsburgs, by blocking their overland transit route from southern to central

Europe in the Val Telline in Switzerland, and by breaking up the aristocratic pro-Spanish camerilla grouped around the Queen Mother—de Medici. Those measures Richelieu made in preparation for his open declaration for the armies of Gustavus Adolphus of Sweden, and against the Hapsburgs in 1631. The work of the *politiques* was the authority Colbert turned to as he began to pull his policies together in 1663.

Thus far, such programs may seem so secular as to be totally irreligious. That view would mistake the trees for the forest. The point is exemplified by considering the paradox which is posed by the juxtaposition of Bodin's notion of a commonwealth, and the instrumentality he devised for implementing that notion. For Bodin, as for all the sixteenth century developers, and followers of the work of Ficino and Pico, man is fundamentally distinguished from the lower beasts through the universal quality of the human mind, the ability to perfect itself. That notion, like the continual references to the work of Thomas More, runs like a thread through his *Six Books of the Commonwealth*.

Yet, for Bodin, as for the other inheritors of that school, the quality of perfection is fixed; "at rest" in the formulation of Ficino. That being the case, how does one activate those universal human qualities to move from present grisly forms of heteronomy to the aspired-for state of perfection? If one decides for a strong central government to override existing heteronomic interests, then what? The question is fundamentally unresolved, as becomes apparent simply by comparing what Richelieu, Mazarin and Colbert did with Bodin's strong state.

Bodin, as with the other developers of these ideas was, of course, acutely aware that there was in fact a paradox to be solved. The intellectual efforts of thinkers from More and Erasmus, through Bodin himself, down to such heroes of the English revolution as John Milton and Cromwell, were directed to the resolution of that paradox.

For Erasmus and the mainline of his followers, the answer is in part provided by education. To that effect, John Colet, Grocyn and Linacre, the direct mediators of Florentine and Paduan influence into England, inspired the beginnings of one of the most relatively massive education programs the world was to see. It was in the formation of that program that Erasmus developed the main intellec-

tual thrust of his life. St. Paul's School in Westminster is the pioneering testament of the effort.

Such figures divided the general strategic approach into two
principal tactics. First, to imbue the rulers, and potential rulers of
the various kingdoms, principalities, etc. with the outlooks of their
own development of Florentine humanism. Second, to educate the
broader layers of the population. It was from that standpoint that
Erasmus wrote his *On the Education of a Christian Prince* in 1516,
appropriately enough for the future Emperor Charles V. He developed the motivation of that pamphlet more forcefully in passages in
his *Adagia,* which was written in 1515.

> Do we not see that noble cities are erected by the people
> and destroyed by the princes? That a state grows rich by
> the industry of its citizens only to be plundered by the
> rapacity of its rulers? That good laws are enacted by the
> representatives of the people and violated by kings? That
> the commonalty loves peace and the monarchs foment war?
> The guardians of a prince aim never to permit him to become
> a man. The nobility, feeding on public corruption, endeav-
> our to make him as effeminate as possible through pleasures,
> lest he learn what a prince ought to know. Villages are burnt,
> fields are devastated, temples pillaged, innocent citizens
> slaughtered, all things spiritual and temporal destroyed
> while the king plays at dice or dances, or amuses himself
> with fools, or in hunting and carousing.

It was such principles which formed the educational background
of rulers such as Henry VIII, his son Edward and daughter Elizabeth
(who was strictly the last English monarch), the leaders of the Netherlands Revolt such as William the Silent and his circle and his successor
Oldenbarnevelde and his ally Grotius, as well as representatives of
the French current such as Bodin, Coligny and DuPlessis Mornay.

England saw the furthest development of the process, in respect
to both aspects of the strategy. At the beginning of the reign of
Elizabeth, there is generally reckoned to have been one Grammar
School for rather more than every 5,000 members of the population
of all ages. The corresponding ratio for the 1860s is generally reckoned as one such school for every 23,000 members of the population.

Thomas More's circle, Erasmus and their followers such as Bishops Cranmer and Latimer, who were burnt at the stake during the brief but hideous reign of Henry VIII's Catholic daughter Mary, the wife of Philip II of Spain (1555–1560), can generally be reckoned as the dynamos of that process. Their principal vehicle was the Church of England, which was charged by law to make available in every parish an English translation of the Bible, selected commentaries, such as Erasmus' *Paraphrases of the Gospel According to St. John,* and the *Book of Common Prayer* as prepared by Cranmer himself. Priests were compelled to read from such texts to their assembled parishioners at least weekly, and were provided with pre-written political sermons to broadcast, in the event that they were unable to develop adequate such texts of their own.

Such efforts, which ensured rapidly expanding literacy levels, were complemented by the curriculum of the Grammar Schools, itself prepared by Erasmus in the form of a revision of the basic grammar text prepared by Colet's collaborator in the establishment of St. Paul's School, Richard Lily. The curriculum thus devised focused on the basic skills of literacy and numeracy in preparation for higher studies between the ages of ten and 15 in the Latin and Greek classics. Hide-bound England still has schools which name their classes after Erasmus and describe their older students as "Grecians." The efforts of Humphrey Gilbert and Thomas Gresham to provide education at the highest levels of contemporary natural science were the most developed expression of that process.

Yet, education, in itself, does not resolve the paradox which presented itself to Bodin, Erasmus and their English associates. How many educated individuals are needed to make a perfected republic? John Milton addressed the problem directly at the height of the constitutional crisis which wracked England in the mid-1650s after the dissolution of what was known as the "Barebones Parliament," as Cromwell and his associates were deliberating on how England should best be governed. In his *Defensio Secunda* he wrote,

It is of no little consequence, O citizens, by what principles you are governed, either in acquiring liberty or in retaining it when acquired. . . . For who would vindicate your right of unrestrained suffrage, or of choosing what representatives you liked best, merely that you might elect the creatures of your own faction whoever they might be, or him, however small might be his worth, who would give you the most lavish feasts, and enable you to drink to the greatest excess? Thus not wisdom and authority, but turbulence and gluttony, would soon exalt the vilest miscreants from our taverns and brothels, from our towns and villages, to the rank and dignity of senators . . . Among such persons, who would be willing either to fight for liberty or to encounter the least peril in its defence? It is not agreeable to the nature of things that such persons should be free . . . You, therefore, who wish to remain free, either instantly be wise, or as soon as possible cease to be fools; if you think slavery an intolerable evil, learn obedience to right reason and the rule of yourselves: and finally bid adieu to your dissensions, your jealousies, your superstitions, your outrages, your rapine, your lusts. Unless you will spare no pains to effect this, you must be judged, by God, man, and your very deliverers, unfit to be entrusted with the possession of liberty, and the administration of the government.

Milton's polemic locates the form of the solution to that fundamentally religious paradox which had plagued the humanist current since the beginning collaboration of More and Erasmus. Republican or commonwealth government is not based on the enlightened outlook of its leaders, nor on a simply educated population, but in a government whose primary task is to evoke and develop those qualities within the population which Ficino, Pico, and their followers had otherwise identified as being perfectible. Yet neither he, nor Cromwell, could provide the means and instrumentality through which such a process of human perfection may be realized on this earth.

However, it is the fundamentally religious current and process we have examined which is the current out of which is born the industrial capitalist outlook associated with the origins of republicanism—as the result of the failure to resolve that apparent paradox.

If the humanist current at that point in its development did not provide the method to overcome the ravages and depredations of heteronomy and greed in a systematic fashion, then such evils were to be suppressed in better-directed motion towards a better state of affairs in this world. To the extent that popular support was won for the forceful expression of such outlooks, and the benefits expected of the same, as was the case with the Tudors, and rather differently with the Dutch, then a relatively positive nationalist outlook was the result of the struggle by the religious-humanist current to equip itself with the intellectual weaponry and material resources which could achieve, and safeguard once achieved, freedom from the bestiality of the House of Hapsburg.

The fundamentally positive content of that struggle can be situated by comparison with works and outlooks of the social contract theorists of the so-called Enlightenment, including in that category Hobbes, and mentioning in that context John Locke, David Hume and Jean-Jacques Rousseau. For that anti-humanist current, heteronomy, along with all the bestial aberrations which flow from it, is a fixed, indeed unchangeable quality in human beings. For such precursors of the morality of George Orwell's *Animal Farm* the task of government is not to evoke, educate and sustain popular aspirations for progress, it is rather to find the negotiated basis for bargaining settlements and agreements between the representatives of contending outlooks and agreements. These clowns are the fears of John Milton writ large, and demonstrate from a different point of view than this, as we have already seen in the field of economics itself, that the body of knowledge forged in the struggle to defeat the Hapsburgs is by and large superior to what are usually considered to be the foremost representatives of eighteenth-century Enlightenment thought, such as the social contract theorists and Adam Smith and the Physiocrats.

The hideous irony that is the result of the religious paradox we have discussed is revealed by the case of the Dutch, and in a different context by Cromwell's England.

The Dutch, who will forever be remembered as the catalyst and focus for the development of the anti-Hapsburg movement as that evolved, themselves adopted the policies of the Hapsburgs' Fugger financiers at the point that they were free of Spanish political and military domination. That fact is reflected positively in their pulling of the financial plug as a weapon against their French allies, the Spanish and the English in 1648. The ensuing bankruptcies of all three kingdoms prevented the French from capitalizing on the advantage they had won over their Spanish Hapsburg opponents at the expense of the inhabitants of the Dutch Republic, who would no more tolerate a French occupying force than they would the Hapsburgs themselves.

This is not to detract in the least from the achievements of the Dutch at that point. The fight for freedom from the chains of Hapsburg oppression created the condition for a flourishing in the arts and sciences comparable only to that enjoyed by the citizens of Florence in the fifteenth century and the citizens of Elizabeth's London in the sixteenth. Rembrandt and Benedict Spinoza were Dutch, after all, and that, in part, at least explains their accomplishment.

Even without the Hapsburgs, the Dutch Republic was caught in a vise. It lived by the proceeds and profits denominated in money of the trade for which it still acted as the entrepôt for Europe as a whole and such colonial appendages of Europe as then existed. Despite the aspirations of the Dutch citizenry themselves, in the absence of an external solution to the apparently paradoxical problem we have identified, there were only two kinds of government which would replace the Spanish rule over the Netherlands.

The one was represented by the military competence of the House of Orange, its mercenary army base, and popular support mobilized either politically and directed against Spain or mobilized like mercenaries through the networks of Calvinist Consistories which distributed Orange patronage to urban inhabitants in the form of bread and doles. (A wretched parody of that method is played out in unhappy Northern Ireland to this day.) The other tendency surfaced in the brief interludes of peace, when the military qualifications and capabilities of the House of Orange could be temporarily dispensed with, on condition that such a period of peace also coincided with the absence of a suitable Orange for their hereditary position, the Stadtholder. Such happier junctures were the merchant-based regimes of John Oldenbarnevelde at the beginning of the seventeenth century and the republic of John de Witt in the 1650s and 1660s, under whose patronage and encouragement Spinoza, outcast from the Amsterdam Jewish community, flourished.

Both were more or less dependent on each other, and on outside support. The merchant interests needed the military capabilities of the Oranges to protect their sources of trade and the practice of that trade; the Oranges needed the merchants' money in the form of tax income to pay their mercenaries. They also needed allies in especially German and Swiss provinces to provide the mercenaries themselves.

Such parameters placed constraining limits on the life expectancy of the two republican governments we have identified, those of Olden-barnevelde and de Witt. At the point that the financial and trading practices of their merchant base brought them into conflict with what would otherwise be their foreign allies, namely their debtors, the military capability of the Oranges would be asserted to maintain the balance.

This outlook was later developed after the Orange coup d'état and counter-revolution in England in 1688 into modern forms of monetarism. Esteemed qualities such as English compromise, moderation and tolerance are the rationalization for periodic political accommodations to such invasions, as with the flatulent House of Hanover in the eighteenth century, and the Rothschilds in the nineteenth. The outlook is otherwise expressed in the fact that Dutch Calvinist bankers, operating from Amsterdam, Paris, Gothenburg, Hamburg and elsewhere, financed both so-called Protestant and Catholic causes in the wars against the Hapsburgs, especially during the so-called Thirty Years War itself.

We can therefore efficiently characterize the period which follows from the conclusion of general hostilities against the Hapsburgs which follows from the Treaty of the Pyrenees signed, as we have seen, in 1659.

The once mighty House of Hapsburg was humbled, its Spanish possessions and territories in hock to a future King of France. The English and the Dutch both momentarily under republican forms of government were plagued by the political implications of the apparent paradox bequeathed them from the humanist past. The rulers of both knew that either they discover a practical political solution to the problem, or the governments they had built at such cost would founder and be dissolved. The French, on the other hand, emerged from that period of bloodshed and warfare with a vastly strengthened and centralized monarchy. To the extent that the humanists' apparent paradox was not resolved, the future of Europe, down to the French and American revolutions in the eighteenth century would be shaped by the fight for hegemony between the political and military power of the French monarchy and its population of approximately 20 million, and the financial and commercial power represented in 1658 by the Dutch merchant oligarchy on the one side, the House of Orange on the other, with the tiny population of the Netherlands sandwiched in between.

Hence we return to Colbert, for he seized on the weapons forged

in the struggle against the Hapsburgs in order to defeat the similar
political problem confronting the French monarchy in the form of
Dutch financial and commercial power. By so doing, Colbert himself
ran headlong into the same apparent paradox faced by the rulers of
both the English and Dutch republics, even if under the altogether
different political constraints of the French monarchical system.
Nonetheless, his efforts to surmount that problem provide an important point of analysis for comparison with Cromwell's efforts to deal
with what was essentially the same problem.

Colbert's Predicament

That problem, and a partial resolution to the apparent antinomy
which confronted the best efforts of the humanist current can be
found in the one word, credit. That one word represents the problem
Colbert could not solve—and actually represents the problem Cromwell would not solve. It is ironic in that regard that Colbert returned
to the subjectivist-voluntarist definitions of credit pioneered by
Gresham—while Cromwell did not.

We have noted that essential features of Colbert's policy of developing an infrastructure in the manufacturing industries and transportation were defined by the perceived need to free France from the
control of Dutch finance and commerce. In the pursuit of that end
it was the question of finance and credit which was key. To solve
it, or attempt to solve it, Colbert, himself of Huguenot stock, returned
to the traditions of Bodin and Gresham as mediated by Henry IV
and his advisor Sully and by Cardinal Richelieu. Such were the
sources and authorities available to him at the point that he began
to deal with the problem of defeating international finance.

There are existent documents which clarify the nature of these
concerns. Again the Municipal Archives in Nantes provide the argu-
mentation for a court case by a lawyer by the name of Hevin. The
argument was presented some time during the course of 1673, after
war had broken out with the Dutch.

> Several years ago His Majesty thought the matter of com-
> merce worthy of his attention and application, since com-
> merce is the gate-way through which abundance enters
> states, and which contributes greatly to the happiness of
> their peoples, and which can only prosper with the assistance

of good laws which extirpate underhanded practices and encourage good faith. One of the principal abuses which was noted at that time was provided by bills of exchange, out of which bankers and merchants had fashioned the art of a cabal. It was a kind of black magic which common people did not understand at all, about which scarcely any law or order of previous kings said a word, and which barely a handful of people at the court itself understood.[7]

The second such document is an explication of legislation passed in the month of March in 1673, which was designed at that point to enable judges to speedily resolve cases involving underhanded dealings between merchants, and to put an end to such practices. The document, in part, attempts to answer the questions raised by Hevin. It reads in extracted form:

All bills of exchange will henceforth only be accepted in writing, purely and simply. The practice of accepting them verbally is abrogated. The holder of a bill of exchange should not be liable at a later date, for a sum larger than that which is written on the bill of exchange. The party who the bill is drawn on is responsible for bad debts, not the holder of the bill. Holders of bills of exchange which should have been accepted, or whose payment falls due on a certain specific day, should be responsible for payment, or they should protest within the ten days after the bill falls due.[8]

It will no doubt not be missed that the latter passage provides a legal loophole for default. Anyone who has read either legislation, or treatises from the Tudor period on the subject of usury, or on the various contemporary instruments of exchange and how such instruments work (such as Thomas Wilson's *Discourse on Usury*, with the valuable introduction by R. H. Tawney), will recognize the parallels immediately. These documents are the tip-off that Colbert was reasserting that specific combination of industrial capitalist nationalist outlook against the Dutch monetarists.

The point is that most of the bills of exchange which circulated

7. Archives Départmentales de la Loire-Atlantique, Côte B168.
8. Archives Départmentales de la Loire-Atlantique, Côte C642(2).

in France in the 1660s and 1670s would have been drawn on primarily Dutch banking establishments, and to a significantly lesser extent on such English-based financial outfits as the Dutch-related companies of Scriveners and Goldsmiths, the founding core of what was to become "the City."

Merchants from, for example, Nantes or St. Malo in Brittany who wanted to sell wines, salted fish or cloth would, through their agents in Amsterdam or London, find a buyer from among the finance houses who would issue paper against anticipated future delivery of the goods themselves. Anticipated delivery in turn provided the basis for further such extensions of paper credit by the finance house, while the note so issued could be discounted and rediscounted for other paper and nominal money profits, or exchanged for goods to be shipped back into French ports themselves. The notes and paper thus issued were, of course, interest-bearing.

But, from such promising beginnings the policy collapsed. By the 1690s and the first decade of the eighteenth century, France was plunged into the chronic financial situation, always verging on bankruptcy, that was to plague it throughout the eighteenth century, just as it had been previously so plagued under Richelieu in the seventeenth century. This time, English-based financial interests were to interfere in the process to the same disastrous effect as the Spanish during the years of the Fronde upsurges which followed Richelieu's death in the late 1640s.

There are two primary, and interrelated features which account for the collapse of that policy, both of which are clarified by reference to the period of Cromwell's Protectorate in England, the political legacy of which was being liquidated by the foolishly ridiculous figure of Charles II and his backers as Colbert himself rose to major importance in France. They are, as we have previously identified, the problem of credit and the vicious heteronomy of the aristocratic-oligarchic faction.

Where Colbert attempted to innovate, to circumvent both problems, Cromwell, of educated rural stock, fell back on the policies of his ancestor, Henry VIII's adviser Thomas Cromwell, and thereby laid the basis for his own undoing. Colbert's innovations were a result of his creative application of the funds available to the royal treasury, and his voluntarist efforts to expand available income to that account. Where Colbert used subsidies, and attacked heteronomic noble privilege to increase the amount available to so extend, Cromwell resorted to the proceeds of confiscation and expropriation, and by so doing built up the interest groupings who were to liquidate his regime.

Treasury income available to Colbert for such purposes was made up from three principal sources: primarily from direct and indirect taxation of which the most notorious representative examples are the property tax known as the "taille," and the income derived from the royal monopoly of salt, known as the "gabelle." Also available was income derived from the wholesale and retail trade in wines and liquors, the proceeds of a multitude of customs and excise duties and tolls, and the income which accrued to the royal treasury through the judicial system and courts. Such income in turn would be apportioned between the crown and its creditors, distributed as a placebo to idle aristocratic interest groups, lest they become more revolting. The budgeted sums for war were subsumed under both categories, for the principal, and most effective way of keeping an idle aristocracy quiet is to pay it to go and get killed in a war. The balance, after such items had been taken care of was the amount available for the commercial and manufacture program.

Worse yet, the funds were not even directly available to the treasury. Income derived and allocated under the headings we have identified was sold in advance to that group known as the tax farmers, who undertook to provide the royal treasury with revenues in exchange for the right to collect the taxes themselves. Such income was in actuality only credit available to the crown at the pleasure of the tax farmer. Obviously they would never withhold such credit altogether for fear of the consequences which would ensure. Equally they had a certain leeway in the terms on which they proposed that the King be pleased to accept the credit they were prepared to so extend. Colbert's ruthless attacks on provincial noble privilege effectively expanded the credit available for the further development of his policies.

Cromwell, in turn, availed himself of two principal sources of income for his treasury: confiscation and expropriations combined with domestic and foreign borrowings to cover the deficit between income from the other sources and expenses. Lands which had previously been held by enemies of the Parliament's cause in the civil war against the treasonous House of Stuart were either sold off to raise liquid cash, or distributed to parliamentary supporters from the war period as a form of payment. Means of subsistence for the army—70,000 strong—which Cromwell had built for the Parliament, and which formed the organized core of his support, were levied by expropriation or contribution from the inhabitants of England's cities.

Colbert attempted to make his program work by finding new and expanded sources of income for the royal treasury. Such new sources were strictly limited in ways which defined constraining limits for the development and implementation of his policy as a whole. Either the monarchy would have to reduce its self-apportioned allocation, or commerce and manufacture would have to be opened up for massive taxation, which would of course be self-defeating, or new sources of income would have to be pried out of the nobles and the church. However, at the point that the latter argument would be advanced seriously, the arguments from the faction representing idle aristocratic privilege, to accomplish by military means the defeat of the Dutch which would otherwise be financed through the holes in their pockets, would become overpowering.

As the example of Brittany shows, Colbert's efforts to find the funding necessary for his program were not in the least cowed by the threats of aristocratic privilege. In this connection the Breton example typifies what was accomplished in other provinces, such as Normandy.

Colbert embarked on a systematic effort to break the local power bases of noble interest groups, to separate such local groupings from foci of overall discontent at the court of Versailles, and to arrogate for the crown the financial proceeds of that process. His ruthlessness to achieve that end is reflected in the fact that he was prepared to unchain the peasants as a revolting battering-ram to force a successful outcome to the political showdown with the previously hegemonic local interests.

From 1665 he embarked on a root-and-branch campaign to rip out and destroy every vestige of an independent power base in that province. Brittany was thereby incorporated into the mainstream of French life, for that province had zealously guarded the independence of its traditional privileges and customs since it had been incorporated as a separate Duchy into the French kingdom during the fifteenth century. Brittany was the kind of feudal "marcher lord" territory otherwise represented by Ireland, the latter whose pacification was such a thorn in the side of Cromwell. Brittany had its own fiscal system. Its nobles, all several thousand of them, each had by traditional right their own seigneurial courts, which formed a parallel judicial, and hence income-gathering system to that of the crown. The monarchy's interests were merely represented by an appointed governor.

Colbert's first target was the independent judicial system. To bust that up he instituted an inquiry into the legitimacy of the Breton nobility. The judicial rights of all those investigated and found wanting reverted to the crown, and the "noble" thus disqualified became a mere subject taxable like the rest. Out of the approximately 1,700 cases examined by the commission only six were found to be genuine.

That healthy blood transfusion into the veins of the common stock enabled political bargaining chips to be piled up on other fronts. Bretons were not taxed as other Frenchmen. The taxes were raised by the provincial assembly known as the Estates in the form of levies on consumption items primarily. Every other year, members of that body would decide how much to levy, and present as little as possible to the crown in the form of a free gift, known as the "don gratuit."

Colbert induced the members of that assembly to raise their gift to ensure that the king would give his attention to the question of repealing the inquiry into the legitimacy of the nobility. At the point at which royal revenues were jacked up to equal the income available to the provincial estates, then new taxes on the consumption of the layer which had been recently disqualified were introduced to ensure that all available revenues were arrogated by the royal treasury without bargaining or complaint.

That point was reached in 1673, as is clear from the accompanying table, and it is at that point that the decision was taken to proceed with the provoked revolt to make the process stick. Two letters from Colbert himself, dated April 7 and September 22, 1673, to D'Argouges, the president of the principal legal and judicial body in Rennes, make that clear.

In the first Colbert writes,

In regard to the execution of the tasks of the notaries, procureurs and sergeants, the King has ordered me to tell you that his Majesty does not want anybody to be afraid of sedition, since he is not persuaded that such a state of affairs could develop and that it is more necessary for the good of his service that no fear be allowed to interrupt the course of procedures which he has resolved on. His authority and his power are in such condition that he neither ought, nor wants to be apprehensive about any bad effects of the will of his peoples, and in case such sedition should develop, he will easily be able to put it down.[9]

In the second such letter Colbert identifies the targets of such mooted repression.

One cannot know where the crazes of the people will lead them as long as such crazes are not repressed as they should be by diligent and thorough magistrates. Only magistrates who would not have discharged their duties would be required to commence such punishment, because the restraint of the excesses of the population is their responsibility.[10]

Beyond that Colbert ensured that there would be a revolt in June of 1675 by sending in detachments of royal troops. *He had previously been informed by the Governor of the province that a revolt would only occur if troops were sent. The night the soldiers arrived in Rennes the revolt started.*

The aftermath of the revolt was as the letters of 1673 indicate. The Parliament was called to account as a body and exiled to the little sea-side town of Vannes, where it was charged with carrying out its responsibilities without accommodations, office facilities, court facilities, etc. Similarly with the Estates; not until well after Colbert's death did the Breton Estates again begin to dispute the amount that they were expected to allocate the crown in the name of the "gratuit," even though the amount extracted from them was more than doubled by means of the process we have described in the span of the years between 1667 and 1675.

As we have already noted, the destruction of the Breton nobility was by no means a one-way conveyor belt for speeding the wealth so

9. P. Clement, *Lettres, Instructions et Mémoires de Colbert*, Volume 1 (of three volumes), Paris, 1882.
10. *Ibid.*

gouged out of such poor provincials into the royal treasury. Corollary measures were underway to develop manufacturing and trading capabilities within the province while strengthening agriculture, especially in so far as horse and cattle rearing is concerned.

Such measures were also, as we have seen, in part successful. But 1673, the high noon of this aspect of Colbert's internal policy so far as Brittany is concerned, with road building projects underway, when the harbor and ship construction program adopted ten years before was beginning to pay off, was also the year in which Louis XIV went to war against John de Witt's Dutch Republic. The outer limits constraining Colbert's policies had been reached.

That war began the process through which Colbert's policies themselves were thrown on the scrap heap by a gaggle of aristocrats at the court. The war actually assisted the overthrow of de Witt's republican administration in favor of the restoration of the House of Orange. More hideously, it began the process of fusion between financial interests of London and Amsterdam and their respective appendages in Germany (the latter included such as the Electors of Brandenburg and Hesse-Cassel, purveyors of mercenaries to the House of Orange), and the Iberian monarchies, which would unleash a new wave of Fuggery on the world in the eighteenth and nineteenth centuries. It is not accidental that the Rothschild family should have emerged as the first modern attempt to replay the insane game of imitating Jacob Fugger, from their humble, and protected origins in the care of the Elector of Hesse-Cassel, the ally of the House of Orange.

From that point on, industrial capitalist outlooks, if one excluded the development of the United States, appear either as a subsumed predicate of monetarism. The industrialization of England, so-called, was a by-product of rent-collecting practices by aristocratic, rural and urban landlords, who were usually the same people. Similarly, later in the nineteenth century, the industrial capitalist's development is a subsumed aspect of largely monetarist stock exchange transactions, and so forth.

The breaking-point had actually been reached in 1654 when Oliver Cromwell went to war against de Witt's Dutch Republic. By 1653 Cromwell, like Colbert after him, had run up against the constraints which bounded his policies. He had an expanding debt, and had run out of lands to confiscate for ready cash. Therefore, as soon as William II of Orange died and was replaced by de Witt, Cromwell proposed that the two republics form a union, in which Holland would have unimpeded access to the territories of the East India Company (of Amsterdam) presumably in exchange for cancelling English debt or granting reciprocal such freedom of access to England in the Western Hemisphere. Further, de Witt was to undertake not to permit the House of Orange and its allies to aid or succour exiled Stuart interests in any attempts at subverting the English Republic or restoring the monarchy. *William II had been notorious for just that practice.*

Holland's financial and merchant community was outraged. The mobs were mobilized. De Witt could not accept.

Cromwell immediately went to war, and in the process relieved the Dutch of their maritime fleet. Both de Witt and Spinoza, no doubt looking over their shoulders at the Oranges, attributed Cromwell's motivation for the war to be an attempt to provide the English population with something else to think about to take their guilty minds off their executed king. They no doubt took such public accounts with a private pinch of proverbial (untaxed) salt.

The irony, as shown by Cromwell's wars against the Dutch, and subsequently against the Spanish in the Caribbean and Mediterranean, is that Cromwell actually represents, if anybody at all does, the monetarist's predicated mercantilist policies we have otherwise identified. His efforts were directed at defeating the commercial supremacy of the Dutch, and in the process his England was taken under their financial and monetary control. The Navigation Acts, which restricted commerce to and from Britain to "British bottoms," and subsequently outlawed the importation of manufactured goods from colonies, a policy whose hideous implications are more fully revealed in the backwardness imposed on pre-revolutionary America, were of his making. And it is under his Protectorate that the horrendous conception of triangular trade, English manufactures-African slaves-American and Caribbean raw materials, was worked out by Maurice Thompson of the East India Company. Such were the desperate measures adopted as a means to secure national independence from Dutch commerce, in the failure to define a practical alternative.

It is easy to decry the hideous implications of Cromwell's policy. It is more appropriate, however, to share his agony over the problem of how to deal with the financial and merchant interests, themselves linked to Dutch outlooks and policies which had made the cause of the Parliament their own during the course of the Civil War, as a result of profoundly different motivations than those for which Milton's pen or the pikes and muskets of the Ironsides in the New Model Army were the executive instruments.

There is another side to all this in which is reflected primarily the rather Physiocratic attitude of Cromwell, the improving farmer. It was under the years of parliamentary rule and the Protectorate that new agricultural methods were adopted which were to see an increase in the amount of grains available to feed urban populations, and improved methods in the cultivation of livestock which would make it possible to raise beef year round without regard to weather conditions and marketing arrangements. They were interconnected by manure. To the extent that rotation crops, such as clover, were made use of, and such associated techniques as water-meadows, then land could be used more intensively, even when left fallow, to raise cattle. The localized dung of the cattle, a necessary by-product of the process, could then be applied to fertilize grain-bearing acreage. Not for nothing was Cromwell's political outlook forged in the fight against Charles I, before the Civil War, to secure an adequate drainage program for that area of eastern England to the north of Cambridge known as the Fens. That land is still to be included in a tally of the richest farming areas of the world.

Equally, Cromwellian England was in the forefront of the introduction of new techniques in the clothing industry. It was under his auspices that the introduction of the stocking-frame, for so long sabotaged by the Stuarts, was finally affected, thereby creating the basis for the highly capitalized, both in machinery and raw materials, silk-stocking industry. He was also responsible for the introduction of the Dutch invention, the ribbon loom. Such concerns again promoted the accelerated development of what were known as the New Draperies: lighter, more finely finished, dyed cloth which replaced the older plain broadcloths and kerseys. The wars against the Dutch and Spanish secured a market for such products in the warmer climates of southern Europe and the Mediterranean Basin, while destroying the role of Holland as the finisher of England's raw manufactured cloths. Such concerns again are the predicates of an orientation to capital-intensive methods of development.

But, it was the two-fold method of raising income for such

policies, from confiscation and expropriation or, where that did not suffice, from loans from the financial and merchant grouping which was otherwise among the prime beneficiaries of the land sales, that constrained the further development of such policies in much the same way that Colbert's policies were also constrained, strait-jacketed and then expunged.

It is those constraints which define the heart-breaking process Cromwell went through to find a stable political settlement for the English Republic's revolution. The vacillations and compromises which mark that process are completely inexplicable when merely set, side-by-side with the genius, resolution and fortitude with which he had conducted the Civil War, and built the political striking force, the New Model Army, whose training, morale and motivation made that victory possible. Cromwell is indeed a figure of tragedy. The committed republican, who, as Milton's *Defensio Secunda* suggests, could not turn directly to the people for support, because he did not know how to replicate the political process he had developed in the ranks of the army for his people as a whole—except through war. The gifted commander-in-chief, whose fear that his assumption of the responsibilities of supreme political power would be a short step away from the restoration of monarchy, created instead the oligarchy whose heteronomy undid all his work.

The elections to Parliament, which had been a feature of Leveller programs in the 1640s, were promised in the Act of Dissolution of the Rump Parliament in 1651, two years before that act itself was scheduled to have the effect of law. The promised elections were not held. The Levellers were sacrificed, along with their leader, John Lilburne, whose missing ears were a testament of Stuart hatred of himself and his ideas—a sacrifice Cromwell undertook to reassure the financiers whose loans propped up Cromwell's treasury. Such were the political problems which shaped Cromwell's doubts as the country, despite the intentions of the Instrument of Government by which he established the Protectorate in 1654, drifted towards either outright military rule or the heteronomic faction of rival oligarchic cliques. Either, as everybody knew, would mark the formal repudiation of the institution of republican government for which the war had been fought, namely the Parliament.

The predicament which Colbert and Cromwell fought to resolve was not to be so resolved until Alexander Hamilton's partial solution during the early years of the American Republic, as represented by his *Proposal for the Establishment of Manufactures* and his *Opinion on the Constitutionality of a Bank*. The Americans both rejoined the line of human intellectual development and progress we have identified as originating in the fifteenth century Florentines, Ficino and Pico della Mirandola. Their solutions make possible the establishment of a political democracy of a new type by junking the apparent paradox which the humanist forebears had passed on to their successors, what we have termed the nationalist-industrial-capitalist current, and which foredoomed their efforts to found stable and durable commonwealth or republican forms of political democracy.

Ironically, the weaponry to solve that problem was, in a sense, available to Cromwell, even though it lay submerged within the morass of expediency and vacillation which characterized the 1650s and was ignored. *The steam engine could have pulled England out of the monetarist swamp to which it was heading.*

Edward Somerset, the Marquis of Worcester, claimed to have invented, and perfected, a functioning steam engine by as early as 1650. As we have noted, that mechanical and scientific problem had first been broached in the last years of Elizabeth I, as a by-product of the determination of her advisers to make full use of coal to replace wood for energy supplies to manufacturing processes wherever that was feasibly achieved. Experimentation had continued on and off in the intervening 50 years.

As the case of the eighteenth century demonstrates, the steam engine, in itself, would of course no more have settled the problem than the introduction of fusion power, in itself, would be the settlement of more contemporary problems. Nonetheless, the heurism of the steam engine illustrates the mediation of the solution to the predicament which both Colbert and Cromwell faced—in the form that predicament is presented by Erasmus' efforts to educate enough citizens, and Milton's concern to evoke what is fundamentally human in the population to build his cherished republic in fact as well as in name.

For the steam engine, if available to Cromwell, could have provided a solution to the problems which the question of credit posed to both himself and Colbert, while simultaneously through the process of capital formation contributed to the development of political democratic outlooks among the population. The scientific and technical challenges thrown up by the application of steam power would, in consequence, have defined the means toward a solution at that point. It is ironical, but nonetheless true that the real means available for such a breakthrough at that point were actually better in the 1650s than in the 1770s and 1780s; the population was better educated, better fed and better accultured for the reception for application of new ideas by the intensive political ferment of the Civil War and its aftermath.

Republican Cromwell, however, did not know what monarchist Colbert knew, nor what Thomas Gresham had discovered in the sixteenth century through the sophisticated conception of economic warfare which he unleashed against the Fuggers. The question of credit is a subjective question. It is a matter for political determination. Gresham did not say to the Fugger, "On what terms are you prepared to buy English manufactured produce and how will that affect your attitude towards our debts?" On the contrary, he said, "The laws by which you have governed the exchange rates to your own profit have been changed. English cloth will henceforth be sold at the following sterling rates against Flemish currency. That will leave so much for our use, and so much for the obligations we have previously incurred on your account. If you don't like it, then invade us."

Such, in essence, was the way in which Colbert improved the credit rating of the royal treasury with the tax farmers who provided the crown with financial resources, by demonstrating his political determination to take on and smash bastions of local noble privilege. Cromwell's problems started before he even reached that point, in his misguided notion that wealth was defined objectively by existent resources of land and previous nominal financial accumulations.

But as the constraints of monarchy and aristocracy imply, Colbert's understanding that the problem of credit was political and subjectively determined did not lead to the elaboration of a durable policy no matter how competent it was in conception, just as the dissolution of Gresham's policies and legacy was prepared by the vicious factional infighting which marked the end of the reign of Elizabeth.

However, as the case is demonstrated by Hamilton, the apparent paradox thus faced is susceptible of a solution, but only in a republican form of government. Indeed it is actually the case, that an effective and stable republican form of government can only be created in the process of resolving that problem, and will only exist so long as that fundamental solution informs such a republic's peoples and policies.

For what is necessary beyond a one-shot assertion of the fact that credit is politically determined, is that such credit once created be applied intensively in the process of capital formation to the net effect that there be available for that society at the end of such a cycle both an increase in the capital available for that society's productive use in the form of plant, raw materials, etc., an increase in the powers of the laboring population to employ such augmented and improved capital equipment effectively, and therefore an increase in the available credit thus generated to repeat the process so initiated at the higher levels of credit input demanded to repeat the process to the same effect.

In outline form, that is the essence of the solution to the apparent paradox left unsolved by the rise of an independent industrially oriented nationalist faction in the sixteenth century, by Hamilton in the documents cited in this text. Anyone who considers the process by which human societies, as defined by their energy sources, have evolved from wood and water, through coal and steam, to electricity and oil, and the beginnings of the era of nuclear power, will see their solution to the apparent antinomies that faced both the early humanists and their more secularly oriented industrial offspring vindicated in the line of human development itself.

For each such energy source defines for a given society a range of raw materials as resources, a spectrum of plant and equipment suitable for the processing of such (raw material) resources, and levels of popular culture and science more or less capable of enabling its population to function productively. The better such a society survives, as measured crudely by population growth, the more it depletes what it defines as its raw material resources, thereby making existing plant and machinery relatively obsolete and discrediting prevailing accepted notions of appropriate culture and science.

To progress, each such progressively more-human society demands of its citizens that they develop those fundamental creative qualities which Ficino otherwise attributed to the "perfected" human soul, and which Milton considered the intellectual attributes of a qualified electorate. Decide to innovate successfully in your methods of thinking and the application of such methods in your daily life or you die. From that standpoint, the human race will look with perpetual gratitude on the contributions of the human beings, including Jean-Baptiste Colbert, who make up the line of development we have examined. It was their effort to solve what appeared to them in the form of a paradox which defined the terms on which republican forms of government could be created and prosper.

Appendix

Letter of Sept. 22, 1673 in which Dutch inventor Huygens reveals Colbert's support for steam engine research:

"A few days ago I let the gentlemen of our Academy and also Monsieur Colbert see a summary of a discovery which was considered very good and from which I should hope for great results, if I were sure that it would be as successful on a large as on a small scale. It concerns a new propulsive power by means of gun-powder and of air pressure. Here is the description of it.

"AB is a tube, well polished within and of unvarying bore, a piston D is in the upper part of the tube, and can move within it but cannot emerge from the top, because a stop is fastened there which prevents it. Within the base of the tube is screwed a little capsule for which leather is used to make it completely tight. At the points EE of the tube are openings, and hoses of moist leather EF are attached to these. Before the capsule C is fastened, a little gunpowder is placed in it with a tiny piece of tinder. After this has been lit at one end, the capsule is fastened. The fire then ignites the powder which flames right up through the tube, filling it and expelling the air through the hoses (or valves) EF, which are soon closed by the pressure of the outer air and pressed flat against the openings, which are furnished with gratings in order that the leather hoses shall not be drawn into the tube. Now while this tube (cylinder) remains in this manner empty or nearly empty, the air presses most powerfully on the piston D and forces it down through the tube, taking with it the rope DK and at the same time the weight G or anything else that is attached to it.

"The strength of this force can easily be calculated by means of our knowledge of the amount of air pressure on a given surface. And if the tube is 1 foot in diameter, the pressure of the air on the piston is 1,800 lb. and correspondingly for other sizes of the surface. But that is only the case if the tube has been completely evacuated of air; a little, however, always remains in the tube. If the diameter of the tube is 2.5 inches, and its length 2 feet, it would be evacuated of air by between .1763 and .2116 oz. (*Avoir du poids*) of gunpowder; but about one sixth of the air would remain in the tube. If the diameter is one foot and the length four feet, it can be evacuated of air by 3/32 oz. (*Avoir du poids*) but still nearly half the air will remain in the tube which very greatly lessens the effectiveness. But I think that this fault arises in part because the openings are much too small to let out the air, which must be definitely settled by further experiments. Meanwhile with this one foot tube that has only half the air evacuated, I have been able to show surprising results by drawing up both men and weights hanging on to the rope H.G. If air could really be removed, it would be quite another matter, and since the tube does not need to be very strong, since it is convex to the pressure of the outer air, and as it could therefore be made very light, it would not be impossible to build a machine in this manner (I do not dare to say for flight) but that would at least raise itself in the air and carry with it anybody who was bold enough to get in it."

A later letter, dated May 24, 1686 and referred to in an anonymous article, describes Colbert's presence at his experiments:

"'I have received the problem communicated by you concerning a new application of gunpowder. In my opinion it may certainly be hoped to attain this end. Seven or eight years ago I showed to Monsieur Colbert an engine which I had built for this very purpose, and which was illustrated in the *Proceedings* of our Academy. It worked as follows; a tiny quantity of gunpowder, about a thimbleful, was able to raise some 1,600 lb. five feet high; and not with such violence as usual, but with moderate and steady power. Four or five servants, whom Monsieur Colbert ordered to pull the rope attached to the engine, were quite easily lifted up into the air. Nevertheless, there was a certain difficulty in constantly reproducing this power.'

"The writer of this letter communicated two quite unusual and really incomparable discoveries;

1. One or two drachmas of gunpowder, a thimbleful, will raise a weight of 1,600 lb. five feet; and furthermore,

2. This occurs without the usual violence, but with moderate and steady power.

"The first of these discoveries arouses admiration, but is in conformity with principles already accepted. The effectiveness of the powder could naturally be increased either by addition of more powder or by improvement of the piston. Nevertheless the second discovery would appear to extend beyond these known principles, and must be the more highly valued since it approaches the miraculous. . . .

"Doubtless therefore all those who are plagued by curiosity to see this simple and really useful experiment could take the trouble to make such a machine or another which is suitable to impel any weight chosen as desired. They should allow themselves to be helped therein by men who are familiar not only with the use and misuse of gunpowder but also with the art of mechanics. Especially they will need for this, the magnificent work of the late Monsieur Bondel. *The Art of Shooting with Iron Balls Filled with Powder,* a work that would perhaps be more correctly entitled *The Art of Thoroughly Understanding the Nature and Characteristics of Natural and Violent Motion.* In it will be found many demonstrations directed toward the aim here mentioned. And there can no longer be any doubt that the fact that a tiny quantity of powder can raise 1,600 lb. so high, can, some day, be put to general use as soon as an inventor turns his attention to solving the many difficulties, especially those which obstruct the repetition of regular action. It remains only to add that at this point besides the description and exhibition, a drawing of the machine itself could very easily have been shown, by means of which its manner of working could have been shown; did not the ease with which this can be manifested and understood seem to make this quite superfluous, especially since its effectiveness has already been more than sufficiently demonstrated. Moreover, gifted investigators have had sufficient reason to believe positively that the making of such experiments, all too rare, each of which needs special consideration, may ultimately lead to a fruitful contribution useful to everyone. Meantime, the decision rests with God alone. He will according to his merciful judgment at the right time make it evident that all creation is appointed for the welfare and service of mankind. It is therefore the duty of man not only to believe this truth, but to work with all his power that he may use and enjoy everything with acknowledgement and gratitude. Praised therefore be the most holy name of Him through whose goodness the first stage of this apparent impossibility (namely the useful application of gunpowder) has been overcome; Praised, say I, be his name to all eternity! Amen."

Bibliographical Notes

The analysis of Colbert's policy both in its overall dimension, and its specific application in Brittany, is based on extensive documentary research in various French archives and the British Museum in London. Archives included the Bibliothèque Nationale, and its collections, the Fonds Français, Petit Fonds Français, Nouvelles Acquisitions Françaises and the Recueil Thoisy. The collections, Mélanges Colbert and Cinq Cents de Colbert, were among the documents most referred to in such collections. The archives of the French Ministry of Foreign Affairs at the Quai D'Orsay and the Ministry of War at Vincennes were also useful. In Brittany, use was made of the Departmental Archives of the Loire-Atlantique at Nantes, and the Ille-et Vilaine at Rennes.

Readers who would pursue the questions identified in the text would be well advised not to start with the writings of contemporary academic historians. Rather, it is preferable to begin one's studies with modern scientific outlook, of which historiography is a properly subsumed aspect. For that reason students should turn first to *Dialectical Economics* by Lyn Marcus (Lyndon H. LaRouche, Jr.), DC Heath and Co. 1975; *The Italy Lectures*, Lyndon H. LaRouche, Jr., Campaigner Publications; *In Defense of Rosa Luxemburg*, Lyndon H. LaRouche, Jr., Campaigner Publications; *Strategic Studies*, Lyndon H. LaRouche, Jr., Campaigner Publications; and *Socialism or Fascism*, Lyndon H. LaRouche, Jr., Campaigner Publications.

Students would then be properly equipped to approach the primary source material identified in this text. For that purpose, there are readily available in cheap editions the writings of Marsilio Ficino, Pico della Mirandola, Thomas More, Erasmus, William Shakespeare and John Milton. Beyond this, there are standard reference works of source material for the period considered here, including R.H. Tawney's three-volume *Tudor Economic Documents*, and C. Elton's *The Tudor Constitution*. Such standard reference works in the form of collections of speeches and writings as well as the proceedings of the various debates within the Army Council, are available for the Cromwellian period. Appropriate such French sources have been identified in the footnotes. Forthcoming articles by Messrs. Barré and Carriègues on François Rabelais and Jean Bodin will shed much important light on this hitherto obscured, but formative period in the development of the humanist tradition in France.

Editor's Note

In the extracts which follow, the editors strove to preserve the original rendering of the works by the author and his printer. The following references occur repeatedly throughout Part I:

d. is an English pence or penny
s. is an English shilling
Li. is an English pound.

The lower case Roman numerals used in the manuscripts often conclude with a "j" which is interchangeable with an "i." Therefore, "iiij" should be read as "4." Otherwise, the reader is referred to the primary source material noted in the Footnotes and Bibliographical Notes to "Jean-Baptiste Colbert and the Origins of Industrial Capitalism," for such additional information as he may require.

The Reign of Henry VIII

The reign of Henry VIII (1503–1547) laid the foundation for the later flourishing of England under his daughter Elizabeth. Henry himself has generally been largely reviled and ridiculed by the commonplace sort of historian on account of his succession of marriage alliances in search of both a male heir to ensure the succession to the throne after his death, and a stable basis for a system of durable anti-Hapsburg foreign alliances.

In such accounts, the actual achievements of Henry's reign are generally reduced to absurdity. The thoughtful reader, desirous of understanding how the giant intellects of Queen Elizabeth's time looked back on the reign of her father could still do no worse than refer to William Shakespeare's last history play, "The Famous History of the Life of King Henry VIII," written in 1612, after the achievements of Elizabeth and her contemporaries had been largely undone by her noxious and idiot successor James Stuart.

"Therefore, for goodness sake, and as you are known
The first and happiest hearers of the town,
Be sad, as we would make ye: think ye see
The very persons of our noble story
As they were living; think ye see them great,
And followed with the general throng and sweat
Of thousand friends; then, in a moment, see
How soon this mightiness meets misery:
And if you can be merry then, I'll say
A man may weep upon his wedding day."

William Shakespeare, The Famous History of
The Life of King Henry VIII, "Prologue."

The reign of Henry in fact sees the first flowering of the later achievements that made England under Elizabeth great. Henry himself is the epitome of that fact: he was no boorish run-of-the-mill monarch, but was educated by England's followers of the Florentine's Ficino and Pico to be imbued with the intellectual fruits of Renaissance humanist culture.

He was to be the incarnation of the humanist prince. Indeed the education of the young Henry became a project in the international development of the humanist political tendency itself, drawing on the best contemporary minds of Italy and Spain as well as Erasmus of Rotterdam and his English mentors such as John Colet, Grocyn and Linacre.

The Chelsea-based intellectual and political circle which surrounded Henry's subsequent Chancellor Thomas More was brought into existence as a by-product of that effort, and More's Utopia, *written in 1515, marks the end of his period of preparation for entry into the royal service. We reproduce below a section of Utopia in which More and his alter ego "Raphael" discuss the political nature of monarchy.*

More's circle included most of the luminaries of contemporary England. Their prime concern, as illustrated by More's Utopia *itself, was to define those internal political and economic arrangements which transform England from being a net exporter of raw wool for the greater benefit of Italian, and subsequently Hapsburg financial interests, into a self-sustaining, self-developing economy. Hence More's implacable hatred of sheep, and a sheep-based agrarian economy: a hatred which no reader of Utopia can miss.*

In the process, More's circle created the conditions for England to become a vital cloth manufacturing center, and a vibrant European intellectual center. Thomas Gresham's father, John, was an associate of More's, as was Thomas Cromwell under whose Chancellorship Henry VIII broke the back of Italian financial control of the English economy as mediated by the papacy. The Acts of 1532 and 1536 printed below express the legal process by which such objectives were completed. Equally significant though is the fact that such lands and facilities as were confiscated under such auspices were more often than not converted into manufacturing processes, such as glass factories and iron foundries.

Additionally, it was More's circle which consciously set about creating the English language as we know that language today. Thomas Elyot, author of The Boke of the Gouvernoure *and a close friend of More's, set himself the task of expanding and perfecting the English language by incorporating such words of especially Latin and Greek derivation as would satisfy those ends. It was likewise the influence of More's circle on the London Merchant Adventurers Company which secured the first translation of the Bible into English by William Tyndale.*

Nothing could misrepresent either More himself, or Henry VIII, more emphatically than the usual stories which surround More's execution by

*the latter. More did not die because he refused to disavow the Pope as
the banal versions have it. More, a convinced Ficinian, could not accept
that the universalizing efforts of his political activities could be subordi-
nated to the mere nationalism that was being forced on Henry by Hapsburg
pressure. Yet, Henry's vigorous measures against such Hapsburg pressure
ensured that both his own and More's successors would have available
the body of knowledge and practice on which to build the achievements
of the reign of Elizabeth I.*

Utopia*

by Thomas Moore
Book One

. . . At this point I get up again, and say that it would be most
unwise as well as most immoral for the King to do any of these
things, because his prestige and security depend less on his own than
on his subjects' wealth.

"Why do you suppose they made you king in the first place?"
I ask him. "Not for your benefit, but for theirs. They meant you to
devote your energies to making their lives more comfortable, and
protecting them from injustice. So your job is to see that they're all
right, not that you are—just as a shepherd's job, strictly speaking,
is to feed his sheep, not himself. As for the theory that peace is best
preserved by keeping the people poor, it's completely contradicted
by the facts. Beggars are far the most quarrelsome section of the
community. Who is more likely to start a revolution than a man
who's discontented with his present living conditions? Who could
have a stronger impulse to turn everything upside down in the hope
of personal profit, than a man who'd got nothing to lose?

"No, if a king is so hated or despised by his subjects that he
can't keep them in order unless he reduces them to beggary by
violence, extortion, and confiscation, he'd far better abdicate. Such
methods of staying in power may preserve the title, but they destroy
the majesty of a king. There's nothing majestic about ruling a nation
of beggars—true majesty consists in governing the rich and prosperous. That's what that admirable character Fabricius meant when he

* Reprinted from the 1965 Penguin Classics translation by Paul Turner (excerpts).

said he'd rather govern rich men than be one. Certainly a man who enjoys a life of luxury while everyone else is moaning and groaning round him can hardly be called a king—he's more like a gaoler.

"In short, it's a pretty poor doctor who can't cure one disease without giving you another, and a king who can't suppress crime without lowering standards of living should admit that he just doesn't know how to govern free men. He should start by suppressing one of his own vices—either his pride or his laziness, for those are the faults most liable to make a king hated or despised. He should live on his own resources, without being a nuisance to others. He should adapt his expenditure to his income. He should prevent crime by sound administration rather than allow it to develop and then start punishing it. He should hesitate to enforce any law which has long been disregarded—especially if people have got on perfectly well without it. And he should never invent a crime as an excuse for imposing a fine—no private person would be allowed to do anything so dishonest."

I then proceed to tell them about a system they have in Happiland, a country not far from Utopia. There the King has to swear a solemn oath at his coronation that he'll never keep more than a thousand pounds of gold in his treasury, or an equivalent amount of silver. Apparently the system was started by an excellent king of theirs, who cared more about his country's welfare than his own. He thought it would prevent the accumulation of royal wealth on such a scale as to cause national poverty, and chose that particular figure because he reckoned it would be enough to suppress a revolution or repel an invasion, but not enough to inspire a king with thoughts of foreign conquest. That was his main idea, but not his only one. He also hoped this arrangement would ensure that there was always enough money in circulation for ordinary purposes of exchange, and that the King would have no motive for raising money unfairly, since he wouldn't be allowed to keep any capital in excess of the statutory limit. Now there you have the type of king who's feared by bad men and loved by good ones—but if I said things like that to people who were quite determined to take the opposite view, do you think they'd listen to me?

More: Of course they wouldn't, and I can't say I'd blame them. Frankly, I don't see the point of saying things like that, or of giving advice that you know they'll never accept. What possible good could it do? How can they be expected to take in a totally unfamiliar line of thought, which goes against all their deepest prejudices? That sort of thing is quite fun in a friendly conversation, but at a Cabinet meeting, where major decisions of policy have to be made, such philosophizing would be completely out of place.

Raphael: That's exactly what I was saying—there's no room at Court for philosophy.

More: There's certainly no room for the academic variety, which says what it thinks irrespective of circumstances. But there is a more civilized form of philosophy which knows the dramatic context, so to speak, tries to fit in with it, and plays an appropriate part in the current performance. That's the sort you should go in for. Otherwise it would be like interrupting some comedy by Plautus, in which a lot of slaves were fooling about, by rushing on to the stage dressed up as a philosopher, and spouting a bit of that scene in the *Octavia* where Seneca is arguing with Nero. Surely it would be better to keep your mouth shut altogether than to turn the thing into a tragicomedy by interpolating lines from a different play? For, even if your contribution were an improvement on what had gone before, the effect would be so incongruous that you'd ruin the whole show. No, do the best you can to make the present production a success—don't spoil the entire play just because you happen to think of another one that you'd enjoy rather more.

The same rule applies to politics and life at Court. If you can't completely eradicate wrong ideas, or deal with inveterate vices as effectively as you could wish, that's no reason for turning your back on public life altogether. You wouldn't abandon ship in a storm just because you couldn't control the winds. On the other hand, it's no use attempting to put across entirely new ideas, which will obviously carry no weight with people who are prejudiced against them. You must go to work indirectly. You must handle everything as tactfully as you can, and what you can't put right you must try to make as little wrong as possible. For things will never be perfect, until human beings are perfect—which I don't expect them to be for quite a number of years!

Raphael: The only advantage of that method would be that I mightn't find it quite so maddening as making a real effort to cure other people's madness. But if I'm to speak the truth, I'll have to say the sort of things that you object to. I don't know whether it's right for a philosopher to tell lies, but it's certainly not my way. Besides, though they might be annoyed by what I said, I don't see why it should be thought so fantastically out of the ordinary. It's not as if I'd recommended the system operated in Plato's imaginary *Republic*, or in Utopia today. Now that, while undoubtedly better than ours, might well strike them as rather odd, because it's based on communal ownership instead of private property.

Of course they wouldn't like my proposals. Having set their hearts on a certain course of action, they'd naturally resent being shown the dangers that lay ahead, and told to give the whole thing up. But apart from that, what did I say that couldn't or shouldn't be said in any company? If we're never to say anything that might be thought unconventional, for fear of its sounding ridiculous, we'll have to hush up, even in a Christian country, practically everything that Christ taught. But that was the last thing He wanted. Didn't He tell His disciples that everything He had whispered in their ears should be proclaimed on the house-tops? And most of His teaching is far more at variance with modern conventions than anything I suggested, except in so far as His doctrines have been modified by ingenious preachers—doubtless on your recommendation!

"We'll never get human behaviour in line with Christian ethics," these gentlemen must have argued, "so let's adapt Christian ethics to human behaviour. Then at least there'll be some connexion between them."

But I can't see what good they've done. They've merely enabled people to sin with a clear conscience—and that's about all I could do at a Cabinet meeting. For I'd either have to vote against my colleagues, which would be equivalent to not voting at all, or else I'd have to vote with them, in which case, like Micio in Terence, I'd be "aiding and abetting insanity."

As for working indirectly, and when things can't be put right, handling them so tactfully that they're as little wrong as possible, I don't quite see what that means. At Court you can't keep your opinions to yourself, or merely connive at other people's crimes. You have to give open support to deplorable policies, and subscribe to utterly monstrous resolutions. If you don't show enough enthusiasm for a bad law, you'll be taken for a spy or even a traitor. Besides, what chance have you got of doing any good, when you're working with colleagues like that? You'll never reform them—they're far

more likely to corrupt you, however admirable a character you are.
By associating with them you'll either lose your own integrity, or
else have it used to conceal their folly and wickedness. So much for
the practical results of your indirect method! . . .

An Act to Repress and Redress the Exactions of Annates or First Fruits (1532:23 Henry VIII, c. 20)*

Forasmuch as it is well perceived by long approved experience that
great and inestimable sums of money be daily conveyed out of this
realm to the impoverishment of the same, and specially such sums
of money as the Pope's Holiness, his predecessors, and the court of
Rome by long time have heretofore taken of all and singular those
spiritual persons which have been named, elected, presented or pos-
tulated to be archbishops or bishops within this realm of England,
under the title of annates, otherwise called first fruits; which annates
or first fruits heretofore have been taken of every archbishopric
or bishopric within this realm by restraint of the Pope's bulls for
confirmations, elections, admissions, postulations, provisions, colla-
tions, dispositions, institutions, installations, investitures, orders
holy, benedictions, palls, or other things requisite and necessary to
the attaining of those their promotions, and have been compelled to
pay before they could attain the same great sums of money, before
they might receive any part of the fruits of the said archbishopric or
bishopric whereunto they were named, elected, presented or postu-
lated; By occasion whereof not only the treasure of this realm hath
been greatly conveyed out of the same, but also it hath happened
many times by occasion of death unto such archbishops and bishops
so newly promoted within two or three years after his or their conse-
cration, that his or their friends by whom he or they have been
holpen to advance and make payment of the said annates or first
fruits have been thereby utterly undone and impoverished; And for
because the said annates have risen, grown and increased by an
uncharitable custom grounded upon no just or good title, and the
payments thereof obtained by restraint of bulls until the same annates

* Stat. Realm, III, 460–1.

or first fruits have been paid or surety made for the same, which declareth the said payments to be exacted and taken by constraint, against all equity and justice; The noblemen therefore of this realm and the wise, sage, politic commons of the same assembled in this present Parliament, considering that the court of Rome ceaseth not to tax, take and exact the said great sums of money under the title of annates or first fruits as is aforesaid to the great damage of the said prelates and this realm, which annates or first fruits were first suffered to be taken within the same realm for the only defence of Christian people against the infidels, and now they be claimed and demanded as mere duty, only for lucre, against all right and conscience, insomuch that it is evidently known that there hath passed out of this realm unto the court of Rome since the second year of the reign of the most noble prince of famous memory King Henry the vijth unto this present time, under the name of annates or first fruits paid for the expedition of bulls of archbishoprics and bishoprics, the sum of eight hundred thousand ducats, amounting in sterling money at the least to eight score thousand pounds, besides other great and intolerable sums which have yearly been conveyed to the said court of Rome by many other ways and means, to the great impoverishment of this realm; And albeit that our said sovereign lord the King and all his natural subjects as well spiritual as temporal be as obedient, devout, Catholic and humble children of God and Holy Church as any people be within any realm christened, yet the said exactions of annates or first fruits be so intolerable and importable to this realm that it is considered and declared by the whole body of this realm now represented by all the estates of the same assembled in this present Parliament that the King's Highness before Almighty God is bound as by the duty of a good Christian prince, for the conservation and preservation of the good estate and commonwealth of this his realm, to do all that in him is to obviate, repress and redress the said abusions and exactions of annates or first fruits; And because that divers prelates of this realm be now in extreme age and in other debilities of their bodies, so that of likelihood bodily death in short time shall or may succeed unto them; by reason whereof great sums of money shall shortly after their deaths be conveyed unto the court of Rome for the unreasonable and uncharitable causes abovesaid, to the universal damage, prejudice and impoverishment of this realm, if speedy remedy be not in due time provided; It is

therefore ordained, established and enacted by authority of this present Parliament that the unlawful payments of annates or first fruits
. . . shall from henceforth utterly cease . . . and that no manner
person or persons hereafter to be named, elected, presented or postu-
lated to any archbishopric or bishopric within this realm shall pay
the said annates or first fruits . . . upon pain to forfeit to our said
sovereign lord the King, his heirs and successors, all manner his
goods and chattels for ever, and all the temporal lands and possessions
of the same archbishopric or bishopric during the time that he or
they which shall offend contrary to this present act shall have, possess
or enjoy the archbishopric or bishopric wherefore he shall so offend
contrary to the form aforesaid.

An Act Whereby All Religious Houses of Monks, Canons and Nuns Which May Not Dispend Manors, Lands, Tenements and Hereditaments Above the Clear Yearly Value Of £200 Are Given to the King's Highness, His Heirs and Successors, For Ever (1536: 27 Henry VIII, c. 28)

Forasmuch as manifest sin, vicious, carnal and abominable living,
is daily used and committed amongst the little and small abbeys,
priories and other religious houses of monks, canons and nuns, where
the congregation of such religious persons is under the number of
12 persons, whereby the governors of such religious houses and
their convent spoil, destroy, consume and utterly waste as well their
churches, monasteries, priories, principal houses, farms, granges,
lands, tenements and hereditaments, as the ornaments of their
churches and their goods and chattels to the high displeasure of
Almighty God, slander of good religion, and to the great infamy of
the King's Highness and the realm if redress should not be had
thereof; and albeit that many continual visitations hath been heretofore had by the space of two hundred years and more for an honest
and charitable reformation of such unthrifty, carnal and abominable

living, yet nevertheless little or none amendment is hitherto had, but their vicious living shamelessly increaseth and augmenteth, and by a cursed custom so rooted and infested that a great multitude of the religious persons in such small houses do rather choose to rove abroad in apostasy than to conform them to the observation of good religion; so that without such small houses be utterly suppressed and the religious persons therein committed to great and honourable monasteries of religion in this realm, where they may be compelled to live religiously for reformation of their lives, there can else be no reformation in this behalf: In consideration whereof the King's most royal Majesty, being supreme head in earth under God of the Church of England, daily finding and devising the increase, advancement and exaltation of true doctrine and virtue in the said Church, to the only glory and honour of God and the total extirping and destruction of vice and sin, having knowledge that the premises be true, as well by the compts of his late visitations as by sundry credible informations, considering also that divers and great solemn monasteries of this realm wherein, thanks be to God, religion is right well kept and observed, be destitute of such full numbers of religious persons as they ought and may keep, hath thought good that a plain declaration should be made of the premises as well to the Lords spiritual and temporal as to other his loving subjects the Commons in this present Parliament assembled; whereupon the said Lords and Commons by a great deliberation finally be resolved that it is and shall be much more to the pleasure of Almighty God and for the honour of this his realm that the possessions of such spiritual religious houses, now being spent, spoiled and wasted for increase and maintenance of sin, should be used and converted to better uses, and the unthrifty religious persons so spending the same to be compelled to reform their lives; and thereupon most humbly desire the King's Highness that it may be enacted by authority of this present Parliament, that his Majesty shall have and enjoy to him and to his heirs for ever all and singular monasteries, priories and other religious houses of monks, canons and nuns, of what kinds or diversities of habits, rules or orders so ever they be called or named, which have not in lands and tenements, rents, tithes, portions and other hereditaments above the clear yearly value of two hundred pounds; and in like manner shall have and enjoy all the sites and circuits of every such religious houses, and all and singular the manors, granges, meses, lands, tenements, reversions, rents, services, tithes, pensions, portions, churches, chapels, advowsons, patronages, annuities, rights, entries, conditions and other hereditaments appertaining or belonging to every such monastery, priory or other religious house not having as is aforesaid above the said clear yearly value of two hundred pounds, in as large and ample manner as the abbots, priors, abbesses, prioresses, or other governors of such monasteries, priories and other religious houses now have or ought to have the same in the right of their houses; and that also his Highness shall have to him and to his heirs all and singular such monasteries, abbeys and priories which, at any time within one year next afore the making of this act, hath been given and granted to his Majesty by any abbot, prior, abbess or prioress under their convent seals, or that otherwise hath been suppressed or dissolved; And all and singular the manors, lands, . . . to the same monasteries, abbeys and priories or to any of them appertaining or belonging; To have and to hold all and singular the premises with all their rights, profits, jurisdictions and commodities, unto the King's Majesty and to his heirs and assigns for ever, to do and use therewith his or their own wills to the pleasure of Almighty God and to the honour and profit of this realm.

The Elizabethans Against
Monetarism and the Fugger

T he following selections of documents establish that the origins of
modern scientific notions of political economy can be dated with
precision to the early years of the reign of Queen Elizabeth, and
were established by the struggle of particularly Thomas Gresham and his
allies to free England from the monetarist grip of the Fugger.

The documents are chosen for two principal reasons. First, to demonstrate the degree of sophistication with which the Tudors understood that
economic processes were subject to human wilful control and were therefore
comprehensible in terms of the actions of even individual human beings.
How refreshing are such Tudor analyses of the activities of the Fugger
and the exchange market he controlled, when set beside modern mealy-
mouthed aberrations such as "market forces," "objective economic conditions" and so forth.

Secondly, the documents demonstrate that the foundation of the Elizabethans' deliberate and wilful approach to solving political economic
problems was the distinction which they drew and maintained for policy
in practice between monetarist exchange and debt manipulations, and
real economic activity in the form of the nation's ability to produce an
expanded output in the form of useful goods and services. Such distinctions
motivated the Elizabethans' search for solutions, as evidenced by the 1576
proposal for the establishment of a public bank.

There is, of course, a school of historiography which defines such
concerns as a relatively reactionary last fling of the essentially medieval
religious concern with usury. The positive achievements of Elizabethan
England relegate such complaints to where they properly belong.

Memorandum on the Exchanges (1564)*

A Conference of the waightes of Bullyone and vallues of the syluere
moneyes of England, and the syluer moneyes of the Lowe Contreyes,

* Harl. Mss., 660., 38, ff. 107 seq. (excerpts).

118

with a Comparrysone of the Exchange used to and froe betweene
the Burse of Anwarpe and Lumbardestreete in London. Whearin is
discussed, not only howe howe muche a pound of Englishe moneye
is worthe of flemyshe moneye, but also howe the sleightes and Cun-
inges of the usage of the Exchange hathe byne, and maybe, to the
greate losse and hinderaunce of the comone wealthe of England, and
howe the same maye be remediede, met withall and turnede to the
benefyte of this Realme of Englande. Written uppon occassyone of
a Commyssione graunted by hir Maiestie unto my lord Tresorore
and to Sir Frauncis Knowles, Sir Waltere Mildmaye, and Sir William
Cordalle, Knightes, for the spessyall Inquiry of the Convenyencyes
of the matteres of the Exchange and the Inconvenyences, and Fyny-
eshed in the monthe of February Anno 1564, and in the 7th yeare
of hir maiestes Raigne.

. . . Nowe that the true vallues of the moneyes and also the
mynte vallues are thus truly discussed, it shalbe necessary to Consydere howe the vsuall Exchange betwene Antewerpe and Lomberdes-
treet hathe differed from the sayd true vallue.

And heare it appearethe that yf our Englishe moneye be of no
bettere vallue then—this laste Comparrison by equall Respecte is set
foarthe, yet synce the Exchange in Lomberdstreete hathe Comonely
gone vntylle this presente shipping all the Queenes Highnes Raigne
at or vnder (22) shillinges (6) d flemyshe for vsance, and since the
gayne in delyuery vppon the Exchange dothe Comonly beate about
and vpon (10) pound in the hondred, therefore our Englishe pounde
hathe byne comonly vnder prised by the Exchange in Lomberdstreete
(9) pence 1/2 penye flemyshe. But yf our Englishe money doe hold
his vallue Respectyvely after the firste Comparrysone afforsayd, then
hathe our Englyshe pounde byne vndere prised by the sayd Exchange
in Lomberdstreete (13) pence flemyshe, because the Exchange thear,
after (10) poundes in the hundred gayne to the delyuerere, shold
have byne (2) pence flemyshe aboue the true vallue of the sterling
Englishe pounde of moneye.

Affore hathe byne declarind the gainefull stelynge ouere of Englishe moneye by the ouer lowe fallinge of the Exchange. But nowe
is also to be Consydered what greater Losse this Realme sustayneth
thearby.

And hear wee muste noat that the Exchange is the gouernere of
prises of all warres enterchangablye vented betweene this Realme

and the Lowe Contreyes, because the greateste quantetye of wares
transported ether outeward or inwarde is boughte by money takene
vppe by Exchange, and also because, althoughe the wares be boughte
with his owne moneye, in sellinge of his hondred poundes worthe
of wares he Consydered what gaynes he myght have made by Exchange of somuche moneye, and he makethe the price of his wares
accordingly or to some Convenyent overpluse.

As for Example, one takethe vppe in Lomberdestreete (100)
pound Englishe for vsance at (22) shillinges (6) pence flemyshe. Nowe
transportynge Englishe warres boughte therwithe into Flaunderes,
he needethe make no greater prise thearof but to Aunswere his
Exchange, which Comethe to (112) pounde (10) shilling flemyshe,
savinge for a Resonable overpluse to beare his Charges and to Answere
his Stocke.

Agayne for Example, one takethe vppe at Antwerpe (110) pound
(16) shillinges (8) pence flemyshe for vsance at 22 s. 2 d. flemishe,
for the Exchange at Anwerpe keepethe about (4) d. flemyshe vnder
the Exchange in Lomberdstreete, and transportethe strange warres
boughte thearwith in to England. Nowe he muste needes raise his
prise thearof, bothe to Answere his Exchange, which is a (100) pounde
Englishe, and also for some reasonable ouerpluse to beare his Charges
and to amend his stocke.

Hearby you maye see the Reason which the Risynge or fallynge
of the Exchange dothe gouerne the prise of wares. And hearvnto it
may be Added that, yf the Exchange at Antwerpe weare kepte vppe
at (23) shillinges (3) pence, which is (3) pence lese then the true
vallue of the Englishe pounde after the firste Comparrysone afforsayd,
which (2) pence muste be defalkede for the Intereste, the Consequently of Strange wares, as for Example, yf flaxe weare at Antewerpe
at (1) peny the pound the Marchante buyenge theare for England
shold have (13) pounde of flaxe moare for every pounde of his sayd
moneye takene vppe by Exchange theare then he Can have so longe
as the Exchange is kept vnder at (22) shillinges (2) pence. Therfore
the Lacke of his (13) pounde of flaxe growinge vppon the same so
lowe fallinge of the Exchange muste needes bee supplyed by sellynge
of the Reste somuche the dearrer.

Thear is good Reasone whie the Exchange at Antewerpe goethe
aboute (4) d. flemyshe lowere at vsance then the price of the Exchange
is in Lomberdstreete, for by the Exchange at Antewerpe the pound

Englishe beinge the valluere as not payd for and Answered vntyll a monthe after the delyuerey of flemishe money for the same, and by Exchange in Lomberdstreete the pound Englishe beinge the valuere is payd a monthe before the deliuery of his vallue in flemyshe money for the same. So that when the Englishe pounde is payd for amonthe before hande, then the prise thearof in Reasone oughte to be the lese; And when the Englishe pounde is not payd for in flemyshe money vntylle a monthe aftere hand, then the price in Reason oughte to be the moare. But heare you maye perceave that this necessaye and faire name Exchange might be truly termed by the odious name of buyenge and sellinge of money for tyme, otherwise Called vsurye.

Here is also to be noted that when the Exchange in Lomberds-treete for vsance goethe at (22) *s.* (6) *d.* flemyshe, and the re-exchange thearof at Antwerpe for vsance goethe at (22) shillinges (2) pence flemyshe, then thearby the Englishe pounde is vallued worthe iuste (22) shillinges (4) pence flemyshe, because the (2) pence more then the value for the Exchange in Lomberdstreete is the hiere and the intereste that the delyuerere dothe bargayne to have for delyueringe and lettynge out of his Englishe pound a monthe before hande, and the (2) *d.* lese then the vallue for the Exchange at Antwerpe is the hiere and Intereste Cutte of by the delyuerere for lettynge oute and delyuereynge of his flemyshe moneye amonthe before hande.

It maye also be Remembered that (2) pence for the Intereste of a pounde for one monthe is (2 *s.*) for the vse of a pounde for (12) monthes, the which (2) shillinges is the tenthe parte of a pounde a vsance, that is to saye for a monthe is aftere (10) pound in the hondred for the whole yeare.

Nowe for as muche as the true vallue of a (100) of Englyshe moneye aftere the fyrste Comparison is worthe (117 *li.* 1 *s.* 9 *d.*) flemyshe, and yet aftere the Exchange of (22) shillinges (6) pence in lomberdstreete and (22 *s.* 2 *d.*) flemishe at Antewerpe the Englishe pounde per medyum is vallued but at (111 *li.* 13 *s.* 4 *d.*) flemyshe, therfore this vnder valluinge exchange aftere the said firste compar-rysone hathe made England to sell Englishe wares vnder the value 5 *li.* 8 *s.* 5 *d.* and 21/79 partes flemyshe in a (100) poundes worthe therof Englishe, and the same Exchange hathe made Englande to paye too deare for a (100) poundes worth Englishe of strange wares by the vallue of 5 *li.* 8 *s.* 8 *d.* and 21/79 partes flemishe also.

Heare now followeth a breefe of the Lose that Englande systaynethe by the fallynge of the Exchange so lowe as to (22 *s.* 6 *d.*) flemyshe in Lomberdstreet and to (22 *s.* 2 *d.*) flemyshe at Antewerpe, sett out in (4) braunches accordinge to the (4) diverse Comparrisones of the moneyes afforsayd. The firste some in Euery Braunche is Englandes Lose in Exchange and Re-Exchange of (100) pounde Englishe transported into wares, the second some in Euery Rowe is Englandes Lose in the Exchange and reexchange of (100,000 *li.*) englishe likewise vented to and froe in wares.

		li.	*s.*	*d.*	*li.*	*s.*	*d.*	
	1st Comparison—	10	16	$10\frac{42}{79}$	—10843	17	$7\frac{51}{79}$	fl.
England losethe aftere the	2nd Comparison—	9	19	$8\frac{10652}{47163}$ —	9984	5	$5\frac{40325}{47163}$	fl.
	3rd Comparison—	9	0	$1\frac{43957}{47163}$ —	9008	0	$11\frac{1084}{47163}$	fl.
	4th Comparison—	8	0	$7\frac{127}{199}$ —	8031	10	$6\frac{38}{199}$	fl.

Nowe you maye perceave that as the smalle lose that England hathe sustayned by the stealynge ouer of Englishe moneye maye be mesured betweene the vnder prise of the Exchange in Lomberdstreete and the prise of Englishe money to be sould at Antwerpe mynte, so Englandes great lose in the Entercourse of wares muste be mesured betweene the vnderprised Exchange outward and homward, and the true vallue of Englishe moneye in flemyshe quoyne tryed by the Equall comparisone of fyne syluer contayned in either of them.

It is also to be noted that the privat gayne by the vnder-valluinge of Englishe moneye in the exchange dothe Consyste in deliuerynge of money vppon the exchange at Antewerpe and in receavinge of money vppon the Exchange in Lomberdstreete, which thinge the Cvnynge Bankeredes and Subtylle money merchantes doe welle vnderstande.

A note also maye be had that the Exchange dothe some tymes rise and fall, as some tyme vppon necessarye occasione and sometymes by Cunynge handlinge, vppon the whiche Risynge and fallynge thes termes are vsed, the exchange goethe Highe or it goethe Lowe; in which exchange the pounde of Englishe money maye be called the vallewer, because the Risynge and fallynge and the goinge highe or Lowe of the Exchange dothe Consyste in the more or the Lese that is delyvered or receavinge of flemyshe money for and in Exchange of a pound of Englyshe moneye.

The Exchange dothe rise in Lomberdstreete vppon necessarye occassyon when many greedy takeres vp of money ther doe teache the delyuerers there to make their owne gayne by Raysynge of the Exchange. The which greedy takynge vp of money thear happenethe espessyally vppon a soddene intellygence that thear wilbe presently a good falle and a greate vente of Englishe ware in the Lowe Contreyes, whervppon Merchantes of all Nacones rune hedlonge to the Exchange for moneye to buye and transport accordingly. A Lyvely Example whearof was in the Late Rysynge of the Exchange in Lomberdstreete vppon the sodene oppenynge of the vente and entercourse in to the Lowe Contreyes.

Contrarywise, the Exchange dothe fall at Antwerpe necessarely occasyoned when the greedy takeres vppe of money theare doe teache the delyuereres theare to make theire owne gayne by fallynge and bringinge downe of the Exchange. So that yf before and vntylle the sayd openynge of the sayd . . .* England had kepte it selfe as barrene of strange wares as Antewerpe and the Lowe Contreyes kepte them of Englyshe wares, then the greedynes of takynge vpe of money at Antewerpe for vente of theire wares countervallynge the greedy takynge vpe of money in Lomberdstreete for vente of our wares wolde have stayed the Exchange from Risynge so highe, for the ferventer occasyone, in whether place soeuer it dothe happen, will force the Exchange in other places to yeld and followe accordingly.

Thear is a contrary Course of the Exchange necessarely happenynge when the greedy delyuereres thearon doe teche the takeres vpe to make theire owne gayne. As yf this greedynes happen in Lomberdstreete by makynge ouere of the Princes money for paymente of debtes beyond the seas or otherwise, then the merchantes will fylle the Exchange ther againe. Yf this greedynes happen at Antwerpe by makenge overe of greate somes of Englishe merchantes money aftere a quicke salle and redy payment therof for their Englyshe wares or otherwise, then the takynge vpe will rayse the Ex-

---

* Blank in manuscript.

change there. And the violent occasyon therof, in whether place soever it happene, will cause the Exchange in the other place to followe accordingly.

The Rysynge and fallynge of the Exchange by Cunynge handlynge dothe spessyally Consyste in the Conspyrasye of the greate Bankeres when thes violente occasyones afforesaid doe not disappoynte them. And because the keepinge of the Exchange Lowe is the Comone benefyte of the Lowe contreyes gayned vppon the Comone detrimente of the Realme of England, therfore it seemethe that the Counsell of the Finaunces in the Lowecontreyes have Contynually spvrred the Bankeres of Antewerpe to keepe the Exchange Lower then the just proportyon of the vallues of the moneyes of eythere Realme hathe duly Required.

The Bankeres doe cunyngly fall the exchange at Antwerpe when foreseeing that shortely a good masse of warre wilbe boughte vppe there for Englande by money takene vppe by exchange. They then forthwith take vpe all the moneye of the Burse to keepe a whyll in their fewe handes, and within fewe dayes aftere, when the tyme of buyinge of ware for Englande dothe drive many to the Exchange for money to buye withall, then the Bankeres, possessinge almoste all the money by their prevensyone, maye by their Consperrasye fall the price of the Exchange thear to their Convenyente gayne.

The Bankeres maye cunyngly rayse the Exchange at Antwerpe when, foreseeinge shortly that a good masse of moneye wilbe made ouer in to Englande by exchange by reason of a quicke salle that presently is in hand of Englishe warres, then they forthwithe delivere out vppon the Exchange all theire moneye in their owne handes and they Refuse to take vppe money at other menes handes, and within fewe dayes aftere, when the tyme of makynge ouere of that good masse of money for England dothe drive many to the Burse to delyuere the same vppon the Exchange, then the bankeres, havinge fylled the Burse with their moneyes and with their forberinge to take moneyes vpone the Exchange, maye by their Conspirarsye Rayese the Exchange theare to their Convenyente gayne.

The Bankeres also vse this pollesye, that when they se good occasyone to have plentye of money at Antewerpe, then they Cause theyre factores in England to make ouer all their money at the syghte, that they maye have it Redy there to serve there foreseene occassyon.

The Bankeres have alwayes this Aduantage, that every man

lightely will delyuer by Exchange in to their handes a peny at the leaste in the pound bettere cheape then they vse to delyuere vnto others, because they are accounted sure mene to delle withealle.

The lyke Connynge to that afforsayd concernyng Raysynge and fallynge of the Exchange may be vsed in Lomberdstreete; savinge that looke what pollesye the Bankeres doe vse for fallynge the Exchange at Antwerpe, the same pollesye the money merchantes muste vse to Raise the Exchange in Lomberdstreete; and Contrarywise, looke what pollesye to bankeres doe vse for Raysynge the Exchange at Antwerpe, the same pollesye the money merchanges muste vse to fall the Exchange in Lomberdstreete.

Remedyes to meete with the devices that doe fall the Exchange and keepe it so farre to Lowe to the great and intollorable lose of the wholle Realme of Englande.

The Cheefeste and the most proffytable Remedy is to gouerne this Realme by good pollecy in suche temperate soarte that the Strange wares vented in to this Realme yearly maye be of lese vallewe then our Englishe wares yearly vented out of the Realme shall amount vnto, the which may esely be brought to pase if wee wold tempere and forbeare the superfluous delycasye of our Expences of Strange wares, and of strange victualles, and withall yf our Englishe warres weare Caused to be wroughte to the beste value before they be vented, and also yf Necessary wares of strange Contreyes weare Caused to be made heare more plentefully; whervppon thes Eventes hearafter rehearsed wold followe.

Fyrste, the ouervallue of our Englyshe wares will yearly bringe in Emperyall and frenche Crownes, for they are Corrante heare; wherby this Realme shalbe enriched and merchantes shall have plenty of money in Englande that is Corrante also in the Lowe Contreyes.

Secondly, because after (6) shillinges Englyshe a frenche Crowne, which is worthe (7) shillinges flemyshe in flaunderes, a pound of Englishe money is worthe (23) shillinges (4 *d*.) flemyshe, therfore when wee have plentye of thes Crownes here, yf the Exchange of Lomberdstreete doe not Rise so highe or to (2 *d*) flemyshe more accordinge to the gayne to (10) pounde in the hondred after the accompte of vsance, then will the Cunynge Merchantes forsacke the Exchange in the streete and convay ouere there money by stelthe in Crownes to serve their turnes therwith at Antwerpe; and so for lacke of ordenary returne by Exchange in Lomberdstreet the bankeres and money merchantes shalbe driven to Raise the Exchange to an Equall vallue to renewe the Recourse therto againe.

Thirdly, when the ouervallue of our Englyshe wares shall from tyme to tyme fyll our Englyshe merchantes purses at Antewerpe, then yf the Bankeres at Antwerpe shall keepe the Exchange downe Lowe, all the gayne shall falle and Redounde vnto the Englyshe merchantes, because they shal become great delyuereres vppon the Exchange there; which occasyon will force the Bankeres to keep vpe the Exchange, to the Comone benefyte of the Realme of England.

Forthely, althoughe frenche Crownes have byne vallued heare amonge merchantes at (4) pence in the pound Englyshe aboue their Corrancy in this Realme, not because they are so worthe but because the Lowe keepynge of the Exchange hath made them so muche worthe to be convayed ouere in to flaunderes, but yf the Exchange wold keepe at (23 s.) 3 (d) flemishe and vpwardes, then he that shoulde buye a french Crowne for more then (6 s.) Englyshe to steale the same to Antewerpe shold be a loosere therby, because (6 s) delivered in the Exchange wold be more worthe to him then a frenche Crowne; wherfore frenche Crownes then wold staye quietly in Englyshe mense purses.

Thus you see that this good principall afforsayd well observed wold by thes Eventes followinge not onely raise or keepe vpe the Exchange Convenyently, but also wold enriche this Realme infynytlye.

An other Remedye to meete withe the Bankeres and to defend or avoyde them to lowe Exchange is to procure and obtayne that Englyshe moneye maybe Corrant either in the Lowecontreyes or else in fraunce according to the Iuste and full vallue thearof duly Comparred to the frenche Crowne, or Phillipes Dollore.

Wher vppon yf this Corrancy shalbe in the Lowe contreyes, forthewith (20 s.) of Englyshe money wilbe worthe currante theare (23 s.) (2 d.) flemishe at the leaste; nowe yf then the Bankeres shall keepe downe the Exchange beneathe the Currancye of Englyshe money theare, all other marchantes will sone fynd what proffyte may be made onely by delyueringe of moneyes vppon the Exchange at Antwerpe, and by stealynge of moneyes agayne out of England instyde of a Retorne by Exchange in Lomberdstreete; so that the Bankeres lackynge heare by takynge vpe of theire moneyes at Antwerpe will soone be driven to Rayse the Exchange, to the Comone benifyte of the Realme of Englande.

Nowe yf this Currancye shalbe in fraunce, wheras nowe all the ouer vallue of our Englyshe warres in Respecte of our Enterchange with flanderes is Convayed or exchanged in to fraunce to Supply the vudervalue of our Englyshe wares . . .* their superfluousely, then will our Englyshe merchantes convaye our Englyshe moneye into fraunce to supply their Lacke thear, and all the frenche Crownes that nowe they convaye or exchange in to fraunce they will then delyuere at Antwerpe vppon the Exchange for England; and when the Bankeres fynd the Englyshe marchantes to become hearby greate delyuereres vppon the Exchange for Englande, then they shalbe driven to Rayse the Exchange, for otherwise the greate proffyte of the Exchange will redound to the Englyshe merchant.

And althoughe England maye seeme hearby to be robbed of Treasure, yet I suppos it is a due meane to save muche Treasure with in England that the Realme hathe of Late byne spoiled of, for yf the Exchange hearby maye be kepte vppe, as the proportyoned vallues of moneyes of Eithere Realme dothe duly require, then will the price of Englyshe wares so Ryse beyond the sease, and the price of strange wares will so falle in England, that our ouervallue gayned thearby in our enterchange of marchandyes will bringe in or save a great delle of Treasure that the fallynge of the Exchange too lowe dothe defraude and spoylle us of.

Some also peradventure wold iudge that, yf Phillips Dollores also shold be currante heare, that the Queenes highenes shold by this Currancye of moneyes entercangably loose some proffyte of hir mynte, by Reasone of the too muche plenty of the strange quoine that wold Come in beinge Currante within this Realme. But I suppos the Cleane Contrary: that yf, by our temperance and polletyque abstenanse from strange wares, Questyonlese then an ouer vallue of strange quoyne shold come in to this Realme to the greate Benefyte thearof, that then Hir Highenes mighte make a private gayne thearof, ethere by Cryenge of it to be bullyone, and so to newe mynte it, orelse by Cryenge it downe Lowere agaynste the Recepte of hir Revenues or other paymentes, as I thinke they doe with strange

---

* Blank in manuscript.

quoynes in flaunderes, crienge it vpe agayne when the prince hathe plentye therof and greate paymentes to make.

Thus I suppos you see that the Currancy of Englyshe money in flaunderes or in fraunce, althoughe Phillipes Dollores weare also Currante in England without any discomodytye thearby, wold Raise the Exchange or keepe it vpe convenyentely to the syngulere benefyte of this Realme.

An other Remedye to meet with the said devisores of fallynge and keepynge the Exchange to lowe is for the Queenes Highenes to have a banke of money of (10000 *li.*) or moare in hir factores handes at Antwerpe.

And to make the matter more playne, it is to be noted that theare be at Antwerpe great Bankeres or money merchantes that vse the Exchange onely for gayne by marchandisynge of money, who lye watching to take advantage of the tyme and occasyone to falle of Raiese the Exchange to their moste proffyte. Thear be also merchantes traffyqueres of warres who vse the Exchange onely for Neede.

Nowe when the merchante Traffyqueres come to the Exchange at Antewerpe to take vppe money to buye strange wares for Englande, then hir highenes factore, havinge suche a greate banque of moneye and dothe Respecte the proffyte of his Contrey more then his owne syngulere gayne, maye Rayse the Exchange by his great delyuerye theron, althoughe all the bankeres conspire to the Contrary; and to Rayse the Exchange thear, when he shalbe the taker vpe, his owne private proffyte and the assente of all the Bankeres will prouoke him.

Agayne hir highenes sayd factore may allso keepe vpe or Rayse the Exchange in Lomberdstreete by taking vpe of money thear at a highe prise when merchante Trafyqueres doe offer to delyuere and make Retornes of their moneyes. As for hir sayd factores Raysinge of the Exchange in Lomberdstreete when he shall delyuere moneye there him selfe, he neede not to be byddene, for private proffyte callethe him thearvnto as well as the Comone welthe of Englande.

Thus have you harde howe hir highenes factore with a great banke of moneye may Raise or keepe vpe the Exchange to the beste Comodyty for Englande, for thear are vnproffytable raisynges.

Another Remedye or meane to raise or keepe vpe the Exchange is to Change and remove our ventynge place from Antewerpe and the Lowe Contreyes vnto Embden and so Estwardes; whervppon thes Eventes hearafter Rehearsed will followe:

Fyrste, the greatest masse of our Englyshe wares shalbe neare to the places wheare they are spent and Consumed then they weare before. The lowecontreyes doe not weare and consume our Englyshe Clothe, and as the further Carryage of our wares dothe aske a great prise for them, so the Bringynge of the sayd wares so neare vnto the Comsumeres of them will make them better able to paye well for them there, because so muche carryadge is saved vnto them, as Antewerpe is further from them, so that hearby some price willbe Raised of our Englyshe wares; espessyally synce many buyeres will Come to them thether that now are served either by their fewe traffyqueres to Antewerpe or onelye by styllyarde mene.

Secondarely, our Englyshe merchantes shalbe neare vnto thos kynde of strange warres that are most necessary for our Realme as Pitche, Tarre, Masts, Clobbord, Seelinge, Dealbord, Corne, etc. And synce our Realme maye hearby be served of pyche and tarre by our own merchantes, whereas nowe onely wee are served almoste onely with a fewe Styllyard mene, it muste needes bringe vs thes strange wares bettere Cheape in to Englande and Cause our merchantes practys further traffycque, to the greate benefyte of our Realme.

Thirdly, as this Raisynge of the price of Englyshe wares and the abatynge of the price of Strange wares is the Effecte of Raisynge of the Exchange for the benefyte of the Realme, so the Lacke of thos Caterpilleres the Bankeres of Antewerpe ther will occasyone our Englishe merchantes heare to beare the moare swaye in the Exchange ther, who will keepe it at suche Convenyent heighte as maye be agreeable to the vallue of our moneyes, to the moste synguler benefyte of our Comon wealle of England.

Forthely, hearby a great number of yonge Englyshe merchantes would be cute of, which nowe thoroughe often lighte gaynes of oftene Retornes of Strange wares into England doe Exercise merchandise withe smalle stockes, who sellinge the strange wares hastelly and needfully Retorne the moneye therof still by delyuerynge the same vppon the Exchange in Lomberdstreete; wherfore they must needes take suche prise thearof as the Takeres vpe, beinge Comonly the money merchantes, will sett vppon them; wherby the Exchange dothe fall or is kept Lowe.

Thus you see howe the Remouinge of our ventynge place forther

of wold occasyon the Exchange to Rise to the greate benefyte of this
Realme. And with all here is to be noted that by this meanes the
Queenes Highenes and this Realme shall not be had in Contempte
of the Lowe Contreyes, nor be in daunger of suche prohibiciones as
of Late hathe byne made, nor yet be in feere of suche Imperious
requests as of Late have byne demaunded, to the perrelous preiudice
of hir Highenes and hir whole Realme.

A fifte remedy for the raisinge the Exchange is to have order
takene by hir Highnes that hir Costomes mayebe more truly
Answered then heretofore they have byne; espesyally of Strange
wares.

Whervppon the price of Strange wares beinge made deerer to
the subiecte will cause the Inferriore soarte to leave the buyenge and
vse of them, and the fraudulent yonge sorte of marchantes beinge
hearby drivene to paye true Costom wilbe so driven to leave their
occupyenge; which wilbe a spessyall occasyone of Raisinge the Exchange to the greate benefyte of this Realme. But hearvnto belongethe
thes orderes followinge.

Fyrste, an opene and Large wharfe muste be made in Londone,
wher the Custom house bothe for Inwarde and outward maye stand;
for otherwise the Costome Cannot be truly and duly Looked vnto,
nether cane the Fravdes thearof be avoyded.

Secondly, strange marchantes and also Englishe and their factores muste be remoued and barred from their Lodginge and Fraudulent houses borderinge vppon the Tham wharfe.

Thirdly, the poundage of Strange wares mustbe exacted accordinge to the true value of the said wares.

And to Conclude, trusty men muste be appoynted to the due
ouersighte of the sayd Customes for a year or twoe, and when the
true revenewe maye be nearly Coniectured, the sayd Costomes wold
be Lett to Ferme to hir highnes moste aduantage thorowghe out the
Realme; which fermeres wold see the Costomes more truly payd then
ever hir hir Highenes shall as longe as they are in hir owne offyceres
handes.

Thus you see by the generall discourse afforsayd what is sayd
in Euery point. You see also of howe greate momente the matteres
of the Exchange are, and and you see how necessary it is to have
Chosen men appoynted by comyssyon to Consydere and beate out
thes matteres to the bottom, that the Exchange and the dependances

thervnto may be by their traville vunderstanded; although the Auth-
orety to ordere and Execute the same be lefte to hir Highenes further
pleasure.

The Inconveniences of, And Remedies for Usury (1570?)*

A device for the remedyinge of some parte of the inconveniences
which dayly growe in this realme by usury and drye exchaunge.

The manifold great inconveniences which dayly more and more
growe in this Realme by the insatiable vice of usury, notwithstandinge
the often and earnest admonitions given in sermons against the sayd
vice by the zealous sinceare preachers of goddes wourde, hath caused
me ofte tymes to wisshe that it might please god to move their hartes
to set penne to the booke in the devisinge of remedye for the sayd
inconvenience, whome he hath indued with moost plentifull giftes
of knowledge howe the same is to be reformed: what they have don
which can do best herein I am utterly ignorant. But, being zealous
that some better successe may followe so godly preachinge, I Have
of remedye to the sayd inconvenience followed thexample of the
poore widowe which offered two mytes towardes the buyldinge of
the temple of Jerusalem. Before I shall enter into the device for the
remedye, I think it consonant with reason that I declare what I
accompte to be usury, and what other practises be as hurtfull to the
comon wealth as is usury, notwithstanding that the practisers thereof
can not by lawe for any usury be impeached.

Phillipp Melanchthon in his booke called *Epitome Philosophie
moralis* in the title *de contractibus* diffineth usury to be that gayne
which is taken above the thinge lent for the only acte of lendinge;
for, sayth he, when more is payd then is borrowed when the borrower
hath geven manifest cause of damage to the lender, that overplus is
not usury nor unlawfull; but that increase is usury and unlawfull
which we covenaunt to receive for the acte of lendinge when the
borrower giveth no cause of any losse. He utterly condemneth usury
which is coloured by pretence of interest, but the takinge and makinge
covenaunt to have trewe and ryghtfull interest he alloweth. His

* S.P.D., Eliz., Vol. LXXV., No. 54.

wourdes be these: "longissime differunt interesse et usura, leges ipse indicant equissimam et honestissimam esse compensationem eius quod interest. Commune et aequum interesse venit in omni contractu, concludo igitur quod liceat stipulari quanti interest damni emergentis ante moram. Nam verum interesse soluere non est usura, et h(a)ec compensatio deberetur iudicio boni viri etiamsi non interessisset stipulatio, nemo enim debet dare efficacem causam damni. Etsi altem obscurior est ratio de lucro cessante ante moram, tamen, si sit probabilis ratio, etiam concedendum est quod liceat stipulari quanti interest ante moram lucri cessantis."* Yt also appeareth as well by the difinition which Hostiensis maketh of usury, as likewyse by the difinition which Thomas Aquinas maketh, that trewe and unfayned interest is no usury; for Hostiensis saythe: "Usura est quodqunque solutioni rei mutuate accedit, ipsius rei usus gratia, pactione interposita."** And Thomas Acquinas sayth: "Usura est quicquid preter sortem accedit sine iusto titulo siu sit (in) mutuis siue in contractibus."† And if trewe and unfayned interest be not usury, but dewe unto the lender by the lawe of nature, as not only Melanchthon but also the Doctores which he hath redde, as he sayth, do affirme, yt semeth to me that the Jewes were not forbidden by the xxij chapter of Exodus to take such interest even of their owne nation, for the wourdes thear be but these: "Si pecuniam mutuam dederis populo meo pauperi qui habitat tecum, non urgebis eum quasi exactor, nec usuris opprimes."‡ But if the borrower ought by the lawe of nature to yeld unto the lender his unfayned interest, the lender, notwithstan-

---

* Interest and usury have the widest possible differences, and the laws themselves cite a thing's interest to be its most fair and honest compensation. A mutual and fair interest occurs in every contract, therefore I conclude that it is allowed to stipulate how much of a loss is at interest (at stake) which would arise before a lapse of time. For truly to pay off interest is not usury and this compensation is owed in the judgment of a good man even if the condition of interest had not been stipulated, for no one ought to give an efficient cause for loss. Even if the reason for a diminishing value before a lapsed period of time were rather obscure, nevertheless if there is a probable reason, even then one must concede that it is allowed to stipulate how much a diminishing value is at interest (at stake) before the lapse of time.

** Usury is whatever happens for the payment of something by exchange for the sake of the use itself of the thing after an agreement has been interposed.

† Usury is whatever occurs outside of chance without just title whether it is done in exchange or spelled out in contracts.

‡ If you give money at exchange to my poor people who live with you, you will not hound them in the manner of an exactor nor oppress them with usuries.

dinge this commaundement, might lawfully receive it, bycause that such unfayned interest is no usury.

But albeit that it alwayes hath ben and is lawfull unto the subiectes of other Christin nations, which be ruled by the civill lawe, to make their contractes in their lendinge of mony to have their lawfull unfayned interest, yet at this daye, and ever sith the first day of maye in the vjth yeare of the Raigne of Kinge Edward the vjth, it hath not ben lawfull unto any Subiecte of this Realme to lend, give, set owt, deliver or forbeare any somme of mony to any person or persons for any interest to be had, received or hoped for, over and above the somme or sommes so lent, gevin, set owt, delivered or forborne, by reason of a statute intituled an acte against usury made in the vth and vjth yeare of the sayd kinge. And althoughe it is not to be doughted but that the good meaninge of the makers and preferrers of that acte was to take awaye that usury which, under pretext of interest beinge not above tenne in the hundreth, might than be committed unpunisshed, bycause the same was lefte at large to the conscience of the lender, unpunisshable by a former statute, intituled also an acte against usury, made in the xxxvijth yeare of Kinge Henry theight, yet, since the makinge of the sayde last acte inhibiting the takinge of such interest and levinge skoope for practisinge as evell practises, farre more inconveniences have growen both in London and els wheare, partely by practisinge of fore bytinge usurye and corrupte chevisans, but cheifflye by open usinge of drye exchaunge under colour of marchauntes exchaunge, as well as it is now used, and as fore bytinge for the moost parte is as playne usurye, and also as unlawfull, for that it is directlye against diuerse and sundry good, godly and profitable statutes heretofore made by aucthoritie of parliament, and farre degenerate from marchauntes naturall exchaunge, which was first diuised and used by the trewe dealinge marchauntes immediately after that princes did inhibit the cariadge of gould and silver out of their Realmes.

For before that tyme there was very litle or no other exchaunge used in England, but only thexchaunge then called the kinges exchaunge, which was made by the kinges exchaungers; that is to saye, to have presentlye delivered by thexchaungers in any place in this Realme whear the sayd exchaunge was keapt the coyne of this Realme for any foreyne coynes either of gould or silver, or for any molten bullyon lykewyse thear presently delivered, according to the iust

value of the gould and silver conteyned in the sayd foreyne coynes
or bullyon, allowinge only unto the sayd exchaungers a certeyne
(sum) for the coynage and other necessary chardges. But thinhibitinge
of the cariadge of gould and silver did cause an other exchaunge to
be frequented; and that was when any man was willinge to have a
somme of mony exchaunged owt of one country wheras he had mony,
into an other country whearas he would have it, he would seke for
a marchaunt which had or should have mony dewe or growinge to
be dewe for wares in the cuntrye whereunto he would make his
exchaunge, and deliver unto the sayd marchaunt a certeyne somme
of mony of the princes coyne whear he delivereth his mony, to have
therfore such like somme of mony or nighe thereaboutes to be payd
of the princes coyne whear he would laye his exchaunge, as the
somme of mony delivered, if he should have caryed the same thither,
woulde yeld at the princes mynte or place of exchaunge whereas he
would have his mony by exchaunge to be layed. And althoughe the
deliverer in such exchaunge receive agayne more or les nomber of
ounces of fyne silver, or more or lesse carectes of fyne gould in thone
coyne than he delivered in thother princes coyne, yet thexchaunge
may for other considerations be agreable with equitie and not unworthy the name of marchauntes naturall and lawfull exchaunge, yf such
exchaunge were not, as it is, by acte of parliament prohibited for
the surer advoydinge of the drye exchaunge.

Dry exchaunge is to deliver mony by exchaunge in one Realme
to be payd in another Realme, whear the deliverer seaketh not to
imploye his monyee either upon wares or otherwyse but only to
exchaunge his sayd mony home agayne with lucre. For the advoydinge of this drye exchaunge diuerse and sundry statutes wear made
in the tymes of the Raignes of Kinge Richard the second, Henry the
iiijth, Henry the vth, and Henry the vjth, byndinge the receivers of
the mony here by exchaunge to imploye the same within a certeyne
tyme into wolles, clothes, lead, tynne, or other comodities of the
Realme. But forasmuchas the marchauntes did still continewe to
defrawde the good meaninge of the sayd statutes, one other statute
was made in the third yeare of the Raigne of King Henry the vijth,
that no man should make any exchaunge without the Kynges licence,
nor make any exchaunge or rechaunge of mony to be payd within
this land, but only such as the kinge should depute thereunto to
keape, make and aunswere such exchaunges and rechanges, upon

the paynes in the statute of sayd kinge Richard contayned, which was the forfaycture of the value of the mony exchaunged. And it appeareth by diuerse and sundry recordes that in the tyme of the Raigne of the sayd kinges diuerse persons wear sued in thexchequer for deliveringe of mony by such exchaunge withowt the kinges licence, and wear driven to obtayne their pardonnes for the sayd offences. Seinge than that the cariadge of mony from one Realme to an other is forbidden, it is necessarye for the trade of marchauntdice that there should be an exchaunge from one realme to an other, and forasmuch as all persons be inhibited to make such exchaunge without lycence, it is requisite that the prince should give lycence under some bodye to make such exchaunge, and so I suppose that Kinge Henry the vijth mynded to do when the sayd acte was made.

There have ben of late some usurers which, for lack of learned Councell in makinge of writinges and devises for the clokinge of their usurye, have ben impeched in thexchequer upon the statute of usurye, and therby driven to greatt chardge in learned Councell and otherwyse for the defence of their corrupt causes. Whearby all the old vsurers are now become so ware, wylye and subtyle, that they will not lightly come in the daunger of that vsury which is punisshable by the statute of vsury, but do converte their mony either to drye exchaunge or else to corrupte chevisans, that is in buyinge of wares to thonly intent to sell the same wares agayne in shiftes with dayes of payment at unreasonable prices unto theim which seke to make shifte for mony. The preachers do inveighe agaynst usury, and these old usurers now beinge only practisers in such dry exchaunge and corrupte chevisans do heare theim, and perswade theim selves that they do not nowe commit any usury bycause they have devised to escape the usury punisshable by the statute; so as they continewe their practises and the preachers their invectives agaynst usury, to the greatt greiffe of the audience, conceivinge that the wourd of god pronounced by the preachers is litle regarded, and to the further alienatinge of the hartes of thenymies of our religion, seinge no better sequell followe so much preachinge. And of the aforesayd ungodly practises these inconveniences must nedes followe if remedye be not therin provided. The riches of the cytie of London and in effecte of all this Realme shalbe in short tyme in the handes of a fewe men havinge unmercifull hartes and beinge unnecessary members of the comon wealth. And a greatt nomber of the rest of the subiectes of this Realme, being in their diuerse vocations necessary members of the comon wealth, by the unmercifull dealinge of these usurers, dry exchaungers and corrupt chevancers, shalbe either driven to banckrowting, or els so impoverisshed, that they shall not be able to do unto the quenes maiestie and unto the realme in tyme of warres any such service as they would willingly do if they wear of habilitie.

Usury and trewe interest be thinges as contrary as falshed is to trewth. For usury contayneth in it selfe inequalitie and unnaturall dealinge, and trewe interest observeth equitie and naturall dealinge. Usury tendeth to the destruction of the comon wealth, but the borrowinge of mony or any other thinge, yeldinge to the lender his trewe and iust interest, is one of the comodities which insue by the societie of man. And forasmuchas this interest is permitted by the Civill lawe as a thinge moost lawfull and very necessary and agreable to nature, it is comonly used in Flaunders and in other realmes whear the Englissh nation do traffike. And although it can not be denyed but that usury under pretence of interest is thear often tymes practised, yet that usury, by reason of their admittinge of contracte for interest, is nothinge so fore bytinge as is either our usury or our sellinge of wares in shiftes with dayes of payment, or as is our dry exchaunge. And therefore their smale usury is not so much against their comon wealthes as our bytinge usury, our sellinge of wares upon dayes of payment and our dry exchaunge is against our comon wealth, no(r) their smale usury do not their comon wealth so much hurt as their sufferinge of contractes for interest doth profight their comon wealth. For by reason that they do admitte contractes for interest, mony is thear to be borrowed and lent unto their own nation for viij, ix or x in the hundreth, whearby their marchauntes may be greatt gayners by givinge dayes of payment in the sellinge of their wares unto our marchauntes, they makinge accompt in the prysinge of their wares after the rate of xij, xiij, or xiiij in the hundreth for the forbearinge of their payment. And the greattest nomber of our marchauntes, dealinge farre deaper upon creadit than upon ready mony, arr driven rather to take wares upon creadit at the handes of the sayd Straungers than at the handes of the englisshe men, bycause they be at lesse losse by takinge wares at dayes of payment at the sayd Straungers handes than at Englisshe mens handes; for that Straunger which is thear of good creadit, although he be not wourth above one thousand pound of his owne goodes, may have v or vj thousand poundes in

his handes of his cuntrye mens mony at very smale interest by reason
of the sayd permission of contractes for interest, and therby inhabled
in the sellinge of his wares unto our nation to give dayes of payment.
Yf the makinge of contractes for interest wear universally forbidden,
as well unto those nations with whome we traffike as it is unto us,
it should not be so hurtefull unto our comon wealth as it nowe is,
being forbidden only unto us and lawfull unto theim. For, as the
case nowe standeth, althoughe we spende in this Realme no more
value yearly in foreyne wares then the wares be in value which we
send yearly into foreyne realmes (both our wares and their wares
being accompted at such rate as they be wourth to be sould for ready
mony), yet by reason that their marchauntes do gayne so much of
the greattest nomber of marchauntes in sellinge their wares dearer
than they be wourth for givinge dayes of payment, and with their
dayly deliveringe of mony unto our sayd porer sorte of marchauntes
upon the dry exchaunge, our Realme is by such meanes yearly impoverisshed of very greatt sommes of mony and their Realme so much
yearly inriched, and we lydelye hereafter to have farre more banck-
rowtes than they.

For remedye of which inconveniences, althoughe I shall
perchaunce neither hitt the marke nor yet perhappes come so nighe
the marke as some other may do which shall shote at it hereafter,
yet to the intent to provoke others to shote at it I will declare my
device. Which is that it might please the Quenes maiestie, for the
causes before recited, to set such a proclamation for the puttinge in
execution of the sayd statute of her highnes graundfather kinge Henry
the vijth, and therupon to depute exchaungers both in london and
at Hamborrowe, and in such other places whear our marchauntes
have moost frequented traffike and whear exchaunge comonly lyeth,
to make all exchaunge and rechaunge to and from England and the
sayd places. And though her maiestie did but freely lycence a certeyne
nomber of discreat and likely men, that it should be lawful unto
theim and such other as they shall thinke good to associate unto
theim to make exchaunge and rechaunge to and from all parties of
beyond the seas at such rates and with such like orders and condicions
as herein shalbe expressed, yt should remedye the moost parte of
the inconveniences before recited. But if her maiestie would take the
sayd exchaunge into her highnes owne handes, it should not only
remedy the sayd inconvenience, but also be a greatt strengthninge

of her maiestie, both against all sodeyne attempes of foreyne enemyes and also against all attemptes of Rebells, yi any hereafter should happen to rebell.

To accomplisshe this device a very great masse of mony must of necessitie be therin imployed. But the greatter that the bancke shall be, the stronger shall her highnes force be at all sodeynes against her enymyes by reason of the habilitie of spedy furniture of mony. But if so be that her highnes have not otherwyse to furnissh that bancke, it may be raysed either by morgaginge of landes unto her highnes subiectes, lettinge theim inioye the rentes after the rate of xx yeares purchase, or by sellinge of Tenementes and cotages havinge therto no landes and whearwith her highnes is chardged with reparacions: for I suppose that smale profight hath come and lesse will come unto her maiestie by keapinge of such tenementes and cotages, the value of the tymber allowed for such reparations and thother charges required for such repayres beinge rightly considered.

First, that ther be in every place whereas this exchaunge shall be made three personns to be always named by her maiestie, which shalbe called the quenes exchaungers or coferors of the quenes threasour for exchaunge, which coferors shall ioyntly kepe the threasour under three severall lockes, and stand ioyntle chardged unto her maiestie for all the threasour which shall come to their handes by reason of their sayd offices.

And that they deliver owt no mony aforehand unto any person by exchaunge but unto such good and sufficient men as they upon the consideracions hereafter to be expressed will aunswere for.

And that the sayd exchaungers be not compellable to deliver any mony in exchaunge aforehand unto any person, except the same person do either deliver a sufficient gage into the handes of the sayd exchaungers, or els be and remayne so sufficiently bounden unto her maiestie in obligation with such other suerties as the sayd exchaungers shall have good lykinge of, to aunswere all such mony as he shall take by exchaunge.

The sayd exchaungers as well to receive as also deliver mony by exchaunge, to be payd either at usans, dowble usans or treble usans, accordinge to the agreament betwene the sayd exchaungers and the takers or deliverers by exchaunge. And, for the mony which they shall deliver, they to take two bylles in such sort as heretofore have been accustomed in marchauntes exchaunge subscribed by the hand of the taker. And, for the mony which shall be by theim beforehand received to be repayed agayne by exchaunge, they lykewyse to make two billes subscribed with the three coferors handes to be delivered to the deliverer of the mony to theim by exchaunge.

And that it be ordered that at whatsoever reconinge her maiesties sayd exchaungers shall deliver any some of mony by exchaunge at dowble usans, if the taker shall fortune not to paye or cause to be payd the mony agreed upon by his bill at the tyme and place by his bill apointed, yet nevertheles, if at thende of iiij monthes next after the takinge of the mony by exchaunge he, the sayd taker by exchaunge, or any other for him, shall repaye unto the sayd exchaungers in the same place whear he received the mony the like some of mony as he the sayd taker by exchaunge before received, and after the rate of iii *li.* vi *s.* viii *d.* in the hundreth pound for the interest and losse which the exchaungers shall sustayne for the not payment at the day and place apointed, the taker nor his suerties not to forfeite their bonde, not to lose any pledge or gage for that cause taken, not to sustayne any further losse or any discreadit.

And that it be also ordered that at whatsoeuer reconninge her highnes sayd exchaungers shall deliver any some of mony by exchaunge at treble usans, if the taker shall fortune not to paye or cause to be payd the some of mony agreed upon by his bill at the tyme and place by his bill to be apointed, yet nevertheles, if at thende of vj monethes next after the takinge of the mony by exchaunge he, the sayd taker by exchaunge, or any other for him. shall at the place where he before received the mony repaye unto the sayd exchaungers the like somme of mony as he the sayd taker by exchaunge before received, and after the rate of v *li.* in the c *li.* for the interest and losse which thexchaungers shall sustayne for the not payment at the day and place apointed, the taker nor his suerties not to forfeite their bonde, nor lose any their pledge or gage for that cause taken, nor sustayne any further losse nor any discreadit.

But if her maiesties exchaungers shall not paye or cause to be payd their billes of exchaunge for the mony by theim aforehand received, either at the iust day of payment or the next day after at the furthest, they to stand chardged to pay unto the deliverer duble the some of mony by theim received and to be compelled trewly to paye the same.

And for any somme of mony which her maiesties exchaungers

in London shall receive to paye the value therof at Hamborowe at dowble usans, her highnes sayd exchaungers to deliver their billes of exchaunge after the rate of xxiiij *s.* vi *d.* at the least for every pound here by theim received.

And the sayd exchaungers not to take above xxiiij *s.* viij *d.* of the currant mony at Hamborowe, for the pound currant money by theim delivered in London to be repayde for the same at dowble usans in Hamborowe.

And the sayd Quenes exchaungers at Hamborrowe to deliver their billes thear to pay in London xx *s.* currant mony of England for every xxiij *s.* x *d.* of the currant mony at Hamborowe by theim thear received to be repayed in London at dowble usans.

Nor they at any tyme to deliver under xxiij *s.* viij *d.* of currant mony at Hamborowe in exchaunge for the pound currant in England to be therfor repayd at dowble usans in London.

And for any somme of mony which her highnes sayd exchaungers in london shall receive to paye the value thereof at Hamborowe at treble usans, the sayd exchaungers to deliver their billes of exchaunge after the rate of xxiiij *s.* vii *d.* at the least for every pound here by theim so received.

And the sayd exchaungers not to take above xxiiij *s.* ix *d.* of the currant mony at Hamborowe for the pound currant mony by theim delivered in London to be repayd for the same at treble usans in Hamborowe.

And her highnes sayd exchaungers at Hamborowe to deliver their billes thear to paye in London xx *s.* of currant mony of England for every xxiij *s.* ix *d.* of the currant mony at Hamborowe by theim thear received to be repayd in london at treble usans.

Nor they at any tyme to deliver under xxiij *s.* vii *d.* of the currant mony in Hamborowe in exchaunge for the pound currant in England to be therfore repayd in London at treble usans.

And for every vi *s.* here by the sayd exchaungers received in exchaunge for Rone, Paris or Lyons, they to paye thear the french crowne within one moneth.

And for every French crowne received by the sayd exchaungers at Rone, Paris or Lyons, they to paye heare within one moneth after vj *s.* of the currant mony of England.

And the sayd exchaungers to be accomptable yearly unto her maieste and to aunswere here maiestie, besydes the full somme of her highnes threasour to theim delivered in bancke, x *li*. yearly for every c *li*. which they shall have of her maiesties in their bancke, and to aunswere also her maiestie the moytie of the residewe of their gaynes which shalbe gayned above x *li*. in the c *li*. And they the sayd exchaungers to inioye the moitie of the residewe above x in the c to their owne uses, for their adventure, bearinge and standinge to all losses and bearinge all chardges. And thus shall they be well and largely rewarded for their travell, her maiestie as well recompenced for the losinge of the rentes of her highnes landes, a great nomber of her highnes subiectes releved, eased and saved from impoverisshinge by borrowing upon usury, the Realme yearly inriched and a greatt masse of threasour allwayes with very short warninge in a readiness for any her highnes weightie affayres.

Mr. Tavernor.

How a Public Bank Will Contribute To the Alleviation of Usury (1576?)*

1. Theise feauwe yeares that I have binne within this Realme, I haue moste soughte to haunte and haunted the compane of all honeste sorte of Inglisshmenne, and sought with kare and diligence to fynde whatt thing and wheare in the common people of this Realme moste fyndethe them selfs borthened and greved withall; and also what thing here is moste repugnante and contrary to the noble trafficque of marchaundys, wiche kausethe all realmes and prouincis to florisshe wheare hitt hathe fre and royall course. I fynde, that (amonge other trafficques and manners of doing wiche people nouwe in theise daies moste do vse) vsery to be an abomynable synne before godde, and contrary to all common weales, and is thatt wich moste greuethe and annoyethe the common people, and wyll also (if in tyme good and decent meanes for remedy be nott fownde) nott only ouer throuwe the trade and trafficque of marchaundys nouwe florisshing with in this Realme, butt in prosses of tyme more and more trobble and annoye the common people and common wheale of this Realme, by the giust giuggement of godde, who (aboue all other) detestethe and abborrethe this abominable sinne of vsery. And for thatt I moste

* S.P.D. Eliz. Vol. CX., No. 57.

desyre with all by lettle powre and industry to shouwe thaffection
and good wyll I have to sarue the Quenes magestie, and spesshally
by the derecktion and good meanes of your honnour (of whome I
have alwayes fownde favor and good direcktion), I have thought hitt
my dute to imploye thatt little talent and tyme wich godde hathe
geven me here to fynde owte somme lawfull, good and polleticque
wayes, by the wiche (through your honnours good helpe and favor)
siche dammegable practyses shortely may be vtterly rooted owt of
this Realme, to the great ease and contentement of the common
people, all thoughe this wyll perchaunce mislyke somme particular
parsons, that have neither charrete norre feare of godde; the wiche
in my simple giuggement arre lettle to be waied to discontente and
hinder theire gaine (beinge but a small nomber of vnsaciable persons)
in respeckt of the whole generall commonweales commodite, and
aboue all thatt thus godde shalbe best pleased.

And for that I will nott be longer tedious to your honnour, I
will entre to the matter, moste humbly besechinge your honnour
with pacience and good affection to reade and waie theise articles
here follouwing, wheare in I brefly sheuwe the wayes and meanes
to avoyde and remedy the horte before eckspressed, and shall deliver
to her magestie a greater bennefette then I meane at this tyme to
eckspresse, and to the common people in generall geve verry greate
contentement, and besydes vnto your honnour Immortall fame, thatt
in your tyme and by your honnours meanes siche a benefisshall and
necessary pollise hathe binne instituted with in this her magesties
Realme, wiche I beseche almighty godde allwayes to presarue and
mantayne and your honnour att all tyme prosper in all honnour and
felissete.

2. Nouwe to enter forther in the matter, and distengktly to
declare the ende of myne intencion, and concerninge therecktion of
the foresaid inuencion and meanes, wheare by with good demonstracions and conuenient inductions greate sommes of monney maye
verry easely be levyed amongeste the people with theire owne good
contentacion. Of the wiche sommes of monney the one thirde parte,
to my simple giuggement, shalbe a sufficient masse and sarue to putt
in ecksecusshon the meanes whearby the aforesaid vsery maye be
cleane abolisshed, and the other 2 partes, ressyduwe of the said
monney, for her magestie to vse att her ouwne wyll and pleasure.
Hitt shalbe good also in my simple giuggement, and onder your

honnours correction, to make theise demonstracions follouwinge vnto the people. And firste:

3. The Quenes magestie maye ordayne certain of her magesties counsaill to infourme and instruckte all officers of her dominions, spirituall and temporall, as bishops, Deans, Maiors, Aldermenne, baylyfs, Constables, giustices, treasorers, and all other manner of officers, and consequently theise by degrees to enfourme and instruckte the common people, of thorders and pollecys wiche her magestie hathe ordeyned and is detarmined they shalbe put in ecksecusshon: aswell for the repayring of decaied havens and fronture places within her magesties dominions, as also for the prouisshon of munisshons and other thinges appartaining for defence in tyme of warre, thinges in theise trobbelsomme dayes thought verry necessary. Beesydes that, her magestie hathe a great desyre and good wyll to helpe and ease her subgieckts of the great dommages and eckstorcions they dayly receave by ecksessif interresses wiche they be dreven to paie to a nomber of insatiable vserers (wiche gnauweth the poore people Dayly to the verry bones) when by necessite they be dreven to seake wopon theim. And nouwe by this good ordre and meanes shall so be prouydeth for as nott only all menne shall in theire necessite knouwe houwe and wheare to go to be eased, but withowt any interest more then euery one of his fre good wyll shalbe willing to geue aswell in consyderacion of the pleasure receaved in his necessite, as also for the helpe and maintenauns of thofficers and other chardges about this worke.

4. The said counsaillers to sheuwe and declaire vnto all the abouesaid officers, and the said officers vnto the common people, houwe the Quenes magestie, of her ouwne good wyll towardes the ayde and aduauwncement of this necessary good and godly workes, is contente to be the firste to geue and contrybute frely (to inriche and increase the masse of monney to this effeckt necessary) all siche confiscations as hcr mcgcstic is acostomcd to gcvc and nouwe from hens forthe shall fall in her magesties good wyll to geve, and, moreover, to beare all manner of chardges towards therecktion and maintenaunce of this matter. And for as miche as siche confiscations seldom happen to befaull in reddy monney, butt moste mouables orre siche lyke, thearefore the Quenes magestie hathe thought good to shuewe vnto her subgiecktes the meanes houwe euery one in his degre withowt losse or discommodite, but easely and with commod-

ite, shall also sheuwe the affection and charrete towardes his neighbour and him self, in contributinge to this intente in manner hereafter follouwinge, that is to saie:

5. Thatt all manner of parsons having in farme any manner of thinge, temporall orre spirituall, as houses, laundes, orre anny manner of thinge whattsoeuer, painge nott onder xx s. by the yeare, shall towardes thinstitusshon of this good worke, att one tyme only and no morre, lende xij d. for euery xx s. he paiethe yearly to his Lorde, and the said xij d. to be paied to the treasorer orre receauer for this appointed, euery one in his diocis.

6. And for euery li. wiche the proprietary orre laundlord hathe orre dothe receaue of the tennaunt orre farmer, for the find of the lease of siche his orre theire housis, launds orre other tenementes whatt soeuer, shall paie 2 d. att one tyme only.

7. Thatt all manner of officers of whatt soeuer degre, aswell ecclesiasticall as temporall, havinge theyre offices for tearme of lyf orre otherwyse, shall also lende towardes the erection of this worke xij d. of euery li. that the fee of the said office is yearly worthe vnto him.

8. And to thintente thatt no farmer shall have cause to complaine of anny losse sostained by lendinge anny monney towardes the erecktion of siche a good and charrytable worke, butt thatt euery of theim in tyme shalbe repaied againe, nott withstandinge the greate commoditie wiche euery manne shall hereby fynde in all his necessites, hitt hathe thearefore thought good to the Quenes magestie (as allso her grace dothe nott doubte butt thatt her magesties officers and people wyll lyke of and allouwe) thatt all tenauntes att thende of yeares shalbe allouwed to him or his heyres siche monney as he to this intente hathe desborsed by siche as after him or his shall sucksede to him orre his heires, and so sucksessifly one after another; onles anny siche tennementes, laundes, houses, orre what soeuer happen to stande voyde the space of 6 monthes: in siche kace, the laundlorde shall repaie vnto the saide tennaunte all siche sommes of monney as heretofore for this intente he hathe desborsed.

9. Hitt hathe also thoughte good vnto the Quenes magestie thatt all manner of officers, aswell ecclesiasticall as temporall, having offices by tearme of lyf orre otherwyse, having desborsed as abouesaide, shall of siche monney be reinboursed orre paied againe by theyre successors in theyre saide office; onles the saide office happen to

befaull to anny of his heyres, the wiche shalbe ecksempt to repaie anny of the desborsed monney.

Hereafter followeth certain articles, concerning thorder to be obsarued in the thecksecuting the aforesaid worke for the vsery.

10. In primis, the gouernors and officers of this worke, in London orre else wheare in the Quenes magesties dominions, shalbe bownde to sarve euery parson whatt soeuer onder that dioces, and having necessite and that to theim declared, of siche somme of monney as his nede shall requyre, nott passinge the somme of 200 *li.*, nor being onder xx *s.*, withowt taking anny interest more then the parte serued shall thinke reasonable in recompence of the bennefytte he hathe receaved in his necessite. Prouyded allwayes thatt the partes borrouwing anny sommes of monney shalbe bownde to geue sufficient assuraunce to the gouernours and officers of this worke, and to the contentacion and estimacion of certain officers thatt for the estimacion and valluwinge shalbe appointed and sworne.

11. And the said gouernors and officers shalbe bownde to lende vnto the borrouwer alwayes thre partes of that his goodes orre laundes shalbe worthe, wiche he pleaggethe for assurance for the monney he borroweth, and the said goodes and laundes so pleagged to be praysed by the abouesaide gouernors and officers, wiche shall vnto the parte geue a byll indented theare in spessefyinge the parcels pleaggehed, the moneey theare wopon borrouwed, and the tyme of repayement: the said byll indentid safly to be kept, and for lacke of the said byll the pleagge to be forfaicte, onles sufficient cawse be shouwed of the lacke theareof orre good proof that the pleagged goodes arre hys.

12. Item, the gouernors and officers of this saide worke shalbe bownde to lende vnto alle menne as aforesaide wopon sufficient assuraunce, and euery one in his dioces, from xx *s.* opwarde vntyll the somme of 10 *li.* and nott onder norre more (onles hitt be his wyll) for the space of tenne wekes, condisshonally that euery parsonne shalbe bownde to redeme his pleagge within the said tyme of 10 wekes; and if faute theareof be made, the abouesaide officers shall have powre and autorite openly to sell the said pleagge in siche place as theare vnto shalbe apointed vnto siche as moste shall offer, and

the ouerplus of the monney theareof made to be paied immediatly vnto the parte vnto whome the goodes do appartayne.

13. Item, the abouesaid officers shalbe bownde to lende vnto all parsons Inhabitinge within theire diocis fromme 10 *li.* opwarde vnto 20 *li.*, for the space of 15 wekes, as aboue.

14. Item, from 20 *li.* to 40 *li.* for the space of 20 wekes, as aboue.

15. Item, from 40 *li.* to 80 *li.* for the space of 30 wekes, as aboue.

16. Item, from 80 *li.* to 200 *li.* for the space of 12 moneths, as aboue. Thatt is to saye, that iff att anny of the preficksed tymes the pleaggis be nott redemed, thatt the officers shall and maie sell them as aboue is rehearsyd.

17. Item, the gouernors and officers aboue saide shalbe bownde to kepe theyre housis here vnto appointed open for all menne thre dayes in the weke, and no more, onles they otherwyse wyll, thatt is to saye, the mondaye, weddensdaye, orre saterdaye in London, orre els in euery other place wopon siche dayes as the marketes in the placis do faull, orre by common consente shalbe thoughte moste conuenient; and to sitt euery daye 4 oures, thatt is to saye, in the foure none from 8 of the clocke vntyll 10, and in the afternone fromme 2 of the clocke vntyll 4.

Conclusion

18. If then thus euidently maie appeare whatt greate comodite all persons generally shall receaue in their necessite by the abouesaide ordre and institusshon, whatt officer, manne of reason orre concience, wyll refuse with all dute, zele and affection, nott only to be the firste to agre and consent to this abouesaid matter, butt also to vse all his eckstremete and force to induce the comon people to the same? And who is he amonge the commons, seinge the officers giustly and truly administringe theire office, and being by them wel perswaded to the good intente of this matter, and of the good ende hitt tendethe vnto, thatt wyll nott also follouwe willingly the others, in lendinge frely and with a good hartte as aforesaide? What parson wyll respeckt the smaulnes of his lone for only one tyme, for to be frustrated of helpe when by necessite he wheare constrained to seke hitt, besydes that he standethe in sure possybillete in tyme to recouer his principall and firste desborsed monney? Who wyll nott consether the intollerable borthen and charge wiche heretofore hathe binne borne by sondry when by necessite they have binne dreven to seke and crepe to their

otter ondoing the onsaciable and gredy vserers, wiche thought neuer anny interest sufficient to satisfye theyre gredy appetyd? Who wyll more (this ones putt in ecksecusshon) paie to theim anny more siche ecksessif interest in tyme to come? Hitt is certain no one manne. More over, who is he of anny giuggement thatt wyll nott regioyce in consethering houwe the noble trafficque of marchaundyse shall florisshe and retourne in his vigor, when this horrible vsery shalbe abolisshed, whearby the common people shall receaue great ease and comodite, and the said trafficque his fre course? Hitt is certain thatt no parson kann otherwyse giugge orre saie, butt that this inuencion was by the holly goste inspyred in the Quenes magesties moste noble harrette, and to be as nessessary to be maintained among the common people, for the common wealth of this Realme, as any other nessessary fode; so thatt, all this being wel consethered, shalbe fownde that a multytude of vserers nouwe rayguyng among the poore people, onfyt for anny common wealth and only for theim selfs, shalbe with gods healpe, and by meanes of this good institusshon, cleane from hens forwarde eckstinguisshed, and frustrated from me theyre damnable practyses and games, to the greate conforte and ease in generall of all the people, to the immortall honnour and glory of her Magestie and her honnorable counsaill, who in her Magesties tyme hathe ereckted siche an honeste, godlye and polletyque worke in her Magesties Realme, wiche the Lorde long prosper and mantayne.

Stephan Parrottes

The Activities of Thomas Gresham: Gresham's Instructions on Being Sent into Spain (1554)*

A memoriall gyven by the Quene's hyhnes vnto hir trusty and welbe-loved servaunt Thomas Gresham, esquier, hir Majestie agent in Flanders, for the purposes ensuing, xii Junii 1554.

Fyrst, where as the sayd Thomas Gresham hath for vs. and to our use, bargayned with dyvers persones in Andwerpe for sundrie sumes of monny, for which he hath receyved theyr bylls of exchange to be payd in Spaine—that is to say, of Anthony Fugger the sume

---

* J.W. Burgon, *The Life and Times of Sir Thomas Gresham*, Vol. I, pp. 472–75.

of cxii^m vii^c l. ducats, to be receyved at the fayre of Villalon lxij^m ducats, and the reste in the fayre of May; of Jasper Schetz and his bretherne the sume of lxv^m ducats, to be receyved in the fayre of October; more of the sayd Schetz and his bretherne the sume of xxxv^m ducats, to be receyved in the fayre of Villalon; of Octavian Lomelino, the sume of xxxij^m ducats, to be receyved at the fayre of Villalon xxxij^m ducats, and the rest in the fayre of May; of John de Mantansse, the sume of xv^m ducats to be receyved in the fayre of Villalon; of John Lopez de Gallo the sume of xxiiij^m ducats, to be receyved in the fayre of Villalon; of Anthony Spynnole and Frederigo Imperialle the sume of xvii^m ducats, to be received in the fayre of May: amounting in the hole to the totall sum of iij^c thowsand vij^c l. ducats. The sayd Thomas Gresham, taking with hym this memorial, and themperors letters of lecense, with suche other things as ar prepared for hym, shall for the receipt of the sayd money make his repayre with as convenient spede as he may towards Spaine; embarking hymsellf at our ports either of Darmouth or Plimouth, where we have caused a vessel to be put in a redynes for his transportacion; from whence he shall procede on his voyage as sone as wynde and wether shall gyve hym leave.

And for the better and more surer conveyance hither owt of Spaine of the sayd money, our pleasure is that the sayd Thomas Gresham shall, before his departure, common with suche marchaunts in London, ether Englyshemen or straungers, as doo trafficque in to Spaine; procuring, yf he by any meanes may, to bargayne with them or any of them for the delyvery here vnto our vse of suche sumes of money as they shall have occasion to employe in Spayne: whiche shall be there by hym repayed againe vnto them owt of the said mony that is to be receyved to our vse, foreseing that we be not of this bargaine burdened with any losse of exchange or interest.

Item, at his coming in to Spayne, in caasa our dearest cousin the Prince of Spaine shall not be departed from thence before the money that is fyrst payable shall be receyved, the sayd Thomas Gresham shall then conferre with our right trusty and right welbeloved cousin and counsellour the Earle of Bedforde, keper of our privie seale, and opening vnto hym the hole circumstance of this matter, shall, by his advise and counsell, distribute amongst the best and most surest shippes of the flete that shall cume in cumpany of our sayd derest cousin the Prince of Spaine, so muche of the sayd mony as he shall have receyved: so as he adventure not above the sume of fyve thowsand pounds sterling in any one botome. And yf it shall fortune our sayd dearest cousin the prince of Spaine to be come from thence before the sayd mony can be receyved, in that caase our pleasur is that the sayd Thomas Gresham procure to sende over by way of exchaunge, to be delyvered there, and repayed againe vnto us here or at Andwerpe vppon sight, so muche of our sayd mony as he can; foreseing that we be not burdened with any losse of exchaunge, and that the persones to whome the mony shalbe delyvered be sure and substanciall.

As for the rest of the sayd mony that cannot be sent over in suche sorte as is aforesayd, our pleasur is that, for the more saffer transportacion thereof, the sayd Thomas Gresham shall abyde the coming from thence of sume convenient flete of shippes, emongst the best and surest of whiche he shall distribute the rest of the sayd mony so remaynyng; so as he adventure not above the sum of eight thowsond pownds in any one botome; using for the convoyannce of our sayd treasure this wayes all the best meanes and pollicie that he can devise.

And finally, for as muche as we have occasion to employe sume masse of treasure within our realme of Ireland, our pleasur is that the sayd Thomas Gresham shall devise sume good and sure way, yf he can, to send vnto our sayd realme of Ireland the sume of tenne thowsand pounds ster., to be delyvered there into thands of the deputie of our sayd realme. In whiche we wolde he employed his best industry and diligence; and bothe herein, and in the rest, to have speciall regarde, as nere as he may, to the strength of the shippes and the honnesty of the persones that shall have the conveyance of the sayd mony; vsing all the secrecie he can in the shipping and sending away thereof.

And where heretofore we appointed vnto the sayd Thomas Gresham towards his diets and entertainement in our service the sume of xx s. by the day, considering now that he shall by this present service be occasioned to be at sume further expence then hitherto he hath byn, we have thought convenient to enlarge his sayd diet, and to give him, till his return out of Spayne, x s. by the day, from the date of thes instructions, ouer and above his former dietts of xx s. the day: which sumes our pleasure is he shall receyve and pay to hymsellf owt of such our treasure as shall from tyme to tyme cume to his hands.

And after he shall have dispached our business in Spaine presently committed to his charge, we ar pleased that he doo make his returne vnto our presence ether by see or by land, as may bee most for his suertye, and shall seme most convenient vnto hym.

The Activities of Thomas Gresham: Gresham to Elizabeth On the Fall of the Exchanges (1558)*

Information of Sir Thomas Gresham, Mercer, towching the fall of the exchaunge, MDLVIII.

To the Quenes most excellant maiestye.

Ytt may please your majesty to understande, thatt the firste occasion off the fall of the exchainge did growe by the Kinges majesty, your latte Father, in abasinge his quoyne Frome vj ounces fine too iij ounces fine. Wheruppon the exchainge fell Frome xxvi s. viii d. to xiii s. iv d. which was the occasion thatt all your Fine goold was convayd ought of this your realme.

Secondly, by reason off his wars, the Kinges majestie Fell into greatt debt in Flanders. And For the paymentt therof thay had no other device butt paye itt by exchainge, and to carry over his Fine gowlde For the paymentt of the same.

Thirdly, the greatt Freadome of the Stillyarde and grantinge of licence For the carringe off your woll and other comodytes ought off your reallme, which is nowe on off the cheffest pointes thatt your majestie hathe to forsee in this your comon well; thatt you neavir restore the steydes called the Stillyarde againe to ther privelydge, which hath bine the cheffest poyntte off the undoinge off this your reallme, and the marchants off the same.

Now, for redresse off thes thinges, in *an.* XVᶜ LI (1551-ed.) the Kinges majestie, your latte brother, callide me to bee his agentt, and repossid a more trust in me, as well For the paymentt off his depttes beyond the seas, as For the ressynge off the exchainge—beinge then at xv s. and xvi s. the pounde, and your mony corrantt, as itt is att this presentt, beinge nott in valew x s. First, I practized with the Kinge and my lorde off Northomberlande to overthrowe the Stilly-

* J.W. Burgon, *The Life and Times of Sir Thomas Gresham*, Vol. I. pp. 483–86.

arde, or else ytt coulde nott be brought to passe, For thatt thay woold kepp downe the exchainge by this consideration: wher as your owne mere marchantes payeth outtwardes xiv *d.* upon a cloth custome, thay pay butt ix *d.;* and like wisse, For all such wairs as was brought into your reallme, your owne mere marchantes payeth xii *d.* upon the pounde, the Stillyarde payd butt iii *d.* upon the pounde, which is v *s.* difference uppon the hundreth: and as they wear men thatt raine all uppon the exchainge For the byenge of ther comodytes, whatt did thay passe to give a lowar price then your owne marchantes, when thaye gotte v *l.* in the hundreth by your custome; which in processe off time woulde have undone your whole reallme, and youre marchantes of the same.

Secondarely, I practissed with the Kinges majestie, your brother, to come in creditt with his owne mer marchantes; and when time servid, I practised with theme att a sett shippinge, the exchainge beinge still att xvi *s.*, thatt every man showld paye the Kinge xv *s.* upon a cloth in Anwarppe, to paye att doble usans xx *s.* in London; which the Kinges majestie payd theme riallye, which did amountte to the some of lx^m *l.* Ande so, vi monthes after, I practissed the licke upon ther comodyties For the some off lxx^m *l.* to paye For every pounde starlinge xxii *s.*: so by thes meanes I maide plenty off mony and scarstie, and brought into the Kinges handes, which raised the exchainge to xxiii *s.* iv *d.* And by thes meanes I did nott only bringe the Kinges majestie, your brother, outt off deptt, wherby I savide hime vi or vii *s.* upon the pounde, but savid his tresore within the reallme, as ther in Mr. Secretary Sissile was most privie unto.

Thirdly, I didd likewise cause all forraine quoynes to bee unvalewed, wherby itt might be brought into the minte to his Majesties most fordlle; att which time the kinge your brother dyed, and for my rewarde of servize, the Bishoppe of Winchester sought to undoe me, and whatsoever I sayd in thes matters I should not be creditted; and againste all wisdome, the sayd bishoppe went and vallewid the French crowne at vi *s.* iv *d.*, and the pistolett at vi *s.* ii *d.*, and the silver rialle at vi *d.* *Ob.* Wheruppon, imediattlye, the exchange fell to xx *s.* vi *d.* and xxi *s.*, and ther hath kept ever sithence. And so consequently aftire this ratte and manor, I brought the quenes majestie your sister out of debtt of the some of ccccxxxv^m *l.*

Fowerthlye, by this itt maye playnely appear to your hightnes,

as the exchainge is the thinge that eatts ought all princes, to the
wholl destruction of ther comon well, if itt be nott substantially loked
unto; so likewise the exchainge is the cheffest and richist thinge only
above all other, to restore your Majestie and your reallme to fine
gowld and sillvar, and is the meane thatt makes all forraine comodit-
ties and your owne comodites with all kinde of vittalles good cheapp,
and likewise kepps your fine golde and sillvar with in your reallme.
As, for exsample to your hightnes, the exchainge beinge att this
present att xxii s., all marchantes seeckes to bringe into your reallme
fine gollde and silver; for if hee should deliver itt by exchainge, he
disbursis xxii s. Flemishe to have xx s. sterlinge: and to bringe itt
in gowlde and sillver he shall make theroff xxi s. ivd., wherby he
saves viii d. in the pounde: which proffitte, if the exchainge showlde
kepp but after this ratte of xxii s., in a fewe years you showld have
a welthi reallme, for her the treasur showld continew for ever; for
thatt all men showlde finde more profytte by v l. in the hundreth
to deliver itt by exchainge, then to carry itt over in mony. So
consequenttly the higar the exchainge riseth, the mor shall your
Majestie and your reallme and common well florrish, which thinge
is only keppt up by artte and Godes providence; for the quoyne
of this your reallme doeth nott corresponde in finnes nott x s.
the pounde.

Finally, and itt please your majestie to restore this your reallme
into such estatt, as hertofore itt hath bine; first, your hyghtnes hath
non other wayes, butt when time and opertunyty serveth, to bringe
your basse mony into fine of xi ounces fine, and so gowlde after the
ratte.

Secondly, nott to restore the Stillyarde to ther usorpid privel-
idges.

Thirdly, to grantt as fewe licences as you cane.

Fowerthly, to come in as small debtt as you can beyond seays.

Fiftly, to kepp your creditt, and specially with your owne merchants, for it is thaye must stand by youe att all eventes in your
necessity. And thus I shall most hombly beseech your majestie to
exceptt this my partte; wherin I shall from time to time, as opertunity
doeth serve, putt your hyghtnes in rememberance, accordinge to the
trust your Majestie hath repposside in me; becechinge the Lorde to
give me the grace and fortune thatt my servis may allwais bee ex-
ceptable to your hightnes; as knoweth our Lorde, whome preserve

your noble Majestie in health, and longe to raigne over us with increasse of honor.

By your Majesties most homble and faythefull obedientt
subject
Thomas Gresham, Mercer.

The Activities of Thomas Gresham; Gresham to Cecil Suggesting that the Merchant Adventurers Should Be Used To Pay the Queen's Foreign Creditors (March 1, 1559)*

. . . It maye like your honnor to understande, that xxx^m *li.* sterling, aftyr xxiij *s.* iiij *d.*, makyth flemyshe xxxiiij^m viii^c xxxiij *li.* vi *s.* viii *d*; and aftyr xxii *s.*, (as the exchange now goythe in Lombarde Streate), xxxiij^m *li.*: wych ys the halfe of the Quene's Majestie's detts that be owing in Aprill and May next. And for the payment thereof, and for keeping uppe of the Exchange, the Quene's Majestie hathe none other ways and helpe but to use her Merchant adventurers. Wherein I doo right well knowe they will stande very stowte in the matter, by the reason of this new costome; as also for the xx^m *li.* that her Hyghnes doth owe them. Nevertheless, considering how moche yt doth import the Quene's Majestie's credit, of force she must use her Merchants; and for the compassing thereof, her highnes shall have good opportewnity both to bargayn and to bringe them to what price her Majestie and yow shall think most convenient; as the like proof was made in King Edwarde her late brother's time.

First, yt is to be considered that our Inglishe marchaunts have at the least 1 or xl^m cloths and kerseys lying upon their hands, reddy to be shipped; whiche they will begynne to ship, when they shall knowe to what poynte they shall trust for their custome.

Secondly, this matter must be kept secreat, that yt maye not come to the marchaunts knowlege that you do intend to use them; and to laye sure wait when their last daye of shipping shall be, and to understand perfectly at the customer's hands, at the same day,

---

* J.W. Burgon, *The Life and Times of Sir Thomas Gresham*, Vol. I. pp. 257–62.

whether all the cloths and kerseys be entreyed and shipped and water-borne. And being once all water-borne, then to make a stay of all the fleete, that none shall depart till further the Quene's Majestie's pleasure be known.

Thyrdly, that being once done, to comande the customer to bring you in a perfect book of all such cloths, kerseys, cottons, lead, tynne, and all other commodities, and the merchauntes' names; particularly what nomber every man hath shipped, and the just and total sum of the whole shipping. And thereby you shall know the nomber, and who be the great doers.

Forthely, apon the view of the customers' booke, you shall send for my Lord Mayre, Sir Rowlond Hill, Sir William Garrat, Sir William Chester, Mr. Alldyrman Martynne, Mr. Alldyrman Baskefylld, Lyonell Dockat, William Bowrde, Rowland Heywood, Waltyr Marller, Harry Becher, Thomas Ryvet: and to move unto them that, "Whereas you have shipped to the number of A, B, wyche be ready to depart to the mart, so it is that the Quene's Majestie ys indetted in Flandyrs for no small some; for the wyche yow, my Lorde Mayre and the cytty, do stand bownd for the payment thereof. And for that yt shall apere unto you that her highness ys not unmyndful for the payment of the same, hath thought good to use you, (as heretofore King Edward her brother dyd): whereby the Exchange may be kept up and raised, and to inrich this realme of fine gold, here to remain; as likewise we maye have our commodities, and forrayne, at some reasonable prices. Whereby you merchants maye flourish in the commenwell, as heretofore you have done. And for the accomplyshment of the premises, the Quene's Majestie, dowthe requyre at your handes to paye in Flanders xx s. sterling upon every cloth that ys now shipped, after the rate of 25 s. flemysh for the pownd sterling; and her highnes shall paye you here again at double usans. Which sum must be paid in Andwerpe; the one thyrde part the fyrst of May,— and the other thyrde part the last of May."

Upon the utterans hereof, they will grant to nothing, till that they have assembled the Company together. Now, having all their goods in the Quene's power, there ys no doubt but that her Majestie shall bring them to bargayne at such reasonable price as you and the rest of my Lords shall think convenient; wherein you may quallify the price of the Exchange as you shall think most meetest, whereby they may the better willing to serve hereafter; considering how much the Quene's highness is indebted unto them alreddy. Giving your honnor to understand I doo not so much press upon the great price, as I do at this present to bring them to make offer to her highness to serve at some reasonable price.

Finally, you maye not come lower than to have for every pound sterling, xxii *s.* Flemish (for so the Exchange passith at this present). Butt I trust yt will be at 22 *s.* 6 *d.* ere they have fynyshed their shipping. Advertising you, yf the exchange be better in Lombard Street than 22 *s.* in any wise, to make them paye aftyr that rate; or ells they do no service, but for their own lucar and gayen, wiche in no wise I will not have them accustomyd unto at the Quene's Majestie's hands.

To conclude eftsoons, yf you can bringe them to 22 *s.*, and yf the Exchange be better, according as the Exchange goeth to pay there, at the days aforesaid, and here at double usance (which ys two months), it wolle prove a more benyfycyall bargayn to the Quene's Majestie and to this her realme than I will at this present molest you withall; for it will raise the Exchange to a onnest price. As for exsampell: the Exchange in Kinge Edwarde's time (when I beganne this practisse) was but 16 *s.* Dyd I not raise it to 23 *s.*, and paid his whole detts after 20 *s.* and 22 *s.?* Wherby wool fell in price from 26 *s.* 8 *d.* to 16 *s.*, and cloths from lx *li.* a packe to xl and xxxvi *li.* a packe, wythe all other our commodities, and forrayners': whereby a number of clothiers gave over the making of cloths and kerseys. Wherein there was touched no man but the Merchant, for to serve the Prince's turn; which appeared to the face of the world that they were great losers; but to the contrary, in the end, when things were brought to perfection, they were great gainers thereby.

Fifthly, what bargayn soever yow do conclude with the Marchantes, to remember specially that they doo paye their mony in vallewyd money (otherwyse termyd permissyone money); for that the Queene is bounde to pay yt in vallewyd mony; wyche maye not in no wyse be forgotten. For yt may chansse to coste the Queene iii or iiii *li.* apon every hundred pownds, to come by the vallewyd money, soche scarsetty there ys thereof: wyche, in the sales of our commodytes, wolle cost the marchants nothing; for that they may sell their commodytes to pay in permyssione money for the some they shall paye for the Quene, wyche wolle not be xx *s.* permyssion money upon every cloth. Which matter move not to the Merchants until such tyme as you have bargayned and agreed upon the Exchange; that being done, yt maye not be forgotten.

Vaughan's Account of the Kingdom's Debts To the Fuggers and Allied Monetarists (1546)*

Pleaseth it your right honorable lordships to be aduertisyd, how I haue Receyuyd by Nicolas, the Kinges Maiestes post, your lordships letter of the viij of this present, by whiche your honors signyfie at what tymes the same haue appoynted as well the strangers as Englishe marchauntes to make payement of such money as the Fugger shuld haue in this present monethe; bysydes that your honors gave me commaundement at the daye to begyn to make payment to the Fugger and to use therin no mo handes then were usyd in the Recept of the Fuggers money, so as the payment maye be prolonged till suche tyme as I shalbe furnysshed with tyme for the satisfaccion of the debt. For answer wherunto it maye please your right honorable lordeships to vnderstand that for asmuch (like as I lately signyfyed vnto the same) as the merchauntes estrangers haue made theyr money from lyons by exchaunge paiable by the Fugger evyn at the same daye whereat the Kinges maieste debt ys payable unto hym, there ys no Waye to be dyvisyd to haue yt out of his handes to be payd to me, and therfore that money, as it shall not be payde to me, so can yt not occupie any tyme at all, in payment to hym, sith he payeth hym self therwith. I haue in Redy money Receyvid of the Kinges maiestes marchauntes aboutes xxv^m _li_. flem. due by theyr billes payable in June last, in payment wherof I woll drawe out the tyme asmuch as ys possible. And like as I lately signyfied unto your honors, and to Sir William Paget also, all the money that both I now have by me and that also that is exchaunged with the Bonvyc, Bartilmew compaigny, Thomas Cavalcanti and John Gyralde, with that also that ys prolonged with the Fugger and appoynted to be payd by Erasmus Schetz, woll not satisfie thonly debt of the Fugger due in this present month.

There is owing to the Fugger in this month clij^m ciiij^{xx} _li_. flem.

---

* S.P. Hen. VIII., Vol. ccxxiii, f. 101.

Towardes the payment and satisfaccion of the which, together with the prolongacion of lx^m *li*. flem., this following ys thorder that your honors haue taken.

I haue and must Receyve of the Kinges ⎫ xxv^m *li*. flem.
Maiestes marchantes for theyr debt payable ⎬
in June last ⎭

Of theyr debt payable in September next I wryte nothing, bycause I cannot therwith pay the Fugger.

I haue of the marchauntes estrangers pay- ⎱ xlvj^m iiij^c *li*. flem.
able the xx of this month xlvj^m iiij^c *li*. flem. ⎰

I haue to answer the Fugger with for this ⎱ lx^m *li*. flem.
tyme lx^m *li*. flem. by your honours prolonged ⎰
in England.

I haue to answer also the Fugger with ⎫ xx^m *li*. flem.
by your honors order taken with the some of ⎬
Erasmus Schetz. ⎭

Summa totalis clj^m iiij^c *li*. flem.

So wantethe there to paye the hole debt due and owing in this monthe of August   vij^c iiij^{xx} *li*. flem.

Then haue I that I Receyvyd from Mr. Dymok for the sale of corne   m vj^c and one *li*. flem.

I haue also Receyued this daye for the sale of the corne which was lately arrested at Camfyre   c iiij^{xx} and one *li*. flem.

Thus appereth it that, the Fugger being payde, I shall haue on my handes but a small rest at this tyme.

By my lettres lately wrytten to your honors I haue signyfied what other Somes of money the Kinges Maieste oweth, which I shall eftsones signyfie ageyn, to thintent the same maye geve order for the payment therof.

There ys owing to Jeronimo and Mighel ⎫ ix^m *l*. flem.
Dyodacy the v of September next upon thc ⎪
credence of Antony Bonvyc xxx^m Crownes of ⎬
vj *s*. the crown some ⎪

Ther ys also owing to Baldassar Guynygy ⎫ vj^m *l*. flem.
and John Balbany the xv of September next ⎪
vpon the credence of Antony Vivald and Ar- ⎬
rego Salvago xx^m crownes of vj *s*. the crown. ⎭

Ther ys also owing to Bartilmew Com-   vj^m *l*. flem.

paigny the xv of October next by your honors
prolonged 3 months from the xv of July last
to the sayd xv of October next, bysydes thint-
erest for the prolongacion of the sayd some
for 3 monthes

    Ther ys owing to John Carolo the xv of   vj^m *li*. flem.
October next upon the credence of John Gy-
rald prolonged from the xv of Aprell last to
the xv of October next, which ys vi monthes

    Summa of all this debt due in September   xxvij^m *li*. flem.
and October next.

    Towardes the payment of this some your honors have gevyn
order that the Kynges Maiestes marchauntes shall paye the xv of
September next xv^m *li*. sterling, which maketh after the Rate of xxv
s. flem. for the pounde sterling the somme of xviij^m vij^c l. *li*. flem.

    And so wanteth to paye the Kinges   viij^m ij^{c}l. *li*. flem.
Maiestes debt due in September and October
next

And yet do I not se how the Kinges Maiestes marchauntes shalbe
able to paye theyr money in ij monthes after theyr daye, money ys
here so hard to com by.

    It maye please your honors to note that, where there ys owing
to Jeronymo Diodaci the v of September next and to baldassar Guy-
nygi and John Balbani the xv of the September next betwene them xv^m
li. flem., towardes theyr satisfacion the Kynges Maiestes marchauntes
begyn not to paye till the xv of September, who, as I saye, woll not
be able to paye in two monthes after.

    Upon the complaint of some person made to the Lady Regent,
who I thinke fyndyng evyn now a great lack of money emonges the
marchauntes, and specially of the valued gold coyned by themperors
maieste in these partes, her grace hath sent down a charge to this
town to have all the bookes of the brokers of exchaunge in this town
brought foorthe, to thintent a view maye be taken to whose handes
the sayd valued gold hath from tyme to tyme byn payd, vpon view
wherof it ys certeyn that all those marchauntes that haue Receyved
valued gold maye answer how they haue bestowed, payed or other
wyse employed the same. Some marchauntes estrangers heryng of
this, which haue byn conveyers of valued gold out of these partes,
are fledd, and many ar like to be in great trowble therfore. Truthe

yt ys, like as I lately signyfied to your honors, that all nacions here, feoryng thissue of these warres presently in hande betwene themperors maieste and the protestantes, in which they se a more perell towardes themperor then they dare eyther saye or reporte, haue made a waye theyr money out of these contreys, some to Lyons, some to Italy, some to Venyce, some to Englond, and some otherwayse. Now (as I gesse) Jasper Dowche, who hath alwayse had charge to furnysshe themporors maieste of money in this town, appercyving a great want and lacke of money, and that he fyndeth not men willing in this daungerous warre of themperor to emprunpt money to themperors Maieste, seyng he hath alwayse bosted to the quene that he wold alwayse fynde meanes that themperor should never want money emonges the marchauntes of the burse, and appercyveth that now he ys not able to kepe towch with themperor, for his fayned excuse peraduentur enfourmeth the quene her grace that English marchauntes and others haue conveyed out of these partes the most parte of all the valued gold that was to be founde here. Vpon which he hath cawsyd the quene to geve order and charge here to haue the brokers of exchaunges bookes seen, by sight whereof many men ar like to be trowbled; for, as I also signyfied to your honors, this town was full of Angell nobles, which brought a great suspicion that men had conveyed much valued gold into England and conveyed hether ageyn Angell nobles. This hath byn told the quene, and vpon that I feared leste her grace wold eyther forbyd the paying and Receyving of Angelles and English crownes, orelles upon great paynes call down theyr pryses, which yet I loke for. And this was the cawse why long before I Refusyd to take Angelles or crownes of the Rose of the Kinges Maiestes merchauntes, lest when I had them I shuld not paye them out ageyn. I toke in the begynnyng aboutes vj or viij^c li. flemish in Angelles and crownes of the Rose, which I doubt much I shall not be able to paye out ageyne, and other money ys there not almost to be had here; no man woll here paye any other money to thenglish merchantes, and they ageyn refuse to take them of English men ageyn.

Of the Fuggers new obligacions for the prolongacion of lx^m li. flem., your honors wryte nothing where they be becom; bycause your honors wrott that I shuld Receyve them I lokyd to haue had them by the xv of this month, but bycause they com not I am dryven to think your honours haue dylyueryd them to the Fuggers factor in london, or to some other body. Yt maye please your right honorable lordshipes to lett me know thereof for the having out of the Fuggers handes of thold obligacions. . . .

Your lordships humble and bounden
Vaughan

To the right honorable lordes, my lordes of the Kinges Maiestes most honorable Cownsail.

Vaughan to the counsail xij August 1546.

A Byll Against Usury (5 and 6 Edward VI. c. 20, 1552)*

Where in the xxxvij yere of the Reigne of the late King of famous memorye King Henry theight, father to our Soveraigne Lorde the King that now is, amongest other Actes and Statutes then made, it was enacted by auctoritye of Parlament that no parsone or parsons, at anny tyme after the last daye of January in the saide xxxvij yere, sholde have, receive, accept or take in lucre or gaynes, for the Lone, forbearing or giving daye of payment of anny somme of moneye for one hole yere above the somme of tenne pownde in the hundred, and so after that rate and not above of and for a more or lesse somme or for a longer or shorter tyme, uppon the paynes and forfaitures in the saide Acte mentyoned and conteyned; The which Acte was not ment or intended for mayntenaunce and allowaunce of Usurie, as dyvers parsons, blynded with inordinat love of themselfes, have and yet doo mistake the same, but rather was made and intendid against all sortes and kyndes of Usurie as a thing unlawfull, as by the tytle and preamble of the saide Acte it doth playnely appeare, And yet neverthelesse the same was by the saide Act permitted for the avoyding of a more yll and inconvenyence that before that tyme was used and exercysed; But Forasmuche as Usurie is by the worde of God utterly prohibited, as a vyce moste odyous and detestable, as in dyvers places of the hollie Scripture it is evydent to be seen, which thing by no godly teachinges and perswations can syncke in to the hartes of dyvers gredie, uncharitable and couvetous parsons of this Realme, nor yet by anny terrible threatninges of Goddes wrathe and vengeaunce that justly hangeth over this Realme for the great and

---

* Stats. of the Realm, Vol. IV, Pt. I, p. 155.

open Usurie therein dailye used and practysed they will forsake such filthie gayne and lucre, onles some temporall punishment be provyded and ordeyned in that bihalfe: For Reformacion whereof, Be it enacted by thauctoritie of this present Parlament, That from the firste daye of Maye which shalbe in the yere of our Lorde God a thousande fyve hundred fiftie and twoo, the saide Acte and Statute concerning onely Usurie, Lucre or Gaynes of or for the Lone, forbearing or geving dayes of anny somme or sommes of moneye, be utterly abrogate, voyde and repealed.

And furthermore be it enacted by thauctoritye aforesaide, that from and after the saide first daye of Maye next comminge, no parsone or parsons of what Estate, degree, qualitie or condicion so ever he or they be, by anny corrupt, colourable or disceitfull conveyaunce, sleight or engyne, or by anny waye or meane, shall lende, give, sett owte, delyver or forbeare anny somme or sommes of moneye, to anny parsone or parsons, or to anny Corporacion or Bodie Politike, to or for anny manner of Usurie, encreace, lucre, gayne or interest to be had, receyved or hoped for, over and above the somme or sommes so lent, given, sett owt, delyvered or forborne; uppon payne of forfaiture the valewe aswell of the somme or sommes so lent, given, sett owt, delyvered or forborne, as allso of the Usurie, encreace, lucre, gayne or interest thereof, and allso uppon payne of emprysonement of the bodye or bodyes of every such offendour or offendours, and allso to make fyne and rawnsome at the Kinges will and pleasure; the moytie of which forfaiture of the saide vallewe shalbe to the King, and thother moitye to the partie that will sue for the same in anny of the Kinges Courtes of Recorde by actyon of Debte, Bill, Playnte or Informacion, wherin no wager of Lawe, Essoyne or Protectyon shalbe allowed or admitted.

Proclamation to Establish Royal Control of the Exchanges (1576)*

September xxvij Anno xviij Regina Elizabethe.

The Orders appoynted for the gouernment and order of the Eschaunge, that the same maie be vsed and kept according to the

---

* Harl. Mss., No. 38, Art. 29, ff. 228–29.

lawes and statutes of this Realme, which are now ordeyned to be
obserued by the Queenes majestes proclamacion.

First, all Marchauntes, English and Strangers, and all other her
Majestes subiectes are to vnderstand that by the lawes and statutes
of this Realme no man ought to make anie eschaunge or rechaunge
of money, but such as her Majestie shall authorise, or their leeful
deputies, to keepe, make, and answere for such eschaunges and
rechaunges, vpon paines conteyned in the same Statutes.

And to the intent the same maie be vsed for the necessarie vses
of leeful eschaunge and rechaunge in cases requisite, it is att this
present time ordered for the vsage thereof that Edmond Calthrop,
Thomas Maston, of the citie of London, Haberdashers, and John
Wanton of the same citie, Grocer, men well acquainted with the
manner of eschaunges and rechaunges from and to the Citie of London and to and from forraigne partes, shall and maie make and giue
sufficient warrant to all persons for eschaunge and reeschaunge, in
such sort as shalbe agreable to the obseruacion of the lawes for
that purpose ordeyned. And therefore from henceforth all billes of
eschange or rechaunge endorsed or subscribed with the name and
handwriting of them, or anie one of them, shalbe sufficient warrant
both for the deliuerer and taker. And whensoeuer anie others shalbe
appointed to occupie and exercise the same roomes, for the keeping
of the same eschaunge, there shalbe thereof from time to time notice
publiquelie giuen in places thereto requisite.

Item, it is to be regarded that none goe about any anie fraudulent
colour or device to alter or to discontinue the auntient manner of
deliuering or taking of money by eschaunge, whereby either the
intention of the lawes provided therefore, or her Majesties prerogative
for her fines and duties answereable for the same, be abused or
defrauded.

Item, though there hath bine alwaies answered in former times
to her Majestes progenitours and to the Masters and Keepers of the
eschaunge from time to time, as by many recordes is very manifest
to be seene, vpon euerie English Noble of the deliuerer one penny,
and the like of the taker, which was vpon euerie pound Sixe pence;
yet for the more ease and lesse burden of such as shall have necessarie
cause to deliuer or take by eschaunge, there shall not be for this
time, nor vntill greater cause shall moue for her Majestes service,

anie more be taken but one farthing of the said Noble or the value thereof for the deliuerer, and one other farthing of the taker, which shalbe vpon the pound but penny halfpenny.

Item, yt is to be considered that the eschaunge and reeschaunge shalbe so ordered, that as neare as possiblie maie be, and as times of trade maie suffer, the moneys of this Realme maie not be deliuered vnder the iust values of their standerd, neither that anie eschaunges of money be vsed but for the vse of knowne Marchauntes, or for such as otherwise by the Queenes Majestes licence, or leefullie by the lawes and vsages of the Realme, haue or hereafter shall haue for their needful businesse to make their eschaunges of the moneys of this Realme for moneys in forraigne places.

Finally, yf there shall hereafter appeare anie further matter needeful to be ordeyned or declared for the better and more perfect vsage of the eschaunge, or for the avoyding or explanyng of anie doubtes that maie aryse, the same shalbe with advise of wise and expert men in the trade of marchandize and of eschange notified in like tables from time to time, to be seene and read in this place.

God Saue the Queene.

The Elizabethans and Industry

The deliberate implementation of the policy approach towards economics which we have documented above led to a period of rapid industrial growth in sixteenth-century England. The following three documents demonstrate how such a programmatic approach was codified into law.

The Statute of Artificers and the Industrial Programme remained on the statute books of the English legal system until their repeal in the first decades of the nineteenth century. By such time, of course, in the wake of the Congress of Vienna settlement of the Napoleonic Wars, England was well on the way to nonmilitary occupation by the House of Rothschild, in their own conception the nineteenth-century reincarnation of the Fuggers.

Under such conditions as then, these statutes represented the most foul kind of slavery and oppression against the English people; restricting movement within the country, providing hideous slave-labor sorts of make-work, including stone breaking and the notorious okum picking, in efforts principally directed at transferring the wage bill of the local landed gentry to the public treasury in order to maintain the representatives of such bucolic idiocy in their rental income.

These kinds of early nineteenth-century slave labor practices for a long time befogged what the original purposes of such Tudor legislation were. In fact, the Tudors conceived no such slave-labor applications at all. Such measures were primarily designed to maintain the real value of the incomes of the general population whether agrarian or urban during a period of rapidly mounting inflation. Their primary parameter was a concern to secure the benefits of real economic growth and to ensure that the population was adequately maintained in order to participate in the process of securing the fruits of such economic growth.

The programs were primarily the work of Elizabeth's Secretary of State William Cecil, who was also Thomas Gresham's political boss. Cecil's principal orientation in the implementation of his program was to secure the introduction of necessary innovations in manufacturing processes to cheapen domestic production for the benefit of the population as a *whole. It was under Cecil's direction that Elizabethan England adopted its early quest to facilitate the introduction of coal-fired industrial processes, to replace charcoal derived from wood which was itself required for ship construction. The third patent concerning the iron and steel industries is exemplary in this regard.*

Such innovative efforts were broad-based, with the nation's naval defense providing the necessary spur to both scientific and technical researches and applications, with backup in the supporting branches of industry such as steel and iron, and so forth.

These Elizabethan efforts in fact were not excelled until well into the industrial revolution, so-called, of the late eighteenth century.

The Statute of Artificers;
An Industrial Programme
(1559)*

Considerations delivered to the Parliament, 1559.

1559, 1. Vagabonds.—That the Statute 1 Edward VI. chap. iii., concerning idle persons and vagabonds being made slaves now repealed be revived with additions.

2. Labourers and Servants.—That the Statutes 12 Richard II., chap. iii., "that no servant or labourer at the end of his term depart out of the hundred or place where he dwells, etc.," and 13 Richard II. chap. viii., ordering the justices at every session to appoint by proclamation the wages of workers, etc., be confirmed, with the addition 'that no man hereafter receive into service any servant without a testimonial from the master he last dwelt with, sealed with a parish seal kept by the constable or church warden, witnessing he left with the free licence of his master, penalty 10 *l.*' So, by the heed of the masters, servants may be reduced to obedience, which shall reduce obedience to the Prince and to God also, by the looseness of the times no other remedy is left but by awe of law to acquaint men with virtue again, whereby the reformation of religion may be brought in credit, with the amendment of manners, the want whereof hath been imputed as a thing grown by the liberty of the Gospel, etc.

---

* Hist. MSS. Com. MSS. of the Marquis of Salisbury, Vol. I, pp. 162–65.

3. Husbandry.—That the Statutes 4 Henry VII. chap. 9, "for re-edifying houses of husbandry and to avoid the decay of towns and villages," and 5 Edward VI. chap. 5, "for maintenance of husbandry and tillage," be put in execution.

4. Purchase of lands.—No husbandman, yeoman, or artificer to purchase above 5 *l.* by the year of inheritance; no clothier, tanner, or common butcher above 10 *l.* a year, save in cities, towns, and boroughs for their better repair; one mansion house only to be purchased over and above the said yearly value. The common purchasing thereof is the ground of dearth of victuals, raising of rents, etc.

5. Merchants.—No merchant to purchase above 50 *l.* a year of inheritance, except aldermen and sheriffs of London who, because they approach to the degree of knighthood, may purchase to the value of 200 *l.*

6. Apprentices.—None to be received apprentice except his father spend 40 *s.* a year of freehold, nor to be apprenticed to a merchant except his father spend 10 *l.* a year of freehold, or be descended from a gentleman or merchant. Through the idleness of those professions so many embrace them that they are only a cloak for vagabonds and thieves, and there is such a decay of husbandry that masters cannot get skilful servants to till the ground without unreasonable wages, etc.

7. Schoolmasters.—None under the degree of baron to keep any schoolmaster in his house to teach children, for it is the decay of the universities and common schools.

8. Education of the nobility.—That an ordinance be made to bind the nobility to bring up their children in learning at some university in England or beyond the sea from the age of 12 to 18 at least; and that one-third of all the free scholarships at the universities be filled by the poorer sort of gentlemen's sons. The wanton bringing up and ignorance of the nobility forces the Prince to advance new men that can serve, which for the most part neither affecting true honour, because the glory thereof descended not to them, nor yet the common wealth (through coveting to be hastily in wealth and honour), forget their duty and old estate and subvert the noble houses to have their rooms themselves, etc.

9. That none study the laws, temporal or civil, except he be immediately descended from a nobleman or gentleman, for they are the entries to rule and government, and generation is the chiefest foundation of inclination.

10. That the statutes 3 Henry IV. chap. 9, and 3 Henry VII. chap. 8, for keeping gold and silver and for increase of the commodities of the realm, ordaining that any merchant stranger bringing in merchandize sell it within three months and employ the money therefor received in England be exchange upon the commodities of the realm, etc.; and the Statute 1 Richard III. chap. 9, that no stranger host or sojourn with a stranger of another country, be revived and executed. The Italians above all other to taken heed of, for they in all times pass to go to and fro everywhere and for themselves serve all princes at once, and with their perfumed gloves and wanton presents, and gold enough to boot if need be, work what they list and lick the fat even from our beards.

11. Haberdasher's wares.—That the Statue 3 Edward IV. chap. 4, ordaining that no merchant, English or stranger, bring into the realm caps, pins, points, dice, gilt stirrups, etc., be revived; for they are not only false and deceitful wares, rather serving for the gaze than any good use, but for such trifles they filch from us the chief and substantial staple wares of the realm, where the people might be better employed in making them, if we will needs have them, and then for our precious commodities we shall receive things of price again.

12. Wines.—That the Statute 40 Edward III. ch. 8, be revived, ordaining that no Englishman fetch or buy any wines in Gascony or France, but have them brought into the realm by Gascons for the profit of the realm. For they are not able to live two years together without making their vent hither, and we are well able to forbear their wines for ever, whereby our fine gold being yearly 100,000 l. at the least which is carried into France by Englishmen shall be kept still within the realm, and we shall rule the price alike of our commodities and their wines, and so make the French King "afeard" to break friendship with us, etc.

13. Stillyard.—That the Queen's Highness in no wise restore to the Stillyard their liberties, for they not only intercepted much of the English merchants' trade, but by concealment of strangers' goods robbed the Queen of customs 10,000 marks a year at least, which was so sweet to them that, as some of them confess, they gained in Queen Mary's time among solicitors above 10,000 l. in bribes.

14. Staple.—That the Staple be removed from Middleburg, where it is now newly erected, into England, as it was removed from Calais into England in the 14th year of Richard II., and

kept in places appointed by the statute 27 Edward III. ch. 1,
which will be for the reparations and maintenance of the havens
and ports of the realm, without the Queen's charge, which now
that Calais is gone is chiefly to be looked to, and also for the
increase of custom. To have it out of the realm is for the profit
of the Staplers and of the Prince where they keep their staple.
But rather than the reformation should come to pass the Staplers
will shrine some solicitors in gold to take upon them to abuse
the Queen. Merchants have grown so cunning in the trade of
corrupting, and found it so sweet, that since the 1 Henry VIII.
there could never be won any good law or order which touched
their liberty or state; but they stayed it, either in the Commons
or higher House of Parliament or else by the Prince himself, with
either *le roy non veut* or *le roi s'advisera*, and if they get the Prince
to be advised they give him leave to forget it altogether.

16. Licences.—That the Queen be pleased after the example
of the law 21 Richard II. ch. 17, to establish that no special
licences be granted to carry out of the realm any staple wares,
victuals, or other commodities; if any hereafter happen to be
granted, the same to be void. The Prince is thereby abused of
his revenue, corruption full fed, the authority and diligence of
Parliament disgraced, etc.

17. Bankrupts.—That bankruptcy be made felony, and bankrupts goods and lands sold and divided among their creditors after
the Statute 34 Henry VIII. ch.—, provided that if all his creditors
join in petition for his pardon he have it allowed for the first time.
Where a poor thief doth steal a sheep, or pick a purse, they come
away with hundreds and thousands at least, and undo a great many
honest men.

18. Perjury.—Perjuries of juries to be punished by attaint as it
was a common law before the Statute.

19. Iron Mills.—That iron mills be banished out of the realm.
Where wood was formerly sold at the stock at 1 *d.* the load, by
reason of the iron mills it is now at 2 *s.* the load. Formerly Spanish
iron was sold for 5 marks the ton, now there are iron mills English
iron is sold at 9 *l.*

20. Sugar.—That no sugar be made within the realm, for it is
counterfeit and unwholesome; and that none be brought into the
realm but pure and simple as it cometh out of the cane. Where before
it was sold for 4 *d.* the lb., it is now at 14 *d.* the lb.

21. Sheriffs.—None to be sheriff of more than one shire at once; his undersheriff to be resident in his house to answer for his defaults, etc.

22. Leather and shoes.—That provision be made for the price of leather and shoes. A pair of shoes within this half year was at 12 *d.* and now at 20 *d.* and 2 *s.* The remedy to be had by calling a convenient number of the most skilful tanners, curriers, and shoe-makers, each sort apart, before the Queen's Council.

23. That the Queen be pleased not to remit any money penalty, after the example of Henry VII., "for thereby he did enrich himself without exacting of his people, kept law and justice in remembrance, and was both loved and feared."

24. Navy.—If any object against the articles aforesaid touching wine and merchandise, that they will decay the navy, it may be answered that England was never in so great wealth and strength both by sea and land as when those laws were observed; there are new navigations since found out, which will alone maintain as great a navy, e.g. those to Guinea, to Barbary, to Muscovy, yea, the navigation into Flanders, Antwerp and Spain, was not then half so much used as now; besides, there may be still a course into France for their woad, salt and canvas, though if the law made for sowing hemp and flax were executed and provision made for growing woad and madder in the realm, as by some men's diligence it is already practised, which growth is here found better than that from beyond the seas, we should not need to seek into France for it. Besides Flanders has enough; no country robbeth England so much as France.

25. Fishing.—Let the old course of fishing be maintained by the straightest observation of fish days, for policy sake; so that sea coasts shall be strong with men and habitations and the fleet flourish more than ever.

"Considerable in Parliament, 1559."

The Statute of Artificers (1563)*

An Acte towching dyvers Orders for Artificers Laborers Servantes of Husbandrye and Apprentises.

---

* Stats. of the Realm, Vol. IV, Pt. I, pp. 414–22 (excerpts).

Althoughe there remayne and stande in force presentlie a greate nombre of Actes and Statutes concernynge the reteynynge departinge wages and orders of Apprentices Servantes and Laborers, aswell in husbandrye as in diuers other Artes Misteries and occupacions, yet partlye for thimperfeccion and contraritie that is founde and doo appere in sondrie of the saide Lawes, and for the varietie and nombre of them, and chieflie for that the wages and allouances lymytted and rated in many of the said statutes are in dyuerse places to small and not answerable to this tyme, respecting thaduancement of pryses of all thinges belonginge to the saide seruantes and laborers, the saide lawes cannot convenyentlie withoute the great greyfe and burden of the poore laborer and hired man, be put in good and due execution: and as the saide severall Actes and Statutes were at the tyme of the makinge of them thought to be very good and beneficiall for the common welthe of this Realme, as dyvers of them yet are, So yf the substaunce of the manny of the saide lawes as are mete to be contynued shalbe digested and reduced into one sole lawe and statute, And in the same an unyforme ordre prescribed and lymyttted concernynge the wages and other ordres for apprentices seruauntes and laborers, their is good hope that it will come to passe that the same lawe, beinge duelie executed, shoulde bannyshe idlenes, avaunce husbandrie, and yelde unto the hyred persone bothe in the tyme of scarcitie and in the tyme of plentie a convenyent proporcion of Wages.

I. Be it therefore enacted . . . That as moche of all the estatutes heretofore made, and every braunche of them as touche or concerne the hyringe kepinge departinge woorckinge wages or ordre of servantes Workemen Artificers apprentices and laborers, or any of them, and the penalties and forfeytures concernyng the same shalbe from and after the last daye of Septembre nexte ensuynge repealed. . . .

II. And be it further enacted . . . that no manner of persone or persones after the foresaide laste daye of Septembre . . . shall reteyne hyre or take into service, or cause to be reteyned hyred or taken into service, nor any persone shalbee reteyned, or hyred, or taken into service, by any meanes or collour to worcke for anny lesse tyme, or terme, then forr one hoole yere in any of the sciences craftes mysterys or arts of clotheires, wollen clothe wevers, tuckers, fullers, Clothworkers, Sheremen, dyers, hosyers, Taylours, shomakers, Tanners, Pewterers, Bakers, Brewers, Glovers, Cutlers, Smythes, Ferroers, Curryers, Sadlers, spurryers, Turners, Cappers, Hatmakers or feltemakers, Bowyers, fletchers, arrowhedmakers, Butchers, Cookes, or Myllers.

III. . . . That every person being unmarryed, and every other person being under thage of thirtie yeres, that after the Feaste of Easter next shall marrye, and havinge bene brought upp in anny of the saide Artes, craftes or sciences, or that hath used or exercysed anny of them by the space of three yeres or more, and not havinge landes, Tenementes, Rentes or Heredyamentes, Copyholde or Freholde, of one estate of inherytaunce, or for terme of anny Lyfe or lyves of the clere value of xl s., nor beinge worth of his owen Goodes the clere value of x poundes, and so allowed by twoo Justices of the peace of the Countie (etc.) . . . nor beinge reteyned with anny person in husbondrie, or in anny of thaforesaide Artes . . . nor llaufullie reteyned in anny other Arte or Science, nor . . . in housholde, or in anny office with anny noble man gentle man or others, accordinge to the lawes of this Realme, nor havinge a convenyent ferme, or other holdinge in tyllage, whereupon he maye employe his Labor, shall, duringe the tyme that he or they shall so be unmarryed, or under the saide Age of xxx yeres, uppon request made by anny person usinge the Arte or mystery, wherin the saide person so required hath beyne exercised as is aforesaide, be reteyned and shall not refuse to serue accordinge to the tenor of this statute, upon the payne and penaltie hereafter mencioned.

IV. . . . That no person which shall retayne anny servaunte shall putt away his or her said seruaunte and that no person reteyned accordinge to this statute shall departe from his Master, Mistress or Dame before the ende of his or her terme, uppon the payne hereafter mencioned, unles it be for some reasonable and sufficient cause or matter to be allowed before twoo Justices of Peace, or one at the least, within the saide Countie or before the mayor or other chief officer of the citie Burrough or towne corporate, wherin the saide Master (etc.) inhabiteth, to whome anny of the parties greved shall complayne, which saide Justice (etc.) shall haue and take uppon them or hym the hearinge and ordringe of the matter, betwixte the saide Master (etc.) and servaunte accordinge to the equitie of the cause. And that no suche Master (etc.) shall putt awaye anny suche servaunte, at thende of his terme, or that anny suche Servaunte shall departe from his Master (etc.) at thend of his terme, withoute one quarter warnynge gyven before thend of his said terme, either by

the saide Master (etc.), or servaunte the one to the other, uppon the
payne hereafter ensuynge.

V. . . . Every person betwene the age of Twelve yeres and the
age of Threescore yeres, not beinge laufullie reteyned, nor apprentice
with any fysherman or maryner haunting the Seas, nor being in
Service with any Kyddyer or Carryer of any corne grayne or meale
for provision of the cltye of London, nor withe any husbondman in
husbondrie, nor in any Citie, Towne Corporate or Market Towne,
in anny of thartes or Sciences . . . appoynted by this Estatute or
haue or take apprentices, nor beinge reteyned by the yere or half
the yere at the leaste, for the diggynge seeking, fyndinge, gettinge,
meltinge, fynynge, workinge, tryinge, makinge of any Syluer, Tynne,
lede, Iron, Coper, Stone, sea coole, stone coole, moore Coole, or
Cherk cole, nor beinge occupied in or aboute the makinge of any
glasse, nor being a gentleman borne, nor being a student or scoller
in any of the universities or in anny scole, nor havinge landes (etc.
as in Section III.) . . . nor having a ffather or mother then lyvyng,
or other Auncestour whose heire apparent he ys, then having lands
(etc.) of the yerely value of x poundes or above, or Goodes or cattelles
of the value of xl poundes, nor beinge a necessarie or convenyent
officer or servaunt laufullie reteyned as is aforesaid, nor havinge a
convenyent ferme, or holdings wherupon he maye or shall employe
his labor, nor being otherwise lawfully reteyned according to the
true meanyng of this Statute, shall . . . by virtue of this estatute, be
compelled to be reteyned to serve in husbandrye by the yere, withe
any person that kepeth husbandrie, and will require anny suche
person so to serve within the same shire wher he shalbee so requyred.

VI. . . . (Penalty on masters unduly dismissing servants, 40 s.;
on servants unduly departing or refusing to serve, imprisonment.)

VII. . . . That none of the saide reteyned persons in husbandrye
or in eny the artes or sciences above remembred, after the tyme of
his reteynor expired, shall departe fourth of one citie towne or parishe
to another, nor oute of the . . . Hundred, nor oute of the Countie
or Shire where he last served, to serve in any other Citie . . . or
Countie, unles he have a testymonyall under the Seale of the saide
citie . . . or of the Constable or constables or other head officer and
of twoo other honest house holders of the Citie Towne or parishe
where he last served declaring his lawfull departure . . ., which
Sertificatt or Testymonyall shalbe wrytten and delyvered unto the

said servaunte and also registred by the Parson Vicar or Curate of
the Parishe where suche Master (etc.) doth or shall dwell. . . .

VIII. . . . Upon the payne that every suche Servante so departing
withoute suche Certificate or Testymonyall shalbe imprysoned untill
he procure a testymonyall . . ., the whiche if he cannot doo within
the space of xxj dayes next after the first daye of his ymprysonment,
then the sayde persone to be whipped and used as a vagabunde
. . .; and that every person reteynyng any suche servaunte withoute
showinge suche testymonyall . . . shall forfaite for every suche of-
fence v *li*. Any yf any such person shalbe taken withe any countrefeyte
or forged Testymonyall, then to be whipped as a Vacabounde.

IX. . . . That all Artificers and laborers being hyred for wages
for the Daye or weeke shall, betwixt the myddest of the monethes
of Marche and September, be and continue at there worke at or
before v of the clock in the mornyng and contynewe at worke and
not Departe untyll betwixt vij and viij of the Cloke at night, except
it be in the tyme of breakefast Dynner or Drincking, the which
tymes at the most shall not excede above ij howers and a half in the
daye, That is to saye at every drynkyng one halfe howre, for his
Dynner one hower, and for his Slepe when he is allowed to slepe,
the which is from the middest of May to the mydest of August, halfe
an houre at the most, and and at every Breakefast one halfe hower;
and all the saide Artificers and laborers betwene the middest of
September and the myddst of Marche, shalbe and contynewe at there
worke from the springe of the daye in the mornynge until the nyght
of the same daye, except it be in tyme afore appoynted for breakefast
and dynner, upon payne to lose and forfeit one penny for every
howers absence, to be deducted . . . oute of his wages that shall so
offende.

X. . . . that every artificer and Laborer . . . shall contynewe and
not departe from the same worke . . . before the fynyshyng of the
said worke, upon payne of ymprysonement by one monethe withoute
bayle . . . and the forfeyture of the somme of fyve powndes to the
partie from whom he shall so departe. . . .

XI. . . . And for the declaracion and lymytacion what wages
servauntes laborers and Artyficers either by the yere or daye or
otherwyse shall have and receyve: Bee it enacted . . . that the Justices
of Peace of every shire . . . within the lymytes of their severall
comyssions, or the more parte of them being then resident within

the same, and the sherife of that countie if he conveniently may, and every mayour, bailyf or other hed officer within any citie . . . wherein is any justice of peace within the lymittes of the said Citie . . . shall before the tenthe day of June next commyng, and afterwarde shall yerely at every general sessions first to be holden and kept after Easter or at some time convenyent within six wekes next followinge every of the said Feastes of Easter, assembel . . . and callinge unto them suche discreate and grave persons of the said Countie or of the said Citie or Towne Corporate as they shall thinke mete, and conferrynge togither respectynge the plentie or scarcity of the tyme and other circumstaunces, necessaryly to be considered, shall have authorytie by vertue herof, within the lymytes and Precinctes of their severall comyssions, to lymyt rate and appoynte the wage as well of Suche and so many of the said Artyficers Handycraftesmen . . . or any other laborer, servante or woorkemen whose wages in tyme past hath bynn by any lawe or statute rated and appoynted, as also the wages of all other laborers . . . which have not been rated, as they . . . shall thinke mete by their discresions to be rated . . . by the yere or by the Daye, Weke, Monethe, or otherwyse, with meate and Drincke or without Meate and Drincke, and what Wages every Workman or laborer shall take by the greate for mowinge, reapinge or thresheinge of corne and grayne, and for mowinge or makinge of heye . . . and for any other kynde of reasonable Laboures or Service: and shall yerely before the xij daye of Iuly next after the said assesse-ment rate so appointed and made, certifie the same . . . with the consideracions and causes therof . . . into the . . . Courte of Chaunc-erey, wheruppon it shalbe lawfull to the lorde chauncellor Englande or Lorde keper . . . upon Declaracion therof to the queenes majestie . . . to cause to be prynted and sent downe, before the first daye of September next after the said Certificat, into every County . . . x or xij Proclamacions or more conteynyng in every of them the severall rates appoynted . . . with commaundement . . . straightly tobserve the same and to all Iustices (etc.) . . . to se the same duelie and severely observed . . .; uppon receyte wherof the saide Shirefes Ius-tices etc. shall cause the same proclamacion to be entred of record . . . and . . . shall fourthewithe in open Markettes upon the market dayes before mychhelmas then ensuynge, cause the same proclama-cion to be proclaymed . . . and to be fixed in some convenient Place . . .; And if the saide shrifes Iustices (etc.) shall at there saide generall

Sessions, or at any tyme after within vj wekes then following . . .
thinke it convenyent to reteyne and kepe for the yere then to come
the rates of Wages that they certefied the yere before or to chaunge
. . . them, . . . they shall before the saide xij day of Iuly yerely
certyfie into the saide Courte of chauncerey theire resoluciones . . .
to thintente that proclamacions may accordingly be renewed and
sent downe; And if yt shall happen that ther be no nede of any . . .
alteracion of the rates . . . then the proclamacions for the yere past
shall remayne in force.

XII. . . . That yf all the said justices . . . doo not . . . assemble
. . . and rate the Wages . . . or be negligent . . . then every Justice
. . . by some credible person assessed and taxed in the Booke of
Subsidie . . . to the clere value of Fyve Poundes at the least, or by
such other person as the most part of such Justices shall allow and
accept to take suche othe, shall for such Negligence forfeite unto
her queenes majestie . . . Tenne Pounds.

XIII. (Penalty for giving wages higher than the rate, ten days
imprisonment and fine of 5 *l.;* for receiving the same, twenty-one
days' imprisonment.)

XIV. (Penalty on servants, etc., assaulting masters, etc., one
years' imprisonment.)

XV. Prouided . . . that in the tyme of hey or corne harvest, the
Iustices of Pease . . . and also the cunstable or other hed officer of
every towneshipe, vpon request and for thavoydinge of the losse of
any corne grayne or heye, shall and may cause all suche artyficers
and persons as be mete to labour . . . to serve by the daye for the
mowinge reapinge . . . inning or corne, grayne and hey . . ., and
that none of the saide persons shall refuse so to do vpon paine to
suffer ymprysonment in the stockes by the space of twoo daies and
one nyght . . .

XVI. . . . all persons of the Counties where they haue accustomed to go into other Shires for Harvest worke and havinge at the
tyme no Harvest worke sufficient in the same towne nor cuntie . . .
bringinge . . . a testimoniall . . . may repayre . . . unto any other
place or countie for the onely mowynge, reapinge, (etc.).

XVII. . . . That twoo Iustices of Pease, the Mayor or other Hed
Officer of any Citie (etc.) and twoo aldermen, or twoo other discrete
burgesses . . . yf there be no aldermen, shall and may by vertue
herof appoynt any suche woman as is of thage of xij yeres and vnder

thage of xl yeres and vnmaryed and furthe of service . . . to be reteyned or serve by the yere or by the weke or day, for suche wages and in such reasonable sorte and maner as they shall thinke mete: And if any suche woman shall refuse so to serve, then it shalbe lawfull for the saide Iustices (etc.) to commyt suche woman to warde untill she shalbe bounden to serve as is aforesaide.

XVIII. And for the better advuncement of Husbondry and till-age, and to thintente that suche as are fyt to be made apprentices to Husbondry may be bounden therevnto . . . That every person beinge an housholder and havinge and usinge halfe a ploughe land at the least in tillage, may have and receyve as an apprentice any person above thage of tenne yeres and under thage of xviij yeres to serve in husbandry untill his Age of xxj yeres at the least, or until thage of xxiiij yeres as the parties can agree . . .

XIX. . . . That every person being an Housholder and xxiiij yeres olde at the least, dwelling . . . in any cytie or towne Corporate, and usinge and exercising any arte mysterye or manuell occupacion there, shall and may after the Feast of St John Baptist next comynge . . . reteyn the sonne of any freman not occupying husbandry nor beinge a laborer and inhabyting in the same or in any other citie or towne . . . incorporate, to serve and be bounde as an apprentice after the Custome and Order of the Citie of Iondon for seven yeres at the least, so as the tearme and yeares of such apprentice Do not expire or determyn afore suche apprentice shalbe of thage of xxiiij yeres at the leaste.

XX. Provided . . . that it shall not be lawfull to any person dwellinge in any Citie or Towne Corporate usinge exercysinge any of the mystereis or craftes of a merchante trapheiquinge by trapheke or trade into any partes beyonde the seae, mercer, draper, goldsmith, ironmonger, Inbroderer or clothear that dothe or shall put clothe to makynge and saile, to take any Apprentice or Servaunte to be en-structed or taughte in any of the artes . . . which they . . . exercise, except such Servaunt or Apprentice be his Son, orels that the Father or Mother of Suche Apprentice or Servaunte shall have . . . landes, tenementes (etc.) of the clere yerely value of xl *s.* of one estate of inheritance or freeholde at the leaste . . .

XXI. . . . That frome and After the said Feast of St John the baptist nexte, yt shalbe Lawfull to every person beynge an housholder and xxiiij yeres Olde at the least, and not occupienge Husbondry,

nor beynge a laborer Dwellinge . . . in any Towne not beynge incor-
porat, that now is or hereafter shalbe A markytt Towne . . ., and
exercysinge any arte mysterye or Manuell Occupacion . . ., to have
in lyke maner to Apprentyes the Childe or Children of any other
artificer . . . not occupienge husbondrye nor beyinge a laborer,
whiche . . . shall Inhabyte . . . in the same or in any other suche
markytt Towne within the same shyre, to serve as Apprentice . . .
as is aforesaid, to any suche Arte (etc.) as hath bene usually exercysed
In any suche markytt Towne where such Apprentice shalbe
bounde. . . .

XXII. Provided . . . that yt shall not be Lawfull to any person
Dwellinge . . . in any suche markytt Towne, exercysinge the feate
mystery or arte of a merchant traphecquinge . . . into the parties
beyond the seaes, Mercer (etc., as in Section XX.) to take any Apprentyce or in any wyse to teache or Instructe Any person in thartes
. . . last before recyted, after the feast of St. John baptist aforesayd,
except suche Servaunte or Apprentice shalbe his son or elles that the
father or mother of suche Apprentice shall have landes (etc.) . . . of
the clere yerely value of three poundes of one estate of inheritance
or freeholde at the least. . . .

XXIII. . . . That frome and after the said feast yt shalbe Lawfull
to any person . . . exercysynge tharte . . . of a Smythe whelwright,
plowewright, mylewright, carpenter, Roughe mayson, playsterer,
sawyer, lymeburner, bryckemaker, bryke layer, Tyler, Slater, helyer,
Tylemaker, lynnen wever, turner, Cowper, Myllers, Earthen potters,
wollenwevers weaving huswyfies or householde clothe only and none
other, Clothe Fuller otherwyse called Tucker or walker, Burner of
Ore and Woade ashes, thatcher or Shingler, wheresoever he or they
shall dwell . . . to have . . . the sonne of any person as
Apprentyce. . . . Albeyt the father or mother of any suche Apprentyce have not any Landes, Tenementes nor hereditamentes.

XXIV. . . . That after the first daye of Maye next commyng yt
shall not be lawfull to any person or persons other then suche as
nowe do Lawfully use or exercyse any arte mystery or manuall Occupacion to sett up occupye use or exercyse any crafte . . . nowe used
or occupyed within the Realme of England or Wales excepte he shall
have bene brought uppe therin Seven yeres at the least as Apprentyce,
in maner and forme abovesaid, nor to sett anye person on worke in
suche . . . Occupacion beinge not a workeman at this day, except

he shall have bene apprentyce as is aforesaid, orels having servyd as an Apprentyce . . . will becomme a Jorneyman or be hyred by the yere : Apon paine that every person willingly offendinge or doynge the contrary shall forfett . . . for every Default x*ls*. for every moneth.

XXV. Provided . . . that no person . . . exercysinge the arte or mystery of a wollen Clothe wever other then suche as be inhabitinge within the counties of cumberlande, westmerlande, lancaster and wales, weavinge Fryzes Cottons or houswyfes clothe only, makinge and weavinge wollen clothe comonly solde or to be solde by any clotherman or clotheor shall . . . have any Apprentyce or shall . . . instructe any person . . . in the Scyence . . . of weaving aforesaid in any village towne or Place, (Cities Townes corporate and market Townes only except) etc. . . . unles suche person bee his Sonne, or els that the father or mother of such apprentyce or servaunte shall . . . have landes (etc.) to the clere yerely value of three poundes at the leaste of an estate of Inheritance or freehold . . . upon paine of forfeyture of xx*s*. for every monethe. . . .

XXVI. . . . That all and every person or persons that shall have Three Apprentices in any of the said craftes . . . of a clothemaker, fuller, shereman, weaver, tailor or shomaker, shall reteyne and kepe one Jorneyman and for every other Apprentyce above the number of the said three Apprentyces one other Jorneyman, upon paine for every defaulte therein tenne pounds.

XXVII. . . . That this act . . . shall not extende to prejudice the companye . . . or worstedmakers . . . of Norwyche. . . .

XXVIII. . . . That yf any person shalbe required by any housholder havinge and usinge halfe a Ploughelande at the least in tillage to be an Apprentyce and to serve in Husbandry as in any other kynde of arte (etc.) before expressed, and shall refusse so to doo, that then upon the Complaynt of suche houskeaper made to one Iustice of peace of the countie wherin the said refusall is or shalbe made, or of such housholder Inhabyting in any Cytty towne corporate or markytt Towne to the mayor and bailiefes or hede officer of the said cytty (etc.) . . . they shall have full poure . . . to sende for the same person so refusing, And yf the said Iustice (etc.) shall thynke the saide person meate . . . to serve as an apprentyce in that arte . . . the said Iustic . . . or hede officer shall have powre . . . to commit him unto Warde, there to remayne untill he be . . . bounden to serve as an apprentise shoulde serve . . .; And yf any suche Master shall mysuse or evill

intreat his apprentyce . . . or thapprentyce do not his deiutie to his
Master, Then the said Master or Prentyce, beyinge grevyd . . . shall
repaire unto one Iustice of peas (etc.) . . . who shall by his wysdome
and dyscreasion take suche order and direction betwene the said Master
and his Apprentyce as thequitie of the cause shall require : and yf for
wante of good conformitie in the said Master the said Iustice (etc.) or
hedd officer cannot compound and Agree the matter betwene hym and
his Apprentyce, then the said Iustice (etc.) or Hedd officer shall take
bande of the said Master to Appere at the next sessyons then to bee
holden in the said Countrie within the said Cytty (etc.) . . ., and uppon
his Apparance and heringe of the matter . . . yf yt be thought mete
unto theme to dyscharge the said Apprentyce of his Apprenticehodd,
That then the said Iustices or fowere of them at the least, wherof one
to be of the quorum, or the said . . . hedd officer, with the consent of
thre other of his Bretherne or Men of beste Reputacion within the said
Cytty (etc.) shall have powre. . . . to pronownce (etc.) that they have
dyscharged the said Apprentyce of his apprenticehode; . . . and yf the
Defaulte shalbe founde to be in the Apprentyce then the said Iustices
etc. or hedd offycer with thassistentes aforesaid, shall cause suche Due
correction and Punishment to be mynestred unto hym, as by their wisdome and dyscreacions shalbe thought mete.

    XXIX. Provided . . . that no person shall be force (etc.) of this
Estatute be bounden to enter into any apprenticeshipe other then
suche as be under thage of xxi yeres.

    XXX. And to thende that this Estatute maye from tyme to tyme
be carefully . . . put in good execusion. . . . Be it enacted . . . that
the Iustices of peas of every countie Devydinge themeselves into
severall lymyttes, and lykewyse every maiar and hed officer of any
cytty or towne corporat, shall yerely betwene the feast of St michell
tharchangell and the nativitee of our lord, and betwene the Feast of
the Annuncyacion of our lady and the feaste of the Nativity of St. John
baptist . . . make a speciall and dyligent inquirie of the Braunches and
articles of this Estatut, and of the good executione of the same, and
where they shall finde any defaultes to see the same severely corrected
and punyshed without favore . . . or dyspleasur.

    XXXI. . . . That every Iustice of peace, Maior and Hedd officer
for every Day that he shall sytte in and Aboutt thexecution of this
Estatut shall have allowed unto hyme fyve shillinges to be (etc.) payde
. . . of the Fynes (etc.) . . . due . . . by force of this Estatut. . . .

XXXII. (Procedure for recovery of penalties.)

XXXIII. Provided . . . that this act . . . shall not be prejuidiciall or hurtfull to the Cytties of London and norwiche or to the lawfull lyberties (etc.) of the same Cytties, for (etc.) the havinge (etc.) of any Apprentice. . . .

XXXIV. (Contracts of apprenticeship contrary to this Act to be void, and a penalty of £10.)

XXXV. (Contracts of apprenticeship to hold good though made while the apprentice is under age.)

XXXVI. (Proviso for the Town of Godalming, Surrey.)

XXXVII. (Application of Penalties in Cities and Towns Corporate.)

XXXVIII. (Proviso for Contracts already made.)

XXXIX. (Servants departing from their masters into other shires to be apprehended and imprisoned until "they shall finde sufficient suretie well and honestlye to serve their master," etc.)

XL. Provided alwayes that it shalbe lawfull to the highe Constables of hundredes in everys here to holde keape and continiwe petye Sessyons otherwise Statute Sessyons within the lymettes of their auctarytes in al sheres wherein suche Sessyons have byn used to be keapte, in such manner and forme as heretofore hathe byn used and accustomed, so as nothinge be by them done therein contrarie or repugnant to this present acte.

A Patent to Make Iron and Steel Using a Coal-Fired Reduction Process (Oct. 9, 1589)*

Elizabeth (etc.) to all to whome it shall apperteyne greetinge.

Whereas wee are crediblye gyven to understande that in many and sundrye places in this our Realme of Englande there bee erected divers and sundrie Mylles for the makinge of Steele and Iron, the which no doubte be of great momente and of no smale benifytt to this our said Realme of Englande yf they may bee used in their righte kinde and Order.

And whereas also many of our trustye and welbeloued subiectes, of a comendable mynde seekinge meanes to woorke publique benifytt

* Lansdowne MSS., No. 59, Art. 73, ff. 196–99b (excerpts).

of this our said realme, haue to their greate costes and charges ende-
vored them selves for the erectinge of the same, and yet contrarye
to their well disposed myndes have encurred the pennaltie of our
lawes and statutes by the fellinge, hewinge and cuttinge downe many
and sundry tymber trees, And in convertinge them to Coale for the
making of Iron and Steele and for the meltinge of Leade, Aswell to
the great hinderance of our shippinge, Thee cheeffest fortresse and
strengthening of this our said Realme, As also to the vtter decay and
distruction of other woodes, wherby our Navye is not onlye lyke To
decaye in contynewaunce of tyme, But also throughe the excessyve
spoylinge and consuminge of Tymber and other woodes for Cole,
the makinge of Iron Steele and Leade shall lykewyse surcease, to
the greate detryment of this our said Realme and the vndoinge of
many our lovinge subiectes.

Knowe yee therfore that wee, of our Princelye mynde and care
that wee haue for the benifytt of our lovinge subiectes and preserva-
cion of this our realme, Forecastinge the greate hurte and Inconvenience that maye befall this our saide realme by the Excessive spoyle
of tymber and other woodes which are converted into Coale for the
makinge of Iron Steele and Leade, And therewithall beinge desyrous
how to prevente and remedye the same, And yet neverthelesse to
mayntayne the makinge of Iron Steele and Leade, Beeinge crediblye
gyven to understande that our faithfull and lovinge subiect Thomas
Proctor of Warssell in the county of Yorke Esquire, havinge spente
muche tyme in the said Arte, Hath by his practise industrye and
indevor to his greate coste and charges Founde out a rare waye and
meanes by vsinge of Earthcoale Seacoale Turffe Peate or some of
them To make as much Iron Steele or leade with one Loade of
woodcoale As hath been hertofore and is now vsuallye maide with
Fower loades of woodcoale, So that by this good and industrius
meanes in every Fower loades of woodcoale There shalbe for ever
heareafter three Loades saved, which, consideringe the greate
quantytie of Iron Steele and Leade that is maide within our saide
realme, Will not onlye bee a marvilous sparinge of woode and tym-
mber in this our sayde realme, Wherbye our Navye may be the better
maynteigned to the inestimable benifytt of our posterytie, But be a
meane also for the contynewance of Iron steele and leade within this
our said realme, which otherwyse (within processe of tyme) for wante
of woodcoale were lyke to decaye.

And consideringe with our selves that everye industrius Act

which shall tende to the benifytt of our Common wealthe is not to
be commended onlye but to be rewarded, And beinge desyrous aswell
to gratyfye the labor and travell, as also to recompence the greate
coste and chardges which our sayde lovinge subiectes hath bestowed
in the findinge out of this secret, And also for the better incour-
agemente of others our lovinge subiectes to imploye their tyme in
like workes commodeous for this our saide Realme, Haue of our
meare mocion, especiall grace, and certen science, gyven leaue and
graunted And by this our present lettres patentes Do gyve leave and
graunte to our trusty and welbeloued subiectes Thomas Proctor and
William Peterson onlye and to their lawfull assigne and Assignes and
everye of them, To effectuate exercyse and vse the said meanes and
way to make Iron steel or Leade By vsinge of Earthcoale Seacoale
Turffe Peate or some of them which to him or them shall seeme for
that purpose most fytt and necessarye, at such tyme and tymes and
in suche place or places within this our said realme as to them or
any of them shall seeme convenient, Duringe the terme of seaven
yeares next and imediatlye insuinge the date of theis presentes, Yeldinge and payinge to vs our heires and Successors duringe the said
tearme of seaven yeares the some of ij *s.* vj *d.* of currant money of
this our saide realme For everye tonn of Iron so hereafter to be
maide, and vj *s.* viij *d.* of lyke currant money for every tonne of
Steele so heareafter to be maide into barres or gaddes, and sixpence
of lyke currant money for every Tonne or foddre of lead so herafter
to be maide in this our said realme By the said Thomas Proctor and
William Peterson or eather of them their assigne or assignes Or any
other person or persons to whome the said Thomas Proctor and
William Peterson or any of them Shall, by vertue of theis our lettres
Patentes, give leaue or lycence to make exercyse vse or effectuate
the same, To be paid yerelye duringe the saide tearme to our Receavor
generall for the tyme beinge of every shyer within this our said realme
wherin the same Iron shalbe so made, Or into the receipt of our
Exchequor yerelye at the feast of St. Mychaell tharchaungell and
thanunciacion of our Ladye or wythin fortye dayes after the same
feastes.

(No person to make iron, steel or lead with sea coal, etc., during
the next seven years without licence of the patentees, on pain of
forfeiture of ten pounds, one half to the Crown and one half to the
patentees, and on pain of such other penalties as may be imposed.)

Provyded alwayes that theis our present letters patentes be not any-
wayes preiudiciall or hurtfull to any person or persons for the making
of Iron steele or Leade by any such vsuall devise or meanes as they
or any of them haue heretofore commonlye vsed, or which they by
their industrie have invented heretofore put vsually in practyse: Any
thinge in theis our lettres patentes conteyned to the contrarye notwithstandinge.

And wheras our said lovinge subiectes Thomas Proctor hath
founde out this secret of makinge of Iron with Seacoale Turffe and
Peate, Tendinge as well to an uniuersall benifytt of our whole realme
in sparing of wood and Timmber, as also to vs in yeldinge in imposi-
cion of vj *s.* viij *d.* the Tonne of Steele And ij *s.* vj *d.* Iron and vj *d.*
Leade, is in theis our present lettres patentes streightted and tyed
to a certaine iust proporcion and rate of three partes at the least of
Seacoale Turffe or Peate And but one parte woodcoale and no more
to be expended about the premisses: Forasmuche as wee are credibly
geven to vnderstande by our said lovinge subiectes that all Seacoale
is not of lyke goodnes nor all Iron stoane of lyke quallytie to bee
cast blowne or wrought, And therfore in some place Iron may be
made very well with Seacoale onlye without any woodcoale at all,
To our greate benefytt, And in some other places cannot be performed
but with a mixture of sea coale turffe or peate and some quantytie
of woodcoale: And further that in divers places of our said realme
vsuall springe wood or fier wood may be very well spared for the
benifytt of the owners, which keepe the same for that purpose onlye:
Our will and pleasure is that in such places only and no other our
said lovinge subiectes, vsinge and takinge the best or most parte of
seacoale Turffe or Peate, shall not be tyed or apporcioned to three
partes of Seacoale Turffe or peate, or in about the premisses, But
shall neverthelesse vse their best and dutyfull endevor in makinge
of Iron as afforesaid; Any thinge herin before conteigned to the
contrarye therof notwithstandinge.

(The patentees to deliver twice yearly a certificate of the number
of tons of iron, steel and lead made, on penalty of ten shillings for
every ton omitted.)

(The patent may be revoked by the Privy Council if at any time
it appear prejudicial.)

Although expresse mencion of the true yerelye value or certayntie
of the premisses or of any of them, or of any other gyftes or grauntes

by vs or any of our progenitors vnto the said Thomas Proctor and William Peterson before this tyme maide, in theis presentes is not maide, or any statute, Act, ordinance, provicion, or restrainte therof to the contrarye maide, had, ordened or provided, or any oth(er th)inge, cawse, or matter whatsoever notwithstandinge. In wytnes wherof wee have caused theis our lettres to be maide patentes. Witnes our selfe, Westminster, the ix day of October in the one and thirty yere of our Raygne.

Per breve de priuato sigillo etc. Powle.

This is a trewe Coppy of the lettres pattentes gravntid to Thomas Proctor and William Peterson. Examined ovt of Mr Petersons lettres pattents fyrst gravnted and ther Orrigenall gravnt, which doth re-mayne in Mr Petersons hande.

Before vs: Ryc. Topclyffe, Gawin Smith, Thomas Proct(or), William Peterson.

A trewe Coppye of the fyrst lettres pattentes gravnted to Mr Thomas Procter and Mr William Petersonn. For making of Iron without spoyle of woode.

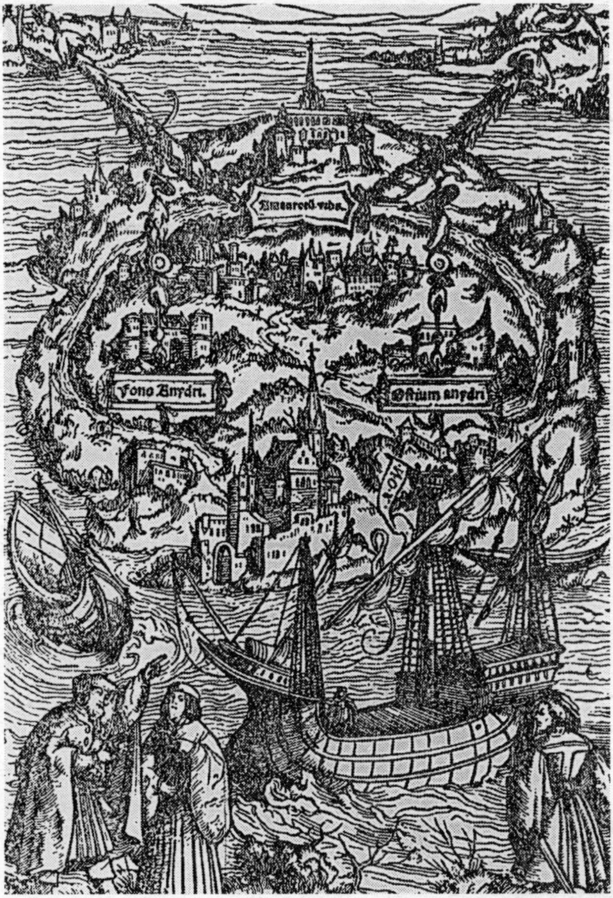

Prints and Photographs Division/Library of Congress

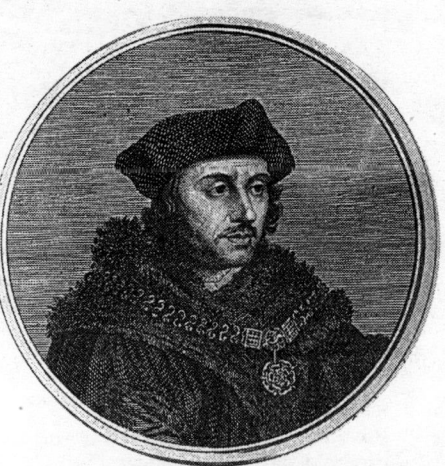

A woodcut depicting Thomas More's fictional island kingdom, Utopia, from a 1518 edition of the famous dialogue.

Prints and Photographs Division/Library of Congress

Sir Thomas More (1478-1535) was a representative of the Golden Renaissance circles in England, who contributed to the founding of the United States.

The English philosopher and economist Adam Smith, shown here as he was depicted in an 1803 edition of his *Wealth of Nations,* was an enemy, not an inspiration, to the infant American republic.

The English philosopher David Hume (1711-1776) represented the school of British empiricism, against which Americans rebelled.

English philospher John Locke (1632-1704) is lyingly portrayed as an inspiration for the American Revolution, but his actual role was to promote slavery and oligarchy.

The universal genius, Gottfried Wilhelm Leibniz
(1646-1716), founded a school of political economy
which inspired the American System of Economics.

The Granger Collection

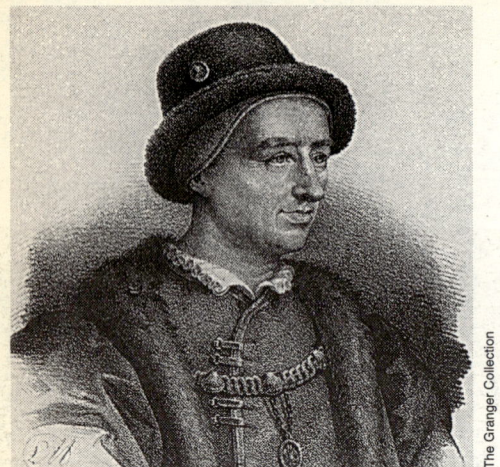

Louis XI, King of France from 1461-1483, shown here in a nineteenth century engraving, established the first sovereign nation-state.

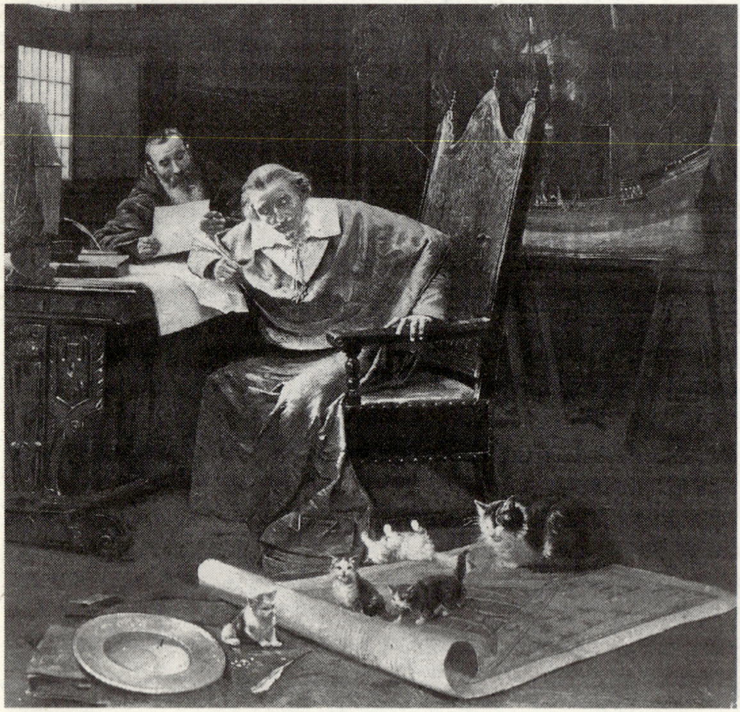

The Bettmann Archive

Cardinal Richelieu (1585-1642), shown here in a painting by Charles DeLort, mediated the tradition of Jean Bodin to Louis XIV's finance minister, Jean Baptiste Colbert.

Jean Baptiste Colbert (1619-1683), finance minister to King Louis XIV of France, is shown here guiding the king on a tour of the French Academy of Sciences. Colbert's Academy subsidized scientists like Leibniz, and Christiaan Huyghens.

Henry VII (1457-1509) promoted nation-building during his reign as King of England.

Elizabeth I (1534-1603) launched an industrial policy during her reign as Queen of England.

Robert Cecil (1563-1612) advised Queen Elizabeth in her industrial policy.

Sir Thomas Gresham (1519-1579) helped lead the fight to free England from the monetarist grip of the Fuggers.

Denis Papin (1647-1712) was part of the Europeanwide circle
of scientists and inventors. Working in correspondence with
Leibniz, he invented the first steam engine.

John Milton (1608-1674), the famous
English poet, played a highly political
role in the Commonwealth period.

Oliver Cromwell (1599-1658) briefly defeated the
British monarchs, but did not establish a successful
industrial republic.

Cromwell's Commonwealth

T he short passages published here from the period of the Commonwealth, and its antecedent Civil War (1641–1660), establish
beyond a shadow of a doubt the crucial difference between Cromwell's effort to establish a durable republican form of government, and
the origins of his efforts in Tudor England.

The effects of the literacy levels developed among the population by
Tudor religious and educational programs, the religious passion so hideously denounced in Thomas Hobbes's account of the war and its aftermath, Behemoth, are nowhere better revealed than in the prose or poetry
of John Milton, who lost his eyesight writing to defend the republican
institutions he so cherished.

Yet, as the Levellers' programmatic approach so eloquently attests,
the seventeenth-century Commonwealth men had not inherited the lessons
in political economy pioneered by their Tudor predecessors. And therein
is located the tragedy of England's brief experiment with political republicanism. The war was won, but could not be translated into similarly
successful policies to safeguard the peace.

From *The Second Defence of the English People* by John Milton (1654)

To these men, whose talents are so splendid, and whose worth has
been so thoroughly tried, you would without doubt do right to commit the protection of our liberties. . . . Then I trust that you will
leave the Church to its own government . . . and no longer suffer
two powers (so different as the civil and the ecclesiastical) . . . by
their mutual and delusive aids in appearance to strengthen, but in
reality to weaken and finally to subvert each other. . . . Then, since
there are often in a state men who have the same itch for making a
multiplicity of laws as some poetasters have for making many verses,

and since laws are usually worse in proportion as they are more numerous, I trust that you will not enact so many new laws as you abrogate old ones which do not operate so much as warnings against evil but rather as impediments in the way of good; and that you will retain only those which are necessary, which do not confound the distinctions of good and evil, and which, while they prevent the frauds of the wicked, do not prohibit the innocent freedoms of the good, which punish crimes without interdicting those things which are lawful, only on account of the abuses to which they may occasionally be exposed. For the intention of laws is to check the commission of vice; but liberty is the best school of virtue, and affords the strongest encouragements to its practice. Then, I trust that you will make a better provision for the education of our youth . . .; that you will prevent the promiscuous instruction of the docile and the indocile, of the idle and the diligent, at the public cost, and reserve the rewards of learning for the learned, and of merit for the meritorious. I trust that you will permit the free discussion of truth without any hazard to the author, or any subjection to the caprice of an individual, which is the best way to make truth flourish and knowledge abound. . . . If there be any one who thinks that this is not liberty enough, he appears to me to be rather inflamed with the lust of ambition, or of anarchy, than with the love of a genuine and well-regulated liberty. . . .

It is of no little consequence, O citizens, by what principles you are governed, either in acquiring liberty or in retaining it when acquired. . . . For who would vindicate your right of unrestrained suffrage, or of choosing what representatives you liked best, merely that you might elect the creatures of your own faction whoever they might be, or him, however small might be his worth, who would give you the most lavish feasts, and enable you to drink to the greatest excess? Thus not wisdom and authority, but turbulence and gluttony, would soon exalt the vilest miscreants from our taverns and our brothels, from our towns and villages, to the rank and dignity of senators. . . . Who could believe that the masters and the patrons of a banditti could be the proper guardians of liberty? . . . Among such persons, who would be willing either to fight for liberty or to encounter the least peril in its defence? It is not agreeable to the nature of things that such persons ever should be free. However much they may brawl about liberty, they are slaves both at home and abroad, but without perceiving it; and when they do perceive it, like unruly horses that are impatient of the bit, they will endeavour to throw off the yoke, not from the love of genuine liberty (which a good man only loves and knows how to obtain), but from the impulses of pride and little passions. But though they often attempt it by arms, they will make no advances to the execution; they may change their masters, but will never be able to get rid of their servitude. . . . Instead of resentment, or thinking that you can lay the blame on anyone but yourselves, know that to be free is the same as to be pious, to be wise, to be temperate and just, to be frugal with your own goods, and abstinent from another's, and, lastly, to be magnanimous and brave; so to be the opposite of all these is the same as to be a slave. . . .

You, therefore, who wish to remain free, either instantly be wise, or as soon as possible cease to be fools; if you think slavery an intolerable evil, learn obedience to right reason and the rule of yourselves; and finally bid adieu to your dissensions, your jealousies, your superstitions, your outrages, your rapine, your lusts. Unless you will spare no pains to effect this, you must be judged, by God, man, and your very deliverers, unfit to be entrusted with the possession of liberty and the administration of the government. . . .

From *The Defence of the English People* by John Milton (1651)

Having proved sufficiently, that the kings of the Jews were subjected to the same laws that the people were; that there are no exceptions made in their favour in scripture; that it is a most false assertion, grounded upon no reason, nor warranted by any authority, to say . . . that God has exempted them from punishment by the people, and reserved thcm to his own tribunal only; let us now consider whether the Gospel preach up any such doctrine, and enjoin that blind obedience which the Law was so far from doing, that it commanded the contrary. Let us consider whether or no the Gospel, that heavenly promulgation, as it were, of Christian liberty, reduce us to a condition of slavery to kings and tyrants, from whose imperious rule even the old Law, that mistress of slavery, discharged the people of God, when it obtained. Your first argument you take from the person of Christ himself. But, alas! who does not know, that he put himself into the condition, not of a subject only, but even of a servant, that we might be free? Nor is this to be understood of some internal liberty only, as opposed to civil liberty; how inconsistent else would that song of his mother's be with the design of his coming into the world: *He hath scattered the proud in the imagination of their heart. He hath put down the mighty from their seat, and hath exalted the humble and meek!* How ill-suited to their occasion would these expressions be, if the coming of Christ rather established and strengthened a tyrannical government, and made a blind subjection the duty of all Christians! He himself having been born, and lived, and died under a tyrannical government, has purchased all due liberty for us. And as he gives us his grace to submit patiently to a condition of slavery, if there be a necessity of it, so if by any honest ways and means we can rid ourselves, and obtain our liberty, he is so far from restraining us, that he encourages us so to do. Hence it is that St. Paul not only of an evangelical, but also of a civil liberty, pronounces (I Cor. 7.21): *Art thou called, being a servant? Care not for it; but if thou mayst be made free, use it rather, you are bought with a price; be not ye servants of men.* So that you are very impertinent in endeavouring to argue us into slavery by the example of our Saviour, who, by submitting to such a condition himself, has confirmed even our civil liberties. He took upon him indeed in our stead the form of a servant, but he always retained his purpose of being a deliverer; and thence it was, that he taught us a quite different notion of the right of kings than this that you endeavour to make good: you, I say, that preach up not kingship, but tyranny, and that in a commonwealth, by enjoining not only a necessary, but a religious subjection to whatever tyrant gets into the chair, whether he come to it by succession or by conquest, or chance, or anyhow. . . . It is evident that our Saviour's principles concerning government were not agreeable to the humour of princes. . . . He asked for the tribute-money. "Whose image and superscription is it?" says he. They tell him it was Caesar's. *Give then to Caesar,* says he, *the things that are Caesar's.* . . . Our liberty is not Caesar's. It is a blessing we have received from God himself. It is what we are born to. To lay this down at Caesar's feet, which we derive not from him, which we are not beholden to him for, were an unworthy action, and a degrading of our very nature. If one should consider attentively the countenance of a man, and inquire after whose image so noble a creature were framed, would not any one that did so presently make answer that he was made after the image of God himself? Being therefore peculiarly God's own, that is, truly free, we are consequently to be subjected to him alone, and cannot, without the greatest sacrilege imaginable, be reduced into a condition of slavery to any man, especially to a wicked, unjust, cruel tyrant. . . . Absolute lordship and Christianity are inconsistent. . . .

On Christian Liberty
by John Milton (1659)*

Many are the ministers of God, and their offices no less many. None more different than state and church government . . .

The main plea (of those who assert the contrary—ed.) is . . . that of the kings of Judah. . . .

But to this I return . . .: that the state of religion under the Gospel is far differing from what it was under the Law. Then was the state of rigour, childhood, bondage, and works; to all which force was not unbefitting. Now is the state of grace, manhood, freedom, and faith; to all which belongs willingness and reason, not force. The Law was then written on tables of stone, and to be performed according to the letter, willingly or unwillingly; the Gospel, our new covenant, upon the heart of every believer, to be interpreted only by the sense of charity and inward persuasion. The Law had no distinct government or governors of church and commonwealth, but the priests and Levites judged in all causes, not ecclesiastical only, but civil (Deut. 17. 8, etc.); which under the Gospel is forbidden to all church ministers, as a thing which Christ their master in his ministry disclaimed (Luke 12. 14), as a thing beneath them (I Cor. 6.4), and by many other statutes, as to them who have a peculiar and far-differing government of their own.

I have shown that the civil power neither hath right nor can do right by forcing religious things. I will now show the wrong it doth by violating the fundamental privilege of the Gospel, the new birthright of every true believer, Christian liberty. 2 Cor. 3. 17: *Where the Spirit of the Lord is, there is liberty. Gal. 4. 26: Jerusalem which is*

---

* excerpts from *Of Civil Power in Ecclesiastical Causes.*

above is free; which is the mother of us all; and 31: *We are not children of the bondwoman, but of the free.* It will be sufficient in this place to say no more of Christian liberty than that it sets us free not only from the bondage of those ceremonies, but also from the forcible imposition of those circumstances, place and time in the worship of God, which though by him commanded in the old Law, yet in respect of that verity and freedom which is evangelical, St. Paul comprehends—both kinds alike, that is to say, both ceremony and circumstance—under one and the same contemptuous name of *weak and beggarly rudiments* (Gal. 4. 3, 9, 10; Col. 2. 8 with 16), conformable to what our Saviour himself taught (John 4. 21, 23): *Neither in this mountain, nor yet at Jerusalem. In spirit and in truth; for the Father seeketh such to worship him.* . . .

They who would seem more knowing, confess that these things are indifferent, but for that very cause by the magistrate may be commanded. As if God of his special grace in the Gospel had to this end freed us from his own commandments in these things, that our freedom should subject us to a more grievous yoke, the commandments of men! As well may the magistrate call that common or unclean which God hath cleansed . . .; as well may he loosen that which God hath straitened or straiten that which God hath loosened, as he may enjoin those things in religion which God hath left free, and lay on that yoke which God hath taken off. For he hath not only given us this gift as a special privilege and excellence of the free Gospel above the servile Law, but strictly also hath commanded us to keep it and enjoy it. Gal. 5. 13: *You are called to liberty.* I Cor. 7. 23: *Be not made the servants of men.* Gal. 5. 1: *Stand fast therefore in the liberty wherewith Christ hath made us free; and be not entangled again with the yoke of bondage.*

Neither is this a mere command, but for the most part in these forecited places, accompanied with the very weightiest and inmost reasons of Christian religion. Rom. 14. 9, 10: *For to this end Christ both died and rose and revived, that he might be Lord both of the dead and living. But why dost thou judge thy brother? etc.* How presumest thou to be his lord, to be whose only Lord, at least in these things, Christ both died and rose and lived again. *We shall all stand before the judgment seat of Christ.* Why then dost thou not only judge, but persecute in these things for which we are to be accountable to the tribunal of Christ only, our Lord and law-giver? I Cor. 7. 23: *Ye are bought with a price: be not made the servants of men.* Some trivial price belike, and for some frivolous pretences paid in their opinion, if— bought and by him redeemed, who is God, from what was once the service of God—we shall be enthralled again and forced by men to what now is but the service of men! Gal. 4. 31, with 5. 1: *We are not children of the bondwoman, etc. Stand fast therefore, etc.* Col. 2. 8: *Beware lest any man spoil you, etc., after the rudiments of the world, and not after Christ.* Solid reasons whereof are continued through the whole chapter. Verse 10: *Ye are complete in him, which is the head of all principality and power.* Not completed therefore, or made the more religious, by those ordinances of civil power from which Christ their head hath discharged us, *blotting out the handwriting of ordinances that was against us, which was contrary to us, and took it out of the way, nailing it to his cross* (verse 14). Blotting out ordinances written by God himself, much more those so boldly written over again by men! Ordinances which were against us, that is, against our frailty, much more those which are against our conscience! *Let no man therefore judge you in respect of, etc.* (verse 16). Gal. 4. 3, *etc.: Even so we, when we were children, were in bondage under the rudiments of the world. But when the fulness of time was come, God sent forth his Son, etc., to redeem them that were under the Law, that we might receive the adoption of sons, etc. Wherefore thou art no more a servant, but a son, etc. But now, etc., how turn ye again to the weak and beggarly rudiments, whereunto ye desire again to be in bondage? Ye observe days, etc.* Hence it plainly appears, that if we be not free, we are not sons, but still servants unadopted; and if we are not free—yea, though willingly, and with a misguided conscience, we desire to be in bondage to them. How much more then, if unwillingly and against our conscience?

Ill was our condition changed from legal to evangelical, and small advantage gotten by the Gospel, if for the spirit of adoption to freedom promised us, we receive again the spirit of bondage to fear; if our fear, which was then servile towards God only, must be now servile in religion towards men. Strange also and preposterous fear, if when and wherein it hath attained by the redemption of our Saviour to be filial only towards God, it must be now servile towards the magistrate. Who, by subjecting us to his punishment in these things, brings back into religion that law of terror and satisfaction belonging now only to civil crimes; and thereby in effect abolishes the Gospel, by establishing again the Law to a far worse yoke of servitude upon us

than before. It will therefore not misbecome the meanest Christian
to put in mind Christian magistrates, and so much the more freely
by how much the more they desire to be thought Christian—for they
will be thereby, as they ought to be in these things, the more our
brethren and the less our lords—that they meddle not rashly with
Christian liberty, the birthright and outward testimony of our adoption; lest while they little think it—nay, think they do God service—
they themselves, like the sons of that bondwoman, be found persecut-
ing them who are freeborn of the Spirit, and by a sacrilege of not
the least aggravation, bereaving them of that sacred liberty which
our Saviour with his own blood purchased for them. . . .

The Levellers' Appeal to Parliament (March 1647)*

But such is our misery, that after the expense of so much precious
time, blood, and treasure, and the ruin of so many thousands of
honest families, in recovering our liberty, we still find the nation
oppressed with grievances of the same destructive nature as formerly,
though under other notions, and which are so much the more grievous
unto us because they are inflicted in the very time of this present
Parliament, under God the hope of the oppressed.

For as then all the men and women in England were made liable
to the summons, attachments, sentences, and imprisonments of the
Lords of the Council-board, so we find by woeful experience, and
the suffering of many particular persons, that the present Lords do
assume and exercise the same power, than which nothing can be
more repugnant and destructive to the Commons' just liberty.

As then the unjust power of the Star Chamber was exercised in
compelling men and women to answer to interrogatories tending to
accuse themselves and others, so is the same now frequently practised
upon divers persons, even your cordial friends, that have been, and
still are, punished for refusing to answer questions against themselves
and nearest relations.

As then the great oppression of the High Commission was most
evident in molesting of godly, peaceable people for nonconformity,

---

* Excerpts from the *Large Petition of the Levellers*.

or different opinion or practice in religion, in judging all who were contrary-minded to themselves to be heretics, sectaries, schismatics, seditious, factious, enemies to the state and the like, and under great penalties forbidding all persons, not licensed by them, to preach or publish the Gospel: even so now at this day, the very same, if not greater, molestations are set on foot and violently prosecuted by the instigation of a clergy no more infallible than the former, to the extreme discouragement and affliction of many thousands of your faithful adherents, who are not satisfied that controversies in religion can be trusted to the compulsive regulation of any, and after the bishops were suppressed did hope never to have seen such a power assumed by any in this nation any more.

And although all new illegal patents are by you abolished, yet the oppressive monopoly of Merchant Adventurers and others do still remain, to the great abridgment of the liberty of the people, and to the extreme prejudice of all such industrious people as do depend on clothing or woolen manufacture (it being the staple commodity of this kingdom and nation), and to the great discouragement and disadvantage of all sorts of tradesmen, seafaring men, and hindrance of shipping and navigation.

Also the old tedious and chargeable way of deciding controversies or suits in law is continued to this day, to the extreme vexation and utter undoing of multitudes of families—a grievance as great and palpable as any in the world. (And) that old and most unequal punishment of malefactors is still continued, whereby men's lives and liberties are liable to the law's corporal pains (as much inflicted for small as for great offences, and that most unjustly) upon the testimony of one witness, contrary both to the Law of God and common equity—a grievance very great, but little regarded.

And also tithes and other enforced maintenance are still continued, though there be no ground for either under the Gospel, and though the same have occasioned multitudes of suits, quarrels, and debates both in former and latter times.

In like manner multitudes of people, poor distressed prisoners for debt, lie still unregarded in a most miserable and woeful condition throughout the land, to the great reproach of this nation.

Likewise, prison-keepers or gaolers are as presumptuous as ever they were both in receiving and detaining of prisoners illegally committed, (and are) as cruel and inhumane to all, especially to such as are well-affected, as oppressive and extorting in their fees, and are attended with under-officers of such vile and unchristian demeanour as is most abominable.

Also thousands of men and women are permitted to live in beggary and wickedness all their life long, and to breed their children to the same idle and vicious course of life; and no effectual means used to reclaim either, or to reduce them to any virtue of industry.

And last, as those who found themselves aggrieved formerly at the burdens and oppressions of those times, that did not conform to the church-government then established, refused to pay ship-money or yield obedience to unjust patents, were reviled and reproached with nicknames of Puritans, heretics, schismatics, sectaries, or were termed factious or seditious, men of turbulent spirits, despisers of government, and disturbers of the public peace: even so it is at this day in all respects with those that show any sensibility of the fore-recited grievances, or move in any manner or measure for remedy thereof; all the reproaches, evils, and mischiefs that can be devised, are thought too few or too little to be laid upon them, as Roundheads, sectaries, Independents, heretics, schismatics, factious, seditious, rebellious, disturbers of the public peace, destroyers of all civil relations and subordinations. Yea, and beyond what was formerly, nonconformity is now judged a sufficient cause to disable any person (though of known fidelity) from bearing any offices of trust in the commonwealth, whiles neuters, malignant and disaffected, are admitted and countenanced. And though it be not now made a crime to mention a Parliament, yet it is little less to mention the supreme power of this honourable House. So that in all these respects this nation remains in a very sad and disconsolate condition, and the more because it is thus with us after so long a session of so powerful and so free a Parliament, and (one that) that been so made and maintained by the abundant love, and liberal effusion of the blood, of the people. And therefore . . . we . . . do most earnestly entreat that you will stir up your affections to a zealous love and tender regard of the people who have chosen and trusted you, that you will seriously consider that the end of your trust was freedom and deliverance from all kind of grievances and oppressions.

1. And that, therefore, in the first place, you will be exceeding careful to preserve your just authority from all prejudices of a negative voice in any person or persons whatsoever, which may disable you

from making that happy return unto the people which they justly expect, and that you will not be induced to lay by your strength till you have satisfied your understandings in the undoubted security of yourselves and of those who have voluntarily and faithfully adhered to you in all your extremities, and until you have secured and settled the commonwealth in settled peace and true freedom, which is the end of the primitive institution of all government.

2. Secondly, that you will take off all sentences, fines, and imprisonments imposed on commoners by any whomsoever, without due course of law or judgment of their equals, and to give due reparations to all those who have been so injuriously dealt withal, and for preventing the like for the time to come, that you will enact all such arbitrary proceedings to be capital crimes.

3. Thirdly, that you permit no authority whatsoever to compel any person or persons to answer to any questions against themselves or nearest relations, except in cases of private interest between party and party in a legal way, and to release such as suffer by imprisonment or otherwise, for refusing to answer to such interrogatories.

4. Fourthly, that all statutes, oaths, and covenants may be repealed so far as they tend, or may be construed, to the molestation and ensnaring of religious, peaceable, and well-affected people, for non-conformity or difference of opinion or practice in religion.

5. Fifthly, that no man for preaching or publishing his opinion in religion in a peaceable way, may be punished or persecuted as heretical, by judges that are not infallible but may be mistaken as well as other men in their judgments, lest upon pretence of suppressing errors, sects, or schisms, the most necessary truths, and sincere professions thereof, may be suppressed, as upon the like pretence it hath been in all ages.

6. Sixthly, that you will for the encouragement of industrious people, dissolve that oppressive company of Merchant Adventurers, and the like, and prevent all such others by great penalties for ever.

7. Seventhly, that you will settle a just, speedy, plain, and unburdensome way for deciding of controversies and suits in law, and reduce all laws to the nearest agreement with Christianity, and publish them in the English tongue, and that all processe(s) and proceedings therein may be true, and also in English, and in the most usual character of writing without any abbreviation, that each one who can read may the better understand their own affairs, and that the

duties of all judges, officers, and practisers in the law, and of all magistrates and officers in the commonwealth, may be prescribed, their fees limited under strict penalties, and published in print to the knowledge and view of all men; by which just and equitable means this nation shall be for ever freed of an oppression more burdensome and troublesome than all the oppressions hitherto by this Parliament removed.

8. Eighthly, that the life of no person may be taken away (but) under the testimony of two witnesses at least, of honest conversation; and that in an equitable way you will proportion punishment to offences, so that no man's life be taken away, his body punished, nor his estate forfeited, but upon such weighty and considerable causes as justly deserve such punishment; and that all prisoners may have a speedy trial, that they be neither starved nor their families ruined by long and lingering imprisonment; and that imprisonment may be used only for safe custody until time of trial, and not as a punishment for offences.

9. Ninthly, that tithes and all other enforced maintenances may be for ever abolished, and nothing in place thereof imposed, but that all ministers may be paid only by those who voluntarily choose them, and contract with them for their labours.

10. Tenthly, that you will take some speedy and effectual course to relieve all such prisoners for debt as are altogether unable to pay, that they may not perish in prison through the hard-heartedness of their creditors; and that all such who have any estates may be enforced to make payment accordingly, and not shelter themselves in prison to defraud their creditors.

11. Eleventhly, that none may be prison-keepers but such as are of approved honesty; and that they be prohibited under great penalties to receive or detain any person or persons without lawful warrant; that their usage of prisoners may be with gentleness and civility, their fees moderate and certain; and that they may give security for the good behaviour of their under-officers.

12. Twelfthly, that you will provide some powerful means to keep men, women, and children from begging and wickedness, that this nation may be no longer a shame to Christianity therein.

13. Thirteenthly, that you will restrain and discountenance the malice and impudency of impious persons in their reviling and re-proaching the well-affected with the ignominious titles of Round-

heads, factious, seditious, and the like, whereby your real friends have been a long time, and still are, exceedingly wronged, discouraged, and made obnoxious to rude and profane people; and that you will not exclude any of approved fidelity from bearing office of trust in the commonwealth for nonconformity, but rather neuters, and such as manifest disaffection or opposition to common freedom, the admission and continuation of such being the chief cause of all our grievances. . . .

The Free People of England Call On All the Soldiers of the Army (Attributed to John Wildman, Oct. 29, 1647)*

Take heed of crafty politicians and subtle Machiavelians, and be sure to trust to no man's painted words; it being high time now to see actions, yea, and those constantly upright too. If any man (by bringing forth unexpected bitter fruits) hath drawn upon himself a just suspicion, let him justly bear his own blame . . .

One of the surest marks of deceivers is to make fair, long and eloquent speeches, but a trusty or true-hearted man studieth more to do good actions than utter deceitful orations. And one of the surest tokens of confederates in evil is not only, when one of his fellows is vehement, fiery or hot in any of their pursuits, to be patient, cold or moderate, to pacify his partner, and like deceitful lawyers before their clients to qualify matters, but sometimes seem to discord or fall out, and quarrel in counsels, reasonings and debates, and yet nevertheless in the end to agree in evil; which they do purposely to hold upright men in a charitable (though doubtful) opinion, that if such and such a man be not godly and upright, they know not whom in the world to trust, whiles in the meantime under the vizards of great professions, gilded with some religious actions, they both deceive the world and bring their wicked designs and self-interests to pass.

Those of you that use your Thursday General Councils of late

---

* Excerpts.

might have observed so much of this kind of juggling, falsehood, and double dealing, as might have served to some good use at this point of extremity. But truly most that have been there have been deluded, to our great grief, which appeareth by the unreasonable proceedings of that court, as in many things, so especially in their debates about the aforesaid *Case of the Army*, now published and subscribed by you. Wherein though the General was so ingenuous as to move for the public reading thereof, yet the Commissary-General Ireton and Lieutenant-General Cromwell, yea, and most of the court, would and did proceed to censure and judge both it and the authors and promoters thereof, without reading it, and ever since do impudently boast and glory in that their victory. . . .

In the Council they held forth to you the bloody flag of threats and terrors, talked of nothing but faction, dividing principles, anarchy, of hanging, punishing, yea, and impudently maintained that your regiments were abused and the aforesaid *Case* not truly subscribed, and did appoint a Committee *ad terrorem*. And abroad they hold forth the white flag of accomodation and satisfaction, and of minding the same thing which ye mind, and to be flesh of your flesh and bone of your bone, and to invite you to their headquarters, where they hope either to work upon you as they have most lamentably done upon others, even to betray your trust, confound both your understandings and counsels, corrupt your judgments, and blast your actions. And though they should not prevail with you, yet there they keep so great a state and distance that they suppose ye will not dare to make good the things ye have published. . . .

If ye do adventure to go thither, beware that ye be not frighted by the word *anarchy*, unto a love of *monarchy*, which is but the gilded name for *tyranny*; for anarchy had never been so much as once mentioned amongst you had it not been for that wicked end. 'Tis an old threadbare trick of the profane Court and doth amongst discreet men show plainly who is for the Court and against the liberties of the people, who, whensoever they positively insist for their just freedoms, are immediately flapped in the mouths and with these most malignant reproaches: 'Oh, ye are for anarchy. Ye are against all government. Ye are sectaries, seditious persons, troublers both of church and state, and so not worthy to live in a commonwealth. There shall be a speedy course taken both against you and such as you. Away with all such from Parliament-doors and Headquarters!'

And if ye can escape these delusions (as through God's assistance, we trust, ye will), and not be satisfied with half or quarter remedies, or things holding a shadow only of good without the substance, we cannot in the least doubt of your good success, being firmly resolved to stand by you and to live and die with you.

Ye had need to be well armed and fortified against the devices that will be put upon you. Ireton (ye know) hath already scandalized *The Case of the Army* in the General Council. Where, by his own and his confederate's craft and policy, he reigneth as sole master, insomuch as those friends ye have there (which we hope ye will see in due time not to be few) find it to little purpose to show themselves active in opposing him. And as he undertook so hath he answered your *Case;* wherein he showeth himself so full of art and cunning, smooth delusion (being skilled in nothing more), and if ye did not sensibly know the things to be really and experimentally true, which ye have therein expressed and published, 'tis ten to one but he would deceive you.

This is certain. In the House of Commons both he and his father Cromwell do so earnestly and palpably carry on the King's design that your best friends there are amazed thereat, and even ready to weep for grief to see such a sudden and dangerous alteration. And this they do in the name of the whole Army, certifying the House that if they do not make further address to the King, they cannot promise that the Army will stand by them if they should find opposition. And what is this but as much in effect as in the name of the whole Army to threaten the House into a compliance with the King, your most deadly enemy, and who, if things go on thus, will deceive both you and them, yea, and all that act most for him?

To what purpose then should you either debate, confer, or treat with such false sophisters or treacherous deceivers as these, who, like the former courtiers, can always play the hypocrites without any check of conscience? To what end should ye read or spend time to consider what they either write or speak, it being so evident that as they did intend so they proceed to hold you in hand till their work be done?

But if you will show yourselves wise, stop your ears against them. *Resist the devil and he will fly from you.* Hold not parley with them, but proceed with that just work ye have so happily begun, without any more regarding one word they speak. For their con-

sciences being at liberty to say or do anything which may advance
their own ends, they have great advantage against you whose consciences will not permit you to say or do anything but what is just
and true and what ye mean to perform, they having shamefully
proved themselves to be large promisers, thereby to deceive both
you and all the people, but the worst performers that ever lived.

And therefore, certainly, ye have no warrant from God to treat
either with them or their deceitful instruments, who will be speedily
(in great numbers) sent amongst you. But as ye know most of them
for evil, so are ye to avoid them as the most venomous serpents, and
fail not in this your just enterprise to cast yourselves chiefly upon
God in the use of all the knowledge, experience, means, and power,
wherewith he hath furnished you; and secondly upon the poeple,
who will be ready with all their might and strength to assist you
whilst ye are faithful and real for them. Join and be one with them
in heart and hand, with all possible speed, in some substantial and
firm Agreement for just freedom and common right, that this nation
may no longer float upon such wavering, uncertain, and sandy foundations of government, which have been one of the greatest causes
both of all your and our predecessors' miseries. . . .

Your Adjutators, we hear, are esteemed but as a burden to the
chief officers, which we judge to be the reason that all things now
are in such a languishing condition. Our hopes die daily within us,
and we fear ye will too soon give yourselves and us, with our joint
and just cause, into their hands. Ye should have considered that they
a long time staggered before they engaged with you, and certainly
had never engaged but that they saw no other way nor means to shelter
and preserve themselves from the power of Hollis and Stapleton, with
their confederates. . . .

We beseech you, . . . commanders and soldiers that are yet
untainted in your integrity and have not yet bowed your knees to
Baal, that ye will not betray yourselves, your just cause and us, so
unworthily, nor seem to distrust that power and wisdom of God by
which ye have done so great and mighty works, but that now ye will
be bold and courageous for your God and for his people, and for
justice against all ungodliness and unrighteousness of men without
respect of persons.

And before it be too late, deal plainly with Ireton, by whose
cowardly or ambitious policy Cromwell is betrayed into these mischie-

vous practices, and by whose craft the power of your Adjutators is brought to nothing, and by whose dissimulation many of them are corrupted and become treacherous unto you. None but flatterers, tale-bearers, and turn-coats are countenanced by him. Let him know ye know him and hate his courses. Your General Councils, by his imperious carriage, are like unto Star Chambers. A plain man is made an offender for a word.

And if Cromwell instantly repent not and alter his course, let him know also that ye loved and honoured just, honest, sincere, and valiant Cromwell that loved his country and the liberties of the people above his life, yea, and hated the King as a man of blood, but that Cromwell ceasing to be such, he ceaseth to be the object of your love.

And since there is no remedy, ye must begin your work anew. Ye are as ye were at Bury. Ye are no strangers to the way; ye have already made a good beginning, wherein we rejoice. Ye have men amongst you as fit to govern as others to be removed. *And with a word ye can create new officers.* Necessity hath no law, and against it there is no plea. The safety of the people is above all law. And if ye be not very speedy, effectual, and do your work thoroughly, and not by halves as it hath been, ye and we perish inevitably.

What your General is ye best know, but 'tis too late to live by hopes or to run any more hazards. None can deceive you but whom ye trust upon doubtful terms. Beware of the flattery and sophistry of men, bargain with your officers not to court it in fine or gaudy apparel, nor to regard titles, fine fare, or compliments. Those that do are much more liable to temptations than other men. A good conscience is a continual feast, and let your outside testify that ye delight not to be soldiers longer than necessity requires.

Draw yourselves into an exact council, and get amongst you the most judicious and truest lovers of the people ye can find to help you, and let your end be justice without respect of persons, and peace and freedom to all sorts of peaceable people. Establish a free Parliament by expulsion of the usurpers. Free the people from all burdens and oppressions, speedily and without delay. Take an exact account of the public treasure, that public charges may be defrayed by subsidies, tithes abolished, the laws, and proceedings therein, regulated, and free-quarter abandoned.

Let nothing deter you from this, so just and necessary a work.

None will oppose you therein, or so long as ye continue sincere and uncorrupted. For all sorts of people have been abused: kings have abused them, parliaments have abused them, and your chief officers have most grossly deceived the honest party. Be confident none will oppose, and be as confident that thousands and ten thousands are ready and ripe to assist you.

Be strong therefore, our dear true-hearted brethren and fellow Commoners, and be of good courage, and the Lord our God will direct you by his wisdom, who never yet failed you in your greatest extremities. Stay for no farther, look for no other call; for the voice of necessity is the call of God. All other ways for your indemnity are but delusive; and if ye trust to any other under the fairest promises, ye will find yourselves in a snare.

Whom can ye trust, who hath not hitherto deceived you? Trust only to justice; for God is a God of justice, and those that promote the same shall be preserved. Free the Parliament from those incendiaries with all your might. The true and just patriots (yea, all but deceivers) therein, long for your assistance, and, that being effectually done, ye may safely put yourselves and the whole nation upon them both for provision, indemnity, and just liberty. . . .

Sonnet XVI, To the Lord Generall Cromwell by John Milton (May 1652)

Cromwell, our chief of men who through a cloud
Not of warr onely, but detractions rude,
Guided by faith and matchless Fortitude
To peace and truth thy glorious way hast plough'd,
And on the neck of crowned Fortune proud
Hast reard Gods Trophies and his work pursu'd,
While Darwen stream with blood of Scotts imbru'd,
And Dunbarr field resounds thy praises loud,
And Worsters laureat wreath, yet much remaines
To conquer still; peace hath her victories
No less renown'd than warr, new foes arise
Threatening to bind our souls with secular chaines:
Helpe us to save free Conscience from the paw
Of hireling wolves whose Gospell is their maw.

Six Books Of The Commonwealth* by Jean Bodin (1576)

Jean Bodin (1530–96) was one of the earliest founders of the school of national economy, and was the leader of a faction in France known as "les politiques." His influence was worldwide, but was especially seminal on all the great French nation-builders who followed him: King Henri IV (reigned from 1589, until his assassination in 1610), Louis XIV's minister of economics, Jean-Baptiste Colbert (1619–83), and the post-revolution architects of modern France, Gaspard Monge and Lazare Carnot. His most often-quoted polemic was that, contrary to those who believed in land as the source of all wealth, "there is no wealth but men."

In his 1566 work, Historic Method, Bodin resolves the theological "dilemma" posed by the artificial categorization of God as either "omniscient" or "omnipotent," but incapable of both. "It is said that, in creating the world, God would have passed from rest to motion, which would have introduced in him a change, a thing contrary to divine perfection. . . . But God was never in this state of rest: His essence is that of eternal activity . . . which reflects itself in history."

Bodin also rose up against the Venetian-inspired religious wars fomented throughout Europe, but especially France at this time, to call on France's monarch to place himself above the Catholic vs. Protestant strife: "The prince is the sovereign judge; if he takes sides, he becomes no more than a party leader and runs the risk of perishing in the struggle. Without trying to determine which of the religions is the better, let the prince forswear violence." As a result of his writings against religious wars, Bodin was almost killed during the night of the Saint Bartholomew's Massacre in 1572, and had to flee Paris.

Like Leibniz after him, Bodin believed in a harmony of sovereign

* Excerpted.

203

*republics, engaging in mutually beneficial foreign trade, while protecting
domestic manufactures. He invited the French King to tax the export of
raw materials, so that they would remain at the disposal of French
manufacturers, "in order that they might increase their value by being
worked," and to reinvest the result of those taxes in long term, low interest
credit to entrepreneurs, "and thus by this means preventing the financiers
from looting the public."*

Bodin wrote the Six Books of the Commonwealth *in 1576, and
then translated them into Latin himself to make his writings available to
all the scholars of Europe.*

BOOK ONE

I. The Final End of the Well-Ordered Commonwealth

A commonwealth may be defined as the rightly ordered government
of a number of families, and of those things which are their common
concern, by a sovereign power. We must start in this way with a
definition because the final end of any subject must first be understood
before the means of attaining it can profitably be considered, and
the definition indicates what that end is. If then the definition is not
exact and true, all that is deduced from it is valueless. One can, of
course, have an accurate perception of the end, and yet lack the
means to attain it, as has the indifferent archer who sees the bull's-
eye but cannot hit it. With care and attention however he may come
very near it, and provided he uses his best endeavours, he will not
be without honour, even if he cannot find the exact centre of the
target. But the man who does not comprehend the end, and cannot
rightly define his subject, has no hope of finding the means of attaining it, any more than the man who shoots at random into the air
can hope to hit the mark.

Let us consider more particularly the terms of this definition.
We say in the first place *right* ordering to distinguish a commonwealth
from a band of thieves or pirates. With them one should have neither
intercourse, commerce, nor alliance. Care has always been taken in
well-ordered commonwealths not to include robber-chiefs and their
followers in any agreements in which honour is pledged, peace
treated, war declared, offensive or defensive alliances agreed upon,
frontiers defined, or the disputes of princes and sovereign lords

submitted to arbitration, except under the pressure of an absolute necessity. Such desperate occasions however do not come within the bounds of normal conventions. The law has always distinguished robbers and pirates from those who are recognized to be enemies legitimately at war, in that they are members of some commonwealth founded upon that principle of justice that brigands and pirates seek to subvert. For this reason brigands cannot claim that the conventions of war, recognized by all peoples, should be observed in their case, nor are they entitled to those guarantees that the victors normally accord to the vanquished. . . .

It is true that we see brigands living amicably and sociably together, sharing the spoil fairly among themselves. Nevertheless the terms *amity, society, share* cannot properly be used of such associations. They should rather be called *conspiracies, robberies*, and *spoliations*. Such associations lack that which is the true mark of a community, a rightly ordered government in accordance with the laws of nature. This is why the ancients define a commonwealth as a society of men gathered together for the good and happy life. This definition however falls short on the one hand, and goes beyond the mark on the other. It omits the three principal elements of a commonwealth, the family, sovereign power, and that which is of common concern, while the term "happy," as they understood it, is not essential. If it were, the good life would depend on the wind always blowing fair, a conclusion no right-thinking man would agree to. A commonwealth can be well-ordered and yet stricken with poverty, abandoned by its friends, beset by its enemies, and brought low by every sort of misfortune. Cicero saw this happen to the city of Marseilles in Provence, yet he thought it the best-ordered and most civilized city, without exception, of any in the world. On the same showing the commonwealth that is well-situated, wealthy, populous, respected by its allies, feared by its enemies, invincible in war, impregnable, furnished with splendid buildings, and of great reputation, must be considered well-ordered, even if given over to every wickedness and abandoned to vicious habits. But there is surely no more fatal enemy to virtue than worldly success of this sort, fortunate as it is accounted to be, for they are contraries not to be reconciled. Therefore we do not include the term "happy" as an essential term in our definition. We aim higher in our attempt to attain, or at least approximate, to the true image of a rightly ordered government. Not that we intend to describe a purely ideal and unrealizable commonwealth, such as that imagined by Plato, or Thomas More the Chancellor of England. We intend to confine ourselves as far as possible to those political forms that are practicable. We cannot therefore be blamed if we do not succeed in describing the state which is rightly ordered absolutely, any more than the pilot, blown out of his course by a storm, or the doctor defeated by a mortal disease, is to be blamed, provided he has managed his ship or his patient in the right way.

The conditions of true felicity are one and the same for the commonwealth and the individual. The sovereign good of the commonwealth in general, and of each of its citizens in particular lies in the intellective and contemplative virtues, for so wise men have determined. It is generally agreed that the ultimate purpose, and therefore sovereign good, of the individual, consists in the constant contemplation of things human, natural, and divine. If we admit that this is the principal purpose whose fulfilment means a happy life for the individual, we must also conclude that it is the goal and the condition of well-being in the commonwealth too. Men of the world and princes however have never accepted this, each measuring his own particular well-being by the number of his pleasures and satisfactions. Even those who have agreed that the sovereign good of the individual is contemplation, have not always agreed that the good of the individual and good of the commonwealth are identical, and that to be a good man is also to be a good citizen. For this reason there has always been a great variety of laws, customs, and policies attendant on the desires and passions of princes and governors. Since however the wise man is the measure of justice and of truth, and those reputed wise have always agreed that the end of the individual and the end of the commonwealth are one, without distinction of the good man and the good citizen, we also must conclude that contemplation is the end and form of the good to which the government of the commonwealth should be directed.

Aristotle was not always consistent in what he had to say on the subject. At times he compromised with the views of various people, coupling now riches, now power, now health, with virtue, in order to take into account commonly received opinions. But in moments of greatest insight he made contemplation the height of felicity. It may have been similar considerations which prompted Marcus Varro to say that human felicity springs from the union of action and contemplation. To my mind this is so, because whereas the well-being of a simple organism may be simple in character, that of a dual organism, composed of diverse elements, must itself be of a dual nature. The well-being of the body comes from health, strength, vigour, and the beauty of well-proportioned members. The well-being of the active principle of the soul, which is the link between body and soul, consists in the subordination of appetite to reason, in other words, the exercise of the moral virtues. The well-being of the intellective part of the soul lies in the intellectual virtues of prudence, knowledge, and faith. By the first we distinguish good and evil, by the second truth and falsehood, and by the third piety and impiety, and what is to be sought and what avoided. These are the sum of true wisdom, which is the highest felicity attainable in this world.

If one turns from the microcosm to the macrocosm, it follows by parity of argument that the commonwealth should have a territory which is large enough, and sufficiently fertile and well stocked, to feed and clothe its inhabitants. It should have a mild and equable climate, and an adequate supply of good water for health. If the geography of the country is not in itself its best defence, it should have sites capable of fortification against the danger of attack. These are the basic needs which are the first objects of concern in all commonwealths. These secured, one looks for such luxuries as minerals, medicinal plants, and dyes. Offensive weapons must also be provided if one would extend one's frontiers and subjugate the enemy, for the appetites of men being for the most part insatiable, they desire to secure great abundance not only of what is necessary and useful, but of what is pleasant merely, and redundant. But just as one does not think of educating a child until it is grown and capable of instruction, so commonwealths do not concern themselves with the moral and mental sciences, still less with philosophy, till they are amply furnished with all that they regard as necessities. They are contented to cultivate that modest degree of prudence, which is sufficient for the defence of the state against its enemies, the prevention of disorders among its subjects, and the reparation of injuries.

A man of good disposition however who finds himself well provided with the necessities and comforts of life, secure and at peace, turns away from unworthy companions and seeks the society of wise and virtuous men. When he has purged his soul of troubling passions and desires, he is free to give his attention to observing his fellows, and interests himself in the difference that age and temperament makes between them, the causes of the greatness of some and the failure of others, and of the fluctuations of states. From men he turns to the contemplation of nature, and considers the great chain of being, minerals, plants, and animals in their hierarchical order, the forms, qualities, and virtues of all generated things, and their mutual attractions and repulsions. From the world of material things he moves forward to the contemplation of the immaterial world of the heavens, where the splendour, beauty, and power of the stars is manifested in their proud, remote, and majestic movements, comprehending the whole universe in a single harmony. The ecstasy of this vision inspires him with a perpetual longing to penetrate to the first cause and author of this perfect creation. But there he must pause, for the greatness, the power, the wisdom, and goodness of the Supreme Being, being infinite, must for ever remain inscrutable in its essence. By such a progression a wise and thoughtful man reaches the concept of the one infinite and eternal God, and thereby as it were attains the true felicity of mankind.

If such a man is adjudged both wise and happy, so also will be the commonwealth which has many such citizens, even though it be neither large nor rich, for in it the pomps and vanities of proud citizens, given over to pleasure, are contemned. But it must not be assumed from this account that felicity comes from a confusion of many elements. Man is made up of a mortal body and an immortal soul, but his final good pertains to the more noble part of himself . . . For though those activities such as eating and drinking by which life is supported are necessary, no thoughtful man finds in them his sovereign good. The habit of good deeds is of the first importance, for the soul that is not illumined and purified by the moral virtues cannot enjoy the fruits of contemplation. The moral virtues are therefore ordained to the intellectual. Felicity cannot be found in that imperfect state in which there is still some good yet to be realized; that which is less noble is ordained to that which is more noble as its final end, body to spirit, spirit to intellect, appetite to reason, living to right living. Therefore when Varro found felicity in both contemplation and action, he would have done better, in my opinion, to have said that a man has need of both action and contemplation in this life, but that his sovereign good lies in contemplation. Never-theless it is certain that a commonwealth is not rightly ordered which neglects altogether, or even for any length of time, mundane activities such as the administration of justice, the defence of the subject, the provision of the necessary means of subsistence, any more than a man whose soul is so absorbed in contemplation that he forgets to eat and drink can hope to live long. . . .

The same principles hold good for the well-ordered common-wealth. It is ordained to the contemplative virtues as its final end, and those things which are least in order of dignity come first in order of necessity. Those material things necessary to the sustenance and defence of the subject must first be secured. Nevertheless such activities are ordained to moral activities, and moral activities to intellectual, or the contemplation of the noblest subjects within the scope of men's imaginations. . . .

BOOK FIVE

II. How to Prevent those Disorders which spring from Excessive Wealth and Excessive Poverty

The commonest cause of disorders and revolutions in common-wealths has always been the too great wealth of a handful of citizens, and the too great poverty of the rest. The histories are full of occasions on which those who have given all sorts of reasons for their discon-tents have taken the first opportunity that offered of dispoiling the rich of the their possessions . . . For this reason Plato called riches and poverty the two original plagues of the commonwealth, not only because of the misery that hunger occasions, but the shame, and shame is a very evil and dangerous malady. To remedy this condition of things, it has been suggested that there should be an equality of possessions. This suggestion has been strongly supported, and it has been claimed that it would prove a source of peace and amity among subjects, whereas inequality is the source of enmity, faction, hatred, and prejudice. He who has more than another, and is conscious of being richer in possessions, thinks he should also enjoy a greater measure of honour, luxury, pleasure, have more food and more clothes. He thinks he should be looked up to by the poor whom he despises and treads underfoot. The poor, for their part, suffer acute envy and jealously in considering themselves just as worthy or even more worthy of riches, yet oppressed by hunger, poverty, misery, and contempt. Therefore many architects of republics in the ancient world advocated an equal division of property among all subjects. Even within living memory Thomas More, the Chancellor of England, in his *Republic* laid down that a necessary condition of general well-being was that men should enjoy a community of goods, which is not possible where there are private property rights . . . Lycurgus accomplished this at the risk of his life, for after having prohibited the circulation of gold and silver, he made an equal division of all lands . . . The Romans as a people were more equitable and had more understanding of the principles of justice than any other. They often decreed a general remission of debts, sometimes to the amount of one quarter, or one third, sometimes even the whole amount. This was the best and quickest way they found of composing disorders and discontents. . . .

On the other side it can be argued that equality of possessions is subversive of the commonwealth. The surest foundation of a commonwealth is public confidence, for without it neither justice, nor any sort of lasting association is possible. Confidence only arises where promises and legal obligations are honoured. If these obligations are cancelled, contracts annulled, debts abolished, what else can one expect but the total subversion of the state, for none would any longer have any confidence in his fellows . . . But if the inconveniences of such abolitions are obvious, still more unfortunate is the equal division of lands and possessions which are neither rightful inheritances, or justly acquired. In the case of debts, one can make the excuse of usury. But this cannot be alleged against lands legitimately inherited. Such partitions of the goods of another is robbery in the name of equality. Moreover to say that equality is the mother of amity is to abuse the ignorant, for there is no hatred so bitter, or enmity so deadly as that between equals. Jealousy of equals one of another is the source of unrest, disorder, and civil war. On the other hand the poor, the weak, and the unprotected defer to and obey their betters, the rich and the powerful, most willingly, with a view to their assistance, and the advantages they hope will accrue. . . .

Besides, what Lycurgus intended in dividing up property among individuals to preserve equality of heritages in perpetuity was a thing impossible of achievement. He could see for himself that the original equality between individuals was almost immediately upset by the fact that some parents had twelve or fifteen children, and others one or two, or even none at all . . . Some, like Hippodamus the Milesian lawgiver, have tried to solve this difficulty by limiting the citizen body to ten thousand . . . Sir Thomas More, the English Chancellor, thought that no family should consist of less than ten or more than sixteen children, as if he could command nature . . . But one should never be afraid of having too many subjects or too many citizens, for the strength of the commonwealth consists in men. Moreover the greater the multitude of citizens, the greater check there is on factious seditions. For there will be many in an intermediate position between the rich and the poor, the good and the bad, the wise and the foolish. There is nothing more dangerous to the commonwealth than that its subjects should be divided into two factions, with none to mediate between them. This is the normal situation in a small commonwealth of few citizens. Let us therefore reject the schemes of those who wish to introduce equality of property in commonwealths already founded, by taking a man's property from him, instead of securing to each that which belongs to him, for this is the only way of establishing natural justice. Let us also reject the idea of limiting the number of citizens, and conclude that there should be no partition of inheritances except on the foundation of a new commonwealth in a conquered country. In each case the division should be by families and not by individuals, and a certain pre-eminence should be accorded to one particular family, and an order of priority established within each family. . . .

The law of God shows us plainly how matters should be arranged . . . By that law the principle of an exact equality is not sustained, for some are assigned more, some less than others. The tribe of Levi apart, there was an even distribution of lands among the twelve tribes. In the family there was an equal division of property among the younger sons, saving the right of the first-born (to a double portion). He was not allowed even four-fifths or two-thirds, much less the whole of the inheritance. This was for fear that so great a degree of inequality might occasion fratricides, quarrels between the tribes, or conflicts and civil wars between subjects. But in order to maintain this balance between too much or too little, alienation either to living persons, or by will, must not be prohibited, as it is in some places, provided that the provisions of the law of God are observed.

That is to say all alienated inheritances revert to the house or family from which they have been withdrawn after fifty years. In this way those who get into difficulties, and have to sell their heritages in order to provide for the necessities of life, can redeem them any time within fifty years, at which term they will return to them or their heirs. In this way bad managers are not able to dissipate their estates permanently, and the avarice of successful managers is kept in check.

As to the abolition of debts, such a proceeding sets a very bad example, as already said. This is not so much because of the loss to creditors, for this is a matter of little moment by comparison with the public interest. What is more serious is the excuse it affords of violating legitimate agreements, and the encouragement it gives to dissatisfied persons to make trouble, in the hope of promoting a remission of debts. . . .

What is most to be feared is that one of the estates of the commonwealth, and that the weakest and least numerous, should become as rich as all the rest put together. This was once the position of the estate of the clergy. An estate of the commonwealth which numbered only one hundredth part of the subjects, collected tithes of all sorts, and, in defiance of the decrees of the primitive Church, as the popes themselves confessed, secured testamentary bequests of both movables and real estate, duchies, counties, baronies, fiefs, castles, houses in town and country, rents all over the place, and sold or exchanged them, and acquired and pledged the revenues of benefices to use the money for further acquisitions. Moreover all this property was exempt from taxes, imposts, and charges of all sorts. It was in the end found necessary to issue an injunction requiring ecclesiastics to surrender inheritances and real estate left to the Church, within a certain time on pain of confiscation, as was done in England by a statute of King Edward I . . . I am not concerned as to whether this property was employed as it ought to have been. What I do say is that so unequal a distribution was perhaps the cause of the disorders and revolts against the estate of the clergy which broke out over practically all Europe, though all was done under the pretext of religion. But if that pretext had not been to hand, another would have been found, as was the case earlier when attacks were made on the Order of the Temple, and on the Jews. . . .

It would seem however that where the eldest son succeeds of right to the whole estate, as was the rule with the seven thousand

Spartan citizens, the splendour and dignity of ancient families is much better preserved and their decline prevented. This, it is argued, benefits the whole estate of the realm, for it is the more firmly established and more stable for being founded on old-established families as upon great and immovable pillars. The weight of a great building cannot be borne by slender columns, even if they are numerous. In fact it appears that the greatness of the kingdoms of France and Spain is largely due to their noble and illustrious houses, and on their ancient guilds and corporations, which once dismembered would lose their value.

But this argument appears more convincing than it is, except where the state is an aristocracy. What the monarch, especially the despotic or tyrannical monarch, has most to fear, are the noble houses and powerful guilds and corporations. As for the popular state, based as it is upon the principle of equality in all things, how can it allow so great an inequality within families that one inherits all and the rest starve? All the rebellions that vexed Greece and Rome arose out of this circumstance. But in the aristocratic state, where the rulers are in principle not the equals of ordinary folk, the custom of primogeniture is preservative, as it was in the aristocratic state of Sparta. . . .

Gottfried Wilhelm Leibniz

Gottfried Wilhelm Leibniz was one of the universal minds of the late 17th and early 18th century. Best known for his work in philosophy and physics, Leibniz was also a lawyer, statesman, and economist. He worked in numerous German courts, and sought to instill a concept of statecraft that is still applicable in principle today.

The following two excerpts are among the most direct statements of economic principle by Leibniz. Both were written during the period when he was in Paris, working under the sponsorship of Jean-Baptiste Colbert and the court of King Louis XIV.

Taken together with Leibniz's work in physics, these memoranda qualify him as the founder of the school of physical economy, which has been taken up again today by the LaRouche movement.

Both have been translated from the German by John Chambless.

Outline of a Memorandum: On the Establishment of a Society In Germany for the Promotion of The Arts and Sciences (1671)

1. The topics of this memorandum are (1) whether and (2) how to set it up. Although, what we have to say about how to set it up, will serve to show that it is to be set up. To the extent that we think about its nature and characteristics, to that extent we must give an account of examples of its operation and usefulness.

2. If it is asked, whether it is to be set up, the answer is, *yes,* and, indeed, as much for the sake of the founders themselves as for the common good. Those who found it I take to be so constituted that, because of their distinguished position, power, and reputation, they have no need of anything other than a good conscience and immortal glory with those judges who cannot be deceived: God and posterity. Both will, of course, only render their judgment in the future; yet even in this life, for persons of high standing and especially

214

for generous men—who are not pressed by necessity and who pay no heed, out of regard of their conscience and their health, to the pleasures of the body beyond necessity—there is nothing sweeter and nothing which promotes health more than that contentment, that joy, that peace of mind and, in a word, that heaven on earth, which gives a truthful foretaste of the future blessedness now, which is otherwise to be believed and hoped for from God and posterity, and which portrays to the mind in a glimpse, as it were, concentrated in a moment, the fruits of eternity. Thus it may be concluded that such a society is to be founded for the sake of (1) the good conscience and (2) the immortal glory of the founders, and also (3) for the common good. Although the common benefit of such a praiseworthy work, agreeable to both God and men, establishes the merit of the founders, their good conscience as well as their immortal name, is the true and infallible reason. Which is now to be shown, point by point.

3. A good conscience is, as I, so to speak, define it, a joy of the mind because of hope for eternal blessedness. So much, that is, and this is self-evident, as the assurance of that is within human power, if a man does all that is possible, and leaves the rest to the infallible, promised grace of God, who is fundamentally good and at the same time just.

4. Hope is faith concerning the future, exactly as faith is, so to speak, a hope concerning the past. For faith amounts to the hope that the past is truly as we say. But true faith, and true hope are not merely a matter of talk, nor even of mere thought, but of thinking in action, that is, action as if it were true. To believe in God, to place hope in God, is to believe that God loves us and that his love offers to awaken in us a reciprocal love through our Savior and Mediator; and to hope that if we love Him in return with our whole heart, that therefore there will arise an indissolvable friendship, and a true and eternal friendship, that there will follow an inexpressible infinite joy in the life to come.

5. Thus hope and faith are founded on love, and all three on knowledge. Love is a joy of the mind arising out of contemplation of the beauty or excellence of another. All beauty consists in a harmony and proportion; the beauty of minds, or of creatures who possess reason, is a proportion between reason and power, which in this life is also the foundation of the justice, the order, and the merits

and even the form of the Republic, that each may understand of what he is capable, and be capable of as much as he understands. If power is greater than reason, then the one who has that is either a simple sheep (in the case where he does not know how to use his power), or a wolf and a tyrant (in the case where he does not know how to use it well). If reason is greater than power, then he who has that is to be regarded as oppressed. Both are useless, indeed even harmful. If, then, the beauty of the mind lies in the proportionality between reason and power, then the beauty of the complete and infinite mind consists in an infinity of power as well as wisdom, and consequently the love of God, the highest good, consists in the incredible joy which one (even now present, without the beatific vision) draws out of the contemplation of that beauty or proportion which is the infinity of omnipotence and omniscience.

6. Again: Faith, hope, and love are wonderfully strengthened through the knowledge and certainty of the omnipotence and omniscience of God. For because He is the highest wisdom, then it is certain that He is so just and good, and has truly loved us his creatures, that He has done everything possible (that is, as much as the universal harmony of things allows, and which can be done without harm to our free will) in order to assure that we love Him, on which faith rests; but if He is also at the same time the highest power, so it is certain that He is powerful enough to allow those who love Him in return to enjoy His love, that is, to make them eternally happy. Which consideration is the foundation of hope, and if it is taken truly to heart, it alone is enough to make men blissful and to make even misfortune, poverty, persecution, contempt, sickness, torment, and death for them as nothing—indeed, even sweet.

7. But just as faith and hope are not a mere formality, but rather practical thought, which is to act as if it were true (above, Section 4) that God loves us, so is the love of God also not merely formal, but is the will in action: which is, to do everything within our power to make it true and real that we also love Him to the utmost. The reality of love consists in our doing what pleases the beloved. What pleases God is again given by knowledge, in so far as it is within our power. For just as the knowledge that He is omnipotent and omniscient is the reason (above, Section 6) why we are to love Him, so is the knowledge that He knows all and is omnipotent, as much as we can attain to that, the guiding principle according to which we are to really love Him.

8. The knowledge of the Divine Nature is naturally to be derived out of nothing other than the true demonstration of His existence. Such must principally be taken from the fact that it is not possible without Him to furnish a reason (and yet nothing is without a reason) why things which might not exist really do exist; and further, why things which could be confused and chaotic are in such a beautiful, inexpressible harmony. The former establishes that He must be the ultimate reason of things and therefore the highest power; the latter, that He must be the ultimate harmony of things, and thus the greatest wisdom.

9. From this it follows inexorably that charity, the love of God above all, and true contrition, on which the assurance of blessedness depends, is nothing other than that love of the public good and of universal harmony; or rather, on that account, the glory of God and to understand are the same, and how great it is in itself to make greater, for there is no more distinction between universal harmony and the glory of God, than between body and shadow, person and picture, between a direct and reflected ray of light, since the one is what is in fact, the other what is in the soul of him who knows it. For God creates rational creatures for no other reason but that they should serve as a mirror, in which His infinite harmony would be infinitely multiplied in some respects. From which must arise in due course the completed knowledge and love of God, in the beatific vision or the incomprehensible joy which the mirroring, and to a certain degree the concentrating of the infinite beauty in a small point in our souls, must bring with it. And thus, a burning mirror or burning glass is the natural image here.

10. If then the love of God above all, contrition, and eternal beatitude arise from the fact that each comprehends the beauty of God and the universal harmony according to his own rational ability, and reflects it back onto others; and additionally, according to the proportion of his ability, promotes and increases that shining forth in men and other creatures; then it follows from that, that all of those to whom the somewhat sparing nature, in order to shade the world with variety, gave a lesser degree of reason and power, so that they must serve others as instruments and means, do enough if they let themselves be used as instruments for the glory of God and, what is the same thing, for the common good, and for the nourishment, ease of labor, comfort, instruction, and enlightenment of their fellow man, for discovery, research, and improvement of creatures, ac-

cording to the limitations of ability and knowledge. Thus they satisfy their conscience.

11. Those who are provided by God with reason without power are appropriately advisers, just as those to whom power is given, should appropriately pay kind attention, and not throw out good proposals, but should rather consider that someday the good, but scorned adviser, will stand before the omniscient Judge, to their dismay, with reproaches, even if silent, of idleness or sinfulness. On the other hand, the disdained, but intelligent advisers are not to attempt to go beyond advising, but are to consider that God reserves a good plan for a better time, and out of His hidden deliberations has not given them a power equal to their reason, and therefore they should in no way attempt to achieve such, in order to carry out their good advice through prohibited words and deeds and machinations which disturb the state.

12. Those to whom God has given reason and power together in the highest degree, are the heroes whom God has created for the execution of his will, as the principal instruments; but whose invaluable talent, if hidden away, will be extremely difficult for them. The corruption and the putrefaction of the best from excessive idleness is worst of all. It is a crucial point, on which blessedness and mortal justice depends, to properly use one's reason and power for God's glory. Thus, I believe a conscientious man should not accept the Philosopher's Stone—to which is attached that difficult condition, which invariably attaches to all great power—without fear and trembling, so that he may never hear the harsh words, "Be damned with all your wealth!"

13. Now reason and power can be used for the glory of God principally in three sorts of ways, exactly as I can meet a man in three sorts of ways; that is, with good words, good thoughts, and good works, or, as the latter are called among men, kindnesses. With God, it is, firstly, praise and sacrifice, next, hope with faith, and finally, good works or obedience, or effective charity. Charity is better than mere faith, obedience is better than sacrifice, faith is better than the feigned sacrifices and praises of those who honor God only with their lips. Hence, we serve God either as orators and priests, or as natural philosophers, or as moralists and politicians.

14. Consequently, those who worship God with praise and sacrifice are orators and priests (setting aside those who care for souls and sacraments, so that they may thus be of benefit to the souls and

who belong to the third class, and also not to mention that among the ancients, those who were priests were philosophers at the same time, and those who guide public affairs and for many reasons should still rightfully be so regarded). Now, orators are those who serve with words, priests with ceremonies. But this involves a great and glorious work, to proclaim the glory of God, and at the same time to enkindle everyone with love of Him. Thus, that which is so established, one is wont to say is established absolutely for the glory of God, for although all good is directed to the glory of God, this goes to glorify God both visibly and audibly for the common man, because it refers directly to the glory of God with the words in which it consists. Also, that which is so established, will be called generally most excellent and absolutely a good work. And what is dedicated as a means to pleasing sacrifice to God, to preaching and music, the composing of gloriously moving songs of praise (in which the ancient Hebrews and even the pagans so exceeded what we enjoy and do), to decorous ceremonies and church ornaments, to glorious temples and churches (which serve to awaken even greater veneration), if these are well used, then they are without doubt to be considered well constructed. And thus it occurs to me that—with the establishment among the French of an academy or society, created by Cardinal Richelieu for the improvement and elaboration of the French language—that one pious man desired to see instituted among other things in the rules, that each member should be responsible for composing something every year to the praise of God; which, however, I know not why, was not done.

15. And among philosophers, those honor God who discover a new harmony in nature and art, and thus make His omnipotence and wisdom visible. Thus Moses, Job, David and others were accustomed for the most part to take the material for their songs of praise from the natural wonders which God implanted in creation, as much as from that which He had done for the salvation of His people: how He set limits to the sea, arched over the heavens, traveled far above the clouds, sounding His thunder, giving rise to rivers, growing plants, and having the animals find, at the proper time, their nourishment and food.

16. Therefore, it is certain that to the extent that one knows a wonder of nature, just to that extent he possesses in his heart images of the majesty of God, if only he refers them thus back to their original: and for that reason the glorious thoughts of an excellent

man of the *Patris Spee Soc. Ies.* are to be praised, who proposed that one should refer to almost nothing without reflecting as much as possible on the glory of God; far less the glorious wonders with which the creatures silently manifest and praise Him.

17. And therefore, I am of the opinion, that even the great moralists and politicians, who are not, however, naturalists, and who are neither conversant with nor pay attention to the wonders of nature, are missing a great part of the proper awe, the true knowledge and the devout love of God, and thus the perfection of their souls, to the point that their art of knowing and ruling men is not made good through excellent science and good practices. Therefore, no one can praise God with more zeal and greater energy than he who, with his eloquence and poetry, and also in true philosophy, goes beyond the boundaries of common knowledge.

18. Especially are those among men to be esteemed, however, who doubtless stand in the grace of God, who with the good intention of praising the Creator and of being of service to their neighbor, discover a glorious wonder of nature or art—it may only be an experiment, or a well-established harmony, and, as it were, just through that, honor God with perorating and poeticizing; just as empirical scientists are to be esteemed higher than orators or historians, and theorists higher than real poets, because the former conceive certain experiments which agree with nature—the latter only fictions—and conceive of rhyming hypotheses on the basis of experiments, and with that harmony praise the wisdom of God.

19. As often as a new structure is discovered by means of experiment by the now industrious anatomists, or a hitherto unknown function of a long-known structure is conceived by means of hypotheses, just so often will the omnipotence and wisdom of God, as it were, be illuminated with living colors, and a rational man will be moved to an awe of the wisdom, a fear of the power, and to a love of the harmony of both, which is the beauty and goodness of his Creator, far more than he is through a thousand speeches, songs, and, indeed, even sometimes lectures and homilies. Correspondingly, one such discovery can be the material and source of more than a thousand beautiful songs of praise.

20. Therefore, any truth, any experiment or theorem, which is admirable and worthy of consideration, even if no problem could be made of it (which is seldom), even if it were not lucrative but only

luciferous, is, as such, to be considered as a new-found mirror of the beauty of God, and to be esteemed as invaluable and more noble than the costliest diamond, and therefore also, what is used among honorable, God-fearing and rational people to the perfection of nature and the real arts, must be considered for the most holy cause and to the benefaction of the inexhaustible true glory of God.

20a. Which is not even to mention, that most would have a benefit for human life, if our evil institutions, carelessnesses, and distractions did not make all our real and useful discoveries, of which there have been not a few in our century, worthless to us. As thus medicine is hardly improved at all by the newly discovered lacteal and lymphatic vessels, of circulation, and so many other ducts, nor by the light which was kindled by chemistry and thrown onto nature, and the methods of medicine remain in the same bad condition with practioners, who are only greedy for money, as it has always been in the past.

21. For that reason, the third way to seek the glory of God, namely those who serve Him as moralists, as politicians, as those who guide public affairs, is the most perfect, since those not only endeavor to find the radiance of God's glory in nature, but also seek to emulate Him through imitation; and thus seek to honor Him not only through praise and devotion, or with words and thoughts, but also with good works, not only to consider the good He has done, but to sacrifice themselves to Him and offer themselves as an instrument and through that to do more good for society and in particular for the human race, as the best of all visible creatures, in those things which we have the power to effect, and for which we are ordered and created.

22. These are the ones who apply the discovered wonders of nature and art to medicine, to mechanics, to the comfort of life, to materials for work and sustenance of the poor, to keeping people from idleness and vice, to the operation of justice, and to reward and punishment, to preservation of the common peace, to the increase and welfare of the fatherland, to the elimination of times of shortage, disease, and war (insofar as it is in our power and is our responsibility), to the propagation of true religion and fear of God, indeed, to the happiness of the human race; and who endeavor to imitate in their domain what God has done in the world.

23. Such happiness of the human race were possible if a general

agreement and understanding were not to be counted as chimeras, and placed along with More's *Utopia*, Campenella's *Civitate Solis*, and Bacon's *Atlantis*, and in general were not commonly too distant from the most powerful Lord Councillors of the common welfare. Nevertheless, it follows from reason, justice, and conscience that each does in his sphere of activity that by which he may be justified before God and the tribunal of his own conscience. If we are not able to do what we want, then we want what we can do. Perhaps through finding means, which though apparently of no great importance and involving no great costs, yet are for the common good, for the stimulus of the nation, for the support and maintenance of many men, for the glory of God and the discovery of His wonders, great results could be accomplished.

24. Among such means, one of the easiest and most important will be the establishment of a society or academy, well grounded although small at the start. Through that, the natural genius of the Germans will be inspired, according to the examples of all their neighbors, which it is hoped they will excel:

• an increased agreement and closer correspondence of skilled people will be aroused, creating opportunity and arrangements for many excellent and useful thoughts, inventions, and experiments, which are often lost, because now those having them will have the confidence to communicate and then to receive them back again;

• to supply and make useful resources and funds, and other things lacking, on a large scale;

• joining theory and experiment in a happy marriage, the one supplying the deficiencies of the other;

• establish a school of inventors and, as it were, an official laboratory, in which each could readily work out his tests and concepts; discover the kinds and advantages of experiences which increase of themselves not in the least by chance (even if in the beginning there is only a small number);

• indeed, means will be supplied to maintain the nourishment of the people, to establish manufacturing and consequently draw in commerce, and in time to establish workhouses and houses of discipline for the idle and criminal in which to work;

• erect warehouses filled with necessities for emergencies, and even in the future form a safe bank for rentiers who wish to invest their money;

- to enter into companies, enter into negotiations with those formed;
- to encourage the Germans to commerce on the sea, joining up with the Hanseatic cities;
- to improve the schools, furnishing the youth with exercises, languages, and the reality of the sciences before they unfortunately travel, and establish Gentlemen's Schools as well;
- to faciliate the crafts through improvements and tools, through always inexpensive fire and motion;
- to test and be able to work out everything in chemistry and mechanics, to work with glass, to create telescopes, machines, water devices, clocks, lathes, painting studios, presses, paint companies, weaving factories, steel and iron works, and even some quite useful things which, when done in a small way without organization are unfruitful;
- to support private laws in land before all else except for new inventions;
- to get support from high places, to support foundations and organizations for curiosities, to form a theater of nature and the arts or chamber of arts, rarities and anatomy for easy learning of all things not in the now-established herbal and other gardens and libraries;
- to summarize books and manuscripts and posthumous works, to bring together scattered reports, experiments, and letters of correspondence, to have everything in order and indexed;
- to support poor students and at the same time create institutions for their work which will be useful both to them and to society;
- to support impoverished eccentrics who have ruined themselves through extravagance, and merchants, ruined through misfoturne as well, helping both for their own benefit and that of society;
- to support useful people on the land (who only wish to have provisions and materials for their nourishment, who for the most part, when they sense something is wrong in the world, leave the land and go over to foreign rule, much to the harm of themselves and the ruined fatherland, some falling into a life of dissipation, running off to war and destroying themselves or being cut off or removed in their first bloom, when they and others like them could people the land with families and thus be useful); to put them to work; to preserve them from beggary, to nourish them with their

wife and family; to guard them and theirs from sin, disgrace, and ruination of the soul.

On the basis, but without determining a definite time and place, rather everything being undertaken in a leisurely manner, this stratagem must be brought into motion with a small fund and some small advantages.

25. This is the constant, indeed continuous charity, which will grow endlessly and increase of itself and be of benefit to many thousands of men, which is circumscribed by no limit in advance; which will not be like other foundations, with which the continuance, support, and even the goal are not always closely connected with the interests of the members and directors, and thus are subject to abuses; and which will not be easily ruined through war or death or other plagues of the country once it gets started; which is directed to the absolutely real things, to the highest glory of God and to universal approval and eternal benediction and gratitude of posterity, which will come after and will perhaps be able to enjoy it over a long period of time; for that purpose God has given many beautiful circumstances, on which to allow delay would be irresponsible; which God hopefully will bless, indeed, in order to carry out what begins so piously, will reward us with health and long life and, finally, which all rational men most highly wish for, with eternal blessedness for our immortal souls and the prayers and blessings and witnesses of so many souls, who have been taken thereby from misery and ruination and at last can receive a decent wage. And in conclusion, this point: that whoever has the power to do something on this work, should not, for the glory of God and the sake of his own conscience, fail to reflect upon it.

Society and Economy, 1671

Monopoly is avoided, since this Society always desires to give commodities at their fair price, or even more cheaply in many cases, by causing manufactured goods to be produced locally rather than having them imported. It will especially preclude the formation of any monopoly of merchants or a cartel of artisans, along with any excessive accumulation of wealth by the merchants or excessive poverty of the artisans—which is particularly the case in Holland, where the majority of merchants are riding high, whereas the artisans are kept in continual poverty and toil. This is harmful to the republic, since even Aristotle maintains that artisanship ought to be one of the worthiest occupations. *Nam Mercaturs transfert tantum, Manufactura gignit.* [For trade can carry only as much as the factories produce.] And why, indeed, should so many people be poor and miserable for the benefit of such a small handful? After all, is not the entire purpose of Society to release the artisan from his misery? The farmer is not in need, since he is sure of his bread, and the merchant has more than enough. The remaining people are either destitute or government servants. Society can likewise satisfy all the farmer's own needs, providing it always buys from him at a reliably fair price, whether that be cheap or dear. We can thereby ensure for all eternity against natural food shortages, since Society can then have what amounts to a general grain reserve.

Through establishment of such a Society, we eliminate a deep-seated drawback within many republics, which consists in allowing each and all to sustain themselves as they please, allowing one individual to become rich at the expense of a hundred others, or allowing him to collapse, dragging down with him the hundreds who have put themselves under his care. An individual may or may not ruin his own family, and then may or may not run through his own and other's funds.

Objection: Should money be invested in other countries? By no means. Each country shall, on the contrary, supply itself with those necessary commodities and manufactured goods which previously came from abroad, so that it will not have to procure from others what it can have for itself; each country shall be shown how properly to use its own domestic resources. In a country which has sufficient wool, manufacturing shall be established for the preparation of cloth; a country with an abundance of flax shall occupy its populace with the production of clothing; and so forth. And thus no country among those which permit Society the proper degree of freedom, will be favored over the other; rather, each shall be made to flourish in those areas in which God and Nature have allowed it to excel.

Manufacturing, therefore, shall always take place at the commodities' point of origin; whereas commerce, in accordance with its nature, shall be located at the rivers and oceans—an arrangement which only becomes disrupted (manufacturing being placed near commercial centers, far from its raw materials) when the necessary

Society and cohesiveness is lacking in many locations, especially where there are no republics.

A great drawback of many republics and countries is that many places have more scholars (not to mention idle people) than they have artisans. But this Society has something for everyone to do, and it needs its scholars for continual conferences and joyous discoveries. This Society can have others adopt the profession of assuming responsibility for providing for unfortunates—e.g., the confinement of criminals, which is of great benefit to the republic.

One might object that artisans today work out of necessity; if all their needs were satisfied, then they would do no work at all. I, however, maintain the contrary, that they would be glad to do more than they now do out of necessity. For, first of all, if a man is unsure of his sustenance, he has neither the heart nor the spirit for anything; will only produce as much as he expects to sell (which is not very much given his few customers); concerns himself with trivialities; and does not have the heart to undertake anything new and important. He thus earns little, must often drink to excess merely in order to dull his own sense of desperation and drown his sorrows, and is tormented by the malice of his journeymen. But it will be different there: Each will be glad to work, because he knows what he has to do. Never will he be involuntarily idle, as he is now, since no one will work for himself, but rather jointly; and if one has too much and the other not enough, then one will give to the other.

On the other hand, no artisan will be suddenly obliged—as he sometimes is now—to torture himself and his men half to death with excessive work, since the amount of work will always remain more or less the same. The journeymen will work together, joyously vying with one another in the public factories, the masters themselves taking care of the work that requires more understanding. No master need be annoyed that an intelligent journeyman might desire to become a master himself, for how does this harm the master? Journeymen's room, board, and necessities will be provided free to all workers. No master will need to worry about how he is to provide for his children or marry them off respectably. The education of children will be taken care of by Society; parents shall be relieved of the task of educating their own children: All children, while they are small, shall be rigorously brought up by women in public facilities. And scrupulous attention will be paid that they do not become overcrowded, are kept clean, and that no diseases arise. How could anyone live more happily than that? Artisans will work together happily in the company's large rooms, singing and conversing, except for those whose work requires more concentration.

Most of the work will be done in the morning. Pains will be taken to provide for pleasures other than drinking—for example, discussions of their craft and the telling of all sorts of funny stories, whereby they must be provided with something to quench their thirst, such as *acida*. There is no greater pleasure for a thoughtful man, or indeed for any man once he becomes accustomed, than being in a company where pleasant and useful things are being discussed; and thus every group, including the artisans, should have someone to write down any useful remarks that may be made. But the Society's highest rule shall be to foster true love and trustfulness among its members, and not to express anything irritating, scornful, or insulting to others. Indeed, even rulers should eschew all insults unless nothing else is effective, since such behavior precludes the establishment of trust. No man shall be derided for a mistake, even if it be a serious one; rather, he should be gently admonished in a brotherly way, and at the same time, immediately and appropriately punished. Punishment shall consist in increased and heavier work, such as making a master work like a journeyman, or a journeyman like an apprentice.

The moral virtues shall be promulgated to their utmost and, as far as possible, according to the principle *Octavii Pisani per gradus* [of Octavius Pisa, by steps]. If it is observed that two people cannot settle their own dispute, they shall be separated. Lies will also be punished. *Sed haec non omnia statim initio publicanda.* [Let this, even though uncompleted, be published as a beginning.]

PART II

The Founding Fathers

The Declaration of Independence

In Congress, July 4, 1776
The Unanimous Declaration of the Thirteen United States of America

(handwritten margin note: created equal ~ in freedom / segregation)

When, in the course of human events, it becomes necessary for one people to dissolve the political bands which have connected them with another, and to assume, among the powers of the earth, the separate and equal station to which the laws of nature and of nature's God entitle them, a decent respect to the opinions of mankind requires that they should declare the causes which impel them to the separation.

We hold these truths to be self-evident: that all men are created equal; that they are endowed by their Creator with certain unalienable rights; that among these are life, liberty, and the pursuit of happiness. That, to secure these rights, governments are instituted among men, deriving their just powers from the consent of the governed. That, whenever any form of government becomes destructive of these ends, it is the right of the people to alter or to abolish it and to institute new government, laying its foundation on such principles and organizing its powers in such form as to them shall seem most likely to effect their safety and happiness. Prudence, indeed, will dictate that governments long established should not be changed for light and transient causes; and accordingly all experience hath shown that mankind are more disposed to suffer, while evils are sufferable, than to right themselves by abolishing the forms to which they are accustomed. But when a long train of abuses and usurpations, pursuing invariably the same object, evinces a design to reduce them under absolute despotism, it is their right, it is their duty, to throw off such government, and to provide new guards for their future security. Such has been the patient sufferance of these colonies; and such is now the necessity which constrains them to alter their former systems of government. The history of the present king of Great Britain is a history of repeated injuries and usurpations, all having in direct object the establishment of an absolute tyranny over these states. To prove this, let facts be submitted to a candid world.

He has refused his assent to laws, the most wholesome and necessary for the public good.

He has forbidden his governors to pass laws of immediate and pressing importance, unless suspended in their operation till his assent should be obtained; and, when so suspended, he has utterly neglected to attend to them.

He has refused to pass other laws for the accommodation of large districts of people, unless those people would relinquish the right of representation in the legislature, a right inestimable to them and formidable to tyrants only.

He has called together legislative bodies at places unusual, uncomfortable, and distant from the depository of their public records, for the sole purpose of fatiguing them into compliance with his measures.

He has dissolved representative houses repeatedly, for opposing with manly firmness his invasions on the rights of the people.

He has refused for a long time, after such dissolutions, to cause others to be elected; whereby the legislative powers, incapable of annihilation, have returned to the people at large for their exercise; the state remaining in the meantime exposed to all the dangers of invasion from without, and convulsions within.

He has endeavored to prevent the population of these states; for that purpose obstructing the laws for naturalization of foreigners, refusing to pass others to encourage their migration hither, and raising the conditions of new appropriations of lands.

He has obstructed the administration of justice by refusing his assent to laws for establishing judiciary powers.

He has made judges dependent on his will alone, for the tenure of their offices, and the amount and payment of their salaries.

He has erected a multitude of new offices, and sent hither swarms of officers to harass our people, and eat out their substance.

He has kept among us, in times of peace, standing armies, without the consent of our legislatures.

He has affected to render the military independent of, and superior to, the civil power.

He has combined with others to subject us to a jurisdiction foreign to our constitution and unacknowledged by our laws, giving his assent to their acts of pretended legislation:

For quartering large bodies of armed troops among us;

For protecting them, by a mock trial, from punishment for any murders which they should commit on the inhabitants of these states;

For cutting off our trade with all parts of the world;

For imposing taxes on us without our consent;

For depriving us, in many cases, of the benefits of trial by jury;

For transporting us beyond seas to be tried for pretended offenses;

For abolishing the free system of English laws in a neighboring province, establishing therein an arbitrary government, and enlarging its boundaries so as to render it at once an example and fit instrument for introducing the same absolute rule into these colonies;

For taking away our charters, abolishing our most valuable laws, and altering fundamentally the forms of our governments;

For suspending our own legislatures, and declaring themselves invested with power to legislate for us in all cases whatsoever.

He has abdicated government here, by declaring us out of his protection and waging war against us.

He has plundered our seas, ravaged our coasts, burned our towns, and destroyed the lives of our people.

He is at this time transporting large armies of foreign mercenaries to complete the works of death, desolation, and tyranny, already begun with circumstances of cruelty and perfidy scarcely paralleled in the most barbarous ages, and totally unworthy the head of a civilized nation.

He has constrained our fellow-citizens taken captive on the high seas to bear arms against their country, to become the executioners of their friends and brethren, or to fall themselves by their hands.

He has excited domestic insurrections amongst us, and has endeavored to bring on the inhabitants of our frontiers, the merciless Indian savages, whose known rule of warfare is an undistinguished destruction of all ages, sexes, and conditions.

In every stage of these oppressions we have petitioned for redress in the most humble terms: Our repeated petitions have been answered only by repeated injury. A prince, whose character is thus marked by every act which may define a tyrant is unfit to be the ruler of a free people.

Nor have we been wanting in attentions to our British brethren. We have warned them from time to time of attempts by their legislature to extend an unwarrantable jurisdiction over us. We have reminded them of the circumstances of our emigration and settlement here. We have appealed to their native justice and magnanimity, and we have conjured them by the ties of our common kindred to disavow these usurpations which would inevitably interrupt our connections and correspondence. They too have been deaf to the voice of justice and of consanguinity. We must, therefore, acquiesce in the necessity, which denounces our separation, and hold them, as we hold the rest of mankind, enemies in war, in peace friends.

We, therefore, the Representatives of the United States of America, in General Congress assembled, appealing to the Supreme Judge of the world for the rectitude of our intentions, do, in the name, and by authority of the good people of these colonies, solemnly publish and declare, That these United Colonies are, and of right ought to be, free and independent states; that they are absolved from all allegiance to the British crown, and that all political connection between them and the state of Great Britain, is and ought to be, totally dissolved; and that, as free and independent states, they have full power to levy war, conclude peace, contract alliances, establish commerce, and to do all other acts and things which independent states may of right do. And for the support of this declaration, with a firm reliance on the protection of Divine Providence, we mutually pledge to each other our lives, our fortunes, and our sacred honor.

The Constitution of the United States

We the people of the United States, in Order to form a more perfect Union, establish Justice, insure domestic Tranquility, provide for the common defence, promote the general Welfare, and secure the Blessings of Liberty to ourselves and our Posterity, do ordain and establish this Constitution for the United States of America. — So the constitution is provisional? As is the government according to the Dec. of Ind. —

Article I The Constitution suggests term-limits should be determined [...]

Section 1. All legislative Powers herein granted shall be vested in a Congress of the United States, which shall consist of a Senate and House of Representatives.

Section 2. The House of Representatives shall be composed of Members chosen every second Year by the People of the several States, and the Electors in each State shall have Qualifications requisite for Electors of the most numerous Branch of the State Legislature.

No Person shall be a Representative who shall not have attained to the Age of twenty-five Years, and been seven Years a Citizen of the United States, and who shall not, when elected, be an Inhabitant of that State in which he shall be chosen.

Representatives and direct Taxes shall be apportioned among the several States which may be included within this Union, according to their respective Numbers, which shall be determined by adding to the whole Number of free Persons, including those bound to Service for a Term of Years, and excluding Indians not taxed, three fifths of all other Persons. The actual Enumeration shall be made within three Years after the first Meeting of the Congress of the United States, and within every subsequent Term of ten Years, in such Manner as they shall by Law direct. The Number of Representatives shall not exceed one for every thirty Thousand, but each State shall have at Least one Representative; and until such enumeration shall be made, the State of New Hampshire shall be entitled to chuse three, Massachusetts eight, Rhode-Island and Providence Plantations one, Connecticut five, New-York six, New Jersey four, Pennsylvania eight, Delaware one, Maryland six, Virginia ten, North Carolina five, South Carolina five, and Georgia three.

When vacancies happen in the Representation from any State, the Executive Authority thereof shall issue Writs of Election to fill such Vacancies.

The House of Representatives shall chuse their Speaker and other Officers; and shall have the sole Power of Impeachment.

Section 3. The Senate of the United States shall be composed of two Senators from each State, chosen by the Legislature thereof, for six Years; and each Senator shall have one Vote.

Immediately after they shall be assembled in Consequence of the first Election, they shall be divided as equally as may be into three Classes. The Seats of the Senators of the first Class shall be vacated at the Expiration of the second Year, of the second Class at the Expiration of the fourth Year, and of the third Class at the Expiration of the sixth Year, so that one-third may be chosen every second Year; and if Vacancies happen by Resignation, or otherwise, during the Recess of the Legislature of any State, the Executive thereof may make temporary Appointments until the next Meeting of the Legislature, which shall then fill such Vacancies.

No Person shall be a Senator who shall not have attained to the Age of thirty Years, and been nine Years a Citizen of the United States, and who shall not, when elected, be an Inhabitant of that State in which he shall be chosen.

The Vice President of the United States shall be President of the Senate, but shall have no vote, unless they be equally divided.

The Senate shall chuse their other Officers, and also a President pro tempore, in the absence of the Vice President, or when he shall exercise the Office of the President of the United States.

The Senate shall have the sole Power to try all Impeachments. When sitting for that purpose, they shall be on Oath or Affirmation. When the President of the United States is tried, the Chief Justice shall preside: And no person shall be convicted without the Concurrence of two thirds of the Members present.

Judgment in Cases of Impeachment shall not extend further than to removal from Office, and disqualification to hold and enjoy any

Office of honor, Trust, or Profit under the United States: but the Party convicted shall nevertheless be liable and subject to Indictment, Trial, Judgment, and Punishment, according to Law.

Section 4. The Times, Places and Manner of holding Elections for Senators and Representatives, shall be prescribed in each state by the Legislature thereof; but the Congress may at any time by Law make or alter such Regulations, except as to the Places of Chusing Senators.

The Congress shall assemble at least once in every Year, and such Meeting shall be on the first Monday in December, unless they shall by Law appoint a different Day.

Section 5. Each House shall be the Judge of the Elections, Returns and Qualifications of its own Members, and a Majority of each shall constitute a Quorum to do Business; but a smaller number may adjourn from day to day, and may be authorized to compel the Attendance of absent Members, in such Manner, and under such Penalties, as each House may provide.

Each House may determine the Rules of its Proceedings, punish its Members for disorderly Behavior, and, with the Concurrence of two thirds, expel a Member.

Each House shall keep a Journal of its Proceedings, and from time to time publish the same, excepting such Parts as may in their Judgment require Secrecy; and the Yeas and Nays of the Members of either House on any question shall, at the Desire of one fifth of those Present, be entered on the Journal.

Neither House, during the Session of Congress, shall, without the Consent of the other, adjourn for more than three days, nor to any other Place than that in which the two Houses shall be sitting.

Section 6. The Senators and Representatives shall receive a Compensation for their Services, to be ascertained by Law, and paid out of the Treasury of the United States. They shall in all Cases, except Treason, Felony, and Breach of the Peace, be privileged from Arrest during their Attendance at the Session of their respective Houses, and in going to and returning from the same; and for any Speech or Debate in either House, they shall not be questioned in any other Place.

No Senator or Representative shall, during the Time for which he was elected, be appointed to any civil Office under the Authority of the United States, which shall have been created, or the Emoluments whereof shall have been increased, during such time; and no Person holding any Office under the United States shall be a Member of either House during his continuance in Office.

Section 7. All Bills for raising Revenue shall originate in the House of Representatives; but the Senate may propose or concur with Amendments as on other bills.

Every Bill which shall have passed the House of Representatives and the Senate, shall, before it become a Law, be presented to the President of the United States; If he approve he shall sign it, but if not he shall return it, with his Objections, to that House in which it shall have originated, who shall enter the Objections at large on their Journal, and proceed to reconsider it. If after such Reconsideration two thirds of that House shall agree to pass the bill, it shall be sent, together with the objections, to the other House, by which it shall likewise be reconsidered, and if approved by two thirds of that House, it shall become a Law. But in all such Cases the Votes of both Houses shall be determined by Yeas and Nays, and the Names of the Persons voting for and against the Bill shall be entered on the Journal of each House respectively. If any Bill shall not be returned by the President within ten Days (Sundays excepted) after it shall have been presented to him, the Same shall be a Law, in like Manner as if he had signed it, unless the Congress by their Adjournment prevent its Return, in which Case it shall not be a Law.

Every Order, Resolution, or Vote to which the Concurrence of the Senate and House of Representatives may be necessary (except on a question of Adjournment) shall be presented to the President of the United States; and before the Same shall take Effect, shall be approved by him, or being disapproved by him, shall be repassed by two thirds of the Senate and House of Representatives, according to the Rules and Limitations prescribed in the Case of a Bill.

Section 8. The Congress shall have Power To lay and collect Taxes, Duties, Imposts and Excises, to pay the Debts and provide for the common Defence and general Welfare of the United States; but all Duties, Imposts and Excises shall be uniform throughout the United States;

To borrow money on the credit of the United States;

To regulate Commerce with foreign Nations, and among the several States, and with the Indian Tribes;

To establish an uniform Rule of Naturalization, and uniform Laws on the subject of Bankruptcies throughout the United States;

To provide for the Punishment of counterfeiting the Securities and current Coin of the United States;

To establish Post Offices and post Roads;

To promote the Progress of Science and useful Arts, by securing for limited Times to Authors and Inventors the exclusive Right to their respective Writings and Discoveries;

To constitute Tribunals inferior to the Supreme Court;

To define and punish Piracies and Felonies committed on the high Seas, and Offences against the Law of Nations;

To declare War, grant Letters of Marque and Reprisal, and make Rules concerning Captures on Land and Water;

To raise and support Armies, but no Appropriation of Money to that Use shall be for a longer Term than two Years;

To provide and maintain a Navy;

To make Rules for the Government and Regulation of the land and naval forces;

To provide for calling forth the Militia to execute the Laws of the Union, suppress Insurrections and repel Invasions;

To provide for organizing, arming, and disciplining the Militia, and for governing such Part of them as may be employed in the Service of the United States, reserving to the States respectively, the Appointment of the Officers, and the Authority of training the Militia according to the discipline prescribed by Congress;

To exercise Legislation in all Cases whatsoever, over such District (not exceeding ten Miles square) as may, by Cession of particular States, and the acceptance of Congress, become the Seat of Government of the United States, and to exercise like Authority over all Places purchased by the Consent of the Legislature of the State in which the Same shall be, for the Erection of Forts, Magazines, Arsenals, dock-Yards, and other needful Buildings;—And

To make all Laws which shall be necessary and proper for carrying into Execution the foregoing Powers, and all other Powers vested by this Constitution in the Government of the United States, or in any Department or Officer thereof.

Section 9. The Migration or Importation of such Persons as any of the States now existing shall think proper to admit, shall not be prohibited by the Congress prior to the Year one thousand eight hundred and eight, but a tax or duty may be imposed on such Importation, not exceeding ten dollars for each Person.

The privilege of the Writ of Habeas Corpus shall not be suspended, unless when in Cases of Rebellion or Invasion the public Safety may require it.

No Bill of Attainder or ex post facto Law shall be passed.

No capitation, or other direct, Tax shall be laid unless in Proportion to the Census or Enumeration herein before directed to be taken.

No Tax or Duty shall be laid on Articles exported from any State.

No Preference shall be given by any Regulation of Revenue to the Ports of one State over those of another: nor shall Vessels bound to, or from, one State, be obliged to enter, clear, or pay Duties in another.

No Money shall be drawn from the Treasury, but in Consequence of Appropriations made by Law; and a regular Statement and Account of the Receipts and Expenditures of all public Money shall be published from time to time.

No Title of Nobility shall be granted by the United States: And no Person holding any Office of Profit or Trust under them, shall, without the Consent of the Congress, accept of any present, Emolument, Office, or Title, of any kind whatever, from any King, Prince, or foreign State.

Section 10. No State shall enter into any Treaty, Alliance, or Confederation; grant Letters of Marque and Reprisal; coin Money; emit Bills of Credit; make any Thing but gold and silver Coin a Tender in Payment of Debts; pass any Bill of Attainder, ex post facto Law, or Law impairing the Obligation of Contracts, or grant any Title of Nobility.

No State shall, without the Consent of the Congress, lay any Imposts or Duties on Imports or Exports, except what may be absolutely necessary for executing its inspection Laws: and the net Produce of all Duties and Imposts, laid by any State on Imports or Exports, shall be for the Use of the Treasury of the United States; and all such Laws shall be subject to the Revision and Control of the Congress.

No State shall, without the Consent of Congress, lay any duty of Tonnage, keep Troops, or Ships of War in time of Peace, enter into any Agreement or Compact with another State, or with a foreign Power, or engage in War, unless actually invaded, or in such imminent Danger as will not admit of delay.

Article II

Section 1. The executive Power shall be vested in a President of the United States of America. He shall hold his Office during the Term of four years, and, together with the Vice-President, chosen for the same Term, be elected, as follows:

Each State shall appoint, in such Manner as the Legislature thereof may direct, a Number of Electors, equal to the whole Number of Senators and Representatives to which the State may be entitled in the Congress; but no Senator or Representative, or Person holding an Office of Trust or Profit under the United States, shall be appointed an Elector.

The Electors shall meet in their respective States, and vote by Ballot for two persons, of whom one at least shall not be an Inhabitant of the same State with themselves. And they shall make a List of all the Persons voted for, and of the Number of Votes for each; which List they shall sign and certify, and transmit sealed to the Seat of the Government of the United States, directed to the President of the Senate. The President of the Senate shall, in the Presence of the Senate and House of Representatives, open all the Certicates, and the Votes shall then be counted. The Person having the greatest Number of Votes shall be the President, if such Number be a Majority of the whole Number of Electors appointed; and if there be more than one who have such Majority, and have an equal Number of Votes, then the House of Representatives shall immediately chuse by Ballot one of them for President; and if no Person have a Majority, then from the five highest on the List the said House shall in like Manner chuse the President. But in chusing the President, the Votes shall be taken by States, the Representation from each State having one Vote; a quorum for this Purpose shall consist of a Member or Members from two-thirds of the States, and a Majority of all the States shall be necessary to a Choice. In every Case, after the Choice of the President, the Person having the greatest Number of Votes of the Electors shall be the Vice President. But if there should remain two or more who have equal votes, the Senate shall chuse from them by Ballot the Vice-President.

The Congress may determine the Time of chusing the Electors, and the Day on which they shall give their votes; which Day shall be the same throughout the United States.

No person except a natural-born Citizen, or a Citizen of the United States, at the time of the Adoption of this Constitution, shall be eligible to the Office of President; neither shall any Person be eligible to that Office who shall not have attained to the Age of thirty-five years, and been fourteen Years a Resident within the United States.

In Case of the Removal of the President from Office, or of his Death, Resignation, or Inability to discharge the Powers and Duties of the said Office, the same shall devolve on the Vice President, and the Congress may by Law provide for the Case of Removal, Death, Resignation, or Inability, both of the President, and Vice President, declaring what Officer shall then act as President, and such Officer shall act accordingly, until the disability be removed, or a President shall be elected.

The President shall, at stated Times, receive for his Services a Compensation, which shall neither be increased nor diminished during the Period for which he shall have been elected, and he shall not receive within that Period any other Emolument from the United States, or any of them.

Before he enter on the execution of his Office, he shall take the following Oath or Affirmation:—"I do solemnly swear (or affirm) that I will faithfully execute the Office of President of the United States, and will, to the best of by Ability, preserve, protect, and defend the Constitution of the United States."

Section 2. The President shall be Commander in Chief of the Army and Navy of the United States, and of the Militia of the several States, when called into the actual Service of the United States; he may require Opinion, in writing, of the principal Officer in each of the executive Departments, upon any subject relating to the Duties of their respective Offices, and he shall have Power to Grant Reprieves and Pardons for Offences against the United States except in Cases of Impeachment.

He shall have Power, by and with the Advice and Consent of the Senate, to make Treaties, provided two thirds of the Senators present concur; and he shall nominate, and by and with the Advice and Consent of the Senate, shall appoint Ambassadors, other public Ministers and Consuls, Judges of the supreme Court, and all other Officers of the United States, whose Appointments are not herein otherwise provided for, and which shall be established by Law: but the Congress may by Law vest the Appointment of such inferior Officers, as they think proper, in the President alone, in the Courts of Law, or in the Heads of Departments.

The President shall have Power to fill up all Vacancies that may happen during the Recess of the Senate, by granting Commissions which shall expire at the End of their next Session.

Section 3. He shall from time to time give to the Congress Information of the State of the Union, and recommend to their Consideration such Measures as he shall judge necessary and expedient; he may, on extraordinary occasions, convene both Houses, or either of them, and in Case of Disagreement between them, with respect to the Time of Adjournment, he may adjourn them to such Time as he shall think proper; he shall receive Ambassadors and other public Ministers; he shall take Care that the Laws be faithfully executed, and shall Commission all the Officers of the United States.

Section 4. The President, Vice President and all civil Officers of the United States, shall be removed from Office on Impeachment for, and Conviction of, Treason, Bribery, or other high Crimes and Misdemeanors.

Article III

Section 1. The judicial Power of the United States, shall be vested in one supreme Court, and in such inferior Courts as the Congress may from time to time ordain and establish. The Judges, both of the supreme and inferior Courts, shall hold their Offices during good Behaviour, and shall, at stated Times, receive for their Services, a Compensation, which shall not be diminished during their Continuance in Office.

Section 2. The judicial Power shall extend to all Cases, in Law and Equity, arising under this Constitution, the Laws of the United States, and treaties made, or which shall be made, under their Authority;—to all Cases affecting ambassadors, other public ministers and consuls;—to all cases of admiralty and maritime Jurisdiction;—to Controversies to which the United States shall be a Party;—to Controversies between two or more States;—between a State and Citizens of another State; between Citizens of different States,—between Citizens of the same State claiming Lands under Grants of different States, and between a State, or the Citizens thereof, and foreign States, Citizens or Subjects.

In all Cases affecting Ambassadors, other public Ministers and Consuls, and those in which a State shall be Party, the supreme Court shall have original Jurisdiction. In all the other Cases before mentioned, the supreme Court shall have appellate Jurisdiction, both as to Law and Fact, with such Exceptions, and under such Regulations as the Congress shall make.

The trial of all Crimes, except in Cases of Impeachment, shall be by Jury; and such Trial shall be held in the State where the said Crimes shall have been committed; but when not committed within any State, the Trial shall be at such Place or Places as the Congress may by Law have directed.

Section 3. Treason against the United States, shall consist only in levying War against them, or in adhering to their Enemies, giving them Aid and Comfort. No Person shall be convicted of Treason unless on the Testimony of two Witnesses to the same overt Act, or on Confession in open Court.

The Congress shall have power to declare the Punishment of Treason, but no Attainder of Treason shall work Corruption of Blood, or Forfeiture except during the Life of the Person attainted.

Article IV

Section 1. Full Faith and Credit shall be given in each State to the public Acts, Records, and judicial Proceedings of every other State. And the Congress may by general Laws prescribe the Manner in which such Acts, Records and Proceedings shall be proved, and the Effect thereof.

Section 2. The Citizens of each State shall be entitled to all Privileges and Immunities of Citizens in the several States.

A Person charged in any State with Treason, Felony, or other Crime, who shall flee from Justice, and be found in another State, shall on demand of the executive Authority of the State from which he fled, be delivered up, to be removed to the State having Jurisdiction of the crime.

No Person held to Service or Labour in one State, under the Laws thereof, escaping into another, shall, in Consequence of any Law or Regulation, therein, be discharged from such Service or Labour but shall be delivered up on Claim of the Party to whom such Service or Labour may be due.

Section 3. New States may be admitted by the Congress into this Union; but no new State shall be formed or erected within the Jurisdiction of any other State; nor any State be formed by the Junction of two or more States, or parts of States, without the Consent of the Legislatures of the States concerned as well as the Congress.

The Congress shall have Power to dispose of and make all needful Rules and Regulations respecting the Territory or other Property belonging to the United States; and nothing in this Constitution shall be so construed as to Prejudice any Claims of the United States, or of any particular State.

Section 4. The United States shall guarantee to every State in this Union a Republican Form of Government, and shall protect each of them against Invasion; and on Application of the Legislature, or of the Executive (when the Legislature cannot be convened) against domestic Violence.

Article V

The Congress, whenever two-thirds of both Houses shall deem it necessary, shall propose Amendments to this Constitution, or, on the Application of the Legislatures of two-thirds of the several States, shall call a Convention for proposing Amendments, which, in either Case, shall be valid to all Intents and Purposes, as part of this Constitution, when ratified by the Legislatures of three-fourths of the several States, or by Conventions in three-fourths thereof, as the one or the other Mode of Ratification may be proposed by the Congress; Provided that no Amendment which may be made prior to the Year One thousand eight hundred and eight shall in any Manner affect the first and fourth Clauses in the Ninth Section of the first Article; and that no State, without its Consent, shall be deprived of its equal Suffrage in the Senate.

Article VI

All Debts contracted and Engagements entered into, before the Adoption of this Constitution, shall be as valid against the United States under this Constitution, as under the Confederation.

This Constitution, and the Laws of the United States which shall be made in Pursuance thereof; and all Treaties made, or which shall be made, under the Authority of the United States, shall be the supreme Law of the Land; and the Judges in every State shall be bound thereby, any Thing in the Constitution or Laws of any State to the Contrary notwithstanding.

The Senators and Representatives before mentioned, and the Members of the several State Legislatures, and all executive and judicial Officers, both of the United States and of the several States, shall be bound by Oath or Affirmation to support this Constitution;

but no religious Test shall ever be required as a qualification to any Office or public Trust under the United States.

Article VII

The Ratification of the Conventions of nine States shall be sufficient for the Establishment of this Constitution between the States so ratifying the same.

Done in Convention by the Unanimous Consent of the States present the Seventeenth Day of September in the Year of our Lord one thousand seven hundred and Eighty seven, and of the Independence of the United States of America the Twelfth. In Witness whereof We have hereunto subscribed our Names.

George Washington, President, and deputy from Virginia.

New Hampshire—John Langdon, Nicholas Gilman.

Massachusetts—Nathaniel Gorham, Rufus King.

Connecticut—William Samuel Johnson, Roger Sherman.

New York—Alexander Hamilton.

New Jersey—William Livingston, David Brearley, William Paterson, Jonathan Dayton.

Pennsylvania—Benjamin Franklin, Thomas Mifflin, Robert Morris, George Clymer, Thomas Fitzsimons, Jared Ingersoll, James Wilson, Gouverneur Morris.

Delaware—George Read, Gunning Bedford, Junior, John Dickinson, Richard Bassett, Jacob Broom.

Maryland—James M'Henry, Daniel Jenifer, of St. Thomas, Daniel Carroll.

Virginia—John Blair, James Madison, Junior.

North Carolina—William Blount, Richard Dobbs Spaight, Hugh Williamson.

South Carolina—John Rutledge, Charles Cotesworth Pinckney, Charles Pinckney, Pierce Butler.

Georgia—William Few, Abraham Baldwin.

Attest. William Jackson, Secretary.

Benjamin Franklin

In 1729, *Benjamin Franklin wrote* A Modest Inquiry Into the Nature and Necessity of Paper Currency *in response to Britain's moves against colonial currencies. It not only foreshadows Hamilton's arguments during the post-Revolutionary War fight for a national economic system, but also roundly refutes those who have dared call Franklin a Malthusian.*

Franklin's A Proposal for Promoting Useful Knowledge Among the British Plantations in America *was issued from Philadelphia in 1743. Its aim—the communication, promotion and social use of scientific ideas—was continued in the American Philosophical Society and in the Constitution itself.*

Testifying before the British House of Commons in 1766 for the repeal of the American Stamp Act, Franklin distinguished between the merely looting policies of Britain and the nature of Parliamentary legislation that would be conducive to the economic development of the American Colonies. At this early date, Franklin admonished Parliament that there would be revolt in the colonies if they persisted in these policies, putting the lie to revisionist stories about "Royalist" Franklin.

Finally, Franklin's correspondence with Priestley was spread over decades and encompassed a wide range of scientific inquiry. The following letter, written during Franklin's deployment as American Ambassador to France, is representative of his viewpoint throughout.

We also include an undated essay by Franklin which was translated from a French edition of Franklin's writings, and published in a collection of American writings on political economy. Likely, the paper was written in France, either during or immediately after the end of the Revolutionary War.

A Modest Inquiry Into the Nature And Necessity of Paper Currency

There is no science, the study of which is more useful and commendable than the knowledge of the true interest of one's country; and

247

perhaps there is no kind of learning more abstruse and intricate, more difficult to acquire in any degree of perfection than this, and therefore none more generally neglected. Hence it is, that we every day find men in conversation contending warmly on some point in politics, which, although it may nearly concern them both, neither of them understands any more than they do each other.

Thus much by way of apology for this present *Inquiry into the Nature and Necessity of a Paper Currency*. And if any thing I shall say may be a means of fixing a subject, that is now the chief concern of my countrymen, in a clearer light, I shall have the satisfaction of thinking my time and pains well employed.

To proceed, then,

There is a certain proportionate quantity of money requisite to carry on the trade of a country freely and currently; more than which would be of no advantage in trade, and less, if much less, exceedingly detrimental to it.

This leads us to the following general considerations.

First. *A great want of money, in any trading country, occasions interest to be at a very high rate.* And here it may be observed, that it is impossible by any laws to restrain men from giving and receiving exorbitant interest, where money is suitably scarce. For he that wants money will find out ways to give ten per cent, when he cannot have it for less, although the law forbids to take more than six per cent. Now the interest of money being high is prejudicial to a country several ways. It makes land bear a low price, because few men will lay out their money in land, when they can make a much greater profit by lending it out upon interest. And much less will men be inclined to venture their money at sea, when they can, without risk or hazard, have a great and certain profit by keeping it at home; thus trade is discouraged. And if in two neighbouring countries the traders of one, by reason of a greater plenty of money, can borrow it to trade with at a lower rate than the traders of the other, they will infallibly have the advantage, and get the greatest part of that trade into their own hands; for he that trades with money he hath borrowed at eight or ten per cent, cannot hold market with him that borrows his money at six or four. On the contrary, *a plentiful currency will occasion interest to be low;* and this will be an inducement to many to lay out their money in lands, rather than put it out to use, by which means land will begin to rise in value and bear a better price.

And at the same time it will tend to enliven trade exceedingly, because people will find more profit in employing their money that way than in usury; and many that understand business very well, but have not a stock sufficient of their own, will be encouraged to borrow money to trade with, when they can have it at a moderate interest.

Secondly. *Want of money in a country reduces the price of that part of its produce which is used in trade;* because, trade being discouraged by it as above, there is a much less demand for that produce. And this is another reason why land in such a case will be low, especially where the staple commodity of the country is the immediate produce of the land; because, that produce being low, fewer people find an advantage in husbandry, or the improvement of the land. On the contrary, *a plentiful currency will occasion the trading produce to bear a good price;* because, trade being encouraged and advanced by it, there will be a much greater demand for that produce; which will be a great encouragement of husbandry and tillage, and consequently make land more valuable, for that many people would apply themselves to husbandry, who probably might otherwise have sought some more profitable employment.

As we have already experienced how much the increase of our currency, by what paper money has been made, has encouraged our trade, particularly to instance only in one article, *ship-building*, it may not be amiss to observe under this head, what a great advantage it must be to us as a trading country, that has workmen and all the materials proper for that business within itself, to have ship-building as much as possible advanced; for every ship, that is built here for the English merchants, gains the province her clear value in gold and silver, which must otherwise have been sent home for returns in her stead; and likewise every ship, built in and belonging to the province, not only saves the province her first cost, but all the freight, wages, and provisions she ever makes or requires as long as she lasts; provided care is taken to make this her *pay-port*, and that she always takes provisions with her for the whole voyage, which may easily be done. And how considerable an article this is yearly in our favor, every one, the least acquainted with mercantile affairs, must needs be sensible; for, if we could not build ourselves, we must either purchase so many vessels as we want from other countries, or else hire them to carry our produce to market, which would be more expensive than purchasing, and on many other accounts exceedingly to our loss. Now as trade in general will decline where there is not a plentiful currency, so ship-building must certainly of consequence decline where trade is declining.

Thirdly. *Want of money in a country discourages laboring and handicraftsmen (who are the chief strength and support of a people) from coming to settle in it, and induces many that were settled to leave the country, and seek entertainment and employment in other places, where they can be better paid.* For what can be more disheartening to an industrious laboring man than this, that, after he hath earned his bread with the sweat of his brows, he must spend as much time, and have near as much fatigue in getting it, as he had to earn it? *And nothing makes more bad paymasters than a general scarcity of money.* And here again is a third reason for land's bearing a low price in such a country, because land always increases in value in proportion with the increase of the people settling on it, there being so many more buyers; and its value will infallibly be diminished, if the number of its inhabitants diminish. On the contrary, *a plentiful currency will encourage great numbers of laboring and handicraftsmen to come and settle in the country,* by the same reason that a want of it will discourage and drive them out. Now the more inhabitants, the greater demand for land (as is said above), upon which it must necessarily rise in value, and bear a better price. The same may be said of the value of house-rent, which will be advanced for the same reasons; and, by the increase of trade and riches, people will be enabled to pay greater rents. Now, the value of house-rent rising, and interest becoming low, many, that in a scarcity of money practised usury, will probably be more inclined to building; which will likewise sensibly enliven business in any place; it being an advantage not only to brickmakers, bricklayers, masons, carpenters, joiners, glaziers, and several other trades immediately employed by building, but likewise to farmers, brewers, bakers, tailors, shoemakers, shopkeepers, and, in short, to every one that they lay their money out with.

Fourthly. *Want of money in such a country as ours, occasions a greater consumption of English and European goods, in proportion to the number of the people, than there would otherwise be.* Because merchants and traders, by whom abundance of artificers and laboring men are employed, finding their other affairs require what money they can get into their hands, oblige those who work for them to take one half or perhaps two-thirds goods in pay. By this means a greater quantity of goods are disposed of, and to a greater value; because working-men and their families are thereby induced to be more profuse and extravagant in fine apparel and the like, than they would be if they were obliged to pay ready money for such things after they had earned and received it, or if such goods were not imposed upon them, of which they can make no other use. For such people cannot send the goods they are paid with to a foreign market, without losing considerably by having them sold for less than they stand them in here; neither can they easily dispose of them at home, because their neighbours are generally supplied in the same manner. But how unreasonable would it be, if some of those very men who *have been a means* of thus forcing people into unnecessary expense, should be the first and most earnest in accusing them of *pride and prodigality*. Now, though this extraordinary consumption of foreign commodities may be a profit to particular men, yet the country in general grows poorer by it apace. On the contrary, as *a plentiful currency will occasion a less consumption of European goods, in proportion to the number of the people,* so it will be a means of making the balance of our trade more equal than it now is, if it does not give it in our favor; because our own produce will be encouraged at the same time. And it is to be observed, that, though less foreign commodities are consumed in proportion to the number of people, yet this will be no disadvantage to the merchant, because the number of people increasing, will occasion an increasing demand of more foreign goods in the whole.

Thus we have seen some of the many heavy disadvantages a country (especially such a country as ours) must labor under, when it has not a sufficient stock of running cash to manage its trade currently. And we have likewise seen some of the advantages which accrue from having money sufficient, or a plentiful currency.

The foregoing paragraphs being well considered, we shall naturally be led to draw the following conclusions with regard to what persons will probably be for or against emitting a large additional sum of paper bills in this province.

1. Since men will always be powerfully influenced in their opinions and actions by what appears to be their particular interest, therefore all those, who, wanting courage to venture in trade, now practise lending money on security for exorbitant interest, which, in a scarcity of money will be done, notwithstanding the law, I say all such will probably be against a large addition to our present stock

of paper money; because a plentiful currency will lower interest, and make it common to lend on less security.

2. All those who are possessors of large sums of money, and are disposed to purchase land, which is attended with a great and sure advantage in a growing country as this is; I say, the interest of all such men will incline them to oppose a large addition to our money. Because their wealth is now continually increasing by the large interest they receive, which will enable them (if they can keep land from rising) to purchase more some time hence than they can at present; and in the mean time all trade being discouraged, not only those who borrow of them, but the common people in general will be impoverished, and consequently obliged to sell more land for less money than they will do at present. And yet, after such men are possessed of as much land as they can purchase, it will then be their interest to have money made plentiful, because that will immediately make land rise in value in *their* hands. Now it ought not to be wondered at, if people from the knowledge of a man's interest do sometimes make a true guess at his designs; for *interest*, they say, *will not lie*.

3. Lawyers, and others concerned in court business, will probably many of them be against a plentiful currency; because people in that case will have less occasion to run in debt, and consequently less occasion to go to law and sue one another for their debts. Though I know some even among these gentlemen, that regard the public good before their own apparent private interest.

4. All those who are any way dependents on such persons as are above mentioned, whether as holding offices, as tenants, or as debtors, must at least *appear* to be against a large addition; because, if they do not, they must sensibly feel their present interest hurt. And besides these, there are, doubtless, many well-meaning gentlemen and others, who, without any immediate private interest of their own in view, are against making such an addition, through an opinion they may have of the honesty and sound judgment of some of their friends that oppose it (perhaps for the ends aforesaid), without having given it any thorough consideration themselves. And thus it is no wonder if there is a *powerful* party on that side.

On the other hand, those who are lovers of trade, and delight to see manufactures encouraged, will be for having a large addition to our currency. For they very well know, that people will have little heart to advance money in trade, when what they can get is scarce sufficient to purchase necessaries, and supply their families with provisions. Much less will they lay it out in advancing new manufactures; nor is it possible new manufactures should turn to any account, where there is not money to pay the workmen, who are discouraged by being paid in goods, because it is a great disadvantage to them.

Again. Those, who are truly for the proprietor's interest (and have no separate views of their own that are predominant), will be heartily for a large addition. Because, as I have shown above, plenty of money will for several reasons make land rise in value exceedingly. And I appeal to those immediately concerned for the proprietor in the sale of his lands, whether land has not risen very much since the first emission of what paper currency we now have, and even by its means. Now we all know the proprietary has great quantities to sell.

And since a plentiful currency will be so great a cause of advancing this province in trade and riches, and increasing the number of its people; which, though it will not sensibly lessen the inhabitants of Great Britain, will occasion a much greater vent and demand for their commodities here; and allowing that the crown is the more powerful for its subjects increasing in wealth and number, I cannot think it the interest of England to oppose us in making as great a sum of paper money here, as we, who are the best judges of our own necessities, find convenient. And if I were not sensible that the gentlemen of trade in England, to whom we have already parted with our silver and gold, are misinformed of our circumstances, and therefore endeavour to have our currency stinted to what it now is, I should think the government at home had some reasons for discouraging and impoverishing this province, which we are not acquainted with.

It remains now that we inquire, *whether a large addition to our paper currency will not make it sink in value very much*. And here it will be requisite that we first form just notions of the nature and value of money in general.

As Providence has so ordered it, that not only the different countries, but even different parts of the same country, have their peculiar most suitable productions; and likewise that different men have geniuses adapted to a variety of different arts and manufactures; therefore *commerce,* or the exchange of one commodity or manufacture for another, is highly convenient and beneficial to mankind. As for instance, A may be skilful in the art of making cloth, and B understand the raising of corn. A wants corn, and B cloth; upon which they make an exchange with each other for as much as each has occasion for, to the mutual advantage and satisfaction of both.

But as it would be very tedious, if there were no other way of general dealing, but by an immediate exchange of commodities; because a man that had corn to dispose of, and wanted cloth for it, might perhaps, in his search for a chapman to deal with, meet with twenty people that had cloth to dispose of, but wanted no corn; and with twenty others that wanted his corn, but had no cloth to suit him with; to remedy such inconveniences, and facilitate exchange, men have invented *money*, properly called a *medium of exchange*, because through or by its means labor is exchanged for labor, or one commodity for another. And whatever particular thing men have agreed to make this medium of, whether gold, silver, copper, or tobacco, it is, to those who possess it (if they want any thing), that very thing which they want, because it will immediately procure it for them. It is cloth to him that wants cloth, and corn to those that want corn; and so of all other necessaries, it *is* whatsoever it will procure. Thus he who had corn to dispose of, and wanted to purchase cloth with it, might sell his corn, for its value in this general medium, to one who wanted corn but had no cloth; and with this medium he might purchase cloth of him that wanted no corn, but perhaps some other thing, as iron it may be, which this medium will immediately procure, and so he may be said to have exchanged his cloth for iron; and thus the general change is soon performed, to the satisfaction of all parties, with abundance of facility.

For many ages, those parts of the world which are engaged in commerce, have fixed upon gold and silver as the chief and most proper materials for this medium; they being in themselves valuable metals for their fineness, beauty, and scarcity. By these, particularly by silver, it has been usual to value all things else. But as silver itself is of no certain permanent value, being worth more or less according to its scarcity or plenty, therefore it seems requisite to fix upon something else, more proper to be made a *measure of values*, and this I take to be *labor*.

By labor may the value of silver be measured as well as other things. As, suppose one man employed to raise corn, while another is digging and refining silver; at the year's end, or at any other period of time, the complete produce of corn, and that of silver, are the natural price of each other; and if one be twenty bushels, and the other twenty ounces, then an ounce of that silver is worth the labor of raising a bushel of that corn. Now if by the discovery of some nearer, more easy or plentiful mines, a man may get forty ounces of silver as easily as formerly he did twenty, and the same labor is still required to raise twenty bushels of corn, then two ounces of silver will be worth no more than the same labor of raising one bushel of corn, and that bushel of corn will be as cheap at two ounces, as it was before at one, *cæteris paribus*.

Thus the riches of a country are to be valued by the quantity of labor its inhabitants are able to purchase, and not by the quantity of silver and gold they possess; which will purchase more or less labor, and therefore is more or less valuable, as is said before, according to its scarcity or plenty. As those metals have grown much more plentiful in Europe since the discovery of America, so they have sunk in value exceedingly; for, to instance in England, formerly one penny of silver was worth a day's labor, but now it is hardly worth the sixth part of a day's labor; because not less than sixpence will purchase the labor of a man for a day in any part of that kingdom; which is wholly to be attributed to the much greater plenty of money now in England than formerly. And yet perhaps England is in effect no richer now than at that time; because as much labor might be purchased, or work got done of almost any kind, for one hundred pounds then, as will now require or is now worth six hundred pounds.

In the next place let us consider the nature of *banks* emitting *bills of credit*, as they are at this time used in Hamburgh, Amsterdam, London, and Venice.

Those places being seats of vast trade, and the payment of great sums being for that reason frequent, *bills of credit* are found very convenient in business; because a great sum is more easily counted in them, lighter in carriage, concealed in less room, and therefore safer in travelling or laying up, and on many other accounts they are very much valued. The banks are the general cashiers of all gentlemen, merchants, and great traders in and about these cities; there they deposit their money, and may take out bills to the value, for which they can be certain to have money again at the bank at any time. This gives the bills a credit; so that in England they are never less valuable than money, and in Venice and Amsterdam they are generally worth more. And the bankers, always reserving money in hand to answer more than the common run of demands (and some people constantly putting in while others are taking out), are able besides to lend large sums, on good security, to the government or others, for a reasonable interest, by which they are paid for their care and trouble; and the money, which otherwise would have lain dead in their hands, is made to circulate again thereby among the people. And thus the running cash of the nation is, as it were, doubled; for all great payments being made in bills, money in lower trade becomes much more plentiful. And this is an exceeding great advantage to a trading country, that is not overstocked with gold and silver.

As those, who take bills out of the banks in Europe, put in money for security; so here, and in some of the neighbouring provinces, we engage our land. Which of these methods will most effectually secure the bills from actually sinking in value, comes next to be considered.

Trade in general being nothing else but the exchange of labor for labor, the value of all things is, as I have said before, most justly measured by labor. Now suppose I put my money into a bank, and take out a bill for the value; if this bill at the time of my receiving it, would purchase me the labor of one hundred men for twenty days, but some time after will only purchase the labor of the same number of men for fifteen days, it is plain the bill has sunk in value one fourth part. Now, silver and gold being of no permanent value, and as this bill is founded on money, and therefore to be esteemed as such, it may be that the occasion of this fall is the increasing plenty of gold and silver, by which money is one fourth part less valuable than before, and therefore one fourth more is given of it for the same quantity of labor; and, if land is not become more plentiful by some proportionate decrease of the people, one fourth part more of money is given for the same quantity of land; whereby it appears, that it would have been more profitable to me to have laid that money out in land which I put into the bank, than to place it there and take a bill for it. And it is certain that the value of money has been continually sinking in England for several ages past, because it has been continually increasing in quantity. But, if bills could be taken out of a bank in Europe on a land security, it is probable the value of such bills would be more certain and steady, because the number of inhabitants continues to be near the same in those countries from age to age.

For, as bills issued upon money security are money, so bills issued upon land, are in effect *coined land*.

Therefore, (to apply the above to our own circumstances) if land in this province was falling, or any way likely to fall, it would behove the legislature most carefully to contrive how to prevent the bills issued upon land from falling with it. But, as our people increase exceedingly, and will be further increased, as I have before shown, by the help of a large addition to our currency, and as land in consequence is continually rising, so, in case no bills are emitted but what are upon land security, the money-acts in every part punctually enforced and executed, and payments of principal and interest being duly and strictly required, and the principal *bonâ fide* sunk according to law, it is absolutely impossible such bills should ever sink below their first value, or below the value of the land on which they are founded. In short, there is so little danger of their sinking, that they would certainly rise as the land rises, if they were not emitted in a proper manner for preventing it. That is, by providing in the act, *that payment may be made, either in those bills, or in any other bills made current by any act of the legislature of this province;* and that the interest, as it is received, may be again emitted in discharge of public debts; whereby circulating, it returns again into the hands of the borrowers, and becomes part of their future payments; and thus, as it is likely there will not be any difficulty for want of bills to pay the office, they are hereby kept from rising above their first value. For else, supposing there should be emitted upon mortgaged land its full present value in bills, as in the banks in Europe the full value of the money deposited is given out in bills; and supposing the office would take nothing but the same sum in those bills in discharge of the land, as, in the banks aforesaid, the same sum in their bills must be brought in, in order to receive out the money; in such case the bills would most surely rise in value as the land rises; as certainly as the bank bills founded on money would fall, if that money was falling. Thus, if I were to mortgage to a loan-office, or bank, a parcel of land now valued at one hundred pounds in silver, and receive for it the like sum in bills, to be paid in again at the expiration of a certain term of years, before which my land, rising in value, becomes worth one hundred and fifty pounds in silver; it is plain, that if I have not these bills in possession, and the office will take nothing but these bills, or else what it is now become worth in silver, in discharge of my land; I say it appears plain, that those bills will now be worth one hundred and fifty pounds in silver to the possessor; and if I can purchase them for less, in order to redeem my land, I shall by so much be a gainer.

I need not say any thing to convince the judicious that our bills have not yet sunk, though there is and has been some difference between them and silver; because it is evident, that that difference is occasioned by the scarcity of the latter, which is now become a merchandise, rising and falling, like other commodities, as there is a greater or less demand for it, or as it is more or less plenty.

Yet farther, in order to make a true estimate of the value of money, we must distinguish between money as it is bullion, which is merchandise, and as by being coined it is made a currency. For its value as a merchandise, and its value as a currency, are two distinct things; and each may possibly rise and fall in some degree independent of the other. Thus, if the quantity of bullion increases in a country, it will proportionably decrease in value; but if at the same time the quantity of current coin should decrease, (supposing payments may not be made in bullion) what coin there is will rise in value as a currency; that is, people will give more labor in manufactures for a certain sum of ready money.

In the same manner must we consider a *paper currency* founded on land; as it is land, and as it is a currency.

Money as bullion, or as land, is valuable by so much labor as it costs to procure that bullion or land.

Money, as a currency, has an additional value by so much time and labor as it saves in the exchange of commodities.

If, as a currency, it saves one fourth part of the time and labor of a country; it has, on that account, one fourth added to its original value.

When there is no money in a country, all commerce must be by exchange. Now, if it takes one fourth part of the time and labor of a country, to exchange or get their commodities exchanged; then, in computing their value, that labor of exchanging must be added to the labor of manufacturing those commodities. But if that time or labor is saved by introducing money sufficient, then the additional value on account of the labor of exchanging may be abated, and things sold for only the value of the labor in making them; because the people may now in the same time make one fourth more in quantity of manufactures than they could before.

From these considerations it may be gathered, that in all the degrees between having no money in a country, and money sufficient for the trade, it will rise and fall in value as a currency, in proportion to the decrease or increase of its quantity. And if there may be at some time more than enough, the overplus will have no effect towards making the currency, as a currency, of less value than when there was but enough; because such overplus will not be used in trade, but be some other way disposed of.

If we inquire, *how much per cent interest ought to be required upon the loan of these bills,* we must consider what is the natural standard of usury. And this appears to be, where the security is undoubted, at least the rent of so much land as the money lent will buy. For it cannot be expected, that any man will lend his money for less than it would fetch him in as rent if he laid it out in land, which is the most secure property in the world. But if the security is casual, then a kind of insurance must be interwoven with the simple natural interest, which may advance the usury very conscionably to any height below the principal itself. Now, among us, if the value of land is twenty years' purchase, five per cent is the just rate of interest for money lent on undoubted security. Yet, if money grows scarce in a country, it becomes more difficult for people to make punctual payments of what they borrow, money being hard to be raised; likewise, trade being discouraged and business impeded for want of a currency, abundance of people must be in declining circumstances, and by these means security is more precarious than where money is plenty. On such accounts it is no wonder if people ask a greater interest for their money than the natural interest; and what is above is to be looked upon as a kind of *premium* for the insurance of those uncertainties, as they are greater or less. Thus we always see, that where money is scarce, interest is high, and low where it is plenty. Now it is certainly the advantage of a country to make interest as low as possible, as I have already shown; and this can be done no other way than by making money plentiful. And since, in emitting paper money among us, the office has the best of security, the titles to the land being all skilfully and strictly examined and ascertained; and as it is only permitting the people by law to coin their own land, which costs the government nothing, the interest being more than enough to pay the charges of printing, officers' fees, etc., I cannot see any good reason why four per cent to the loan-office should not be thought fully sufficient. As a low interest may incline more to take money out, it will become more plentiful in trade; and this may bring down the common usury, in which security is more dubious, to the pitch it is determined at by law.

If it should be objected, *that emitting it at so low an interest, and on such easy terms, will occasion more to be taken out than the trade of the country really requires;* it may be answered, that, as has already been shown, there can never be so much of it emitted as to make it fall below the land it is founded on; because no man in his senses will mortgage his estate for what is of no more value to him than that he has mortgaged, especially if the possession of what he receives is more precarious than of what he mortgages, as that of paper money is when compared to land. And if it should ever become so plenty by indiscreet persons continuing to take out a large overplus, above what is necessary in trade, so as to make people imagine it would become by that means of less value than their mortgaged lands, they would immediately of course begin to pay it in again to the office to redeem their land, and continue to do so till there was no more left in trade than was absolutely necessary. And thus the proportion would find itself (though there were a million too much in the office to be let out), without giving any one the trouble of calculation.

It may, perhaps, be objected to what I have written concerning the advantages of a large addition to our currency, *that, if the people of this province increase, and husbandry is more followed, we shall over-stock the markets with our produce of flour, etc.* To this it may be answered, that we can never have too many people (nor too much money.) For, when one branch of trade or business is overstocked with hands, there are the more to spare to be employed in another. So, if raising wheat proves dull, more may (if there is money to support and carry on new manufactures) proceed to the raising and manufacturing of hemp, silk, iron, and many other things the country is very capable of, for which we only want people to work, and money to pay them with.

Upon the whole it may be observed, that it is the highest interest of a trading country in general to make money plentiful; and that it can be a disadvantage to none that have honest designs. It cannot hurt even the usurers, though it should sink what they receive as interest; because they will be proportionably more secure in what they lend; or they will have an opportunity of employing their money to greater advantage, to themselves as well as to the country. Neither can it hurt those merchants, who have great sums outstanding in debts in the country, and seem on that account to have the most plausible reason to fear it; to wit, because a large addition being made to our currency will increase the demand of our exporting produce, and by that means raise the price of it, so that they will not be able to purchase so much bread or flour with one hundred pounds when they shall receive it after such an addition, as they now can, and may if there is no addition. I say it cannot hurt even such, because they will get in their debts just in exact proportion so much the easier and sooner as the money becomes plentier; and therefore, considering the interest and trouble saved, they will not be losers; because it only sinks in value as a currency, proportionally as it becomes more plenty. It cannot hurt the interest of Great Britain, as has been shown; and it will greatly advance the interest of the proprietor. It will be an advantage to every industrious tradesman, etc., because his business will be carried on more freely, and trade be universally enlivened by it. And as more business in all manufactures will be done, by so much as the labor and time spent in exchange is saved, the country in general will grow so much the richer.

It is nothing to the purpose to object the wretched fall of the bills in New England and South Carolina, unless it might be made evident that their currency was emitted with the same prudence, and on such good security, as ours is; and it certainly was not.

As this essay is wrote and published in haste, and the subject in itself intricate, I hope I shall be censured with candor, if, for want of time carefully to revise what I have written, in some places I should appear to have expressed myself too obscurely, and in others am liable to objections I did not foresee. I sincerely desire to be acquainted with the truth, and on that account shall think myself obliged to any one, who will take the pains to show me, or the public, where I am mistaken in my conclusions. And as we all know there are among us several gentlemen of acute parts and profound learning, who are very much against any addition to our money, it were to be wished that they would favor the country with their sentiments on this head in print; which, supported with truth and good reasoning, may probably be very convincing. And this is to be desired the rather because many people, knowing the abilities of those gentlemen to manage a good cause, are apt to construe their silence in this, as an argument of a bad one. Had any thing of that kind ever yet appeared, perhaps I should not have given the public this trouble. But, as those ingenious gentlemen have not yet (and I doubt never will) think it worth their concern to enlighten the minds of their erring countrymen in this particular, I think it would be highly commendable in every one of us, more fully to bend our minds to the study of *what is the true interest of Pennsylvania;* whereby we may be enabled, not only to reason pertinently with one another; but, if occasion requires, to transmit home such clear representations, as must inevitably convince our superiors of the reasonableness and integrity of our designs.

Philadelphia, April 3, 1729.

A Proposal for Promoting Useful Knowledge Among the British Plantations in America

The English are possessed of a long tract of continent, from Nova Scotia to Georgia, extending north and south through different climates, having different soils, producing different plants, mines, and minerals, and capable of different improvements, manufactures, etc.

The first drudgery of settling new colonies, which confines the attention of people to mere necessaries, is now pretty well over; and there are many in every province in circumstances that set them at ease, and afford leisure to cultivate the finer arts and improve the common stock of knowledge. To such of these who are men of speculation, many hints must from time to time arise, many observations occur, which, if well examined, pursued, and improved, might produce discoveries to the advantage of some or all of the British plantations, or to the benefit of mankind in general.

But as from the extent of the country such persons are widely separated, and seldom can see and converse or be acquainted with each other, so that many useful particulars remain uncommunicated, die with the discoverers, and are lost to mankind; it is, to remedy this inconvenience for the future, proposed,

That one society be formed of *virtuosi* or ingenious men,

residing in the several colonies, to be called *The American Philosophical Society*, who are to maintain a constant correspondence.

That Philadelphia, being the city nearest the center of the continent colonies, communicating with all of them northward and southward by post, and with all the islands by sea, and having the advantage of a good growing library, be the center of the society.

That at Philadelphia there be always at least seven members, viz., a physician, a botanist, a mathematician, a chemist, a mechanician, a geographer, and a general natural philosopher, besides a president, treasurer, and secretary.

That these members meet once a month, or oftener, at their own expense, to communicate to each other their observations and experiments, to receive, read, and consider such letters, communications, or queries as shall be sent from distant members; to direct the dispersing of copies of such communications as are valuable, to other distant members, in order to procure their sentiments thereupon.

That the subjects of the correspondence be: all new-discovered plants, herbs, trees, roots, their virtues, uses, etc.; methods of propagating them, and making such as are useful, but particular to some plantations, more general; improvements of vegetable juices, as ciders, wines, etc.; new methods of curing or preventing diseases; all new-discovered fossils in different countries, as mines, minerals, and quarries; new and useful improvements in any branch of mathematics; new discoveries in chemistry, such as improvements in distillation, brewing, and assaying of ores; new mechanical inventions for saving labour, as mills and carriages, and for raising and conveying of water, draining of meadows, etc.; all new arts, trades, and manufactures, that may be proposed or thought of; surveys, maps and charts of particular parts of the seacoasts or inland countries; course and junction of rivers and great roads, situation of lakes and mountains, nature of the soil and productions; new methods of improving the breed of useful animals; introducing other sorts from foreign countries; new improvements in planting, gardening, and clearing land; and all philosophical experiments that let light into the nature of things, tend to increase the power of man over matter, and multiply the conveniences or pleasures of life.

That a correspondence, already begun by some intended members, shall be kept up by this society with the Royal Society of London and with the Dublin Society.

That every member shall have abstracts sent him quarterly, of everything valuable communicated to the society's secretary at Philadelphia; free of all charge except the yearly payment hereafter mentioned.

That, by permission of the postmaster-general, such communications pass between the secretary of the society and the members, postage-free.

That, for defraying the expense of such experiments as the society shall judge proper to cause to be made, and other contingent charges for the common good, every member send a piece of eight per annum to the treasurer, at Philadelphia, to form a common stock, to be disbursed by the order of the president with the consent of the majority of the members that can conveniently be consulted thereupon, to such persons and places where and by whom the experiments are to be made, and otherwise as there shall be occasion; of which disbursements an exact account shall be kept, and communicated yearly to every member.

That, at the first meetings of the members at Philadelphia, such rules be formed for regulating their meetings and transactions for the general benefit, as shall be convenient and necessary; to be afterward changed and improved as there shall be occasion, wherein due regard is to be had to the advice of distant members.

That, at the end of every year, collections be made and printed, of such experiments, discoveries, and improvements, as may be thought of public advantage; and that every member have a copy sent him.

That the business and duty of the secretary be to receive all letters intended for the society, and lay them before the president and members at their meetings; to abstract, correct, and methodize such papers as require it, and as he shall be directed to do by the president, after they have been considered, debated, and digested by the society; to enter copies thereof in the society's books, and make out copies for distant members; to answer their letters by direction of the president, and keep records of all material transactions of the society.

Benjamin Franklin, the writer of this proposal, offers himself to serve the society as their secretary, till they shall be provided with one more capable.

Philadelphia, May 14, 1743

The Examination of Doctor Benjamin Franklin In the British House of Commons, Relative To the Repeal of the American Stamp Act (1766)

In 1766, Benjamin Franklin was summoned to the British House of Commons to give testimony concerning the American colonies' opposition to the Stamp Act. In the short sections of that testimony excerpted here, Franklin is explicit in his denunciation of Britain's policy of looting the American colonies of wealth. The exchange between Parliament and Franklin is a continuous effort on the part of the examiner to determine whether there are any circumstances under which the colonists will accept the imposition of an internal tax. At each point, Franklin distinguishes between the purely looting function of such a tax, imposed without colonial representation in the Parliament, and the intent of an external tax to regulate commerce. In the process, he delineates for Parliament a program of agricultural and industrial development for the colonies, and the American colonists' determination to see that program realized—with or without the assistance of Britain.

... Q. Did the Americans ever dispute the controling power of Parliament to regulate commerce?

A. No.

Q. Can anything less than a military force carry the Stamp Act into execution?

A. I do not see how a military force can be applied to that purpose.

Q. Why may it not?

A. Suppose a military force sent into America, they will find nobody in arms; what are they then to do? They cannot force a man to take stamps who chooses to do without them. They will not find a rebellion; they may indeed make one.

Q. If the act is not repealed, what do you think will be the consequences?

A.   A total loss of the respect and affection the people of America bear to this country, and of all the commerce that depends on that respect and affection.

Q.   How can the commerce be affected?

A.   You will find that, if the act is not repealed, they will take very little of your manufactures in a short time.

Q.   Is it in their power to do without them?

A.   I think they may very well do without them.

Q.   Is it their interest not to take them?

A.   The goods they take from Britain are either necessaries, mere conveniences, or superfluities. The first, as cloth, etc., with a little industry they can make at home; the second they can do without till they are able to provide them among themselves; and the last, which are much the greatest part, they will strike off immediately. They are mere articles of fashion, purchased and consumed because the fashion in a respected country; but will now be detested and rejected. The people have already struck off, by general agreement, the use of all goods fashionable in mournings, and many thousand pounds worth are sent back as unsalable. . . .

. . . Q. Would the repeal of the Stamp Act be any discouragement of your manufactures? Will the people that have begun to manufacture decline it?

A.   Yes, I think they will; especially if, at the same time, the trade is opened again, so that remittances can be easily made. I have known several instances that make it probable. In the war before last, tobacco being low, and making little remittance, the people of Virginia went generally into family manufactures. Afterward, when tobacco bore a better price, they returned to the use of British manufactures. So fulling mills were very much disused in the last war in Pennsylvania, because bills were then plenty and remittances could easily be made to Britain for English cloth and other goods.

Q.   If the Stamp Act should be repealed, would it induce the assemblies of America to acknowledge the rights of parliament to tax them, and would they erase their resolutions?

A.   No, never.

Q.   Are there no means of obliging them to erase those resolutions?

A.   None that I know of; they will never do it, unless compelled by force of arms.

Q.   Is there a power on earth that can force them to erase them?

A.   No power, how great soever, can force men to change their opinions.

Q.   Do they consider the post office as a tax, or as a regulation?

A.   Not as a tax, but as a regulation and conveniency; every assembly encouraged it, and supported it in its infancy, by grants of money, which they would not otherwise have done; and the people have always paid the postage.

Q.   When did you receive the instructions you mentioned?

A.   I brought them with me, when I came to England, about 15 months since.

Q.   When did you communicate that instruction to the minister?

A.   Soon after my arrival, while the stamping of America was under consideration, and before the bill was brought in.

Q.   Would it be most for the interest of Great Britain to employ the hands of Virginia in tobacco, or in manufactures?

A.   In tobacco, to be sure.

Q.   What used to be the pride of the Americans?

A.   To indulge in the fashions and manufactures of Great Britain.

Q.   What is now their pride?

A.   To wear their old clothes over again, till they can make new ones.

Letter to Joseph Priestley
Passy 8, Feb., 1780

Dear Sir,

Your kind letter of Sept. 27 came to hand but very lately, the bearer having stayed long in Holland. I always rejoice to hear of your being still employed in experimental researches into nature, and of the success you meet with. The rapid progress true science now makes occasions my regretting sometimes that I was born too soon. It is impossible to imagine the height to which may be carried, in a 1000 years, the power of man over matter. We may perhaps learn to deprive large masses of their gravity, and give them absolute levity for the sake of easy transport. Agriculture may diminish its labor and double its produce; all diseases may by sure means be prevented or cured, not excepting even that of old age, and our lives lengthened at pleasure even beyond the antediluvian standard. O that mortal science were in as fair a way of improvement, that men would cease to be wolves to one another, and that human beings would at length learn what they now improperly call humanity!

I am glad my little paper on the Aurora Borealis pleased you. If it should occasion further inquiry, and so produce a better hypothesis, it will not be wholly useless. I am ever, with the greatest and most sincere esteem, dear Sir, etc.

B. Franklin

Reflections on the Augmentation of Wages, Which Will Be Occasioned in Europe by the American Revolution

THE independence and prosperity of the United States of America will raise the price of wages in Europe, an advantage of which I believe no one has yet spoken.

The low rate of wages is one of the greatest defects in the political associations of Europe, or rather of the old world.

If the term *wages* be taken in its widest signification, it will be found that almost all the citizens of a large state receive and pay wages. I shall confine my remarks, however, to one description of wages, the only one with which government should intermeddle, or which requires its care. I mean the wages of the lowest class, those men without property, without capital, who live solely by the labor of their hands. This is always the most numerous class in a state; and, consequently, that community cannot be pronounced happy, in which, from the lowness and insufficiency of wages, the laboring class procure so scanty a subsistence, that, barely able to provide for their own necessities, they have not the means of marrying and rearing a family, and are reduced to beggary, whenever employment fails them, or age and sickness oblige them to give up work.

Further, the wages under consideration ought not to be estimated by their amount in money, but by the quantity of provisions, clothing, and other commodities, which the laborer can procure for the money which he receives.

Unhappily, in all the political states of the old world, a numerous class of citizens have nothing to live upon but their wages, and these are inadequate to their support. This is the real cause of the misery of so many day-laborers, who work in the fields, or in manufactories in towns; of pauperism, an evil which is spreading every day, more and more, because governments attempt to check it by feeble remedies only; of depravity of morals; and of almost every crime. The policy of tyranny and of commerce has overlooked and disguised these truths. The horrible maxim, that the people must be poor, in order that they may remain in subjection, is still held by many persons of hard hearts and perverted understanding, with whom it were useless to contend. Others, again, think that the people should be poor, from a regard for the supposed interests of commerce. They believe that to increase the rate of wages would raise the price of the productions of the soil, and especially of industry, which are sold to foreign nations, and thus that exportation and the profits arising from it would be diminished. But this motive is at once cruel and ill-founded.

It is cruel; for, whatever may be the advantages of foreign commerce, if, in order to possess them, half the nation must languish in misery, we cannot without crime endeavour to obtain them, and it becomes the duty of a government to relinquish them. To desire to keep down the rate of wages, with the view of favoring the exportation of merchandise, is to seek to render the citizens of a state miserable, in order that foreigners may purchase its productions at a cheaper rate; it is, at most, attempting to enrich a few merchants by impoverishing the body of the nation; it is taking the part of the stronger in that contest, already so unequal, between the man who can pay wages, and him who is under the necessity of receiving them; it is, in one word, to forget, that the object of every political society ought to be the happiness of the largest number.

This motive is, moreover, ill-founded; for, in order to secure to a nation a profitable export for the products of its agriculture and manufactures, it is not necessary that the rate of wages should be reduced so extremely low, as we find it in almost all the countries of Europe. It is not the wages of the workman, but the price of the merchandise, that should be lowered, in order that this merchandise may be sold to foreign nations. But men have always neglected to make this distinction. The wages of the laborer are the price of his day's work. The price of merchandise is the sum it costs to gather the produce of the soil, or prepare any product of industry. The price of this production may be very moderate, while the laborer may receive good wages, that is, the means of procuring a comfortable subsistence. The labor necessary to gather or prepare the article to be sold may be cheap, and the wages of the workman good. Although the workmen of Manchester and Norwich, and those of Amiens and Abbeville, are employed in the same kind of labor, the former receive considerably higher wages than the latter; and yet the woollen fabrics of Manchester and Norwich, of the same quality, are not so dear as those of Amiens and Abbeville.

It would occupy too much time fully to develope this principle. I will only observe here, that it results in a great measure from the fact, that the price of labor in the arts, and even in agriculture, is wonderfully diminished by the perfection of the machinery employed in them, by the intelligence and activity of the workmen, and by the judicious division of labor. Now these methods of reducing the price of manufactured articles have nothing to do with the low wages of the workman. In a large manufactory, where animals are employed instead of men, and machinery instead of animal power, and where that judicious division of labor is made, which doubles, nay, increases tenfold, both power and time, the article can be manufactured and sold at a much lower rate, than in those establishments, which do not enjoy the same advantages; and yet the workmen in the former may receive twice as much as in the latter.

It is, undoubtedly, an advantage for a manufactory to obtain workmen at a moderate price; and excessively high wages are an obstacle to the foundation of large manufacturing establishments. This high price of wages, as I shall presently explain, is one reason for the opinion which is entertained, that it will many years before the manufactures of the United States of America can rival those of Europe. But we must not conclude from this, that manufactures cannot prosper, unless the wages of the workmen are reduced as low as we find them in Europe. And, moreover, the insufficiency of wages occasions the decline of a manufactory, as its prosperity is promoted by a high rate of wages.

High wages attract the most skilful and most industrious work-men. Thus the article is better made; it sells better; and, in this way, the employer makes a greater profit, than he could do by diminishing the pay of the workmen. A good workman spoils fewer tools, wastes

less material, and works faster, than one of inferior skill; and thus
the profits of the manufacturer are increased still more.

The perfection of machinery in all the arts is owing, in a great
degree, to the workmen. There is no important manufacture, in
which they have not invented some useful process, which saves time
and materials, or improves the workmanship. If common articles of
manufacture, the only ones worthy to interest the statesman, if woollen, cotton, and even silk stuffs, articles made of iron, steel, copper,
skins, leather, and various other things, are generally of better quality, at the same price, in England than in other countries, it is because
workmen are there better paid.

The low rate of wages, then, is not the real cause of the advantages
of commerce between one nation and another; but it is one of the
greatest evils of political communities.

Let us now inquire what is the situation of the United States in
this respect. The condition of the day-laborer, in these states, is
infinitely better than in the wealthiest countries in the old world,
and particularly England, where, however, wages are higher than in
any other part of Europe. In the state of New York, the lowest class
of workmen and those employed in the most ordinary kinds of labor
usually gain "three shillings and sixpence currency, equal to two
shillings sterling, a day; ship-carpenters, ten shillings and sixpence
currency, with a pint of rum, equal in all to five shillings and sixpence
sterling; house-carpenters and brick-layers, eight shillings currency,
equal to four shillings and sixpence sterling; journeymen tailors,
five shillings currency, equal to about two shillings and ten pence
sterling."

These prices, much higher than those of London, are quite as
high in other parts of the United States as in New York. I have taken
them from Adam Smith's *Wealth of Nations*.

An intelligent observer, who travelled through a part of the
United States in 1780, gives us a still more favorable idea of the price
that is paid there for work.

"At Farmington," says he, "I saw them weaving a kind of cam-
blet, and also a blue and white striped woollen cloth, for women's
clothing. These fabrics are all sold at three shillings and sixpence
per ell, in the currency of the country, equal to about forty-five *sous
tournois*. The sons and the grandsons of the master of the house were

working at the business. One workman can easily make five ells of this cloth a day; and as the original material costs but a shilling, he can earn ten or twelve shillings by his day's labor."

But this fact is so well known, that it is superfluous to attempt to prove it by further examples.

The causes of the high price of labor in our American States must then continue to operate more and more powerfully; since agriculture and population advance there with such rapidity, that labor of every description is increased in proportion.

Nor is this all. The high rate of wages paid them in money proves, that they are even better than one would suppose them at first view; and, in order to estimate them correctly, an important circumstance should be known. In every part of North America, the necessaries of life are cheaper than in England. Scarcity is unknown there. In the least productive seasons, the harvest is always sufficient for the supply of the inhabitants, and they are only obliged to diminish the exportation of their produce. Now, the price of labor in money being higher there than in England, and provisions cheaper, the actual wages, that is, the amount of necessary articles, which the day laborer can buy, is so much the greater.

It remains for me to show how the high rate of wages in America will increase their rate in Europe.

Two distinct causes will unite in producing this effect. The first is the greater quantity of labor, that Europe will have to perform, in consequence of the existence of another great nation in the commercial world, and of its continual increase; and the second, the emigration of European workmen, or the mere possibility of their emigrating, in order to go to America, where labor is better paid.

It is certain, that the amount of labor in the various branches of agriculture, manufactures, commerce, and navigation, must be augmented in Europe, by the addition of several millions of men to the commercial world. Now, the amount of annual labor being increased, labor will be somewhat better paid, and the rate of daily wages received by the workman will be raised by this concurrence of circumstances. For example, if the additional supply of one hundred thousand pieces of cloth, twenty thousand casks of wine, and ten thousand casks of brandy, is to be furnished to the Americans, not only will the persons necessarily employed in the production or manufacture of these commodities receive higher wages, but the price of all other kinds of labor will be augmented.

The rate of wages in Europe will be raised by yet another circumstance, with which it is important to be acquainted. I have already said, that the value of wages ought not to be estimated solely by the amount of money, nor even by the quantity of subsistence, which the workman receives per day, but also by the number of days in which he is employed; for it is by such a calculation alone, that we can find out what he has for each day. Is it not evident, that he who should be paid at the rate of forty pence a day, and should fail of obtaining work half the year, would really have but twenty pence to subsist upon, and that he would be less advantageously situated than the man, who, receiving but thirty pence, could yet be supplied with work every day? Thus the Americans, occasioning in Europe an increased demand and necessity for labor, would also necessarily cause there an augmentation of wages, even supposing the price of the day's work to remain at the same rate.

Perhaps it will be objected to what I have said, that this new nation will contain within itself as many laboring people as it can employ; and that thus, adding nothing to the quantity of work to be performed in Europe, it will be no advantage to the men who perform this work. But I reply, that it is impossible but that the United States of America, in their present condition, and much more when their population and wealth shall be doubled, nay, quadrupled, should employ the labor of Europeans in one way or another. It is impossible, because in this respect the Americans are not differently situated from other nations, who all have need of each other. The fertility of the American soil, the abundance and variety of its productions, the activity and industry of its inhabitants, and the unrestricted commerce, which will sooner or later be established in Europe in consequence of the American Independence, secure the relations of America with other countries; because she will furnish to other nations such of her productions, as they may require; and, as each country possesses some productions peculiar to itself, the demand and advantage will be reciprocal.

The second cause, which I have said must cooperate in producing an augmentation of wages in Europe, is emigration, or the mere possibility of emigrating to America, where labor is better paid. It is easy to conceive, that, when this difference is generally known, it will draw to the United States many men, who, having no means of subsistence but their labor, will flock to the place where this labor is best recompensed. Since the last peace, the Irish have been continually emigrating to America. The reason of this is, that in Ireland wages are much less than in England, and that the lower classes are consequently great sufferers. Germany has also furnished new citizens to the United States; and all these laborers must, by leaving Europe, have raised the price of work for those who remain.

This salutary effect will be produced even without emigration, and will result from the mere possibility of emigrating, at least in those states of Europe whose inhabitants are not compelled to leave their own country by excessive taxation, bad laws, and the intolerance of government.

In order to raise the rate of wages, it is enough that higher can be obtained in any place to which the workman, who depends upon them, can remove. It has been wisely remarked in the discussions, which have arisen upon the corn trade, that the simple liberty of exporting grain would keep up and even raise its price, without the actual exportation of a single bushel. The case is the same with wages. As European workmen can so easily remove to America to procure higher wages, they will oblige those who purchase their labor to pay them more for it.

Hence it follows, that these two causes of the rise of wages, actual emigration and the mere possibility of emigrating, will concur to produce the same effect. Each acting at first in an inconsiderable degree, there will be some emigration. Then wages will be raised, and the laborer, finding his gains increase, will no longer have a sufficiently powerful motive to emigrate.

But the rise of wages will not be equally felt by the different nations of Europe. It will be more or less considerable, in proportion to the greater or less facilities for emigration, which each affords. England, whose manners, language, and religion are the same with those of America, must naturally enjoy this advantage in a higher degree than any other European state. We may assert, that she already owes much to America; for her relations with that country, the market which she has found there for her merchandise, and which has raised the wages of the day-laborers employed in her agriculture and manufactures, are among the principal causes of her wealth, and of the political influence we find her exerting.

But, to say nothing of other advantages, which may ultimately accrue from the rise of wages, this augmentation has already produced one most valuable result in England. It has ameliorated the condition of that class of men, who live by the labor of their hands alone, that is, the most numerous portion of society. This class, elsewhere reduced to the most scanty subsistence, are much better off in England. They there obtain by their labor the necessaries of life in greater abundance than in many other parts of Europe; and there can be no doubt, that this springs from the influence of American commerce on the rate of wages.

I know it may be said, that, notwithstanding the increase of labor and of subsistence in Europe, and notwithstanding the emigration which may take place, the same causes which we have mentioned, and which have reduced wages so low, will continue to operate, because they are inherent in the constitutions of European states, whose defects will not be remedied by the liberty and prosperity of America. Perhaps it may be said, also, that the number of proprietors and capitalists, a number very small compared with that of the men, who, having no landed property nor capital, are compelled to live upon wages, will remain the same, because the causes which accumulate landed property and capital in their hands will not change, and consequently that they will reduce, or rather keep wages very low. Finally, it may be said, that the tyranny of the feudal laws, the mode of taxation, the excessive increase of the public revenue, and the laws of commerce, will always produce the same effect of diminishing wages, and that, should Europe derive any real advantage, in this respect, from American independence, it would not be permanent.

To these suggestions, many things may be said in reply. I will observe, in the first place, that, if the governments of Europe endeavour to counteract the salutary effects, which the independence of America would naturally produce in respect to them, it is not the less interesting to endeavour to ascertain what these effects would be. Better days may come, when, the true principles of the happiness of nations being better understood, there will be some sovereign sufficiently enlightened and just to put them in operation. The causes, which tend continually to accumulate and concentrate landed property and wealth in a few hands, may be diminished. The remains of the feudal system may be abolished, or, at least, rendered less oppressive. The mode of taxation may be changed, and its excess moderated. And, lastly, bad commercial regulations may be amended. The tendency of all these improvements will be, to enable the working classes to profit by the favorable change, which the American Revolution must naturally produce.

But, admitting that all the causes, which have just been mentioned, should concur to keep the wages, which the day-laborer receives for his work in Europe, at a low rate, they could, however, only weaken the influence exerted by the prosperity of America, and not wholly destroy it. If every thing else remained in the same state, there would still be a greater consumption, and consequently more labor to be performed. Now, this consumption and labor continually increasing in the same ratio with the increase of population and wealth in the New World, an augmentation of wages in Europe will be the necessary result; for the counteracting causes will not operate more powerfully than they now do.

George Washington

T*he following writings of George Washington came late in his career—the* Will *in July of 1799, and the two* Farewell Addresses *in 1796. They reflect his concern with education and industrial growth as the mainstays of a safe and growing nation, as well as the warnings against "entangling alliances" and faction which are so often quoted.*

The first Farewell Address *was written by the first President in September of 1796, in order to explain why he intended to withdraw from public life, and not stand for re-election. It is the one which was worked over by Alexander Hamilton, and was published in* American Daily Advertiser *of Sept. 19.*

The second Farewell Address *is Washington's eighth annual address to Congress, which was delivered before a joint session on Dec. 7, 1796.*

Farewell Address
(United States, September 19, 1796)

Friends, and Fellow-Citizens: The period for a new election of a Citizen, to Administer the Executive government of the United States, being not far distant, and the time actually arrived, when your thought must be employed in designating the person, who is to be cloathed with that important trust, it appears to me proper, especially as it may conduce to a more distinct expression of the public voice, that I should now apprise you of the resolution I have formed, to decline being considered among the number of those, out of whom a choice is to be made.

I beg you, at the same time, to do me that justice to be assured, that this resolution has not been taken, without a strict regard to all the considerations appertaining to the relation, which binds a dutiful citizen to his country, and that, in with drawing the tender of service which silence in my situation might imply, I am influenced by no diminution of zeal for your future interest, no deficiency of grateful respect for your past kindness; but am supported by a full conviction that the step is compatible with both.

The acceptance of, and continuance hitherto in, the office to which your Suffrages have twice called me, have been a uniform sacrifice of inclination to the opinion of duty, and to a deference for what appeared to be your desire. I constantly hoped, that it would have been much earlier in my power, consistently with motives, which I was not at liberty to disregard, to return to that retirement, from which I had been reluctantly drawn. The strength of my inclination to do this, previous to the last Election, had even led to the preparation of an address to declare it to you; but mature reflection on the then perplexed and critical posture of our Affairs with foreign Nations, and the unanimous advice of persons entitled to my confidence, impelled me to abandon the idea.

I rejoice, that the state of your concerns, external as well as internal, no longer renders the pursuit of inclination incompatible with the sentiment of duty, or proprietary; and am persuaded whatever partiality may be retained for my services, that in the present circumstances of our country, you will not disapprove my determination to retire.

The impressions, with which I first undertook the arduous trust, were explained on the proper occasion. In the discharge of this trust, I will only say, that I have, with good intentions, contributed towards the Organization and Administration of the government, the best exertions of which a very fallible judgment was capable. Not unconscious, in the outset, of the inferiority of my qualifications, experience in my own eyes, perhaps still more in the eyes of others, has strengthened the motives to diffidence of myself; and every day the encreasing weight of years admonishes me more and more, that the shade of retirement is as necessary to me as it will be welcome. Satisfied that if any circumstances have given peculiar value to my services, they were temporary, I have the consolation to believe, that while choice and prudence invite me to quit the political scene, patriotim does not forbid it.

In looking forward to the moment, which is intended to terminate the career of my public life, my feelings do not permit me to suspend the deep acknowledgment of that debt of gratitude wch. I owe to my beloved country, for the many honors it has conferred upon me; still more for the stedfast confidence with which it has supported me; and for the opportunities I have thence enjoyed of manifesting my inviolable attachment, by services faithful and persevering, though in usefulness unequal to my zeal. If benefits have resulted to our country from these services, let it always be remembered to your praise, and as an instructive example in our annals, that, under circumstances in which the Passions agitated in every direction were liable to mislead, amidst appearances sometimes dubious, viscissitudes of fortune often discouraging, in situations in which not unfrequently want of Success has countenanced the spirit of criticism, the constancy of your support was the essential prop of the efforts, and a guarantee of the plans by which they were effected. Profoundly penetrated with this idea, I shall carry it with me to my grave, as a strong incitement to unceasing vows that Heaven may continue to you the choicest tokens of its beneficence; that your Union and brotherly affection may be perpetual; that the free constitution, which is the work of your hands, may be sacredly maintained; that its Administration in every department may be stamped with wisdom and Virtue; that, in fine, the happiness of the people of these States, under the auspices of liberty, may be made complete, by so careful a preservation and so prudent a use of this blessing as will acquire to them the glory of recommending it to the applause, the affection, and adoption of every nation which is yet a stranger to it.

Here, perhaps, I ought to stop. But a solicitude for your welfare, which cannot end but with my life, and the apprehension of danger, natural to that solicitude, urge me on an occasion like the present, to offer to your solemn contemplation, and to recommend to your frequent review, some sentiments; which are the result of much reflection, of no inconsiderable observation, and which appear to me all important to the permanency of your felicity as a People. These will be offered to you with the more freedom, as you can only see in them the disinterested warnings of a parting friend, who can possibly have no personal motive to biass his counsel. Nor can I forget, as an encouragement to it, your endulgent reception of my sentiments on a former and not dissimilar occasion.

Interwoven as is the love of liberty with every ligament of your hearts, no recommendation of mine is necessary to fortify or confirm the attachment.

The Unity of Government which constitutes you one people is also now dear to you. It is justly so; for it is a main Pillar in the

Edifice of your real independence, the support of your tranquility
at home; your peace abroad; of your safety; of your prosperity; of
that very Liberty which you so highly prize. But as it is easy to
foresee, that from different causes and from different quarters, much
pains will be taken, many artifices employed, to weaken in your
minds the conviction of this truth; as this is the point in your political
fortress against which the batteries of internal and external enemies
will be most constantly and actively (though often covertly and
insidiously) directed, it is of infinite moment, that you should properly estimate the immense value of your national Union to your
collective and individual happiness; that you should cherish a cordial,
habitual and immoveable attachment to it; accustoming yourselves
to think and speak of it as of the Palladium of your political safety
and prosperity; watching for its preservation with jealous anxiety;
discountenancing whatever may suggest even a suspicion that it can
in any event be abandoned, and indignantly frowning upon the first
dawning of every attempt to alienate any portion of our Country
from the rest, or to enfeeble the sacred ties which now link together
the various parts.

For this you have every inducement of sympathy and interest.
Citizens by birth or choice, of a common country, that country has
a right to concentrate your affections. The name of AMERICAN, which
belongs to you, in your national capacity, must always exalt the just
pride of Patriotism, more than any appellation derived from local
discriminations. With slight shades of difference, you have the same
Religeon, Manners, Habits and political Principles. You have in a
common cause fought and triumphed together. The independence
and liberty you possess are the work of joint councils, and joint
efforts; of common dangers, sufferings and successes.

But these considerations, however powerfully they address themselves to your sensibility are greatly outweighed by those which apply
more immediately to your Interest. Here every portion of our country
finds the most commanding motives for carefully guarding and preserving the Union of the whole.

The *North*, in an unrestrained intercourse with the *South*, protected by the equal Laws of a common government, finds in the
productions of the latter, great additional resources of Maratime
and commercial enterprise and precious materials of manufacturing
industry. The *South* in the same Intercourse, benefitting by the

Agency of the *North,* sees its agriculture grow and its commerce expand. Turning partly into its own channels the seamen of the *North,* it finds its particular navigation envigorated; and while it contributes, in different ways, to nourish and increase the general mass of the National navigation, it looks foward to the protection of a Maratime strength, to which itself is unequally adapted. The *East,* in a like intercourse with the *West,* already finds, and in the progressive improvement of interior communications, by land and water, will more and more find a valuable vent for the commodities which it brings from abroad, or manufactures at home. The *West* derives from the *East* supplies requisite to its growth and comfort, and what is perhaps of still greater consequence, it must of necessity owe the *secure* enjoyment of indispensable *outlets* for its own productions to the weight, influence, and the future Maritime strength of the Atlantic side of the Union, directed by an indissoluble community of Interest as *one Nation.* Any other tenure by which the *West* can hold this essential advantage, whether derived from its own seperate strength, or from an apostate and unnatural connection with any foreign Power, must be intrinsically precarious.

While then every part of our country thus feels an immediate and particular Interest in Union, all the parts combined cannot fail to find in the united mass of means and efforts greater strength, greater resource, proportionably greater security from external danger, a less frequent interruption of their Peace by foreign Nations; and, what is of inestimable value! they must derive from Union an exemption from those broils and Wars between themselves, which so frequently afflict neighbouring countries, not tied together by the same government; which their own rivalships alone would be sufficient to produce, but which opposite foreign alliances, attachments and intriegues would stimulate and imbitter. Hence likewise they will avoid the necessity of those overgrown Military establishments, which under any form of Government are inauspicious to liberty, and which are to be regarded as particularly hostile to Republican Liberty: In this sense it is, that your Union ought to be considered as a main prop of your liberty, and that the love of the one ought to endear to you the preservation of the other.

These considerations speak a persuasive language to every reflecting and virtuous mind, and exhibit the continuance of the UNION as a primary object of Patriotic desire. Is there a doubt, whether a common government can embrace so large a sphere? Let experience solve it. To listen to mere speculation in such a case were criminal. We are authorized to hope that a proper organization of the whole, with the auxiliary agency of governments for the respective Sub divisions, will affaord a happy issue to the experiment. 'Tis well worth a fair and full experiment. With such powerful and obvious motives to Union, affecting all parts of our country, while experience shall not have demonstrated its impracticability, there will always be reason, to distrust the patriotism of those, who in any quarter may endeavor to weaken its bands.

In contemplating the causes wch. may disturb our Union, it occurs as matter of serious concern, that any ground should have been furnished for characterizing parties by *Geographical* discriminations: *Northern* and *Southern*; *Altnatic* and *Western*; whence designing men may endeavour to excite a belief that there is a real difference of local interests and views. One of the expedients of Party to acquire influence, within particular districts, is to misrepresent the opinions and aims of other Districts. You cannot shield yourselves too much against the jealousies and heart burnings which spring from these misarepresentations. They tend to render Alien to each other those who ought to be bound together by fraternal affection. The Inhabitants of our Western country have lately had a useful lesson on this head. They have seen, in the Negociation by the Executive, and in the unanimous ratification by the Senate, of the Treaty with Spain, and in the universal satisfaction at that event, throughout the United States, a decisive proof how unfounded were the suspicions propagated among them of a policy in the General Government and in the Atlantic States unfriendly to their Interests in regard to the MISSISSIPPI. They have been witnesses to the formation of two Treaties, that with G: Britain and that with Spain, which secure to them every thing they could desire, in respect to our Foreign relations, towards confirming their prosperity. Will it not be their wisdom to rely for the preservation of [*sic*] these advantages on the UNION by wch. they were procured? Will they not henceforth be deaf to those advisers, if such there are, who would sever them from their Brethren and connect them with Aliens?

To the efficacy and permanency of Your Union, a Government for the whole is indispensable. No Alliances however strict between the parts can be adequate substitute. They must inevitably experience the infractions and interruptions which all Alliances in all times have experienced. Sensible of this momentous truth, you have improved upon your first essay, by the adoption of a Constitution of Government, better calculated than your former for an intimate Union, and for the efficacious management of your common concerns. This government, the offspring of our own choice uninfluenced and unawed, adopted upon full investigation and mature deliberation, completely free in its principles, in the distribution of its powers, uniting security with energy, and containing within itself a provision for its own amendment, has a just claim to your confidence and your support. Respect for its authority, compliance with its Laws, acquiescence in its measures, are duties enjoined by the fundamental maxims of true Liberty. The basis of our political systems is the right of the people to make and to alter their Constitutions of Government. But the Constitution which at any time exists, 'till changed by an explicit and authentic act of the whole People, is sacredly obligatory upon all. The very idea of the power and the right of the People to establish Government presupposes the duty of every Individual to obey the established Government.

All obstructions to the execution of the Laws, all combinations and Associations, under whatever plausible character, with the real design to direct, controul counteract, or awe the regular deliberation and action of the Constituted authorities are distructive of this fundamental principle and of fatal tendency. They serve to organize faction, to give it an artificial and extraordinary force; to put in the place of the delegated will of the Nation, the will of a party; often a small but artful and enterprizing minority of the Community; and, according to the alternate triumphs of different parties, to make the public administration of the Mirror of the ill concerted and incongruous projects of faction, rather than the organ of consistent and wholesome plans digested by common councils and modefied by mutual interests. However combinations or Associations of the above description may now and then answer popular ends, they are likely, in the course of time and things, to become potent engines, by which cunning, ambitious and unprincipled men will be enabled to subvert the Power of the People, and to usurp for themselves the reins of Government; destroying afterwards the very engines which have lifted them to unjust dominion.

Towards the preservation of your Government and the permanency of your present happy state, it is requisite, not only that you steadily discountenance irregular oppositions to its acknowledged authority, but also that you resist with care the spirit of innovation upon its principles however specious the pretexts. one method of assault may be to effect, in the forms of the Constitution, alterations which will impair the energy of the system, and thus to undermine what cannot be directly overthrown. In all the changes to which you may be invited, remember that time and habit are at least as necessary to fix the true character of Governments, as of other human institutions; that experience is the surest standard, by which to test the real tendency of the existing Constitution of a country; that facility in changes upon the credit of mere hypotheses and opinion exposes to perpetual change, from the endless variety of hypotheses and opinion; and remember, especially, that for the efficient management of your common interests, in a country so extensive as ours, a Government of as much vigour as is consistent with the perfect security of Liberty is indispensable. Liberty itself will find in such a Government, with powers properly distributed and adjusted, its surest Guardian. It is indeed little else than a name, where the Government is too feeble to withstand the enterprises of faction, to confine each member of the Society within the limits prescribed by the laws and to maintain all in the secure and tranquil enjoyment of the rights of person and property.

I have already intimated to you the danger of Parties in the State, with particular reference to the founding of them on Geographical discriminations. Let me now take a more comprehensive view, and warn you in the most solemn manner against the baneful effects of the Spirit of Party, generally.

This spirit, unfortunately, is inseperable from our nature, having its root in the strongest passions of the human Mind. It exists under different shapes in all Governments, more or less stifled, controuled, or repressed; but, in those of the popular form it is seen in its greatest rankness and is truly their worst enemy.

The alternate domination of one faction over another, sharpened by the spirit of revenge natural to party dissention, which in different ages and countries has perpetrated the most horrid enormities, is itself a frightful despotism. But this leads at length to a more formal and permanent despotism. The disorders and miseries, which result, gradually incline the minds of men to seek security and repose in the absolute power of an Individual: and sooner or later the chief of some prevailing faction more able or more fortunate than his competitors, turns this disposition to the purposes of his own elevation, on the ruins of Public Liberty.

Without looking forward to an extremity of this kind (which nevertheless ought not to be entirely out of sight) the common and continual mischiefs of the spirit of Party are sufficient to make it the interest and the duty of a wise People to discourage and restrain it.

It serves always to distract the Public Councils and enfeeble the Public administration. It agitates the Community with ill founded jealousies and false alarms, kindles the animosity of one part against another, foments occasionally riot and insurrection. It opens the door to foreign influence and corruption, which find a facilitated access to the government itself through the channels of party passions. Thus the policy and [sic] the will of one country, are subjected to the policy and will of another.

There is an opinion that parties in free countries are useful checks upon the Administration of the Government and serve to keep alive the spirit of Liberty. This within certain limits is probably true, and in Governments of a Monarchical cast Patriotism may look with endulgence, if not with favour, upon the spirit of party. But in those of the popular character, in Governments purely elective, it is a spirit not to be encouraged. From their natural tendency, it is certain there will always be enough of that spirit for every salutary purpose. And there being constant danger of excess, the effort ought to be, by force of public opinion, to mitigate and assuage it. A fire not to be quenched; it demands a uniform vigilance to prevent its bursting into a flame, lest instead of warming it should consume.

It is important, likewise, that the habits of thinking in a free Country should inspire caution in those entrusted with its administration, to confine themselves within their respective Constitutional spheres; avoiding in the exercise of the Powers of one department to encroach upon another. The spirit of encroachment tends to consolidate the powers of all the departments in one, and thus to create whatever the form of government, a real despotism. A just estimate of that love of power, and proneness to abuse it, which predominates in the human heart is sufficient to satisfy us of the truth of this position. The necessity of reciprocal checks in the exercise of political power; by dividing and distributing it into different depositories, and constituting each the Guardian of the Public Weal against invasions by the others, has been evinced by experiments ancient and modern; some of them in our country and under our own eyes. To preserve them must be as necessary as to institute them. If in the opinion of the People, the distribution or modification of the Constitutional powers be in any particular wrong, let it be corrected by an amendment in the way which the Constitution designates. But let there be no change by usurpation; for though this, in one instance, may be the instrument of good, it is the customary weapon by which free governments are destroyed. The precedent must always greatly overbalance in permanent evil any partial or transient benefit which the use can at any time yield.

Of all the dispositions and habits which lead to political prosperity, Religion and morality are indispensable supports. In vain would that man claim the tribute of Patriotism, who should labour to subvert these great Pillars of human happiness, these firmest props of the duties of Men and citizens. The mere Politician, equally with the pious man ought to respect and to cherish them. A volume could not trace all their connections with private and public felicity. Let it simply be asked where is the security for property, for reputation, for life, if the sense of religious obligation *desert* the oaths, which are the instruments of investigation in Courts of Justice? And let us with caution indulge the supposition, that morality can be maintained without religion. Whatever may be conceded to the influence of refined education on minds of peculiar structure, reason and experience both forbid us to expect that National morality can prevail in exclusion of religious principle.

'Tis substantially true, that virtue or morality is a necessary spring of popular government. The rule indeed extends with more or less force to every species of free Government. Who that is a sincere friend to it, can look with indifference upon attempts to shake the foundation of the fabric.

Promote then as an object of primary importance, Institutions for the general diffusion of knowledge. In proportion as the structure of a government gives force to public opinion, it is essential that public opinion should be enlightened.

As a very important source of strength and security, cherish public credit. One method of preserving it is to use it as sparingly as possible: avoiding occasions of expence by cultivating peace, but remembering also that timely disbursements to prepare for danger frequently prevent much greater disbursements to repel it; avoiding likewise the accumulating of debt, not only by shunning occasions of expence, but by vigorous exertions in time of Peace to discharge the Debts which unavoidable wars may have occasioned, not ungenerously throwing upon posterity the burthen which we ourselves ought to bear. The execution of these maxims belongs to your Representatives, but it is necessary that public opinion should cooperate. To facilitate to them the performance of their duty, it is essential that you should practically bear in mind, that towards the payment of debts there must be Revenue; that to have Revenue there must be taxes; that no taxes can be devised which are not more or less inconvenient and unpleasant; that the intrinsic embarrassment inseperable from the selection of the proper objects (which is always a choice of difficulties) ought to be a decisive motive for a candid construction of the Conduct of the Government in making it, and for a spirit of acquiescence in the measures for obtaining Revenue which the public exigencies may at any time dictate.

Observe good faith and justice towds. all Nations. Cultivate peace and harmony with all. Religion and morality enjoin this conduct; and can it be that good policy does not equally enjoin it? It will be worthy of a free, enlightened, and, at no distant period, a great Nation, to give to mankind the magnanimous and too novel example of a People always guided by an exalted justice and benevolence. Who can doubt that in the course of time and things the fruits of such a plan would richly repay any temporary advantages wch. might be lost by a steady adherence to it? Can it be, that Providence has not connected the permanent felicity of a Nation with its virtue? The experiment, at least, is recommended by every sentiment which ennobles human Nature. Alas! is it rendered impossible by its vices?

In the execution of such a plan nothing is more essential than that permanent, inveterate antipathies against particular Nations and passionate attachments for others should be excluded; and that in place of them just and amicable feelings towards all should be cultivated. The Nation, which indulges towards another an habitual hatred, or an habitual fondness, is in some degree a slave. It is a slave to its animosity or to its affection, either of which is sufficient to lead it astray from its duty and its interest. Antipathy in one Nation against another, disposes each more readily to offer insult and injury, to lay hold of slight causes of umbrage, and to be haughty and intractable, when accidental or trifling occasions of dispute occur. Hence frequent collisions, obstinate envenomed and bloody contests. The Nation, prompted by illwill and resentment sometimes impels to War the Government, contrary to the best calculations of policy. The Government sometimes participates in the national propensity, and adopts through passion what reason would reject; at other times, it makes the animosity of the Nation subservient to projects of hostility instigated by pride, ambition and other sinister and pernicious motives. The peace often, sometimes perhaps the Liberty, of Nations has been the victim.

So likewise, a passionate attachment of one Nation for another produces a variety of evils. Sympathy for the favourite nation, facilitating the illusion of an imaginary common interest, in cases where no real common interest exists, and infusing into one the enmities of the other, betrays the former into a participation in the quarrels and Wars of the latter, without adequate inducement or justification: It leads also to concessions to the favourite Nation of priviledges denied to others, which is apt doubly to injure the Nation making the concessions; by unnecessarily parting with what ought to have been retained; and by exciting jealousy, ill will, and a disposition to retaliate, in the parties from whom eql. priviledges are withheld: And it gives to ambitious, corrupted, or deluded citizens (who devote themselves to the favourite Nation) facility to betray, or sacrifice the interests of their own country, without odium, sometimes even with popularity; gilding with appearances of a virtuous sense of obligation a commendable deference for public opinion, or a laudable zeal for public good, the base or foolish compliances of ambition corruption or infatuation.

As avenues to foreign influence in innumerable ways, such attachments are particularly alarming to the truly enlightened and independent Patriot. How many opportunities do they afford to tamper with domestic factions, to practice the arts of seduction, to mislead public opinion, to influence or awe the public Councils! Such an attachment of a small or weak, towards a great and powerful Nation, dooms the former to be the satellite of the latter.

Against the insidious wiles of foreign influence, (I conjure you to believe me fellow citizens) the jealousy of a free people ought to be *constantly* awake; since history and experience prove that foreign influence is one of the most baneful foes of Republican Government. But that jealousy to be useful must be impartial; else it becomes the instrument of the very influence to be avoided, instead of a defence against it. Excessive partiality for one foreign nation and excessive dislike of another, cause those whom they actuate to see danger only on one side, and serve to veil and even second the arts of influence on the other. Real Patriots, who may resist the intriegues of the favourite, are liable to become suspected and odious; while its tools and dupes usurp the applause and confidence of the people, to surrender their interests.

The Great rule of conduct for us, in regard to foreign Nations is in extending our commercial relations to have with them as little *political* connection as possible. So far as we have already formed engagements let them be fulfilled, with perfect good faith. Here let us stop.

Europe has a set of primary interests, which to us have none, or a very remote relation. Hence she must be engaged in frequent controversies, the causes of which are essentially foreign to our concerns. Hence therefore it must be unwise in us to implicate ourselves, by artificial ties, in the ordinary vicissitudes of her politics, or the ordinary combinations and collisions of her friendships, or enmities:

Our detached and distant situation invites and enables us to pursue a different course. If we remain one People, under an efficient government, the period is not far off, when we may defy material injury from external annoyance; when we may take such an attitude as will cause the neutrality we may at any time resolve upon to be scrupulously respected; when belligerent nations, under the impossibility of making acquisitions upon us, will not lightly hazard the giving us provocation; when we may choose peace or war, as our interest guided by our justice shall Counsel.

Why forego the advantages of so peculiar a situation? Why quit our own to stand upon foreign ground? Why, by interweaving our destiny with that of any part of Europe, entangle our peace and prosperity in the toils of European Ambition, Rivalship, Interest, Humour or Caprice?

'Tis our true policy to steer clear of permanent Alliances, with any portion of the foreign world. So far, I mean, as we are now at liberty to do it, for let me not be understood as capable of patronising infidility to existing engagements (I hold the maxim no less applicable to public than to private affairs, that honesty is always the best policy). I repeat it therefore, let those engagements be observed in their genuine sense. But in my opinion, it is unnecessary and would be unwise to extend them.

Taking care always to keep ourselves, by suitable establishments, on a respectably defensive posture, we may safely trust to temporary alliances for extraordinary emergencies.

Harmony, liberal intercourse with all Nations, are recommended by policy, humanity and interest. But even our Commercial policy should hold an equal and impartial hand: neither seeking nor granting exclusive favours or preferences; consulting the natural course of things; diffusing and deversifying by gentle means the streams of Commerce, but forcing nothing; establishing with Powers so dis-posed; in order to give to trade a stable course, to define the rights of our Merchants, and to enable the Government to support them; conventional rules of intercourse, the best that present circumstances and mutual opinion will permit, but temporary, and liable to be from time to time abandoned or varied, as experience and circum-stances shall dictate; constantly keeping in view, that 'tis folly in one Nation to look for disinterested favors from another; that it must pay with a portion of its Independence for whatever it may accept under that character; that by such acceptance, it may place itself in the condition of having given equivalents for nominal favours and yet of being reproached with ingratitude for not giving more. There can be no greater error than to expect, or calculate upon real favours from Nation to Nation. 'Tis an illusion which experience must cure, which a just pride ought to discard.

In offering to you, my Countrymen these counsels of an old and affectionate friend, I dare not hope they will make the strong and lasting impression, I could wish; that they will controul the usual current of the passions, or prevent our Nation from running the course which has hitherto marked the Destiny of Nations: But if I may even flatter myself, that they may be productive of some partial benefit, some occasional good; that they may now and then recur to moderate the fury of party spirit, to warn against the mischiefs of foreign Intriegue, to guard against the Impostures of pretended patriotism; this hope will be a full recompence for the solicitude for your welfare, by which they have been dictated.

How far in the discharge of my Official duties, I have been

guided by the principloes which have been delineated, the public Records and other evidences of my conduct must Witness to You and to the world. To myself, the assurance of my own conscience is, that I have at least believed myself to be guided by them.

In relation to the still subsisting War in Europe, my Proclamation of the 22d. of April 1793 is the index to my Plan. Sanctioned by your approving voice and by that of Your Representatives in both Houses of Congress, the spirit of that measure has continually governed me; uninfluenced by any attempts to deter or divert me from it.

After deliberate examination with the aid of the best lights I could obtain I was well satisfied that our Country, under all the circumstances of the case, had a right to take, and was bound in duty and interest, to take a Neutral position. Having taken it, I determined, as far as should depend upon me, to maintain it, with modertaion, perseverence and firmness.

The considerations, which respect the right to hold this conduct, it is not necessary on this occasion to detail. I will only observe, that according to my understanding of the matter, that right, so far from being denied by any of the Belligerent Powers has been virtually admitted by all.

The duty of holding a Neutral conduct may be inferred, without any thing more, from the obligation which justice and humanity imposse on every Nation, in cases in which it is free to act, to maintain inviolate the relations of Peace and amity towards other Nations.

The inducements of interest for observing that conduct will best be referred to your own reflections and experience. With me, a predominant motive has been to endeavour to gain time to our country to settle and mature its yet recent institutions, and to progress without interruption, to that degree of strength and consistency, which is necessary to give it, humanly speaking, the command of its own fortunes.

Though in reviewing the incidents of my Administration, I am unconscious of intentional error, I am nevertheless too sensible of my defects not to think it probable that I may have committed many errors. Whatever they may be I fervently beseech the Almighty to avert or mitigate the evils to which they may tend. I shall also carry with me the hope that my Country will never cease to view them with indulgence; and that after forty five years of my life dedicated to its Service, with an upright zeal, the faults of incompetent abilities will be consigned to oblivion, as myself must soon be to the Mansions of rest.

Relying on its kindness in this as in other things, and actuated by that fervent love towards it, which is so natural to a Man, who views in it the native soil of himself and his progenitors for several Generations; I anticipate with pleasing expectation that retreat, in which I promise myself to realize, without alloy, the sweet enjoyment of partaking, in the midst of my fellow Citizens, the benign influence of good Laws under a free Government, the ever favourite object of my heart, and the happy reward, as I trust, of our mutual cares, labours and dangers.

Farewell Address to Congress (December 7, 1796)

Fellow Citizens of the Senate and the House of Representatives: In recurring to the internal situation of our Country, since I had last the pleasure to Address you, I find ample reason for a renewed expression of that gratitude to the ruler of the Universe, which a continued series of prosperity has so often and so justly called forth.

The Acts of the last Session, which required special arrangements, have been, as far as circumstances would admit, carried into operation.

Measures calculated to insure a continuance of the friendship of the Indians, and to preserve peace along the extent of our interior frontier, have been digested and adopted. In the framing of these, care has been taken to guard on the one hand, our advanced Settlements from the predatory incursions of those unruly Individuals, who cannot be restrained by their Tribes; and on the other hand, to protect the rights secured to the Indians by Treaty; to draw them nearer to the civilized state; and inspire them with correct conceptions of the Power, as well as justice of the Government.

The meeting of the deputies from the Creek Nation at Colerain, in the State of Georgia, which had for a principal object the purchase of a parcel of their land, by that State, broke up without its being accomplished; the Nation having, previous to their departure, instructed them against making any Sale; the occasion however has been improved, to confirm by a new Treaty with the Creeks, their pre-existing engagements with the United States; and to obtain their consent, to the establishment of Trading Houses and Military Posts within their boundary; by means of which, their friendship, and the general peace, may be more effectually secured.

The period during the late Session, at which the appropriation was passed, for carrying into effect the Treaty of Amity, Commerce, and Navigation, between the United States and his Britannic Majesty, necessarily procrastinated the reception of the Posts stipulated to be delivered, beyond the date assigned for that event. As soon however as the Governor General of Canada could be addressed with propriety on the subject, arrangements were cordially and promptly concluded for their evacuation; and the United States took possession of the principal of them, comprehending Oswego, Niagara, Detroit, Michelimackina, and Fort Miami; where, such repairs, and additions have been ordered to be made, as appeared indispensible.

The Commissioners appointed on the part of the United States and of Great Britain, to determine which is the river St. Croix, mentioned in the Treaty of peace of 1783, agreed in the choice of Egbert Benson Esqr. of New York, for the third Commissioner. The whole met at St. Andrews, in Passamaquoddy Bay, in the beginning of October; and directed surveys to be made of the Rivers in dispute; but deeming it impracticable to have these Surveys completed before the next Year, they adjourned, to meet at Boston in August 1797, for the final decision of the question.

Other Commissioners appointed on the part of the United States, agreeably to the seventh Article of the Treaty with Great Britain, relative to captures and condemnations of Vessels and other property, met the Commissioners of his Britannic Majesty in London, in August last, when John Trumbull, Esqr. was chosen by lot, for the fifth Commissioner. In October following the Board were to proceed to business. As yet there has been no communication of Commissioners on the part of Great Britain, to unite with those who have been appointed on the part of the United States, for carrying into effect the sixth Article of the Treaty.

The Treaty with Spain, required, that the Commissioners for running the boundary line between the territory of the United States, and his Catholic Majesty's Provinces of East and West Florida, should meet at the Natchez, before the expiration of six Months after the exchange of the ratifications, which was effected at Aranjuez on the 25th. day of April; and the troops of his Catholic Majesty occupying any Posts within the limits of the United States, were within the same period to be withdrawn. The Commissioner of the United States therefore, commenced his journey for the Natchez in September; and troops were ordered to occupy the Posts from which the Spanish Garrisons should be withdrawn. Information has been recently received, of the appointment of a Commissioner on the part of his Catholic Majesty for running the boundary line, but none of any appointment, for the adjustment of the claims of our Citizens, whose Vessels were captured by the Armed Vessels of Spain.

In pursuance of the Act of Congress, passed in the last Session, for the protection and relief of American Seamen, Agents were appointed, one to reside in Great Britain, and the other in the West Indies. The effects of the Agency in the West Indies, are not yet fully ascertained; but those which have been communicated afford grounds to believe, the measure will be beneficial. The Agent destined to reside in Great Britain, declining to accept the appointment, the business has consequently devolved on the Minister of the United States in London; and will command his attention, until a new Agent shall be appointed.

After many delays and disappointments, arising out of the European War, the final arrangements for fulfilling the engagements made to the Dey and Regency of Algiers, will, in all present appearance, be crowned with success: but under great, tho' inevitable disadvantages, in the pecuniary transactions, occasioned by that War; which will render a further provision necessary. The actual liberation of all our Citizens who were prisoners in Algiers, while it gratifies every feeling heart, is itself an earnest of a satisfactory termination of the whole negotiation. Measures are in operation for effecting Treaties with the Regencies of Tunis and Tripoli.

To an active external Commerce, the protection of a Naval force is indispensable. This is manifest with regard to Wars in which a State itself is a party. But besides this, it is in our own experience, that the most sincere Neutrality is not a sufficient guard against the depredations of Nations at War. To secure respect to a Neutral Flag, requires a Naval force, organized, and ready to vindicate it, from insult or aggression. This may even prevent the necessity of going to War, by discouraging belligerent Powers from committing such violations of the rights of the Neutral party, as may first or last, leave no other option. From the best information I have been able to obtain, it would seem as if our trade to the mediterranean, without a protecting force, will always be insecure; and our Citizens exposed to the calamities from which numbers of them have but just been relieved.

These considerations invite the United States, to look to the means, and to set about the gradual creation of a Navy. The increasing progress of their Navigation, promises them, at no distant period, the requisite supply of Seamen; and their means, in other respects, favour the undertaking. It is an encouragement, likewise, that their particular situation, will give weight and influence to a moderate Naval force in their hands. Will it not then be adviseable, to begin without delay, to provide, and lay up the materials for the building and equipping of Ships of War; and to proceed in the Work by degrees, in proportion as our resources shall render it practicable without inconvenience; so that a future War of Europe, may not find our Commerce in the same unprotected state, in which it was found by the present.

Congress have repeatedly, and not without success, directed their attention to the encouragement of Manufactures. The object is of too much consequence, not to insure a continuance of their efforts, in every way which shall appear eligible. As a general rule, Manufactures on public account, are inexpedient. But where the state of things in a Country, leaves little hope that certain branches of Manufacture will, for a great length of time obtain; when these are of a nature essential to the furnishing and equipping of the public force in time of War, are not establishments for procuring them on public account, *to the extent of the ordinary demand for the public service,* recommended by strong considerations of National policy, as an exception to the general rule? Ought our Country to remain in such cases, dependant on foreign supply, precarious, because liable to be interrupted? If the necessary Articles should, in this mode cost more in time of peace, will not the security and independence thence arising, form an ample compensation? Establishments of this sort, commensurate only with the calls of the public service in time of peace, will, in time of War, easily be extended in proportion to the exigencies of the Government; and may even perhaps be made to yield a surplus for the supply of our Citizens at large; so as to mitigate the privations from the interruption of their trade. If adopted, the plan ought to exclude all those branches which are already, or likely soon to be, established in the Country; in order that there may be no danger of interference with pursuits of individual industry.

It will not be doubted, that with reference either to individual, or National Welfare, Agriculture is of primary importance. In proportion as Nations advance in population, and other circumstances of maturity, this truth becomes more apparent; and renders the cultivation of the Soil more and more, an object of public patronage. Institutions for promoting it, grow up, supported by the public purse: and to what object can it be dedicated with greater propriety? Among the means which have been employed to this end, none have been attended with greater success than the establishment of Boards, composed of proper characters, charged with collecting and diffusing information, and enabled by premiums, and small pecuniary aids, to encourage and assist a spirit of discovery and improvement. This species of establishment contributes doubly to the increase of improvement; by stimulating to enterprise and experiment, and by drawing to a common centre, the results everywhere of individual skill and observation; and spreading them thence over the whole Nation. Experience accordingly has shewn, that they are very cheap Instruments, of immense National benefits.

I have heretofore proposed to the consideration of Congress, the expediency of establishing a National University; and also a Military Academy. The desirableness of both these Institutions, has so constantly increased with every new view I have taken of the subject, that I cannot omit the opportunity of once for all, recalling your attention to them.

The Assembly to which I address myself, is too enlightened not to be fully sensible how much a flourishing state of the Arts and Sciences, contributes to National prosperity and reputation. True it is, that our Country, much to its honor, contains many Seminaries of learning highly respectable and useful; but the funds upon which they rest, are too narrow, to command the ablest Professors, in the different departments of liberal knowledge, for the Institution contemplated, though they would be excellent auxiliaries.

Amongst the motives to such an Institution, the assimilation of the principles, opinions and manners of our Country men, but the common education of a portion of our Youth from every quarter, well deserves attention. The more homogeneous our Citizens can be made in these particulars, the greater will be our prospect of permanent Union; and a primary object of such a National Institution should be, the education of our Youth in the science of *government*. In a Republic, what species of knowledge can be equally important? and what duty, more pressing on its Legislature, than to patronize a plan for communicating it to those, who are to be the future guardians of the liberties of the Country?

The Institution of a Military Academy, is also recommended by cogent reasons. However pacific the general policy of a Nation may be, it ought never to be without an adequate stock of Military knowledge for emergencies. The first would impair the energy of its character, and both would hazard its safety, or expose it to greater evils when War could not be avoided. Besides that War, might often, not depend upon its own choice. In proportion, as the observance of pacific maxims, might exempt a Nation from the necessity of practising the rules of the Military Art, ought to be its care in preserving, and transmitting by proper establishments, the knowledge of that Art. Whatever argument may be drawn from particular examples, superficially viewed, a thorough examination of the subject will evince, that the Art of War, is at once comprehensive and complicated; that it demands much previous study; and that the possession of it, in its most improved and perfect state, is always of great moment to the security of a Nation. This, therefore, ought to be a serious care of every Government: and for this purpose, an Academy, where a regular course of Instruction is given, is an obvious expedient, which different Nations have successfully employed.

The compensations to the Officers of the United States, in various instances, and in none more than in respect to the most important stations, appear to call for Legislative revision. The consequences of a defective provision, are of serious import to the Government. If private wealth, is to supply the defect of public retribution, it will greatly contract the sphere within which, the selection of Characters for Office, is to be made, and will proportionally diminish the probability of a choice of Men, able, as well as upright: Besides that it would be repugnant to the vital principles of our Government, virtually to exclude from public trusts, talents and virtue, unless accompanied by wealth.

While in our external relations, some serious inconveniences and embarrassments have been overcome, and others lessened, it is with much pain and deep regret I mention, that circumstances of a very unwelcome nature, have lately occurred. Our trade has suffered, and is suffering, extensive injuries in the West Indies, from the Cruisers, and Agents of the French Republic; and communications have been received from its Minister here, which indicate the danger of a further disturbance of our Commerce, by its authority; and which are, in other respects, far from agreeable.

It has been my constant, sincere, and earnest wish, in conformity with that of our Nation, to maintain cordial harmony, and a perfectly friendly understanding with that Republic. This wish remains unabated; and I shall persevere in the endeavour to fulfil it, to the utmost extent of what shall be consistent with a just, and indispensable regard to the rights and honour of our Country; nor will I easily cease to cherish the expectation, that a spirit of justice, candour and friendship, on the part of the Republic, will eventually ensure success.

In pursuing this course however, I cannot forget what is due to the character of our Government and Nation; or to a full and entire confidence in the good sense, patriotism, self-respect, and fortitude of my Countrymen.

I reserve for a special Message a more particular communication on this interesting subject.

Gentlemen of the House of Representatives: I have directed an estimate of the Appropriations, necessary for the service of the ensuing year, to be submitted from the proper Department; with a view of the public receipts and expenditures, to the latest period to which an account can be prepared.

It is with satisfaction I am able to inform you, that the Revenues of the United States continue in a state of progressive improvement.

A reinforcement of the existing provisions for discharging our public Debt, was mentioned in my Address at the opening of the last Session. Some preliminary steps were taken towards it, the maturing of which will, no doubt, engage your zealous attention during the present. I will only add, that it will afford me, heart felt satisfaction, to concur in such further measures, as will ascertain to our Country the prospect of a speedy extinguishment of the Debt. Posterity may have cause to regret, if, from any motive, intervals of tranquility are left unimproved for accelerating this valuable end.

Gentlemen of the Senate, and of the House of Representatives:

My solicitude to see the Militia of the United States placed on an efficient establishment, has been so often, and so ardently expressed, that I shall but barely recall the subject to your view on the present occasion; at the same time that I shall submit to your inquiry, whether our Harbours are yet sufficiently secured.

The situation in which I now stand, for the last time, in the midst of the Representatives of the People of the United States, naturally recalls the period when the Administration of the present form of Government commenced; and I cannot omit the occasion, to congratulate you and my Country, on the success of the experiment; nor to repeat my fervent supplications to the Supreme Ruler of the Universe, and Sovereign Arbiter of Nations, that his Providential care may still be extended to the United States; that the virtue and happiness of the People, may be preserved; and that the Government, which they have instituted, for the protection of their liberties, may be perpetual.

Last Will and Testament (July 1799)

Item—Whereas by a law of the Commonwealth of Virginia enacted in the year 1785, the legislature thereof was pleased (as an evidence of its approbation of the services I had rendered the public during the Revolution—and partly, I believe in consideration of my having suggested the vast advantages which the community would derive from the extension of its Inland navigation, under legislative patronage) to present me with one one hundred shares of one hundred dollars each, in the incorporated company established for the purpose of extending the navigation of James River from the tide-water to the mountains; and also with fifty shares of one hundred pounds sterling each in the corporation of another company likewise established for the similar purpose of opening the navigation of the River Potomac from tide water to Fort Cumberland; the acceptance of which, although the offer was highly honorable and grateful to my feelings, was refused, as inconsistent with a principle which I had adopted, and had never departed from, namely, not to receive pecuniary compensation for any services I could render my country in its arduous struggle with Great Britain for its Right; and because I had

evaded similar propositions from other States in the Union—adding
to this refusal, however, an intimation, that, if it should be the
pleasure of the legislature to permit me to appropriate the said shares
to public uses, I would receive them on those terms with due sensibility—and this having consented to in flattering terms, as will appear
by a subsequent law and sundry resolutions, in the most ample and
honorable manner, I proceed after this recital for the more correct
understanding of the case to declare—that it has always been a source
of serious regret with me to see the youth of these United States sent
to foreign countries for the purpose of education, often before their
minds were formed or they had imbibed any adequate ideas of the
happiness of their own, contracting too frequently not only habits of
dissipation and extravagance, but principles unfriendly to Republican
Governm't and to the true and genuine liberties of mankind, which
hereafter are rarely overcome—for these reasons it has been my
ardent wish to see a plan devised on a liberal scale which would have
a tendency to spread systematic ideas through all parts of this rising
Empire, thereby to do away local attachments and state prejudices
as far as the nature of things would, or indeed ought to admit, from
our national councils—looking anxiously forward to the accomplishment of so desirable an object as this is, (in my estimation) my mind
has not been able to contemplate any plan more likely to effect the
measure than the establishment of a University in a central part of
the United States to which the youth of fortune and talent from all
parts thereof might be sent for the completion of their education in
all the branches of polite literature, in arts and sciences—in acquiring
knowledge in the principles of Politics and good Government and
(as a matter of infinite importance in my judgment) by associating
with each other and forming friendships in Juvenile years, be enabled
to free themselves in a proper degree from those local prejudices and
habitual jealousies which have just been mentioned and which when
carried to excess are never failing sources of disquietude to the Public
mind and pregnant of mischievous consequences to this country:—
under these impressions so fully dilated,—

  Item—I give and bequeath in perpetuity the fifty shares which
I hold in the Potomac Company (under the aforesaid Acts of the
Legislature of Virginia) towards the endowment of a university to
be established within the limits of the District of Columbia, under
the auspices of the General Government, if that Government should

incline to extend a fostering hand towards it,—until such seminary be established, and the funds arising on these shares shall be required for its support, my further will and desire is that the profit accruing therefrom shall whenever the dividends are made be laid out in purchasing stock in the Bank of Columbia or some other Bank at the discretion of my Executors, or by the Treasurer of the United States for the time being under the direction of Congress, provided that Honorable body should patronize the measure. And the dividends proceeding from the purchase of such stock is to be vested in more stock and so on until a sum adequate to the accomplishment of the object is obtained, of which I have not the smallest doubt before many years pass away, even if no aid or encouragement is given by Legislative authority or from any other source.

Item—The hundred shares which I held in the James River Company I have given and now confirm in perpetuity to and for the use and benefit of Liberty Hall Academy in the County of Rockbridge, in the Commonwealth of Virginia.

Thomas Paine

T *homas Paine's distorted reputation as a radical anti-Federalist has rested primarily on works such as the* Rights of Man *and* Common Sense. *In addition to such tours de force, however, Paine wrote constantly on the key nuts and bolts issues of putting together a free nation. One of the most critical of these issues was economic program, and it is economics and its relationship to a republican government that Paine takes up in the following* Dissertation, *which was written in 1786 to convince the Pennsylvania Legislature to restore the charter of the Bank of North America.*

As the somewhat edited version of the Dissertation *shows, Paine was not only a diehard Federalist, but one who was exceedingly competent in capitalist political economy. His acute understanding of the vulnerabilities of the British imperial system led him to propose a strategy of bankrupting the British pound in 1796, a strategy that, like the wave of revolutionary ferment his writings evoked across Britain in the 1790s, languished for lack of a strong political leadership to carry it through.*

Dissertations on Government; the Affairs Of the Bank; and Paper Money

Preface

I here present the public with a new performance. Some parts of it are more particularly adapted to the state of Pennsylvania, on the present state of its affairs: but there are others which are on a larger scale. The time bestowed on this work has not been long, the whole of it being written and printed during the short recess of the assembly.

As to parties, merely considered as such, I am attached to no particular one. There are such things as right and wrong in the world, and so far as these are parties against each other, the signature of *Common Sense* is properly employed.

Thomas Paine

Philadelphia, Feb. 18, 1786

Every government, let its form be what it may, contains within itself a principle common to all, which is, that of a sovereign power, or a power over which there is no control, and which controls all others: and as it is impossible to construct a form of government in which this power does not exist, so there must of necessity be a place, if it may be so called, for it to exist in.

In despotic monarchies this power is lodged in a single person, or sovereign. His will is law; which he declares, alters or revokes as he pleases, without being accountable to any power for so doing. Therefore, the only modes of redress, in countries so governed, are by petition or insurrection. And this is the reason we so frequently hear of insurrections in despotic governments; for as there are but two modes of redress, this is one of them.

Perhaps it may be said that as the united resistance of the people is able, by force, to control the will of the sovereign, that therefore, the controlling power lodges in them; but it must be understood that I am speaking of such powers only as are constituent parts of the government, not of those powers which are externally applied to resist and overturn it.

In republics, such as those established in America, the sovereign power, or the power over which there is no control, and which controls all others, remains where nature placed it—in the people; for the people in America are the fountain of power. It remains there as a matter of right, recognized in the constitutions of the country, and the exercise of it is constitutional and legal. This sovereignty is exercised in electing and deputing a certain number of persons to represent and act for the whole, and who, if they do not act right, may be displaced by the same power that placed them there, and others elected and deputed in their stead, and the wrong measures of former representatives corrected and brought right by this means. Therefore the republican form and principle leaves no room for insurrection, because it provides and establishes a rightful means in its stead. . . .

. . . The administration of a republic is supposed to be directed by certain fundamental principles of right and justice, from which there cannot, because there ought not to be any deviation; and whenever any deviation appears, there is a kind of stepping out of the republican principle, and an approach towards the despotic one. This administration is executed by a select number of persons, periodically chosen by the people, who act as representatives and in behalf of the whole, and who are supposed to enact the same laws, and pursue the same line of administration, as the people would do were they all assembled together.

The *public good* is to be their object. It is therefore necessary to understand what public good is.

Public good is not a term opposed to the good of individuals; on the contrary, it is the good of every individual collected. It is the good of all, because it is the good of every one: for as the public body is every individual collected, so the public good is the collected good of those individuals.

The foundation-principle of public good is justice, and wherever justice is impartially administered the public good is promoted; for as it is to the good of every man that no injustice be done to him, so likewise it is to his good that the principle which secures him should not be violated in the person of another, because such a violation weakens *his* security, and leaves to chance what ought to be to him a rock to stand on.

But in order to understand more minutely, how the public good is to be promoted, and the manner in which the representatives are to act to promote it, we must have recourse to the original or first principles, on which the people formed themselves into a republic.

When a people agree to form themselves into a republic (for the word *republic* means the *public good,* or the good of the whole, in contradistinction to the despotic form, which makes the good of the sovereign, or of one man, the only object of the government), when I say, they agree to do this, it is to be understood, that they mutually resolve and pledge themselves to each other, rich and poor alike, to support and maintain this rule of equal justice among them. They therefore renounce not only the despotic form, but the despotic principle, as well of governing as of being governed by mere will and power, and substitute in its place a government of justice.

By this mutual compact, the citizens of a republic put it out of their power, that is, they renounce, as detestable, the power of exercising, at any future time, any species of despotism over each other, or doing a thing not right in itself, because a majority of them may have strength of numbers sufficient to accomplish it.

In this pledge and compact[1] lies the foundation of the republic: and the security to the rich and the consolation to the poor is, that what each man has is his own; that no despotic sovereign can take it from him, and that the common cementing principle which holds all the parts of a republic together, secures him likewise from the

---

1 This pledge and compact is contained in the declaration of rights prefixed to the constitution (of Pennsylvania—Ed.), and is as follows:

I. That all men are born equally free and independent, and have certain natural, inherent and unalienable rights, amongst which are, the enjoying and defending life and liberty, acquiring, possessing and protecting property, and pursuing and obtaining happiness and safety.

II. That all men have a natural and unalienable right to worship almighty God, according to the dictates of their own consciences and understanding: and that no man ought or of right can be compelled to attend any religious worship, or erect or support any place of worship, or maintain any ministry, contrary to, or against, his own free will and consent: nor can any man, who acknowledges the being of a God, be justly deprived or abridged of any civil right as a citizen, on account of his religious sentiments or peculiar mode of religious worship: and that no authority can or ought to be vested in, or assumed by, any power whatever, that shall in any case interfere with, or in any manner control, the right of conscience in the free exercise of religious worship.

III. That the people of this state have the sole, exclusive and inherent right of governing and regulating the internal police of the same.

IV. That all power being originally inherent in, and consequently derived from, the people; therefore, all officers of government, whether legislative or executive, are their trustees and servants, and at all times accountable to them.

V. That government is, or ought to be, instituted for the common benefit, protection and security of the people, nation or community; and not for the particular emolument or advantage of any single man, family, or set of men, who are a part only of that community: and that the community hath an indubitable, unalienable and indefeasible right to reform, alter or abolish government in such manner as shall be by that community judged most conducive to the public weal.

VI. That those who are employed in the legislative and executive business of the state may be restrained from oppression, the people have a right, at such periods as they may think proper, to reduce their public officers to a private station, and supply the vacancies by certain and regular elections.

VII. That all elections ought to be free; and that all free men having a sufficient evident common interest with, and attachment to the community, have a right to elect officers, or to be elected into office.

VIII. That every member of society hath a right to be protected in the enjoyment of life, liberty and property, and therefore is bound to contribute his proportion towards the expense of that protection, and yield his personal service when necessary, or an equivalent thereto; but no part of a man's property can be justly taken from him, or applied to public uses, without his own consent, or that of his legal representatives: nor can any man who is conscientiously scrupulous of bearing arms, be justly compelled thereto, if he will pay such equivalent: nor are the people bound by any laws, but such as they have in like manner assented to, for their common good.

IX. That in all prosecutions for criminal offences, a man hath a right to be heard by himself and his counsel, to demand the cause and nature of his accusation, to be

despotism of numbers: for despotism may be more effectually acted by many over a few, than by one man over all.

Therefore, in order to know how far the power of an assembly, or a house of representatives can act in administering the affairs of a republic, we must examine how far the power of the people extends under the original compact they have made with each other; for the power of the representatives is in many cases less, but never can be greater than that of the people represented; and whatever the people in their mutual original compact have renounced the power of doing towards, or acting over each other, the representatives cannot assume the power to do, because, as I have already said, the power of the representatives cannot be greater than that of the people they represent.

---

confronted with the witnesses, to call for evidence in his favour, and a speedy public trial, by an impartial jury of the country, without the unanimous consent of which jury he cannot be found guilty: nor can he be compelled to give evidence against himself ; nor can any man be justly deprived of his liberty, except by the laws of the land, or the judgment of his peers.

X. That the people have a right to hold themselves, their houses, papers, and possessions free from search or seizure ; and therefore warrants without oaths or affirmations, first made, affording a sufficient foundation for them, and whereby any officer or messenger may be commanded or required to search suspected places, or to seize any person or persons, his or their property, not particularly described, are contrary to that right, and ought not to be granted.

XI. That in controversies respecting property, and in suits between man and man, the parties have the right to trial by jury, which ought to be held sacred.

XII. That the people have a right to freedom of speech, and of writing and publishing their sentiments: therefore the freedom of the press ought not to be restrained.

XIII. That the people have a right to bear arms for the defence of themselves and the state—and as standing armies, in the time of peace, are dangerous to liberty, they ought not to be kept up—and that the military should be kept under a strict subordination to, and governed by, the civil power.

XIV. That a frequent recurrence to fundamental principles, and a firm adherence to justice, moderation, temperance, industry and frugality are absolutely necessary to preserve the blessings of liberty and keep a government free—the people ought therefore to pay particular attention to these points in the choice of officers and representatives, and have a right to exact a due and constant regard to them, from their legislators, and magistrates, in the making and executing such laws as are necessary for the good government of the state.

XV. That all men have a natural inherent right to emigrate from one state to another that will receive them, or to form a new state in vacant countries, or in such countries as they can purchase, whenever they think that thereby they may promote their own happiness.

XVI. That the people have a right to assemble together, to consult for their common good, to instruct their representatives, and to apply to the legislature for redress of grievances, by address, petition, or remonstrance.

The Saugus Ironworks, shown above, was founded in Saugus, Massachusetts during the 1640s by John Winthrop, and reflected the advanced concept of economic development which the Massachusetts founders held—a concept which led to the War of Independence.

Benjamin Franklin, the most universal Founding Father of the American Republic, is shown here in a public monument in Glendale, California, looking over the Constitution he helped create.

George Washington, the citizen-soldier who won the Revolutionary War and led the new Republic, is shown here in a Newark, New Jersey memorial.

The printing press used by Benjamin Franklin as a journeyman printer in London in 1726. Franklin spurred publications and correspondence throughout the colonies, to build the revolutionary movement.

The paper currency issued by the Continental Congress, to finance the Revolution, became worthless because there was no strong national government.

This cartoon, "Join or Die," was published by Franklin in the *Pennsylvania Gazette* in 1754, as a way of urging the colonies to unite.

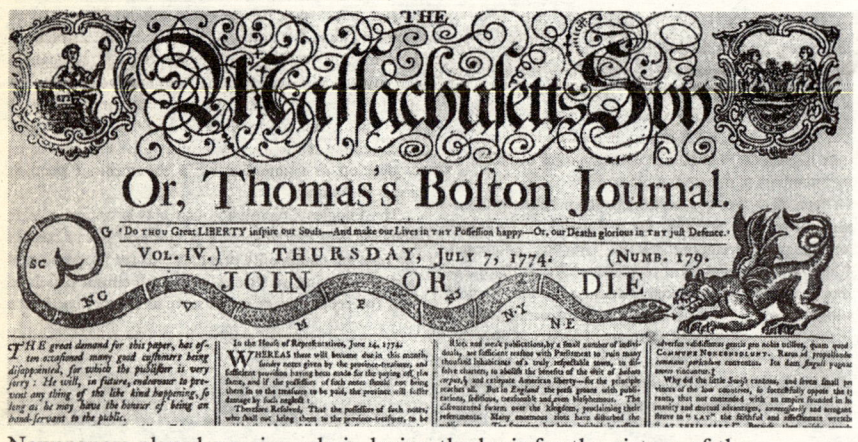

Newspapers played a major role in laying the basis for the victory of the American Revolution. Above is the masthead of the *Massachusetts Spy*, a major patriotic paper of the 1770s.

Thomas Paine, best known for authoring the war mobilization pamphlet *Common Sense*, was part of the Franklin network, and a fighter for economic development as well as against the monarchy.

COMMON SENSE;

ADDRESSED TO THE

INHABITANTS

OF

AMERICA,

On the following interesting

SUBJECTS.

I. Of the Origin and Design of Government in general, with concise Remarks on the English Constitution.

II. Of Monarchy and Hereditary Succession.

III. Thoughts on the present State of American Affairs.

IV. Of the present Ability of America, with some miscellaneous Reflections.

Man knows no Master save creating HEAVEN,
Or those whom choice and common good ordain.
THOMSON.

PHILADELPHIA;

Printed, and Sold, by R. BELL, in Third-Street.

MDCCLXXVI.

Paine's *Common Sense*, written in 1776, when the Revolutionary War looked bleak indeed, provided a crucial rallying cry for continuing the fight.

Thomas Jefferson (left) and Alexander Hamilton (right) worked together with Washington, but had a major falling-out over the need for an industrial economic policy. Hamilton's industrial approach won, with the formation of the First National Bank of the United States, which still stands in Philadelphia today (see below).

King George III, shown here, attempted to prevent the American colonies from expanding and industrializing—a course that led straight to the Revolution.

On July 9, 1776, after Washington's army had reached New York from Boston, and the Declaration of Independence was read to the troops, citizens moved to tear down the equestrian statue of George III. The statue was later melted down into bullets for the American army.

There was massive
celebration when the new
Constitution of the United
States was adopted in
1788. Here is depicted the
arrival of the good ship
Hamilton, at New York
harbor festivities.

It was a national
tragedy when Aaron
Burr assassinated
Alexander Hamilton in
Weehawken, New
Jersey in July of 1804.
This is an artist's
illustration of the event.

In this place it naturally presents itself that the people in their original compact of equal justice or first principles of a republic, renounced, as despotic, detestable and unjust, the assuming a right of breaking and violating their engagements, contracts and compacts with, or defrauding, imposing or tyrannizing over each other, and therefore the representatives cannot make an act to do it for them, and any such kind of act would be an attempt to depose not the personal sovereign, but the sovereign principle of the republic, and to introduce despotism in its stead.

It may in this place be proper to distinguish between that species of sovereignty which is claimed and exercised by despotic monarchs, and that sovereignty which the citizens of a republic inherit and retain. The sovereignty of a despotic monarch assumes the power of making wrong right, or right wrong, as he pleases or as it suits him. The sovereignty in a republic is exercised to keep right and wrong in their proper and distinct places, and never suffer the one to usurp the place of the other. A republic, properly understood, is a sovereignty of justice, in contradistinction to a sovereignty of will.

Our experience in republicanism is yet so slender, that it is much to be doubted, whether all our public laws and acts are consistent with, or can be justified on, the principles of a republican government.

We have been so much habited to act in committees at the commencement of the dispute, and during the interregnum of government, and in many cases since, and to adopt expedients warranted by necessity, and to permit to ourselves a discretionary use of power, suited to the spur and exigency of the moment, that a man transferred from a committee to a seat in the legislature, imperceptibly takes with him the ideas and habits he has been accustomed to, and continues to think like a committee-man instead of a legislator, and to govern by the spirit rather than by the rule of the constitution and the principles of the republic.

Having already stated that the power of the representatives can never exceed the power of the people whom they represent, I now proceed to examine more particularly, what the power of the representatives is.

It is, in the first place, the power of acting as legislators in making laws—and in the second place, the power of acting in certain cases, as agents or negotiators for the commonwealth, for such purposes as the circumstances of the commonwealth require.

A very strange confusion of ideas, dangerous to the credit, stability, and the good and honor of the commonwealth, has arisen, by confounding those two distinct powers and things together, and blending every act of the assembly, of whatever kind it may be, under one general name, of *Laws of the Commonwealth*, and thereby creating an opinion (which is truly of the despotic kind) that every succeeding assembly has an equal power over every transaction, as well as law, done by a former assembly.

All laws are acts, but all acts are not laws. Many of the acts of the assembly are acts of agency or negociation, that is they are acts of contract and agreement, on the part of the state, with certain persons therein mentioned, and for certain purposes therein recited. An act of this kind, after it has passed the house, is of the nature of a deed or contract, signed, sealed and delivered; and subject to the same general laws and principles of justice as all other deeds and contracts are: for in a transaction of this kind, the state stands as an individual, and can be known in no other character in a court of justice.

By "*laws*," as distinct from the agency transactions, or matters of negociation, are to be comprehended all those public acts of the assembly or commonwealth, which have a universal operation, or apply themselves to every individual of the commonwealth. Of this kind are the laws for the distribution and administration of justice, for the preservation of the peace, for the security of property, for raising the necessary revenue by just proportions, etc. . . .

. . . Acts of this kind are distinguishable into two classes:—

First, Those wherein the matters inserted in the act have already been settled and adjusted between the state on one part, and the persons therein mentioned on the other part. In this case the act is the completion and ratification of the contract or matters therein recited. It is in fact a deed signed, sealed and delivered.

Second, Those acts wherein the matters have not been already agreed upon, and wherein the act only holds forth certain propositions and terms to be accepted of and acceded to.

I shall give an instance of each of those acts. First, the state wants the loan of a sum of money—certain persons make an offer to government to lend that sum, and send in their proposals: the government accepts these proposals, and all the matters of the loan and the payment are agreed on; and an act is passed according to the usual form of passing acts, ratifying and confirming this agreement. This act is final.

In the second case,—the state, as in the preceding one, wants a loan of money—the assembly passes an act holding forth the terms on which it will borrow and pay: this act has no force until the propositions and terms are accepted of and acceded to by some person or persons, and when those terms are accepted of and complied with, the act is binding on the state.—But if at the meeting of the next assembly, or any other, the whole sum intended to be borrowed, should not be borrowed, that assembly may stop where they are, and discontinue proceeding with the loan, or make new propositions and terms for the remainder; but so far as the subscriptions have been filled up, and the terms complied with, it is, as in the first case, a signed deed: and in the same manner are all acts, let the matters in them be what they may, wherein, as I have before mentioned, the state on one part, and certain individuals on the other part, are parties in the act.

If the state should become a bankrupt, the creditors, as in all cases of bankruptcy, will be sufferers; they will have but a dividend for the whole: but this is not a dissolution of the contract, but an accommodation of it, arising from necessity. And so in all cases of this kind, if an inability takes place on either side, the contract cannot be performed, and some accomodation must be gone into, or the matter falls through of itself.

It may likewise, though it ought not to, happen that in performing the matters, agreeably to the terms of the act, inconveniences, unforeseen at the time of making the act, may arise to either or both parties: in this case, those inconveniences may be removed by the mutual consent and agreement of the parties, and each finds its benefit in so doing: for in a republic it is the harmony of its parts that constitutes their several and mutual good.

But the acts themselves are legally binding, as much as if they had been made between two private individuals. The greatness of one party cannot give it a superiority or advantage over the other. The state, or its representatives, the assembly, has no more power over an act of this kind, after it has passed, than if the state was a private person. It is the glory of a republic to have it so, because it secures the individual from becoming the prey of power, and prevents *might* from overcoming *right*.

If any difference or dispute arise afterwards between the state and the individuals with whom the agreement is made respecting the contract, or the meaning, or extent of any of the matters contained in the act, which may affect the property or interest of either, such difference or dispute must be judged of, and decided upon, by the laws of the land, in a court of justice and trial by jury; that is, by the laws of the land already in being at the time such act and contract was made.—No law made afterwards can apply to the case, either directly, or by construction or implication: for such a law would be a retrospective law, or a law made after the fact, and cannot even be produced in court as applying to the case before it for judgment.

That this is justice, that it is the true principle of republican government, no man will be so hardy as to deny.—If, therefore, a lawful contract or agreement, sealed and ratified, cannot be affected or altered by any act made afterwards, how much more inconsistent and irrational, despotic and unjust would it be, to think of making an act with the professed intention of breaking up a contract already signed and sealed.

That it is possible an assembly, in the heat and indiscretion of party, and meditating on power rather than on the principle by which all power in a republican government is governed, that of equal justice, may fall into the error of passing such an act, is admitted;— but it would be an actless act, an act that goes for nothing, an act which the courts of justice, and the established laws of the land, could know nothing of.

Because such an act would be an act of one party only, not only without, but against the consent of the other; and, therefore, cannot be produced to affect a contract made between the two.—That the violation of a contract should be set up as a justification to the violator, would be the same thing as to say, that a man by breaking his promise is freed from the obligation of it, or that by transgressing the laws, he exempts himself from the punishment of them.

Besides the constitutional and legal reasons why an assembly cannot, of its own act and authority, undo or make void a contract made between the state (by a former assembly) and certain individuals, may be added what may be called the natural reasons, or those reasons which the plain rules of common sense point out to every man. Among which are the following:

The principals, or real parties in the contract, are the state and the persons contracted with. The assembly is not a party, but an agent in behalf of the state, authorised and empowered to transact its affairs.

Therefore it is the state that is bound on one part and certain individuals on the other part, and the performance of the contract, according to the conditions of it, devolves on succeeding assemblies, not as principals, but as agents.

Therefore, for the next or any other assembly to undertake to dissolve the state from its obligation is an assumption of power of a novel and extraordinary kind.—It is the servant attempting to free his master.

The election of new assemblies following each other makes no difference in the nature of the thing. The state is still the same state. The public is still the same body. These do not annually expire though the time of an assembly does. These are not new-created every year, nor can they be displaced from their original standing; but are a perpetual, permanent body, always in being and still the same.

But if we adopt the vague, inconsistent idea that every new assembly has a full and complete authority over every act done by the state in a former assembly, and confound together laws, contracts, and every species of public business, it will lead us into a wilderness of endless confusion and insurmountable difficulties. It would be declaring an assembly despotic for the time being.—Instead of a government of established principles administered by established rules, the authority of government by being strained so high, would, by the same rule, be reduced proportionably as low, and would be no other than that of a committee of the state, acting with discretionary powers for one year. Every new election would be a new revolution, or it would suppose the public of the former year dead and a new public in its place.

Having now endeavoured to fix a precise idea to, and distinguish between legislative acts and acts of negociation and agency, I shall proceed to apply this distinction to the case now in dispute, respecting the charter of the bank.

The charter of the bank, or what is the same thing, the act for incorporating it, is to all intents and purposes an act of negociation and contract, entered into, and confirmed between the state on one part, and certain persons mentioned therein on the other part. The purpose for which the act was done on the part of the state is therein recited, *viz.* the support which the finances of the country would derive therefrom. The incorporating clause is the condition or obligation on the part of the state; and the obligation on the part of the bank, is "that nothing contained in that act shall be construed to authorise the said corporation to exercise any powers in this state repugnant to the laws or constitution thereof."

Here are all the marks and evidences of a contract. The parties—the purport—and the reciprocal obligations.

That this is a contract, or a joint act, is evident from its being in the power of either of the parties to have forbidden or prevented its being done. The state could not force the stockholders of the bank to be a corporation, and therefore as their consent was necessary to the making the act, their dissent would have prevented its being made; so on the other hand, as the bank could not force the state to incorporate them, the consent or dissent of the state would have had the same effect to do, or to prevent its being done; and as neither of the parties could make the act alone, for the same reason can neither of them dissolve it alone: but this is not the case with a law or act of legislation, and therefore the difference proves it to be an act of a different kind.

The bank may forfeit the charter by delinquency, but the delinquency must be proved and established by a legal process in a court of justice and trial by jury: for the state, or the assembly, is not to be a judge in its own case, but must come to the laws of the land for judgment; for that which is law for the individual, is likewise law for the state.

Before I enter further into this affair, I shall go back to the circumstances of the country, and the condition the government was in, for some time before, as well as at the time it entered into this engagement with the bank, and this act of incorporation was passed: for the government of this state, and I suppose the same of the rest, were then in want of two of the most essential matters which governments could be destitute of—money and credit.

In looking back to those times, and bringing forward some of the circumstances attending them, I feel myself entering on unpleasant and disagreeable ground; because some of the matters which the attacks on the bank now make it necessary to state, in order to bring the affair fully before the public, will not add honour to those who

have promoted that measure and carried it through the late house
of assembly; and for whom, though my own judgment and opinion
on the case oblige me to differ from, I retain my esteem, and the
social remembrance of times past. But, I trust, those gentlemen will
do me the justice to recollect my exceeding earnestness with them,
last spring, when the attack on the bank first broke out; for it clearly
appeared to me one of those overheated measures, which, neither
the country at large, nor their own constituents, would justify them
in, when it came to be fully understood; for however high a party
measure may be carried in an assembly, the people out of doors are
all the while following their several occupations and employments,
minding their farms and their business, and take their own time and
leisure to judge of public measures; the consequence of which is,
that they often judge in a cooler spirit than their representatives act
in.

It may be easily recollected that the present bank was preceded
by, and rose out of a former one, called the Pennsylvania bank which
began a few months before; the occasion of which I shall briefly
state.

In the spring of 1780, the Pennsylvania assembly was composed
of many of the same members, and nearly all of the same connexion,
which composed the late house that began the attack on the bank.
I served as clerk of the assembly of 1780, which station I resigned
at the end of the year, and accompanied a much lamented friend,
the late colonel John Laurens, on an embassy to France.

The spring of 1780 was marked with an accumulation of misfortunes. The reliance placed on the defence of Charleston failed, and
exceedingly lowered or depressed the spirits of the country. The
measures of the government, from the want of money, means and
credit, dragged on like a heavy loaded carriage without wheels, and
were nearly got to what a countryman would understand by a dead
pull.

The assembly of that year met, by adjournment, at an unusual
time, the 10th of May, and what particularly added to the affliction,
was, that so many of the members, instead of spiriting up their
constituents to the most nervous exertions, came to the assembly
furnished with petitions to be exempt from paying taxes. How the
public measures were to be carried on, the country defended, and
the army recruited, clothed, fed, and paid, when the only resource,

and that not half sufficient, that of taxes, should be relaxed to almost nothing, was a matter too gloomy to look at. A language very different from that of petitions ought at this time to have been the language of every one. A declaration to have stood forth with their lives and fortunes, and a reprobation of every thought of partial indulgence would have sounded much better than petitions.

While the assembly was sitting, a letter from the commander-in-chief was received by the executive council and transmitted to the house. The doors were shut, and it fell officially to me to read.

In this letter the naked truth of things was unfolded. Among other informations, the general said, that notwithstanding his confidence in the attachment of the army to the cause of the country, the distress of it, from the want of every necessary which men could be destitute of, had arisen to such a pitch, that the appearances of mutiny and discontent were so strongly marked on the countenance of the army, that he dreaded the event of every hour.

When the letter was read, I observed a despairing silence in the house. Nobody spoke for a considerable time. At length a member, of whose fortitude to withstand misfortunes I had a high opinion, rose: "If," said he, "the account in that letter is a true state of things, and we are in the situation there represented, it appears to me in vain to contend the matter any longer. We may as well give up at first as at last."

The gentleman who spoke next, was (to the best of my recollection) a member of Bucks county, who, in a cheerful note, endeavored to dissipate the gloom of the house—"Well, well," said he, "don't let the house despair, if things are not so well as we wish, we must endeavour to make them better." And on a motion for adjournment, the conversation went no further.

There was now no time to lose, and something absolutely necessary to be done, which was not within the immediate power of the house to do; for what with the depreciation of the currency, and slow operation of taxes, and the petitions to be exempted therefrom, the treasury was moneyless, and the government creditless.

If the assembly could not give the assistance which the necessity of the case immediately required, it was very proper the matter should be known by those who either could or would endeavor to do it. To conceal the information within the house, and not provide the relief which that information required, was making no use of the knowledge, and endangering the public cause. The only thing that now remained, and was capable of reaching the case, was private credit, and the voluntary aid of individuals; and under this impression, on my return from the house, I drew out the salary due to me as clerk, enclosed five hundred dollars to a gentleman in this city, in part of the whole, and wrote fully to him on the subject of our affairs.

The gentleman to whom this letter was addressed is Mr. Blair M'Clenaghan. I mentioned to him, that notwithstanding the current opinion that the enemy were beaten from before Charleston, there were too many reasons to believe the place was then taken and in the hands of the enemy: the consequence of which would be, that a great part of the British force would return, and join at New York. That our own army required to be augmented, ten thousand men, to be able to stand against the combined force of the enemy. I informed Mr. M'Clenaghan of general Washington's letter, the extreme distresses he was surrounded with, and the absolute occasion there was for the citizens to exert themselves at this time, which there was no doubt they would do, if the necessity was made known to them; for that the ability of government was exhausted. I requested Mr. M'Clenaghan to propose a voluntary subscription among his friends, and added, that I had enclosed five hundred dollars as my mite thereto, and that I would increase it as far as the last ability would enable me to go.[2]

The next day Mr. M'Clenaghan informed me that he had communicated the contents of the letter at a meeting of gentlemen at the coffee-house, and that a subscription was immediately began; that Mr. Robert Morris and himself had subscribed two hundred pounds each, in hard money, and that the subscription was going on very successfully. This subscription was intended as a donation, and to be given in bounties to promote the recruiting service. It is dated June 8, 1780. The original subscription list is now in my possession—it amounts to four hundred pounds hard money, and one hundred and one thousand three hundred and sixty pounds continental.

While this subscription was going forward, information of the

2 Mr. M'Clenaghan being now returned from Europe, has my consent to show this letter to any gentleman who may be inclined to see it.

loss of Charleston arrived,[3] and on a communication from several members of congress to certain gentlemen of this city, of the increasing distresses and dangers then taking place, a meeting was held of the subscribers, and such other gentlemen who chose to attend, at the city tavern. This meeting was on the 17th of June, nine days after the subscriptions had begun.

At this meeting it was resolved to open a security-subscription, to the amount of three hundred thousand pounds, Pennsylvania currency, in real money; the subscribers to execute bonds to the amount of their subscriptions, and to form a bank thereon for supplying the army. This being resolved on and carried into execution, the plan of the first subscriptions was discontinued, and this extended one established in its stead.

By means of this bank the army was supplied through the campaign, and being at the same time recruited, was enabled to maintain its ground; and on the appointment of Mr. Morris to be superintendent of the finances the spring following, he arranged the system of the present bank, styled the bank of North America, and many of the subscribers of the former bank transferred their subscriptions into this.

Towards the establishment of this bank, congress passed an ordinance of incorporation, December 21, which the government of Pennsylvania recognized by sundry matters: and afterwards, on an application of the president and directors of the bank, through the mediation of the executive council, the assembly agreed to, and passed the state act of incorporation April 1, 1782.

Thus arose the bank—produced by the distresses of the times and the enterprising spirit of patriotic individuals.—Those individuals furnished and risked the money, and the aid which the government contributed was that of incorporating them.—It would have been well if the State had made all its bargains and contracts with as much true policy as it made this: for a greater service for so small a consideration, that only of an act of incorporation, has not been obtained since the government existed.

Having now shown how the bank originated, I shall proceed with my remarks.

---

3 Colonel Tennant, aid to general Lincoln, arrived the 14th of June, with despatches of the capitulation of Charleston.

The sudden restoration of public and private credit, which took place on the establishment of the bank, is an event as extraordinary in itself as any domestic occurence during the progress of the revolution.

How far a spirit of envy might operate to produce the attack on the bank during the sitting of the late assembly, is best known and felt by those who began or promoted the attack. The bank had rendered services which the assembly of 1780 could not, and acquired an honour which many of its members might be unwilling to own, and wish to obscure.

But surely every government, acting on the principles of patriotism and public good, would cherish an institution capable of rendering such advantages to the community. The establishment of the bank in one of the most trying vicissitudes of the war, its zealous services in the public cause, its influence in restoring and supporting credit, and the punctuality with which all its business has been transacted, are matters, that so far from meriting the treatment it met with from the late assembly, are an honour to the state, and what the body of her citizens may be proud to own.

But the attack on the bank, as a chartered institution, under the protection of its violators, however criminal it may be as an error of government, or impolitic as a measure of party, is not to be charged on the constituents of those who made the attack. It appears from every circumstance that has come to light, to be a measure which that assembly contrived of itself. The members did not come charged with the affair from their constituents. There was no idea of such a thing when they were elected or when they met. The hasty and precipitate manner in which it was hurried through the house, and the refusal of the house to hear the directors of the bank in its defence, prior to the publication of the repealing bill for public consideration, operated to prevent their constituents comprehending the subject: therefore, whatever may be wrong in the proceedings lies not at the door of the public. The house took the affair on its own shoulders, and whatever blame there is, lies on them.

The matter must have been prejudged and predetermined by a majority of the members out of the house, before it was brought into it. The whole business appears to have been fixed at once, and all reasoning or debate on the case rendered useless.

Petitions from a very inconsiderable number of persons, suddenly procured, and so privately done, as to be a secret among the

few that signed them, were presented to the house and read twice
in one day, and referred to a committee of the house to *inquire* and
report thereon. I here subjoin the petition[4] and the report, and shall
exercise the right and privilege of a citizen in examining their merits,
not for the purpose of opposition, but with a design of making an
intricate affair more generally and better understood.

4 Minutes of the assembly, March 21, 1785. Petitions from a considerable number
of the inhabitants of *Chester* county were read, representing that the bank established
at *Philadelphia* has fatal effects upon the community; that whilst men are enabled,
by means of the bank, to receive near three times the rate of common interest, and
at the same time receive their money at very short warning, whenever they have
occasion for it, it will be impossible for the husbandman or mechanic to borrow
on the former terms of legal interest and distant payments of the principal; that
the best security will not enable the person to borrow: that experience clearly
demonstrates the mischevious consequences of this institution to the fair trader;
that imposters have been enabled to support themselves in a fictitious credit, by
means of a temporary punctuality at the bank, until they have drawn in their honest
neighbours to trust them with their property, or to pledge their credit as sureties,
and have been finally involved in ruin and distress; that they have repeatedly seen
the stopping of discounts at the bank operate on the trading part of the community,
with a degree of violence scarcely inferior to that of a stagnation of the blood in
the human body, hurrying the wretched merchant who hath debts to pay into the
hands of griping usurers: that the directors of the bank may give such preference
in trade, by advances of money, to their particular favourites, as to destroy that
equality which ought to prevail in a commercial country; that paper money has
often proved beneficial to the state, but the bank forbids it, and the people must
acquiesce: therefore, and in order to restore public confidence and private security,
they pray that a bill may be brought in and passed into a law for repealing the law
for incorporating the bank.
March 28. The report of the committee, read March 25, on the petitions from the
counties of *Chester* and *Berks*, and the city of *Philadelphia* and its vicinity, praying
the act of the assembly, whereby the bank was established at *Philadelphia*, may be
repealed, was read the second time as follows—*viz.*
The committee to whom was referred the petitions concerning the bank established
at *Philadelphia*, and who were instructed to inquire whether the said bank be compatible with the public safety, and that equality which ought ever to prevail between the
individuals of a republic, beg leave to report, that it is the opinion of this committee
that the said bank, as at present established, is in every view incompatible with the
public safety—that in the present state of our trade, the said bank has a direct tendency
to banish a great part of the specie from the country, so as to produce a scarcity of
money, and to collect into the hands of the stockholders of the said bank, almost the
whole of the money which remains amongst us. That the accumulation of enormous
wealth in the hands of a society, who claim perpetual duration, will necessarily produce
a degree of influence and power, which cannot be intrusted in the hands of any set
of men whatsoever, without endangering the public safety. That the said bank, in its
corporate capacity, is empowered to hold estates to the amount of ten millions of
dollars, and by the tenor of the present charter, is to exist forever, without being
obliged to yield any emolument to the government, or to be at all dependent upon

So far as my private judgment is capable of comprehending the subject, it appears to me, that the committee were unacquainted with, and have totally mistaken, the nature and business of a bank, as well as the matter committed to them, considered as a proceeding of government.

They were instructed by the house to *inquire* whether the bank established at Philadelphia was compatible with the public safety. It is scarcely possible to suppose the instructions meant no more than that they were to inquire of one another. It is certain they made no inquiry at the bank, to inform themselves of the situation of its affairs, how they were conducted, what aids it had rendered the public cause, or whether any; nor do the committee produce in their report a single fact or circumstance to show that they made any inquiry at all, or whether the rumours then circulated were true or false; but content themselves with modelling the insinuations of the petitions into a report and giving an opinion thereon. It would appear from the report, that the committee either conceived that the house had already determined how it would act without regard to the case,

---

it. That the great profits of the bank which will daily increase as money grows scarcer, and which already far exceed the profits of European banks, have tempted foreigners to vest their money in this bank, and thus to draw from us large sums for interest. That foreigners will doubtless be more and more induced to become stockholders, until the time may arrive when this enormous engine of power may become subject to foreign influence; this country may be agitated with the politics of European courts, and the good people of America reduced once more into a state of subordination, and dependance upon some one or other of the European powers. That at best, if it were even confined to the hands of Americans, it would be totally destructive of that equality which ought to prevail in a republic. We have nothing in our free and equal government capable of balancing the influence which this bank must create—and we see nothing, which in the course of a few years, can prevent the directors of the bank from governing Pennsylvania. Already we have felt its influence indirectly interfering in the measures of the legislature. Already the house of assembly, the representatives of the people, have been threatened, that the credit of our paper currency will be blasted by the bank ; and if this growing evil continues, we fear the time is not very distant, when the bank will be able to dictate to the legislature, what laws to pass and what to forbear.

Your committee therefore beg leave further to report the following resolution to be adopted by the house—*viz.*

Resolved, that a committee be appointed to bring in a bill to repeal the act of assembly passed the 1st day of April, 1782, entitled, "An act to incorporate the subscribers to the bank of North-America :" and also to repeal one other act of assembly, passed the 18th of March, 1782, entitled, "An act for preventing and punishing the counterfeiting of the common seal, bank bills and bank notes of the president, directors and company, of the bank of North-America, and for other purposes therein mentioned."

and that they were only a committee for form sake, and to give a colour of inquiry without making any, or that the case was referred to them, *as law-questions are sometimes referred to law-officers for an opinion only.*

This method of doing public business serves exceedingly to mislead a country.—When the constituents of an assembly hear that an inquiry into any matter is directed to be made, and a committee appointed for that purpose, they naturally conclude that the inquiry *is made,* and that the future proceedings of the house are in consequence of the matters, facts, and information obtained by means of that inquiry.—But here is a committee of inquiry making no inquiry at all, and giving an opinion on a case without inquiring into the merits of it. This proceeding of the committee would justify an opinion that it was not their wish to *get,* but to *get over* information, and lest the inquiry should not suit their wishes, omitted to make any. The subsequent conduct of the house, in resolving not to hear the directors of the bank, on their application for that purpose, prior to the publication of the bill for the consideration of the people, strongly corroborates this opinion: for why should not the house hear them, unless it was apprehensive that the bank, by such a public opportunity, would produce proofs of its services and usefulness, that would not suit the temper and views of its oppressors?

But if the house did not wish or choose to hear the defence of the bank, it was no reason that their constituents should not. The constitution of this state, in lieu of having two branches of legislature, has substituted, that, "to the end that laws before they are enacted may be more *maturely considered,* and the inconvenience of *hasty determinations* as much as possible prevented, all bills of a public nature shall be printed for the consideration of the people."[5] The people, therefore, according to the constitution, stand in the place of another house; or, more properly speaking, are a house in their own right. But in this instance, the assembly arrogates the whole power to itself, and places itself as a bar to stop the necessary information spreading among the people. The application of the bank to be heard before the bill was published for public consideration had two objects. First, to the house,—and secondly, through the house to

5 Constitution, sect. 15th.

the people, who are as another house. It was as a defence in the first
instance, and as an appeal in the second. But the assembly absorbs
the right of the people to judge; because, by refusing to hear the
defence, they barred the appeal. Were there no other cause which
the constituents of that assembly had for censuring its conduct, than
the exceeding unfairness, partiality, and arbitrariness with which its
business was transacted, it would be cause sufficient.

Let the constituents of assemblies differ, as they may, respecting
certain peculiarities in the *form* of the constitution, they will all agree
in supporting its *principles*, and in reprobating unfair proceedings and
despotic measures.—Every constituent is a member of the republic,
which is a station of more consequence to him than being a member
of a party, and though they may differ from each other in their choice
of persons to transact the public business, it is of equal importance
to all parties that the business be done on right principles; otherwise
our laws and acts, instead of being founded in justice, will be founded
in party, and be laws and acts of retaliation; and instead of being a
republic of free citizens, we shall be alternately tyrants and slaves.
But to return to the report.

The report begins by stating that, "The committee to whom was
referred the petitions concerning the bank established at Philadelphia, and who were instructed to *inquire* whether the said bank be
compatible with the public safety, and that equality which ought
ever to prevail between the individuals of a republic, beg leave to
report" (not that they have made any *inquiry*, but) "that it is the
opinion of this committee, that the said bank, as at present established,
is, in every view, incompatible with the public safety." But why is
it so? Here is an opinion unfounded and unwarranted. The committee
have begun their report at the wrong end; for an opinion, when
given as a matter of judgment, is an action of the mind which follows
a fact, but here it is put in the room of one.

The report then says, "that in the present state of our trade, the
said bank has a direct tendency to banish a great part of the specie from
the country, and to collect into the hands of the stockholders of the
bank, almost the whole of the money which remains among us."

Here is another mere assertion, just like the former, without a
single fact or circumstance to show why it is made, or whereon it is
founded. Now the very reverse of what the committee asserts is the
natural consequence of a bank. Specie may be called the stock in trade

of the bank, it is therefore its interest to prevent it from wandering out of the country, and to keep a constant standing supply to be ready for all domestic occasions and demands. Were it true that the bank has a direct tendency to banish the specie from the country, there would soon be an end to the bank; and, therefore, the committee have so far mistaken the matter, as to put their fears in the place of their wishes: for if it is to happen as the committee states, let the bank alone and it will cease of itself, and the repealing act need not have been passed.

It is the interest of the bank that people should keep their cash there, and all commercial countries find the exceeding great convenience of having a general depository for their cash. But so far from banishing it, there are no two classes of people in America who are so much interested in preserving hard money in the country as the bank and the merchant. Neither of them can carry on their business without it. Their opposition to the paper money of the late assembly was because it has a direct effect, as far as it is able, to banish the specie, and that without providing any means for bringing more in.

The committee must have been aware of this, and therefore chose to spread the first alarm, and, groundless as it was, to trust to the delusion.

As the keeping the specie in the country is the interest of the bank, so it has the best opportunities of preventing its being sent away, and the earliest knowledge of such a design. While the bank is the general depository of cash, no great sums can be obtained without getting it from thence, and as it is evidently prejudicial to its interest to advance money to be sent abroad, because in this case the money cannot by circulation return again, the bank, therefore, is interested in preventing what the committee would have it suspected of promoting.

It is to prevent the exportation of cash, and to retain it in the country, that the bank has, on several occasions, stopped the discounting notes till the danger has been passed.[6] The first part, there-

---

6 The petitions say, "That they have frequently seen the stopping of discounts at the bank operate on the trading part of the community, with a degree of violence scarcely inferior to that of a stagnation of the blood in the human body, hurrying the wretched merchant who hath debts to pay into the hands of griping usurers." As the persons who say or signed this live somewhere in Chester county, they are not, from situation, certain of what they say. Those petitions have every appearance

fore, of the assertion, that of banishing the specie, contains an apprehension as needless as it is groundless, and which, had the committee understood, or been the least informed of the nature of a bank, they could not have made. It is very probable that some of the opposers of the bank are those persons who have been disappointed in their attempts to obtain specie for this purpose, and now disguise their opposition under other pretences.

I now come to the second part of the assertion, which is, that when the bank has banished a great part of the specie from the country, "it will collect into the hands of the stockholders almost the whole of the money which remains among us." But how, or by what means, the bank is to accomplish this wonderful feat, the committee have not informed us. Whether people are to give their money to the bank for nothing, or whether the bank is to charm it from them as a rattlesnake charms a squirrel from a tree, the committee have left us as much in the dark about as they were themselves.

Is it possible the committee should know so very little of the matter, as not to know that no part of the money which at any time may be in the bank belongs to the stockholders? Not even the original capital which they put in is any part of it their own, until every person who has a demand upon the bank is paid, and if there is not

---

of being contrived for the purpose of bringing the matter on. The petitions and the report have strong evidence in them of being both drawn by the same person: for the report is as clearly the echo of the petitions as ever the address of the British parliament was the echo of the king's speech.

Besides the reason I have already given for occasionally stopping discounting notes at the bank, there are other necessary reasons. It is for the purpose of settling accounts: short reckonings make long friends. The bank lends its money for short periods, and by that means assists a great many different people: and if it did not sometimes stop discounting as a means of settling with the persons it has already lent its money to, those persons who would find a way to keep what they had borrowed longer than they ought, and prevent others being assisted. It is a fact, and some of the committee know it to be so, that sundry of those persons who then opposed the bank acted this part.

The stopping the discounts do not, and cannot, operate to call in the loans sooner than the time for which they were lent, and therefore the charge is false that "it hurries men into the hands of griping usurers": and the truth is, that it operates to keep them from them.

If petitions are to be contrived to cover the design of a house of assembly, and give a pretence for its conduct, or if a house is to be led by the nose by the idle tale of any fifty or sixty signers to a petition, it is time for the public to look a little closer into the conduct of its representatives.

a sufficiency for this purpose, on the balance of loss and gain, the original money of the stockholders must make up the deficiency.

The money, which at any time may be in the bank, is the property of every man who holds a bank note, or deposits cash there, or who has a just demand upon it from the city of Philadelphia up to fort Pitt, or to any part of the United States; and he can draw the money from it when he pleases. Its being in the bank, does not in the least make it the property of the stockholders, any more than the money in the state treasury is the property of the state treasurer. They are only stewards over it for those who please to put it, or let it remain there: and, therefore, this second part of the assertion is somewhat ridiculous.

The next paragraph in the report is, "that the accumulation of *enormous wealth* in the hands of a *society* who claim perpetual duration, will necessarily produce a degree of influence and power which cannot be entrusted in the hands of any set of men whatsoever" (the committee I presume excepted) "without endangering public safety." There is an air of solemn fear in this paragraph which is something like introducing a ghost in a play to keep people from laughing at the players.

I have already shown that whatever wealth there may be, at any time, in the bank, is the property of those who have demands upon the bank, and not the property of the stockholders. As a society they hold no property, and most probably never will, unless it should be a house to transact their business in, instead of hiring one. Every half year the bank settles its accounts, and each individual stockholder takes his dividend of gain or loss to himself, and the bank begins the next half year in the same manner it began the first, and so on. This being the nature of a bank, there can be no accumulation of wealth among them as a society.

For what purpose the word "*society*" is introduced into the report I do not know, unless it be to make a false impression upon people's minds. It has no connexion with the subject, for the bank is not a society, but a company, and denominated so in the charter. There are several religious societies incorporated in this state, which hold property as the right of those societies, and to which no person can belong that is not of the same religious profession. But this is not the case with the bank. The bank is a company for the promotion and convenience of commerce, which is a matter in which all the state is interested, and holds no property in the manner which those societies do.

But there is a direct contradiction in this paragraph to that which goes before it. The committee, there, accuses the bank of banishing the specie, and here, of accumulating enormous sums of it. So here are two enormous sums of specie; one enormous sum going out, and another enormous sum remaining. To reconcile this contradiction, the committee should have added to their report, *that they suspected the bank had found out the philosopher's stone, and kept it a secret.*

The next paragraph is, "that the said bank, in its corporate capacity, is empowered to hold estates to the amount of ten millions of dollars, and by the tenor of the present charter is to exist for ever, without being obliged to yield any emolument to the government, or be in the least dependant on it."

The committee have gone so vehemently into this business, and so completely shown their want of knowledge in every point of it, as to make, in the first part of this paragraph, a fear of what, the greater fear is, will never happen. Had the committee known any thing of banking, they must have known, that the objection against banks has been (not that they held great estates but) that they held none; that they had no real, fixed, and visible property, and that it is the maxim and practice of banks not to hold any.

The honourable chancellor Livingston, late secretary for foreign affairs, did me the honour of showing, and discoursing with me on, a plan of a bank he had drawn up for the state of New York. In this plan it was made a condition or obligation, that whatever the capital of the bank amounted to in specie, there should be added twice as much in real estates. But the mercantile interest rejected the proposition.

It was a very good piece of policy in the assembly which passed the charter act, to add the clause to empower the bank to purchase and hold real estates. It was as an inducement to the bank to do it, because such estates being held as the property of the bank would be so many mortgages to the public in addition to the money capital of the bank.

But the doubt is that the bank will not be induced to accept the opportunity. The bank has existed five years, and has not purchased a shilling of real property: and as such property or estates cannot be purchased by the bank but with the interest money which the stock produces, and as that is divided every half year among the stockholders, and each stockholder chooses to have the management of his own dividend, and if he lays it out in purchasing an estate to have that estate his own private property, and under his own immediate management, there is no expectation, so far from being any fear, that the clause will be accepted.

Where knowledge is a duty, ignorance is a crime; and the committee are criminal in not understanding this subject better. Had this clause not been in the charter, the committee might have reported the want of it as a defect, in not empowering the bank to hold estates as a real security to its creditors: but as the complaint now stands, the accusation of it is, that the charter empowers the bank to *give real security* to its creditors. A complaint never made, heard of, or thought of before.

The second article in this paragraph is, "that the bank, according to the tenor of the present charter, is to exist for ever." Here I agree with the committee, and am glad to find that among such a list of errors and contradictions there is one idea which is not wrong, although the committee have made a wrong use of it.

As we are not to live for ever ourselves, and other generations are to follow us, we have neither the power nor the right to govern them, or to say how they shall govern themselves. It is the summit of human vanity, and shows a covetousness of power beyond the grave, to be dictating to the world to come. It is sufficient that we do that which is right in our own day, and leave them with the advantage of good examples.

As the generations of the world are every day both commencing and expiring, therefore, when any public act, of this sort, is done, it naturally supposes the age of that generation to be then beginning, and the time contained between coming of age, and the natural end of life, is the extent of time it has a right to go to, which may be about thirty years; for though many may die before, others will live beyond; and the mean time is equally fair for all generations.

If it was made an article in the constitution, that all laws and acts should cease of themselves in thirty years, and have no legal force beyond that time, it would prevent their becoming too numerous and voluminous, and serve to keep them within view in a compact compass. Such as were proper to be continued, would be enacted again, and those which were not, would go into oblivion. There is the same propriety that a nation should fix a time for a full settlement of its affairs, and begin again from a new date, as that an individual should; and to keep within the distance of thirty years would be a convenient period.

The British, from the want of some general regulation of this kind, have a great number of obsolete laws; which, though out of use and forgotten, are not out of force, and are occasionally brought up for particular purposes, and innocent, unwary persons trapanned thereby.

To extend this idea still further,—it would probably be a considerable improvement in the political system of nations, to make all treaties of peace for a limited time. It is the nature of the mind to feel uneasy under the idea of a condition perpetually existing over it, and to excite in itself apprehensions that would not take place were it not from that cause.

Were treaties of peace made for, and renewable every seven or ten years, the natural effect would be, to make peace continue longer than it does under the custom of making peace for ever. If the parties felt, or apprehended, any inconveniences under the terms already made, they would look forward to the time when they should be eventually relieved therefrom, and might renew the treaty on improved conditions. This opportunity periodically occurring, and the recollection of it always existing, would serve as a chimney to the political fabric, to carry off the smoke and fume of national fire. It would naturally abate and honorably take off the edge and occasion for fighting: and however the parties might determine to do it, when the time of the treaty should expire, it would then seem like fighting in cool blood: the fighting temper would be dissipated before the fighting time arrived, and negotiation supply its place. To know how probable this may be, a man need do no more than observe the progress of his own mind on any private circumstance similar in its nature to a public one. But to return to my subject.

To give limitation is to give duration: and though it is not a justifying reason, that because an act or contract is not to last for ever, that it shall be broken or violated to-day, yet, where no time is mentioned, the omission affords an opportunity for the abuse. When we violate a contract on this pretence, we assume a right that belongs to the next generation; for though they, as a following generation, have the right of altering or setting it aside, as not being concerned in the making it, or not being done in their day, we, who made it, have not that right; and, therefore, the committee, in this part of their report, have made a wrong use of a right principle; and as this clause in the charter might have been altered by the consent of the parties, it cannot be produced to justify the violation. And were it not altered there would be no inconvenience from it. The term "for ever" is an absurdity that would have no effect. The next age will think for itself, by the same rule of right that we have done, and not admit any assumed authority of ours to encroach upon the system of their day. Our *for ever* ends, where their *for ever* begins.

The third article in this paragraph is, that the bank holds its charter "without being obliged to yield any emolument to the government."

Ingratitude has a short memory. It was on the failure of the government to support the public cause, that the bank originated. It stepped in as a support, when some of the persons then in the government, and who now oppose the bank, were apparently on the point of abandoning the cause, not from disaffection, but from despair. While the expenses of the war were carried on by emissions of continental money, any set of men, in government, might carry it on. The means being provided to their hands, required no great exertions of fortitude or wisdom; but when this means failed, they would have failed with it, had not a public spirit awakened itself with energy out of doors. It was easy times to the governments while continental money lasted. The dream of wealth supplied the reality of it; but when the dream vanished, the government did not awake.

But what right has the government to expect any emolument from the bank? Does the committee mean to set up acts and charters for sale, or what do they mean? Because it is the practice of the British ministry to grind a toll out of every public institution they can get a power over, is the same practice to be followed here?

The war being now ended, and the bank having rendered the service expected, or rather hoped for, from it, the principal public use of it, at this time, is for the promotion and extension of commerce. The whole community derives benefit from the operation of the bank. It facilitates the commerce of the country. It quickens the means of purchasing and paying for country produce, and hastens on the exportation of it. The emolument, therefore, being to the community, it is the office and duty of government to give protection to the bank.

Among many of the principal conveniences arising from the bank, one of them is, that it gives a kind of life to, what would otherwise be, dead money. Every merchant and person in trade, has always in his hands some quantity of cash, which constantly remains with him; that is, he is never entirely without: this remnant money, as it may be called, is of no use to him till more is collected to it.— He can neither buy produce nor merchandize with it, and this being the case with every person in trade, there will be (though not all at the same time) as many of those sums lying uselessly by, and scattered throughout the city, as there are persons in trade, besides many that are not in trade.

I should not suppose the estimate overrated, in conjecturing, that half the money in the city, at any one time, lies in this manner. By collecting those scattered sums together, which is done by means of the bank, they become capable of being used, and the quantity of circulating cash is doubled, and by the depositors alternately lending them to each other, the commercial system is invigorated: and as it is the interest of the bank to preserve this money in the country for domestic uses only, and as it has the best opportunity of doing so, the bank serves as a sentinel over the specie.

If a farmer, or a miller, comes to the city with produce, there are but a few merchants that can individually purchase it with ready money of their own; and those few would command nearly the whole market for country produce; but, by means of the bank, this monopoly is prevented, and the chance of the market is enlarged. It is very extraordinary that the late assembly should promote monopolizing; yet such would be the effect of suppressing the bank; and it is much to the honour of those merchants, who are capable by their fortunes of becoming monopolizers, that they support the bank. In this case, honour operates over interest. They were the persons who first set up the bank, and their honour is now engaged to support what it is their interest to put down.

If merchants, by this means, or farmers, by similar means, among themselves, can mutually aid and support each other, what has the government to do with it? What right has it to expect emolument from associated industry, more than from individual industry? It would be a strange sort of government, that should make it illegal for people to assist each other, or pay a tribute for doing so.

But the truth is, that the government has already derived emoluments, and very extraordinary ones. It has already received its full share, by the services of the bank during the war; and it is every day receiving benefits, because whatever promotes and facilitates commerce, serves likewise to promote and facilitate the revenue.

The last article in this paragraph is, "that the bank is not the least dependant on the government."

Have the committee so soon forgotten the principles of republican government, and the constitution, or are they so little acquainted with them, as not to know, that this article in their report partakes of the nature of treason? Do they not know, that freedom is destroyed by dependance, and the safety of the state endangered thereby? Do they not see, that to hold any part of the citizens of the state, as yearly pensioners on the favour of an assembly, is striking at the root of free elections?

If other parts of their report discover a want of knowledge on the subject of banks, this shows a want of principle in the science of government.

Only let us suppose this dangerous idea carried into practice, and then see what it leads to. If corporate bodies are, after their incorporation, to be annually dependant on an assembly for the continuance of their charter, the citizens which compose those corporations, are not free. The government holds an authority and influence over them, in a manner different from what it does over other citizens, and by this means destroys that equality of freedom, which is the bulwark of the republic and the constitution.

By this scheme of government any party, which happens to be uppermost in a state, will command all the corporations in it, and may create more for the purpose of extending that influence. The dependant borough towns in England are the rotten parts of their government and this idea of the committee has a very near relation to it.

"If you do not do so and so," expressing what was meant, "take care of your charter," was a threat thrown out against the bank. But as I do not wish to enlarge on a disagreeable circumstance, and hope that what is already said is sufficient to show the anti-constitutional conduct and principles of the committee, I shall pass on to the next paragraph in the report.—Which is—

"That the great profits of the bank, which will daily increase as money grows scarcer, and which already far exceeds the profits of European banks, have tempted foreigners to vest their money in this bank, and thus to draw from us large sums for interest."

Had the committee understood the subject, some dependance might be put on their opinion which now cannot. Whether money will grow scarcer, and whether the profits of the bank will increase, are more than the committee know, or are judges sufficient to guess at. The committee are not so capable of taking care of commerce, as commerce is capable of taking care of itself. The farmer understands farming, and the merchant understands commerce; and as riches are equally the object of both, there is no occasion that either should fear that the other will seek to be poor. The more money the merchant has, so much the better for the farmer who has produce to sell; and the richer the farmer is, so much the better for the merchant, when he comes to his store.

As to the profits of the bank, the stockholders must take their chance for it. It may some years be more and others less, and upon the whole may not be so productive as many other ways that money may be employed. It is the convenience which the stockholders, as commercial men, derive from the establishment of the bank, and not the mere interest they receive, that is the inducement to them. It is the ready opportunity of borrowing alternately of each other that forms the principal object: and as they pay as well as receive a great part of the interest among themselves, it is nearly the same thing, both cases considered at once, whether it is more or less.

The stockholders are occasionally depositors and sometimes borrowers of the bank. They pay interest for what they borrow, and receive none for what they deposit; and were a stockholder to keep a nice account of the interest he pays for the one and loses on the other, he would find, at the year's end, that ten per cent. on his stock would probably not be more than common interest on the whole, if so much.

As to the committee complaining "that foreigners by vesting their money in the bank will draw large sums from us for interest," it is like a miller complaining, in a dry season, that so much water runs into his dam some of it runs over.

Could those foreigners draw this interest without putting in any capital, the complaint would be well founded; but as they must first put money in before they can draw any out, as they must draw many years before they can draw even the numerical sum they put in at first, the effect for at least twenty years to come, will be directly contrary to what the committee states; because we draw *capital* from them and they only *interest* from us, and as we shall have the use of

the money all the while it remains with us, the advantage will always
be in our favour.—In framing this part of the report, the committee
must have forgotten which side of the Atlantic they were on, for the
case would be as they state it if we put money into their bank instead
of their putting it into ours.

I have now gone through, line by line, every objection against
the bank, contained in the first half of the report; what follows
may be called, *The lamentations of the committee*, and a lamentable,
pusillanimous, degrading thing it is.—It is a public affront, a reflection upon the sense and spirit of the whole country. . . .

. . . There is something in this sequel to the report that is perplexed and obscure.

Here are two acts to be repealed. One is, the incorporating act.
The other, the act for preventing and punishing the counterfeiting
of the common seal, bank bills, and bank notes of the president,
directors and company of the bank of North-America.

It would appear from the committee's manner of arranging them
(were it not for the difference of their dates) that the act for punishing
the counterfeiting the common seal, etc. of the bank, followed the
act of incorporation, and that the common seal there referred to is
a common seal which the bank held in consequence of the aforesaid
incorporating act.—But the case is quite otherwise. The act for
punishing the counterfeiting the common seal, etc. of the bank, was
passed prior to the incorporating act, and refers to the common seal
which the bank held in consequence of the charter of congress, and
the style which the act expresses, of president, directors and company
of the bank of North-America, is the corporate style which the bank
derives under the congress charter.

The punishing act, therefore, hath two distinct legal points. The
one is, an authoritative public recognition of the charter of congress.
The second is, the punishment it inflicts on counterfeiting.

The legislature may repeal the punishing part, but it cannot
undo the recognition, because no repealing act can say that the state
has not recognized. The recognition is a mere matter of fact, and no
law or act can undo a fact, or put it, if I may so express it, in the
condition it was before it existed. The repealing act therefore does
not reach the full point the committee had in view; for even admitting
it to be a repeal of the state charter, it still leaves another charter
recognized in its stead.—The charter of congress, standing merely

on itself, would have a doubtful authority, but recognition of it by the state gives it legal ability. The repealing act, it is true sets aside the punishment, but does not bar the operation of the charter of congress as a charter recognized by the state, and therefore the committee did their business but by halves.

I have now gone entirely through the report of the committee, and a more irrational, inconsistent, contradictory report will scarcely be found on the journals of any legislature of America.

How the repealing act is to be applied, or in what manner it is to operate, is a matter yet to be determined. For admitting a question of law to arise, whether the charter, which that act attempts to repeal, is a law of the land in the manner which laws of universal operation are, or of the nature of a contract made between the public and the bank, (as I have already explained in this work,) the repealing act does not and cannot decide the question, because it is the repealing act that makes the question, and its own fate is involved in the decision. It is a question of law and not a question of legislation, and must be decided on in a court of justice and not by a house of assembly.

But the repealing act, by being passed prior to the decision of this point, assumes the power of deciding it, and the assembly in so doing erects itself unconstitutionally into a tribunal of judicature, and absorbs the authority and right of the courts of justice into itself.

Therefore the operation of the repealing act, in its very outset, requires injustice to be done. For it is impossible on the principles of a republican government and the constitution, to pass an act to forbid any of the citizens the right of appealing to the courts of justice on any manner in which his interest or property is affected; but the first operation of this act goes to shut up the courts of justice and holds them subservient to the assembly. It either commands or influences them not to hear the case, or to give judgment on it on the mere will of one party only.

I wish the citizens to awaken themselves on this subject. Not because the bank is concerned, but because their own constitutional rights and privileges are involved in the event. It is a question of exceeding great magnitude; for if an assembly is to have this power, the laws of the land and the courts of justice are but of little use.

Having now finished with the report, I proceed to the third and last subject—that of paper money.

I remember a German farmer expressing as much in a few words as the whole subject requires; *"money is money, and paper is paper."*—All the invention of man cannot make them otherwise. The alchymist may cease his labours, and the hunter after the philosopher's stone go to rest, if paper can be metamorphosed into gold and silver, or made to answer the same purpose in all cases.

Gold and silver are the emissions of nature: paper is the emission of art. The value of gold and silver is ascertained by the quantity which nature has made in the earth. We cannot make that quantity more or less than it is, and therefore the value being dependant upon the quantity, depends not on man.—Man has no share in making gold or silver; all that his labours and ingenuity can accomplish is, to collect it from the mine, refine it for use and give it an impression, or stamp it into coin.

Its being stamped into coin adds considerably to its convenience but nothing to its value. It has then no more value than it had before. Its value is not in the impression but in itself. Take away the impression and still the same value remains. Alter it as you will, or expose it to any misfortune that can happen, still the value is not diminished. It has a capacity to resist the accidents that destroy other things. It has, therefore, all the requisite qualities that money can have, and is a fit material to make money of; and nothing which has not all those properties, can be fit for the purpose of money.

Paper, considered as a material whereof to make money, has none of the requisite qualities in it. It is too plentiful, and too easily come at. It can be had any where, and for a trifle.

There are two ways in which I shall consider paper.

The only proper use for paper, in the room of money, is to write promissory notes and obligations of payment in specie upon. A piece of paper, thus written and signed, is worth the sum it is given for, if the person who gives it is able to pay it; because in this case, the law will oblige him. But if he is worth nothing, the paper note is worth nothing. The value, therefore, of such a note, is not in the note itself, for that is but paper and promise, but in the man who is obliged to redeem it with gold or silver.

Paper, circulating in this manner, and for this purpose, continually points to the place and person where, and of whom, the money is to be had, and at last finds its home; and, as it were, unlocks its master's chest and pays the bearer.

But when an assembly undertake to issue paper *as* money, the whole system of safety and certainty is overturned, and property set afloat. Paper notes given and taken between individuals as a promise of payment is one thing, but paper issued by an assembly *as* money is another thing. It is like putting an apparition in the place of a man; it vanishes with looking at it, and nothing remains but the air.

Money, when considered as the fruit of many years industry, as the reward of labour, sweat and toil, as the widow's dowry and children's portion, and as the means of procuring the necessaries and alleviating the afflictions of life, and making old age a scene of rest, has something in it sacred that is not to be sported with, or trusted to the airy bubble of paper currency.

By what power or authority an assembly undertakes to make paper money, is difficult to say. It derives none from the constitution, for that is silent on the subject. It is one of those things which the people have not delegated, and which, were they at any time assembled together, they would not delegate. It is, therefore, an assumption of power which an assembly is not warranted in, and which may, one day or other, be the means of bringing some of them to punishment.

I shall enumerate some of the evils of paper money and conclude with offering means for preventing them.

One of the evils of paper money is, that it turns the whole country into stock jobbers. The precariousness of its value and the uncertainty of its fate continually operate, night and day, to produce this destructive effect. Having no real value in itself it depends for support upon accident, caprice and party, and as it is the interest of some to depreciate and of others to raise its value, there is a continual invention going on that destroys the morals of the country.

It was horrid to see, and hurtful to recollect, how loose the principles of justice were left, by means of the paper emissions during the war. The experience then had, should be a warning to any assembly how they venture to open such a dangerous door again.

As to the romantic, if not hypocritical, tale that a virtuous people need no gold and silver, and that paper will do as well, it requires no other contradiction than the experience we have seen. Though some well meaning people may be inclined to view it in this light, it is certain that the sharper always talks this language.

There are a set of men who go about making purchases upon credit, and buying estates they have not wherewithal to pay for;

and having done this, their next step is to fill the newspapers with paragraphs of the scarcity of money and the necessity of a paper emission, then to have a legal tender under the pretence of supporting its credit, and when out, to depreciate it as fast as they can, get a deal of it for a little price, and cheat their creditors; and this is the concise history of paper money schemes.

But why, since the universal custom of the world has established money as the most convenient medium of traffic and commerce, should paper be set up in preference to gold and silver? The productions of nature are surely as innocent as those of art; and in the case of money, are abundantly, if not infinitely, more so. The love of gold and silver may produce covetousness, but covetousness, when not connected with dishonesty, is not properly a vice. It is frugality run to an extreme.

But the evils of paper money have no end. Its uncertain and fluctuating value is continually awakening or creating new schemes of deceit. Every principle of justice is put to the rack, and the bond of society dissolved: the suppression, therefore, of paper money might very properly have been put into the act for preventing vice and immorality.

The pretence for paper money has been, that there was not a sufficiency of gold and silver. This, so far from being a reason for paper emissions, is a reason against them.

As gold and silver are not the productions of North America, they are, therefore, articles of importation; and if we set up a paper manufactory of money, it amounts, as far as it is able, to prevent the importation of hard money, or to send it out again as fast as it comes in; and by following this practice we shall continually banish the specie, till we have none left, and be continually complaining of the grievance instead of remedying the cause.

Considering gold and silver as articles of importation, there will in time, unless we prevent it by paper emissions, be as much in the country as the occasions of it require, for the same reasons there are as much of other imported articles. But as every yard of cloth manufactured in the country occasions a yard the less to be imported, so it is by money, with this difference, that in the one case we manufacture the thing itself and in the other we do not. We have cloth for cloth, but we have only paper dollars for silver ones.

As to the assumed authority of any assembly in making paper money, or paper of any kind, a legal tender, or in other language, a compulsive payment, it is a most presumptuous attempt at arbitrary power. There can be no such power in a republican government: the people have no freedom, and property no security where this practice can be acted: and the committee who shall bring in a report for this purpose, or the member who moves for it, and he who seconds it merit impeachment, and sooner or later may expect it.

Of all the various sorts of base coin, paper money is the basest. It has the least intrinsic value of any thing that can be put in the place of gold and silver. A hobnail or a piece of wampum far exceeds it. And there would be more propriety in making those articles a legal tender than to make paper so.

It was the issuing base coin, and establishing it as a tender, that was one of the principal means of finally overthrowing the power of the Stuart family in Ireland. The article is worth reciting as it bears such a resemblance to the process practised in paper money.

> Brass and copper of the basest kind, old cannon, broken bells, household utensils were assiduously collected; and from every pound weight of such vile materials, valued at four-pence, pieces were coined and circulated to the amount of five pounds normal value. By the first proclamation they were made current in all payments to and from the king and the subjects of the realm, except in duties on the importation of foreign goods, money left in trust, or due by mortgage, bills or bonds; and James promised that when the money should be decried, he would receive it in all payments, or make full satisfaction in gold and silver. The nominal value was afterwards raised by subsequent proclamations, the original restrictions removed, and this base money was ordered to be received in all kinds of payments. As brass and copper grew scarce, it was made of still viler materials, of tin and pewter, and old debts of one thousand pounds were discharged by pieces of vile metal amounting to thirty shillings in intrinsic value.[7]

Had king James thought of paper, he needed not to have been at the trouble or expense of collecting brass and copper, broken bells, and household utensils.

7 Leland's *History of Ireland*, Vol. IV, p. 265.

The laws of a country ought to be the standard of equity, and calculated to impress on the minds of the people the moral as well as the legal obligations of reciprocal justice. But tender laws, of any kind, operate to destroy morality, and to dissolve, by the pretence of law, what ought to be the principle of law to support, reciprocal justice between man and man: and the punishment of a member who should move for such a law ought to be *death*.

When the recommendation of congress, in the year 1780, for repealing the tender laws was before the assembly of Pennsylvania, on casting up the votes, for and against bringing in a bill to repeal those laws, the numbers were equal, and the casting vote rested on the speaker, colonel Bayard. "I give my vote," said he, "for the repeal, from a consciousness of justice; the tender laws operate to establish iniquity by law." But when the bill was brought in, the house rejected it, and the tender laws continued to be the means of fraud.

If any thing had, or could have, a value equal to gold and silver, it would require no tender law: and if it had not that value it ought not to have such a law; and, therefore, all tender laws are tyrannical and unjust, and calculated to support fraud and oppression.

Most of the advocates for tender laws are those who have debts to discharge, and who take refuge in such a law, to violate their contracts and cheat their creditors. But as no law can warrant the doing an unlawful act, therefore the proper mode of proceeding, should any such laws be enacted in future, will be to impeach and execute the members who moved for and seconded such a bill, and put the debtor and creditor in the same situation they were in, with respect to each other, before such a law was passed. Men ought to be made to tremble at the idea of such a barefaced act of injustice. It is in vain to talk of restoring credit, or complain that money cannot be borrowed at legal interest, until every idea of tender laws is totally and publicly reprobated and extirpated from among us.

As to paper money, in any light it can be viewed, it is at best a bubble. Considered as property, it is inconsistent to suppose that the breath of an assembly, whose authority expires with the year, can give to paper the value and duration of gold. They cannot even engage that the next assembly shall receive it in taxes. And by precedent, (for authority there is none,) that one assembly makes paper money, another may do the same, until confidence and credit are totally expelled, and all the evils of depreciation acted over again. The amount, therefore, of paper money is this, that it is the illegitimate offspring of assemblies, and when their year expires, they leave a vagrant on the hands of the public.

Having now gone through the three subjects proposed in the title to this work, I shall conclude with offering some thoughts on the present affairs of the state.

My idea of a single legislature was always founded on a hope, that whatever personal parties there might be in the state, they would all unite and agree in the general principles of good government— that these party differences would be dropped at the threshold of the statehouse, and that the public good, or the good of the whole, would be the governing principle of the legislature within it.

Party dispute, taken on this ground, would only be, who should have the honour of making the laws; not what the laws should be. But when party operates to produce party laws, a single house is a single person, and subject to the haste, rashness and passion of individual sovereignty. At least, it is an aristocracy.

The form of the present constitution is now made to trample on its principles, and the constitutional members are anti-constitutional legislators. They are fond of supporting the form for the sake of the power, and they dethrone the principle to display the sceptre.

The attack of the late assembly on the bank, discovers such a want of moderation and prudence, of impartiality and equity, of fair and candid inquiry and investigation, of deliberate and unbiassed judgment, and such a rashness of thinking and vengeance of power, as is inconsistent with the safety of the republic. It was judging without hearing, and executing without trial.

By such rash, injudicious and violent proceedings, the interest of the state is weakened, its prosperity diminished, and its commerce and its specie banished to other places. Suppose the bank had not been in an immediate condition to have stood such a sudden attack, what a scene of instant distress would the rashness of that assembly have brought upon this city and state. The holders of bank notes, whoever they might be, would have been thrown into the utmost confusion and difficulties. It is no apology to say the house never thought of this, for it was their duty to have thought of every thing.

But by the prudent and provident management of the bank, (though unsuspicious of the attack,) it was enabled to stand the run upon it without stopping payment a moment, and to prevent the evils and mischiefs taking place which the rashness of the assembly had a direct tendency to bring on; a trial that scarcely a bank in Europe, under a similar circumstance, could have withstood.

I cannot see reason sufficient to believe that the hope of the house to put down the bank was placed on the withdrawing the charter, so much as on the expectation of producing a bankruptcy of the bank, by starting a run upon it. If this was any part of their project it was a very wicked one, because hundreds might have been ruined to gratify a party spleen.

But this not being the case, what has the attack amounted to, but to expose the weakness and rashness, the want of judgment as well as justice, of those who made it, and to confirm the credit of the bank more substantially than it was before?

The attack, it is true, has had one effect, which is not in the power of the assembly to remedy; it has banished many thousand hard dollars from the state. By the means of the bank, Pennsylvania had the use of a great deal of hard money belonging to citizens of other states, and that without any interest, for it laid here in the nature of deposit, the depositors taking bank notes in its stead. But the alarm called those notes in and the owners drew out their cash.

The banishing the specie served to make room for the paper money of the assembly, and we have now paper dollars where we might have had silver ones. So that the effect of the paper money has been to make less money in the state than there was before. Paper money is like dram-drinking, it relieves for a moment by deceitful sensation, but gradually diminishes the natural heat, and leaves the body worse than it found it. Were not this the case, and could money be made of paper at pleasure, every sovereign in Europe would be as rich as he pleased. But the truth is, that it is a bubble and the attempt vanity. Nature has provided the proper materials for money, gold and silver, and any attempt of ours to rival her is ridiculous.

But to conclude. If the public will permit the opinion of a friend who is attached to no party, and under obligation to none, nor at variance with any, and who through a long habit of acquaintance with them has never deceived them, that opinion shall be freely given.

The bank is an institution capable of being made exceedingly beneficial to the state, not only as the means of extending and facilitating its commerce, but as a means of increasing the quantity of hard money in the state. The assembly's paper money serves directly to banish or crowd out the hard, because it is issued *as* money and put in the place of hard money. But bank notes are of a very different kind, and produce a contrary effect. They are promissory notes payable on demand, and may be taken to the bank and exchanged for gold or silver without the least ceremony or difficulty.

The bank, therefore, is obliged to keep a constant stock of hard money sufficient for this purpose; which is what the assembly neither does, nor can do by their paper; because the quantity of hard money collected by taxes into the treasury is trifling compared with the quantity that circulates in trade and through the bank.

The method, therefore, to increase the quantity of hard money would be to combine the security of the government and the bank into one. And instead of issuing paper money that serves to banish the specie, to borrow the sum wanted of the bank in bank notes, on the condition of the bank exchanging those notes at stated periods and quantities, with hard money.

Paper issued in this manner, and directed to this end, would, instead of banishing, work itself into gold and silver; because it will then be both the advantage and duty of the bank, and of all the mercantile interests connected with it, to procure and import gold and silver from any part of the world, to give in exchange for the notes. The English bank is restricted to the dealing in no other articles of importation than gold and silver, and we may make the same use of our bank if we proceed properly with it.

Those notes will then have a double security, that of the government and that of the bank: and they will not be issued *as* money, but as hostages to be exchanged for hard money, and will, therefore, work the contrary way to what the paper of the assembly, uncombined with the security of the bank, produces: and the interest allowed the bank will be saved to government, by a saving of the expenses and charges attending paper emissions.

It is, as I have already observed in the course of this work, the harmony of all the parts of a republic, that constitutes their several and mutual good. A government that is constructed only to govern, is not a republican government. It is combining authority with usefulness, that in a great measure distinguishes the republican system from others.

Paper money appears, at first sight, to be a great saving, or rather

that it costs nothing; but it is the dearest money there is. The ease with
which it is emitted by an assembly at first, serves as a trap to catch
people in at last. It operates as an anticipation of the next year's taxes.
If the money depreciates, after it is out, it then, as I have already remarked, has the effect of fluctuating stock, and the people become
stock-jobbers, to throw the loss on each other. If it does not depreciate,
it is then to be sunk by taxes at the price of *hard money;* because the
same quantity of produce, or goods, that would procure a paper dollar
to pay taxes with, would procure a silver one for the same purpose.
Therefore, in any case of paper money, it is dearer to the country than
hard money, by all the expense which the paper, printing, signing,
and other attendant charges come to, and at last goes into the fire.

Suppose one hundred thousand dollars in paper money to be
emitted every year by the assembly, and the same sum to be sunk
every year by taxes, there will then be no more than one hundred
thousand dollars out at any one time. If the expense of paper and
printing, and of persons to attend the press while the sheets are
striking off, signers, etc. be five per cent. it is evident that in the
course of twenty years' emissions, the one hundred thousand dollars
will cost the country two hundred thousand dollars. Because the
papermaker's and printer's bills, and the expense of supervisors and
signers, and other attendant charges, will in that time amount to as
much as the money amounts to; for the successive emissions are but
a re-coinage of the same sum.

But gold and silver require to be coined but once, and will last
an hundred years, better than paper will one year, and at the end
of that time be still gold and silver. Therefore, the saving to government, in combining its aid and security with that of the bank in
procuring hard money, will be an advantage to both, and to the
whole community.

The case to be provided against, after this, will be, that the
government do not borrow too much of the bank, nor the bank lend
more notes than it can redeem; and, therefore, should any thing of
this kind be undertaken, the best way will be to begin with a moderate
sum, and observe the effect of it. The interest given the bank operates
as a bounty on the importation of hard money, and which may not
be more than the money expended in making paper emissions.

But nothing of this kind, nor any other public undertaking, that
requires security and duration beyond the year, can be gone upon

under the present mode of conducting government. The late assembly, by assuming a sovereign power over every act and matter done by the state in former assemblies, and thereby setting up a precedent of overhauling, and overturning, as the accident of elections shall happen or party prevail, have rendered government incompetent to all the great objects of the state. They have eventually reduced the public to an annual body like themselves; whereas the public are a standing, permanent body, holding annual elections.

There are several great improvements and undertakings, such as inland navigation, building bridges, opening roads of communication through the state, and other matters of a public benefit, that might be gone upon, but which now cannot, until this governmental error or defect is remedied. The faith of government, under the present mode of conducting it, cannot be relied on. Individuals will not venture their money in undertakings of this kind, on an act that may be made by one assembly and broken by another. When a man can say that he cannot trust the government, the importance and dignity of the public is diminished, sapped and undermined; and, therefore, it becomes the public to restore their own honour by setting these matters to rights.

Perhaps this cannot be effectually done until the time of the next convention, when the principles, on which they are to be regulated and fixed, may be made a part of the constitution.

In the mean time the public may keep their affairs in sufficient good order, by substituting prudence in the place of authority, and electing men into the government, who will at once throw aside the narrow prejudices of party, and make the good of the whole the ruling object of their conduct. And with this hope, and a sincere wish for their prosperity, I close my book.

Alexander Hamilton

W hile Alexander Hamilton's political writings began as early as 1775, he reached his height during the period of the Constitutional Convention and during his term as secretary of the treasury from 1789–1794. In the Federalist Papers included here, The Federalist No. 10 and No. 11, *the explicit constitutional basis for his notions of industrial progress, and the government's role in promoting it, is laid out clearly. Hamilton had in mind at the time the implementation measures on public credit, a national bank, and manufactures that he presented to the Congress a few years later. His co-author Madison, however, failed to follow through on his own concepts with an economic program based on the total national interest.*

We excerpt a relatively short section from the Report on Public Credit *(1790), present in full the* Report on the National Bank *(1790), and reproduce nearly the entirety of Hamilton's* Report on Manufactures, *presented in 1791. Hamilton's reports were intended as educational treatises not only for the Congressmen, but also for their constituencies. In them, he develops more fully than his predecessor Franklin the notion of* total surplus value *by spelling out the role of mechanization and the division of labor in increasing that value and the quality of the human mind.*

From the Report on Public Credit (January 1790)

To the Speaker of the House of Representatives:

The Secretary of the Treasury, in obedience to the resolution of the House of Representatives, of the twenty-first day of September last, has, during the recess of Congress, applied himself to the consideration of a proper plan for the support of the Public Credit, with all the attention which was due to the authority of the House, and to the magnitude of the object.

In the discharge of this duty, he has felt, in no small degree, the anxieties which naturally flow from a just estimate of the difficulty

344

of the task, from a well-founded diffidence of his own qualifications for executing it with success, and from a deep and solemn conviction of the momentous nature of the truth contained in the resolution under which his investigations have been conducted, "That an *adequate* provision for the support of the Public Credit, is a matter of high importance to the honor and prosperity of the United States."

With an ardent desire that his well-meant endeavors may be conducive to the real advantage of the nation, and with the utmost deference to the superior judgment of the House, he now respectfully submits the result of his enquiries and reflections, to their indulgent construction.

In the opinion of the Secretary, the wisdom of the House, in giving their explicit sanction to the proposition which has been stated, cannot but be applauded by all, who will seriously consider, and trace through their obvious consequences, these plain and undeniable truths.

That exigencies are to be expected to occur, in the affairs of nations, in which there will be a necessity for borrowing.

That loans in times of public danger, especially from foreign war, are found an indispensable resource, even to the wealthiest of them.

And that in a country, which, like this, is possessed of little active wealth, or in other words, little monied capital, the necessity for that resource, must, in such emergencies, be proportionably urgent.

And as on the one hand, the necessity for borrowing in particular emergencies cannot be doubted, so on the other, it is equally evident, that to be able to borrow upon *good terms*, it is essential that the credit of a nation should be well established.

For when the credit of a country is in any degree questionable, it never fails to give an extravagant premium, in one shape or another, upon all the loans it has occasion to make. Nor does the evil end here; the same disadvantage must be sustained upon whatever is to be bought on terms of future payment.

From this constant necessity of *borrowing* and *buying dear*, it is easy to conceive how immensely the expences of a nation, in a course of time, will be augmented by an unsound state of the public credit.

To attempt to enumerate the complicated variety of mischiefs in the whole system of the social economy, which proceed from a neglect of the maxims that uphold public credit, and justify the solicitude manifested by the House on this point, would be an improper intrusion on their time and patience.

In so strong a light nevertheless do they appear to the Secretary, that on their due observance at the present critical juncture, materially depends, in his judgment, the individual and aggregate prosperity of the citizens of the United States; their relief from the embarrassments they now experience; their character as a People; the cause of good government.

If the maintenance of public credit, then, be truly so important, the next enquiry which suggests itself is, by what means it is to be effected? The ready answer to which question is, by good faith, by a punctual performance of contracts. States, like individuals, who observe their engagements, are respected and trusted: while the reverse is the fate of those, who pursue an opposite conduct.

Every breach of the public engagements, whether from choice or necessity, is in different degrees hurtful to public credit. When such a necessity does truly exist, the evils of it are only to be palliated by a scrupulous attention, on the part of the government, to carry the violation no farther than the necessity absolutely requires, and to manifest, if the nature of the case admits of it, a sincere disposition to make reparation, whenever circumstances shall permit. But with every possible mitigation, credit must suffer, and numerous mischiefs ensue. It is therefore highly important, when an appearance of necessity seems to press upon the public councils, that they should examine well its reality, and be perfectly assured, that there is no method of escaping from it, before they yield to its suggestions. For though it cannot safely be affirmed, that occasions have never existed, or may not exist, in which violations of the public faith, in this respect, are inevitable; yet there is great reason to believe, that they exist far less frequently than precedents indicate; and are oftenest either pretended through levity, or want of firmness, or supposed through want of knowledge. Expedients might often have been devised to effect, consistently with good faith, what has been done in contravention of it. Those who are most commonly creditors of a nation, are, generally speaking, enlightened men; and there are signal examples to warrant a conclusion, that when a candid and fair appeal is made to them, they will understand their true interest too well to refuse their concurrence in such modifications of their claims, as any real necessity may demand.

While the observance of that good faith, which is the basis of public credit, is recommended by the strongest inducements of political expediency, it is enforced by considerations of still greater authority. There are arguments for it, which rest on the immutable principles of moral obligation. And in proportion as the mind is disposed to contemplate, in the order of Providence, an intimate connection between public virtue and public happiness, will be its repugnancy to a violation of those principles.

This reflection derives additional strength from the nature of the debt of the United States. It was the price of liberty. The faith of America has been repeatedly pledged for it, and with solemnities, that give peculiar force to the obligation. There is indeed reason to regret that it has not hitherto been kept; that the necessities of the war, conspiring with inexperience in the subjects of finance, produced direct infractions; and that the subsequent period has been a continued scene of negative violation, or non-compliance. But a diminution of this regret arises from the reflection, that the last seven years have exhibited an earnest and uniform effort, on the part of the government of the union, to retrieve the national credit, by doing justice to the creditors of the nation; and that the embarrassments of a defective constitution, which defeated this laudable effort, have ceased.

From this evidence of a favorable disposition, given by the former government, the institution of a new one, cloathed with powers competent to calling forth the resources of the community, has excited correspondent expectations. A general belief, accordingly, prevails, that the credit of the United States will quickly be established on the firm foundation of an effectual provision for the existing debt. The influence, which this has had at home, is witnessed by the rapid increase, that has taken place in the market value of the public securities. From January to November, they rose thirty-three and a third per cent, and from that period to this time, they have risen fifty per cent more. And the intelligence from abroad announces effects proportionably favourable to our national credit and consequence.

It cannot but merit particular attention, that among ourselves the most enlightened friends of good government are those, whose expectations are the highest.

To justify and preserve their confidence; to promote the encreasing respectability of the American name; to answer the calls of justice; to restore landed property to its due value; to furnish new resources both to agriculture and commerce; to cement more closely the union of the states; to add to their security against foreign attack; to establish public order on the basis of an upright and liberal policy. These are the great and invaluable ends to be secured, by a proper and adequate provision, at the present period, for the support of public credit.

To this provision we are invited, not only by the general considerations, which have been noticed, but by others of a more particular nature. It will procure to every class of the community some important advantages, and remove some no less important disadvantages.

The advantage to the public creditors from the increased value of that part of their property which constitutes the public debt, needs no explanation.

But there is a consequence of this, less obvious, though not less true, in which every other citizen is interested. It is a well known fact, that in countries in which the national debt is properly funded, and an object of established confidence, it answers most of the purposes of money. Transfers of stock or public debt are there equivalent to payments in specie; or in other words, stock, in the principal transactions of business, passes current as specie. The same thing would, in all probability happen, here, under the like circumstances.

The benefits of this are various and obvious.

First. Trade is extended by it; because there is a larger capital to carry it on, and the merchant can at the same time, afford to trade for smaller profits; as his stock, which, when unemployed, brings him in an interest from the government, serves him also as money, when he has a call for it in his commercial operations.

Secondly. Agriculture and manufactures are also promoted by it: For the like reason, that more capital can be commanded to be employed in both; and because the merchant, whose enterprize in foreign trade, gives to them activity and extension, has greater means for enterprize.

Thirdly. The interest of money will be lowered by it; for this is always in a ratio, to the quantity of money, and to the quickness of circulation. This circumstance will enable both the public and individuals to borrow on easier and cheaper terms.

And from the combination of these effects, additional aids will be furnished to labour, to industry, and to arts of every kind.

But these good effects of a public debt are only to be looked for, when, by being well funded, it has acquired an *adequate* and *stable* value. Till then, it has rather a contrary tendency. The fluctuation and insecurity incident to it in an unfunded state, render it a mere commodity, and a precarious one. As such, being only an object of occasional and particular speculation, all the money applied to it is so much diverted from the more useful channels of circulation, for which the thing itself affords no substitute: So that, in fact, one serious inconvenience of an unfunded debt is, that it contributes to the scarcity of money.

This distinction which has been little if at all attended to, is of the greatest moment. It involves a question immediately interesting to every part of the community; which is no other than this—Whether the public debt, by a provision for it on true principles, shall be rendered a *substitute* for money; or whether, by being left as it is, or by being provided for in such a manner as will wound those principles, and destroy confidence, it shall be suffered to continue, as it is, a pernicious drain of our cash from the channels of productive industry.

The effect, which the funding of the public debt, on right principles, would have upon landed property, is one of the circumstances attending such an arrangement, which has been least adverted to, though it deserves the most particular attention. The present depreciated state of that species of property is a serious calamity. The value of cultivated lands, in most of the states, has fallen since the revolution from 25 to 50 per cent. In those farthest south, the decrease is still more considerable. Indeed, if the representations, continually received from that quarter, may be credited, lands there will command no price, which may not be deemed an almost total sacrifice.

This decrease, in the value of lands, ought, in a great measure, to be attributed to the scarcity of money. Consequently whatever produces an augmentation of the monied capital of the country, must have a proportional effect in raising that value. The beneficial tendency of a funded debt, in this respect, has been manifested by the most decisive experience in Great Britain.

The proprietors of lands would not only feel the benefit of this increase in the value of their property, and of a more prompt and better sale, when they had occasion to sell; but the necessity of selling would be, itself, greatly diminished. As the same cause would contribute to the facility of loans, there is reason to believe, that such of them as are indebted, would be able through that resource, to satisfy their more urgent creditors.

It ought not however to be expected, that the advantages, described as likely to result from funding the public debt, would be instantaneous. It might require some time to bring the value of stock to its natural level, and to attach to it that fixed confidence, which is necessary to its quality as money. Yet the late rapid rise of the public securities encourages an expectation, that the progress of stock to the desireable point, will be much more expeditious than could have been foreseen. And as in the mean time it will be increasing in value, there is room to conclude, that it will, from the outset, answer many of the purposes in contemplation. Particularly it seems to be probable, that from creditors, who are not themselves necessitous, it will early meet with a ready reception in payment of debts, at its current price.

Having now taken a concise view of the inducements to a proper provision for the public debt, the next enquiry which presents itself is, what ought to be the nature of such a provision? This requires some preliminary discussions.

It is agreed on all hands, that that part of the debt which has been contracted abroad, and is denominated the foreign debt, ought to be provided for, according to the precise terms of the contracts relating to it. The discussions, which can arise, therefore, will have reference essentially to the domestic part of it, or to that which has been contracted at home. It is to be regretted, that there is not the same unanimity of sentiment on this part, as on the other.

The Secretary has too much deference for the opinions of every part of the community, not to have observed one, which has, more than once, made its appearance in the public prints, and which is occasionally to be met with in conversation. It involves this question, whether a discrimination ought not to be made between original holders of the public securities, and present possessors, by purchase. Those who advocate a discrimination are for making a full provision for the securities of the former, at their nominal value; but contend, that the latter ought to receive no more than the cost to them, and the interest: And the idea is sometimes suggested of making good the difference to the primitive possessor.

In favor of this scheme, it is alledged, that it would be unreasonable to pay twenty shillings in the pound, to one who had not given more for it than three or four. And it is added, that it would be hard to aggravate the misfortune of the first owner, who, probably through necessity, parted with his property at so great a loss, by obliging him to contribute to the profit of the person, who had speculated on his distresses.

The Secretary, after the most mature reflection on the force of this argument, is induced to reject the doctrine it contains, as equally unjust and impolitic, as highly injurious, even to the original holders of public securities; as ruinous to public credit.

It is inconsistent with justice, because in the first place, it is a breach of contract; in violation of the rights of a fair purchaser.

The nature of the contract in its origin, is, that the public will pay the sum expressed in the security, to the first holder, or his *assignee*. The *intent*, in making the security assignable, is, that the proprietor may be able to make use of his property, by selling it for as much as it *may be worth in the market*, and that the buyer may be *safe* in the purchase.

Every buyer therefore stands exactly in the place of the seller, has the same right with him to the identical sum expressed in the security, and having acquired that right, by fair purchase, and in conformity to the original *agreement* and *intention* of the government, his claim cannot be disputed, without manifest injustice.

That he is to be considered as a fair purchaser, results from this: Whatever necessity the seller may have been under, was occasioned by the government, in not making a proper provision for its debts. The buyer had no agency in it, and therefore ought not to suffer. He is not even chargeable with having taken an undue advantage. He paid what the commodity was worth in the market, and took the risks of reimbursement upon himself. He of course gave a fair equivalent, and ought to reap the benefit of his hazard; a hazard which was far from inconsiderable, and which, perhaps, turned on little less than a revolution in government.

That the case of those, who parted with their securities from necessity, is a hard one, cannot be denied. But whatever complaint of injury, or claim of redress, they may have, respects the government solely. They have not only nothing to object to the persons who relieved their necessities, by giving them the current price of their property, but they are even under an implied condition to contribute to the reimbursement of those persons. They knew, that by the terms of the contract with themselves, the public were bound to pay to those, to whom they should convey their title, the sums stipulated to be paid to them; and, as citizens of the United States, they were to bear their proportion of the contribution for that purpose. This, by the act of assignment, they tacitly engage to do; and if they had an option, they could not, with integrity or good faith, refuse to do it, without the consent of those to whom they sold.

But though many of the original holders sold from necessity, it does not follow, that this was the case with all of them. It may well be supposed, that some of them did it either through want of confidence in an eventual provision, or from the allurements of some profitable speculation. How shall these different classes be discriminated from each other? How shall it be ascertained, in any case, that the money, which the original holder obtained for his security, was not more beneficial to him, than if he had held it to the present time, to avail himself of the provision which shall be made? How shall it be known, whether if the purchaser had employed his money in some other way, he would not be in a better situation, than by having applied it in the purchase of securities, though he should now receive their full amount? And if neither of these things can be known, how shall it be determined whether a discrimination, independent of the breach of contract, would not do a real injury to purchasers; and if it included a compensation to the primitive proprietors, would not give them an advantage, to which they had no equitable pretension.

It may well be imagined, also, that there are not wanting instances, in which individuals, urged by a present necessity, parted with the securities received by them from the public, and shortly after replaced them with others, as an indemnity for their first loss. Shall they be deprived of the indemnity which they have endeavoured to secure by so provident an arrangement?

Questions of this sort, on a close inspection, multiply themselves without end, and demonstrate the injustice of a discrimination, even on the most subtile calculations of equity, abstracted from the obligation of contract.

The difficulties too of regulating the details of a plan for that purpose, which would have even the semblance of equity, would be found immense. It may well be doubted whether they would not be insurmountable, and replete with such absurd, as well as inequitable consequences, as to disgust even the proposers of the measure.

As a specimen of its capricious operation, it will be sufficient to notice the effect it would have upon two persons, who may be supposed two years ago to have purchased, each, securities at three shillings in the pound, and one of them to retain those bought by him, till the discrimination should take place; the other to have parted with those bought by him, within a month past, at nine shillings. The former, who had had most confidence in the government, would in this case only receive at the rate of three shillings and the interest; while the latter, who had had less confidence would receive *for what cost him the same money* at the rate of nine shillings, and his representative, *standing in his place*, would be entitled to a like rate.

The impolicy of a discrimination results from two considerations; one, that it proceeds upon a principle destructive of that *quality* of the public debt, or the stock of the nation, which is essential to its capacity for answering the purposes of money—that is the *security* of *transfer;* the other, that as well on this account, as because it includes a breach of faith, it renders property in the funds less valuable; consequently induces lenders to demand a higher premium for what they lend, and produces every other inconvenience of a bad state of public credit.

It will be perceived at first sight, that the transferable quality of stock is essential to its operation as money, and that this depends on the idea of complete security to the transferree, and a firm persuasion, that no distinction can in any circumstances be made between him and the original proprietor.

The precedent of an invasion of this fundamental principle, would of course tend to deprive the community of an advantage, with which no temporary saving could bear the least comparison.

And it will as readily be perceived, that the same cause would operate a diminution of the value of stock in the hands of the first, as well as of every other holder. The price, which any man, who should incline to purchase, would be willing to give for it, would be in a compound ratio to the immediate profit it afforded, and to the chance of the continuance of his profit. If there was supposed to be any hazard of the latter, the risk would be taken into the calculation, and either there would be no purchase at all, or it would be at a proportionably less price.

For this diminution of the value of stock, every person, who should be about to lend to the government, would demand a compensation; and would add to the actual difference, between the nominal and the market value, and equivalent for the chance of greater decrease; which, in a precarious state of public credit, is always to be taken into the account.

Every compensation of this sort, it is evident, would be an absolute loss to the government.

In the preceding discussion of the impolicy of a discrimination, the injurious tendency of it to those, who continue to be the holders of the securities, they received from the government, has been explained. Nothing need be added, on this head, except that this is an additional and interesting light, in which the injustice of the measure may be seen. It would not only divest present proprietors by purchase, of the rights they had acquired under the sanction of public faith, but it would depreciate the property of the remaining original holders.

It is equally unnecessary to add any thing to what has been already said to demonstrate the fatal influence, which the principle of discrimination would have on the public credit.

But there is still a point in view in which it will appear perhaps even more exceptionable, than in either of the former. It would be repugnant to an express provision of the Constitution of the United States. This provision is, that "all debts contracted and engagements entered into before the adoption of that Constitution shall be as valid against the United States under it, as under the confederation," which amounts to a constitutional ratification of the contracts respecting the debt, in the state in which they existed under the confederation. And resorting to that standard, there can be no doubt, that the rights of assignees and original holders, must be considered as equal.

In exploding thus fully the principle of discrimination, the Secretary is happy in reflecting, that he is the only advocate of what has been already sanctioned by the formal and express authority of the government of the Union, in these emphatic terms—"The remaining class of creditors (say Congress in their circular address to the states, of the 26th of April 1783) is composed, partly of such of our fellow-citizens as originally lent to the public the use of their funds, or have since manifested *most confidence* in their country, by receiving transfers from the lenders; and partly of those, whose property has been either advanced or assumed for the public service. To *discriminate* the merits of these several descriptions of creditors, would be a task equally unnecessary and invidious. If the voice of humanity plead more loudly in favor of some than of others, the voice of policy, no less than of justice, pleads in favor of all. A *wise nation* will never permit those who relieve the wants of their country, or who *rely most* on its *faith,* its *firmness,* and its *resources,* when either of them is distrusted, to suffer by the event."

The Secretary concluding, that a discrimination, between the different classes of creditors of the United States, cannot with propriety be *made,* proceeds to examine whether a difference ought to be permitted to *remain* between them, and another description of public creditors—Those of the states individually.

The Secretary, after mature reflection on this point, entertains a full conviction, that an assumption of the debts of the particular states by the union, and a like provision for them, as for those of the union, will be a measure of sound policy and substantial justice.

It would, in the opinion of the Secretary, contribute, in an eminent degree, to an orderly, stable and satisfactory arrangement of the national finances. . . .

Report on a National Bank
(December 13, 1790)

To the Speaker of the House of Representatives:

In obedience to the order of the House of Representatives of the ninth day of August last, requiring the Secretary of the Treasury to prepare and report on this day such further provision as may, in his opinion, be necessary for establishing the public Credit.

The said Secretary further respectfully reports

That from a conviction (as suggested in his report No. I herewith presented) That a National Bank is an Institution of primary importance to the prosperous administration of the Finances, and would be of the greatest utility in the operations connected with the support of the Public Credit, his attention has been drawn to devising the plan of such an institution, upon a scale which will intitle it to the confidence, and be likely to render it equal to the exigencies of the Public.

Previously to entering upon the detail of this plan, he entreats the indulgence of the House, towards some preliminary reflections naturally arising out of the subject, which he hopes will be deemed, neither useless, nor out of place. Public opinion being the ultimate arbiter of every measure of Government, it can scarcely appear improper, in deference to that, to accompany the origination of any new proposition with explanations, which the superior information of those, to whom it is immediately addressed, would render superfluous.

It is a fact well understood, that public Banks have found admission and patronage among the principal and most enlightened commercial nations. They have successively obtained in Italy, Germany, Holland, England and France, as well as in the United States. And it is a circumstance, which cannot but have considerable weight in a candid estimate of their tendency, that after an experience of centuries, there exists not a question about their util(ity) in the countries in which they have been so long established. Theories and men of business unite in the acknowledgement of it.

Trade and industry, wherever they have been tried, have been indebted to them for important aid. And Government has been repeatedly under the greatest obligations to them, in dangerous and distressing emergencies. That of the United States, as well in some of the most critical conjunctures of the late war, as since the peace has received assistance from those established among us, with which it could not have dispensed.

With this two fold evidence before us, it might be expected, that there would be a perfect union of opinions in their favour. Yet doubts have been entertained; jealousies and prejudices have circulated: and though the experiment is every day dissipating them within the spheres in which effects are best known; yet there are still persons by whom they have not been intirely renounced. To give a full and accurate view of the subject would be to make a Treatise of a report; but there are certain aspects in which it may be cursorily exhibited, which may perhaps conduce to a just impression of its merits. These will involve a comparison of the advantages, with the disadvantages, real or supposed, of such institutions.

The following are among the principal advantages of a Bank.

First. The augmentation of the active or productive capital of a country. Gold and Silver, when they are employed merely as the instruments of exchange and alienation, have been not improperly denominated dead Stock; but when deposited in Banks, to become the basis of a paper circulation, which takes their character and place, as the signs or representatives of value, they then acquire life, or, in other words, an active and productive quality. This idea, which appears rather subtil and abstract, in a general form, may be made obvious and palpable, by entering into a few particulars. It is evident, for instance, that the money, which a merchant keeps in his chest, waiting for a favourable opportunity to employ it, produces nothing 'till that opportunity arrives. But if instead of locking it up in this manner, he either deposits it in a Bank, or invests it in the Stock of a Bank, it yields a profit, during the interval; in which he partakes, or not, according to the choice he may have made of being a depositor or a proprietor; and when any advantageous speculation offers, in order to be able to embrace it, he has only to withdraw his money, if a depositor, or if a proprietor to obtain a loan from the Bank, or to dispose of his Stock; an alternative seldom or never attended with difficulty, when the affairs of the institution are in a prosperous train. His money thus deposited or invested, is a fund, upon which himself and others can borrow to a much larger amount. It is a well established fact, that Banks in good credit can circulate a far greater sum than the actual quantum of their capital in Gold and Silver. The extent of the possible excess seems indeterminate; though it has been conjecturally stated at the proportions of two and three to one. This faculty is produced in various ways. First. A great proportion of the notes, which are issued and pass current as Cash, are indefinitely suspended in circulation, from the confidence which each holder has, that he can at any moment turn them into gold and silver. Secondly, Every loan, which a Bank makes is, in its first shape, a credit given to the borrower on its books, the amount of which it stands ready to pay, either in its own notes, or in gold or silver, at his option. But, in a great number of cases, no actual payment is made in either. The Borrower frequently, by a check or order, transfers his credit to some other person, to whom he has a payment to make; who, in his turn, is as often content with a similar credit, because he is satisfied, that he can, whenever he pleases, either convert it into cash, or pass it to some other hand, as an equivalent for it. And in this manner the credit keeps circulating, performing in every stage the office of money, till it is extinguished by a discount with some person, who has a payment to make to the Bank, to an equal or greater amount. Thus large sums are lent and paid, frequently through a variety of hands, without the intervention of a single piece of coin. Thirdly, There is always a large quantity of gold and silver in the repositories of the Bank, besides its own Stock, which is placed there, with a view partly to its safe keeping and partly to the accommodation of an institution, which is itself a source of general accommodation. These deposits are of immense consequence in the operations of a Bank. Though liable to be redrawn at any moment, experience proves, that the money so much oftener changes proprietors than place, and that what is drawn out is generally so speedily replaced as to authorise the counting upon the sums deposited, as an *effective fund;* which, concurring with the Stock of the Bank, enables it to extend its loans, and to answer all the demands for coin, whether in consequence of those loans, or arising from the occasional return of its notes.

These different circumstances explain the manner, in which the ability of a bank to circulate a greater sum, than its actual capital in coin, is acquired. This however must be gradual; and must be preceded by a firm establishment of confidence; a confidence which may be bestowed on the most rational grounds; since the excess in question will always be bottomed on good security of one kind or another. This, every well conducted Bank carefully requires, before it will consent to advance either its money or its credit; and when there is an auxiliary capital (as will be the case in the plan hereafter submitted) which, together with the capital in coin, define the boundary, that shall not be exceeded by the engagements of the Bank, the security may, consistently with all the maxims of a reasonable circumspection be regarded as complete.

The same circumstances illustrate the truth of the position, that it is one of the properties of Banks to increase the active capital of a country. This, in other words is the sum of them. The money of one individual, while he is waiting for an opportunity to employ it by being either deposited in the Bank for safe keeping, or invested in its Stock, is in a condition to administer to the wants of others without being put out of his own reach, when occasion presents. This yields an extra profit, arising from what is paid for the use of his money by others, when he could not himself make use of it and keeps the money itself in a state of incessant activity, in the almost infinite vicissitudes and competitions of mercantile enterprise, there never can be danger of an intermission of demand, or that the money will remain for a moment idle in the vaults of the Bank. This additional employment given to money, and the faculty of a bank to lend and circulate a greater sum than the amount of its stock in coin are to all the purposes of trade and industry an absolute increase of capital. Purchases and undertakings, in general, can be carried on by any given sum of bank paper or credit, as effectually as by an equal sum of gold and silver. And thus by contributing to enlarge the mass of industrious and commercial enterprise, banks become nurseries of national wealth: a consequence, as satisfactorily verified by experience, as it is clearly deducible in theory.

Secondly, Greater facility to the Government in obtaining pecuniary aids, especially in sudden emergencies. This is another and an undisputed advantage of public banks: one, which as already remarked, has been realised in signal instances, among ourselves. The reason is obvious: The capitals of a great number of individuals are, by this operation, collected to a point, and placed under one direction. The mass, formed by this union, is in a certain sense magnified by the credit attached to it: And while this mass is always ready, and can at once be put in motion, in aid of the Government, the interest of the bank to afford that aid, independent of regard to the public safety and welfare, is a sure pledge for its disposition to go as far in its compliances, as can in prudence be desired. There is in the nature of things, as will be more particularly noticed in another place, an intimate connection of interest between the government and the Bank of a Nation.

Thirdly. The facilitating of the payment of taxes. This advantage is produced in two ways. Those who are in a situation to have access to the Bank can have the assistance of loans to answer with punctuality the public calls upon them. This accommodation has been . . . felt in the payment of the duties heretofore laid, by those who reside where establishments of this nature exist. This however, though an extensive, is not a universal benefit. The other way, in which the effect here contemplated is produced, and in which the benefit is general, is the encreasing of the quantity of circulating medium and the quickening of circulation. The manner in which the first happens has already been traced. The last may require some illustration. When payments are to be made between different places, having an intercourse of business with each other, if there happen to be no private bills, at market, and there are no Bank notes, which have a currency in both, the consequence is, the coin must be remitted. This is attended with trouble, delay, expense and risk. If on the contrary, there are bank notes current in these places, the transmission of these by the post, or any other speedy, and convenient conveyance answers the purpose; and these again, in the alternations of demand, are frequently returned, very soon after, to the place from whence they were first sent: Whence the transportation and retransportation of the metals are obviated; and a more convenient and more expeditious medium of payment is substituted. Nor is this all. The metals, instead of being suspended from their usual functions, during this process of vibration from place to place continue in activity, and administer still to the ordinary circulation; which of course is prevented from suffering either diminution or stagnation. These circumstances are additional causes of what, in a practical sense or to the purposes of business, may be called greater plenty of money. And it is evident, that whatever enhances the quantity of circulating money adds to the ease, with which every industrious member of the community may acquire that portion of it, of which he stands in need; and enables him the better to pay his taxes, as well as to supply his other wants. Even where the circulation of the bank paper is not general, it must still have the same effect, though in a less degree. For whatever furnishes additional supplies to the channels of circulation, in one quarter, naturally contributes to keep the stream fuller elsewhere. This last view of the subject serves both to demonstrate the position, that Banks tend to facilitate the payment of taxes; and to exemplify their utility to business of every kind in which money is an agent.

It would be to intrude too much on the patience of the house to prolong the details of the advantages of Banks; especially since those, which might still be particularized are readily to be referred as consequences from those, which have been enumerated. Their disadvantages, real or supposed, are now to be reviewed. The most serious of the charges which have been brought against them are—

That they serve to increase usury:

That they tend to prevent other kinds of lending:

That they furnish temptations to overtrading:

That they afford aid to ignorant adventurers who disturb the natural and beneficial course of trade:

That they give to bankrupt and fraudulent traders a fictitious credit, which enables them to maintain false appearances and to extend their impositions: And lastly

That they have a tendency to banish gold and silver from the country.

There is great reason to believe, that on a close and candid survey, it will be discovered, that these charges are either destitute of foundation; or that, as far as the evils, they suggest, have been found to exist, they have proceeded from other, or partial, or temporary states, are not inherent in the nature and permanent tendency of such institutions; or are more than counterbalanced by opposite advantages. This survey shall be had, in the order in which the charges have been stated.

The first of them is, that Banks serve to increase usury.

It is a truth, which ought not to be denied, that the method of conducting business, which is essential to bank operations, has among us, in particular instances, given occasion to usurious transactions. The punctuality, in payments, which they necessarily exact is sometimes obliged those, who have adventured beyond both their capital and their *credit* to procure money, at any price, and consequently to resort to usurers for aid.

But experience and practice gradually bring a cure to this evil. A general habit of punctuality among traders is the natural consequence of the necessity of observing it with the Bank; a circumstance which itself more than compensates for any occasional ill, which may have sprung from that necessity, in the particular, under consideration. As far therefore as Traders depend on each other for pecuniary supplies, they can calculate their expectations with greater certainty; and are in proportionably less danger of disappointments, which might compel them to have recourse to so pernicious an expedient, as that of borrowing at usury; the mischiefs from which, after a few examples, naturally inspire great care, in all such men of desperate circumstances, to avoid the possibility of becoming subjected to them. One, and not the least of the evils incident to the use of that expedient, if the fact be known or even strongly suspected, is loss of credit with the bank itself.

The Directors of a bank too, though in order to extend its business and its popularity, in the infancy of an institution, they may be tempted to go further in accommodations, than the strict rules of prudence will warrant, grow more circumspect of course, as the affairs become better established, and as the evils of too great facility are experimentally demonstrated. They become more attentive to the situation and conduct of those, with whom they deal; they observe more narrowly their operations and pursuits, they economise the credit, they give to those of suspicious solidity; they refuse it to those whose career is more manifestly hazardous. In a word, in the course of practice, from the very nature of things, their *interest* will make it the *policy* of a Bank, to succour the wary and industrious; to discredit the rash and unthrifty; to discountenance both usurious lenders and usurious borrowers.

There is a leading view, in which the tendency of banks will be seen to be, to abrige rather than to promote usury. This relates to their property of increasing the quantity and quickening the circulation of money. If it be evident, that usury will prevail or diminish according to the proportion which the demand for borrowing bears to the quantity of money at market to be lent; whatever has the property just mentioned, whether it be in the shape of paper or of coin, by contributing to render the supply more equal to the demand, must tend to counteract the progress of usury.

But bank-lending, it is pretended, is an impediment to other kinds of lending; which, by confining the resource of borrowing to a particular class, leaves the rest of the community more destitute, and therefore more exposed to the extortions of usurers. As the profits of bank stock exceed the legal rate of interest, the possessors of money, it is argued, prefer investing it in that article to lending it at this rate; to which there are the additional motives of a very prompt command of the capital, and of more frequent and exact returns, without trouble or perplexity in the collection. This constitutes the second charge, which has been enumerated.

The fact on which this charge rests is not to be admitted without several qualifications; particularly in reference to the state of things in this country. First. The great bulk of the Stock of a bank will consist of the funds of men in trade, among ourselves, and monied foreigners; the former of whom could not spare their capitals out of their reach, to be invested in loans, for long periods, on mortgages, or personal security; and the latter of whom would not be willing to be subjected to the casualties, delays and embarassments of such a disposition of their money in a distant country. Secondly. There will always be a considerable proportion of those, who are properly the money lenders of a Country, who from that spirit of caution, which usually characterises this description of men will incline rather to vest their funds in mortgages on real estate, than in the Stock of a Bank, which they are apt to consider as a more precarious security.

These considerations serve in a material degree to narrow the foundation of the objection, as to the point of fact. But there is a more satisfactory answer to it. The effect supposed, as far as it has existence, is temporary. The reverse of it takes place, in the general and permanent operation of the thing.

The capital of every public bank will of course be restricted within a certain defined limit. It is the province of legislative prudence so to adjust this limit, that while it will not be too contracted for the demand, which the course of business may create, and for the security, which the public ought to have for the solidity of the paper, which may be issued by the bank, it will still be within the compass of the pecuniary resources of the community; so that there may be an easy practicability of completing the subscriptions by it. When this is once done, the supposed effect of necessity ceases. There is then no longer room for the investment of any additional capital. Stock may indeed change hands by one person selling and another buying; but the money, which the buyer takes out of the common mass to purchase the stock, the seller receives, and restores to it. Hence the future surplusses, which may accumulate, must take their natural course, and lending at interest must go on, as if there were no such institution.

It must indeed flow in a more copious stream. The Bank furnishes an extraordinary supply for borrowers, within its immediate sphere. A larger supply consequently remains for borrowers elsewhere. In proportion, as the circulation of the Bank is extended, there is an augmentation of the aggregate mass of money, for answering the aggregate mass of demand. Hence a greater facility in obtaining it for every purpose.

It ought not to escape without a remark, that as far as the citizens of other countries become adventurers in the Bank, there is a positive increase of the gold and silver of the Country. It is true, that from this a half yearly rent is drawn back, accruing from the dividends upon the Stock. But as this rent arises from the employment of the capital, by our own citizens, it is probable, that it is more than replaced by the profits of that employment. It is also likely, that a part of it is, in the course of trade, converted into the products of our Country: And it may even prove an incentive, in some cases, to emigration to a country, in which the character of citizen is as easy to be acquired, as it is estimable and important. This view of the subject furnishes an answer to an objection, which has been deduced from the circumstance here taken notice of, namely the income resulting to foreigners from the part of the Stock, owned by them, which has been represented as tending to drain the country of its specie. In this objection, the original investment of the capital, and the constant use of it afterwards seem both to have been overlooked.

That Banks furnish temptations to overtrading is the third of the enumerated objections. This must mean, that by affording additional aids to mercantile enterprise, they induce the merchant sometimes to adventure beyond the prudent or salutary point. But the very statement of the thing shews, that the subject of the charge is an occasional ill, incident to a general good. Credit of every kind (as a species of which only can bank lending have the effect supposed) must be in different degrees, chargeable with the same inconvenience. It is even applicable to gold and silver, when they abound in circulation. But would it be wise on this account to decry the precious metals, to root out credit; or to proscribe the means of that enterprise, which is the main spring of trade and a principal source of national wealth, because it now and then runs into excesses, of which overtrading is one?

If the abuses of a beneficial thing are to determine its condemnation, there is scarcely a source of public prosperity, which will not speedily be closed. In every case, the evil is to be compared with the good; and in the present case such a comparison will issue in this, that the new and increased energies derived to commercial enterprise, from the aid of banks, are a source of general profit and advantage; which greatly outweigh the partial ills of the overtrading of a few individuals, at particular times, or of numbers of particular conjunctures.

The fourth and fifth charges may be considered together. These relate to the aid, which is sometimes afforded by banks to unskilful adventurers and fraudulent traders. These charges also have some degree of foundation; though far less than has been pretended, and they add to the instances of partial ills, connected with more extensive and overbalancing benefits.

The practice of giving fictitious credit to improper persons is one of those evils, which experience guided by interest speedily corrects. The bank itself is in so much jeopardy of being a sufferer by it, that it has the strongest of all inducements to be on its guard. It may not only be injured immediately by the delinquencies of the persons, to whom such credit is given; but eventually, by the incapacities of others, whom their impositions, or failures may have ruined.

Nor it there much danger of a bank's being betrayed into this error, from want of information. The Directors, themselves, being, for the most part, selected from the class of Traders are to be expected to possess individually an accurate knowledge of the characters and situations of those, who come within that description. And they have, in addition to this, the course of dealing of the persons themselves with the bank to assist their judgment, which is in most cases a good index of the state, in which those persons are. The artifices and shifts, which those in desperate or declining circumstances are obliged to employ, to keep up the countenance, which the rules of the Bank require, and the train of their connections, are so many prognostics, not difficult to be interpreted, of the fate which awaits them. Hence it not unfrequently happens, that Banks are the first to discover the unsoundness of such characters, and, by withholding credit, to announce to the public, that they are not intitled to it.

If banks, in spite of every precaution, are sometimes betrayed into giving a false credit to the persons described; they more frequently enable honest and industrious men, of small or perhaps of no capital to undertake and prosecute business, with advantage to themselves and to the community; and assist merchants of both capital and credit, who meet with fortuitous and unforeseen shocks, which might without such helps prove fatal to them and to others; to make head against their misfortunes, and finally to retrieve their affairs: Circumstances, which form no inconsiderable encomium on the utility of Banks.

But the last and heaviest charge is still to be examined. This is, that Banks tend to banish the gold and silver of the Country.

The force of this objection rests upon their being an engine of paper credit, which by furnishing a substitute for the metals, is supposed to promote their exportation. It is an objection, which if it has any foundation, lies not against Banks, peculiarly, but against every species of paper credit.

The most common answer given to it is, that the thing supposed is of little, or no consequence; that it is immaterial what serves the purpose of money, whether paper or gold and silver; that the effect of both upon industry is the same; and that the intrinsic wealth of a nation is to be measured, not by the abundance of the precious metals, contained in it, but by the quantity of the productions of its labor and industry.

This answer is not destitute of solidity, though not intirely satisfactory. It is certain, that the vivification of industry, by a full circulation, with the aid of a proper and well regulated paper credit, may more than compensate for the loss of a part of the gold and silver of a Nation; if the consequence of avoiding that loss should be a scanty or defective circulation.

But the positive and permanent increase or decrease of the precious metals, in a Country, can hardly ever be a matter of indifference. As the commodity taken in lieu of every other, it is a species of the most effective wealth; and as the money of the world, it is of great concern to the state, that it possess a sufficiency of it to face any demands, which the protection of its external interests may create.

The objection seems to admit of another and a more conclusive answer, which controverts the fact itself. A nation, that has no mines of its own, must derive the precious metals from others; generally speaking, in exchange for the products of its labor and industry. The quantity, it will possess, will therefore, in the ordinary course of things, be regulated by the favourable, or unfavourable balance of its trade; that is, by the proportion between its abilities to supply foreigners, and its wants of them; between the amount of its exportations and that of its importations. Hence the state of its agriculture and manufactures, the quantity and *quality* of its labor and industry must, in the main, influence and determine the increase or decrease of its gold and silver.

If this be true, the inference seems to be, that well constituted Banks favour the increase of the precious metals. It has been shewn, that they augment in different ways, the active capital of the country. This, it is, which generates employment; which animates and expands labor and industry. Every addition, which is made to it, by contributing to put in motion a greater quantity of both, tends to create a greater quantity of the products of both: And, by furnishing more materials for exportation, conduces to a favourable balance of trade and consequently to the introduction and increase of gold and silver.

This conclusion appears to be drawn from solid premises. There are however objections to be made to it.

It may be said, that as Bank paper affords a substitute for specie, it serves to counteract that rigorous necessity for the metals, as a medium of circulation, which in the case of a wrong balance, might restrain in some degree their exportation; and it may be added, that from the same cause, in the same case, it would retard those oeconomical and parsimonious reforms, in the manner of living, which the scarcity of money is calculated to produce, and which might be necessary to rectify such wrong balance.

There is perhaps some truth in both these observations; but they appear to be of a nature rather to form exceptions to the generality of the conclusion, than to overthrow it. The state of things, in which the *absolute exigencies* of circulation can be supposed to resist with any effect the urgent demands for specie, which a wrong balance of trade may occasion, presents an *extreme case*. And a situation in which a too expensive manner of living of a community, compared with its means, can stand in need of a corrective, from distress or necessity, is one, which perhaps rarely results, but from extraordinary and adventitious causes: such for example, as a national revolution, which unsettles all the established habits of a people, and inflames the appetite for extravagance, by the illusions of an ideal wealth, engendered by the continual multiplication of a depreciating currency or some similar cause. There is good reason to believe, that where the laws are wise and well executed, and the inviolability of property and contracts maintained, the oeconomy of a people will, in the general course of things, correspond with its means.

The support of industry is probably in every case, of more consequence towards correcting a wrong balance of trade, than any practicable retrenchments, in the expences of families, or individuals: And the stagnation of it would be likely to have more effect, in prolonging, than any such savings in shortening its continuance. That stagnation is a natural consequence of an inadequate medium, which, without the aid of Bank circulation, would in the cases supposed, be severely felt.

It also deserves notice, that as the circulation is always in a compound ratio to the fund, upon which it depends, and to the demand for it, and as that fund is itself affected by the exportation of the metals, there is no danger of its being overstocked, as in the case of paper issued at the pleasure of the Government; or of its preventing the consequences of any unfavourable balance from being sufficiently felt, to produce the reforms alluded to, as far as circumstances may require and admit.

Nothing can be more fallible, than the comparisons, which have been made between different countries, to illustrate the truth of the position under consideration. The comparative quantity of gold and silver, in different countries, depends upon an infinite variety of facts and combinations, all of which ought to be known, in order to judge, whether the existence or non existence of paper currencies has any share in the relative proportions they contain. The *mass* and *value* of the productions of the labor and industry of each, compared with its wants; the nature of its establishments abroad; the kind of wars in which it is usually engaged; the relations it bears to the countries, which are the original possessors of those metals; the privileges it enjoys in their trade; these and a number of other circumstances are all to be taken into the account, and render the investigation too complex to justify any reliance on the vague and general surmises, which have been hitherto hazarded on the point.

In the foregoing discussion, the objection has been considered as applying to the permanent expulsion and diminution of the metals. Their temporary exportation, for particular purposes, has not been contemplated. This, it must be confessed is facilitated by Banks, from the faculty they possess of supplying their place. But their utility is in nothing more conspicuous, than in these very cases. They enable the Government to pay its foreign debts, and to answer any exigencies, which the external concerns of the community may have produced. They enable the Merchant to support his credit, (on which the prosperity of trade depends) when special circumstances prevent remittances in other modes. They enable him also to prosecute enterprises, which ultimately tend to an augmentation of the species of wealth in question. It is evident, that gold and silver may often be employed in procuring commodities abroad; which, in a circuitous commerce, replace the original fund, with considerable addition. But it is not to be inferred from this facility given to temporary exportation, that Banks, which are so friendly to trade and industry, are in their general tendency, inimical to the increase of the precious metals.

These several views of the subject appear sufficient to impress a full conviction, of the utility of Banks, and to demonstrate that they are of great importance, not only in relation to the administration of the finances, but in the general system of the political oeconomy.

The judgment of many concerning them has no doubt been perplexed, by the misinterpretation of appearances, which were to be ascribed to other causes. The general devastation of personal property, occasioned by the late war, naturally produced, on the one hand, a great demand for money, and on the other a great deficiency of it to answer the demand. Some injudicious laws, which grew out of the public distresses, by impairing confidence and causing a part of the inadequate sum in the country to be locked up, aggravated the evil: The dissipated habits, contracted by many individuals, during the war, which after the peace plunged them into expences beyond their incomes: The number of adventurers without capital and in many instances, without information, who at that epoch rushed into trade, and were obliged to make any sacrifices to support a transient credit; the employment of considerable sums in speculations upon the public debt, which from its unsettled state was incapable of becoming itself a substitute: All these circumstances concurring necessarily led to usurious borrowing, produced most of the inconveniences, and were the true causes of most of the appearances; which, where the Banks were established, have been by some erroneously placed to their account: a mistake, which they might easily have avoided, by turning their eyes towards places, where there were none, and where, nevertheless, the same evils would have been perceived to exist, even in a greater degree, than where those institutions had obtained.

These evils have either ceased, or been greatly mitigated. Their more complete extinction may be looked for, from that additional security to property, which the constitution of the United States happily gives (a circumstance of prodigious moment in the scale both of public and private prosperity) from the attraction of foreign capital, under the auspices of that security, to be employed upon objects and in enterprises, for which the state of this country opens a wide and inviting field, from the consistency and stability, which the public debt is fast acquiring, as well in the public opinion, at home and abroad, as in fact; from the augmentation of capital, which that circumstance and the quarter yearly payment of interest will afford; and from the more copious circulation, which will be likely to be created by a well constituted National Bank.

The establishment of Banks in this country seems to be recommended by reasons of a peculiar nature. Previously to the revolution circulation was in a great measure carried on by paper emitted by the several local governments. In Pennsylvania alone the quantity of it was near a million and a half of dollars. This auxiliary may be said to be now at an end. And it is generally supposed, that there has been for some time past, a deficiency of circulating medium. How far that deficiency is to be considered as real or imaginary is not susceptible of demonstration, but there are circumstances and appearances, which, in relation to the country at large, countenance the supposition of its reality.

The circumstances are, besides the fact just mentioned respecting paper emissions the vast tracts of waste land, and the little advanced state of manufactures. The progressive settlement of the former, while it promises ample retribution, in the generation of future resources, diminishes or obstructs, in the mean time, the *active* wealth of the country. It not only draws off a part of the circulating money, and places it in a more passive state, but it diverts into its own channels a portion of that species of labor and industry, which would otherwise be employed, in furnishing materials for foreign trade, and which by contributing to a favourable balance, would assist the introduction of specie. In the early periods of new settlements, the settlers not only furnish no surplus for exportation, but they consume a part of that which is produced by the labour of others. The same thing is a cause, that manufactures do not advance or advance slowly. And notwithstanding some hypotheses to the contrary, there are many things to induce a suspicion, that the precious metals will not abound, in any country, which has not mines or variety of manufactures. They have been sometimes acquired by the sword, but the modern system of war has expelled this resource, and it is one upon which it is to be hoped the United States will never be inclined to rely.

The appearances, alluded to, are, greater prevalency of direct barter, in the more interior districts of the country, which however has been for some time past gradually lessening; and greater difficulty, generally, in the advantageous alienation of improved real estate; which, also, has, of late, diminished, but is still seriously felt in different parts of the Union. The difficulty of getting money, which has been a general complaint, is not added to the number;

because it is the complaint of all times, and one, in which imagination must ever have too great scope, to permit an appeal to it.

If the supposition of such a deficiency be in any degree founded, and some aid to circulation be desireable, it remains to inquire what ought to be the nature of that aid.

The emitting of paper money by the authority of Government is wisely prohibited to the individual States, by the National Constitution. And the spirit of that prohibition ought not to be disregarded, by the Government of the United States. Though paper emissions, under a general authority, might have some advantages, not applicable, and be free from some disadvantages, which are applicable, to the like emissions by the States separately; yet they are of a nature so liable to abuse, and it may even be affirmed so certain of being abused, that the wisdom of the Government will be shewn in never trusting itself with the use of so seducing and dangerous an expedient. In times of tranquility, it might have no ill consequence, it might even perhaps be managed in a way to be productive of good; but in great and trying emergencies, there is almost a moral certainty of its becoming mischievous. The stamping of paper is an operation so much easier than the laying of taxes, that a government, in the practice of paper emissions, would rarely fail in any such emergency to indulge itself too far, in the employment of that resource, to avoid as much as possible one less auspicious to present popularity. If it should not even be carried so far as to be rendered an absolute bubble, it would at least be likely to be extended to a degree, which would occasion an inflated and artificial state of things incompatible with the regular and prosperous course of the political oeconomy.

Among other material differences between a paper currency, issued by the mere authority of Government, and one issued by a Bank, payable in coin, is this—That in the first case, there is no standard to which an appeal can be made, as to the quantity which will only satisfy, or which will surcharge the circulation; in the last, that standard results from the demand. If more should be issued, than is necessary, it will return upon the bank. Its emissions, as elsewhere intimated, must always be in a compound ratio to the fund and to the demand: Whence it is evident, that there is a limitation in the nature of the thing: While the discretion of the government is the only measure of the extent of the emissions, by its own authority.

This consideration further illustrates the danger of emissions of that sort, and the preference, which is due to Bank paper.

The payment of the interest of the public debt, at thirteen different places, is a weighty reason, peculiar to our immediate situation, for desiring a Bank circulation. Without a paper, in general currency, equivalent to gold and silver, a considerable proportion of the specie of the country must always be suspended from circulation and left to accumulate, preparatorily to each day of payment; and as often as one approaches, there must in several cases be an actual transportation of the metals at both expence and risk, from their natural and proper reservoirs to distant places. This necessity will be felt very injuriously to the trade of some of the States; and will embarrass not a little the operations of the Treasury in those States. It will also obstruct those negociations, between different parts of the Union, by the instrumentality of Treasury bills, which have already afforded valuable accommodations to Trade in general.

Assuming it then as a consequence, from what has been said, that a national bank is a desireable institution; two inquiries emerge. Is there no such institution, already in being, which has a claim to that character, and which supersedes the propriety, or necessity of another? If there be none, what are the principles upon which one ought to be established?

There are at present three banks in the United States. That of North America, established in the city of Philadelphia; that of New York, established in the city of New York; that of Massachusetts, established in the city of Boston. Of these three, the first is the only one, which has at any time had a direct relation to the Government of the United States.

The Bank of North America originated in a resolution of Congress of the 26th of May 1781, founded upon a proposition of the Superintendant of finance, which was afterwards carried into execution, by an ordinance of the 31st of december following, entitled, "An Ordinance to incorporate the Subscribers to the Bank of North America."

The aid afforded to the United States, by this institution, during the remaining period of the war, was of essential consequence, and its conduct towards them since the peace, has not weakened its title to their patronage and favour. So far its pretensions to the character in question are respectable; but there are circumstances, which militate against them; and considerations, which indicate the propriety of an establishment on different principles.

The Directors of this Bank, on behalf of their constituents, have since *accepted* and *acted* under a new charter from the State of Pennsylvania, materially variant from their original one; and which so narrows the foundation of the institution, as to render it an incompetent basis for the extensive purposes of a National Bank.

The limit assigned by the ordinance of Congress to the Stock of the Bank is ten millions of Dollars. The last charter of Pennsylvania confines it to two millions. Questions naturally arise, whether there be not a direct repugnancy between two charters so differently circumstanced; and whether the acceptance of the one is not to be deemed a virtual surrender of the other. But perhaps it is neither adviseable nor necessary to attempt a solution of them.

There is nothing in the Acts of Congress, which imply an exclusive right in the institution, to which they relate, except during the term of the war. There is therefore nothing, if the public good require it, which prevents the establishment of another. It may however be incidentally remarked, that in the general opinion of the citizens of the United States, the Bank of North America has taken the station of a bank of Pennsylvania only. This is a strong argument for a new institution, or for a renovation of the old, to restore it to the situation in which it originally stood, in the view of the United States.

But though the ordinance of Congress contains no grant of exclusive privileges, there may be room to allege, that the Government of the United States ought not, in point of candour and equity, to establish any rival or interfering institution, in prejudice of the one already established; especially as this has, from services rendered, well founded claims to protection and regard.

The justice of such an observation ought within proper bounds to be admitted. A new establishment of the sort ought not to be made, without cogent and sincere reasons of public good. And in the manner of doing it every facility should be given to a consolidation of the old with the new, upon terms not injurious to the parties concerned. But there is no ground to maintain, that in a case, in which the Government has made no condition restricting its authority, it ought voluntarily to restrict it, through regard to the interests of a particular institution, when those of the state dictate a different course; especially too after such circumstances have intervened, as characterise the actual situation of the Bank of North America.

The inducements, to a new disposition of the thing are now to be considered. The first of them which occurs is, the, at least ambiguous, situation, in which the Bank of North America has placed itself, by the acceptance of its last charter. If this has rendered it the mere Bank of a particular State, liable to dissolution at the expiration of fourteen years, to which term the act of that state has restricted its duration, it would be neither fit nor expedient to accept it, as an equivalent for a Bank of the United States.

The restriction of its capital also, which according to the same supposition, cannot be extended beyond two millions of dollars, is a conclusive reason for a different establishment. So small a capital promises neither the requisite aid to government, nor the requisite security to the community. It may answer very well the purposes of local accommodation, but is an inadequate foundation for a circulation coextensive with the United States, embracing the whole of their revenues, and affecting every individual, into whose hands the paper may come.

And inadequate as such a capital would be to the essential ends of a National Bank, it is liable to being rendered still more so, by that principle of the constitution of the Bank of North America, contained equally in its old and in its new charter, which leaves the increase of the *actual* capital at any time (now far short of the allowed extent) to the discretion of the Directors, or Stockholders. It is naturally to be expected, that the allurements of an advanced price of Stock and or large dividends may disincline those, who are interested, to an extension of capital; from which they will be apt to fear a diminution of profits. And from this circumstance, the interest and accommodation of the public (as well individually as collectively) are made more subordinate to the interest, real or imagined, of the Stockholders, than they ought to be. It is true, that unless the latter be consulted, there can be no bank (in the sense at least in which institutions of this kind, worthy of confidence, can be established in this Country) but it does not follow, that this is alone to be consulted, or that it even ought to be paramount. Public utility is more truly the object of public Banks, than private profit. And it is the business of Government, to constitute them on such principles, that while the latter will result, in a sufficient degree, to afford competent motives to engage in them, the former be not made subservient to it. To effect this, a principal object of attention ought to be to give free scope to the creation of an ample capital; and with this view, fixing the bounds, which are deemed safe and convenient, to leave no discretion either to stop short of them or to overpass them. The want of this precaution, in the establishment of the Bank of North America, is a further and an important reason for desiring one differently constituted.

There may be room, at first sight, for a supposition, that as the profits of a Bank will bear a proportion to the extent of its operations, and as, for this reason, the interest of the Stockholders will not be disadvantageously affected, by any necessary augmentations of capital, there is no cause to apprehend, that they will be indisposed to such augmentations. But most men in matters of this nature, prefer the certainties, they enjoy, to probabilities depending on untried experiments; especially when these promise rather, that they will not be injured, than that they will be benefited.

From the influence of this principle, and a desire of enhancing its profits, the Directors of a Bank will be more apt to over-strain its faculties, in the attempt to face the additional demands, which the course of business may create, than to set on foot new subscriptions, which may hazard a diminution of the profits, and even a temporary reduction of the price of Stock.

Banks are among the best expedients for lowering the rate of interest, in a country; but to have this effect, their capitals must be completely equal to all the demands of business, and such as will tend to remove the idea, that the accomodations they afford, are in any degree favours; an idea very apt to accompany the parsimonious dispensation of contracted funds. In this, as in every other case, the plenty of the commodity ought to beget a moderation of the price.

The want of a principle of rotation, in the constitution of the Bank of North America, is another argument for a variation of the establishment. Scarcely one of the reasons, which militate against this principle in the constitution of a country, is applicable to that of a Bank; while there are strong reasons in favour of it, in relation to the one, which do not apply to the other. The knowledge, to be derived from experience, is the only circumstance common to both, which pleads against rotation in the directing officers of a Bank.

But the objects of the Government of a nation, and those of the government of a bank are so widely different, as greatly to weaken the force of that consideration, in reference to the latter. Almost every important case of legislation requires, towards a right decision, a general and an accurate acquaintance with the affairs of the state; and habits of thinking seldom acquired, but from a familiarity with public concerns. The administration of a bank, on the contrary, is regulated, by a few simple fixed maxims, the application of which is not difficult to any man of judgment, especially if instructed in the principles of trade. It is in general a constant succession of the same details.

But though this be the case, the idea of the advantages of experience is not to be slighted. Room ought to be left for the regular transmission of official information: And for this purpose the head of the direction ought to be excepted from the principle of rotation. With this exception, and with the aid of the information of the subordinate officers, there can be no danger of any ill effects from want of experience, or knowledge; especially as the periodical exclusion ought not to reach the whole of the Directors at one time.

The argument in favour of the principle of rotation is this, that by lessening the danger of combinations among the Directors, to make the institution subservient to party views, or to the accommodation, preferably, of any particular set of men, it will render the public confidence more firm, stable and unqualified.

When it is considered, that the Directors of a Bank are not elected by the great body of the community, in which a diversity of views will naturally prevail, at different conjunctures, but by a small and select class of men, among whom it is far more easy to cultivate a steady adherence to the same persons and objects; and that those Directors have it in their power so immediately to conciliate, by obliging the most influential of this class, it is easy to perceive, that without the principle of rotation, changes in that body can rarely happen, but as a concession which they may themselves think it expedient to make to public opinion.

The continual administration of an institution of this kind, by the same persons, will never fail, with, or without, cause, from their conduct, to excite distrust and discontent. The necessary secrecy of their transactions gives unlimited scope to imagination to infer that something is, or may be wrong. And this *inevitable* mystery is a solid reason, for inserting in the constitution of a Bank the necessity of a change of men. As neither the mass of the parties interested nor the public in general can be permitted to be witnesses of the interior management of the Directors, it is reasonable, that both should have that check upon their conduct, and that security against the prevalency of a partial or pernicious system, which will be produced by the certainty of periodical changes. Such too is the delicacy of the credit of a Bank, that every thing, which can fortify confidence and repel suspicion, without injuring its operations, ought carefully to be sought after in its formation.

A further consideration in favour of a change, is the improper rule, by which the right of voting for Directors is regulated in the plan, upon which the Bank of North America was originally constituted, namely a vote for each share, and the want of a rule in the last charter; unless the silence of it, on that point, may signify that every Stockholder is to have an equal and a single vote, which would be a rule in a different extreme not less erroneous. It is of importance that a rule should be established, on this head, as it is one of those things, which ought not to be left to discretion; and it is consequently, of equal importance, that the rule should be a proper one.

A vote for each share renders a combination, between a few principal Stockholders, to monopolise the power and benefits of the Bank too easy. An equal vote to each Stockholder, however great or small his interest in the institution, allows not that degree of weight to large stockholders, which it is reasonable they should have, and which perhaps their security and that of the bank require. A prudent mean is to be preferred. A conviction of this has produced a bye-law of the corporation of the bank of North America, which evidently aims at such a mean. But a reflexion arises here, that a like majority with that which enacted this law, may at any moment repeal it.

The last inducement, which shall be mentioned, is the want of precautions to guard against a foreign influence insinuating itself into the Direction of the Bank. It seems scarcely reconcileable with a due caution to permit, that any but citizens should be eligible as Directors of a National Bank, or that non-resident foreigners should be able to influence the appointment of Directors by the votes of their proxies. In the event however of an incorporation of the Bank of North America in the plan, it may be necessary to qualify this principle, so as to leave the right of foreigners, who now hold shares of its stock unimpaired; but without the power of transmitting the privilege in question to foreign alienees.

It is to be considered, that such a Bank is not a mere matter of private property, but a political machine of the greatest importance to the State.

There are other variations from the Constitution of the Bank of North America, not of inconsiderable moment, which appear desireable, but which are not of magnitude enough to claim a preliminary discussion. These will be seen in the plan, which will be submitted in the sequel.

If the objections, which have been stated to the constitution of the Bank of North America, are admitted to be well founded, they will nevertheless not derogate from the merit of the main design, or of the services which that bank has rendered, or of the benefits which it has produced. The creation of such an institution, at the time it took place, was a measure dictated by wisdom. Its utility has been amply evinced by its fruits. American Independence owes much to it. And it (is) very conceivable, that reasons of the moment may have rendered those features in it inexpedient which a revision, with a permanent view, suggests as desireable.

The order of the subject leads next to an inquiry into the principles, upon which a national Bank, ought to be organised.

The situation of the United States naturally inspires a wish, that the form of the institution could admit of a plurality of branches. But various considerations discourage from pursuing this idea. The complexity of such a plan would be apt to inspire doubts, which might deter from adventuring in it. And the practicability of a safe and orderly administration, though not to be abandoned as desparate cannot be made so manifest in perspective, as to promise the removal of those doubts, or to justify the Government in adopting the idea as an original experiment. The most that would seem adviseable, on this point, is to insert a provision, which may lead to it hereafter; if experience shall more clearly demonstrate its utility, and satisfy those, who may have the Direction, that it may be adopted with safety. It is certain, that it would have some advantages both peculiar and important. Besides more general accommodation, it would lessen the danger of a run upon the bank.

The argument, against it, is, that each branch must be under a distinct, though subordinate direction; to which a considerable latitude of discretion must of necessity be entrusted. And as the property of the whole institution would be liable for the engagements of each part, that and its credit would be at stake, upon the prudence of the Directors of every part. The mismanagement of either branch, might hazard serious disorder in the whole.

Another wish, dictated by the particular situation of the country, is, that the Bank could be so constituted as to be made an immediate instrument of loans to the proprietors of land; but this wish also yields to the difficulty of accomplishing it. Land is alone an unfit fund for a bank circulation. If the notes issued upon it were not to be payable in coin, on demand, or at a short date; this would amount to nothing more than a repetition of the paper emissions, which are now exploded by the general voice. If the notes are to be payable in coin, the land must first be converted into it by sale, or mortgage. The difficulty of effecting the latter is the very thing, which begets the desire of finding another resource, and the former would not be practicable on a sudden emergency, but with sacrifices which would make the cure worse than the disease. Neither is the idea of constituting the fund partly of coin and partly of land free from impediments. These two species of property do not for the most part unite in the same hands. Will the monied man consent to enter into a partnership with the landholder by which *the latter* will share in the profits *which will be* made *by the money of the former?* The money it is evident will be the agent or efficient cause of the profits. The land can only be regarded as an additional security. It is not difficult to foresee, that an union, on such terms, will not readily be formed. If the landholders are to procure the money by sale or mortgage of a part of their lands, this they can as well do, when the Stock consists wholly of money, as if it were to be compounded of money and land.

To procure for the landholders the assistance of loans is the great desideratum. Supposing other difficulties surmounted, and a fund created, composed partly of coin and partly of land, yet the benefit contemplated could only then be obtained, by the banks advancing them its notes for the whole or part of the value of the lands, they had subscribed to the Stock. If this advance was small, the relief aimed at would not be given; if it was large, the quantity of notes issued would be a cause of *distrust*, and, if received at all, they would be likely to return speedily upon the Bank for payment; which, after exhausting its coin, might be under a necessity of turning its lands into money, at any price, that could be obtained for them, to the irreparable prejudice of the proprietors.

Considerations of public advantage suggest a further wish, which is, that the Bank could be established upon principles, that would cause the profits of it to redound to the immediate benefit of the State. This is contemplated by many, who speak of a National Bank, but the idea seems liable to insuperable objections. To attach full confidence to an institution of this nature, it appears to be an essential ingredient in its structure, that it shall be under a *private* not a *public* Direction, under the guidance of *individual interest*, not of *public policy;* which would be supposed to be, and in certain emergencies, under a feeble or too sanguine administration would, really, be, liable to being too much influenced by *public necessity.* The suspicion of this would most probably be a canker, that would continually corrode the vitals of the credit of the Bank, and would be most likely to prove fatal in those situations, in which the public good would require, that they should be most sound and vigorous. It would indeed be little less, than a miracle, should the credit of the Bank be at the disposal of the Government, if in a long series of time, there was not experienced a calamitous abuse of it. It is true, that it would be the real interest of the Government not to abuse it; its genuine policy to husband and cherish it with the most guarded circumspection as an inestimable treasure. But what Government ever uniformly consulted its true interest, in opposition to the temptations of momentary exigencies? What nation was ever blessed with a constant succession of upright and wise Administrators?

The keen, steady, and, as it were, magnetic sense, of their own interest, as proprietors, in the Directors of a Bank, pointing invariably to its true pole, the prosperity of the institution, is the only security, that can always be relied upon, for a careful and prudent administration. It is therefore the only basis on which an enlightened, unqualified and permanent confidence can be expected to be erected and maintained.

The precedents of the Banks established in several cities of Europe, Amsterdam, Hamburgh and others, may seem to militate against this position. Without a precise knowledge of all the peculiarities of their respective constitutions, it is difficult to pronounce how far this may be the case. That of Amsterdam, however, which we best know, is rather under a municipal than a governmental direction.

Particular magistrates of the city, not officers of the republic, have
the management of it. It is also a Bank of deposit, not of loan, or
circulation; consequently less liable to abuse, as well as less useful.
Its general business consists in receiving money for safekeeping;
which if not called for within a certain time becomes a part of its
Stock and irreclaimable: But a Credit is given for it on the books of
the Bank, which being transferable, answers all the purposes of
money.

The Directors being Magistrates of the city, and the Stockholders
in general, its most influential citizens, it is evident, that the principle
of private interest must be prevalent in the management of the Bank.
And it is equally evident, that from the nature of its operations, that
principle is less essential to it, than to an Institution constituted with
a view to the accommodation of the Public and Individuals by direct
loans and a paper circulation.

As far as may concern the aid of the Bank, within the proper
limits, a good government has nothing more to wish for, than it will
always possess; though the management be in the hands of private
individuals. As the institution, if rightly constituted, must depend for
its renovation from time to time on the pleasure of the Government, it
will not be likely to feel a disposition to render itself, by its conduct,
unworthy of public patronage. The Government too in the administration of its finances, has it in its power to reciprocate benefits to
the Bank, of not less importance, than those which the bank affords
to the Government, and which besides are never unattended with
an immediate and adequate compensation. Independent of these
more particular considerations, the natural weight and influence of
a good Government will always go far towards procuring a compliance
with its desires; and as the Directors will usually be composed of
some of the most discreet, respectable and well informed citizens,
it can hardly ever be difficult to make them sensible of the force of
the inducements, which ought to stimulate their exertions.

It will not follow, from what has been said, that the State may
not be the holder of a part of the Stock of a Bank, and consequently
a sharer in the profits of it. It will only follow, that it ought not to
desire any participation in the Direction of it, and therefore ought
not to own the whole or a principal part of the Stock; for if the mass
of the property should belong to the public, and if the direction of
it should be in private hands, this would be to commit the interests

of the State to persons, not interested, or not enough interested in their proper management.

There is one thing, however, which the Government owes to itself and to the community; at least to all that part of it, who are not Stockholders; which is to reserve to itself a right of ascertaining, as often as may be necessary, the state of the Bank, excluding however all pretension to controul. This right forms an article in the primitive constitution of the Bank of North America. And its propriety stands upon the clearest reasons. If the paper of a Bank is to be permitted to insinuate itself into all the revenues and receipts of a country; if it is even to be tolerated as the substitute for gold and silver, in all the transactions of business, it becomes in either view a national concern of the first magnitude. As such the ordinary rules of prudence require, that the Government should possess the means of ascertaining, whenever it thinks fit, that so delicate a trust is executed with fidelity and care. A right of this nature is not only desireable, as it respects the Government; but it ought to be equally so to all those, concerned in the institution; as an additional title to public and private confidence; and as a thing which can only be formidable to practices, that imply mismanagement. The presumption must always be, that the characters who would be entrusted with the exercise of this right, on behalf of the Government, will not be deficient in the discretion, which it may require; at least the admitting of this presumption cannot be deemed too great a return of confidence for that very large portion of it, which the Government is required to place in the Bank.

Abandoning, therefore, ideas, which however agreeable or desireable, are neither practicable nor safe, the following plan for the constitution of a National Bank is respectfully submitted to the consideration of the House.

I. The capital Stock of the Bank shall not exceed ten Millions of Dollars, divided into Twenty five thousand shares, each share being four hundred Dollars; to raise which sum, subscriptions shall be opened on the first monday of april next, and shall continue open, until the whole shall be subscribed. Bodies politic as well as individuals may subscribe.

II. The amount of each share shall be payable, one fourth in gold and silver coin, and three fourths in that part of the public debt, which according to the loan proposed by the Act making provision for the debt of the United States, shall bear an accruing interest at the time of payment of six per centum per annum.

III. The respective sums subscribed shall be payable in four equal parts, as well specie as debt, in succession, and at the distance of six calendar months from each other; the first payment to be made at the time of subscription. If there shall be a failure in any subsequent payment, the party failing shall lose the benefit of any dividend which may have accrued, prior to the time for making such payment, and during the delay of the same.

IV. The Subscribers to the Bank and their successors shall be incorporated, and shall so continue until the final redemption of that part of its stock, which shall consist of the public debt.

V. The capacity of the corporation to hold real and personal estate shall be limited to fifteen millions of Dollars, including the amount of its capital, or original stock. The lands and tenements, which it shall be permitted to hold, shall be only such as shall be requisite for the immediate accommodation of the institution; and such as shall have been bona fide mortgaged to it by way of security, or conveyed to it in satisfaction of debts previously contracted, in the usual course of its dealings, or purchased at sales upon judgments which shall have been obtained for such debts.

VI. The totality of the debts of the company, whether by bond, bill, note, or other contract, (credits for deposits excepted) shall never exceed the amount of its capital stock. In case of excess, the Directors, under whose administration it shall happen, shall be liable for it in their private or separate capacities. Those who may have dissented may excuse themselves from this responsibility by immediately giving notice of the fact and their dissent to the President of the United States, and to the Stockholders, at a general meeting to be called by the President of the Bank at their request.

VII. The Company may sell or demise its lands and tenements, or may sell the whole, or any part of the public Debt, whereof its Stock shall consist; but shall *trade* in nothing, except bills of exchange, gold and silver bullion, or in the sale of goods pledged for money lent: nor shall take more than at the rate of six per centum, per annum, upon its loans or discounts.

VIII. No loan shall be made by the bank, for the use or on account of the Government of the United States, or of either of them to an amount exceeding fifty thousand Dollars, or of any foreign prince or State; unless previously authorised by a law of the United States.

IX. The Stock of the Bank shall be transferable according to such rules as shall be instituted by the Company in that behalf.

X. The affairs of the Bank shall be under the management of Twenty five Directors, one of whom shall be the President. And there shall be on the first monday of January, in each year, a choice of Directors, by plurality of suffrages of the Stockholders, to serve for a year. The Directors at their first meeting, after each election, shall choose one of their number as President.

XI. The number of votes, to which each Stockholder shall be entitled, shall be according to the number of shares he shall hold in the proportions following, that is to say, for one share and not more than two shares one vote; for every two shares, above two and not exceeding ten, one vote; for every four shares above ten and not exceeding thirty, one vote; for every six shares above thirty and not exceeding sixty, one vote; for every eight shares above sixty and not exceeding one hundred, one vote; and for every ten shares above one hundred, one vote; but no person, copartnership, or body politic, shall be entitled to a greater number than thirty votes. And after the first election, no share or shares shall confer a right of suffrage, which shall not have been holden three calendar months previous to the day of election. Stockholders actually resident within the United States and none other may vote in elections by proxy.

XII. Not more than three fourths of the Directors in office, exclusive of the President, shall be eligible for the next succeeding year. But the Director who shall be President at the time of an election may always be reelected.

XIII. None but a Stockholder being a citizen of the United States, shall be eligible as a Director.

XIV. Any number of Stockholders not less than sixty, who together shall be proprietors of two hundred shares, or upwards, shall have power at any time to call a general meeting of the Stockholders, for purposes relative to the Institution; giving at least six weeks notice in two public gazettes of the place where the Bank is kept and specifying in such notice the object of the meeting.

XV. In case of the death, resignation, absence from the United States, or removal of a Director by the Stockholders, his place may be filled by a new choice for the remainder of the year.

XVI. No Director shall be entitled to any emolument, unless the same shall have been allowed by the Stockholders at a General meeting. The Stockholders shall make such compensation to the President, for his extraordinary attendance at the Bank, as shall appear to them reasonable.

XVII. Not less than seven Directors shall constitute a Board for the transaction of business.

XVIII. Every Cashier, or Treasurer, before he enters on the duties of his office shall be required to give bond, with two or more sureties, to the satisfaction of the Directors, in a sum not less than twenty thousand Dollars, with condition for his good behaviour.

XIX. Half yearly dividends shall be made of so much of the profits of the Bank as shall appear to the Directors adviseable: And once in every three years the Directors shall lay before the Stockholders, at a General Meeting, for their information, an exact and particular statement of the debts, which shall have remained unpaid, after the expiration of the original credit, for a period of treble the term of that credit; and of the surplus of profit, if any, after deducting losses and dividends.

XX. The bills and notes of the Bank originally made payable, or which shall have become payable on demand, in gold and silver coin, shall be receivable in all payments to the United States.

XXI. The Officer at the head of the Treasury Department of the United States, shall be furnished from time to time, as often as he may require, not exceeding once a week, with statements of the amount of the capital Stock of the Bank and of the debts due to the same; of the monies deposited therein; of the notes in circulation, and of the Cash in hand; and shall have a right to inspect such general account in the books of the bank as shall relate to the said statements; provided, that this shall not be construed to imply a right of inspecting this account of any private individual or individuals with the Bank.

XXII. No similar institution shall be established by any future act of the United States, during the continuance of the one hereby proposed to be established.

XXIII. It shall be lawful for the Directors of the Bank to establish offices, wheresoever they shall think fit, within the United States, for the purposes of discount and deposit only, and upon the same terms, and in the same manner, as shall be practiced at the Bank; and to commit the management of the said offices, and the making of the said discounts, either to Agents specially appointed by them, or to such persons as may be chosen by the Stockholders residing at the place where any such office shall be, under such agreements and subject to such regulations as they shall deem proper; not being contrary to law or to the Constitution of the Bank.

XXIV. And lastly. The President of the United States shall be authorised to cause a subscription to be made to the Stock of the said Company, on behalf of the United States, to an amount not exceeding two Millions of Dollars, to be paid out of the monies which shall be borrowed by virtue of either of the Acts, the one entitled "an Act making provision for the debt of the United States," and the other entitled "An Act making provision for the reduction of the Public Debt"; borrowing of the bank an equal sum, to be applied to the purposes for which the said monies shall have been procured, reimbursable in ten years by equal annual instalments; or at any time sooner, or in any greater proportions, that the Government may think fit.

The reasons for the several provisions contained in the foregoing plan, have been so far anticipated, and will, for the most part, be so readily suggested, by the nature of those provisions, that any comments, which need further be made, will be both few and concise.

The combination of a portion of the public Debt in the formation of the Capital, is the principal thing, of which an explanation is requisite. The chief object of this is, to enable the creation of a capital sufficiently large to be the basis of an extensive circulation, and an adequate security for it. As has been elsewhere remarked, the original plan of the Bank of North America contemplated a capital of ten millions of Dollars, which is certainly not too broad a foundation for the extensive operations, to which a National Bank is destined. But to collect such a sum in this country, in gold and silver into one depository, may, without hesitation, be pronounced impracticable. Hence the necessity of an auxiliary which the public debt at once presents.

This part of the fund will be always ready to come in aid of the specie. It will more and more command a ready sale; and can therefore expeditiously be turned into coin if an exigency of the Bank should at any time require it. This quality of prompt convertibility into coin, renders it an equivalent for that necessary agent of Bank circulation; and distinguished it from a fund in land of which the sale would generally be far less compendious and at great disadvantage. The quarter yearly receipts of interest will also be an actual addition to the specie fund during the intervals between them and the half yearly dividends of profits. The objection to combining land with specie, resulting from their not being generally in possession of the same persons, does not apply to the debt which will always be found in considerable quantity among the monied and trading people.

The debt composing part of the capital, besides its collateral effect in enabling the Bank to extend its operations, and consequently to enlarge its profits, will produce a direct annual revenue of six per centum from the Government, which will enter into the half yearly dividends received by the Stockholders.

When the present price of the public debt is considered, and the effect which its conversion into Bank Stock, incorporated with a specie fund, would in all probability have to accelerate its rise to the proper point, it will easily be discovered, that the operation presents in its outset a very considerable advantage to those who may become subscribers; and from the influence, which that rise would have on the general mass of the Debt, a proportional benefit to all the public creditors, and, in a sense, which has been more than once adverted to, to the community at large.

There is an important fact, which exemplifies the fitness of the public Debt, for a bank fund, and which may serve to remove doubts in some minds on this point. It is this, that the Bank of England in its first erection rested wholly on that foundation. The subscribers to a Loan to Government of one million two hundred thousand pounds sterling were incorporated as a Bank; of which the Debt created by the Loan, and the interest upon it, were the sole fund. The subsequent augmentations of its capital, which now amounts to between eleven and twelve millions of pounds sterling, have been of the same nature.

The confining of the right of the Bank to contract debts to the amount of its capital is an important precaution, which is not to be found in the constitution of the Bank of North America, and which, while the fund consists wholly of coin, would be a restriction attended with inconveniencies, but would be free from any if the composition of it should be such as is now proposed. The restriction exists in the establishment of the Bank of England, and as a source of security is worthy of imitation. The consequence of exceeding the limit there is, that each Stockholder is liable to the excess, in proportion to his interest in the Bank. When it is considered, that the Directors owe their appointments to the choice of the Stockholders, a responsibility of this kind, on the part of the latter, does not appear unreasonable. But, on the other hand, it may be deemed a hardship upon those, who may have dissented from the choice. And there are many among us, whom it might perhaps discourage from becoming concerned in the institution. These reasons have induced the placing of the responsibility upon the Directors, by whom the limit prescribed should be transgressed.

The interdiction of loans on account of the United States, or of any particular State, beyond the moderate sum specified, or of any foreign power, will serve as a barrier to executive incroachments; and to combinations inauspicious to the safety or contrary to the policy of the Union.

The limitation of the rate of interest is dictated by the consideration, that different rates prevail in different parts of the Union; and as the operations of the Bank may extend through the whole, some rule seems to be necessary. There is room for a question, whether the limitation ought not rather to be to five than to six per cent, as proposed. It may with safety be taken for granted, that the former rate would yield an ample dividend; perhaps as much as the latter, by the extension which it would give to business. The natural effect of low interest is to increase trade and industry; because undertakings of every kind can be prosecuted with greater advantage. This is a truth generally admitted; but it is requisite to have analised the subject, in all its realtions, to be able to form a just conception of the extent of that effect. Such an analysis cannot but satisfy an intelligent mind, that the difference of one per cent, in the rate at which money may be had, is often capable of making an essential change for the better in the situation of any country or place.

Every thing, therefore, which tends to lower the rate of interest is peculiarly worthy of the cares of Legislators. And though laws which violently sink the legal rate of interest greatly below the market level are not to be commended, because they are not calculated to answer their aim, yet whatever has a tendency to effect a reduction, without violence to the natural course of things, ought to be attended to and pursued. Banks are among the means most proper to accomplish this end; and the moderation of the rate at which their discounts are made, is a material ingredient towards it; with which their own interest, viewed on an enlarged and permanent scale, does not appear to clash.

But as the most obvious ideas are apt to have greater force, than those which depend on complex and remote combinations, there would be danger, that the persons whose funds must constitute the Stock of the Bank would be diffident of the sufficiency of the profits to be expected, if the rate of loans and discounts were to be placed below the point to which they have been accustomed; and might on this account be indisposed to embarking in the plan. There is, it is true, one reflection, which in regard to men actively engaged in trade ought to be a security against this danger; it is this, that the accommodations which they might derive in the way of their business, at a low rate, would more than indemnify them for any difference in the dividend, supposing even that some diminution of it were to be the consequence. But upon the whole, the hazard of contrary reasoning among the mass of monied men is a powerful argument against the experiment. The institutions of the kind already existing add to the difficulty of making it. Maturer reflection and a large capital may of themselves lead to the desired end.

The last thing, which will require any explanatory remark, is the authority proposed to be given to the President to subscribe to the amount of two millions of Dollars on account of the public. The main design of this is to enlarge the specie fund of the Bank, and to enable it to give a more early extension to its operations. Though it is proposed to borrow with one hand what is lent with the other, yet the disbursement of what is borrowed will be progressive, and Bank notes may be thrown into circulation, instead of the gold and silver. Besides, there is to be an annual reimbursement of a part of the sum borrowed, which will finally operate as an actual investment of so much specie. In addition to the inducements to this measure, which results from the general interest of the Government, to enlarge the sphere of the utility of the Bank, there is this more particular consideration, to wit, that as far as the dividend on the Stock shall exceed the interest paid on the loan, there is a positive profit.

The Secretary begs leave to conclude, with this general observation, that if the Bank of North America shall come forward with any propositions, which have for object the ingrafting upon that institution the characteristics, which shall appear to the Legislature necessary to the due extent and safety of a National Bank, there are, in his judgment, weighty inducements to giving every reasonable facility to the measure. Not only the pretensions of that institution, from its original relation to the Government of the United States, and from the services it has rendered, are such as to claim a disposition favourable to it, if those who are interested in it are willing on their part to place it on a footing satisfactory to the Government, and equal to the purposes of a Bank of the United States; but its cooperation would materially accelerate the accomplishment of the great object, and the collision, which might otherwise arise, might, in a variety of ways, prove equally disagreeable and injurious. The incorporation or union here contemplated, may be effected in different modes, under the auspices of an Act of the United States, if it shall be desired by the Bank of North America, upon terms, which shall appear expedient to the Government.

All which is humbly submitted

Alexander Hamilton
Secretary of the Treasury

From the Report
On the Subject of Manufactures
(December 5, 1791)

To the Speaker of the House of Representatives:

The Secretary of the Treasury in obedience to the order of ye House of Representatives, of the 15th day of January 1790, has applied his attention, at as early a period as his other duties would permit, to the subject of Manufactures; and particularly to the means of promoting such as will tend to render the United States, independent on foreign nations, for military and other essential supplies. And he there (upon) respectfully submits the following Report.

The expediency of encouraging manufactures in the United States, which was not long since deemed very questionable, appears at this time to be pretty generally admitted. The embarrassments, which have obstructed the progress of our external trade, have led to serious reflections on the necessity of enlarging the sphere of our domestic commerce: the restrictive regulations, which in foreign markets abrige the vent of the increasing surplus of our Agricultural produce, serve to beget an earnest desire, that a more extensive demand for that surplus may be created at home: And the complete success, which has rewarded manufacturing enterprise, in some valuable branches, conspiring with the promising symptoms, which attend some less mature essays, in others, justify a hope, that the obstacles to the growth of this species of industry are less formidable than they were apprehended to be; and that it is not difficult to find, in its further extension; a full indemnification for any external disadvantages, which are or may be experienced, as well as an accession of resources, favourable to national independence and safety.

There still are, nevertheless, respectable patrons of opinions, unfriendly to the encouragement of manufactures. The following are, substantially, the arguments by which these opinions are defended.

"In every country (say those who entertain them) Agriculture is the most beneficial and *productive* object of human industry. This position, generally, if not universally true, applies with peculiar emphasis to the United States, on account of their immense tracts of fertile territory, uninhabited and unimproved. Nothing can so afford so advantageous an employment for capital and labour, as the conversion of this extensive wilderness into cultivated farms. Nothing equally with this, can contribute to the population, strength and real riches of the country."

"To endeavor by the extraordinary patronage of Government, to accelerate the growth of manufactures, is in fact, to endeavor, by force and art, to transfer the natural current of industry, from a more to a less beneficial channel. Whatever has such a tendency must necessarily be unwise. Indeed it can hardly ever be wise in a government, to attempt to give a direction to the industry of its citizens. This under the quicksighted guidance of private interest, will, if left to itself, infallibly find its own way to the most profitable employment: and 'tis by such employment, that the public prosperity will be most effectually promoted. To leave industry to itself, therefore, is, in almost every case, the soundest as well as the simplest policy."

"This policy is not only recommended to the United States, by considerations which affect all nations, it is, in a manner, dictated to them by the imperious force of a very peculiar situation. The smallness of their population compared with their territory—the constant allurements to emigration from the settled to the unsettled parts of the country—the facility, with which the less independent condition of an artisan can be exchanged for the more independent condition of a farmer, these and similar causes conspire to produce, and for a length of time must continue to occasion, a scarcity of hands for manufacturing occupation, and dearness of labor generally. To these disadvantages for the prosecution of manufactures, a deficiency of pecuniary capital being added, the prospect of a successful competition with the manufactures of Europe must be regarded as little less than desperate. Extensive manufactures can only be the offspring of a redundant, at least of a full population. Till the latter shall characterise the situation of this country, 'tis vain to hope for the former."

"If contrary to the natural course of things, an unseasonable and premature spring can be given to certain fabrics, by heavy duties, prohibitions, bounties, or by other forced expedients; this will only be to sacrifice the interests of the community to those of particular classes. Besides the misdirection of labour, a virtual monopoly will be given to the persons employed on such fabrics; and an enhancement of price, the inevitable consequence of every monopoly, must be defrayed at the expence of the other parts of society. It is far preferable, that those persons should be engaged in the cultivation of the earth, and that we should procure, in exchange for its productions, the commodities, with which foreigners are able to supply us in greater perfection, and upon better terms."

This mode of reasoning is founded upon facts and principles, which have certainly respectable pretensions. If it had governed the conduct of nations, more generally than it has done, there is room to suppose, that it might have carried them faster to prosperity and greatness, than they have attained, by the pursuit of maxims too widely opposite. Most general theories, however, admit of numerous exceptions, and there are few, if any, of the political kind, which do not blend a considerable portion of error, with the truths they inculcate.

In order to an accurate judgement how far that which has been just stated ought to be deemed liable to a similar imputation, it is necessary to advert carefully to the considerations, which plead in favour of manufactures, and which appear to recommend the special and positive encouragement of them; in certain cases, and under certain reasonable limitations.

It ought readily to be conceded, that the cultivation of the earth—as the primary and most certain source of national supply—as the immediate and chief source of subsistence to man—as the principal source of those materials which constitute the nutriment of other kinds of labor—as including a state most favorable to the freedom and independence of the human mind—one, perhaps, most conducive to the multiplication of the human species—has *intrinsically a strong claim to preeminence over every other kind of industry*.

But, that it has a title to any thing like an exclusive predilection, in any country, ought to be admitted with great caution. That it is even more productive than every other branch of Industry requires more evidence, than has yet been given in support of the position. That its real interests, precious and important as without the help of exaggeration, they truly are, will be advanced, rather than injured by the due encouragement of manufactures, may, it is believed, be satisfactorily demonstrated. And it is also believed that the expediency of such encouragement in a general view may be shewn to be recommended by the most cogent and persuasive motives of national policy.

It has been maintained, that Agriculture is, not only, the most productive, but the only productive species of industry. The reality of this suggestion in either aspect, has, however, not been verified by any accurate detail of facts and calculations; and the general arguments, which are adduced to prove it, are rather subtil and paradoxical, than solid or convincing.

Those which maintain its exclusive productiveness are to this effect.

Labour, bestowed upon the cultivation of land produces enough, not only to replace all the necessary expences incurred in the business, and to maintain the persons who are employed in it, but to afford together with the *ordinary profit* on the stock or capital of the Farmer, a nett surplus, or *rent* for the landlord or proprietor of the soil. But the labor of Artificers does nothing more, than replace the Stock which employs them (or which furnishes materials tools and wages) and yield the *ordinary profit* upon that Stock. It yields nothing equivalent to the *rent* of land. Neither does it add any thing to the *total value* of the *whole annual produce* of the land and labour of the country. The additional value given to those parts of the produce of land, which are wrought into manufactures, is counterbalanced by the value of those other parts of that produce, which are consumed by the manufacturers. It can therefore only be by saving, or *parsimony* not by the positive *productiveness* of their labour, that the classes of Artificers can in any degree augment the revenue of the Society.

To this it has been answered—

I. "That inasmuch as it is acknowleged, that manufacturing labour reproduces a value equal to that which is expended or consumed in carrying it on, and continues in existence the original Stock or capital employed—it ought on that account alone, to escape being considered as wholly unproductive: That though it should be admitted, as alleged, that the consumption of the produce of the soil, by the classes of Artificers or Manufacturers, is exactly equal to the value added by their labour to the materials upon which it is exerted; yet it would not thence follow, that it added nothing to the Revenue of the Society, or to the aggregate value of the annual produce of its land and labour. If the consumption for any given period amounted to a *given sum* and the *increased* value of the produce manufactured, in the same period, to a *like sum,* the total amount of the consumption and production during that period, would be equal to the *two sums,* and consequently double the value of the agricultural produce consumed. And though the increment of value produced by the classes of Artificers should at no time exceed the value of the produce of the land consumed by them, yet there would be at every moment, in consequence of their labour, a greater value of goods in the market than would exist independent of it."

II. "That the position, that Artificers can augment the revenue of a Society, only by parsimony, is true in no other sense, than in one, which is equally applicable to Husbandmen or Cultivators. It may be alike affirmed of all these classes, that the fund acquired by their labor and destined for their support is not, in an ordinary way, more than equal to it. And hence it will follow, that augmentations of the wealth or capital of the community (except in the instances of some extraordinary dexterity or skill) can only proceed, with respect to any of them, from the savings of the more thrifty and parsimonious."

III. "That the annual produce of the land and labour of a country can only be encreased, in two ways—by some improvement in the *productive powers* of the useful labour, which actually exists within it, or by some increase in the quantity of such labour: That with regard to the first, the labour of Artificers being capable of greater subdivision and simplicity of operation, than that of Cultivators, it is susceptible, in a proportionably greater degree, of improvement in its *productive powers*, whether to be derived from an accession of Skill, or from the application of ingenious machinery; in which particular, therefore, the labour employed in the culture of land can pretend to no advantage over that engaged in manufactures: That with regard to an augmentation of the quantity of useful labour, this, excluding adventitious circumstances, must depend essentially upon an increase of *capital*, which again must depend upon the savings made out of the revenues of those, who furnish or manage *that*, which is at any time employed, whether in Agriculture, or in Manufactures, or in any other way."

But while the *exclusive* productiveness of Agricultural labour has been thus denied and refuted, the superiority of its productiveness has been conceded without hesitation. As this concession involves a point of considerable magnitude, in relation to maxims of public administration, the grounds on which it rests are worthy of a distinct and particular examination.

One of the arguments made use of, in support of the idea may be pronounced both quaint and superficial. It amounts to this—That in the productions of the soil, nature co-operates with man; and that the effect of their joint labour must be greater than that of the labour of man alone.

This however, is far from being a necessary inference. It is very conceivable, that the labor of man alone laid out upon a work, requiring great skill and art to bring it to perfection, may be more productive, *in value*, than the labour of nature and man combined, when directed towards more simple operations and objects: And when it is recollected to what an extent the Agency of nature, in the application of the mechanical powers, is made auxiliary to the prosecution of manufactures, the suggestion, which has been noticed, loses even the appearance of plausibility.

It might also be observed, with a contrary view, that the labour employed in Agriculture is in a great measure periodical and occasional, depending on seasons, liable to various and long intermissions; while that occupied in many manufactures is constant and regular, extending through the year, embracing in some instances night as well as day. It is also probable, that there are among the cultivators of land more examples of remissness, than among artificers. The farmer, from the peculiar fertility of his land, or some other favorable circumstance, may frequently obtain a livelihood, even with a considerable degree of carelessness in the mode of cultivation; but the artisan can with difficulty effect the same object, without exerting himself pretty equally with all those, who are engaged in the same pursuit. And if it may likewise be assumed as a fact, that manufactures open a wider field to exertions of ingenuity than agriculture, it would not be a strained conjecture, that the labour employed in the former, being at once more *constant*, more uniform and more ingenious, than that which is employed in the latter, will be found at the same time more productive.

But it is not meant to lay stress on observations of this nature— they ought only to serve as a counterbalance to those of a similar complexion. Circumstances so vague and general, as well as so abstract, can afford little instruction in a matter of this kind.

Another, and that which seems to be the principal argument offered for the superior productiveness of Agricultural labour, turns upon the allegation, that labour employed in manufactures yields nothing equivalent to the rent of land; or to that nett surplus, as it is called, which accrues to the proprietor of the soil.

But this distinction, important as it has been deemed, appears rather *verbal* than *substantial*.

It is easily discernible, that what in the first instance is divided into two parts under the denominations of the *ordinary profit* of the Stock of the farmer and *rent* to the landlord, is in the second instance united under the general appellation of the *ordinary profit* on the Stock of the Undertaker; and that this formal or verbal distribution constitutes the whole difference in the two cases. It seems to have been overlooked, that the land is itself a Stock or capital, advanced or lent by its owner to the occupier or tenant, and that the rent he receives is only the ordinary profit of a certain Stock in land, not managed by the proprietor himself, but by another to whom he lends or lets it, and who on his part advances a second capital to stock and improve the land, upon which he also receives the usual profit. The rent of the landlord and the profit of the farmer are therefore nothing more than the *ordinary profits* of *two* capitals belonging to *two* different persons, and united in the cultivation of a farm: As in the other case, the surplus which arises upon any manufactory, after replacing the expences of carrying it on, answers to the profits of *one* or *more* capitals engaged in the prosecution of such manufactory. It is said *one* or *more* capitals; because in fact, the same thing which is contemplated, in the case of the farm, sometimes happens in that of a manufactory. There is one, who furnishes a part of the capital, or lends a part of the money, by which it is carried on, and another, who carries it on, with the addition of his own capital. Out of the surplus, which remains, after defraying expences, an interest is paid to the money lender for the portion of the capital furnished by him which exactly agrees with the rent paid to the landlord; and the residue of that surplus constitutes the profit of the undertaker or manufacturer, and agrees with what is denominated the ordinary profits on the Stock of the farmer. Both together make the ordinary profits of two capitals (employed in a manufactory; as in the other case the rent of the landlord and the revenue of the farmer compose the ordinary profits of two Capitals) employed in the cultivation of a farm.

The rent therefore accruing to the proprietor of the land, far from being a criterion of *exclusive* productiveness, as has been argued, is no criterion even of superior productiveness. The question must still be, whether the surplus, after defraying expences, of a *given capital*, employed in the *purchase* and *improvement* of a piece of land, is greater or less, than that of a like capital employed in the prosecution of a manufactory: or whether the *whole value produced* from a *given capital* and a *given quantity of labour*, employed in one way, be greater or less, than the *whole value produced* from an *equal capital* and an *equal quantity of labour* employed in the other way: or rather, perhaps whether the business of Agriculture or that of Manufactures will yield the greatest product, according to a *compound ratio* of the quantity of the Capital and the quantity of labour, which are employed in the one or in the other.

The solution of either of these questions is not easy; it involves numerous and complicated details, depending on an accurate knowledge of the objects to be compared. It is not known that the comparison has every yet been made upon sufficient data properly ascertained and analised. To be able to make it on the present occasion with satisfactory precision would demand more previous enquiry and investigation, than there has been hitherto either leisure or opportunity to accomplish.

Some essays however have been made towards acquiring the requisite information; which have rather served to throw doubt upon, than to confirm the Hypothesis, under examination: But it ought to be acknowledged, that they have been too little diversified, and are too imperfect, to authorise a definitive conclusion either way; leading rather to probable conjecture than to certain deduction. They render it probable, that there are various branches of manufactures, in which a given Capital will yield a greater *total* product, and a considerably greater *nett* product, than an equal capital invested in the purchase and improvement of lands; and that there are also *some* branches, in which both the *gross* and *nett* produce will exceed that of Agricultural industry; according to a compound ratio of capital and labour: But it is on this last point, that there appears to be the greatest room for doubt. It is far less difficult to infer generally, that the *nett produce* of Capital engaged in manufacturing enterprises is greater than that of Capital engaged in Agriculture.

In stating these results, the purchase and improvement of lands, under previous cultivation are alone contemplated. The comparison is more in favour of Agriculture, when it is made with reference to the settlement of new and waste lands; but an argument drawn from so temporary a circumstance could have no weight in determining the general question concerning the permanent relative productiveness of the two species of industry. How far it ought to influence the policy of the United States, on the score of particular situation, will be adverted to in another place.

The foregoing suggestions are *not designed to inculcate an opinion that manufacturing industry is more productive than that of Agriculture*. They are intended rather to shew that the reverse of this proposition is not ascertained; that the general arguments which are brought to establish it are not satisfactory; and consequently that a supposition of the superior productiveness of Tillage ought to be no obstacle to listening to any substantial inducements to the encouragement of manufactures, which may be otherwise perceived to exist, through an apprehension, that they may have a tendency to divert labour from a more to a less profitable employment.

It is extremely probable, that on a full and accurate devellopment of the matter, on the ground of fact and calculation, it would be discovered that there is no material difference between the aggregate productiveness of the one, and of the other kind of industry; and that the propriety of the encouragements, which may in any case be proposed to be given to either ought to be determined upon considerations irrelative to any comparison of that nature.

II. But without contending for the superior productiveness of Manufacturing Industry, it may conduce to a better judgment of the policy, which ought to be pursued respecting its encouragement, to contemplate the subject, under some additional aspects, tending not only to confirm the idea, that this kind of industry has been improperly represented as unproductive in itself; but (to) evince in addition that the establishment and diffusion of manufactures have the effect of rendering the total mass of useful and productive labor in a community, *greater than it would otherwise be*. In prosecuting this discussion, it may be necessary briefly to resume and review some of the topics, which have been already touched.

To affirm, that the labour of the Manufacturer is unproductive, because he consumes as much of the produce of land, as he adds value to the raw materials which he manufactures, is not better founded, than it would be to affirm, that the labour of the farmer, which furnishes materials to the manufacturer, is unproductive, *because he consumes an equal value of manufactured articles*. Each furnishes a certain portion of the produce of his labor to the other, and each destroys a correspondent portion of the produce of the labour of the other. In the mean time, the maintenance of two Citizens, instead of one, is going on; the State has two members instead of one; and they together consume twice the value of what is produced from the land.

If instead of a farmer and artificer, there were a farmer only, he would be under the necessity of devoting a part of his labour to the fabrication of cloathing and other articles, which he would procure of the artificer, in the case of there being such a person; and of course he would be able to devote less labor to the cultivation of his farm; and would draw from it a proporitionably less product. The whole quantity of production, in this state of things, in provisions, raw materials and manufactures, would certainly not exceed in value the amount of what would be produced in provisions and raw materials only, if there were an artificer as well as a farmer.

Again—if there were both an artificer and a farmer, the latter would be left at liberty to pursue exclusively the cultivation of his farm. A greater quantity of provisions and raw materials would of course be produced—equal at least—as has been already observed, to the whole amount of the provisions, raw materials and manufactures, which would exist on a contrary supposition. The artificer, at the same time would be going on in the production of manufactured commodities; to an amount sufficient not only to repay the farmer, in those commodities, for the provisions and materials which were procured from him, but to furnish the Artificer himself with a supply of similar commodities for his own use. Thus then, there would be two quantities or values in existence, instead of one; and the revenue and consumption would be double in one case, what it would be in the other.

If in place of both these suppositions, there were supposed to be two farmers, and no artificer, each of whom applied a part of his labour to the culture of land, and another part to the fabrication of Manufactures—in this case, the portion of the labour of both bestowed upon land would produce the same quantity of provisions and raw materials only, as would be produced by the intire sum of the labour of one applied in the same manner, and the portion of the labour of both bestowed upon manufactures, would produce the same quantity of manufactures only, as would be produced by the intire sum of the labour of one applied in the same manner. Hence the produce of the labour of the two farmers would not be greater than the produce of the labour of the farmer and artificer; and hence, it results, that the labour of the artificer is as possitively productive as that of the farmer, and, as positively, augments the revenue of the Society.

The labour of the Artificer replaces to the farmer that portion of his labour, with which he provides the materials of exchange with the Artificer, and which he would otherwise have been compelled to apply to manufactures: and while the Artificer thus enables the farmer to enlarge his stock of Agricultural industry, a portion of which he purchases for his own use, *he also supplies himself with the manufactured articles of which he stands in need.*

He does still more—Besides this equivalent which he gives for the portion of Agricultural labour consumed by him, and this supply of manufactured commodities for his own consumption—he furnishes still a surplus, which compensates for the use of the Capital advanced either by himself or some other person, for carrying on the business. This is the ordinary profit of the stock employed in the manufactory, and is, in every sense, as effective an addition to the income of the Society, as the rent of land.

The produce of the labour of the Artificer consequently, may be regarded as composed of three parts; one by which the provisions for his subsistence and the materials for his work are purchased of the farmer, one by which he supplies himself with manufactured necessaries, and a third which constitutes the profit on the Stock employed. The two last portions seem to have been overlooked in the system, which represents manufacturing industry as barren and unproductive.

In the course of the preceding illustrations, the products of equal quantities of the labour of the farmer and artificer have been treated as if equal to each other. But this is not to be understood as intending to assert any such precise equality. It is merely a manner of expression adopted for the sake of simplicity and perspicuity. Whether the value of the produce of the labour of the farmer be somewhat more or less, than that of the artificer, is not material to the main scope of the argument, which hitherto has only aimed at shewing, that the one, as well as the other, occasions a possitive augmentation of the total produce and revenue of the Society.

It is now proper to proceed a step further, and to enumerate the principal circumstances, from which it may be inferred—That manufacturing establishments not only occasion a possitive augmentation of the Produce and Revenue of the Society, but that they contribute essentially to rendering them greater than they could possibly be, without such establishments. These circumstances are—

1. The division of Labour.

2. An extension of the use of Machinery.

3. Additional employment to classes of the community not-ordinarily engaged in the business.

4. The promoting of emigration from foreign Countries.

5. The furnishing greater scope for the diversity of talents and dispositions which discriminate men from each other.

6. The affording a more ample and various field for enterprize.

7. The creating in some instances a new, and securing in all, a more certain and steady demand for the surplus produce of the soil.

Each of these circumstances has a considerable influence upon the total mass of industrious effort in a community. Together, they add to it a degree of energy and effect, which are not easily conceived.

Some comments upon each of them, in the order in which they have been stated, may serve to explain their importance.

I. As to the Division of Labour.

It has justly been observed, that there is scarcely any thing of greater moment in the economy of a nation, than the proper division of labour. The seperation of occupations causes each to be carried to a much greater perfection, than it could possible acquire, if they were blended. This arises principally from three circumstances.

First. The greater skill and dexterity naturally resulting from a constant and undivided application to a single object. It is evident, that these properties must increase, in proportion to the separation and simplification of objects and the steadiness of the attention devoted to each; and must be less, in proportion to the complication of objects, and the number among which the attention is distracted.

Second. The economy of time—by avoiding the loss of it, incident to a frequent transition from one operation to another of a different nature. This depends on various circumstances—the transition itself—the orderly disposition of the impliments, machines and materials employed in the operation to be relinquished—the preparatory steps to the commencement of a new one—the interruption of the impulse, which the mind of the workman acquires, from being engaged in a particular operation—the distractions hesitations and reluctances, which attend the passage from one kind of business to another.

Third. An extension of the use of Machinery. A man occupied on a single object will have it more in his power, and will be more naturally led to exert his imagination in devising methods to facilitate and abrige labour, than if he were perplexed by a variety of independent and dissimilar operations. Besides this, the fabrication of Machines, in numerous instances, becoming itself a distinct trade, the Artist who follows it, has all the advantages which have been enumerated, for improvement in his particular art; and in both ways the invention and application of machinery are extended.

And from these causes united, the mere separation of the occupation of the cultivator, from that of the Artificer, has the effect of augmenting the *productive powers* of labour, and with them, the total mass of the produce or revenue of a Country. In this single view of the subject, therefore, the utility of Artificers or Manufacturers, towards promoting an increase of productive industry, is apparent.

II. As to an extension of the use of Machinery a point which though partly anticipated requires to be placed in one or two additional lights.

The employment of Machinery forms an item of great importance in the general mass of national industry. 'Tis an artificial force brought in aid of the natural force of man; and, to all the purposes of labour, is an increase of hands; an accession of strength, *unincumbered too by the expence of maintaining the laborer*. May it not therefore be fairly inferred, that those occupations, which give greatest scope to the use of this auxiliary, contribute most to the general Stock of industrious effort, and, in consequence, to the general product of industry?

It shall be taken for granted, and the truth of the position referred to observation, that manufacturing pursuits are susceptible in a greater degree of the application of machinery, than those of Agriculture. If so all the difference is lost to a community, which, instead of manufacturing for itself, procures the fabrics requisite to its supply from other Countries. The substitution of foreign for domestic manufactures is a transfer to foreign nations of the advantages accruing from the employment of Machinery, in the modes in which it is capable of being employed, with most utility and to the greatest extent.

The Cotton Mill invented in England, within the last twenty years, is a signal illustration of the general proposition, which has been just advanced. In consequence of it, all the different processes for spining Cotton are performed by means of Machines, which are put in motion by water, and attended chiefly by women and Children; (and by a smaller) number of (persons, in the whole, than are) requisite in the ordinary mode of spinning. And it is an advantage of great moment that the operations of this mill continue with convenience, during the night, as well as through the day. The prodigious affect of such a Machine is easily conceived. To this invention is to be attributed essentially the immense progress, which has been so suddenly made in Great Britain in the various fabrics of Cotton.

III. As to the additional employment of classes of the community, not ordinarily engaged in the particular business.

This is not among the least valuable of the means, by which manufacturing institutions contribute to augment the general stock of industry and production. In places where those institutions prevail, besides the persons regularly engaged in them, they afford occasional and extra employment to industrious individuals and families, who are willing to devote the leisure resulting from the intermissions of their ordinary pursuits to collateral labours, as a resource of multiplying their acquisitions or (their) enjoyments. The husbandman himself experiences a new source of profit and support from the encreased industry of his wife and daughters; invited and stimulated by the demands of the neighboring manufactories.

Besides this advantage of occasional employment to classes having different occupations, there is another of a nature allied to it (and) of a similar tendency. This is—the employment of persons who would otherwise be idle (and in many cases a burthen on the community), either from the byass of temper, habit, infirmity of body, or some other cause, indisposing, or disqualifying them for the toils of the Country. It is worthy of particular remark, that, in general, women and Children are rendered more useful and the latter more early useful by manufacturing establishments, than they would otherwise be. Of the number of persons employed in the Cotton Manufactories of Great Britain, it is computed that 4/7 nearly are women and children; of whom the greatest proportion are children and many of them of a very tender age.

And thus it appears to be one of the attributes of manufactures, and one of no small consequence, to give occasion to the exertion of a greater quantity of Industry, even by the *same number* of persons, where they happen to prevail, than would exist, if there were no such establishments.

IV. As to the promoting of emigration from foreign Countries.

Men reluctantly quit one course of occupation and livelihood for another, unless invited to it by very apparent and proximate advantages. Many, who would go from one country to another, if they had a prospect of continuing with more benefit the callings, to which they have been educated, will often not be tempted to change their situation, by the hope of doing better, in some other way. Manufacturers, who listening to the powerful invitations of a better price for their fabrics, or their labour, of greater cheapness of provisions and raw materials, of an exemption from the chief part of the taxes burthens and restraints, which they endure in the old world, of greater personal independence and consequence, under the operation of a more equal government, and of what is far more precious than mere religious toleration—a perfect equality of religious privileges; would probably flock from Europe to the United States to pursue their own trades or professions, if they were once made sensible of the advantages they would enjoy, and were inspired with an assurance of encouragement and employment, will, with difficulty, be induced to transplant themselves, with a view to becoming Cultivators of Land.

If it be true then, that it is the interest of the United States to open every possible (avenue to) emigration from abroad, it affords a weighty argument for the encouragement of manufactures; which for the reasons just assigned, will have the strongest tendency to multiply the inducements to it.

Here is perceived an important resource, not only for extending the population, and with it the useful and productive labour of the country, but likewise for the prosecution of manufactures, without deducting from the number of hands, which might otherwise be drawn to tillage; and even for the indemnification of Agriculture for such as might happen to be diverted from it. Many, whom Manufacturing views would induce to emigrate, would afterwards yield to the temptations, which the particular situation of this Country holds out to Agricultural pursuits. And while Agriculture would in other respects derive many signal and unmingled advantages, from the growth of manufactures, it is a problem whether it would gain or lose, as to the article of the number of persons employed in carrying it on.

V. As to the furnishing greater scope for the diversity of talents and dispositions, which discriminate men from each other.

This is a much more powerful mean of augmenting the fund of national Industry than may at first sight appear. It is a just observation, that minds of the strongest and most active powers for their proper objects fall below mediocrity and labour without effect, if confined to uncongenial pursuits. And it is thence to be inferred, that the results of human exertion may be immensely increased by diversifying its objects. When all the different kinds of industry obtain in a community, each individual can find his proper element, and can call into activity the whole vigour of his nature. And the community is benefitted by the services of its respective members, in the manner, in which each can serve it with most effect.

If there be anything in a remark often to be met with—namely that there is, in the genius of the people of this country, a peculiar aptitude for mechanic improvements, it would operate as a forcible reason for giving opportunities to the exercise of that species of talent, by the propagation of manufactures.

VI. As to the affording a more ample and various field for enterprise.

This also is of greater consequence in the general scale of national exertion, than might perhaps on a superficial view be supposed, and has effects not altogether dissimilar from those of the circumstance last noticed. To cherish and stimulate the activity of the human mind, by multiplying the objects of enterprise, is not among the least considerable of the expedients, by which the wealth of a nation may be promoted. Even things in themselves not positively advantageous, sometimes become so, by their tendency to provoke exertion. Every new scene, which is opened to the busy nature of man to rouse and exert itself, is the addition of a new energy to the general stock of effort.

The spirit of enterprise, useful and prolific as it is, must necessarily be contracted or expanded in proportion to the simplicity or variety of the occupations and productions, which are to be found in a Society. It must be less in a nation of mere cultivators, than in a nation of cultivators and merchants; less in a nation of cultivators and merchants, than in a nation of cultivators, artificers and merchants.

VII. As to the creating, in some instances, a new, and securing in all a more certain and steady demand, for the surplus produce of the soil.

This is among the most important of the circumstances which have been indicated. It is a principal mean, by which the establishment of manufactures contributes to an augmentation of the produce or revenue of a country, and has an immediate and direct relation to the prosperity of Agriculture.

It is evident, that the exertions of the husbandman will be steady or fluctuating, vigorous or feeble, in proportion to the steadiness or fluctuation, adequateness, or inadequateness of the markets on which he must depend, for the vent of the surplus, which may be produced by his labour; and that such surplus in the ordinary course of things will be greater or less in the same proportion.

For the purpose of this vent, a domestic market is greatly to be preferred to a foreign one; because it is in the nature of things, far more to be relied upon.

It is a primary object of the policy of nations, to be able to supply themselves with subsistence from their own soils; and manufacturing nations, as far as circumstances permit, endeavor to procure, from the same source, the raw materials necessary for their own fabrics. This disposition, urged by the spirit of monopoly, is sometimes even carried to an injudicious extreme. It seems not always to be recollected, that nations, who have neither mines nor manufactures, can only obtain the manufactured articles, of which they stand in need, by an exchange of the products of their soils; and that, if those who can best furnish them with such articles are unwilling to give a due course to this exchange, they must of necessity make every possible effort to manufacture for themselves, the effect of which is that the manufacturing nations abrige the natural advantages of their situation, through an unwillingness to permit the Agricultural countries to enjoy the advantages of theirs, and sacrifice the interests of a mutually beneficial intercourse to the vain project of *selling every thing* and *buying nothing*.

But it is also a consequence of the policy, which has been noted, that the foreign demand for the products of Agricultural Countries, is, in a great degree, rather casual and occasional, than certain or constant. To what extent injurious interruptions of the demand for some of the staple commodities of the United States, may have been experienced, from that cause, must be referred to the judgment of those who are engaged in carrying on the commerce of the country; but it may be safely assumed, that such interruptions are at times very inconveniently felt, and that cases not unfrequently occur, in which markets are so confined and restricted, as to render the demand very unequal to the supply.

Independently likewise of the artificial impediments, which are created by the policy in question, there are natural causes tending to render the external demand for the surplus of Agricultural nations a precarious reliance. The differences of seasons, in the countries, which are consumers make immense differences in the produce of their own soils, in different years; and consequently in the degrees of their necessity for foreign supply. Plentiful harvests with them, especially if similar ones occur at the same time in the countries, which are the furnishers, occasion of course a glut in the markets of the latter.

Considering how fast and how much the progress of new settlements in the United States must increse the surplus produce of the soil, and weighing seriously the tendency of the system, which prevails among most of the commercial nations of Europe; whatever dependence may be placed on the force of natural circumstances to counteract the effects of an artificial policy; there appear strong reasons to regard the foreign demand for that surplus as too uncertain a reliance, and to desire a substitute for it, in an extensive domestic market.

To secure such a market, there is no other expedient, than to promote manufacturing establishments. Manufacturers who constitute the most numerous class, after the Cultivators of land, are for that reason the principal consumers of the surplus of their labour.

This idea of an extensive domestic market for the surplus produce of the soil is of the first consequence. It is of all things, that which most effectually conduces to a flourishing state of Agriculture. If the effect of manufactories should be to detach a portion of the hands, which would otherwise be engaged in Tillage, it might possibly cause a smaller quantity of lands to be under cultivation but by their tendency to procure a more certain demand for the surplus produce of the soil, they would, at the same time, cause the lands which were in cultivation to be better improved and more productive. And while, by their influence, the condition of each individual farmer would be meliorated, the total mass of Agricultural production would probably be increased. For this must evidently depend as much, if not more, upon the degree of improvement; than upon the number of acres under culture.

It merits particular observation, that the multiplication of manufactories not only furnishes a Market for those articles, which have been accustomed to be produced in abundance, in a country; but it likewise creates a demand for such as were either unknown or produced in considerable quantities. The bowels as well as the surface of the earth are ransacked for articles which were before neglected. Animals, Plants and Minerals acquire an utility and value, which were before unexplored.

The foregoing considerations seem sufficient to establish, as general propositions, That it is the interest of nations to diversify the industrious pursuits of the individuals, who compose them. That the establishment of manufactures is calculated not only to increase the general stock of useful and productive labour; but even to improve the state of Agriculture in particular; certainly to advance the interests of those who are engaged in it. There are other views, that will be hereafter taken of the subject, which, it is conceived, will serve to confirm these inferences.

Previously to a further discussion of the objections to the encouragement of manufactures which have been stated, it will be of use to see what can be said, in reference to the particular situation of the United States, against the conclusions appearing to result from what has been already offered.

It may be observed, and the idea is of no inconsiderable weight, that however true it might be, that a State, which possessing large tracts of vacant and fertile territory, was at the same time secluded from foreign commerce, would find its interest and the interest of Agriculture, in diverting a part of its population from Tillage to Manufactures; yet it will not follow, that the same is true of a State, which having such vacant and fertile territory, has at the same time ample opportunity of procuring from abroad, on good terms, all the fabrics of which it stands in need, for the supply of its inhabitants. The power of doing this at least secures the great advantage of a division of labor; leaving the farmer free to pursue exclusively the culture of his land, and enabling him to procure with its products the manufactured supplies requisite either to his wants or to his enjoyments. And though it should be true, that in settled countries, the diversification of Industry is conducive to an increase in the productive powers of labour, and to an augmentation of revenue and capital; yet it is scarcely conceivable that there can be any (thing) of so solid and permanent advantage to an uncultivated and unpeopled country as to convert its wastes into cultivated and inhabited districts. If the Revenue, in the mean time, should be less, the Capital, in the event, must be greater.

To these observations, the following appears to be a satisfactory answer—

1. If the system of perfect liberty to industry and commerce were the prevailing system of nations—the arguments which dissuade a country in the predicament of the United States, from the zealous pursuits of manufactures would doubtless have great force. It will not

be affirmed, that they might not be permitted, with few exceptions, to serve as a rule of national conduct. In such a state of things, each country would have the full benefit of its peculiar advantages to compensate for its deficiencies or disadvantages. If one nation were in condition to supply manufactured articles on better terms than another, that other might find an abundant indemnification in a superior capacity to furnish the produce of the soil. And a free exchange, mutually beneficial, of the commodities which each was able to supply, on the best terms, might be carried on between them, supporting in full vigour the industry of each. And though the circumstances which have been mentioned and others, which will be unfolded hereafter render it probable, that nations merely Agricultural would not enjoy the same degree of opulence, in proportion to their numbers, as those which united manufactures with agriculture; yet the progressive improvement of the lands of the former might, in the end, atone for an inferior degree of opulence in the mean time: and in a case in which opposite considerations are pretty equally balanced, the option ought perhaps always to be, in favour of leaving Industry to its own direction.

But the system which has been mentioned, is far from characterising the general policy of Nations. (The prevalent one has been regulated by an opposite spirit.)

The consequence of it is, that the United States are to a certain extent in the situation of a country precluded from foreign Commerce. They can indeed, without difficulty obtain from abroad the manufactured supplies, of which they are in want; but they experience numerous and very injurious impediments to the emission and vent of their own commodities. Nor is this the case in reference to a single foreign nation only. The regulations of several countries, with which we have the most extensive intercourse, throw serious obstructions in the way of the principal staples of the United States.

In such a position of things, the United States cannot exchange with Europe on equal terms; and the want of reciprocity would render them the victim of a system, which should induce them to confine their views to Agriculture and refrain from Manufactures. A constant and encreasing necessity, on their part, for the commodities of Europe, and only a partial and occasional demand for their own, in return, could not but expose them to a state of impoverishment, compared with the opulence to which their political and natural advantages authorise them to aspire.

Remarks of this kind are not made in the spirit of complaint. 'Tis for the nations, whose regulations are alluded to, to judge for themselves, whether, by aiming at too much they do not lose more than they gain. 'Tis for the United States to consider by what means they can render themselves least dependent, on the combinations, right or wrong of foreign policy.

It is no small consolation, that already the measures which have embarrassed our Trade, have accelerated internal improvements, which upon the whole have bettered our affairs. To diversify and extend these improvements is the surest and safest method of indemnifying ourselves for any inconveniences, which those or similar measures have a tendency to beget. If Europe will not take from us the products of our soil, upon terms consistent with our interest, the natural remedy is to contract as fast as possible our wants of her.

2. The conversion of their waste into cultivated lands is certainly a point of great moment in the political calculations of the United States. But the degree in which this may possibly be retarded by the encouragement of manufactories does not appear to countervail the powerful inducements to affording that encouragement.

An observation made in another place is of a nature to have great influence upon this question. If it cannot be denied, that the interests even of Agriculture may be advanced more by having such of the lands of a state as are occupied under good cultivation, than by having a greater quantity occupied under a much inferior cultivation, and if Manufactories, for the reasons assigned, must be admitted to have a tendency to promote a more steady and vigorous cultivation of the lands occupied than would happen without them—it will follow, that they are capable of indemnifying a country for a diminution of the progress of new settlements; and may serve to increase both the capital (value) and the income of its lands, even though they should abrige the number of acres under Tillage.

But it does, by no means, follow, that the progress of new settlements would be retarded by the extension of Manufactures. The desire of being an independent proprietor of land is founded on such strong principles in the human breast, that where the opportunity of becoming so is as great as it is in the United States, the proportion will be small of those, whose situations would otherwise lead to it, who would be diverted from it towards Manufactures. And it is highly probable, as already intimated, that the accessions of foreigners, who originally drawn over by manufacturing views would afterwards abandon them for Agricultural, would be more than equivalent for those of our own Citizens, who might happen to be detached from them.

The remaining objections to a particular encouragement of manufactures in the United States now require to be examined.

One of these turns on the proposition, that Industry, if left to itself, will naturally find its way to the most useful and profitable employment: whence it is inferred, that manufactures without the aid of government will grow up as soon and as fast, as the natural state of things and the interest of the community may require.

Against the solidity of this hypothesis, in the full latitude of the terms, very cogent reasons may be offered. These have relation to—the strong influence of habit and the spirit of imitation—the fear of want of success in untried enterprises—the intrinsic difficulties incident to first essays towards a competition with those who have previously attained to perfection in the business to be attempted—the bounties premiums and other artificial encouragements, with which foreign nations second the exertions of their own Citizens in the branches, in which they are to be rivalled.

Experience teaches, that men are often so much governed by what they are accustomed to see and practice, that the simplest and most obvious improvements, in the (most) ordinary occupations, are adopted with hesitation, reluctance and by slow gradations. The spontaneous transition to new pursuits, in a community long habituated to different ones, may be expected to be attended with proportionably greater difficulty. When former occupations ceased to yield a profit adequate to the subsistence of their followers, or when there was an absolute deficiency of employment in them, owing to the superabundance of hands, changes would ensue; but these changes would be likely to be more tardy than might consist with the interest either of individuals or of the Society. In many cases they would not happen, while a bare support could be ensured by an adherence to ancient courses; though a resort to a more profitable employment might be practicable. To produce the desireable changes, as early as may be expedient, may therefore require the incitement and patronage of government.

The apprehension of failing in new attempts is perhaps a more serious impediment. There are dispositions apt to be attracted by the mere novelty of an undertaking—but these are not always those best calculated to give it success. To this, it is of importance that the confidence of cautious sagacious capitalists both citizens and foreigners, should be excited. And to inspire this description of persons with confidence, it is essential, that they should be made to see in any project, which is new, and for that reason alone, if, for no other, precarious, the prospect of such a degree of countenance and support from government, as may be capable of overcoming the obstacles, inseperable from first experiments.

The superiority antecedently enjoyed by nations, who have pre-occupied and perfected a branch of industry, constitutes a more formidable obstacle, than either of those, which have been mentioned, to the introduction of the same branch into a country, in which it did not before exist. To maintain between the recent establishments of one country and the long matured establishments of another country, a competition upon equal terms, both as to quality and price, is in most cases impracticable. The disparity in the one, or in the other, or in both, must necessarily be so considerable as to forbid a successful rivalship, without the extraordinary aid and protection of government.

But the greatest obstacle of all to the successful prosecution of a new branch of industry in a country, in which it was before unknown, consists, as far as the instances apply, in the bounties premiums and other aids which are granted, in a variety of cases, by the nations, in which the establishments to be imitated are previously introduced. It is well known (and particular examples in the course of this report will be cited) that certain nations grant bounties on the exportation of particular commodities, to enable their own workmen to undersell and supplant all competitors, in the countries to which those commodities are sent. Hence the undertakers of a new manufacture have to contend not only with the natural disadvantages of a new undertaking, but with the gratuities and remunerations which other governments bestow. To be enabled to contend with success, it is evident, that the interference and aid of their own government are indispensible.

Combinations by those engaged in a particular branch of business in one country, to frustrate the first efforts to introduce it into another, by temporary sacrifices, recompensed perhaps by extraordinary indemnifications of the government of such country, are believed to have existed, and are not to be regarded as destitute of probability.

The existence or assurance of aid from the government of the country, in which the business is to be introduced, may be essential to fortify adventurers against the dread of such combinations, to defeat their effects, if formed and to prevent their being formed, by demonstrating that they must in the end prove fruitless.

Whatever room there may be for an expectation that the industry of a people, under the direction of private interest, will upon equal terms find out the most beneficial employment for itself, there is none for a reliance, that it will struggle against the force of unequal terms, or will of itself surmount all the adventitious barriers to a successful competition, which may have been erected either by the advantages naturally acquired from practice and previous possession of the ground, or by those which may have sprung from positive regulations and an artificial policy. This general reflection might alone suffice as an answer to the objection under examination; exclusively of the weighty considerations which have been particularly urged.

The objections to the pursuit of manufactures in the United States, which next present themselves to discussion, represent an impracticability of success, arising from three causes—scarcity of hands—dearness of labour—want of capital.

The two first circumstances are to a certain extent real, and, within due limits, ought to be admitted as obstacles to the success of manufacturing enterprize in the United States. But there are various considerations, which lessen their force, and tend to afford an assurance that they are not sufficient to prevent the advantageous prosecution of many very useful and extensive manufactories.

With regard to scarcity of hands, the fact itself must be applied with no small qualification to certain parts of the United States. There are large districts, which may be considered as pretty fully peopled; and which notwithstanding a continual drain for distant settlement, are thickly interspersed with flourishing and increasing towns. If these districts have not already reached the point, at which the complaint of scarcity of hands ceases, they are not remote from it, and are approaching fast towards it: And having perhaps fewer attractions to agriculture, than some other parts of the Union, they exhibit a proportionably stronger tendency towards other kinds of industry. In these districts, may be discerned, no inconsiderable maturity for manufacturing establishments.

But there are circumstances, which have been already noticed with another view, that materially diminish every where the effect of a scarcity of hands. These circumstances are—the great use which can be made of women and children; on which point a very pregnant and instructive fact has been mentioned—the vast extension given by late improvements to the employment of Machines, which substituting the Agency of fire and water, has prodigiously lessened the necessity for manual labor—the employment of persons ordinarily engaged in other occupations, during the seasons, or hours of leisure; which, besides giving occasion to the exertion of a greater quantity of labour by the same number of persons, and thereby encreasing the general stock of labour, as has been elsewhere remarked, may also be taken into the calculation, as a resource for obviating the scarcity of hands—lastly the attraction of foreign emigrants. Whoever inspects, with a careful eye, the composition of our towns will be made sensible to what an extent this resource may be relied upon. This exhibits a large proportion of ingenious and valuable workmen, in different arts and trades, who, by expatriating from Europe, have improved their own condition, and added to the industry and wealth of the United States. It is a natural inference from the experience, we have already had, that as soon as the United States shall present the countenance of a serious prosecution of Manufactures—as soon as foreign artists shall be made sensible that the state of things here affords a moral certainty of employment and encouragement—competent numbers of European workmen will transplant themselves, effectually to ensure the success of the design. How indeed can it otherwise happen considering the various and powerful inducements, which the situation of this country offers; addressing themselves to so many strong passions and feelings, to so many general and particular interests?

It may be affirmed therefore, in respect to hands for carrying on manufactures, that we shall in great measure trade upon a foreign Stock; reserving our own, for the cultivation of our lands and the manning of our Ships; as far as character and circumstances (shall) incline. It is not unworthy of remark, that the objection to the success of manufactures, deduced from the scarcity of hands, is alike applicable to Trade and Navigation; and yet these are perceived to flourish, without any sensible impediment from that cause.

As to the dearness of labor (another of the obstacles alledged) this has relation principally to two circumstances, one that which has been just discussed, or the scarcity of hands, the other, the greatness of profits.

As far as it is a consequence of the scarcity of hands, it is mitigated by all the considerations which have been adduced as lessening that deficiency.

It is certain too, that the disparity in this respect, between some of the most manufacturing parts of Europe and a large proportion of the United States, is not nearly so great as is commonly imagined. It is also much less in regard to Artificers and manufacturers than in regard to country labourers; and while a careful comparison shews, that there is, in this particular, much exaggeration; it is also evident that the effect of the degree of disparity, which does truly exist, is diminished in proportion to the use which can be made of machinery.

To illustrate this last idea—Let it be supposed, that the difference of price, in two Countries, of a given quantity of manual labour requisite to the fabrication of a given article is as 10; and that some *mechanic power* is introduced into both countries, which performing half the necessary labour, leaves only half to be done by hand, it is evident, that the difference in the cost of the fabrication of the article in question, in the two countries, as far as it is connected with the price of labour, will be reduced from 10. to 5, in consequence of the introduction of that *power*.

This circumstance is worthy of the most particular attention. It diminishes immensely one of the objections most strenuously urged, against the success of manufactures in the United States.

To procure all such machines as are known in any part of Europe, can only require a proper provision and due pains. The knowledge of several of the most important of them is already possessed. The preparation of them here, is in most cases, practicable on nearly equal terms. As far as they depend on Water, some superiority of advantages may be claimed, from the uncommon variety and greater cheapness of situations adapted to Mill seats, with which different parts of the United States abound.

So far as the dearness of labour may be a consequence of the greatness of profits in any branch of business, it is no obstacle to its success. The Undertaker can afford to pay the price.

There are grounds to conclude that undertakers of Manufacturers in this Country can at this time afford to pay higher wages to the workmen they may employ than are paid to similar workmen in

Europe. The prices of foreign fabrics, in the markets of the United States, which will for a long time regulate the prices of the domestic ones, may be considered as compounded of the following ingredients—The first cost of materials, including the Taxes, if any, which are paid upon them where they are made: the expence of grounds, buildings machinery and tools: the wages of the persons employed in the manufactory: the profits on the capital or Stock employed: the commissions of Agents to purchase them where they are made; the expence of transportation to the United States (including insurance and other incidental charges;) the taxes on duties, if any (and fees of office) which are paid on their exportation: the taxes or duties (and fees of office) which are paid on their importation.

As to the first of these items, the cost of materials, the advantage upon the whole, is at present on the side of the United States, and the difference, in their favor, must increase, in proportion as a certain and extensive domestic demand shall induce the proprietors of land to devote more of their attention to the production of those materials. It ought not to escape observation, in a comparison on this point, that some of the principal manufacturing Countries of Europe are much more dependent on foreign supply for the materials of their manufactures, than would be the United States, who are capable of supplying themselves, with a greater abundance, as well as a greater variety of the requisite materials.

As to the second item, the expence of grounds buildings machinery and tools, an equality at least may be assumed; since advantages in some particulars will counterbalance temporary disadvantages in others.

As to the third item, or the article of wages, the comparison certainly turns against the United States, though as before observed not in so great a degree as is commonly supposed.

The fourth item is alike applicable to the foreign and to the domestic manufacture. It is indeed more properly a *result* than a particular, to be compared.

But with respect to all the remaining items, they are alone applicable to the foreign manufacture, and in the strictest sense extraordinaries; constituting a sum of extra charge on the foreign fabric, which cannot be estimated, at less than (from 15 to 30) Per Cent. on the cost of it at the manufactory.

This sum of extra charge may confidently be regarded as more than a Counterpoise for the real difference in the price of labour; and is a satisfactory proof that manufactures may prosper in defiance of it in the United States. To the general allegation, connected with the circumstances of scarcity of hands and dearness of labour, that extensive manufactures can only grow out of a redundant or full population, it will be sufficient, to answer generally, that the fact has been otherwise—That the situation alleged to be an essential condition of success, has not been that of several nations, at periods when they had already attained to maturity in a variety of manufactures.

The supposed want of Capital for the prosecution of manufactures in the United States is the most indefinite of the objections which are usually opposed to it.

It is very difficult to pronounce any thing precise concerning the real extent of the monied capital of a Country, and still more concerning the proportion which it bears to the objects that invite the employment of Capital. It is not less difficult to pronounce how far the *effect* of any given quantity of money, as capital, or in other words, as a medium for circulating the industry and property of a nation, may be encreased by the very circumstance of the additional motion, which is given to it by new objects of employment. That effect, like the momentum of descending bodies, may not improperly be represented, as in a compound ratio to *mass* and *velocity*. It seems pretty certain, that a given sum of money, in a situation, in which the quick impulses of commercial activity were little felt, would appear inadequate to the circulation of as great a quantity of industry and property, as in one, in which their full influence was experienced.

It is not obvious, why the same objection might not as well be made to external commerce as to manufactures; since it is manifest that our immense tracts of land occupied and unoccupied are capable of giving employment to more capital than is actually bestowed upon them. It is certain, that the United States offer a vast field for the advantageous employment of Capital; but it does not follow, that there will not be found, in one way or another, a sufficient fund for the successful prosecution of any species of industry which is likely to prove truly beneficial.

The following considerations are of a nature to remove all inquietude on the score of want of Capital.

The introduction of Banks, as has been shewn on another occasion, has a powerful tendency to extend the active Capital of a Country. Experience of the Utility of these Institutions is multiplying them in the United States. It is probable that they will be established wherever they can exist with advantage; and wherever, they can be supported, if administered with prudence, they will add new energies to all pecuniary operations.

The aid of foreign Capital may safely, and, with considerable latitude be taken into calculation. Its instrumentality has been long experienced in our external commerce; and it has begun to be felt in various other modes. Not only our funds, but our Agriculture and other internal improvements have been animated by it. It has already in a few instances extended even to our manufactures.

It is a well known fact, that there are parts of Europe, which have more Capital, than profitable domestic objects of employment. Hence, among other proofs, the large loans continually furnished to foreign states. And it is equally certain that the capital of other parts may find more profitable employment in the United States, than at home. And notwithstanding there are weighty inducements to prefer the employment of capital at home even at less profit, to an investment of it abroad, though with greater gain, yet these inducements are overruled either by a deficiency of employment or by a very material difference in profit. Both these Causes operate to produce a transfer of foreign capital to the United States. 'Tis certain, that various objects in this country hold out advantages, which are with difficulty to be equalled elsewhere; and under the increasingly favorable impressions, which are entertained of our government, the attractions will become more and More strong. These impressions will prove a rich mine of prosperity to the Country, if they are confirmed and strengthened by the progress of our affairs. And to secure this advantage, little more is now necessary, than to foster industry, and cultivate order and tranquility, at home and abroad.

It is not impossible, that there may be persons disposed to look with a jealous eye on the introduction of foreign Capital, as if it were an instrument to deprive our own citizens of the profits of our own industry: But perhaps there never could be a more unreasonable jealousy. Instead of being viewed as a rival, it ought to be Considered as a most valuable auxiliary; conducing to put in Motion a greater Quantity of productive labour, and a greater portion of useful enterprise than could exist without it. It is at least evident, that in a

Country situated like the United States, with an infinite fund of resources yet to be unfolded, every farthing of foreign capital, which is laid out in internal ameliorations, and in industrious establishments of a permanent nature, is a precious acquisition.

And whatever be the objects which originally attract foreign Capital, when once introduced, it may be directed towards any purpose of beneficial exertion, which is desired. And to detain it among us, there can be no expedient so effectual as to enlarge the sphere, within which it may be usefully employed: Though induced merely with views to speculations in the funds, it may afterwards be rendered subservient to the Interests of Agriculture, Commerce and Manufactures.

But the attraction of foreign Capital for the direct purpose of Manufactures ought not be deemed a chimerial expectation. There are already examples of it, as remarked in another place. And the examples, if the disposition be cultivated can hardly fail to multiply. There are also instances of another kind, which serve to strengthen the expectation. Enterprises for improving the Public Communications, by cutting canals, opening the obstructions in Rivers and erecting bridges, have received very material aid from the same source.

When the Manufacturing Capitalist of Europe shall advert to the many important advantages, which have been intimated, in the Course of this report, he cannot but perceive very powerful inducements to a transfer of himself and his Capital to the United States. Among the reflections, which a most interesting peculiarity of situation is calculated to suggest, it cannot excape his observation, as a circumstance of Moment in the calculation that the progressive population and improvement of the United States insure a continually increasing domestic demand for the fabrics which he shall produce, not to be affected by any external casualties or vicissitudes.

But while there are Circumstances sufficiently strong to authorise a considerable degree of reliance on the aid of foreign Capital towards the attainment of the object in view, it is satisfactory to have good grounds of assurance, that there are domestic resources of themselves adequate to it. It happens, that there is a species of Capital actually existing within the United States, which relieves from all inquietude on the score of want of Capital—This is the funded Debt.

The effect of a funded debt, as a species of Capital, has been

Noticed upon a former Occasion; but a more particular elucidation of the point seems to be required by the stress which is here laid upon it. This shall accordingly be attempted.

Public Funds answer the purpose of Capital, from the estimation in which they are usually held by Monied men; and consequently from the Ease and dispatch with which they can be turned into money. This capacity of prompt convertibility into money causes a transfer of stock to be in a great number of Cases equivalent to a payment in coin. And where it does not happen to suit the party who is to receive, to accept a transfer of Stock, the party who is to pay, is never at a loss to find elsewhere a purchaser of his Stock, who will furnish him in lieu of it, with the Coin of which he stands in need. Hence in a sound and settled state of the public funds, a man possessed of a sum in them can embrace any scheme of business, which offers, with as much confidence as if he were possessed of an equal sum in Coin.

This operation of public funds as capital is too obvious to be denied; but it is objected to the Idea of their operating as an *augmentation* of the Capital of the community, that they serve to occasion the *destruction* of some other capital to an equal amount.

The Capital which alone they can be supposed to destroy must consist of—The annual revenue, which is applied to the payment of Interest on the debt, and to the gradual redemption of the principal— The amount of the Coin, which is employed in circulating the funds, or, in other words, in effecting the different alienations which they undergo.

But the following appears to be the true and accurate view of this matter.

First. As to the point of the Annual Revenue requisite for Payment of interest and redemption of principal.

As a determinate proportion will tend to perspicuity in the reasoning, let it be supposed that the annual revenue to be applied, corresponding with the modification of the 6 per Cent stock of the United States, is in the ratio of eight upon the hundred, that is in the first instance six on Account of interest, and two on account of Principal.

Thus far it is evident, that the Capital destroyed to the capital created, would bear no greater proportion, than 8 to 100. There would be withdrawn from the total mass of other capitals a sum of eight dollars to be paid to the public creditor; while he would be possessed of a sum of One Hundred dollars, ready to be applied to any purpose, to be embarked in any enterprize, which might appear to him eligible. Here then the *Augmentation* of Capital, or the excess of that which is produced, beyond that which is destroyed is equal to Ninety two dollars. To this conclusion, it may be objected, that the sum of Eight dollars is to be withdrawn annually, until the whole hundred is extinguished, and it may be inferred, that in process of time a capital will be destroyed equal to that which is at first created.

But it is nevertheless true, that during the whole of the interval, between the creation of the Capital of 100 dollars, and its reduction to a sum not greater than that of the annual revenue appropriated to its redemption—there will be a greater active capital in existence than if no debt had been Contracted. The sum drawn from other Capitals *in any one year* will not exceed eight dollars; but there will be *at every instant of time* during the whole period, in question a sum corresponding *with so much of the principal,* as remains *unredeemed,* in the hands of some person, or other, employed, or ready to be employed in some profitable undertaking. There will therefore constantly be more capital, in capacity to be employed, than capital taken from employment. The excess for the first year has been stated to be Ninety two dollars; it will diminish yearly, but there always will be an excess, until the principal of the debt is brought to a level with the *redeeming annuity,* that is, in the case which has been assumed by way of example, to *eight dollars.* The reality of this excess becomes palpable, if it be supposed, as often happens, that the citizen of a foreign Country imports into the United States 100 dollars for the purchase of an equal sum of public debt. Here is an absolute augmentation of the mass of Circulating Coin to the extent of 100 dollars. At the end of a year the foreigner is presumed to draw back eight dollars on account of his Principal and Interest, but he still leaves, Ninety two of his original Deposit in circulation, as he in like manner leaves Eighty four at the end of the second year, drawing back then also the annuity of Eight Dollars: And thus the Matter proceeds; The capital left in circulation diminishing each year, and coming nearer to the level of the annuity drawnback. There are however some differences in the ultimate operation of the part of the debt, which is purchased by foreigners, and that which remains in the hands of citizens. But the general effect in each case, though in different degrees, is to add to the active capital of the Country.

Hitherto the reasoning has proceeded on a concession of the position, that there is a destruction of some other capital, to the extent of the annuity appropriated to the payment of the Interest and the redemption of the principal of the debt but in this, too much has been conceded. There is at most a temporary transfer of some other capital, to the amount of the Annuity, from those who pay to the Creditor who receives; which he again restores to the circulation to resume the offices of a capital. This he does either immediately by employing the money in some branch of Industry, or mediately by lending it to some other person, who does so employ it or by spending it on his own maintenance. In either supposition there is no destruction of capital, there is nothing more than a suspension of its motion for a time; that is, while it is passing from the hands of those who pay into the Public coffers, and thence through the public Creditor into some other Channel of circulation. When the payments of interest are periodical and quick and made by instrumentality of Banks the diversion or suspension of capital may almost be denominated momentary. Hence the deduction on this Account is far less, than it at first sight appears to be.

There is evidently, as far as regards the annuity no destruction nor transfer of any other Capital, than that portion of the income of each individual, which goes to make up the Annuity. The land which furnishes the Farmer with the sum which he is to contribute remains the same; and the like may be observed of other Capitals. Indeed as far as the Tax, which is the object of contribution (as frequently happens, when it does not oppress, by its weight) may have been a Motive to *greater exertion* in any occupation; it may even serve to encrease the contributory Capital: This idea is not without importance in the general view of the subject.

It remains to see, what further deduction ought to be made from the capital which is created, by the existence of the Debt; on account of the coin, which is employed in its circulation. This is susceptible of much less precise calculation, than the Article which has just been discussed. It is impossible to say what proportion of coin is necessary to carry on the alienations which any species of property usually undergoes. The quantity indeed varies according to circumstances. But it may still without hesitation be pronounced, from the quickness of the rotation, or rather of the transitions, that the *medium* of circulation always bears but a small proportion to the amount of the *property* circulated. And it is thence satisfactorily deducible, that the coin employed in the Negociations of the funds and which serves to give them activity, as capital, is incomparably less than the sum of the debt negotiated for the purposes of business.

It ought not however, to be omitted, that the negotiation of the funds becomes itself a distinct business; which employs, and by employing diverts a portion of the circulating coin from other pursuits. But making due allowance for this circumstance there is no reason to conclude, that the effect of the diversion of coin in the whole operation bears any considerable proportion to the amount of the Capital to which it gives activity. The sum of the debt in circulation is continually at the Command, of any useful enterprise—the coin itself which circulates it, is never more than momentarily suspended from its ordinary functions. It experiences an incessant and rapid flux and reflux to and from the Channels of industry to those of speculations in the funds.

There are strong circumstances in confirmation of this Theory. The force of Monied Capital which has been displayed in Great Britain, and the height to which every species of industry has grown up under it, defy a solution from the quantity of coin which that kingdom has ever possessed. Accordingly it has been Coeval with its funding system, the prevailing opinion of the men of business, and of the generality of the most sagacious theorists of that country, that the operation of the public funds as capital has contributed to the effect in question. Among ourselves appearances thus far favour the same Conclusion. Industry in general seems to have been reanimated. There are symptoms indicating an extension of our Commerce. Our navigation has certainly of late had a Considerable spring, and there appears to be in many parts of the Union a command of capital, which till lately, since the revolution at least, was unknown. But it is at the same time to be acknowledged, that other circumstances have concurred, (and in a great degree) in producing the present state of things, and that the appearances are not yet sufficiently decisive, to be intirely relied upon.

In the question under discussion, it is important to distinguish between an *absolute increase of Capital, or an accession of real wealth,* and *an artificial increase of Capital,* as an engine of business, or as an instrument of industry and Commerce. In the first sense, a funded debt has no pretensions to being deemed an increase of Capital; in the last, it has pretensions which are not easy to be controverted.

Of a similar nature is bank credit and in an inferior degree, every species of private credit.

But though a funded debt is not in the first instance, an absolute increase of Capital, or an augmentation of real wealth; yet by serving as a New power in the operation of industry, it has within certain bounds a tendency to increase the real wealth of a Community, in like manner as money borrowed by a thrifty farmer, to be laid out in the improvement of his farm may, in the end, add to his Stock of real riches.

There are respectable individuals, who from a just aversion to an accumulation of Public debt, are unwilling to concede to it any kind of utility, who can discern no good to alleviate the ill with which they suppose it pregnant; who cannot be persuaded that it ought in any sense to be viewed as an increase in capital lest it should be inferred, that the more debt the more capital, the greater the burthens the greater the blessings of the community.

But it interests the public Councils to estimate every object as it truly is; to appreciate how far the good in any measure is compensated by the ill; or the ill by the good, Either of them is seldom unmixed.

Neither will it follow, that an accumulation of debt is desireable, because a certain degree of it operates as capital. There may be a plethora in the political, as in the Natural body; There may be a state of things in which any such artificial capital is unnecessary. The debt too may be swelled to such a size, as that the greatest part of it may cease to be useful as a Capital, serving only to pamper the dissipation of idle and dissolute individuals: as that the sums required to pay the Interest upon it may become oppressive, and beyond the means, which a government can employ, consistently with its tranquility, to raise them; as that the resources of taxation, to face the debt, may have been strained too far to admit of extensions adequate to exigencies, which regard the public safety.

Where this critical point is, cannot be pronounced, but it is impossible to believe, that there is not such a point.

And as the vicissitudes of Nations beget a perpetual tendency to the accumulation of debt, there ought to be in every government a perpetual, anxious and unceasing effort to reduce that, which at any time exists, as fast as shall be practicable consistently with integrity and good faith.

Reasonings on a subject comprehending ideas so abstract and complex, so little reducible to precise calculation as those which enter into the question just discussed, are always attended with a danger of runing into fallacies. Due allowance ought therefore to be made for this possibility. But as far as the Nature of the subject admits of it, there appears to be satisfactory ground for a belief, that the public funds operate as a resource of capital to the Citizens of the United States, and, if they are a resource at all, it is an extensive one.

To all the arguments which are brought to evince the impracticability of success in manufacturing establishments in the United States, it might have been a sufficient answer to have referred to the experience of what has been already done. It is certain that several important branches have grown up and flourished with a rapidity which surprises: affording an encouraging assurance of success in future attempts: of these it may not be improper to enumerate the most considerable.

I of Skins.	Tanned and tawed leather dressed skins, shoes, boots and Slippers, harness and sadlery of all kinds. Portmanteau's and trunks, leather breeches, gloves, muffs and tippets, parchment and Glue.
II of Iron.	Barr and Sheet Iron, Steel, Nail-rods and Nails, implements of husbandry, Stoves, pots and other household utensils, the steel and Iron work of carriages and for Shipbuilding, Anchors, scale beams and Weights and Various tools of Artificers, arms of different kinds; though the manufacture of these last has of late diminished for want of demand.
III of Wood.	Ships, Cabinet Wares and Turnery, Wool and Cotton cards and other Machinery for manufactures and husbandry, Mathematical instruments, Coopers wares of every kind.
IV of Flax and Hemp.	Cables, sail-cloth, Cordage, twine and pack-thread.

V   Bricks and coarse tiles and Potters Wares.

VI   Ardent Spirits and malt liquors.

VII Writing and printing Paper, sheathing and wrapping Paper, pasteboards, fillers or press papers, paper hangings.

VIII Hats of furr and Wool and of mixtures of both, Womens Stuff and Silk shoes.

IX   Refined Sugars

X   Oil of Animals and seeds; Soap, Spermaceti and Tallow Candles.

XI   Copper and brass wares, particularly utensils for distillers, Sugar refiners and brewers, And—Irons and other Articles for household Use, philosophical apparatus

XII Tin Wares, for most purposes of Ordinary use.

XIII Carriages of all kinds

XIV Snuff, chewing and smoking Tobacco.

XV   Starch and Hairpowder.

XVI Lampblack and other painters colours,

XVII Gunpowder

Besides manufactories of these articles which are carried on as regular Trades, and have attained to a considerable degree of maturity, there is a vast scene of household manufacturing, which contributes more largely to the supply of the Community, than could be imagined; without having made it an object of particular enquiry. This observation is the pleasing result of the investigation, to which the subject of the report has led, and is applicable as well to the Southern as to the middle and Northern States; great quantities of coarse cloths, coatings, serges, and flannels, linsey Woolseys, hosiery of Wool, cotton and thread, coarse fustians, jeans and Muslins, checked and striped cotton and linen goods, bed ticks, Coverlets and Counterpanes, Tow linens, coarse shirtings, sheetings, toweling and table linen, and various mixtures of wool and cotton, and of Cotton and flax are made in the household way, and in many instances to an extent not only sufficient for the supply of the families in which they are made, but for sale, and (even in some cases) for exportation. It is computed in a number of districts that 2/3, 3/4 and even 4/5 of all the clothing of the Inhabitants are made by themselves. The importance of so great a progress, as appears to have been made in family Manufactures, within a few years, both in a moral and political view, renders the fact highly interesting.

Neither does the above enumeration comprehend all the articles that are manufactured as regular Trades. Many others occur, which are equally well established, but which not being of equal importance have been omitted. And there are many attempts still in their Infancy, which though attended with very favorable appearances, could not have been properly comprized in an enumeration of manufactories already established. There are other articles also of great importance, which tho' strictly speaking manufactures are omitted, as being immediately connected with husbandry: such are flour, pot and pearl ash, Pitch, tar, turpentine and the like.

There remains to be noticed an objection to the encouragement of manufactures, of a nature different from those which question the probability of success. This is derived from its supposed tendency to give a monopoly of advantages to particular classes at the expence of the rest of the community, who, it is affirmed, would be able to procure the requisite supplies of manufactured articles on better terms from foreigners, than from our own Citizens, and who it is alledged, are reduced to a necessity of paying an enhanced price for whatever they want, by every measure, which obstructs the free competition of foreign commodities.

It is not an unreasonable supposition, that measures, which serve to abridge the free competition of foreign Articles, have a tendency to occasion an enhancement of prices and it is not to be denied that such is the effect in a number of Cases; but the fact does not uniformly correspond with the theory. A reduction of prices has in several instances immediately succeeded the establishment of a domestic manufacture. Whether it be that foreign Manufacturers endeavour to supplant by underselling our own, or whatever else be the cause, the effect has been such as is stated, and the reverse of what might have been expected.

But though it were true, that the immediate and certain effect of regulations controlling the competition of foreign with domestic fabrics was an increase of price, it is universally true, that the contrary is the ultimate effect with every successful manufacture. When a domestic manufacture has attained to perfection, and has engaged in the prosecution of it a competent number of Persons, it invariably becomes cheaper. Being free from the heavy charges, which attend the importation of foreign commodities, it can be afforded, and accordingly seldom or never fails to be sold Cheaper, in process of time, than was the foreign Article for which it is a substitute. The internal competition, which takes place, soon does away every thing like Monopoly, and by degrees reduces the price of the Article to the *minimum* of a reasonable profit on the Capital employed. This accords with the reason of the thing and with experience.

Whence it follows, that it is the interest of a community with a view to eventual and permanent economy, to encourage the growth of manufactures. In a national view, a temporary enhancement of price must always be well compensated by a permanent reduction of it.

It is a reflection, which may with propriety be indulged here, that this eventual diminution of the prices of manufactured Articles; which is the result of internal manufacturing establishments, has a direct and very important tendency to benefit agriculture. It enables the farmer, to procure with a smaller quantity of his labour, the manufactured produce of which he stands in need, and consequently increases the value of his income and property.

The objections which are commonly made to the expediency of encouraging, and to the probability of succeeding in manufacturing pursuits, in the United states, having now been discussed; the Considerations which have appeared in the Course of the discussion, recommending that species of industry to the patronage of the Government, will be materially strengthened by a few general and some particular topics, which have been naturally reserved for subsequent Notice.

I. There seems to be a moral certainty, that the trade of a country which is both manufacturing and Agricultural will be more lucrative and prosperous, than that of a Country, which is, merely Agricultural.

One reason for this is found in that general effort of nations (which has been already mentioned) to procure from their own soils, the articles of prime necessity requisite to their own consumption and use; and which serves to render their demand for a foreign supply of such articles in a great degree occasional and contingent. Hence, while the necessities of nations exclusively devoted to Agriculture, for the fabrics of manufacturing states are constant and regular, the wants of the latter for the products of the former, are liable to very considerable fluctuations and interruptions. The great inequalities resulting from difference of seasons, have been elsewhere remarked: This uniformity of demand on one side, and unsteadiness of it, on the other, must necessarily have a tendency to cause the general course of the exchange of commodities between the parties to turn to the disadvantage of the merely agricultural States. Peculiarity of situation, a climate and soil adapted to the production of peculiar commodities, may, sometimes, contradict the rule; but there is every reason to believe that it will be found in the Main, a just one.

Another circumstance which gives a superiority of commercial advantage to states, that manufacture as well as cultivate, consists in the more numerous attractions, which a more diversified market offers to foreign Customers, and greater scope, which it affords to mercantile enterprise. It is a position of indisputable truth in Commerce, depending too on very obvious reasons, that the greatest resort will ever be to those marts where commodities, while equally abundant, are most various. Each difference of kind holds out an additional inducement. And it is a position not less clear, that the field of enterprise must be enlarged to the Merchants of a Country, in proportion to the variety as well as the abundance of commodities which they find at home for exportation to foreign Markets.

A third circumstance, perhaps not inferior to either of the other two, conferring the superiority which has been stated has relation to the stagnations of demand for certain commodities which at some time or other interfere more or less with the sale of all. The Nation which can bring to Market, but few articles is likely to be more quickly and sensibly affected by such stagnations, than one, which is always possessed of a great variety of commodities. The former frequently finds too great a proportion of its stock of materials, for sale or exchange, lying on hand—or is obliged to make injurious sacrifices to supply its wants of foreign articles, which are *Numerous* and *urgent,* in proportion to the smallness of the number of its own. The latter commonly finds itself indemnified, by the high prices of some articles, for the low prices of others—and the Prompt and advantageous sale of those articles which are in demand enables its merchant the better to wait for a favorable change, in respect to those which are not. There is ground to believe, that a difference of situation, in this particular, has immensely different effects upon the wealth and prosperity of Nations.

From these circumstances collectively, two important inferences are to be drawn, one, that there is always a higher probability of a favorable balance of Trade, in regard to countries in which manufactures founded on the basis of a thriving Agriculture flourish, than in regard to those, which are confined wholly or almost wholly to Agriculture; the other (which is also a consequence of the first) that countries of the former description are likely to possess more pecuniary wealth, or money, than those of the latter.

Facts appear to correspond with this conclusion. The importations of manufactured supplies seem invariably to drain the merely Agricultural people of their wealth. Let the situation of the manufacturing countries of Europe be compared in this particular, with that of Countries which only cultivate, and the disparity will be striking. Other causes, it is true, help to Account for this disparity between some of them; and among these causes, the relative state of Agriculture; but between others of them, the most prominent circumstance of dissimilitude arises from the Comparative state of Manufactures. In corroboration of the same idea, it ought not to escape remark, that the West India Islands, the soils of which are the most fertile, and the Nation, which in the greatest degree supplies the rest of the world, with the precious metals, exchange to a loss with almost every other Country.

As far as experience at home may guide, it will lead to the same conclusion. Previous to the revolution, the quantity of coin, possessed by the colonies, which now compose the United states, appeared, to be inadequate to their circulation; and their debt to Great-Britain was progressive. Since the Revolution, the States, in which manufactures have most increased, have recovered fastest from the injuries of the late War, and abound most in pecuniary resources.

It ought to be admitted, however in this as in the preceding case, that causes irrelative to the state of manufactures account, in a degree, for the Phoenomena remarked. The continual progress of new settlements has a natural tendency to occasion an unfavorable balance of Trade; though it indemnifies for the inconvenience, by that increase of the national capital which flows from the conversion of waste into improved lands: And the different degrees of external commerce, which are carried on by the different States, may make material differences in the comparative state of their wealth. The first circumstance has reference to the deficiency of coin and the increase of debt previous to the revolution; the last to the advantages which the most manufacturing states appear to have enjoyed, over the others, since the termination of the late War.

But the uniform appearance of an abundance of specie, as the concomitant of a flourishing state of manufactures and of the reverse, where they do not prevail, afford a strong presumption of their favourable operation upon the wealth of a Country.

Not only the wealth; but the independence and security of a Country, appear to be materially connected with the prosperity of manufactures. Every nation, with a view to those great objects, ought to endeavour to possess within itself all the essentials of national supply. These comprise the means of *Subsistence habitation clothing* and *defence*.

The possession of these is necessary to the perfection of the body politic, to the safety as well as to the welfare of the society; the want of either, is the want of an important organ of political life and Motion; and in the various crises which await a state, it must severely feel the effects of any such deficiency. The extreme embarrassments of the United States during the late War, from an incapacity of supplying themselves, are still matter of keen recollection: A future war might be expected again to exemplify the mischiefs and dangers of a situation, to which that incapacity is still in too great a degree applicable, unless changed by timely and vigorous exertion. To effect this change as fast as shall be prudent, merits all the attention and all the Zeal of our Public Councils; 'tis the next great work to be accomplished.

The want of a Navy to protect our external commerce, as long as it shall Continue, must render it a peculiarly precarious reliance, for the supply of essential articles, and must serve to strengthen prodigiously the arguments in favour of manufactures.

To these general Considerations are added some of a more particular nature.

Our distance from Europe, the great fountain of manufactured supply, subjects us in the existing state of things, to inconvenience and loss in two Ways.

The bulkiness of those commodities which are the chief productions of the soil, necessarily imposes very heavy charges on their transportation, to distant markets. These charges, in the Cases, in which the nations, to whom our products are sent, maintain a Competition in the supply of their own markets, principally fall upon us, and form material deductions from the primitive value of the articles furnished. The charges on manufactured supplies, brought from Europe are greatly enhanced by the same circumstance of distance. These charges, again, in the cases in which our own industry maintains no competition, in our own markets, also principally fall upon us; and are an additional cause of extraordinary deduction from the primitive value of our own products; these being the materials of exchange for the foreign fabrics, which we consume.

The equality and moderation of individual property and the growing settlements of new districts, occasion in this country an unusual demand for coarse manufactures; The charges of which being greater in proportion to their greater bulk augment the disadvantage, which has been just described.

As in most countries domestic supplies maintain a very considerable competition with such foreign productions of the soil, as are imported for sale; if the extensive establishment of Manufactories in the United states does not create a similar competition in respect to manufactured articles, it appears to be clearly deducible, from the Considerations which have been mentioned, that they must sustain a double loss in their exchanges with foreign Nations; strongly conducive to an unfavorable balance of Trade, and very prejudicial to their Interests.

These disadvantages press with no small weight, on the landed interest of the Country. In seasons of peace, they cause a serious deduction from the intrinsic value of the products of the soil. In the time of a War, which shou'd either involve ourselves, or another nation, possessing a Considerable share of our carrying trade, the charges on the transportation of our commodities, bulky as most of them are, could hardly fail to prove a grievous burthen to the farmer; while obliged to depend in so great degree as he now does, upon foreign markets for the vent of the surplus of his labour.

As far as the prosperity of the Fisheries of the United states is impeded by the want of an adequate market, there arises another special reason for desiring the extension of manufactures. Besides the fish, which in many places, would be likely to make a part of the subsistence of the persons employed; it is known that the oils, bones and skins of marine animals, are of extensive use in various manufactures. Hence the prospect of an additional demand for the produce of the Fisheries.

One more point of view only remains in which to Consider the expediency of encouraging manufactures in the United states.

It is not uncommon to meet with an opinion that though the promoting of manufactures may be the interest of a part of the Union, it is contrary to that of another part. The Northern and southern regions are sometimes represented as having adverse interests in this respect. Those are called Manufacturing, these Agricultural states; and a species of opposition is imagined to subsist between the Manufacturing and Agricultural interests.

This idea of an opposition between those two interests is the common error of the early periods of every country, but experience gradually dissipates it. Indeed they are perceived so often to succour and to befriend each other, that they come at length to be considered as one: a supposition which has been frequently abused and is not universally true. Particular encouragements of particular manufactures may be of a Nature to sacrifice the interests of landholders to those of manufacturers; But it is nevertheless a maxim well established by experience, and generally acknowledged, where there has been sufficient experience, that the *aggregate* prosperity of manufactures, and the *aggregate* prosperity of Agriculture are intimately connected. In the Course of the discussion which has had place, various weighty considerations have been adduced operating in support of that maxim. Perhaps the superior steadiness of the demand of a domestic market for the surplus produce of the soil, is alone a convincing argument of its truth.

Ideas of a contrariety of interests between the Northern and southern regions of the Union, are in the Main as unfounded as they are mischievous. The diversity of Circumstances on which such contrariety is usually predicated, authorises a directly contrary conclusion. Mutual wants constitute one of the strongest links of political connection, and the extent of these bears a natural proportion to the diversity in the means of mutual supply.

Suggestions of an opposite complexion are ever to be deplored, as unfriendly to the steady pursuit of one great common cause, and to the perfect harmony of all the parts.

In proportion as the mind is accustomed to trace the intimate connexion of interest, which subsists between all the parts of a Society united under the *same* government—the infinite variety of channels which serve to Circulate the prosperity of each to and through the rest—in that proportion will it be little apt to be disturbed by solicitudes and Apprehensions which originate in local discriminations. It is a truth as important as it is agreeable, and one to which it is not easy to imagine exceptions, that every thing tending to establish *substantial* and *permanent order*, in the affairs of a Country, to increase the total mass of industry and opulence, is ultimately beneficial to every part of it. On the Credit of this great truth, an acquiescence may safely be accorded, from every quarter, to all institutions and arrangements, which promise a confirmation of public order, and an augmentation of National Resource.

But there are more particular considerations which serve to fortify the idea, that the encouragement of manufactures is the interest of all parts of the Union. If the Northern and middle states should be the principal scenes of such establishments, they would immediately benefit the more southern, by creating a demand for productions; some of which they have in common with the other states, and others of which are either peculiar to them, or more abundant, or of better quality, than elsewhere. These productions, principally are Timber, flax, Hemp, Cotton, Wool, raw silk, Indigo, iron, lead, furs, hides, skins and coals. Of these articles Cotton and Indigo are peculiar to the southern states; as are hitherto *Lead* and *Coal*. Flax and Hemp are or may be raised in greater abundance there, than in the More

Northern states; and the Wool of Virginia is said to be of better quality than that of any other state: a Circumstance rendered the more probable by the reflection that Virginia embraces the same latitudes with the finest Wool Countries of Europe. The Climate of the south is also better adapted to the production of silk.

The extensive cultivation of Cotton can perhaps hardly be expected, but from the previous establishment of domestic Manufactories of the Article; and the surest encouragement and vent, for the others, would result from similar establishments in respect to them.

If then, it satisfactorily appears, that it is the Interest of the United states, generally, to encourage manufactures, it merits particular attention, that there are circumstances, which Render the present a critical moment for entering with Zeal upon the important business. The effort cannot fail to be materially seconded by a considerable and encreasing influx of money, in consequence of foreign speculations in the funds—and by the disorders, which exist in different parts of Europe.

The first circumstance not only facilitates the execution of manufacturing enterprises; but it indicates them as a necessary mean to turn the thing itself to advantage, and to prevent its being eventually an evil. If useful employment be not found for the Money of foreigners brought to the country to be invested in purchases of the public debt, it will quickly be reexported to defray the expence of an extraordinary consumption of foreign luxuries; and distressing drains of our specie may hereafter be experienced to pay the interest and redeem the principal of the purchased debt.

This useful employment too ought to be of a Nature to produce solid and permanent improvements. If the money merely serves to give a temporary spring to foreign commerce; as it cannot procure new and lasting outlets for the products of the Country; there will be no real or durable advantage gained. As far as it shall find its way in Agricultural ameliorations, in opening canals, and in similar improvements, it will be productive of substantial utility. But there is reason to doubt, whether in such channels it is likely to find sufficient employment, and still more whether many of those who possess it, would be as readily attracted to objects of this nature, as to manufacturing pursuits; which bear greater analogy to those to which they are accustomed, and to the spirit generated by them.

To open the one field, as well as the other, will at least secure a better prospect of useful employment, for whatever accession of money, there has been or may be.

There is at the present juncture a certain fermentation of mind, a certain activity of speculation and enterprise which if properly directed may be made subservient to useful purposes; but which if left entirely to itself, may be attended with pernicious effects.

The disturbed state of Europe, inclining its citizens to emigration, the requisite workmen, will be more easily acquired, than at another time; and the effect of multiplying the opportunities of employment to those who emigrate, may be an increase of the number and extent of valuable acquisitions to the population arts and industry of the Country. To find pleasure in the calamities of other nations, would be criminal; but to benefit ourselves, by opening an asylum to those who suffer, in consequence of them, is as justifiable as it is politic.

A full view having now been taken of the inducements to the promotion of Manufactures in the United states, accompanied with an examination of the principal objections which are commonly urged *in opposition*, it is proper in the next place, to consider the means, by which it may be effected, as introductory to a Specification of the objects which in the present state of things appear the most fit to be encouraged, and of the particular measures which it may be adviseable to adopt, in respect to each.

In order to a better judgment of the Means proper to be resorted to by the United states, it will be of use to Advert to those which have been employed with success in other Countries. The principal of these are.

I. Protecting duties—or duties on those foreign articles which are the rivals of the domestic ones, intended to be encouraged.

Duties of this Nature evidently amount to a virtual bounty on the domestic fabrics since by enhancing the charges on foreign Articles, they enable the National Manufacturers to undersell all their foreign Competitors. The propriety of this species of encouragement need not be dwelt upon; as it is not only a clear result from the numerous topics which have been suggested, but is sanctioned by the laws of the United states in a variety of instances; it has the additional recommendation of being a resource of revenue. Indeed all the duties imposed on imported articles, though with an exclusive view to Revenue, have the effect in Contemplation, and except where

they fall on raw materials wear a beneficent aspect towards the manufactures of the Country.

II. Prohibitions of rival articles or duties equivalent to prohibitions.

This is another and an efficacious mean of encouraging national
manufactures, but in general it is only fit to be employed when a
manufacture, has made such a progress and is in so many hands as
to insure a due competition, and an adequate supply on reasonable
terms. Of duties equivalent to prohibitions, there are examples in
the Laws of the United States, and there are other Cases to which
the principle may be advantageously extended, but they are not
numerous.

Considering a monopoly of the domestic market to its own manufacturers as the reigning policy of manufacturing Nations, a similar
policy on the part of the United states in every proper instance, is
dictated, it might almost be said, by the principles of distributive
justice; certainly by the duty of endeavouring to secure to their own
Citizens a reciprocity of advantages.

III. Prohibitions of the exportation of the materials of manufactures.

The desire of securing a cheap and plentiful supply for the
national workmen, and, where the article is either peculiar to the
Country, or of peculiar quality there, the jealousy of enabling foreign
workmen to rival those of the nation, with its own Materials, are the
leading motives to this species of regulation. It ought not to be
affirmed, that it is no instance proper, but it is certainly one which
ought to be adopted with great circumspection and only in very plain
Cases. It is seen at once, that its immediate operation, is to abridge
the demand and keep down the price of the produce of some other
branch of industry, generally speaking, of Agriculture, to the prejudice of those, who carry it on; and though if it be really essential to
the prosperity of any very important national Manufacture, it may
happen that those who are injured in the first instance, may be
eventually indemnified, by the superior steadiness of an extensive
domestic market, depending on that prosperity: yet in a matter, in
which there is so much room for nice and difficult combinations, in
which such opposite considerations combat each other, prudence
seems to dictate, that the expedient in question, ought to be indulged
with a sparing hand.

IV. Pecuniary bounties.

This has been found one of the most efficacious means of encouraging manufactures, and it is in some views, the best. Though it has not yet been practiced upon by the Government of the United states (unless the allowances on the exportation of dried and pickled Fish and salted meat could be considered as a bounty) and though it is less favored by public opinion than some other modes.

Its advantages, are these—

1. It is a species of encouragement more positive and direct than any other, and for that very reason, has a more immediate tendency to stimulate and uphold new enterprises, increasing the chances of profit, and diminishing the risks of loss, in the first attempts.

2. It avoids the inconvenience of a temporary augmentation of price, which is incident to some other modes, or it produces it to a less degree; either by making no addition to the charges on the rival foreign article, as in the Case of protecting duties, or by making a smaller addition. The first happens when the fund for the bounty is derived from a different object (which may or may not increase the price of some other article, according to the nature of that object) the second, when the fund is derived from the same or a similar object of foreign manufacture. One per cent duty on the foreign article converted into a bounty on the domestic, will have an equal effect with a duty of two per Cent, exclusive of such bounty; and the price of the foreign commodity is liable to be raised, in the one Case, in the proportion of 1 per Cent; in the other, in that of two per Cent. Indeed the bounty when drawn from another source is calculated to promote a reduction of price, because without laying any new charge on the foreign article, it serves to introduce a competition with it, and to increase the total quantity of the article in the Market.

3. Bounties have not like high protecting duties, a tendency to produce scarcity. An increase of price is not always the immediate, though, where the progress of a domestic Manufacture does not counteract a rise, it is commonly the ultimate effect of an additional duty. In the interval, between the laying of the duty and a proportional increase of price, it may discourage importation, by interfering with the profits to be expected from the sale of the article.

4. Bounties are sometimes not only the best, but the only proper expedient, for uniting the encouragement of a new object of agricul-

ture, with that of a new object of manufacture. It is the Interest of the farmer to have the production of the raw material promoted, by counteracting the interference of the foreign material of the same kind. It is the interest of the manufacturer to have the material abundant and cheap. If prior to the domestic production of the Material, in sufficient quantity, to supply the manufacturer on good terms; a duty be laid upon the importation of it from abroad, with a view to promote the raising of it at home, the Interests both of the Farmer and Manufacturer will be disserved. By either destroying the requisite supply, or raising the price of the article, beyond what can be afforded to be given for it, by the Conductor of an infant manufacture, it is abandoned or fails; and there being no domestic manufactories to create a demand for the raw material, which is raised by the farmer, it is in vain, that the Competition of the like foreign article may have been destroyed.

It cannot escape notice, that a duty upon the importation of an article can no otherwise aid the domestic production of it, than giving the latter greater advantages in the home market. It can have no influence upon the advantageous sale of the article produced, in foreign markets; no tendency, therefore to promote its exportation.

The true way to conciliate these two interests, is to lay a duty on foreign *manufactures* of the material, the growth of which is desired to be encouraged, and to apply the produce of that duty by way of bounty, either upon the production of the material itself or upon its manufacture at home or upon both. In this disposition of the thing, the Manufacturer commences his enterprise under every advantage, which is attainable, as to quantity or price, of the raw material: And the Farmer if the bounty be immediately to him, is enabled by it to enter into a successful competition with the foreign material; if the bounty be to the manufacturer on so much of the domestic material as he consumes, the operation is nearly the same; he has a motive of interest to prefer the domestic Commodity, if of equal quality, even at a higher price than the foreign, so long as the difference of price is any thing short of the bounty which is allowed upon the article.

Except the stable and ordinary kinds of household Manufactures, or those for which there are very commanding local advantages, pecuniary bounties are in most cases indispensable to the introduction of a new branch. A stimulus and a support not less powerful and direct is generally speaking essential to the overcoming of the obstacles which arise from the Competitions of superior skill and maturity elsewhere. Bounties are especially essential, in regard to articles, upon which those foreigners, who have been accustomed to supply a Country, are in the practice of granting them.

The continuance of bounties on manufactures long established must almost always be of questionable policy: Because a presumption would arise in every such Case, that there were natural and inherent impediments to success. But in new undertakings, they are as justifiable, as they are oftentimes necessary.

There is a degree of prejudice against bounties from an appearance of giving away the public money, without an immediate consideration, and from a supposition, that they serve to enrich particular classes, at the expence of the Community.

But neither of these sources of dislike will bear a serious examination. There is no purpose, to which public money can be more beneficially applied, than to the acquisition of a new and useful branch of industry; no Consideration more valuable than a permanent addition to the general stock of productive labour.

As to the second source of objection, it equally lies against other modes of encouragement, which are admitted to be eligible. As often as a duty upon a foreign article makes an addition to its price, it causes an extra expence to the Community, for the benefit of the domestic manufacturer. A bounty does no more: But it is the Interest of the society in each case, to submit to a temporary expence, which is more than compensated, by an increase of industry and Wealth, by an augmentation of resources and independence; and by the circumstance of eventual cheapness, which has been noticed in another place.

It would deserve attention, however, in the employment of this species of encouragement in the United states, as a reason for moderating the degree of it in the instances, in which it might be deemed eligible, that the great distance of this country from Europe imposes very heavy charges on all the fabrics which are brought from thence, amounting from 15 to 30 Per Cent on their value, according to their bulk.

A Question has been made concerning the Constitutional right of the Government of the United States to apply this species of encouragement, but there is certainly no good foundation for such a question. The National Legislature has express authority "To lay and Collect taxes, duties, imposts and excises, to pay the debts and provide for the *Common defence* and *general welfare*" with no other qualifications than that "all duties, imposts and excises, shall be *uniform* throughout the United States, that no capitation or other direct tax shall be laid unless in proportion to numbers ascertained by a census or enumeration taken on the principles prescribed in the Constitution," and that "no tax or duty shall be laid on articles exported from any state." These three qualifications excepted, the power to *raise money* is *plenary,* and *indefinite;* and the objects to which it may be *appropriated* are no less comprehensive, than the payment of the public debts and the providing for the common defence and *"general Welfare."* The terms *"general Welfare"* were doubtless intended to signify more than was expressed or imported in those which Preceded; otherwise numerous exigencies incident to the affairs of a Nation would have been left without a provision. The phrase is as comprehensive as any that could have been used; because it was not fit that the constitutional authority of the Union, to appropriate its revenues shou'd have been restricted within narrower limits than the "General Welfare" and because this necessarily embraces a vast variety of particulars, which are susceptible neither of specification nor of definition.

It is therefore of necessity left to the discretion of the National Legislature, to pronounce, upon the objects, which concern the general Welfare, and for which under that description, an appropriation of money is requisite and proper. And there seems to be no room for a doubt that whatever concerns the general Interests of *learning of Agriculture,* of *Manufactures,* and of *Commerce* are within the sphere of the national Councils *as far as regards an application of Money.*

The only qualification of the generallity of the Phrase in question, which seems to be admissible, is this—That the object to which an appropriation of money is to be made be *General* and not *local;* its operation extending in fact, or by possibility, throughout the Union, and not being confined to a particular spot.

No objection ought to arise to this construction from a supposition that it would imply a power to do whatever else should appear to Congress conducive to the General Welfare. A power to appropriate money with this latitude which is granted too in *express terms* would not carry a power to do any other thing, not authorised in the constitution, either expressly or by fair implication.

V. Premiums.

These are of a Nature allied to bounties, though distinguishable from them, in some important features.

Bounties are applicable to the whole quantity of an article produced, or manufactured, or exported, and involve a correspondent expence. Premiums serve to reward some particular excellence or superiority, some extraordinary exertion or skill, and are dispensed only in a small number of cases. But their effect is to stimulate general effort. Contrived so as to be both honorary and lucrative, they address themselves to different passions; touching the chords as well of emulation as of Interest. They are accordingly a very economical mean of exciting the enterprise of a Whole Community.

There are various Societies in different countries, whose object is the dispensation of Premiums for the encouragement of *Agriculture Arts manufactures* and *Commerce;* and though they are for the most part voluntary associations, with comparatively slender funds, their utility has been immense. Much has been done by this mean in great Britain: Scotland in particular owes materially to it a prodigious amelioration of Condition. From a similar establishment in the United states, supplied and supported by the Government of the Union, vast benefits might reasonably be expected. Some further ideas on this head, shall accordingly be submitted, in the conclusion of this report.

VI. The Exemption of the Materials of manufactures from duty.

The policy of that Exemption as a general rule, particularly in reference to new Establishments, is obvious. It can hardly ever be adviseable to add the obstructions of fiscal burthens to the difficulties which naturally embarrass a new manufacture; and where it is matured and in condition to become an object of revenue, it is generally speaking better that the fabric, than the Material should be the subject of Taxation. Ideas of proportion between the quantum of the tax and the value of the article, can be more easily adjusted, in the former, than in the latter case. An argument for exemptions of this kind in the United States, is to be derived from the practice, as far as their necessities have permitted, of those nations whom we are to meet as competitors in our own and in foreign Markets.

There are however exceptions to it; of which some examples will be given under the next head.

The Laws of the Union afford instances of the observance of the policy here recommended, but it will probably be found adviseable to extend it to some other Cases. Of a nature, bearing some affinity to that policy is the regulation which exempts from duty the tools and implements, as well as the books, cloths and household furniture of foreign artists, who come to reside in the United states; an advantage already secured to them by the Laws of the Union, and which, it is in every view, proper to Continue.

VII. Drawbacks of the duties which are imposed on the Materials of Manufactures.

It has already been observed as a general rule that duties on those materials, ought with certain exceptions to be foreborne. Of these exceptions, three cases occur, which may serve as examples— one—where the material is itself, an object of general or extensive consumption, and a fit and productive source of revenue: Another, where a manufacture or a simpler kind (the competition of which with a like domestic article is desired to be restrained,) partakes of the Nature of a raw material, from being capable, by a further process to be converted into a manufacture of a different kind, the introduction or growth of which is desired to be encouraged; a third where the Material itself is a production of the Country, and in sufficient abundance to furnish cheap and plentiful supply to the national Manufacturer.

Under the first description comes the article of Molasses. It is not only a fair object of revenue; but being a sweet, it is just that the consumers of it should pay a duty as well as the Consumers of sugar.

Cottons and linens in their White state fall under the second description. A duty upon such as are imported is proper to promote the domestic Manufacture of similar articles in the same state. A Drawback of that duty is proper to encourage the printing and staining at home of those which are brought from abroad: When the first of these manufactures has attained sufficient maturity in a Country, to furnish a full supply for the second, the utility of the drawback ceases.

The article of Hemp either now does or may be expected soon to exemplify the third Case, in the United states.

Where duties on the materials of manufactures are not laid for the purpose of preventing a competition with some domestic production, the same reasons which recommend, as a general rule, the exemption of those materials from duties, would recommend as a like General rule, the allowance of draw backs, in favor of the manufacturer. Accordingly such drawbacks are familiar in countries which systematically pursue the business of manufactures; which furnishes an argument for the observance of a similar policy in the United states; and the Idea has been adopted by the laws of the Union in the instances of salt and Molasses. It is believed that it will be found advantageous to extend it to some other Articles.

VIII. The encouragement of new inventions and discoveries, at home, and of the introduction into the United States of such as may have been made in other countries; particularly those, which relate to machinery.

This is among the most useful and unexceptionable of the aids, which can be given to manufactures. The usual means of that encouragement are pecuniary rewards, and, for a time, exclusive privileges. The first must be employed, according to the occasion, and the utility of the invention, or discovery: For the last, so far as respects "authors and inventors" provision has been made by Law. But it is desireable in regard to improvements and secrets of extraordinary value, to be able to extend the same benefit to Introducers, as well as Authors and Inventors; a policy which has been practiced with advantage in other countries. Here, however, as in some other cases, there is cause to regret, that the competency of the authority of the National Government to the *good*, which might be done, is not without a question. Many aids might be given to industry; many internal improvements of primary magnitude might be promoted, by an authority operating throughout the Union, which cannot be effected, as well, if at all, by an authority confined within the limits of a single state.

But if the legislature of the Union cannot do all the good, that might be wished, it is at least desirable, that all may be done, which is practicable. Means for promoting the introduction of foreign improvements, though less efficaciously than might be accomplished with more adequate authority, will form a part of the plan intended to be submitted in the close of this report.

It is customary with manufacturing nations to prohibit, under severe penalties, the exportation of implements and machines, which they have either invented or improved. There are already objects for a similar regulation in the United States; and others may be expected to occur from time to time. The adoption of it seems to be dictated by the principle of reciprocity. Greater liberality, in such respects, might better comport with the general spirit of the country; but a selfish and exclusive policy in other quarters will not always permit the free indulgence of a spirit, which would place us upon an unequal footing. As far as prohibitions tend to prevent foreign competitors from deriving the benefit of the improvements made at home, they tend to increase the advantages of those by whom they may have been introduced; and operate as an encouragement to exertion.

IX. Judicious regulations for the inspection of manufactured commodities.

This is not among the least important of the means, by which the prosperity of manufactures may be promoted. It is indeed in many cases one of the most essential. Contributing to prevent frauds upon consumers at home and exporters to foreign countries—to improve the quality and preserve the character of the national manufactures, it cannot fail to aid the expeditious and advantageous Sale of them, and to serve as a guard against successful competition from other quarters. The reputation of the flour and lumber of some states, and of the Pot ash of others has been established by an attention to this point. And the like good name might be procured for those articles, wheresoever produced, by a judicious and uniform system of Inspection; throughout the ports of the United States. A like system might also be extended with advantage to other commodities.

X. The facilitating of pecuniary remittances from place to place is a point of considerable moment to trade in general, and to manufactures in particular; by rendering more easy the purchase of raw materials and provisions and the payment for manufactured supplies. A general circulation of Bank paper, which is to be expected from the institution lately established will be a most valuable mean to this end. But much good would also accrue from some additional provisions respecting inland bills of exchange. If those drawn in one state payable in another were made negotiable, everywhere, and interest and damages allowed in case of protest, it would greatly promote negotiations between the Citizens of different states, by rendering them more secure; and, with it the convenience and advantage of the Merchants and manufacturers of each.

XI. The facilitating of the transportation of commodities.

Improvements favoring this object intimately concern all the domestic interests of a community; but they may without impropriety be mentioned as having an important relation to manufactures. There is perhaps scarcely any thing, which has been better calculated to assist the manufactures of Great Britain, than the ameliorations of the public roads of that Kingdom, and the great progress which has been of late made in opening canals. Of the former, the United States stand much in need; and for the latter they present uncommon facilities.

The symptoms of attention to the improvement of inland Navigation, which have lately appeared in some quarters, must fill with pleasure every breast warmed with a true Zeal for the prosperity of the Country. These examples, it is to be hoped, will stimulate the exertions of the Government and the Citizens of every state. There can certainly be no object, more worthy of the cares of the local administrations; and it were to be wished, that there was no doubt of the power of the national Government to lend its direct aid, on a comprehensive plan. This is one of those improvements, which could be prosecuted with more efficacy by the whole, than by any part or parts of the Union. There are cases in which the general interest will be in danger to be sacrificed to the collission of some supposed local interests. Jealousies, in matters of this kind, are as apt to exist, as they are apt to be erroneous.

The following remarks are sufficiently judicious and pertinent to deserve a literal quotation. "Good roads, canals, and navigable rivers, by diminishing the expence of carriage, put the *remote parts of a country* more nearly upon a level with those in the neighborhood of the town. They are *upon that account* the greatest of all improvements. They encourage the cultivation of the remote, which must always be the most extensive circle of the country. They are advantageous to the Town by breaking down the monopoly of the country in its neighborhood. They are advantageous *even to that part of the Country*. Though they introduce some rival commodities into the old Market, they open many new markets to its produce. Monopoly besides is a great enemy to good management, which can never be universally established, but in consequence of that free and universal competition, which forces every body to have recourse to it for the sake of self defence. It is not more than Fifty years ago that *some of the countries in the neighborhood of London petitioned the Parliament, against the extension of the turnpike roads, into the remoter counties. Those remoter counties, they pretended, from the cheapness of Labor, would be able to sell their grass and corn cheaper in the London Market, than themselves, and they would thereby reduce their rents and ruin their cultivation.* Their rents however have risen and their cultivation has been improved, since that time."

Specimens of a spirit, similar to that which governed the counties here spoken of present themselves too frequently to the eye of an impartial observer, and render it a wish of patriotism, that the body in this Country, in whose councils a local or partial spirit is least likely to predominate, were at liberty to pursue and promote the general interest, in those instances, in which there might be danger of the interference of such a spirit.

The foregoing are the principal of the means, by which the growth of manufactures is ordinarily promoted. It is, however, not merely necessary, that the measures of government, which have a direct view to manufactures, should be calculated to assist and protect them, but that those which only collaterally affect them, in the general course of the administration, should be guarded from any peculiar tendency to injure them.

There are certain species of taxes, which are apt to be oppressive to different parts of the community, and among other ill effects have a very unfriendly aspect towards manufactures. All Poll or Capitation taxes are of this nature. They either proceed, according to a fixed rate, which operates unequally, and injuriously to the industrious poor; or they vest a discretion in certain officers, to make estimates and assessments which are necessarily vague, conjectural and liable to abuse. They ought therefore to be abstained from, in all but cases of distressing emergency.

All such taxes (including all taxes on occupations) which proceed according to the amount of capital *supposed* to be employed in a business, or of profits *supposed* to be made in it are unavoidably hurtful to industry. It is in vain, that the evil may be endeavoured to be mitigated by leaving it, in the first instance, in the option of the party to be taxed, to declare the amount of his capital or profits.

Men engaged in any trade of business have commonly weighty reasons to avoid disclosures, which would expose, with any thing like accuracy, the real state of their affairs. They most frequently find it better to risk oppression, than to avail themselves of so inconvenient a refuge. And the consequence is, that they often suffer oppression.

When the disclosure too, if made, is not definitive, but controulable by the discretion, or in other words, by the passions and prejudices of the revenue officers, it is not only an ineffectual protection, but the possibility of its being so is an additional reason for not resorting to it.

Allowing to the public officers the most equitable dispositions; yet where they are to exercise a discretion, without certain data, they cannot fail to be often misled by appearances. The quantity of business, which seems to be going on, is, in a vast number of cases, a very deceitful criterion of the profits which are made; yet it is perhaps the best they can have, and it is the one, on which they will most naturally rely. A business therefore which may rather require aid, from the government, than be in a capacity to be contributory to it, may find itself crushed by the mistaken conjectures of the Assessors of taxes.

Arbitrary taxes, under which denomination are comprised all those, that leave the *quantum* of the tax to be raised on each person, to the *discretion* of certain officers, are as contrary to the genius of liberty as to the maxims of industry. In this light, they have been viewed by the most judicious observers on government; who have bestowed upon them the severest epithets of reprobation; as constituting one of the worst features usually to be met with in the practice of despotic governments.

It is certain at least, that such taxes are particularly inimical to the success of manufacturing industry, and ought carefully to be avoided by a government, which desires to promote it.

The great copiousness of the subject of this Report has insensibly led to a more lengthy preliminary discussion, than was originally contemplated, or intended. It appeared proper to investigate principles, to consider objections, and to endeavour to establish the utility of the thing proposed to be encouraged; previous to a specification of the objects which might occur, as meriting or requiring encouragement, and of the measures, which might be proper, in respect to each. The first purpose having been fulfilled, it remains to pursue the second. In the selection of objects, five circumstances seem intitled to particular attention; the capacity of the Country to furnish the raw material—the degree in which the nature of the manufacture admits of a substitute for manual labour in machinery—the facility of execution—the extensiveness of the uses, to which the article can be applied—its subserviency to other interests, particularly the great one of national defence. There are however objects, to which these circumstances are little applicable, which for some special reasons, may have a claim to encouragement.

A designation of the principal raw material of which each manufacture is composed will serve to introduce the remarks upon it. As, in the first place—

Iron

The manufactures of this article are entitled to preeminent rank. None are more essential in their kinds, nor so extensive in their uses. They constitute in whole or in part the implements or the materials or both of almost every useful occupation. Their instrumentality is everywhere conspicuous.

It is fortunate for the United States that they have peculiar advantages for deriving the full benefit of this most valuable material, and they have every motive to improve it, with systematic care. It is to be found in various parts of the United States, in great abundance and of almost every quality; and fuel the chief instrument in manufacturing it, is both cheap and plenty. This particularly applies to Charcoal; but there are productive coal mines already in operation, and strong indications, that the material is to be found in abundance, in a variety of other places.

The inquiries to which the subject of this report has led have been answered with proofs that manufactories of Iron, though generally understood to be extensive, are far more so than is commonly supposed. The kinds, in which the greatest progress has been made, have been mentioned in another place, and need not be repeated; but there is little doubt that every other kind, with due cultivation, will rapidly succeed. It is worthy of remark that several of the particular trades, of which it is the basis, are capable of being carried on without the aid of large capitals.

Iron works have very greatly increased in the United States and are prosecuted, with much more advantage than formerly. The average price before the revolution was about Sixty four Dollars Per Ton—at present it is about Eighty; a rise which is chiefly to be attributed to the increase of manufactures of the material.

The still further extension and multiplication of such manufactures will have the double effect of promoting the extraction of the

Metal itself, and of converting it to a greater number of profitable purposes.

Those manufactures too unite in a greater degree, than almost any others, the several requisites, which have been mentioned, as proper to be consulted in the selection of objects.

The only further encouragement of manufactories of this article, the propriety of which may be considered as unquestionable, seems to be an increase of the duties on foreign rival commodities. . . .

(Hamilton continues in this line of development, discussing the current state of manufactories and the requisite measures for their encouragement with respect to the following: steel, copper, lead, fossil coal, wood, skins, grain, flax, hemp, cotton, wool, silk, glass, gunpowder, paper, printed books, refined sugar and chocolate—ed.)

. . . The foregoing heads comprise the most important of the several kinds of manufactures, which have occurred as requiring, and, at the same time, as most proper for public encouragement; and such measures for affording it, as have appeared best calculated to answer the end, have been suggested.

The observations, which have accompanied this delineation of objects, supercede the necessity of many supplementary remarks. One or two however may not be altogether superfluous.

Bounties are in various instances proposed as one species of encouragement.

It is a familiar objection to them that they are difficult to be managed and liable to frauds. But neither that difficulty nor this danger seems sufficiently great to countervail the advantages of which they are productive, when rightly applied. And it is presumed to have been shewn, that they are in some cases, particularly in the infancy of new enterprises indispensable.

It will however be necessary to guard, with extraordinary circumspection, the manner of dispensing them. The requisite precautions have been thought of; but to enter into the detail would swell this report, already voluminous, to a size too inconvenient.

If the principle shall not be deemed inadmissible the means of avoiding an abuse of it will not be likely to present insurmountable obstacles. There are useful guides from practice in other quarters.

It shall therefore only be remarked here, in relation to this point, that any bounty, which may be applied to the *manufacture* of an article, cannot with safety extend beyond those manufactories, at which the making of the article is a *regular trade*.

It would be impossible to annex adequate precautions to a benefit of that nature, if extended to every private family, in which the manufacture was incidentally carried on, and its being a merely incidental occupation which engages a portion of time that would otherwise be lost, it can be advantageously carried on, without so special an aid.

The possibility of a diminution of the revenue may also present itself, as an objection to the arrangements, which have been submitted.

But there is no truth, which may be more firmly relied upon, than that the interests of the revennue are promoted, by whatever promotes an increase of National industry and wealth.

In proportion to the degree of these, is the capacity of every country to contribute to the public treasury; and where the capacity to pay is increased, or even is not decreased, the only consequence of measures, which diminish any particular resource is a change of the object. If by encouraging the manufacture of an article at home, the revenue, which has been wont to accrue from its importation, should be lessened, an indemnification can easily be found, either out of the manufacture itself, or from some other object, which may be deemed more convenient.

The measures however, which have been submitted, taken aggregately, will for a long time to come rather augment than decrease the public revenue.

There is little room to hope, that the progress of manufactures, will so equally keep pace with the progress of population, as to prevent, even, a gradual augmentation of the product of the duties on imported articles.

As, nevertheless, an abolition in some instances, and a reduction in others of duties, which have been pledged for the public debt, is proposed, it is essential, that it should be accompanied with a competent substitute. In order to this, it is requisite, that all the additional duties which shall be laid, be appropriated in the first instance, to replace all defalcations, which may proceed from any such abolition or diminution. It is evident, at first glance, that they will not only be adequate to this, but will yield a considerable surplus.

This surplus will serve.

First. To constitute a fund for paying the bounties which shall have been decreed.

Secondly. To constitute a fund for the operations of a Board, to be established, for promoting Arts, Agriculture, Manufactures and Commerce. Of this institution, different intimations have been given, in the course of this report. An outline of a plan for it shall now be submitted.

Let a certain annual sum, be set apart, and placed under the management of Commissioners, not less than three, to consist of certain Officers of the Government and their Successors in Office.

Let these Commissioners be empowered to apply the fund confided to them—to defray the expences of the emigration of Artists, and Manufacturers in particular branches of extraordinary importance—to induce the prosecution and introduction of useful discoveries, inventions and improvements, by proportionate rewards, judiciously held out and applied—to encourage by premiums both honorable and lucrative the exertions of individuals, and of classes, in relation to the several objects, they are charged with promoting—and to afford such other aids to those objects, as may be generally designated by law.

The Commissioners to render (to the Legislature) an annual account of their transactions and disbursements; and all such sums as shall not have been applied to the purposes of their trust, at the end of every three years, to revert to the Treasury. It may also be enjoined upon them, not to draw out the money, but for the purpose of some specific disbursement.

It may moreover be of use, to authorize them to receive voluntary contributions; making it their duty to apply them to the particular objects for which they may have been made, if any shall have been designated by the donors.

There is reason to believe, that the progress of particular manufactures has been much retarded by the want of skilful workmen. And it often happens that the capitals employed are not equal to the purposes of bringing from abroad workmen of a superior kind. Here, in cases worthy of it, the auxiliary agency of Government would in all probability be useful. There are also valuable workmen, in every branch, who are prevented from emigrating solely by the want of means. Occasional aids to such persons properly administered might be a source of valuable acquisitions to the country.

The propriety of stimulating by rewards, the invention and introduction of useful improvements, is admitted without difficulty. But the success of attempts in this way must evidently depend much on the manner of conducting them. It is probable, that the placing of the dispensation of those rewards under some proper discretionary direction, where they may be accompanied by *collateral expedients,* will serve to give them the surest efficacy. It seems impracticable to apportion, by general rules, specific compensations for discoveries of unknown and disproportionate utility.

The great use which may be made of a fund of this nature to procure and import foreign improvements is particularly obvious. Among these, the article of machines would form a most important item.

The operation and utility of premiums have been adverted to; together with the advantages which have resulted from their dispensation, under the direction of certain public and private societies. Of this some experience has been had in the instance of the Pennsylvania society, (for the Promotion of Manufactures and useful Arts;) but the funds of that association have been too contracted to produce more than a very small portion of the good to which the principles of it would have led. It may confidently be affirmed that there is scarcely any thing, which has been devised, better calculated to excite a general spirit of improvement than the institutions of this nature. They are truly invaluable.

In countries where there is great private wealth much may be effected by the voluntary contributions of patriotic individuals, but in a community situated like that of the United States, the public purse must supply the deficiency of private resource. In what can it be so useful as in prompting and improving the efforts of industry?

All which is humbly submitted

Alexander Hamilton
Secretary of the Treasury

The Federalist No. 11 (Hamilton)

To the People of the State of New York:

The importance of the Union, in a commercial light, is one of those points about which there is least room to entertain a difference of opinion, and which has, in fact, commanded the most general assent of men who have any acquaintance with the subject. This applies as well to our intercourse with foreign countries as with each other.

There are appearances to authorize a supposition that the adventurous spirit, which distinguishes the commercial character of America, has already excited uneasy sensations in several of the maritime powers of Europe. They seem to be apprehensive of our too great interference in that carrying trade, which is the support of their navigation and the foundation of their naval strength. Those of them which have colonies in America look forward to what this country is capable of becoming, with painful solicitude. They foresee the dangers that may threaten their American dominions from the neighborhood of States, which have all the dispositions, and would possess all the means, requisite to the creation of a powerful marine. Impressions of this kind will naturally indicate the policy of fostering divisions among us, and of depriving us, as far as possible, of an *active commerce* in our own bottoms. This would answer the threefold purpose of preventing our interference in their navigation, of monopolizing the profits of our trade, and of clipping the wings by which we might soar to a dangerous greatness. Did not prudence forbid the detail, it would not be difficult to trace, by facts, the workings of this policy to the cabinets of ministers.

If we continue united, we may counteract a policy so unfriendly to our prosperity in a variety of ways. By prohibitory regulations, extending, at the same time, throughout the States, we may oblige foreign countries to bid against each other, for the privileges of our markets. This assertion will not appear chimerical to those who are able to appreciate the importance of the markets of three millions of people—increasing in rapid progression, for the most part exclusively addicted to agriculture, and likely from local circumstances to remain so—to any manufacturing nation; and the immense difference there would be to the trade and navigation of such a nation, between a direct communication in its own ships, and an indirect conveyance of its products and returns, to and from America, in the ships of another country. Suppose, for instance, we had a government in America, capable of excluding Great Britain (with whom we have at present no treaty of commerce) from all our ports; what would be the probable operation of this step upon her politics? Would it not enable us to negotiate, with the fairest prospect of success, for commercial privileges of the most valuable and extensive kind, in the dominions of that kingdom? When these questions have been asked, upon other occasions, they have received a plausible, but not a solid or satisfactory answer. It has been said that prohibitions on our part would produce no change in the system of Britain, because she could prosecute her trade with us through the medium of the Dutch, who would be her immediate customers and paymasters for those articles which were wanted for the supply of our markets. But would not her navigation be materially injured by the loss of the important advantage of being her own carrier in that trade? Would not the principal part of its profits be intercepted by the Dutch, as a compensation for their agency and risk? Would not the mere circumstance of freight occasion a considerable deduction? Would not so circuitous an intercourse facilitate the competitions of other nations, by enhancing the price of British commodities in our markets, and by transferring to other hands the management of this interesting branch of the British commerce?

A mature consideration of the objects suggested by these questions will justify a belief that the real disadvantages to Britain from such a state of things, conspiring with the prepossessions of a great part of the nation in favor of the American trade, and with the importunities of the West India islands, would produce a relaxation in her present system, and would let us into the enjoyment of privileges in the markets of those islands and elsewhere, from which our trade would derive the most substantial benefits. Such a point gained from the British government, and which could not be expected without an equivalent in exemptions and immunities in our markets, would be likely to have a correspondent effect on the conduct of other nations, who would not be inclined to see themselves altogether supplanted in our trade.

A further resource for influencing the conduct of European nations towards us, in this respect, would arise from the establishment of a federal navy. There can be no doubt that the continuance of the Union under an efficient government, would put it in our power, at a period not very distant, to create a navy which, if it could not vie with those of the great maritime powers, would at least be of respectable weight if thrown into the scale of either of two contending parties. This would be more peculiarly the case in relation to operations in the West Indies. A few ships of the line, sent opportunely to the reinforcement of either side, would often be sufficient to decide the fate of a campaign, on the event of which interests of the greatest magnitudes were suspended. Our position is, in this respect, a most commanding one. And if to this consideration we add that of the usefulness of supplies from this country, in the prosecution of military operations in the West Indies, it will readily be perceived that a situation so favorable would enable us to bargain with great advantage for commercial privileges. A price would be set not only upon our friendship, but upon our neutrality. By a steady adherence to the Union, we may hope, erelong, to become the arbiter of Europe in America, and to be able to incline the balance of European competitions in this part of the world as our interest may dictate.

But in the reverse of this eligible situation, we shall discover that the rivalships of the parts would make them checks upon each other, and would frustrate all the tempting advantages which nature has kindly placed within our reach. In a state so insignificant our commerce would be a prey to the wanton intermeddlings of all nations at war with each other; who, having nothing to fear from us, would with little scruple or remorse supply their wants by depredations on our property as often as it fell in their way. The rights of neutrality will only be respected when they are defended by an adequate power. A nation, despicable by its weakness, forfeits even the privilege of being neutral.

Under a vigorous national government, the natural strength and resources of the country, directed to a common interest, would baffle all the combinations of European jealousy to restrain our growth. This situation would even take away the motive to such combinations, by inducing an impracticability of success. An active commerce, an extensive navigation, and a flourishing marine would then be the offspring of moral and physical necessity. We might defy the little arts of the little politicians to control or vary the irresistible and unchangeable course of nature.

But in a state of disunion, these combinations might exist and might operate with success. It would be in the power of the maritime nations, availing themselves of our universal impotence, to prescribe the conditions of our political existence; and as they have a common interest in being our carriers, and still more in preventing our becoming theirs, they would in all probability combine to embarrass our navigation in such a manner as would in effect destroy it, and confine us to a *passive commerce*. We should then be compelled to content ourselves with the first price of our commodities, and to see the profits of our trade snatched from us to enrich our enemies and persecutors. That unequalled spirit of enterprise, which signalizes the genius of the American merchants and navigators, and which is in itself an inexhaustible mine of national wealth, would be stifled and lost, and poverty and disgrace would overspread a country which, with wisdom, might make herself the admiration and envy of the world.

There are rights of great moment to the trade of America which are rights of the Union—I allude to the fisheries, to the navigation of the Western lakes, and to that of the Mississippi. The dissolution of the Confederacy would give room for delicate questions concerning the future existence of these rights; which the interest of more powerful partners would hardly fail to solve to our disadvantage. The disposition of Spain with regard to the Mississippi needs no comment. France and Britain are concerned with us in the fisheries, and view them as of the utmost moment to their navigation. They, of course, would hardly remain long indifferent to that decided mastery, of which experience has shown us to be possessed in this valuable branch of traffic, and by which we are able to undersell those nations in their own markets. What more natural than that they should be disposed to exclude from the lists such dangerous competitors?

This branch of trade ought not to be considered as a partial benefit. All the navigating States may, in different degrees, advantageously participate in it, and under circumstances of a greater extension of mercantile capital, would not be unlikely to do it. As a nursery of seamen, it now is, or, when time shall have more nearly assimilated the principles of navigation in the several States, will become, a universal resource. To the establishment of a navy, it must be indispensable.

To this great national object, a *navy*, union will contribute in various ways. Every institution will grow and flourish in proportion to the quantity and extent of the means concentrated towards its formation and support. A navy of the United States, as it would embrace the resources of all, is an object far less remote than a navy of any single State or partial confederacy, which would only embrace the resources of a single part. It happens, indeed, that different portions of confederated America possess each some peculiar advantage for this essential establishment. The more southern States furnish in greater abundance certain kinds of naval stores—tar, pitch, and turpentine. Their wood for the construction of ships is also of a more solid and lasting texture. The difference in the duration of the ships of which the navy might be composed, if chiefly constructed of Southern wood, would be of signal importance, either in the view of naval strength, or of national economy. Some of the Southern and of the Middle States yield a greater plenty of iron, and of better quality. Seamen must chiefly be drawn from the Northern hive. The necessity of naval protection to external or maritime commerce does not require a particular elucidation, no more than the conduciveness of that species of commerce to the prosperity of a navy.

An unrestrained intercourse between the States themselves will advance the trade of each by an interchange of their respective productions, not only for the supply of reciprocal wants at home, but for exportation to foreign markets. The veins of commerce in every part will be replenished, and will acquire additional motion and vigor from a free circulation of the commodities of every part. Commercial enterprise will have much greater scope, from the diversity in the productions of different States. When the staple of one fails from a bad harvest or unproductive crop, it can call to its aid the staple of another. The variety, not less than the value, of products for exportation contributes to the activity of foreign commerce. It can be conducted upon much better terms with a large number of materials of a given value than with a small number of materials of the same value; arising from the competitions of trade and from the fluctuations of markets. Particular articles may be in great demand at certain periods, and unsalable at others; but if there be a variety of articles, it can scarcely happen that they should all be at one time in the latter predicament, and on this account the operations of the merchant would be less liable to any considerable obstruction or stagnation. The speculative trader will at once perceive the force of these observations, and will acknowledge that the aggregate balance of the commerce of the United States would bid fair to be much more favorable than that of the thirteen States without union or with partial unions.

It may perhaps be replied to this, that whether the States are united or disunited, there would still be an intimate intercourse between them which would answer the same ends, but this intercourse would be fettered, interrupted, and narrowed by a multiplicity of causes which in the course of these papers have been amply detailed. A unity of commercial, as well as political, interests, can only result from a unity of government.

There are other points of view in which this subject might be placed, of a striking and animating kind. But they would lead us too far into the regions of futurity, and would involve topics not proper for a newspaper discussion. I shall briefly observe, that our situation invites and our interests prompt us to aim at an ascendant in the system of American affairs. The world may politically, as well as geographically, be divided into four parts, each having a distinct set of interests. Unhappily for the other three, Europe, by her arms and by her negotiations, by force and by fraud, has, in different degrees, extended her dominion over them all. Africa, Asia, and America, have successively felt her domination. The superiority she has long maintained has tempted her to plume herself as the Mistress of the World, and to consider the rest of mankind as created for her benefit. Men admired as profound philosophers have, in direct terms, attributed to her inhabitants a physical superiority and have gravely asserted that all animals, and with them the human species, degenerate in America—that even dogs cease to bark after having breathed awhile in our atmosphere. Facts have too long supported these arrogant pretensions of the Europeans. It belongs to us to vindicate the honor of the human race, and to teach that assuming brother, moderation. Union will enable us to do it. Disunion will add another victim to his triumphs. Let Americans disdain to be the instruments of European greatness! Let the thirteen States, bound together in a strict and indissoluble Union, concur in erecting one great American system, superior to the control of all transatlantic force or influence and able to dictate the terms of the connection between the old and the new world!

PUBLIUS

Thomas Jefferson

T*he following selections from Thomas Jefferson have been chosen precisely because they are not representative of his views on the path of America's progress throughout his entire career. His 1805 Address to Congress marks a break from his previous belief and practice of using national revenue first and foremost for retiring the national debt. In it, he forms the outlines of the internal improvements program which was to be elaborated and fought for by John Quincy Adams, Henry Clay, and eventually the Republicans under Abraham Lincoln.*

The Report of the Commissioners Appointed to Fix the Site of the University of Virginia, etc. was authored by Jefferson for the twenty other members of the commission in August 1818. The major difference between this piece—of which only excerpts are printed here—and Jefferson's decades-long eloquence on behalf of primary-school-through-university-education is its specific advocacy of "manufactures" and "public industry."

Second Inaugural Address to Congress (1805)

Proceeding, fellow citizens, to that qualification which the constitution requires, before my entrance on the charge again conferred upon me, it is my duty to express the deep sense I entertain of this new proof of confidence from my fellow citizens at large, and the zeal with which it inspires me, so to conduct myself as may best satisfy their just expectations.

On taking this station on a former occasion, I declared the principles on which I believed it my duty to administer the affairs of our commonwealth. My conscience tells me that I have, on every occasion, acted up to that declaration, according to its obvious import, and to the understanding of every candid mind.

In the transaction of your foreign affairs, we have endeavored to cultivate the friendship of all nations, and especially of those with which we have the most important relations. We have done them justice on all occasions, favored where favor was lawful and cherished mutual interests and intercourse on fair and equal terms. We are firmly convinced, and we act on that conviction, that with nations as with individuals, our interests soundly calculated, will ever be found inseparable from our moral duties; and history bears witness to the fact, that a just nation is taken on its word, when recourse is had to armaments and wars to bridle others.

At home, fellow citizens, you best know whether we have done well or ill. The suppression of unnecessary offices, of useless establishments and expenses, enabled us to discontinue our internal taxes. These covering our land with officers, and opening our doors to their intrusions, had already begun that process of domiciliary vexation which, once entered, is scarcely to be restrained from reaching successively every article of produce and property. If among these taxes some minor ones fell which had not been inconvenient, it was because their amount would not have paid the officers who collected them, and because, if they had any merit, the state authorities might adopt them, instead of others less approved.

The remaining revenue on the consumption of foreign articles, is paid cheerfully by those who can afford to add foreign luxuries to domestic comforts, being collected on our seaboards and frontiers only, and incorporated with the transactions of our mercantile citizens, it may be the pleasure and pride of an American to ask, what farmer, what mechanic, what laborer, ever sees a taxgatherer of the United States? These contributions enable us to support the current expenses of the government, to fulfill contracts with foreign nations, to extinguish the native right of soil within our limits, to extend those limits, and to apply such a surplus to our public debts, as places at a short day their final redemption, and that redemption once effected, the revenue thereby liberated may, by a just repartition among the states, and a corresponding amendment of the constitution, be applied, *in time of peace,* to rivers, canals, roads, arts, manufactures, education, and other great objects within each state. *In time of war,* if injustice, by ourselves or others, must sometimes produce war, increased as the same revenue will be increased by population and consumption, and aided by other resources reserved for that crisis, it may meet within the year all the expenses of the year, without encroaching on the rights of future generations, by burdening them with the debts of the past. War will then be but a suspension of useful works, and a return to a state of peace, a return to the progress of improvement.

I have said, fellow citizens, that the income reserved had enabled us to extend our limits; but that extension may possibly pay for itself before we are called on, and in the meantime, may keep down the accruing interest; in all events, it will repay the advances we have made. I know that the acquisition of Louisiana has been disapproved by some, from a candid apprehension that the enlargement of our territory would endanger its union. But who can limit the extent to which the federative principle may operate effectively? The larger our association, the less will it be shaken by local passions; and in any view, is it not better that the opposite bank of the Mississippi should be settled by our own brethren and children, than by strangers of another family? With which shall we be most likely to live in harmony and friendly intercourse?

In matters of religion, I have considered that its free exercise is placed by the constitution independent of the powers of the general government. I have therefore undertaken, on no occasion, to prescribe the religious exercises suited to it; but have left them, as the constitution found them, under the direction and discipline of State or Church authorities acknowledged by the several religious societies.

The aboriginal inhabitants of these countries I have regarded with the commiseration their history inspires. Endowed with the faculties and the rights of men, breathing an ardent love of liberty and independence, and occupying a country which left them no desire but to be undisturbed, the stream of overflowing population from other regions directed itself on these shores; without power to divert, or habits to content against, they have been overwhelmed by the current, or driven before it; now reduced within limits too narrow for the hunter's state, humanity enjoins us to teach them agriculture and the domestic arts; to encourage them to that industry which alone can enable them to maintain their place in existence, and to prepare them in time for that state of society, which to bodily comforts adds the improvement of the mind and morals. We have therefore liberally furnished them with the implements of husbandry and household use; we have placed among them instructors in the arts of first necessity; and they are covered with the aegis of the law against aggressors from among ourselves.

But the endeavors to enlighten them on the fate which awaits their present course of life, to induce them to exercise their reason, follow its dictates, and change their pursuits with the change of circumstances, have powerful obstacles to encounter; they are combated by the habits of their bodies, prejudice of their minds, ignorance, pride, and the influence of interested and crafty individuals among them, who feel themselves something in the present order of things, and fear to become nothing in any other. These persons inculcate a sanctimonious reverence for the customs of their ancestors; that whatsoever they did, must be done through all time; that reason is a false guide, and to advance under its counsel, in their physical, moral or political condition, is perilous innovation; that their duty is to remain as their Creator made them, ignorance being safety, and knowledge full of danger; in short, my friends, among them is seen the action and counteraction of good sense and bigotry; they, too, have their anti-philosophers, who find an interest in keeping things in their present state, who dread reformation, and exert all their faculties to maintain the ascendency of habit over the duty of improving our reason, and obeying its mandates.

In giving these outlines, I do not mean, fellow citizens, to arrogate to myself the merit of the measures; that is due, in the first place, to the reflecting character of our citizens at large, who, by the weight of public opinion, influence and strengthen the public measures; it is due to the sound discretion with which they select from among themselves those to whom they confide the legislative duties; it is due to the zeal and wisdom of the characters thus selected, who lay the foundations of public happiness in wholesome laws, the execution of which alone remains for others; and it is due to the able and faithful auxiliaries, whose patriotism has associated with me in the executive functions.

During this course of administration, and in order to disturb it, the artillery of the press has been levelled against us, charged with whatsoever its licentiousness could devise or dare. These abuses of an institution so important to freedom and science, are deeply to be regretted, inasmuch as they tend to lessen its usefulness, and to sap its safety; they might, indeed, have been corrected by the wholesome punishments reserved and provided by the laws of the several States against falsehood and defamation; but public duties more urgent press on the time of public servants, and the offenders have therefore been left to find their punishment in the public indignation.

Nor was it uninteresting to the world, that an experiment should be fairly and fully made, whether freedom of discussion, unaided by power, is not sufficient for the propagation and protection of truth—whether a government, conducting itself in the true spirit of its constitution, with zeal and purity, and doing no act which it would be unwilling the whole world should witness, can be written down by falsehood and defamation. The experiment has been tried; you have witnessed the scene; our fellow citizens have looked on, cool and collected; they saw the latent source from which these outrages proceeded; they gathered around their public functionaries, and when the constitution called them to the decision by suffrage, they pronounced their verdict, honorable to those who had served them, and consolatory to the friend of man, who believes he may be intrusted with his own affairs.

No inference is here intended, that the laws, provided by the State against false and defamatory publications, should not be enforced; he who has time, renders a service to public morals and public tranquillity, in reforming these abuses by the salutary coercions of the law; but the experiment is noted, to prove that, since truth and reason have maintained their ground against false opinions in league with false facts, the press, confined to truth, needs no other legal restraint; the public judgment will correct false reasonings and opinions, on a full hearing of all parties; and no other definite line can be drawn between the inestimable liberty of the press and its demoralizing licentiousness. If there be still improprieties which this rule would not restrain, its supplement must be sought in the censorship of public opinion.

Contemplating the union of sentiment now manifested so generally, as auguring harmony and happiness to our future course, I offer to our country sincere congratulations. With those, too, not yet rallied to the same point, the disposition to do so is gaining strength; facts are piercing through the veil drawn over them; and our doubting brethren will at length see, that the mass of their fellow citizens, with whom they cannot yet resolve to act, as to principles and measures, think as they think, and desire what they desire; that our wish, as well as theirs, is, that the public efforts may be directed honestly to the public good, that peace be cultivated, civil and religious liberty unassailed, law and order preserved, equality of rights maintained, and that state of property, equal or unequal, which results to every man from his own industry, or that of his fathers. When satisfied of these views, it is not in human nature that they should not approve and support them; in the meantime, let us cherish them with patient affection; let us do them justice, and more than justice, in all competitions of interest; and we need not doubt that truth, reason, and their own interests, will at length prevail, will gather them into the fold of their country, and will complete their entire union of opinion, which gives to a nation the blessing of harmony, and the benefit of all its strength.

I shall now enter on the duties to which my fellow citizens have again called me, and shall proceed in the spirit of those principles which they have approved. I fear not that any motives of interest may lead me astray; I am sensible of no passion which could seduce me knowingly from the path of justice; but the weakness of human nature, and the limits of my own understanding, will produce errors of judgment sometimes injurious to your interests. I shall need, therefore, all the indulgence I have heretofore experienced—the want of it will certainly not lessen with increasing years. I shall need, too, the favor of that Being in whose hands we are, who led our forefathers, as Israel of old, from their native land, and planted them in a country flowing with all the necessaries and comforts of life; who has covered our infancy with his providence, and our riper years with his wisdom and power; and to whose goodness I ask you to join with me in supplications, that he will so enlighten the minds of your servants, guide their councils, and prosper their measures, that whatsoever they do, shall result in your good, and shall secure to you the peace, friendship, and approbation of all nations.

The Report of the Commissioners Appointed to Fix the Site Of the University of Virginia, etc. (August 1818)

. . . 3, 4. In proceeding to the third and fourth duties prescribed by the Legislature, of reporting "the branches of learning, which should be taught in the University, and the number and description of the professorships they will require," the Commissioners were first to consider at what point it was understood that university education should commence? Certainly not with the alphabet, for reasons of expediency and impracticability, as well as from the obvious sense of the Legislature, who, in the same act, make other provision for the primary instruction of the poor children, expecting, doubtless, that in other cases it would be provided by the parent, or become, perhaps, subject of future and further attention of the Legislature. The objects of this primary education determine its character and limits. These objects would be,

To give to every citizen the information he needs for the transaction of his own business;

To enable him to calculate for himself, and to express and preserve his ideas, his contracts and accounts, in writing;

To improve, by reading, his morals and faculties;

To understand his duties to his neighbors and country, and to discharge with competence the functions confided to him by either;

To know his rights; to exercise with order and justice those he retains; to choose with discretion the fiduciary of those he delegates; and to notice their conduct with diligence, with candor, and judgment;

And, in general, to observe with intelligence and faithfulness all the social relations under which he shall be placed.

To instruct the mass of our citizens in these, their rights, interests and duties, as men and citizens, being then the objects of education in the primary schools, whether private or public, in them should be taught reading, writing and numerical arithmetic, the elements of mensuration (useful in so many callings) and the outlines of geography and history. And this brings us to the point at which are to commence the higher branches of education, of which the Legislature require the development; those, for example which are,

To form the statesmen, legislators and judges, on whom public prosperity and individual happiness are so much to depend;

To expound the principles and structure of government, the laws which regulate the intercourse of nations, those formed municipally for our own government, and a sound spirit of legislation, which, banishing all arbitrary and unnecessary restraint on individual action, shall leave us free to do whatever does not violate the equal rights of another;

To harmonize and promote the interests of agriculture, manufactures and commerce, and by well informed views of political economy to give a free scope to the public industry;

To develop the reasoning faculties of our youth, enlarge their minds, cultivate their morals, and instill into them the precepts of virtue and order;

To enlighten them with mathematical and physical sciences, which advance the arts, and administer to the health, the subsistence, and comforts of human life;

And, generally, to form them to habits of reflection and correct action, rendering them examples of virtue to others, and of happiness within themselves.

These are the objects of that higher grade of education, the benefits and blessings of which the Legislature now propose to provide for the good and ornament of their country, the gratification and happiness of their fellow-citizens, of the parent especially, and his progeny, on which all his affections are concentrated.

In entering on this field, the Commissioners are aware that they have to encounter much difference of opinion as to the extent which it is expedient that this institution should occupy. Some good men, and even of respectable information, consider the learned sciences as useless acquirements; some think that they do not better the condition of man; and others that education, like private and individual concerns, should be left to private individual effort; not reflecting that an establishment embracing all the sciences which may be useful and even necessary in the various vocations of life, with the buildings and apparatus belonging to each, are far beyond the reach of individual means, and must either derive existence from public patronage, or not exist at all. This would leave us, then, without those callings which depend on education, or send us to other countries to seek the instruction they require. But the Commissioners are happy in considering the statute under which they are assembled as proof that the Legislature is far from the abandonment of objects so interesting. They are sensible that the advantages of well-directed education, moral, political and economical, are truly above all estimate. Education generates habits of application, of order, and the love of virtue; and controls, by the force of habit, any innate obliquities in our moral organization. We should be far, too, from the discouraging persuasion that man is fixed, by the law of his nature, at a given point; that his improvement is a chimera, and the hope delusive of rendering ourselves wiser, happier or better than our forefathers were. As well might it be urged that the wild and uncultivated tree, hitherto yielding sour and bitter fruit only, can never be made to yield better; yet we know that the grafting art implants a new tree on the savage stock, producing what is most estimable both in kind and degree. Education, in like manner, engrafts a new man on the native stock, and improves what in his nature was vicious and perverse into qualities of virtue and social worth. And it cannot be but that each generation succeeding to the knowledge acquired by all those who preceded it, adding to it their own acquisitions and discoveries, and handing the mass down for successive and constant accumulation, must advance the knowledge and well-being of mankind, not *infinitely*, as some have said, but *indefinitely*, and to a term which no one can fix and foresee. Indeed, we need look back half a century, to times which many now living remember well, and see the wonderful advances in the sciences and arts which have been made within that period. Some of these have rendered the elements themselves subservient to the purposes of man, have harnessed them to the yoke of his labors, and effected the great blessings of moderating his own, of accomplishing what was beyond his feeble force, and extending the comforts of life to a much enlarged circle, to those who had before known its necessaries only. That these are not the vain dreams of sanguine hope, we have before our eyes real and living examples. What, but education, has advanced us beyond the condition of our indigenous neighbors? And what chains them to their present state of barbarism and wretchedness, but a bigotted veneration for the supposed superlative wisdom of their fathers, and the preposterous idea that they are to look backward for better things, and not forward, longing, as it should seem, to return to the days of eating acorns and roots, rather than indulge in the degeneracies of civilization? And how much more encouraging to the achievements of science and improvement is this, than the desponding view that the condition of man cannot be ameliorated, that what has been must ever be, and that to secure ourselves where we are, we must tread with awful reverence in the footsteps of our fathers. This doctrine is the genuine fruit of the alliance between Church and State; the tenants of which, finding themselves but too well in their present condition, oppose all advances which might unmask their usurpations, and monopolies of honors, wealth, and power, and fear every change, as endangering the comforts they now hold. Nor must we omit to mention, among the benefits of education, the incalculable advantage of training up able counsellors to administer the affairs of our country in all its departments, legislative, executive and judiciary, and to bear their proper share in the councils of our national government; nothing more than education advancing the prosperity, the power, and the happiness of a nation.

Encouraged, therefore, by the sentiments of the Legislature, manifested in this statute, we present the following tabular statements of the branches of learning which we think should be taught in the University, forming them into groups, each of which are within the powers of a single professor:

    I.   Languages, ancient: Latin, Greek, Hebrew.

   II.   Languages, modern: French, Spanish, Italian, German, Anglo-Saxon.

  III.   Mathematics, pure: Algebra, Fluxions, Geometry, elementary, transcendal, Architecture, military, naval.

  IV.   Physico-Mathematics: Mechanics, Statics, Dynamics, Pneumatics, Acoustics, Optics, Astronomy, Geography.

   V.   Physics, or Natural Philosophy: Chemistry, Mineralogy.

  VI.   Botany, Zoölogy.

 VII.   Anatomy, Medicine.

VIII.   Government, Political Economy, Law of Nature and Nations, History, being interwoven with Politics and Law.

  IX.   Law, municipal.

   X.   Ideology, General Grammar, Ethics, Rhetoric, Belles Lettres, and the fine arts.

Index

Great Debasement, 77
Greece, ancient, 213; language of, i, iv
Gresham, John, 76, 108
Gresham, Thomas, 53, 61, 75, 76, 77, 78, 79, 83, 88, 100, 108, 164; correspondence with Jean Bodin, 61; as Elizabeth's agent in Antwerp, 147; as Elizabeth's agent in Spain, 147-150; and the English debt, 78; *Memorandum on the Exchange*, 77
"Gresham's Law," 45
Grocyn, William, 81, 108
Grotius, Hugo, 82
Guise faction, 72, 74
Gutenberg, 69

Hamburg, 87, 137, 140
Hamilton, Alexander, ii, v, viii, xv, 1, 3, 7, 8, 11-12, 16-18, 20-31, 40-44, 47, 53, 54, 55, 101, 246, 247, 277, 344; on agriculture, 392-399; on agricultural markets, 406-409; on capital shortages, 417-426; on credit, 344-359, 446; on charges against the National Bank, 360-369; on customs and duties, 438-441, 444-445, 451-452; defends industrial development, 390-400, 415; on division of labor, 401-402, 405-406; economic program of, 11, 28-29, 30-34; on encouragement of inventions, 445-446; on expanded employment, 403-404; on federal government and commerce, 454-461; on federal government and the navy, 458-459; on fisheries, 434-435; foreign policy of, 34-39; on immigration, 404-405, 437; on increased use of machinery, 403; on industrial regulation, 446; on industry's relation with agriculture, 398, 408, 409, 431; on the iron industry, 450-451; on labor power, 393-394, 401-403, 405; on limitations of the Bank of North America, 372-380; on manufacturing and profit, 401; on mechanization, 416; on the National Bank, 355-390; on the National Bank and industry, 355-356; on the National Bank and rate of interest, 375, 388-389; on National Bank and taxes, 359-360; on National Bank and trade, 355-356; on national debt, 346, 354, 386-388,
420-426; on the navy, 433; notion of surplus value, 344; plans for founding of National Bank, 382-386; on premiums, 443-444, 453; on President and national debt, 389; reasons for establishing National Bank, 369-380; on shortage of labor, 415-416; on taxes, 448-449; on transportation, 447; on U.S. commerce, 410, 430-431, 454; on wages, 417; on wealth, 365-366; *The Continentalist*, 20; *Opinion on the Constitutionality of the Bank*, 99; *Report on Public Credit*, 24, 31; *Report on Subject of Manufactures*, ii, 1, 28, 32, 40, 41, 99

H

Hanotaux, Gabriel, 53
Hanover, House of, 35, 87
Happiness, 88, Jefferson on, 464, 465, 467, 468, 470; Leibniz on, 221; Paine on, 305, 306, 347; Washington on, 231, 279, 280, 286, 299, 300
Hapsburg, House of, 54, 55, 61, 67-70, 73-75, 78, 79, 85, 86, 87, 108, 109; bankruptcies of, 73; European policy of, 72; Latin American policy of, 72
Henry V, credit policy of, 133
Henry IV of England, credit policy of, 133
Henry IV of France, 74, 80, 88, 203
Henry VII, 67, 116, 137; and aristocracy, 79; credit policy of, 133-134
Henry VIII, 66, 69, 90, 107, 109, 133, 160; and the aristocracy, 79; and church lands, 66, 77, 115-117; debts of, 150; education of, 82, 108; as humanist prince, 108; mint policy of, 150; monetary policy of, 77; *Valour Ecclesiasticus*, 66
Henry, Patrick, 13
Hesse-Cassel, Elector of, as purveyor of mercenaries, 95
High Commission, 192
Hill, Rowland, 154
Hippodamus, 210
Historiography, 1-7, 29, 47, 61, 67, 118
Hitler, Adolf, 4
Hobbes, Thomas, xiii, 85, 185; *Behemoth*, 185
Hochstetters, 54, 61